Handbook of Self-Help Therapies

Handbook of Self-Help Therapies

Edited by

Patti Lou Watkins ✦ George A. Clum

Routledge
Taylor & Francis Group
New York   London

Lawrence Erlbaum Associates
Taylor & Francis Group
270 Madison Avenue
New York, NY 10016

Lawrence Erlbaum Associates
Taylor & Francis Group
2 Park Square
Milton Park, Abingdon
Oxon OX14 4RN

© 2008 by Taylor & Francis Group, LLC
Lawrence Erlbaum Associates is an imprint of Taylor & Francis Group, an Informa business

Printed in the United States of America on acid-free paper
10 9 8 7 6 5 4 3 2 1

International Standard Book Number-13: 978-0-8058-5171-7 (Hardcover)

Library of Congress Cataloging-in-Publication Data

Handbook of self-help therapies / [edited by] Patti Lou Watkins, George A. Clum.
    p. ; cm.
    Includes bibliographical references and index.
    ISBN 978-0-8058-5171-7 (hardcover)
    1. Self-help techniques. 2. Psychological literature. 3. Self-care, Health. 4. Mental illness--Treatment. I. Watkins, Patti Lou. II. Clum, George A., 1942-
    [DNLM: 1. Self Care. 2. Bibliotherapy. 3. Communications Media. 4. Health Behavior. 5. Patient Education. WB 327 H236 2007]

BF632.H258 2007
158'.9--dc22   2007019575

Visit the Taylor & Francis Web site at
http://www.taylorandfrancis.com

This book is dedicated to the memory of the 32 men and women who lost their lives in the April 16, 2007 shootings at Virgina Tech and to their families and friends. It is further dedicated to the survivors of that attack and to the spirit of the Virginia Tech community, reflected in its motto: *Ut Prosim* – That I may serve.

Contents

Preface

Empirically supported interventions were the hallmark of psychology in the late 1960s as the new science of behavior therapy began to take hold. This was an era characterized by a concern for the betterment of society, and behavior therapy optimistically offered a means of improving the psychological circumstances of the masses (Evans, 1997). Bolstered by the demonstrated success of these latest therapeutic techniques, George Miller, in his 1969 presidential address, encouraged members of the American Psychological Association to "give psychology away" (Rosen, Glasgow, & Moore, 2003). In the nearly 40 years since he issued this charge, psychologists have done just that. Self-help—in the form of books, audio- and videotapes, and most recently computer technologies—has grown beyond the cottage industry it once was into a mammoth force in the marketplace. America's populace has welcomed this gift of self-help with open arms—and open wallets, judging by the near $2.5 billion the business draws per year (Rosen et al., 2003). Unfortunately, all gifts are not of comparable quality. In addition, gifts may fail to come with adequate instructions, may be ill suited to their recipients, and may not even work at all—or worse yet, result in harm to the recipient. Sadly, the motives of the gift-givers may also come into doubt. While Miller's message was an altruistic one, Evans (1997, p. 488) poses the question, "But did we really have ideals of helping people, or did we simply want to have a better product for sale?"

The impetus for the *Handbook of Self-Help Therapies* was to shed light on these and other concerns surrounding this genre. As Floyd, McKendree-Smith, and Scogin (2004) note, self-help programs far outstrip the research base supporting their efficacy. We are in concert with the idea that our task as psychologists is to help people learn to help themselves. However, we firmly believe that the field of self-help needs to incorporate the empiricism that led Miller to make his recommendation in the first place. Rosen et al. (2003, p. 410) concede that "psychologists have contributed to the glut of untested programs more than they have advanced the empirical foundation of self help." We, the editors, scientist-practitioners ourselves—along with the authors who have contributed to this volume—hope to counter this trend by presenting an accumulation of empirical evidence supporting, and sometimes refuting, the effectiveness of self-help interventions across problem areas in psychology, psychiatry, and behavioral medicine.

Whatever one believes about the merits of self-help interventions, Scogin (2003) states, they are unlikely to disappear from the national (and international) landscape in any near future. "Book prescriptions are on the increase and general opinion appears to be in favour of this change" according to Lehane (2005, p. 24), a community psychiatric nurse in Cardiff. Furthermore, as Halliday (1991) documented, many clients access self-help materials on their own. Ballou (1995) underscores the importance of therapists having a thorough grounding in the contents and effectiveness of self-help materials. Therefore, it serves us—whether we are psychologists, counselors, social workers, nurses, nurse practitioners, physicians, physician assistants, and even dentists and dental hygienists, who are on the front lines of detecting and intervening with eating disorders and tobacco use—to understand which self-help materials are empirically valid.

In *The Practitioner*, Williams (2004) advocates the use of self-help, especially in settings where access to traditional modes of therapy is limited. However, Adams and Pitre (2000) point to a lack of systematic research attesting to their usefulness as one reason that the practitioners who they surveyed may hesitate to adopt self-help interventions. Holdsworth, Paxton, Seidel, Thomson, and Shrubb (1996) contend that more primary care practitioners would utilize self-help materials with the myriad of patients who present with mental health problems if only they were aware of effective self-directed interventions. Johnson and Johnson (1998) surveyed master's- and doctoral-level counselors, and those who failed to incorporate self-help books in their practice also cited a lack of awareness regarding which books were appropriate to use. Again, this is a problem that our text attempts to overcome.

Another difficulty highlighted by Johnson and Johnson is the apparent disregard for empirical validation in selecting self-help programs among therapists who do rely on these in their practice. These investigators were struck by the fact that only 30% of the practitioners surveyed actually considered research support to be an important criterion in deciding which self-help materials to prescribe. Consistent with these findings, Adams and Pitre (2000) found that many of the books employed by practitioners in their sample actually advocated treatment techniques with no empirical basis. Of the books that were based on validated intervention methods, only one had been validated when these methods were translated into self-help form. Johnson and Johnson also describe some practitioners dismissing the use of self-help books because they seem trite and superficial. Wilson (2003) addresses this issue, voicing her concerns that the advice industry, fraught with unvalidated products, may degrade or displace the validated interventions that do exist. She states that ignoring this advice industry is like "ignoring a sizeable and growing tumor" (p. 425). Taking this analogy further, she warns that "Not only has the advice industry used the mental health profession as a host, but it has metastasized in ways that threaten to displace the profession itself" (p. 425).

Two decades ago, Starker (1989) noted that the scientific community seemed to ignore self-help books, perhaps because they were considered undeserving of serious attention. Simonds (1992) observed a similar trend, suggesting that this genre—which largely targets women—has been viewed dismissively, as are many facets of "women's culture." Whatever the barriers may have been, we must now move beyond them and turn our scientific attention to this phenomenon of self-help. As Starker (1989) forewarned, "it does not seem wise to ignore an agency" that "addresses a mass audience, offers exact directions for solving problems, claims competence in virtually all aspects of human concern, and is relatively free of external evaluation and regulation" (p. 5).

The *Handbook of Self-Help Therapies* represents a tangible effort to shine an empirical light on this industry. Indeed, Marrs (1995) remarks that practitioners have put greater stock in subjective opinions about which self-help program to use than in the empirical evidence that speaks to these interventions. Likewise, Rosen et al. (2003) assert that it is time to move beyond 1- to 5-star rating systems in judging the worth of self-help materials and, instead, rely on existing and future scientific findings to make these decisions. Pantalon (1998) suggests that if empirically validated self-help books can attain a higher profile (like many that have not undergone such scientific scrutiny), then practitioners who cite lack of awareness as a barrier to usage may gain incentive to adopt them. Additionally, he suggests that clients themselves may be more willing to seek and procure these materials on their own.

Our motivation for assembling this text was to feature self-help programs that have the backing of a body of research attesting to their effectiveness, as well as their potential limitations. In doing so, we hope to achieve praxis, providing a resource that is both helpful to practitioners working directly with clients and inspiring to researchers seeking to extend the data base in this area. Adams and Pitre (2000) surveyed practitioners across disciplines (psychiatry, psychology, counseling, nursing) and levels of training (bachelor's, master's, and doctoral level), finding that nearly 70% recommended self-help books to their clients. While there were no significant differences across discipline or training level, these researchers found that practitioners with 10 or more years of experience were significantly more likely to prescribe self-help books. Adams and Pitre offer that because bibliotherapy is typically not a part of practitioners' training, they are left to discover and experiment with its utility on their own. We encourage practitioners to continue such experimentation and, further, to document and communicate their findings through case study and single case design articles. In addition, we advance the idea that practitioner and researcher education in the helping professions begin to include training specific to the use of self-help therapies. Such education could complement current training in traditional group and individual therapeutic modalities, and the *Handbook of Self-Help Therapies* might serve as a resource in these endeavors.

References

Adams, S. J., & Pitre, N. L. (2000). Who uses bibliotherapy and why? A survey from an underserviced area. *Canadian Journal of Psychiatry, 45*, 645–650.

Ballou, M. (1995). Bibliotherapy. In M. Ballou (Ed.), *Psychological interventions: A guide to strategies* (pp. 55–65). Westport, CT: Praeger.

Evans, I. M. (1997). The effect of values on scientific and clinical judgement in behavior therapy. *Behavior Therapy, 28*, 483–493.

Floyd, M., McKendree-Smith, N. L., & Scogin, F. R. (2004). Remembering the 1978 and 1990 task forces on self-help therapies: A response to Gerald Rosen. *Journal of Clinical Psychology, 60*, 115–117.

Halliday, G. (1991). Psychological self-help books—How dangerous are they? *Psychotherapy, 28*, 678–686.

Holdsworth, N., Paxton, R., Seidel, S., Thomson, D., & Shrubb, S. (1996). Parallel evaluations of new guidance materials for anxiety and depression in primary care. *Journal of Mental Health, 5*, 195–207.

Johnson, B. W., & Johnson, W. L. (1998). Self-help books used by religious practitioners. *Journal of Counseling and Development, 76*, 459–466.

Lehane, M. (2005). Treatment by the book. *Nursing Standard, 19*, 24.

Marrs, R. W. (1995). A meta-analysis of bibliotherapy studies. *American Journal of Community Psychology, 23*, 843–870.

Pantalon, M. V. (1998). Use of self-help books in the practice of clinical psychology. In A. S. Bellack & M. Hersen (Series Eds.) & P. Salkovskis (Vol. Ed.), *Comprehensive clinical psychology: Vol. 6. Adults: Clinical formulation and treatment* (pp. 265–276). New York: Elsevier Science.

Rosen, G. M., Glasgow, R. E., & Moore, T. E. (2003). Self-help therapy: The science and business of giving psychology away. In S. O. Lilienfeld, S. J. Lynn, & J. M. Lohr (Eds.), *Science and pseudoscience in clinical psychology* (pp. 399–424). New York: Guilford.

Scogin, F. R. (2003). Introduction: The status of self-administered treatments. *Journal of Clinical Psychology, 59*, 247–249.

Simonds, W. (1992). *Women and self-help culture: Reading between the lines.* New Brunswick, NJ: Rutgers University Press.

Starker, S. (1989). *Oracle at the supermarket.* New Brunswick, NJ: Transaction Publishers.

Williams, C. J. (2004). Self-help models in cognitive behavioural therapy. *The Practitioner, 248*, 418–430.

Wilson, N. (2003). Commercializing mental health issues: Entertainment, advertising, and psychological advice. In S. O. Lilienfeld, S. J. Lynn, & J. M. Lohr (Eds.), *Science and pseudoscience in clinical psychology* (pp. 425–459). New York: Guilford.

About the Editors

Patti Lou Watkins, Ph.D., is an associate professor in the Women Studies Program at Oregon State University. Her background is in psychology, having obtained her bachelor's degree from West Virginia University, her master's degree in applied behavioral analysis from the University of the Pacific, and her doctoral degree in clinical psychology from Virginia Tech. There, she began her collaboration with her former professor and current coeditor, George Clum, evaluating interventions for panic disorder. Dr. Watkins's areas of interest revolved around adult stress and anxiety disorders, which she pursued during her internship at the University of Mississippi Medical Center/Jackson VAMC and her NHLBI postdoctoral fellowship at Washington University Medical Center in St. Louis. In her research, Dr. Watkins was attentive to gender issues, noting differential manifestations of Type A behavior and differential experiences when seeking professional help for anxiety disorders. She was initially appointed as an assistant professor to the Psychology Department at Oregon State University. However, her rewarding collaboration with OSU Women Studies faculty resulted in her appointment to this program in 2002. As such, Dr. Watkins's research is now more fully informed from a feminist perspective, which is reflected in this volume as well as other recent publications. Dr. Watkins's most contemporary work has examined weight bias, eating disorders, and barriers to physical activity among larger women. Dr. Watkins's current classes include, *Women, Weight, & Body Image* as well as *Violence Against Women*. She is a member of the Association for the Advancement of Behavior Therapy, the Society of Behavioral Medicine, and the National Women's Studies Association.

George A. Clum, Ph.D., is a professor of psychology at Virginia Tech, where he conducts research in the assessment, etiology, and treatment of anxiety and affective disorders and of suicidal behaviors. Dr. Clum received his B.S. from Scranton University in 1963 and his doctorate in clinical psychology from St. John's University in 1968. He interned at the National Naval Medical Center in Bethesda, Maryland, and spent 3 years in the navy conducting research at the Neuropsychiatric Research Unit in San Diego and teaching at the University of San Diego and San Diego State College. He accepted an appointment as assistant professor of psychiatry at the University of Virginia School of Medicine, where he was also director of internship training. He has taught at Virginia Tech for 31 years. He has been conducting treatment outcome studies and meta-analytic studies on the effectiveness of self-administered interventions for the last 10 years. In addition to authoring his own self-help book, *Coping With Panic*, he has helped develop Web-based interventions for reactions to general trauma and combat trauma. He is a diplomate in clinical psychology and has served on the State of Virginia Board of Psychology.

About the Authors

Eileen S. Anderson, Ed.D., is an assistant research professor of psychology specializing in community- and Internet-based health behavioral research with diverse populations. Her research interests include the evaluation of the theoretical foundations of behavior and interventions, computer-based measurement, and multivariate approaches to analysis.

Manuel Barrera, Jr., Ph.D., is a professor of psychology and director of clinical training at Arizona State University. He also is an adjunct senior research scientist at Oregon Research Institute in Eugene, Oregon. He received his doctorate in clinical psychology from the University of Oregon, where he began collaborative work on self-help therapies with Dr. Gerald Rosen and Russell Glasgow. Dr. Barrera has had career-long interests in understanding how naturally occurring social support and social support interventions influence health and psychological distress.

Rebecca Y. Concepcion obtained her Ph.D. from the Department of Nutrition and Exercise Sciences at Oregon State University with an emphasis in sport and exercise psychology. She also obtained her master's degree at OSU after working as health and fitness educator for 10 years. Her area of study includes self-concept, and affect and their relationship to health behaviors, with dissertation work examining weight stigma, self-concept physical activity, and eating behaviors. Additionally, she has served as editorial assistant for the *Journal of Applied Sport Psychology*. She is a member of the Association for Applied Sport Psychology; the American Alliance for Health, Physical Education, Recreation, and Dance; and the North American Society for the Psychology of Sport and Physical Activity.

John Cunningham, Ph.D., received his doctoral degree in experimental psychology from the University of Toronto, Ontario, Canada, in 1995. He has spent his career at the Centre for Addiction and Mental Health and is currently associate professor of psychology and of public health sciences at the University of Toronto. His research is driven by the question, "How do people change from addictive behaviors?" To answer this question, he has combined population research methods with clinical and other research traditions. The findings from these studies have been translated into a series of brief interventions for problem drinkers and other drug users that can be applied in treatment or community settings.

Shawn Currie, Ph.D., is an adjunct associate professor in psychology and psychiatry at the University of Calgary, Alberta, Canada, and a licensed clinical psychologist. He completed his doctoral degree at the University of Ottawa, Ontario, Canada, in 1998 and trained as clinical psychologist in Ontario and Alberta. In 2002, he received the University of Calgary's Faculty of Medicine Research Award and the New Researcher Award from the Canadian Psychological Association. He has authored and coauthored numerous peer-reviewed articles and book chapters on a broad range of topics including the assessment and treatment of insomnia in medical and psychiatric populations, chronic pain, gambling, and other addictions. He lectures at the University of Calgary on psychopathology, assessment, and research design. In 2006 he became director of the Mental Health Information Management and Evaluation Unit in the Calgary Health Region.

Frank Elgar, Ph.D., received his degree at Dalhousie University. He is now an assistant professor in the Department of Psychology at Carleton University, Ottawa, Ontario, Canada. His research on the social determinants of child health addresses parents' influences on the development and treatment of child adjustment problems.

Greg A. R. Febbraro, Ph.D., is a clinical psychologist in private practice at Counseling for Growth & Change, L.C., in Windsor Heights, Iowa. Dr. Febbraro holds a doctorate in clinical psychology from Virginia Tech and has published on the topics of self-administered interventions for anxiety disorders, phobias, self-regulatory processes, and the relationship between suicidality and problem-solving. Prior to entering full-time private practice, Dr. Febbraro was an assistant professor of psychology at Drake University in Des Moines, Iowa. He serves as an ad hoc reviewer for several journals including the *Journal of Clinical Psychology* and the *Journal of Traumatic Studies*. Dr. Febbraro is a member of the American Psychological Association, Association for Advancement of Behavioral and Cognitive Therapies, and the Iowa Psychological Association. His clinical interests include working with anxious, depressed, and traumatized populations.

Edwin B. Fisher, Ph.D., is professor and chair of the Department of Health Behavior and Health Education in the School of Public Health at the University of North Carolina at Chapel Hill. He has served as national program director of the Robert Wood Johnson Foundation's Diabetes Initiative since its inception in 2002. The Diabetes Initiative demonstrates promotion of self-management of diabetes through real-world primary care and community settings. His research addresses (a) management of chronic diseases, including diabetes; (b) health risk reduction, including weight management and smoking cessation; (c) psychosocial aspects of chronic diseases; and (d) social support in health behavior and quality of life. He was president of the Society of Behavioral Medicine 2006–2007. He is a fellow of the American Psychological Association, the American Psychological Society, and the Society of Behavioral Medicine.

Jeanne M. Gabriele is completing her doctorate in clinical psychology at Washington University in St. Louis. Her research interests focus on social support and health promotion and the use of technology in delivering health promotion or disease prevention programs. She has an M.S. in exercise and sport science from the University of North Carolina at Greensboro and an M.A. in clinical psychology from Washington University in St. Louis.

Russell Glasgow, Ph.D., received his degree in clinical psychology at the University of Oregon. He is now Senior Scientist in the Institute for Health Research at Kaiser Permanente Colorado. He has conducted research on patient-centered health behavior change and self-management for the past 20 years. He has contributed conceptual articles, empirical reviews of the literature, outcome studies, and methodological papers on assessment, evaluation, and translation of research into practice issues, many of which use the RE-AIM model (www.re-aim.org). His recent work has focused on health technology aided interventions that work in concert with primary care settings and offer potential for broad dissemination.

Michiyo Hirari, Ph.D., is an assistant professor in the Psychology Department at Washington State University. Her research interests include the etiology, assessment, and cognitive–behavioral treatment of anxiety disorders; application of Web-based assessment and interventions to anxiety disorders; roles of emotions in developing and maintaining pathological fear and anxiety; and cross-cultural issues in anxiety disorders.

Jennifer A. Karpe, M.A., has a bachelor's degree in psychology from the University of Miami and a master's degree in psychology from the University of Alabama. Her master's thesis involved conducting an efficacy study of a self-help treatment for depression. She is currently pursuing a J.D. at the University of Pennsylvania.

Alan Katz, M.B.Ch.B., M.Sc., C.C.F.P., is an associate professor in the Department of Family Medicine at the University of Manitoba, Canada, and researcher at the Manitoba Centre for Health Policy. His research interests include health services research with a focus on primary care and quality of care and patient safety. He is also the Manitoba Medical Service Foundation Clinical Research Professor in population medicine.

Despina D. Konstas, Ph.D., is a graduate of Hofstra University's doctoral program in combined clinical and school psychology. Since graduation, she has been a staff psychologist at Hofstra University's student counseling services for the past 2 years. She is responsible for orienting and supervising psychology interns, running and supervising groups, and providing therapy to Hofstra students and outreach services to the Hofstra community. Her professional interests involve research on addictions and suicide prevention, bereavement counseling, and the cognitive–behavioral treatment of anxiety and mood disorders.

Kyp Kypri, Ph.D., did his undergraduate training in psychology and received his doctoral degree in public health at the University of Otago, New Zealand, in 2003. His research area is the social epidemiology of young people's alcohol use and evaluation of interventions to reduce hazardous drinking. He has a joint appointment as a senior lecturer in population health in the School of Medicine and Public Health at the University of Newcastle, Australia, and as a senior research fellow at the Injury Prevention Research Unit at the University of Otago, New Zealand.

Kristine Luce, Ph.D., is a clinical assistant professor in the Department of Psychiatry and Behavioral Sciences at Stanford University. Dr. Luce's recent research has been in the development and evaluation of Web-based interventions for eating disorders and healthy weight regulation.

Patrick J. McGrath, O.C., Ph.D., is vice president of research at the IWK Health Centre and professor of psychology, pediatrics, and psychiatry at Dalhousie University in Halifax, Nova Scotia, Canada. His research is on innovative delivery of care to families and on pediatric pain.

Gerald M. Rosen, Ph.D., has a private practice in clinical psychology in Seattle, Washington. He holds appointments as clinical professor with the Department of Psychology, University of Washington, and the Department of Psychiatry and Behavioral Sciences, University of Washington Medical School. Since the 1970s, Dr. Rosen has published on professional issues concerning the development of self-help therapies. He chaired task forces on these issues for the American Psychological Association in 1978 and 1990.

Mitchell L. Schare, Ph.D., ABPP, holds the rank of professor and is the director of the doctoral program in clinical psychology at Hofstra University. He completed his doctorate in clinical psychology with a specialization in substance abuse behaviors at the State University of New York—Binghamton in 1985 following an internship at the Brown University Medical School Consortium. He holds a diplomate from the American Board of Cognitive & Behavioral Psychology. He is an active researcher, having published and presented over 100 papers in scientific journals, books, and at national and international conferences. His current research interests include treatment of cigarette cessation through self-help methods, applications of motivational interviewing, and the virtual reality treatment of anxiety disorders.

Forrest Ray Scogin, Jr., Ph.D., is a professor in the Psychology Department at the University of Alabama. His research is in the areas of mental health and aging, the effects of self-administered treatment, and rural mental health. He has published a number of articles, chapters, and books in these areas and has received external funding to support these activities.

Deborah F. Tate, Ph.D., is an assistant professor of health behavior-health education and nutrition at the University of North Carolina in the School of Public Health. The focus of her research is in developing public health alternatives to standard clinical treatments for obesity, incorporating technology and informatics and developing tailored health communications interventions.

C. Barr Taylor, M. D., is a professor in the Department of Psychiatry and Behavioral Sciences at Stanford University. He is currently developing and evaluating innovative electronic and computer-assisted programs to make treatments, proven effective for treating various psychosocial problems, more cost-effective and available. Additionally, he is developing prevention programs for eating disorders involving interactive multimedia interventions.

Jacques van Lankveld, Ph.D., is a clinical psychologist, psychotherapist, and sexologist. He is a professor of sexology in the Department of Clinical Psychological Science at Maastricht University and at ProPsy Sittard in The Netherlands.

Norah Vincent, Ph.D., is a clinical psychologist and associate professor in the Department of Clinical Health Psychology at the University of Manitoba, Canada. She is active in research, teaching, and clinical work, in areas of sleep disorders, eating disorders/obesity, and anxiety disorders. She has a particular interest in how newer technologies can be used to provide self-help treatments to the public in these areas.

John R. Walker, Ph.D., is a clinical psychologist and a professor of clinical health psychology at the University of Manitoba, Canada. He is active in research, teaching, and clinical work, particularly in the areas of anxiety disorders, coping with illness, and epidemiology. With his colleagues, he has published several books over the years, including *Triumph Over Shyness: Conquering Shyness and Social Anxiety* (2001), and *Treating Health Anxiety and Fear of Death* (2006).

Richard A. Winett, Ph.D., is the Heilig Meyers Professor of Psychology at Virginia Tech, where he directs the Center for Research in Health Behavior and has directed the clinical science program. His main interests focus on health behavior, disease prevention interventions in different settings and with different medium, and, more specifically, the problem of maintaining behavior changes.

Sheila G. Winett is the owner of Personal Computer Resources, Inc. (PCR), in Blacksburg, Virginia. PCR developed the software used to implement the Guide-to-Health and Nutrition for a Lifetime projects, both funded by the NCI, and the CD-based computerized assessment tool used by the NIMH-funded Teen Health Project. PCR is currently developing the software that will be used by the new, totally Internet-based Guide to Health program funded by the NCI. In addition to its research work, PCR also creates and manages several commercial Web sites. She is a graduate of Queens College (B.A.), the University of Kentucky (M.S.W.), and Virginia Tech (M.S., computer science).

Andrew Winzelberg, Ph.D., is a researcher in the Department of Psychiatry and Behavioral Sciences at Stanford University. Dr. Winzelberg has been developing and evaluating computer-assisted self-help interventions since 1985. His current research investigates the effectiveness of Internet-delivered interventions to prevent eating disorders and to provide care to those coping with cancer and other chronic illnesses.

Janet R. Wojcik, Ph.D., is director for research and assessment for the ZestQuest Project in the Department of Health and Physical Education at Winthrop University, Rock Hill, South Carolina. Previously, she was a research assistant professor in the Center for Research in Health Behavior, Department of Psychology, Virginia Tech. Her research interests include designing and implementing nutrition and physical activity health behavior interventions, nutrition and physical activity assessments, and developing Internet-based nutrition and physical activity content and logic.

CHAPTER 1

Self-Help Therapies
Past and Present

PATTI LOU WATKINS

What Is Self-Help?

Definitions of self-help seem as varied as the myriad of programs that use this label to describe their contents. First, it may be useful to distinguish between self-help groups and media-based self-help approaches (Gould & Clum, 1993). According to Den Boer, Wiersma, and Van Den Bosch (2004), each of these has a distinct "history of development, methodology, research strategy, and relationship with professionals" (p. 960). In self-help groups, individuals with a shared problem lend support and assist each other in coping with and/or overcoming the problem in question. Den Boer et al. stress that such groups should not be confused with profession-ally led support groups, remarking that lay networks represent the old-est system of care for various maladies. Alcoholics Anonymous and its derivatives epitomize contemporary self-help groups. A number of texts (e.g., Kurtz, 1997; Powell, 1994; Riessman & Carroll, 1995) already exist that attempt to summarize the body of knowledge surrounding self-help groups. Thus, the focus of the current text is on media-based self-help, a relatively new means for individuals to manage both medical and psycho-logical problems.

In their meta-analytic review, Gould and Clum (1993) defined media-based self-help as including books, manuals, audiotapes, videotapes, or some combination of these formats. Over the ensuing decade, computer-based self-help programs have proliferated and now must be considered part of the mix of media-based self-help interventions. For instance, Tate and Zabinski (2004) describe the use of Web-based self-help programs as well as the use of handheld computers to deliver treatment strategies that would otherwise have been implemented by a therapist. Some researchers have used the term *bibliotherapy* as synonymous with media-based self-help. In his meta-analytic review, Marrs (1995) defines bibliotherapy as "the use of written materials or computer programs, or listening/viewing of audio/videotapes for the purpose of gaining understanding or solving problems relevant to a person's developmental or therapeutic needs" (p. 846). Because the modality by which an intervention is delivered (e.g., book vs. Internet) may produce disparate results—or may produce similar results albeit via different mechanisms—we prefer to reserve the term bibliotherapy for interventions that are actually delivered in written form. In essence, bibliotherapy is a subset of the broader term, "media-based self-help," which refers to interventions delivered across the aforementioned modalities. Nevertheless, bibliotherapy—at least for the time being—remains the largest category of media-based self-help. Thus, an examination of the variations within this category seems warranted.

Bibliotherapy

Anderson et al. (2005) assert that, "Self-help is difficult to define but there is consensus that self-help books should aim to guide and encourage the patient to make changes, resulting in improved self-management, rather than just provide information" (p. 387). With similar conviction, Lichterman (1992) defines self-help books as "an enduring, highly popular non-fiction genre" (p. 421). Unfortunately, such consensus is not so easy to come by. A number of scholars would dispute these descriptions, offering a broader definition of self-help books, or bibliotherapy. Campbell and Smith (2003) include both nonfiction and fiction works among self-help books for psychological distress. The former, which correspond to those that Anderson et al. had in mind, typically include specific treatment techniques, often cognitive–behavioral in nature, intended to accomplish certain treatment outcomes. Although the subject of far less research, the latter merits mention in the delineation of bibliotherapy.

Starker (1989) describes a continuum between informational and anecdotal forms of bibliotherapy. At one end of this continuum lie informational sources that are comprised of empirically based directives for behavior. At the other end of the continuum reside anecdotal sources that, instead, rely upon "interesting, amusing, or biographical incidents" (p. 9). Similarly, Riordan, Mullis, and Nuchow (1996) distinguish between didactic and imaginative materials. Didactic bibliotherapy provides suggestions for new behaviors, presumably through specific therapeutic techniques. Imaginative bibliotherapy, on the other hand, incorporates the works of fiction to which Campbell and Smith allude. However, it may also include poetic and other inspirational forms of literature, fiction and nonfiction, that provide insight and understanding to readers. Johnson, Johnson, and Hillman (1997) also describe self-help books as ranging from specific therapeutic procedures to inspirational prose, citing the Bible as perhaps the most long-lived form of motivational bibliotherapy. Sommer (2003) describes the use of autobiographies in overcoming psychological distress. He explains that clients' identification with someone who has suffered the same problem may prove therapeutically beneficial. Pantalon (1998) concurs, stating that biographies and novels may not have been intended as self-help but that some individuals may find characters' attempts to cope with similar problems therapeutic in some fashion. As articulated by Riordan et al. (1996), readers of imaginative bibliotherapy "moved from identification with characters and situations through catharsis to the development of insight which applied to their own condition or issues" (p. 170).

While virtually any written material may be construed as bibliotherapy, nonfiction books, manuals, or pamphlets that provide information while prompting decision-making and problem-solving more aptly typify self-help reading (Campbell & Smith, 2003). Pantalon (1998) offers a useful classification of such materials, which includes; (a) general self-help books, (b) problem-focused self-help books, and (c) technique-focused self-help books. In this scheme, general self-help books are those that address broad-spectrum emotional health and relationship issues rather than specific disorders. Such books may provide general guidelines for well-being, but they do not include assessment or treatment exercises in a systematic approach. *Women Who Love Too Much* (Norwood, 1985) and *Awakening At Midlife: A Guide to Reviving Your Spirit, Recreating Your Life, and Returning to Your Truest Self* (Brehony, 1996) exemplify this category of books. Starker (1989) might call such offerings *descriptive bibliotherapy*, in which authors present a number of wide-ranging suggestions that readers may or may not choose to follow.

In contrast, problem-focused self-help books target a particular disorder (e.g., panic attacks, depression, insomnia, etc.), providing "specific techniques and homework exercises within a structured protocol" (Pantalon, 1998, p. 267). According to Anderson et al. (2005), this form of self-help "fits well with cognitive behavioural therapy, in which patients are encouraged to carry out work in between sessions in order to challenge unhelpful thoughts and behaviours" (p. 388). Pantalon concedes that most books of this ilk derive from a cognitive–behavioral perspective, although he states that problem-focused self-help books may also draw from other psychological orientations. In 1978, Glasgow and Rosen noted that self-help books have been based on Gestalt, rational–emotive, transactional analysis, and hypnotic methods of intervention. In the succeeding decades, however, cognitive–behavioral therapies appear to be the predominant means of intervention (Garvin, Striegel-Moore, Kaplan, & Wonderlich, 2001). Examples of problem-focused bibliotherapy abound throughout this text, as this brand of self-help has been the subject of most empirical research in this area. Finally, Pantalon describes technique-focused self-help books as akin to problem-focused manuals. Both include specific therapeutic techniques; however, in the latter case, these intervention strategies could be applied across problem areas. Pantalon cites *The Relaxation Response* (Benson, 1975), which perhaps best characterizes this form of bibliotherapy. Starker (1989) might describe both problem- and technique-focused manuals as *prescriptive bibliotherapy*, in which authors mandate readers to follow authoritative rules and directives.

Levels of Contact

In attempting to define self-help, a larger issue looms than determining the modality (i.e., book, audiotape, videotape, computer), the content (e.g., type of technique), or the purpose (e.g., providing inspiration vs. eliminating a target behavior) of the work. This issue involves the amount of contact, if any, an individual should have with others for an intervention to truly be considered "self"-help. The others to be considered in this debate include health care practitioners, significant others, and the community of consumers themselves. The role of health care practitioners in the administration and resultant effectiveness of self-help interventions has received the most attention in the literature to date as illustrated by a recent article entitled "Self-Help and Minimal Contact Therapies for Anxiety Disorders: Is Human Contact Necessary for Therapeutic Efficacy?" (Newman, Ericckson, Przeworski, & Dzus, 2003). Thus, contact with practitioners will serve as a starting point for our discussion.

In reality (i.e., outside the confines of research settings), most self-help materials are purchased and used by individuals independent of contact with a practitioner (Johnson et al., 1997). Pantalon (1998) suggests that this is more likely the case with general self-help books, but that problem-focused self-help books are also oft used by individuals apart from any professional contact. Some authors in the self-help arena voice strong opinions as to the appropriateness of independent self-help usage. For instance, Adams and Pitre (2000) state that bibliotherapy "should never entirely replace the therapist" (p. 645), who is viewed as necessary for a variety of functions, including selection of the material itself, interpretation, and subsequent processing. Lehane (2005) advises that self-help books should be seen as only part of a solution, rather than the entire solution to the whole array of clients' problems. Riordan et al. (1996) state similar concerns, prompting readers to consider bibliotherapy as a single tool to be used within a broader therapeutic context. They assert that "To conceive of bibliotherapy as using a book to solve problems is deferring to an 'all or none' thinking pattern" (p. 178). As such, these authors question whether self-help materials should even be examined in isolation (i.e., apart from therapist contact) in research studies.

Perhaps Riordan et al. need not worry, because when self-help programs have been empirically investigated, some level of practitioner contact inevitably takes place, even though said contact is not intended to be therapeutic (e.g., Watkins, 1999). For purposes of their meta-analytic review, Gould and Clum (1993) defined self-help as media-based materials that "are used largely by an individual independent of a helping professional" (p. 170). Even in their "pure" or "unadulterated" classification of studies, Gould and Clum noted that therapist contact occurred, although for assessment purposes only. Interestingly, these researchers found no difference in effectiveness between this condition and a minimal contact condition in which practitioners interacted briefly to monitor progress, clarify procedures, answer questions, and provide general encouragement. Furthermore, these self-help conditions appeared to be as effective as therapist-assisted interventions in this meta-analysis.

The extent to which therapist contact affects treatment outcome in studies of self-help programs is a question of ongoing empirical research— and one that many of the chapters in this text attempt to answer. One might revisit Glasgow and Rosen's (1978) seminal writing on self-help interventions to conceptualize this question. In this article, the authors describe four levels of therapist–patient contact. The first level, dubbed *self-administered* therapy, involves contact solely for assessment purposes. This is synonymous with the condition labeled pure or unadulterated self-help by Gould and Clum (1993). Glasgow and Rosen referred to the second level as minimal contact therapy. This might involve some therapist interaction at the outset to introduce the intervention materials. It may also entail subsequent check-ins, perhaps via telephone, to determine whether clients are enacting the intervention as planned. The third level is known as *therapist-administered* intervention. Here, the therapist plays some active role such as clarifying or elaborating upon the material contained within the self-help program. However, the onus is still on the client to implement treatment strategies. *Facilitated self-help* is a term used by Rogers, Oliver, Bower, Lovell, and Richards (2004) to describe this circumstance in which "the patient receives brief assistance from a therapist to help in implementing programmes and activities in the manuals" (p. 41). Glasgow and Rosen's fourth level of contact is known as *therapist-directed* intervention. This refers to traditional psychotherapy in which the therapist conducts treatment that does not include use of a self-help program. Conceivably, the first three levels in this model might be construed as self-help, not because the individual acts in isolation but because she/he is primarily responsible for implementing the treatment techniques.

Contact with a practitioner may not be the only manner in which consumers of self-help programs potentially derive therapeutic benefit from the presence of others. Lehane (2005) reports that clients have shared their self-help reading with family members and that such interactions are valuable. Simonds (1992) describes the case of a woman who discussed her self-help reading on relationships with her husband. This discussion subsequently led to a processing of feelings and mutual problem-solving behavior. Watkins (1999) presents a case study in which a woman using a self-help manual for panic disorder also interacted with significant others over the material contained therein. Watkins explains that this manual, *Coping with Panic* (Clum, 1990), actually includes explicit instruction for readers to adaptively engage with significant others about their symptoms and the treatment strategies that the manual prescribes. In fact, the manual advises readers to view such communication as a form of coping. Researchers have yet to systematically investigate the extent to which consumers of self-help engage with significant others over these programs or the extent to which such interaction may facilitate treatment outcome. As is the case with therapist contact, this remains a subject for ongoing empirical investigation.

Employing qualitative research, Grodin (1991, 1995) examined the ways in which women utilize self-help reading, interviewing participants as to which elements of this process they found beneficial and which they found dissatisfying. Based on these interviews, Grodin (1995) articulates the notion that female readers of self-help literature "construct a community of others with whom to share a sense of purpose and meaning" (p. 130). This community consists of the women whose stories—similar to the readers' own—are represented as illustrative vignettes within the pages of the books. It may also include other readers of these books who endure the same circumstances. Consistent with this view, Simonds (1992) writes that "Reading about emotions or experiences they had suffered through made women realize that they were not abnormal or alone" (p. 85). Although the others in this scenario reside in the consumer's imagination, they nevertheless impacted the perceived benefit Grodin's and Simond's participants reported. Grodin describes this phenomenon as contrasting to the American therapeutic ideal of autonomy and self-responsibility in which dependence and reliance on others may, in fact, be seen as pathological.

Grodin (1991) contends that women's sense of self "pivots upon a desire for autonomy and a desire for connection to a world beyond the self" (p. 416). Paradoxically, women who read self-help books develop a stronger sense of self, not in isolation but by connecting with their constructed community of others.

In this section, we have touched upon the role that practitioners, significant others, and even imaginal others play in individuals' use of media-based self-help materials. This suggests that the term *self-help* may be somewhat of a misnomer in that a variety of people, professionals and non-professionals alike, may influence the effectiveness of these interventions. Similarly, Garvin et al. (2001) state that "The rhetoric of *self*-help, with its explicit focus on the self, furthers the misconception that self-help only involves the individual" (p. 163). They stress the need to acknowledge the interpersonal aspects of self-help programs, maintaining that the impact of others—therapeutic agents in this case—should remain in the forefront of empirical research. To overlook the potential curative role of the practitioner may constitute a breach of professional standards. While the self may not act in isolation as the term self-help implies, we do not seek to rename this genre. We simply wish to prompt readers to recognize the array of others who may influence outcomes and, perhaps, consider making these connections more explicit when administering self-help materials to clients.

History of Self-Help

Human beings have long turned to the written word for solace in the face of psychological adversity. Ballou (1995) notes that an inscription over the door of a library in ancient Thebes identified it as a "Healing Place of the Soul." Starker (1989) suggests the quest for enlightenment is synonymous with human existence and that, throughout time, individuals have looked to soothsayers, prophets, and gurus in search of advice. In contemporary times, these sources have been supplanted by a new oracle, the self-help book. "The search for the Holy Grail, for spiritual renewal and hope, no longer requires a heroic trip into the distant corners of the kingdom; the object of the quest may be found conveniently in paperback, at the grocery, to the left of the chocolate milk" (p. 1).

Self-help books were one of the first imports to the New World. As Lichterman (1992) states, "[T]hey are a tradition as old as the American Republic" (p. 421). Rosenberg (2003) traces the appearance of self-help books in America to the arrival of the English colonists who transported these texts "like every other European cultural artifact across the Atlantic" (p. 2). Several factors appear to have conspired to explain the proliferation of self-help books since their inception in the United States. Practically speaking, the advent of the printing press and the availability of less expensive materials during the 1800s did much to increase the accessibility of self-help advice across sectors of society. In the 1930s, the development of paperback publishing houses such as Pocket Books further boosted public ease of access (Simonds, 1992; Starker, 1989). The arrival of computer technology and its increasing availability seems the modern-day equivalent of these events.

Cushman (1995, p. 210) points to the "quintessentially American" trend of consumerism as another reason that the self-help movement has flourished over the ensuing years. That is, Americans have been molded into expecting self-fulfillment through the "compulsive purchase and consumption of goods, experiences, and celebrities" (p. 211). Furthermore, advertising suggests that the purchase of a product will heal the empty self. Certainly, self-help products are marketed more heavily today than at any other time in their history (Simonds, 1992). While Cushman's missive helps to explain the widespread presence of self-help goods in today's society, it also harkens to a critique of the self-help genre (i.e., exaggerated claims of effectiveness) that will be revisited later in this chapter.

Thus far, technological advancements and a culture based on consumerism have been implicated as forces behind the formidable self-help movement. Perhaps a more pervasive factor is the concept on which the United States was founded. Starker (1989) traces the roots of American self-help literature to the tenets of the first settlers. This Protestant ethic emphasized individual responsibility and control over one's quality of life. Quinn and Crocker (1999) explain the Protestant ethic as an ideology including the notion that "individual hard work leads to successes and that lack of success is caused by the moral failings of self-indulgence and lack of self-discipline" (p. 403). Thus, as Greenberg (1994) states, self-help therapies blossomed "in a culture that already valued the 'power' of the individual, already held self-containment to be a worthwhile aspiration, and was already optimistic about the individual's prospects of achieving that aspiration" (p. 41).

Seligman (1994) contends that, historically, this belief in the individual's ability to change is relatively recent—that a dogma of implasticity characterized Western thought largely until European colonization of America. In contrast, the early Americans developed a dogma of human plasticity, the notion that individuals are able to transform themselves in whatever manner they desire. "Improving is absolutely central to American ideology," states Seligman (1994, p. 16). Furthermore, the primary agent of change is the self. Brownell (1991) adds that the more capitalistic the country, the greater the responsibility attributed to individuals over their lot in life.

This deep-seated belief in personal control seems to have intensified over time, reaching an all-time high in recent decades. Starker (1989) describes the 1960s and 1970s as the "Me Generation," in which psychological movements of the day (e.g., humanistic psychology) reinforced the primacy of the self. This period saw an explosion of self-help publications, which he explains established and maintained the selfist orientation of the times. Ballou (1995) concurs that the human potential movement accounted for the surge in popularity that self-help books experienced during this period. Progressing into the 1980s, the self-help movement continued to boom. Perhaps a return to "rugged individualism," which Thoresen and Powell (1992) define as "a kind of fiercely autonomous, self-indulgent, and sometimes narcissistic perspective guided by economic, political, and social self-interest" (p. 597), fueled this movement. Brownell (1991) suggests that as governments become more conservative, social programs are weakened, underscoring "the view that personal behavior, not social problems, are the root of many personal problems" (p. 304). With a conservative government largely in place since the 1980s, the obligation for improvement continues to rest on the shoulders of individuals who have turned to the self-help industry in droves. Simonds (1992) agrees that Americans have indeed become increasingly self-involved—and that self-help books have spurred this rejuvenation of the long-held American ideology of personal control.

Marrs (1995) declares that the United States has become an increasingly self-help oriented society, and Seligman (1994) expresses amazement at the numerous qualities that Americans believe they can change. As illustration, he lists dozens of topics that populate the self-improvement literature—assertiveness, weight control, time management, stress management, anxiety reduction, to name just a few. Like self-help consumers today, the early settlers believed that, through individual effort, one could reap whatever rewards were desired. Initially, the rewards were spiritual in nature, and the first American self-help books of the 1600s reflected these goals. Starker (1989) lists titles such as *The Practice of Piety* and *Guide to Heaven* as exemplars of these texts. In the next century, self-help books grew more secular, now containing advice for achieving wealth, social status, and health. In the early 1900s, the emerging fields of psychology and psychiatry pervaded American culture. As such, self-help books became directed toward resolution of interpersonal and psychological conflicts. Over time, self-help books on general emotional health have given way to those addressing a wide array of problems, often defined more specifically in terms of particular behaviors or disorders as Seligman describes. Rosen, Glasgow, and Moore (2003) agree that this trend toward greater specificity, along with newly developed modalities for delivery, helps explains how the self-help industry has evolved into such big business.

Women and Self-Help

In recounting the evolution of self-help in the United States, we would be remiss if we did not address women's place in this *herstory*. Grodin (1991, 1995) reports that, in contemporary society, women are much more likely than men to avail themselves of self-help resources. It should be noted that she speaks primarily of bibliotherapy rather than computer-based self-help. Grodin further asserts that much of today's self-help literature explicitly targets a female audience. DeFrancisco (1995) concurs that "Anyone visiting a bookstore can see that women are the intended readers of this literature" (p. 107). Both Ebben (1995) and Rapping (1996) proclaim that women constitute approximately 80% of the self-help readership. Rapping identifies the many subgroups of women—young mothers, working women, women survivors of abuse, women in menopause, grieving women, women with addictions, women in bad marriages—who are currently targeted for sales of self-help books. Perini and Bayer (1996) suggest that women have gradually assimilated the masculine canon of rugged individualism. As such, they represent a prime audience for the marketing of self-help books.

The first self-help books developed for a female audience were guides on midwifery and childrearing, making their appearance in the early 1800s. Though intended for women, most of these manuals were written by male physicians (Rosenberg, 2003). This trend continued into the 1900s, with Benjamin Spock's (1946, 1968) *Common Sense Book of Baby and Child Care*, perhaps the most popular such guide of all time. The 1800s also saw another type of self-help publication aimed toward women. These guides contained advice concerning relations between the sexes, focusing on issues such as contraception and (the perils of) masturbation. Self-help guides for women's health were also common at this time (Rosenberg, 2003). Starker (1989) lists the following titles, both authored by men, as typifying women's self-help publications during this era: *Ladies Guide in Health and Disease: Girlhood, Maidenhood, Wifehood, Motherhood* and *Chastity: Its Physical, Intellectual and Moral Advantages*.

Decades later, ongoing dissatisfaction with male dictates regarding physical and emotional health gave way to the women's self-help movement of the 1960s. Many women deemed traditional care to be paternalistic, judgmental, misleading, and uninformative. Furthermore, these women saw health care as being bound up in patriarchal concepts of female beauty and sexuality (Dresser, 1996). Arising from this movement was one of the most well-known self-help books of all time, written by women for women. A group of women known as the Boston Women's Health Collective saw the first publication of *Our Bodies, Ourselves* in 1973. This text is now in its eighth edition, published in 2005. It is a comprehensive collection of knowledge and advice, its latest iteration containing 32 chapters that cover health habits, relationships and sexuality, sexual health, reproductive choices, child-bearing, aging, medical problems and procedures, and negotiation of the health care system. The intent of this movement in general, and this book in particular, was to empower women, making them more informed and assertive participants in the maintenance of their health. In fact, the self-help movement of this era viewed the individual, rather than the practitioner, as key to health care.

Although the self-help movement of the 1960s and 1970s viewed the individual as "expert," "resource to self and others," and "decision-maker," the current self-help movement has seen a return to the traditional model of health care (Garvin et al., 2001). Today's self-help purveyors are typically authorities who identify problems as residing within the individual and who subsequently offer mandates for desired outcomes. Within this current structure of self-help, there are two topics that women access with regularity. Perini and Bayer (1996) highlight women's abundant use of resources on diet, fitness, and weight loss. Meanwhile, many researchers (e.g., McLellan, 1995; Rapping, 1996; Simonds, 1992) note that women frequently partake of materials focusing on interpersonal relationships—what some refer to as the codependency literature. These self-help trends among women are not without their attendant critiques, which will be addressed in a subsequent section.

Advantages of Self-Help

Cost Benefits

Cost containment might be the most salient advantage of media-based self-help therapies—and the most long-lived reason for developing such interventions. A historical account proffers that a medical self-help book of 17th-century Europe was written expressly to aid indigent people who could not afford physicians' fees (Ring, 2004). Indeed, Rosenberg (2003) highlights the inexpensiveness of the self-help materials brought to America by English settlers, noting that these could help individuals bypass physicians' costly interventions. Alleviating costs associated with health care appears to be the leading rationale behind self-help treatments today. In a special issue of the *Journal of Clinical Psychology* devoted to self-help, Mains and Scoggins (2003) lament the billions of dollars spent on mental health care alone in the United States. They note that geographical and financial access to treatment is a barrier for many who suffer from psychological disorders. As such, a priority lies in finding effective treatments that are cost efficient. Similarly, Den Boer et al. (2004) ask in the title of their recent article, "Why is self-help neglected in the treatment of emotional disorders?" (p. 959). They, too, cite the exorbitant costs of treating depression and anxiety disorders. Watkins and Lee (1997) note that the majority of anxiety sufferers are women who typically earn less than men and who are less likely to have insurance coverage. Therefore, they promote bibliotherapy as a financially viable means of treating these disorders, especially for women who cannot afford conventional care.

In this age of managed care, interest in self-help programs has risen to the fore. Marrs (1995) asserts that self-help is "pertinent to the country's current struggle with health care costs and delivery systems" (p. 845). Pantalon (1998) recognizes that managed care places limits on the availability of psychotherapy sessions. In a similar vein, Den Boer et al. (2004) stress that the existing health care system lacks the resources for attending to the scores of individuals with emotional disorders. Such is the case in Britain as well (Gega, Kenwright, Mataix-Cols, Cameron, & Marks, 2005; Williams, 2004). Gega et al. note that the majority of people with anxiety and depression are left untreated because the demand for cognitive–behavior therapy delivered in the traditional manner far exceeds its supply. Therefore, they promote the use of computer-based self-help for these problems, along with the use of screening devices to determine which clients may be best suited to this alternative delivery mode.

Given the constraints of the current health care system, psychologists (e.g., Hayes, Barlow, & Nelson-Gray, 1999) have proposed a stepped-care approach to treatment. The stepped-care model is intended to "maximize the effectiveness and efficiency of decisions about allocation of resources in therapy" (Hagga, 2000, p. 547). In this model, clients are first met with the least intrusive, least costly intervention deemed to be effective for their circumstance. If the initial intervention proves ineffective, clients then receive a more intensive version of the intervention. This continues until the client is matched with the level of intervention that most effectively treats her or his presenting complaint.

This stepped-care model dovetails nicely with Glasgow and Rosen's 1978 description of levels of therapeutic contact. For instance, a number of clinical needs might be satisfied by self-administered therapies—books, audio/videotapes, or computer programs that do not require the actual presence of a professional in order to be effective. Mains and Scoggins

(2003) suggest that such self-administered treatments might save time and money for people with relatively mild symptoms who might otherwise (and unnecessarily) undergo more rigorous treatment attempts. At the next step, these resources might be supplemented by minimal contact, in which a professional or paraprofessional introduces the material and maintains contact with the client to ensure proper implementation of the intervention. If clients require more intensive contact with practitioners, then the intervention might be therapist administered, with self-help materials serving as an adjunct to traditional psychotherapy. Thus, self-help programs may have an impact at several levels in a stepped-care model.

In addition, media-based self-help interventions may help maintain treatment gains because clients can readily reaccess intervention strategies at later points in time. Pantalon (1998) suggests telling clients at the outset that the materials may be used in this way, that "learning does not end by the time he or she finishes reading the book" (p. 273). Starker (1989) likens bibliotherapy to having a clinic in every home, which is then easily accessible for repeat visits. Watkins (1999) provides evidence that panic sufferers in this case study used a self-help book in this manner. Here, participants verbalized that they had reexamined intervention strategies in the months following the formal treatment phase. In addition, their self-monitoring and questionnaire data showed maintenance of treatment gains, and in some cases continued improvement, throughout a one-year follow-up period.

Psychological Benefits

Enhanced self-efficacy, the belief in one's own ability to accomplish a task, is considered one of the main psychological benefits of self-help interventions. Pantalon (1998) suggests that self-efficacy increases as clients come to realize that they, rather than a therapist, are responsible for improvements in their condition. Marks (1994) concurs that skill acquisition via self-care can have an empowering effect. Black and Scott (1998) contend that women especially feel empowered and efficacious through the use of self-help interventions. Rogers et al. (2004) cite self-efficacy as a potential mechanism of change in self-help interventions. However, they note a relative lack of research regarding this construct in the self-help arena. In their own study, they interviewed individuals accessing a self-help clinic. The majority of their participants experienced the self-help clinic in a positive way, with many making comments that suggested enhanced self-efficacy compared to pharmacological or therapist-directed treatment. One participant verbalized that "medication masks it, it just numbs you. I think cognitive therapy enables you to identify problems, it doesn't mask it, you can meet the problem, deal with it in such a way that you know why it happened, but you can deal with it, so I much prefer it" (Rogers et al., 2004, p. 44). While such qualitative data are certainly illuminating, some quantitative data also support increased self-efficacy as a function of self-help interventions. Clum and colleagues have developed a self-efficacy questionnaire specific to panic disorder and have noted improvements in this construct as a function of self-help interventions (e.g., Lidren et al., 1994).

Universality, the sense that one is not alone in experiencing a problem, appears to be another psychological benefit of media-based self-help. As Ballou (1995) phrases it:

> Identification with one another (or characters in a story) is a powerful force that can help people cope with the difficulties of life. Just to know that one is not alone in facing adversity can be a comforting thought, even if those with whom the common problem is shared are characters in a book. (p. 58)

Ballou contends that this sense of universality leads to self-acceptance and the sense that one's own problems can be effectively dealt with. In their qualitative studies, Lictherman (1992) and Grodin (1991) provide ample case examples that self-help readers feel a connection with similar others, which may help explain the salutary effects of the materials. Similarly, Simonds (1992) analyzed readers' letters to self-help authors Robin Norwood and Betty Friedan, concluding that their books helped decrease feelings of loneliness and isolation: "Just having her own dilemma there in print, simply having a label to fit on the problem she was experiencing, felt empowering, could make formerly insurmountable problems seem less formidable to a reader" (p. 85).

A final psychological benefit of self-help interventions to be discussed here entails decreases in anxiety and other negative emotions surrounding traditional approaches to care. For instance, the availability of self-help programs may reduce the stigma of seeing a therapist (Garvin et al., 2001; Mains & Scoggin, 2003). Individuals who feel alienated with the current health care system may also find solace in self-help approaches. Watkins and Whaley (2000) suggest that women in particular experience dissatisfaction with the health care system and, therefore, suggest self-help as a potential means of circumventing these negative encounters. Historically, Rosenberg (2003) speaks of self-help as a means of bypassing physicians' deleterious prescriptions. Contemporary treatments may not bear the same risk of those prescribed in the 1800s. Nevertheless, some individuals may still eschew medications due to fear of dependence or unsavory side effects. Thus, the availability of self-help interventions may eliminate these concerns.

Limitations of Self-Help

In a vast understatement, Ballou (1995) remarks that "Self-help materials vary dramatically in quality when considering vital attributes such as thoroughness, knowledge of psychology, and responsibility to the reader" (p. 56). Perhaps the biggest criticism of the self-help genre is that very few of these materials have been subjected to research and shown to be empirically valid. Starker (1989) notes that, unlike pharmacological treatments, self-help books are totally unregulated. Thus, these untested interventions are disseminated to the public with little or no understanding of their effects. Pantalon (1998) adds that the best-selling self-help books are *not* the ones that have undergone scientific evaluation. The lack of empirical evaluation of self-help materials is, in fact, the impetus for this text. The following sections elaborate upon other, related limitations of self-help therapies.

Capitalistic Versus Therapeutic Motives

Long-time investigators in the field of self-help (e.g., Rosen et al., 2003) contend that professional standards have taken a backseat to commercialization factors in marketing self-help products. Thus, the sale of these materials has become the overriding concern, more so than the actual effectiveness of the products (Pantalon, 1998). Aggressive advertising seems to be the key to boosting sales, and scholars are concerned that such advertising contains false and/or exaggerated claims of success. Simonds (1992, p. 119) writes that at times, "Authors statements are so ambitious they sound as if foolproof plans for achieving a state of perfection and bliss will be revealed." Rapping (1996) suggests that in this era of consumerism, self-help books often profess a cult-like certainty about their effects. Based on interview data, Simonds (1992) found that editors often seek self-help books that merely *sound* authoritative, and one editor admitted that self-help books may be deceptive regarding promises of cures. Furthermore, if a number of authors are writing on the same topic, an editor would likely select the one who would be most presentable on television.

Wilson (2003) is particularly critical of the writing and sanctioning of self-help books by celebrities who lack training in the subjects of which they speak. She cites the popularity of Dr. Phil's self-help books, promoted by Oprah Winfrey, as one example, noting that "Legitimate professionals do not make public claims about instant cures or unfailing success" (p. 433). Rapping (1996) laments that books written by uninformed celebrities frequently have greater credibility than those authored by learned professionals.

Apart from presenting overstated claims of effectiveness, self-help advertising is also geared to trigger a sense of inadequacy among potential consumers

(Wilson, 2003). As Greenberg (1994) notes, the only thing standing between the flawed self and its fulfillment is a product that is conveniently available for a certain price. He charges the self-help industry with an abuse of power in that unethical psychotherapists prey upon individuals' despair, prompting them to spend money on techniques of dubious quality. In the end, the self has become an object to be commodified for capitalistic gain.

Submission to Authority versus Self-Efficacy

As noted earlier, the women's self-help movement was born in response to distrust of and dissatisfaction with patriarchal health care institutions. By taking health matters into their own hands, individuals are meant to feel efficacious and empowered. Over the last 40 years, however, this ideal of self-help has changed so that individuals, mostly women, once again find themselves submitting to the authority of an (usually male) expert. Polivy and Herman (2002) state "There is fine irony in the notion that following prescriptions of others constitutes self-help" (p. 678). Greenberg (1994) agrees that the work has already been done by the authority, thus the individual simply consumes the material presented. As with Dorothy in the *Wizard of Oz*, Simonds (1992) says that self-hood is discovered only by means of experts' insights.

Ebben (1995) explains that the current self-help movement draws upon and reproduces medical—as well as religious—conventions. Regarding the latter, Rapping (1996) sardonically suggests that distressed individuals need only turn to God and self-help for relief. Thus, the recent promulgation of self-help products once again expands the power of the expert authority. Garvin et al. (2001) agree that self-help in the 21st century has seen a return to the traditional hierarchy between professional and patient. This is the case even with respect to cognitive–behavioral self-help programs, exemplified by the eating disorder interventions that they review.

Despite this possibility, Ebben (1995) advances the argument that self-help readers may interpret the material in ways that actually *challenge* the author's authority. Grodin (1995) concurs, noting that participants in her qualitative study rarely read books in their entirety—a pattern that, in her estimation, indicated a resistance to the text's authority. Grodin also found that readers generally had low expectations about the utility of self-help books and did not expect them to provide simple solutions to complex problems. Similarly, Simonds (1996) found that the self-help consumers she interviewed "do not merely uncritically, unthinkingly slurp up what they find within its pages" (p. 26). She asserts that, just because consumers may trust in an authority in one instance does not mean that they are gullible or uniformly uncritical. Thus, what happens in actual practice may diverge from the criticisms that professionals put forth.

Self-Harm versus Self-Help

Regrettably, scant research exists on the appropriate selection and implementation of self-help materials (Pantalon, 1998). This circumstance gives rise to the concern that consumers may incur harm through misdiagnosis and misuse of these products. Diagnostically, Greenberg (1994) points to the codependence literature, largely targeted toward women, as having such a broad definition that most readers are likely to meet these criteria. He states that one book even claims a 98% "infection rate" for codependence. One problem with this overly inclusive set of diagnostic indicators is that it implies that all women are, in some way, codependent.

In a similar vein, Wilson (2003) notes that the self-help literature has the tendency to overlook power differences between women and their male partners. As such, therapeutic edicts, for instance in the case of domestic violence, may be harmful if enacted outside of a professional context of support. Ballou (1995) agrees that consumers' reactions to self-help material must be carefully monitored by a trained therapist. She suggests that misinterpretation of information can exacerbate symptoms, especially among socially withdrawn and depressive individuals. She also suggests that false expectations and countereffective role models presented in the material may act to reinforce problems. Lichterman (1992) reports that a participant in his qualitative study became depressed in response to self-help reading because she was ill equipped to deal with the issues that it raised. Starker (1989) indicates that researchers have paid little attention to the reactions of self-help users—especially potentially negative reactions. He relays the results from a now dated survey of psychologists, psychiatrists, and internists regarding their perception of patients' self-help use. Respondents cited benefits associated with this form of intervention more often than problems. However, respondents across all three professions did note that some patients had experienced harm as a result of their self-help reading. Starker writes that a psychiatrist "reported one suicide, and two attempts at suicide, which he explained as follows, 'Depressive patients unable to measure up to magical expectations of self-help'" (p. 155).

Individual versus Sociocultural Focus

Perhaps it is no wonder that those who partake of self-help therapies find themselves unable to adequately resolve their problems or rid themselves of their distress when these interventions, by definition, target the individual apart from the environment that gave rise to their concerns. These programs do not talk about altering social conditions; rather, they deal with altering the individual who suffers from them (Perini & Bayer, 1996).

They instruct readers how to change their lives largely through individual effort and, in doing so, "are an all too popular distraction from a good sociological imagination" (Lichterman, 1992, p. 422). Grodin (1991) cites this as the most frequent feminist critique of the self-help genre—that it is exclusively personal rather than political or cultural in nature. Ballou (1995) adds that "The attention to the surrounding systems as well as their impact on the individual is precisely the focus of feminist psychology" (p. 64). She notes that this is a pitfall with psychotherapy in general, but more so with *self*-help therapy. Mainstream psychologists share these same concerns. Rosen et al. (2003) note that self-help interventions inevitably neglect the sociocultural context in which disorders develop. Seligman (1994) comments that the social sciences were founded on the notion that environments could be changed to alleviate the strife of individual members. However, in this modern age of personal control, individuals are expected to "lift themselves by their own bootstraps" (p. 27).

Feminist writers may have extended the individual versus sociocultural critique by highlighting the terminology of personal blame that the self-help genre engenders. Rapping (1996) illustrates this pattern, noting that self-help books often implore individuals to "get one's life in order," overlooking the fact that "life will still be lived in a context of social reality which therapy, alone, does not address" (p. 165). Greenberg (1994) points to the codependence literature as a prime example of victim-blaming because it basically pathologizes the socially constructed roles of women. Ebben (1995) states that "Expanding conceptions of codependency functions to substitute a critique of gender structures for a critique of the individual" (p. 115). Indeed, as Simonds (1992) recounts, one reader of the codependence classic, *Women Who Love Too Much*, protested, why not a book about men who love too little?! Simonds recognizes that Norwood's book might encourage readers to disregard the injustice of their situation and hold themselves solely culpable for their distress.

Women are particularly susceptible to this tendency to blame the victim given their lack of power and status in society relative to men, asserts McClellan (1995). In her words, "Blame the oppressed for being oppressed and also for their inability to rise above the oppression" (p. 107). She concludes that accepting total responsibility is a heavy burden for those whose traumatic experiences are truly the result of oppression. In concert, Ebben (1995) remarks that individuals, not social institutions with their disparate structures of power and privilege, bear the brunt of criticism and the responsibility for change. Rapping (1996) argues that self-esteem cannot be cultivated in a social vacuum, although self-help books imply that it can develop regardless of one's life's circumstances. Simonds (1996) counters that feminist scholars bell hooks and Gloria Steinem both view self-esteem as a necessary foundation for social change. Nevertheless, Simonds (1992) herself maintains that self-help interventions provide only temporary respite from symptoms and simply an "illusory cure for what ails us, collectively as a culture" (p. 227). Most importantly, they distract from genuine efforts to challenge and change societal institutions. "To change what is objectionable about our culture, we must do more than revamp ourselves" (Simonds, 1996, p. 27).

Taking these words to heart, Yeater and colleagues (Yeater, Naugle, O'Donohue, & Bradley, 2004) explain that the title of their self-help book aiming to prevent sexual assault, *Dating 101: A Practical Guide for Improving Your Relationships With Men*, is in no way intended to blame women for being victimized. The authors make clear that the ultimate goal for society is to "eliminate men's potential to engage in sexually coercive behavior" (p. 610). Since publication of their study, Katz (2006) has released a book, *The Macho Paradox: Why Some Men Hurt Women and How All Men Can Help*, which calls for male responsibility and widespread cultural change to eradicate violence against women. However, until this lofty goal is accomplished, materials such as these are meant to imbue women with requisite skills to keep them safe in the interim. Yeater et al. are to be lauded for empirically assessing this program, finding that bibliotherapy participants reported engaging in fewer risky behaviors and better sexual communication strategies than participants in a waiting-list control condition. Furthermore, participants rated the materials as highly palatable, suggesting future usage.

Summary

This chapter began with an explication of the question "What is self-help?" In doing so, it attempted to integrate elements of various and varying definitions in order to come to a common understanding of the term. Next it revealed that the process of self-help is rarely, if ever, conducted in isolation. As Grodin (1991) explains, self-help is a relatively private act that paradoxically places users in contact with others. Although current research has begun to examine the practitioner's role in the efficacy of self-help interventions, research on the impact of others beyond the professional setting awaits further investigation.

The chapter then explores the origins of self-help in the United States, tracing them to the 1600s. It also examines this genre's increasing popularity over the centuries, attributing this to innovations such as mass production techniques and computer technology. It also ascribes today's glut of self-help products to an increased emphasis on consumerism coupled with more sophisticated marketing strategies. Most saliently, however, it explains that self-help programs are the tangible extension of this country's increasing quest for individualism. In reviewing the history of self-help, the chapter highlights gender differences in both production and usage, with men largely the creators of these materials and women largely the consumers.

The chapter subsequently addresses possible benefits and limitations of self-help interventions. It reviews both practical (e.g., reduced cost) and psychological (e.g., reduced stigmatization) advantages. Greater attention is, however, paid to possible problems associated with self-help programs. Because the consumption of self-help products by far outstrips empirical evidence of their worth, scholars fear that users will succumb to ill effects, blame themselves, or develop a dependence on authorities to resolve their difficulties. Unscrupulous advertising may create or perpetuate these problems. A counterargument to these concerns lies in qualitative studies that found that many who engage with self-help are active, critical consumers rather than passive, credulous recipients. The extent to which the benefits and limitations highlighted here actually exist ultimately remains an empirical question. Finally, the chapter elucidates the inherent drawback of self-help in that it does not offer a solution for changing sociocultural conditions that may have contributed to and support individuals' distress. This, however, is *not* cause to ignore or discard self-help interventions. Rather, researchers should continue to develop empirically informed self-help techniques, scientifically examining their utility, at the same time that broader solutions are sought.

Chapter Points

- Media-based self-help should be distinguished from self-help groups, the former of which is a more recent development that has received less attention in the empirical literature.
- Bibliotherapy is the primary means of media-based self-help, although computer-based approaches are on the rise. Many forms of bibliotherapy exist, but problem-focused approaches that prescribe cognitive–behavioral techniques have received the most empirical attention.
- Self-help materials may be less efficacious when consumed in isolation from others (e.g., therapists, family members, etc.).
- Self-help therapies arrived in America with the first settlers and proliferated, in large part, due to the ideology that persons can improve their circumstances through individual effort; i.e., the notion that one can pull one's self up by one's own bootstraps.
- Women are the primary consumers of self-help products, particularly in the areas of relationship enhancement and diet/weight loss.

- Benefits of self-help programs may include cost effectiveness, especially as they lend themselves to a stepped-care approach to therapy. Self-help programs may also enhance consumers' self-efficacy and reduce the stigma associated with seeking formal treatment.
- Drawbacks of self-help programs may include the marketing of materials with no sound empirical basis, with many programs touting exaggerated claims of effectiveness. Some programs may be ineffective or actually cause harm to the consumer. When programs are ineffective, consumers often blame themselves for failure.
- Self-help programs are limited in their effectiveness to the extent that the sociocultural environment contributes to and maintains the problem in question. Thus, self-help therapies might best be viewed as one of many ways of addressing complex problems. They have great potential as individual interventions but should not serve as substitutes to necessary changes in the broader environment.

References

Adams, S. J., & Pitre, N. L. (2000). Who uses bibliotherapy and why? A survey from an underserviced area. *Canadian Journal of Psychiatry, 45,* 645–650.

Anderson, L., Lewis, G., Araya, R., Elgie, R., Harrison, G., Proudfoot, J., et al. (2005). Self-help books for depression: How can practitioners and patients make the right choice? *British Journal of General Practice, 55,* 387–392.

Ballou, M. (1995). Bibliotherapy. In M. Ballou (Ed.), *Psychological interventions: A guide to strategies* (pp. 55–65), Westport, CT: Praeger.

Benson, H. (1975). *The relaxation response.* New York: Avon.

Black, D. R., & Scott, L. A. (1998). Self-administered interventions. In E. A. Blechman & K. D. Brownell (Eds.), *Behavioral medicine and women: A comprehensive handbook* (pp. 333–342). New York: Guilford.

Boston Women's Health Book Collective (2005). *Our bodies, ourselves: A new edition for a new era.* New York: Simon & Schuster.

Brehony, K. A. (1996). *Awakening at midlife: A guide to reviving your spirit, recreating your life, and returning to your truest self.* New York: Penguin.

Brownell, K. D. (1991). Personal responsibility and control over our bodies: When expectation exceeds reality. *Health Psychology, 10,* 303–310.

Campbell, L. F., & Smith, T. P. (2003). Integrating self-help books into psychotherapy. *Journal of Clinical Psychology/In Session: Psychotherapy in Practice, 59,* 177–186.

Clum, G. A. (1990). *Coping with panic: A drug free approach to dealing with panic attacks.* Pacific Grove, CA: Brookes-Cole.

Cushman, P. (1995). *Constructing the self, constructing America: A cultural history of psychotherapy.* Reading, MA: Addison-Wesley.

DeFrancisco, V. L. (1995). Helping our selves: An introduction. *Women's Studies in Communication, 18,* 107–110.

Den Boer, P. C. A. M., Wiersma, D., & Van Den Bosch, R. J. (2004). Why is self-help neglected in the treatment of emotional disorders? A meta-analysis. *Psychological Medicine, 34*, 959–971.

Dresser, R. (1996). What bioethics can learn from the women's health movement. In S. M. Wolfe (Ed.), *Feminism and bioethics: Beyond reproduction* (pp. 144–159). New York: Oxford University Press.

Ebben, M. (1995). Off the shelf salvation: A feminist critique of self-help. *Women's Studies in Communication, 18*, 111–121.

Garvin, V., Striegel-Moore, R. H., Kaplan, A., & Wonderlich, S. A. (2001). The potential of professionally developed self-help interventions for the treatment of eating disorders. In R. H. Striegel-Moore & L. Smolak (Eds.), *Eating disorders: Innovative directions in research and practice* (pp. 153–172). Washington, DC: American Psychological Association.

Gega, L., Kenwright, M., Mataix-Cols, D., Cameron, R., & Marks, I. M. (2005). Screening people with anxiety and depression for suitability for guided self-help. *Cognitive Behaviour Therapy, 34*, 16–21.

Glasgow, R. E., & Rosen, G. M. (1978). Behavioral bibliotherapy: A review of self-help behavior therapy manuals. *Psychological Bulletin, 85*, 1–23.

Gould, R. A., & Clum, G. A. (1993). A meta-analysis of self-help treatment approaches. *Clinical Psychology Review, 13*, 169–186.

Greenberg, G. (1994). *The self on the shelf: Recovery books and the good life*. Albany: State University of New York Press.

Grodin, D. (1991). The interpretive audience: The therapeutics of self-help book reading. *Critical Studies in Mass Communication, 8*, 404–420.

Grodin, D. (1995). Women reading self-help: Themes of separation and connection. *Women's Studies in Communication, 18*, 123–134.

Hagga, D. A. F. (2000). Introduction to the special section on stepped care models in psychotherapy. *Journal of Consulting and Clinical Psychology, 68*, 547–548.

Hayes, S. C., Barlow, D. H., & Nelson-Gray, R. O. (1999). *The scientist-practitioner: Research and accountability in the age of managed care*. Boston: Allyn & Bacon.

Johnson, B. W., Johnson, W. L., & Hillman, C. (1997). Toward guidelines for the development, evaluation, and utilization of Christian self-help materials. *Journal of Psychology and Theology, 25*, 341–353.

Katz, J. (2006). *The macho paradox: Why some men hurt women and how all men can help*. Naperville, IL: Sourcebooks.

Kurtz, L. F. (1997). *Self-help and support groups: A handbook for practitioners*. Thousand Oaks, CA: Sage.

Lehane, M. (2005). Treatment by the book. *Nursing Standard, 19*, 24.

Lichterman, P. (1992). Self-help reading as a thin culture. *Media, Culture, and Society, 14*, 431–447.

Lidren, D. M., Watkins, P. L., Gould, R. A., Clum, G. A., Asterino, M., & Tulloch, H. L. (1994). A comparison of bibliotherapy and group therapy in the treatment of panic disorder. *Journal of Consulting and Clinical Psychology, 62*, 865–869.

Mains, J. A., & Scoggins, F. R. (2003). The effectiveness of self-administered treatments: A practice friendly review of the research. *Journal of Clinical Psychology/In Session: Psychotherapy in Practice, 59*, 237–246.

Marks, I. M. (1994). Behavior therapy as an aid to self-care. *Current Directions in Psychological Science, 3*, 19–22.

Marrs, R. W. (1995). A meta-analysis of bibliotherapy studies. *American Journal of Community Psychology, 23*, 843–870.

McLellan, B. (1995). *Beyond psychoppression: A feminist alternative therapy.* North Melbourne, Australia: Spinifex.

Newman, M. G., Erickson, T., Przeworski, A., & Dzus, E. (2003). Self-help and minimal contact therapies for anxiety disorders: Is human contact necessary for therapeutic efficacy? *Journal of Clinical Psychology/In Session: Psychotherapy in Practice, 59*, 251–274.

Norwood, R. (1985). *Women who love too much.* New York: Putnam Berkeley Group.

Pantalon, M. V. (1998). Use of self-help books in the practice of clinical psychology. In A. S. Bellack & M. Hersen (Series Eds.) & P. Salkovskis (Vol. Ed.), *Comprehensive clinical psychology: Vol. 6. Adults: Clinical formulation and treatment* (pp. 265–276). New York: Elsevier Science.

Perini, G. M., & Bayer, B. M. (1996). Out of our minds, in our bodies: Women's embodied subjectivity and self-help culture. In C. W. Tolman & F. Cherry (Eds.), *Problems of theoretical psychology* (pp. 291–303). North York, England: Captus Press.

Polivy, J., & Herman, C. P. (2002). If at first you don't succeed: False hopes of self-change. *The American Psychologist, 57*, 677–689.

Powell, T. J. (1994). *Understanding the self-help organization: Frameworks and findings.* Thousand Oaks, CA: Sage.

Quinn, D. M., & Crocker, J. (1999). When ideology hurts: Effects of belief in the Protestant ethic and feeling overweight on the psychological well-being of women. *Journal of Personality and Social Psychology, 77*, 403–414.

Rapping, E. (1996). *The culture of recovery: Making sense of the self-help movement in women's lives.* Boston: Beacon Press.

Riessman, F., & Carroll, D. (1995). *Redefining self-help: Policy and practice.* San Francisco: Jossey-Bass.

Ring, M. E. (2004). Dental writings in a medical self-help book of 1650. *Journal of the History of Dentistry, 52*, 125–129.

Riordan, R. J., Mullis, F., & Nuchow, L. (1996). Organizing for bibliotherapy: The science in the art. *Individual Psychology: Journal of Adlerian Theory, Research, and Practice, 52*, 169–180.

Rogers, A., Oliver, D., Bower, P., Lovell, K., & Richards, D. (2004). People's understanding of a primary care-based mental health self-help clinic. *Patient Education and Counseling, 53*, 41–46.

Rosen, G. M., Glasgow, R. E., & Moore, T. E. (2003). Self-help therapy: The science and business of giving psychology away. In S. O. Lilienfeld, S. J. Lynn, & J. M. Lohr (Eds.), *Science and pseudoscience in clinical psychology* (pp. 399–424). New York: Guilford.

Rosenberg, C. E. (2003). Health in the home: A tradition of print and practice. In C. E. Rosenberg (Ed.), *Right living: An Anglo-American tradition of self-help medicine and hygiene* (pp. 1–20). Baltimore: The Johns Hopkins University Press.

Seligman, M. E. P. (1994). *What you can change and what you can't: The complete guide to successful self-improvement.* New York: Knopf.

Simonds, W. (1992). *Women and self-help culture: Reading between the lines.* New Brunswick, NJ: Rutgers University Press.

Simonds, W. (1996). All consuming selves: Self-help literature and women's identities. In D. Grodin & T. R. Lindlof (Eds.), *Constructing the self in a mediated world* (pp. 15–29). Thousand Oaks, CA: Sage.

Sommer, R. (2003). The use of autobiography in psychotherapy. *Journal of Clinical Psychology/In Session: Psychotherapy in Practice, 59*, 197–205.

Spock, B. (1946). *Common sense book of baby and child care.* New York: Duell, Sloan, & Pearce.

Spock, B. (1968). *Common sense book of baby and child care.* New York: Meredith Press.

Starker, S. (1989). *Oracle at the supermarket.* New Brunswick, NJ: Transaction Publishers.

Tate, D. F., & Zabinski, M. F. (2004). Computer and internet applications for psychological treatment: Update for clinicians. *Journal of Clinical Psychology/In Session, 60*, 209–220.

Thoresen, C. E., & Powell, L. H. (1992). Type A behavior: New perspectives on theory, assessment, and intervention. *Journal of Consulting and Clinical Psychology, 60*, 595–604.

Watkins, P. L. (1999). Manualized treatment of panic disorder in a medical setting: Two illustrative case studies. *Journal of Clinical Psychology in Medical Settings, 6*, 353–372.

Watkins, P. L., & Lee, J. (1997). A feminist perspective on panic disorder and agoraphobia: Etiology and treatment. *Journal of Gender, Culture, & Health, 2*, 65–87.

Watkins, P. L., & Whaley, D. (2000). Gender role stressors and women's health. In R. M. Eisler & M. Hersen (Eds.), *Handbook of gender, culture, and health* (pp. 43–62). Mahwah, NJ: Lawrence Erlbaum.

Williams, C. J. (2004). Self-help models in cognitive behavioural therapy. *The Practitioner, 248*, 421–424.

Wilson, N. (2003). Commercializing mental health issues: Entertainment, advertising, and psychological advice. In S. O. Lilienfeld, S. J. Lynn, & J. M. Lohr (Eds.), *Science and pseudoscience in clinical psychology* (pp. 425–459). New York: Guilford.

Yeater, E. A., Naugle, A. E., O'Donohue, W., & Bradley, A. R. (2004). Sexual assault prevention with college-aged women: A bibliotherapy approach. *Violence and Victims, 19*, 593–612.

CHAPTER 2

Good Intentions Are Not Enough

Reflections on Past and Future
Efforts to Advance Self-Help

GERALD M. ROSEN, MANUEL BARRERA, JR.
AND RUSSELL E. GLASGOW

In recent years, the American Psychological Association revised its *Ethical Principles of Psychologists and Code of Conduct* (APA, 2002). The document begins with this general statement:

> Psychologists are committed to increasing scientific and professional knowledge of behavior and people's understanding of themselves and others and to the use of such knowledge to improve the condition of individuals, organizations, and society. (p. 1062)

Upon reading this introduction, one might think there was no better way to accomplish the ideals of psychology and allied health fields than to develop self-help programs: self-administered treatment programs in the form of books, tapes, and other media that help consumers change problematic behaviors and psychological conditions. As observed by Rosen (1982):

> Psychologists are in a unique position to contribute to the self-help movement. No other professional group combines the clinical and research experiences that are part of the clinical psychologist's educational background. Clinical psychologists are skilled in current therapeutic techniques, they have clinical experience and sensitivity, and they have the training to assess empirically the efficacy of

the programs they develop. Consequently, clinical psychologists are in a position to assess empirically, and thereby distinguish, their self-help programs from previous, untested books of advice. This would represent a most significant and new development in the area of self-help approaches to self-management. (p. 185)

The notion that psychologists and allied health professionals can use their skills to advance self-help calls to mind a past president of the American Psychological Association, who encouraged psychologists, more than 30 years ago, to "give psychology away" (Miller, 1969, p. 1074). Miller employed this phrase at his 1969 presidential address and further stated that psychology's *major social responsibility* was to learn how to help people help themselves.

Miller's urgings helped spur a "revolution" in the 1970s, if by that term we mean a fundamental change in our ways of thinking. This was a time when psychologists had unprecedented involvement in the development, assessment, and marketing of self-help materials. During the 1970s, leading academic psychologists translated their knowledge on clinic-based programs to "do-it-yourself" treatment books. Some of these programs were then tested under totally self-administered or minimal-therapist conditions (see reviews by Glasgow & Rosen, 1978, 1982). A number of studies included controlled comparisons with therapist-administered, no treatment, or even placebo conditions. These studies provided important information on the effectiveness and limits of self-help materials and suggested directions to make future self-help programs more effective.

The 1970s started as a decade of excitement and promise in the field of self-help but ended with the realization that giving psychology away was more complicated than early investigators had thought. Unbridled enthusiasm was tempered by reality, when research demonstrated that not all self-help programs promote the public's welfare.

Lessons Learned

In the 1970s, the foremost instructional modality for self-administering treatments was the self-help book. Glasgow and Rosen (1978, 1982) reviewed over 100 studies and case reports from the 1970s that evaluated behaviorally oriented self-help instructional materials. This impressive body of research generally supported the use of do-it-yourself treatments. Research findings also highlighted the multiple, cost-effective benefits of self-instructional programs. At the same time, a number of sobering findings emerged. For example, Matson and Ollendick (1977) had parents toilet train their children using the self-help book, *Toilet Training in Less Than a Day* (Azrin & Foxx, 1974). This study found that four of five mothers in a therapist-administered condition successfully trained their children, whereas only one of five mothers who used the book in a self-administered condition was successful. Further, unsuccessful efforts were associated with an increase in childrens' problem behaviors and negative emotional side effects between mothers and children. The implications of these findings are great and point to the important issue of unintended negative consequences. If, for example, 100,000 copies of *Toilet Training in Less Than a Day* were self-administered, and Matson and Ollendick's (1977) findings applied, then upwards of 80,000 mothers might be frustrated, if not angry, with their children. After all, on the back jacket of the book, the publisher proclaimed:

> Two noted learning specialists have developed this amazing new training method that—for the average child—requires less than four hours.... Parents report other benefits from the Azrin-Foxx scientifically tested method.... Most children become more responsive to parental instruction in other areas. At least one-third of the children trained by this method stop wetting their beds. Many parents find they have more time for personal interests, and that their child is now a source of increased pride and pleasure.

Azrin and Foxx's self-help book was not the only one that failed to deliver what it promised. Zeiss (1978) conducted a controlled outcome study on the treatment of premature ejaculation by randomly assigning couples to receive either self-administered treatment, minimal therapist contact, or therapist-directed treatment. As in earlier reports (Lowe & Mikulas, 1975; Zeiss, 1977), treatment with minimal therapist contact was effective, but of six couples who self-administered treatment without any therapist contact, none successfully completed the program (Zeiss, 1978). Once again, a highly successful intervention supervised by a therapist did not translate into a helpful do-it-yourself program.

The present authors conducted another set of studies that demonstrated how well-intentioned instructional materials may not be effective. In the first study (Rosen, Glasgow, & Barrera, 1976), we found that subjects highly fearful of snakes could totally self-administer a written desensitization program and significantly reduce their anxiety, with treatment effects maintained at two-year follow-up (Rosen, Glasgow, & Barrera, 1977). Yet, 50% of subjects in the self-administered condition failed to carry out instructional assignments, and these subjects did not improve. Because follow-through was an important concern related to outcome, Barrera and Rosen (1977) attempted to increase adherence with new instructional materials. In a follow-up to the 1976 study, phobic subjects were randomly assigned to the original self-administered program or to a revised program that included a self-reward contracting module, in line with self-management efforts promoted at the time (Mahoney & Thoresen, 1974). Results were surprising and counterintuitive. As in the 1976 study, 50% of subjects completed the original program and substantially reduced their fears. However, in the "new and improved" program, in which self-contracting had been added, not a single subject (0%) followed through with the instructions.

Findings from the studies cited above, and additional research efforts in the 1970s, allowed for several conclusions (Glasgow & Rosen, 1978).

1. Self-help instructional materials can be effective, and they provide a cost-effective alternative to therapist-directed interventions.
2. Some self-help instructional materials are not effective, even when based on empirically validated methods delivered by therapists. Therefore, the effectiveness of a treatment program under one set of conditions cannot be assumed to generalize to all conditions.
3. The effect of *any* change in instructional content, no matter how *well-intentioned*, is an empirical question that must be assessed under the specific conditions for which the materials are intended.

Perhaps the most striking illustration of these conclusions was our own series of studies, which showed that a change in instructional materials led to adherence rates as low as 0%. Despite these findings, one of us revised the desensitization manual yet another time and published *Don't Be Afraid* (Rosen, 1976a). To appreciate fully these findings within a historical perspective, it can be noted that an earlier text entitled *Don't Be Afraid* was published by Edward Cowles in 1941. This older *Don't Be Afraid* differed in content from the *Don't Be Afraid* of 1976: it promoted nerve fatigue theories rather than modern desensitization. Nevertheless, without appropriate research, psychologists and consumers cannot know whether any advance really occurred in the self-treatment of phobic disorders over the span of a quarter century. A similar historical example pertains to the self-help book *Mind-Power* by Zilbergeld and Lazarus (1987). As it turns out, Olston (1903) and Atkinson (1912) published advice books under the same title. Because all three *Mind Power* books lack empirical support, no one knows if the public has benefited over a period of eight decades.

APA's Task Forces on Self-Help Therapies

In 1977, the Committee on Scientific and Professional Ethics and Conduct of the American Psychological Association, after discussions involving the Board of Professional Affairs, invited one of us (G. Rosen) to chair a Task Force on Self-Help Therapies (APA, 1978a, 1978b). The task force was asked to consider whether ethical standards adopted by APA adequately dealt with the recent involvement of psychologists in developing and marketing self-help programs. A report was issued by the task force in October of 1978, in which various principles cited in APA's ethical standards were applied to self-help therapies:

> Self-help therapies can help people to understand themselves, and they may provide one of the most effective instructional modalities for promoting human welfare (Preamble). However, psychologists bear heavy professional responsibilities in developing such programs. This is particularly the case in light of the influence that psychologists may have on the behaviors of others (Principle 1). Accordingly, self-help therapies that are developed by psychologists should meet recognized standards, as is the case for all therapeutic modalities (Principle 2). The development of self-help therapies should not be compromised by financial pressures or other factors (Principle 1). Public statements, announcements, and promotional activities pertaining to a commercially published self-help therapy should be informative. Sensationalism is to be avoided in such statements. The limitations, as well as the benefits, of a self-help therapy should be clearly stated (Principle 4).

The task force noted that most self-help programs were marketed without any attempt to assess their effectiveness. It also was observed that a visit to any bookstore demonstrated frequent violations of APA's ethical standards. The members of the task force cautioned:

> Despite the observed trend for programs to receive inadequate assessment, promotional claims and titles that accompany these programs are increasingly exaggerated and sensationalized. The public is promised total cures and told that a self-help program can eliminate the need for any outside professional help. Such extravagant claims do a disservice to the public by misleading the consumer and by fostering unrealistic expectations. Exaggerated claims do a disservice to the profession of psychology as well. They affect consumer attitudes and discredit professionals and properly developed programs.

Various recommendations were made to the sponsoring committee, including the suggestion that APA publish a set of guidelines for psychologists, similar in intent to the standards that guide developers of psychological tests. For reasons never clarified, only one task force recommendation was enacted: this occurred when the editor of *Contemporary Psychology* adopted guidelines for the review of do-it-yourself programs (Rosen, 1978, 1981b), and established a framework that remains as useful today (e.g., Rosen, 2002) as it was when first adopted (e.g., Rosen, 1981a, 1988).

In 1990, the Board of Professional Affairs constituted a new Task Force on Self-Help Therapies and revisited the same issues considered by the 1978 group. The 1990 task force observed the continuing proliferation of self-help programs in the 1980s, not only in terms of sheer number of programs but also in terms of instructional modalities (i.e., audio cassettes, videotapes, and computerized programs). Recommendations similar to those provided in the late 1970s were again proposed, and these recommendations were again not enacted.

The history of APA's task forces has often been forgotten (Rosen, 1994, 2003), as have numerous publications that analyzed the issues (Barrera, Rosen, & Glasgow, 1981; McMahon & Forehand, 1982; Rosen, 1976b, 1987, 1993). It seems unlikely that the field of self-help will advance, if lessons learned over time are not recalled.

Current Efforts

The fundamental concern of psychologists and allied health professionals interested in advancing self-help has remained the same throughout the years. This fundamental concern is "How can professionals contribute to self-help instructional materials so that today's programs are more effective than yesterday's, and tomorrow's programs will be more effective than today's?" In this context, it is significant that research has continued to demonstrate the effectiveness of self-help programs. For example, George Clum and colleagues have conducted a systematic program of research on the self-help treatment of panic (Febbraro, Clum, Roodman, & Wright, 1999; Gould & Clum, 1995; Gould, Clum, & Shapiro, 1993; Lidren et al., 1994); Forrest Scogin and colleagues have assessed the utility of a depression program for the elderly (Scogin, Jamison, & Davis, 1990; Scogin, Jamison, & Gochneaur, 1989); Isaac Marks has demonstrated that computerized self-help programs are feasible (Marks et al., 2003; Marks, Shaw, & Parkins, 1998); and psychologists have begun to translate instructional materials to an expanding audience on the Internet (e.g., Jerome & Zaylor, 2000; Lange et al., 2003; Strom, Pettersson, & Andersson, 2000, 2004).

Also published in the 1990s were several meta-analytic studies that demonstrated the general effectiveness of tested programs (Gould & Clum, 1993; Kurtzweil, Scogin, & Rosen, 1996; Marrs, 1995; Scogin, Bynum, Stephens, & Calhoon, 1990). These research efforts, and others, have been accompanied by a large number of articles that extol the virtues of self-help therapies and encourage professionals in their usage (e.g., Ganzer, 1995; Johnson & Johnson, 1998; Lanza, 1996; Pardeck, 1990, 1991, 1992; Quackenbush, 1992; Warner, 1992). One of the most enthusiastic papers of this genre was a delightfully titled paper by Norcross (2000), "Here Comes the Self-Help Revolution in Mental Health," in which he observed:

> [T]he self-help revolution is here and it is growing. Psychologists can idly watch with bemused interest—devaluing self-change as shallow, self-help books as trivial, and Internet sites as harmless—as the train roars past us. Alternatively, we can recognize the power and potential of the locomotive and help steer it to valuable destinations for our patients and the populace. (pp. 375–376)

At the same time that enthusiasm for self-help therapies maintained throughout the 1980s and 1990s, very little changed, if anything, for the consumer in need of self-instructional materials. A vast number of programs were marketed, a majority of which remained untested. Clum's book on *Coping With Panic* (Clum, 1990) is an excellent example of one book systematically assessed, but no efforts were made to determine the therapeutic utility of more than a dozen other anxiety reduction programs (e.g., Bourne, 1998; Dupont, Spencer, & DuPont, 1998; Zuercher-White, 1998). Further, there was no basis to know whether self-help books from the 1990s were more effective than similarly intended texts from earlier times. In this sense, the field of self-help has stood still, despite the involvement of professionals over a span of three decades. Untold numbers of new programs have been marketed by their individual authors, and more choices exist for the consumer. But nowhere has systematic research established whether today's instructional materials help consumers more than programs available for purchase years before. Further, while new modalities such as the Internet offer a number of potential advantages, including the ability to deliver deeply tailored and individualized interventions, early evaluations indicate that many users of self-help Internet programs do not follow-through with or complete recommended courses of treatment (Glasgow, Boles, McKay, & Barrera, 2003).

The Ethics of Good Intentions

The key lesson learned from early research on self-help therapies, *that good intentions do not assure effective therapies*, continues to be demonstrated. Ehlers and colleagues randomly assigned motor vehicle accident survivors diagnosed with posttraumatic stress disorder to receive therapist-administered cognitive therapy, a self-help booklet, or repeated assessments (Ehlers et al., 2003). While cognitive therapy was demonstrated to be effective, the self-help booklet was not superior to simple repeated assessments. Of greater concern, outcome for the self-help group was actually worse than for repeated assessments on two measures.

The issues we are discussing in relation to self-help are more broadly based. Glasgow, Lichtenstein, and Marcus (2003) observed that many interventions for health problems that are efficacious in traditional efficacy-based studies do not translate into effective programs when delivered under real-world conditions. They noted several reasons for this and stressed that medical, behavioral, and public health interventions need to be tested with representative samples, in representative settings, under representative conditions of use.

Further, the lesson that sound clinical practice cannot be based on good intentions has been demonstrated in other areas of clinical psychology (see Lilienfeld, Lynn, & Lohr, 2003). Take, for example, the finding that critical incident stress debriefings (CISD) are not effective in the aftermath of trauma, and these methods may actually impede the natural recovery that occurs for most individuals (e.g., Carlier, van Uchelen, Lamberts, & Gersons, 1998; Carlier, Voerman, & Gersons, 2000; Hobbs, Mayou, Harrison, & Worlock, 1996; Mayou, Ehlers, & Hobbs, 2000). Such findings led Mayou et al. (2000) to conclude that "Psychological debriefing is ineffective and has adverse long-term effects. It is not an appropriate treatment for trauma victims" (p. 589). Numerous reviews of the literature have come to similar conclusions (e.g., Bryant, 2004; Rose, Bisson, & Wessely, 2001).

Findings on the ill-advisability of conducting critical incident debriefings with trauma victims came as a surprise to many. Like self-help instructional materials, the concept of early intervention in the aftermath of trauma was based on the best of intentions. Research had demonstrated that the majority of people are resilient after trauma, but a substantial minority can have continuing and severe posttraumatic reactions that meet criteria for PTSD (e.g., Kessler, Sonnega, Bromet, Hughes, & Nelson, 1995; Rothbaum, Foa, Riggs, Murdock, & Walsh, 1992; Yehuda & McFarlane, 1995). Therefore, it was reasoned, early intervention could provide support and information to trauma victims, in the aftermath of their misfortune, possibly reducing the risk of severe problems associated with posttraumatic stress disorder. The model sounded good, but failed the empirical test. In their review of CISD, Devilly and Cotton (2004) reached a conclusion that applies just as well to self-help: "It is becoming clear that 'belief' may indeed be a dangerous emotion when coming to judge the effectiveness of an intervention" (p. 37).

An Alternative Model to Advance Self-Help

Despite all that we learned in the 1970s, the majority of instructional materials sold to the public remain untested, and programs are accompanied with exaggerated claims. One response by many in the field is to remain optimistic and to discount the impact of a small number of studies that have reported negative results. This view is exemplified by Floyd, McKendree-Smith, and Scogin (2004), who recently stated: "Our opinion is that although many self-help books may not lead to lasting improvement (though some do), they are only rarely harmful.... Overall, we have a positive view of self-help books and self-administered treatments" (p. 116).

We agree that one can take a positive view toward self-help books and other instructional modalities that allow for self-administered treatments. Indeed, ever since the 1970s, in peer review journals and in reports by APA committee task forces, the benefits of self-help have been appreciated and the use of these materials encouraged. Yet, the central concern for self-help, the ethical imperative if you will, is a different matter. Rather than professionals assuring themselves that self-help is "at least benign" as they continue to market products, professionals must assure that there is no harm (nonmaleficence) while attempting to develop increasingly effective instructional programs for the public (beneficence). Simply put, the goal is to assure that panic control, fear reduction, weight loss, and other self-help instructional materials published in 2050 are steps ahead of anything we have today. Our point in stating this is not to castigate individual authors but to observe that seemingly logical and well-intentioned materials can have unintended consequences. In line with the movement toward evidence-based psychology and medicine, we need to evaluate our interventions rather than assume that they have desired consequences.

The current framework adopted by psychologists when interfacing with self-help is not achieving the desired goals (Rosen, Glasgow, & Moore, 2003). If we continue along the current paths that have been documented in this chapter, then all we can expect in 2050 is a new set of review articles that praise the usually helpful, and otherwise benign programs of the day. These programs will be written by the current experts, whoever they may be, perhaps under titles such as *Don't Be Afraid*, *Mind Power*, or *Coping with Panic*. And just as we had no way of knowing if the 1976 *Don't Be Afraid* was an improvement on the one published in 1941, so will we have no way of knowing if things are any better in 2050.

Rosen et al. (2003) proposed that the "individualistic" approach to developing and evaluating self-help materials should be replaced by a "team" or "program-based" approach, consistent with public health models of intervention and evaluation (Abrams et al., 1996; Brownson, Remington, & Davis, 1998; Glasgow, Vogt, & Boles, 1999; Winnett, King, & Altman, 1989). Within this framework, responsibility for developing and evaluating a self-help program would not reside with an individual author. Instead, programs would be tested by a variety of individuals, in a variety of settings, under a variety of conditions. Educators, family physicians, other health care professionals, and researchers would collaborate as a team to identify health topics appropriate for self-help intervention. Members of related professional organizations, consortia of clinics, HMOs, or health care systems would then be in a position to coordinate multiple site studies to advance the development of effective instructional materials.

A team approach to developing and evaluating self-help materials would be furthered by the sponsorship of an institution whose commitment would extend beyond the professional career of individual authors. Imagine, for example, that a self-help book on controlling panic was created by an international organization on anxiety disorders, and the author of the book was a team of experts from various health fields who collaborated on the development of instructional materials. The person who might have been devoted to sole authorship of a book would now serve as director of the team effort. Within this framework, the membership of the professional team or work group would change over time, as would the director of the program, but the defined group and its activities would be ongoing, continually refining and improving its program to assure progress from one generation to the next. This is how the Cochrane Collaboration operates when they provide evidence-based reviews and updates (e.g., Rose et al., 2001).

We recognize that individuals will certainly continue to publish programs as they wish. We also recognize that a team and organizational approach to developing self-help programs may be fraught with problems. All working models are subject to financial interests, departures from the methods and values of sound science, and breaches of professional standards. Nevertheless, the real future of empirically supported instructional programs is to be found with program-based methods. This is the next revolution for self-help.

Chapter Points

- No better way exists to accomplish the ideals of psychology and allied health fields than to use the clinical and research expertise of the profession to develop effective self-help programs.
- Effective treatment programs, as administered by a health professional, do not necessarily translate into effective programs when administered in a self-help program. The effectiveness of even small changes in content must be evaluated.
- The individualistic approach to developing self-help materials should be replaced by a team- or program-based approach.

References

Abrams, D. B., Orleans, C. T., Niaura, R. S., Goldstein, M. G., Prochaska, J. O., & Velicer, W. (1996). Integrating individual and public health perspectives for treatment of tobacco dependence under managed care: A combined stepped care and matching model. *Annals of Behavioral Medicine, 18,* 290–304.

American Psychological Association. (1978a). Officers, boards, committees, and representatives of the American Psychological Association: 1978. *American Psychologist, 33,* 573–599.

American Psychological Association. (1978b). Proceedings of the American Psychological Association incorporated for the year 1977: Minutes of the annual meeting of the council of representatives. *American Psychologist, 33,* 544–572.

American Psychological Association. (2002). Ethical principles of psychologists and code of conduct. *American Psychologist, 57,* 1060–1073.

Atkinson, W. W. (1912). *Mind-power: The secret of mental magic.* Chicago: Yogi Publication Society.

Azrin, N. H., & Foxx, R. M. (1974). *Toilet training in less than a day.* New York: Simon & Schuster.

Barrera, M., Jr., & Rosen, G. M. (1977). Detrimental effects of a self-reward contracting program on subjects' involvement in self-administered desensitization. *Journal of Consulting and Clinical Psychology, 45,* 1180–1181.

Barrera, M., Jr., Rosen, G. M., & Glasgow, R. E. (1981). Rights, risks and responsibilities in the development and use of self-help psychotherapies. In J. T. Hannah, R. Clark, & P. Christian (Eds.), *Preservation of client rights* (pp. 204–221). New York: Free Press.

Bourne, E. (1998). *Healing fear: New approaches to overcoming anxiety.* Oakland, CA: New Harbinger Publications.

Brownson, R. C., Remington, P. L., & Davis, J. R. (1998). *Chronic disease epidemiology and control* (2nd ed.). Washington, DC: American Public Health Association.

Bryant, R. A. (2004). In the aftermath of trauma: Normative reactions and early interventions. In G. M. Rosen (Ed.), *Posttraumatic stress disorder: Issues and controversies* (pp. 187–211). Chichester, England: John Wiley & Sons.

Carlier, I. V. E., van Uchelen, J. J., Lamberts, R. D., & Gersons, B. P. R. (1998). Disaster-related posttraumatic stress in police officers: A field study of the impact of debriefing. *Stress Medicine, 14,* 143–148.

Carlier, I. V. E., Voerman, A. E., & Gersons, B. P. R. (2000). The influence of occupational debriefing of post-traumatic stress symptomatology in traumatized police officers. *British Journal of Medical Psychology, 73,* 87–98.

Clum, G. A. (1990). *Coping with panic: A drug-free approach to dealing with anxiety attacks.* Pacific Grove, CA: Brooks/Cole.

Cowles, E. S. (1941). *Don't be afraid!* New York: McGraw-Hill.

Devilly, G. J., & Cotton, P. (2004). Caveat emptor, caveat venditor, and Critical Incident Stress Debriefing/Management (CISD/M). *Australian Psychologist, 39,* 35–40.

DuPont, R. L., Spencer, E., & DuPont, C. M. (1998). *The anxiety cure: An eight-step program for getting well.* New York: John Wiley & Sons.

Ehlers, A., Clark, D. M., Hackmann, A., McManus, F., Fennell, M., Herbert, C., et al. (2003). A randomized controlled trial of cognitive therapy, a self-help booklet, and repeated assessments as early interventions for posttraumatic stress disorder. *Archives General Psychiatry, 60*, 1024–1032.

Febbraro, G. A. R., Clum, G. A., Roodman, A. A., & Wright, J. H. (1999). The limits of bibliotherapy: A study of the differential effectiveness of self-administered interventions in individuals with panic attacks. *Behavior Therapy, 30*, 209–222.

Floyd, M., McKendree-Smith, N. L., & Scogin, F. (2004). Remembering the 1978 and 1990 task forces on self-help therapies: A response to Gerald Rosen. *Journal of Clinical Psychology, 60*, 115–117.

Ganzer, C. (1995). Using literature as an aid to practice. *Families in Society, 75*, 616–623.

Glasgow, R. E., Boles, S. M., McKay, H. G., & Barrera, M. (2003). The D-Net Diabetes Self-Management Program: Long-term implementation, outcomes, and generalization results. *Preventive Medicine, 36*, 410–419.

Glasgow, R. E., Lichtenstein, E., & Marcus, A. C. (2003). Why don't we see more translation of health promotion research to practice? Rethinking the efficacy to effectiveness transition. *American Journal of Public Health, 93*, 1261–1267.

Glasgow, R. E., & Rosen, G. M. (1978). Behavioral bibliotherapy: A review of self-help behavior therapy manuals. *Psychological Bulletin, 85*, 1–23.

Glasgow, R. E., & Rosen, G. M. (1982). Self-help behavior therapy manuals: Recent development and clinical usage. *Clinical Behavior Therapy Review, 1*, 1–20.

Glasgow, R. E., Vogt, T. M., & Boles, S. M. (1999). Evaluating the public health impact of health promotion interventions: The RE-AIM framework. *American Journal of Public Health, 89*, 1322–1327.

Gould, R. A., & Clum, G. A. (1993). A meta-analysis of self-help treatment approaches. *Clinical Psychology Review, 13*, 169–186.

Gould, R. A., & Clum, G. A. (1995). Self-help plus minimal therapist contact in the treatment of panic disorder: A replication and extension. *Behavior Therapy, 26*, 533–546.

Gould, R. A., Clum, G. A., & Shapiro, D. (1993). The use of bibliotherapy in the treatment of panic: A preliminary investigation. *Behavior Therapy, 24*, 241–252.

Hobbs, M., Mayou, R., Harrison, B., & Warlock, P. (1996). A randomised trial of psychological debriefing for victims of road traffic accidents. *British Medical Journal, 313*, 1438–1439.

Jerome, L. W., & Zaylor, C. (2000). Cyberspace: Creating a therapeutic environment for telehealth applications. *Professional Psychology: Research and Practice, 31*, 478–483.

Johnson, B. W., & Johnson, W. L. (1998). Self-help books used by religious practitioners. *Journal of Counseling and Development, 76*, 459–466.

Kessler, R. C., Sonnega, A., Bromet, E., Hughes, M., & Nelson, C. B. (1995). Posttraumatic stress disorder in the National Comorbidity Survey. *Archives of General Psychiatry, 52*, 1048–1060.

Kurtzweil, P. L., Scogin, F., & Rosen, G. M. (1996). A test of the fail-safe N for self-help programs. *Professional Psychology: Research and Practice, 27*, 629–630.

Lange, A., Rietdijk, D., Hudcovicova, M., van de Ven, J.-P., Schrieken, B., & Emmelkamp, P. M. G. (2003). Interapy: A controlled randomized trial of the standardized treatment of posttraumatic stress through the internet. *Journal of Consulting and Clinical Psychology, 71*, 901–909.

Lanza, M. L. (1996). Bibliotherapy and beyond. *Perspective in Psychiatric Care, 32*, 12–14.

Lidren, D. M., Watkins, P. L., Gould, R. A., Clum, G. A., Asterino, M., & Tulloch, H. L. (1994). A comparison of bibliotherapy and group therapy in the treatment of panic disorder. *Journal of Consulting and Clinical Psychology, 62*, 865–869.

Lilienfeld, S. O., Lynn, S. J., & Lohr, J. M. (Eds.). (2003). *Science and pseudoscience in clinical psychology.* New York: Guilford.

Lowe, J. C., & Mikulas, W. L. (1975). Use of written material in learning self-control of premature ejaculation. *Psychological Reports, 37*, 295–298.

Mahoney, M. J., & Thoresen, C. E. (1974). *Self-control: Power to the person.* Monterey, CA: Brooks-Cole.

Marks, I. M., Mataix-Cols, D., Kenwright, K., Cameron, R., Hirsch, S., & Gega, L. (2003). Pragmatic evaluation of computer-aided self help for anxiety and depression. *British Journal of Psychiatry, 183*, 57–65.

Marks, I. M., Shaw, S., & Parkins, R. (1998). Computer-aided treatments of mental health problems. *Clinical Psychology: Science and Practice, 5*, 151–170.

Marrs, R. W. (1995). A meta-analysis of bibliotherapy studies. *American Journal of Community Psychology, 23*, 843–870.

Matson, J. L., & Ollendick, T. H. (1977). Issues in toilet training normal children. *Behavior Therapy, 8*, 549–553.

Mayou, R. A., Ehlers, A., & Hobbs, M. (2000). Psychological debriefing for road traffic accident victims: Three-year follow-up of a randomised controlled trial. *British Journal of Psychiatry, 176*, 589–593.

McKendree-Smith, N. L., Floyd, M., & Scogin, F. R. (2003). Self-administered treatments for depression: A review. *Journal of Clinical Psychology, 59*, 275–288.

Miller, G. A. (1969). Psychology as a means of promoting human welfare. *American Psychologist, 24*, 1063–1075.

Norcross, J. C. (2000). Here comes the self-help revolution in mental health. *Psychotherapy, 37*, 370–377.

Olston, A. R. (1903). *Mind power and privileges.* Boston: Rockwell and Churchill Press.

Pardeck, J. T. (1990). Using bibliotherapy in clinical practice with children. *Psychological Reports, 67*, 1043–1049.

Pardeck, J. T. (1991). Bibliotherapy and clinical social work. *Journal of Independent Social Work, 5*, 53–63.

Pardeck, J. T. (1992). Using books in clinical practice. *Psychotherapy in Private Practice, 9*, 105–119.

Quackenbush, R. L. (1992). The prescription of self-help books by psychologists: A bibliography of selected bibliotherapy resources. *Psychotherapy, 28*, 671–677.

Rose, S., Bisson, J., & Wessely, S. (2001). Psychological debriefing for preventing posttraumatic stress disorder (PTSD) (Cochrane Review). In *The Cochrane Library, Issue 3*, Oxford: Update Software.

Rosen, G. M. (1976a). *Don't be afraid.* Englewood Cliffs, NJ: Prentice-Hall.

Rosen, G. M. (1976b). The development and use of nonprescription behavior therapies. *American Psychologist, 31*, 139–141.

Rosen, G. M. (1978). Suggestions for an editorial policy on the review of self-help treatment books. *Behavior Therapy, 9*, 960.

Rosen, G. M. (1981a). Another miraculous do-it-yourself treatment book. *Contemporary Psychology, 26*, 921–922.

Rosen, G. M. (1981b). Guidelines for the review of do-it-yourself treatment books. *Contemporary Psychology, 26*, 189–190.

Rosen, G. M. (1982). Self-help approaches to self-management. In K. R. Blankstein & J. Polivy (Eds.), *Self-control and self-modification of emotional behavior* (pp. 183–199). New York: Plenum Press.

Rosen, G. M. (1987). Self-help treatment books and the commercialization of psychotherapy. *American Psychologist, 42*, 46–51.

Rosen, G. M. (1988). Multimodal marketing: The selling of Mind Power. *Contemporary Psychology, 33*, 861–863.

Rosen, G. M. (1993). Self-help or hype? Comments on psychology's failure to advance self-care. *Professional Psychology: Research and Practice, 24*, 340–345.

Rosen, G. M. (1994). Self-help task forces revisited: A reply to Dr. Lowman. *Professional Psychology: Research and Practice, 25*, 100–101.

Rosen, G. M. (2002). Review of "Do-it-yourself eye movement technique for emotional healing" by F. Friedberg. *Journal of Behavior Therapy and Experimental Psychiatry, 33*, 59–64.

Rosen, G. M. (2003). Remembering the 1978 and 1990 task forces on self-help therapies. *Journal of Clinical Psychology, 60*, 111–113.

Rosen, G. M., Glasgow, R. E., & Barrera, M., Jr. (1976). A controlled study to assess the clinical efficacy of totally self-administered systematic desensitization. *Journal of Consulting and Clinical Psychology, 44*, 208–217.

Rosen, G. M., Glasgow, R. E., & Barrera, M. (1977). A two-year follow-up on systematic desensitization with data pertaining to the external validity of laboratory fear assessment. *Journal of Consulting and Clinical Psychology, 45*, 1188–1189.

Rosen, G. M., Glasgow, R. E., & Moore, T. E. (2003). Self-help therapy: The science and business of giving psychology away. In S. O. Lilienfeld, S. J. Lynn, & J. M. Lohr (Eds.), *Science and pseudoscience in clinical psychology* (pp. 399–424). New York: Guilford.

Rothbaum, B. O., Foa, E. B., Riggs, D. S., Murdock, T., & Walsh, W. (1992). A prospective examination of post-traumatic stress disorder in rape victims. *Journal of Traumatic Stress, 5*, 455–475.

Scogin, F., Bynum, J., Stephens, G., & Calhoon, S. (1990). Efficacy of self-administered treatment programs: Meta-analytic review. *Professional Psychology: Research and Practice, 21*, 42–47.

Scogin, F., Jamison, C., & Davis, N. (1990). Two-year follow-up of bibliotherapy for depression in older adults. *Journal of Consulting and Clinical Psychology, 58*, 665–667.

Scogin, F., Jamison, C., & Gochneaur, K. (1989). Comparative efficacy of cognitive and behavioral bibliotherapy for mildly and moderately depressed older adults. *Journal of Consulting and Clinical Psychology, 57*, 403–407.

Strom, L., Pettersson, R., & Andersson, G. (2000). A controlled trial of self-help treatment of recurrent headache conducted via the internet. *Journal of Consulting and Clinical Psychology, 68*, 722–727.

Strom, L., Pettersson, R., & Andersson, G. (2004). Internet-based treatment for insomnia: A controlled evaluation. *Journal of Consulting and Clinical Psychology, 72*, 113–120.

Warner, R. E. (1992). Bibliotherapy: A comparison of the prescription practices of Canadian and American psychologists. *Canadian Psychology, 32*, 529–530.

Winnett, R. A., King, A. C., & Altman, D. G. (1989). *Health psychology and public health: An integrative approach.* New York: Pergamon.

Yehuda, R., & McFarlane, A. C. (1995). Conflict between current knowledge about posttraumatic stress disorder and its original conceptual basis. *American Journal of Psychiatry, 152*, 1705–1713.

Zeiss, R. A. (1977). Self-directed treatment for premature ejaculation: Preliminary case reports. *Journal of Behavior Therapy and Experimental Psychiatry, 8*, 87–91.

Zeiss, R. A. (1978). Self-directed treatment for premature ejaculation. *Journal of Consulting and clinical Psychology, 46*, 1234–1241.

Zilbergeld, B., & Lazarus, A. A. (1987). *Mind power.* Boston: Little, Brown.

Zuercher-White, E. (1998). *An end to panic: Breakthrough techniques for overcoming panic disorder* (2nd ed.). Oakland, CA: New Harbinger Publications.

CHAPTER 3

Self-Help Interventions
Mapping the Role of Self-Administered Treatments in Health Care

GEORGE A. CLUM

The last 30 years have witnessed the publication of a torrent of books aimed at transforming the average American citizen into a successful business and financial entrepreneur who is at once thin, muscular, fit, free of illness and disease, and content with life. This transformation is to be achieved at the hands of none other than the average citizen herself, for the vehicle that will provide this metamorphosis is the self-help book or program in the hands of this same citizen. In the health arena, this change guru might be someone who has personally overcome disease or disorder or who has systematized an approach whose change formula will help sufferers overcome their deficiencies. The number of books dedicated to this enterprise has expanded to the point where the *New York Times* provides a separate rating system of the most successful. Clearly, the self-help book has become a major factor in the domain of self-improvement.

The assumption of the majority of these books is that the success stories detailed within will provide the motivational prod to stir the consumer to action and that, once so stirred, the technology advocated will be employed and the intended change produced. The extrapolated message is obvious: " I've been able to do it. Follow my formula and you will too!" or "I've shown that this formula has transformed others. Use it and transform yourself!" Almost without exception, the purveyors of change have failed to examine whether their formula has in fact been read, understood, digested, and implemented, much less whether that implementation has produced the intended change. The author's obligation terminates with the provision of the formula.

More determined or more responsible purveyors of change have begun to ask, and attempt to answer, a series of questions related to their formulas. Who reads, watches, or listens to their message? Is receiving the message sufficient to produce change or must the formula for change actually be applied? What level or degree of application is sufficient to produce change? Are all parts of the formula equally important or even relevant? Can the reader, for example, identify more personally relevant segments, apply only those segments, and experience a level of change identical to that produced by someone who has digested and applied all segments? Are multiple formulae equally successful—do readers simply need a formula and any formula will do?

The present chapter begins by examining similarities and differences in the process encountered in accessing the more general health system and in accessing the self-help arena. A number of discrepancies are noted between how self-help materials are typically accessed and utilized and how the general health system works, discrepancies that may be cause for concern. One of those discrepancies in the self-help arena involves the lack of formal diagnosis prior to selecting a self-help remedy. Trends in the scientific study of self-help are then examined to provide insights into how this area is growing and where deficiencies may lie. Next examined is the overall effectiveness of self-help materials, as revealed in meta-analytic studies summarizing their effectiveness. In this section, estimates of the overall effectiveness of self-help approaches are examined as assessed by dropout rates, treatment outcome comparing self-help to both wait-list and therapist-administered treatments, and long-term outcomes. Where possible, specific comparisons are made between effectiveness rates for self-administered treatments and therapist-administered treatments for specific disorders. Next addressed was the place of self-help treatments in the health arena. In this context we examine the conditions under which self-help treatments could be used as a stand-alone treatment and when their use as an adjunctive treatment should be recommended. Specific approaches to stepped-care models are examined as part of this debate. The chapter concludes by examining the importance of assessment of change for answering a variety of questions on overall treatment effectiveness and changes in treatment tactics linked to expected rates of change for target problems.

Parallels to Help-Seeking in the Health Arena

In the health arena, people seek help when things go wrong—they feel bad (symptoms), notice that something has changed in how their body functions (signs), or receive information that their symptoms or signs deserve further examination. If the object of their attention is behavior—smoking, eating, drinking—individuals usually do not consult experts to diagnose the problem, though their attention may be aroused if someone has labeled their behavior "addicted" or the consequences of their behavior "obese." Problem definition, as this phase is called, can be either self- or other-identified. If the problem in question requires specific definition, the sufferer may seek an expert opinion to provide a diagnosis. In the mental health arena, diagnosis is a complex process that involves not only definition of the identified signs and symptoms, but also definition of additional/accompanying conditions, officially termed comorbid conditions, that may contribute to, complicate, and be associated with the presenting problem that prompted the health search. The process of accurately defining the target problem(s) has been largely ignored in the self-help domain and is a major source of concern for both researchers and authors of self-help materials. Self-help programs designed to treat depression, for example, assume that the problem to be targeted is indeed depression and not another physical disorder with a symptom picture similar to depression. Obviously, a self-administered change program applied by an individual to a problem that does not exist will not work and is also likely to have unintended consequences—not receiving treatment for the disorder that does exist, for example. Individuals who suffer from severe levels of the disorder in question or who have complicating comorbid conditions, e.g., substance dependence *and* depression, may not realize that the self-help program being employed was never intended to be applied to individuals with their level of disorder.

Once a problem is diagnosed, the health expert may turn her attention to what causal factors are involved. At the molar level, this determination might include examining the individual's history for evidence of significant losses or stressors or conducting a lab test to determine thyroid function. The medical treatment recommended would hinge on the formulation of what was causing the depression. Differences in causal formulations also exist within the psychological domain. While professionals are aware of these differences and may prescribe different treatments depending on these formulations, purveyors of self-administered therapies typically advocate for one specific approach. Discriminations between causal agents are considered unimportant or their importance is ignored. This one-size-fits-all approach is applied indiscriminately by the consumer who is likely unaware that different formulations exist. If improvement does not follow upon application of the program, the user is likely to conclude "The program is worthless!" or "I'm worthless for failing to make the program work for me," as opposed to the determination that "This program was not designed for my specific needs."

In the health arena, once a specific treatment for the specific problem is applied, its effectiveness is evaluated. Simply put, the sufferer and the health expert determine whether change occurs. This phase of the intervention is often incorporated into many self-help programs. Various self-administered assessment instruments are often provided and the consumer is encouraged to assess his progress, or lack thereof, on a regular basis. What is not known in the self-help arena is what happens to those people who have not responded to the self-help program. Do they abandon it? Do they try harder? Do they jettison that approach and call their physician or seek other professional services? Information on the fate of failed self-helpers would be useful in recommending changes to the self-administered treatment protocols.

Positioning Self-Help Treatments in the Health Arena

In one sense, the people have voted and self-help materials occupy a place of prominence in the pantheon of treatments for mental health problems. According to Amazon.com, 81,796 self-help books were available to help negotiate life's shoals as of October 2006. Advice on how to deal with specific problems included 522 books on depression, 398 on anxiety, and 425 on various addictions. Children merited 1429 self-help books of their own. One book proclaimed that it was the last self-help book one would ever need. The very fact that so many choices exist is part of the problem because there is little in the way of guidance to help individuals decide which books might be useful for their particular problem, much less specific data on which are effective and which are not.

Were it known which books were effective, a related issue involves how to position self-help materials in the health arena. One possibility is to offer such materials as an alternative to or as an adjunct to professional advice and help. In this scenario, self-help materials would be used very much as they are today. That is, authors would offer various forms of advice, which would be purchased in the marketplace and utilized with various levels of success. Used in this way, self-help programs are only an informal part of the health system, whose impact is difficult, if not impossible, to gauge.

Another approach is to offer self-help materials more formally, as part of the overall process of evaluation and diagnosis by primary and secondary health professionals. Used in this way, individuals with yet-unidentified specific problems would enter the health care system seeking help for signs or symptoms of concern. A formal evaluation would then be conducted and individuals assigned to an appropriate treatment, in some cases a stand-alone self-administered treatment (SAT), in others a therapist-enhanced SAT, in still others treatment provided by a professional. Improvement (or not) would be carefully monitored to determine whether the SAT was proving effective. Essentially, all of the SATs examined in this book utilized this approach. Because all SATs were examined as part of a study, a formal evaluation was conducted to determine whether individuals met the criteria for inclusion in the study. Only then were they assigned to an SAT condition, wherein they were carefully evaluated at, minimally, posttreatment. In a very real sense, what we know about the effectiveness of SATs is based totally on individuals who have received SATs within this model.

Patterns in the Study of SAT Effectiveness

Next examined was the growth of treatment outcome studies of the effectiveness of SATs over the last 30 years. An increase in the number of outcome studies was expected for several reasons: (a) Attention was drawn to the study of the effectiveness of SATs by Glasgow and Rosen's (1978) and Rosen's (1987) articles on the need for such studies as well as the dearth of studies conducted up to the time their papers were written; (b) several meta-analyses (Gould & Clum, 1993; Marrs, 1995) were written, also publicizing the importance of and need for such studies; (c) the growth of the number of books and tapes on self-help approaches was growing rapidly; and (d) a rapid increase in the use of the Internet by the public and a rapid increase in the number of self-help approaches available on the Internet all pointed to the need for such studies.

To illustrate whether this expected proliferation of studies materialized, we examined the references for a number of review and meta-analytic-review studies for eight different target problems (an approach admittedly not leading to an exhaustive review of the literature). We grouped these studies in 5-year increments for the last three decades. These results are shown in Table 3.1. A number of trends stand out in this table. The most obvious trend is that, in spite of an increase in the number of such studies in recent years, there has clearly been no proliferation of research in this area. This conclusion accords with that of (Chapter 2 in this text), who argue that the case for the effectiveness of most self-help offerings in the health arena simply has not been made. There has, however, been a clearly increasing trend in the number of such studies, with a doubling in each successive decade over the previous decade. This increase in controlled outcome studies does seem to have been spurred by the high-profile reviews of this research area. The number of controlled evaluations of Internet-based interventions, on the other hand, has been limited.

A second trend to be seen in the completed studies is that researchers are increasingly willing to evaluate SATs for more difficult mental health problems. For example, studies on the effectiveness of SATs for eating

Table 3.1 Summary of the Number of Controlled Studies Evaluating SATs for Specific Target Problems Over a 30-Year Period

Target problem	5-Year period					
	75–79	80–84	85–89	90–94	95–99	00–04
Eating disorders			1	3	10	12
Sexual dysfunctions	5	4	3			1
Insomnia	1		1	2	2	3
Problem drinking			2	1	3	8
Cigarette smoking		2	1	2	9	1
Depression		3	2	2	6	5
Anxiety disorders	3	1	3	8	7	6
Childhood problems	1	1	1	3	6	1
Totals	10	11	14	21	43	37

disorders has increased greatly in the last decade, this in spite of the fact that eating disorders have been considered difficult to treat and sufferers both resistant to talk about their problems and to take action to change them. In a similar vein, problem drinking and depression both have seen a significant increase in the number of studies that have evaluated the effectiveness of SATs. The belief that therapists must be employed to overcome low levels of motivation of these target populations is being challenged by the success of the evaluated programs. The type of anxiety disorders being targeted has also shifted. In the early part of this 30-year period, speech anxiety and phobias were the target problems. More recently, panic disorder, agoraphobia, obsessive–compulsive disorder, and posttraumatic stress disorder have all been targeted, mostly successfully. This willingness to tackle mental disorders of known difficulty has consistently been preceded by the development of an effective treatment approach that is delivered by a therapist. This sort of progression makes sense, because the technology for delivering treatments already exists and simply awaits the development of content shown to be effective.

Effectiveness of Self-Administered Treatments

The determination of whether SATs are effective must be approached by providing answers to several questions and by drawing parallels to the psychotherapy outcome literature. Recent answers to the question of whether psychotherapy is effective have specified the importance of comparing specific treatments with different control groups, including wait-list (WL) and placebo (PL) controls, and the determination of whether specific treatments for any given disorder or problem yield different outcomes than do other treatments. In the domain of SATs, the questions addressed to date include: (a) whether SATs are more effective than no treatment or WL; and (b) whether SATs are equivalent to treatments offered in individual or group therapy formats (hereafter referred to as therapist-directed treatments [TDTs]). Other questions addressed are whether more individuals drop out of SATs as compared to TDTs and whether any improvements realized are stable over time. A further question is whether effectiveness rates differ depending on the type of problem that is being addressed.

To begin to answer these questions, the literature was examined for meta-analytic summaries of the effectiveness of SATs and TDTs, both for the general outcome literature and for specific disorders/problems. Meta-analytic summaries were chosen for comparison because they offer the best hope of making valid comparisons. These comparisons were further standardized by examining only those effect sizes (ESs) that compared SATs and TDTs to no treatment or WL groups, a decision necessitated by the almost exclusive use of such comparison groups in studies of the efficacy of SATs.

The first question addressed is whether individuals who enter studies that evaluate the effectiveness of SATs do not tolerate the approach being offered and drop out of treatment. Such dropouts could occur for a variety of reasons, including preference for seeing a live therapist or taking medication, failure to see the relevance of the selected SAT to the identified problem, a desire to sample the material rather than consume it in its entirety, or unwillingness to comply with assorted exercises offered in the self-help material. Rosen, Glasgow, and Barrera (1976) identified a number of examples of study participants who failed to conduct exercises, complete the entire treatment package, or dropped out of the study altogether. The question of compliance and how it relates to outcome will be addressed in a later section. The question of what the frequency of study dropouts is from SATs, however, was evaluated by Gould and Clum (1993) in a set of 40 studies. These authors reported that, in the studies that presented such information, the dropout rate was 9.7% for individuals receiving the SAT and 8.6% for individuals in the control condition. This estimate is comparable to the dropout rate of 10% of treated individuals and 9.2% of controls reported by Shapiro and Shapiro (1983) in their meta-analysis of psychotherapy studies where treatment was administered by a therapist. These results indicate that SATs are well-tolerated within the context of outcome studies in which individuals are formally enrolled.

A more recent analysis of dropout rate in SATs was conducted by Hirai and Clum (2006) for individuals seeking help for anxiety problems. These authors reported a dropout rate of 12.3% for individuals in SATs during the treatment period. Individuals dropped out while in the control conditions at somewhat higher rates, with 11.3% of individuals in WL groups, 13.4% in placebo groups, and 18.0% in minimal treatment groups dropping out during the intervention phase of the study. These results support the contention that participation in SATs is well tolerated and that individuals perceive the viability of the approach being offered.

The next question addressed concerns the level of treatment effectiveness of SATs. Several comprehensive meta-analyses have been conducted of the SAT literature, with overall estimates of effectiveness as measured by ESs for comparisons of SATs and WL/no treatment controls ranging from .57 (Marrs, 1995) to .87 (Gould & Clum, 1993). Given that SATs that have been empirically examined almost exclusively utilized cognitive–behavioral treatment (CBT) approaches, prudence requires that the above results be compared with the general effectiveness of CBT treatments delivered by trained experts. Bowers and Clum (1988) conducted such a meta-analytic study, evaluating 69 treatment studies that compared the effectiveness of therapist-administered CBTs to a placebo or attention-control group, with a subset of 40 studies that also utilized a no treatment or WL control. The overall ES comparing TDTs to WL was .76, while the overall ES comparing TDTs to placebo controls was .55. The estimates of ESs from the two general meta-analyses of SATs compare favorably with these estimates of effectiveness for TDTs. Several caveats exist for these comparisons. The Bowers and Clum study was conducted using treatments available 10 years prior to those evaluated in the meta-analytic summaries of SAT effectiveness. Given that SATs are based on standard CBT treatments for various disorders, improvements in treatments could be expected over that 10-year period. Such improvements would then be mirrored in the SATs, which, even when self-administered, could prove superior to older, less sophisticated approaches. In addition, summaries of treatments not aggregated by type of problem may pose additional problems. Gould and Clum (1993), for example, found that treatment effectiveness varied by type of target sample, with anxiety problems being more effectively treated with SATs than depression or habit disturbances. A more valid comparison, therefore, would examine the effectiveness of SATs and TDTs for the same type of target problem.

Accordingly, we next compared treatment effectiveness for different diagnostic groups/target problems. Table 3.2 summarizes these comparisons. An examination of the ESs for SATs indicates that the treatment effects may be described as highly variable, varying from small to large,

Table 3.2 Comparisons of Summary ESs for SATs and TDTs for Specific Types of Target Problems at Posttreatment

	Type of treatment approach	
Target problem	SATs	TDTs
Posttraumatic stress disorder	.45	1.26
Panic disorder/agoraphobia	.56	.87
Generalized anxiety disorder	.92	.82
Depression	.83	.73
Smoking	1.28	1.88
Alcohol abuse	.15	.37

using a standard for ESs developed by Wolf (1986). Thus, SATs are effective for a wide variety of mental health problems, when compared to WL controls, but this effectiveness varies in degree. Moreover, variations in the level of effectiveness mirror somewhat closely variations for TDTs for similar problems. For example, as indicated in Table 3.2, the lowest ESs, whether therapist-directed or self-administered, are for alcohol abuse problems, while the highest ESs are for smoking cessation. Moderate treatment effects are found for both TDTs and SATs for most of the anxiety disorders and depression.

A more accurate determination of whether SATs have approximately the same level of effect or are substantially less effective than TDTs comes from direct comparisons between these two venues in the same study. In these comparisons, more confidence can be placed in the outcomes because individuals with similar levels of the target problem are being treated in both groups. Fewer studies have been conducted that permit these types of comparisons. When they do exist, however, they are instructive. Hirai and Clum (2006), for example, evaluated such comparisons in individuals with various anxiety problems. In these comparisons, TDTs were clearly more effective for specific phobias, social anxiety, posttraumatic stress disorder (PTSD), and obsessive–compulsive disorder (OCD). Similar outcomes were found for panic disorder/agoraphobia and test anxiety. Differences in effectiveness between the two venues were also reported by van Lankveld (Chapter 9 in this text) in the treatment of sexual dysfunctions. van Lankveld reports equal efficacy between SATs and TDTs for problems of premature ejaculation but more efficacy for TDTs for problems of orgasmic dysfunction, especially in women.

Also lacking in the SAT effectiveness literature are follow-up studies that evaluate the duration of treatment effects. In the general meta-analysis by Gould and Clum (1993), only 12 of 40 studies conducted follow-up assessments in a form that allowed the determination of ESs. The ES for those 12 studies was .53, a moderate effect, and compares with an Es of .66 for these same 12 studies at posttreatment. These results suggest that the treatment effects were fairly stable, with some attenuation of the level of improvement. The stability of outcomes varies by type of target problem. Fairly stable results over time exist for social skills and headaches, variable results for smoking, and attenuation of treatment gains for weight loss and depression. Such comparisons are based on very few studies, however, and must be considered tentative. More recent meta-analyses of specific subsets of problems have yielded more reliable results, although based on a limited number of studies. Of 24 studies that compared the effectiveness of SATs to WL controls in the treatment of anxiety disorders, only 7 examined efficacy in a follow-up period. Of studies that compared SATs and TDTs in this same meta-analysis, 11 of 17 studied the comparative effects in a follow-up period. Hirai and Clum (2006) reported that treatment effects tended to be stable in the follow-up period and that differences between SATs and TDTs narrowed. Van Lankveld (Chapter 9 in this text), on the other hand, found that the effects of SATs for sexual dysfunctions tended to be short-lived, with problems in orgasmic dysfunction and pain during sexual activity reverting to levels extant prior to the start of treatment. Again, a caveat must be issued, as most of the SATs studied to date have used very brief follow-up periods to determine the stability of outcomes, with maximum periods infrequently exceeding 6 months.

In summary, individuals who enter treatment studies knowing that one of the approaches offered might be an SAT have dropout rates similar to those for individuals who enter treatment studies knowing that they will either be placed in a TDT or a control condition. Once assigned to an SAT, individuals tend to remain in treatment. For those individuals who complete SATs, outcomes are in the moderate range when compared to WL or placebo but tend to be somewhat less when compared to a TDT. This latter conclusion varies depending on the type of target problem, however, with SATs equivalent to TDTs for some disorders.

Moreover, relapse rates after treatment suggest that the effects of many SATs are stable. Once again, however, stability of effects varies depending on the type of problem being addressed.

Integrating SATs in the Delivery of Treatments for Health Problems

The principle question to be addressed here is whether any SATs have demonstrated sufficient efficacy to warrant their prescription for dealing with any health problems. A related question is how SATs are to be used in the treatment armamentarium—only adjunctively with other treatments offered by a professional, as a first step in a stepped-care approach, or as a stand-alone treatment. Also critical is the question of whether the most familiar approach to using SATs should be employed (i.e., prescribing an empirically validated book, tape, or Web-based intervention) or whether modifications should be recommended in how SATs are utilized (e.g., with regular therapist follow-up and only in the context of an established health care system).

Arguably, those SATs that have shown empirical equivalence to TDTs can be recommended as stand-alone treatments. SATs that are effective compared to WL but less effective than TDTs, on the other hand, would be considered the first step in a stepped-care approach. Stepped-care can be defined as "lower-cost interventions (that) are tried first, with more intensive and costly interventions reserved for those insufficiently helped by the initial intervention" (Haaga, 2000, p. 547). Cognitive behavioral treatment approaches, especially when delivered in group format, have been found to be more cost-efficient for panic disorder (PD) than pharmacologic interventions (Otto, Pollack, & Maki, 2001). Thus, stepped-care interventions might involve SATs alone, SATs in combination with individual or group therapy interventions, psychotherapy alone, and pharmacologic agents. In a special section published in the *Journal of Consulting and Clinical Psychology* devoted to examining stepped-care approaches to psychotherapy, a series of experts recommended SATs or SAT-augmented treatments for generalized anxiety disorder (GAD; Newman, 2001), PD (Otto et al., 2001), eating disorders (Wilson, Vitousek, & Loeb, 2001), and alcohol problems (Sobell & Sobell, 2000).

While SATs have been found effective for a number of diagnosable problems, solutions for implementing their use in stepped-care approaches have yet to be resolved. One approach would be to develop predictive models for who responds to SATs, TDTs, and pharmacotherapies. Differential assignment to these treatments would require different predictive models, a requirement that may prove elusive, given Otto et al.'s (2000) experience with predicting treatment response in individuals with PD. These authors report that severity and comorbidity predict outcome regardless of the treatment venue.

In contrast, Sobell and Sobell (2000) recommend an approach in which assignment to venue of treatment is based on clinical judgment and would include such variables as severity of the problem, the presence of suicide ideation, and the patient's preferences for and biases toward treatment. Decisions to continue or change treatment approaches would be based on evaluations that reflect progress or not. The requirement of involving experts from the beginning of treatment has the added benefit of ensuring that the recommended treatment approach fits the problem definition.

When used adjunctively to individual or group-administered treatments, SATs have another benefit; i.e., they can be used once treatment is over as a reference guide for what to do in case of setbacks or relapse. This approach would reduce therapist time requirements and provide support for the individual's efficacy for solving the problem alone.

Feedback Approaches for Enhancing Outcome

SATs, whether delivered via books or computer-assisted programs, often incorporate continuous assessments to check on progress or the lack of progress. Stepped-care approaches require the use of constant monitoring to determine whether progress is occurring or whether a shift to more traditional treatments is required. As examined to date, SATs have utilized assessments to provide feedback to the individual being treated and to the individual conducting the study to assist with treatment planning.

Feedback mechanisms regarding the progress of individuals in treatment serve to enhance treatment outcome (Chapter 4 in this text). This is true whether the feedback is provided to the individual in treatment or to the therapist working with the individual. In both cases, the mechanisms for producing change are likely similar. Feedback to the individual in treatment informs the individual of her progress, or lack thereof. If informing the individual of progress, feedback serves as both a reward and as information that the individual is acting in ways to produce treatment gains. If informing of lack of progress, feedback serves to motivate and to help the individual change direction and attempt other approaches. Feedback to the therapist may have similar effects. This possibility was explored in a study by Lambert, Hansen, and Finch (2001), who compared the results of a simple feedback system that used color-coding to identify progress and to make simple change-no-change in treatment plan recommendations. Therapists who received such feedback produced more cases with clinically significant change than did therapists not receiving feedback. Other therapist feedback systems have similar goals but their effectiveness has not been evaluated. Ideas regarding how to use feedback in SATs can be gleaned from research on feedback with TDTs.

In spite of the lack of validating data, Lambert (2001) identified a beginning trend to evaluate individual treatment progress as an approach likely to enhance psychotherapy outcomes. In his discussion of this important area, he noted that psychotherapy outcome research has evolved from efficacy research, which establishes differential treatment outcomes for specific modalities under controlled conditions, to effectiveness research, which establishes the effectiveness of various treatment approaches on the front lines, where treatment is being accomplished with individuals of complex diagnostic configurations. More recently, assessing treatment outcomes has been expanded to include evaluating the progress of individuals, in comparison to predicted pathways based on normative data.

In one such model, reported on by Lueger, Howard, Martinovich, Lutz, Anderson, and Grissom (2001), individuals were compared to three dosage levels of outcome and three phases of outcome to determine where they were in terms of psychotherapeutic progress. Howard, Kopta, Krause, and Orlinsky (1986) reported that 50% of patients improved after 8 sessions, 75% improved after 26 sessions, and 85% reached an asymptote after 60 sessions. Variability in this pattern was produced by variations in diagnoses, symptoms, and interpersonal problems. The rate of patient improvement was slower in a study by Anderson and Lambert (2001), who reported that 50% of patients needed 13 sessions of psychotherapy before reporting clinically significant change. Using a phase model to describe how therapy progresses, Howard, Lueger, Maling, and Martinovich (1993) reported three distinct phases—increases in subjective well-being (remoralization), symptom reduction (remediation), and recovery of life functioning (rehabilitation). Improvement in remoralization occurred mostly around the 2nd session, remediation around the 6th session, and life functioning around the 10th session. Deviations from this progression have been linked to less successful treatment outcomes.

Feedback systems such as described in these studies of psychotherapy processes have not been systematically incorporated into therapist-assisted treatments or SATs. The potential for doing so, however, is considerable. Self-help books frequently include a variety of assessment devices with instructions to chart progress on a regular basis. A variety of online programs exist that conduct basic assessments that help individuals identify the types of problems they may have, with recommendations to check such assessments with their therapist or to proceed to the online treatment. Online assessments are capable of much more, given that repeat assessments are relatively easy to perform, as are graphs illustrating change over time. As an example, panicsolutions.com offers a real-time feedback report for individuals who want to evaluate their pre- and posttreatment panic profile and compare themselves to individuals who have completed a self-administered treatment program. Because this assessment incorporates evaluations of the principle symptom domains of PD, coping strategies, and efficacy for performing coping strategies, users of the program can evaluate themselves on factors predictive of and representative of treatment change. Therapists who utilize this system can receive regular updates on their clients' progress. Roodman (1996), in an unpublished study, evaluated a feedback system based on this profile and delivered either in person, by a therapist, or by mail. When compared to assessment only, differential improvement was found for the feedback groups on frequency of full and limited-symptom panic attacks.

Using established assessments for different disorders, the effectiveness of SATs could be examined and rates of change compared. As with the studies completed for TDTs, such assessments could help determine whether change continues to occur or whether an asymptote has been reached. Decisions could then be made to utilize another self-help modality or to switch to a TDT or pharmacologic agent. Participants in the program would also have access to such data and could be a part of the decision process.

Summary and Conclusions

The present chapter began with an evaluation of the scope of self-help approaches to problems of medical and psychological relevance in present-day American society. While the use of various self-help approaches is both undeniable and vast, much less information is available on the effectiveness of these approaches. One of the chief difficulties encountered in examining the role of SATs for reducing health problems in our society is that no information exists as to how individuals identify the problems to be addressed, whether the identified problems exist in a form that can be targeted by SATs, how or whether such self-help vehicles are utilized, and whether any change takes place.

As an alternative to the way in which SATs are currently consumed, an alternative approach was identified, one that parallels how SATs have been evaluated in the scientific literature. In this approach, SATs are considered to have a potentially important role in society's overall approach to health problems. Such a role recognizes the treatment validity of some approaches and calls for the development and testing of others. Critical to the employment of such approaches is the formal diagnostic process that typifies the medical/psychological treatment process when individuals access formal health care modalities. It is not expected that such an approach would replace the current way in which self-help treatments are used, but rather that it would augment the current approach.

For SATs to be incorporated into the current health system, it must first be established that they are in fact effective. Also requisite is the determination of the level of effectiveness. Accordingly, the literature on effectiveness was selectively sampled to provide a sense of the levels at which effectiveness has been tested and the levels of effectiveness so far established. Generally speaking, the number of studies is still low but the frequency with which such approaches are being examined is accelerating. Evidence collected so far paints a picture of a small cadre of approaches validated for a growing number of specific health problems. Furthermore, the evidence suggests that the approaches targeted to date are well tolerated, moderately effective, and generally stable in their effects. Moreover, an examination of the outcome studies that have been conducted leads to the inevitable conclusion that the only information available on effectiveness exists in the context of studies completed after both a thorough evaluation of the problem to be addressed and careful monitoring of the progress found.

Next addressed was the use of SATs in a stepped-care approach to medical and psychological problems. The stepped-care approach, when applied to SATs, is basically a conceptualization of the possible roles SATs could have relative to other treatment approaches. The recommendation was made that SATs could be a valuable first step when their validity has been established and when they are clearly inferior to TDTs. SATs would have alternate treatment status when they were found equivalent to TDTs in treatment effect. Regardless of the history of effectiveness determined in past studies, an important feature of the stepped-care approach is continuous monitoring of the individual's progress for the approach selected. Regular monitoring of treatment progress is considered essential to the determination of treatment effectiveness in the community setting, having established treatment efficacy in controlled studies.

Another approach for the use of continuous assessment of SAT effectiveness was found in a set of studies used to establish norms for change in mental health problems, regardless of the psychological treatment approach employed. This approach seeks to identify common processes across theoretically different treatment approaches as well as to identify typical time periods for patient involvement in each of those processes. While not yet employed in SAT research, the promise exists for finding common therapeutic elements as well as for estimating the time required for various types of change using SATs.

Chapter Points

- The first step in addressing health problems within the health care system is diagnosis, a step often omitted in seeking self-administered solutions to problems.
- Also missing in the application of self-help remedies is an understanding of specific connections between causal factors and the identified problem, a gap that may reduce successful treatment of the problem.
- The place of SATs in the total approach to health delivery systems is largely undefined. The current role of SATs is largely informal,

with neither access nor use tied to diagnosed problems, except when recommended by a health care professional.
- More formal integration of SATs into the health care system is possible. The extant body of empirical literature evaluating the effectiveness of SATs illustrates how formal incorporation of such approaches might work.
- Empirical studies of the effectiveness of SATs has been increasing, as have investigations of more difficult and complex mental health problems.
- The effectiveness of SATs has been demonstrated for a number of different problems, while the level of effectiveness parallels that for TDTs. SATs will continue to be used informally but also might be formally incorporated into the health care system as both stand-alone treatments and as the first step in stepped-care approaches.
- The formal use of SATs requires ongoing assessment of progress, a procedure that both enhances outcome and improves the likelihood of selecting the best treatment approach.

References

Anderson, E. E., & Lambert, M. J. (2001). A survival analysis of clinically significant change in outpatient psychotherapy. *Journal of Clinical Psychology, 57*, 875–888.

Bowers, T., & Clum, G. A. (1988). The relative contribution of specific and non-specific treatment effects: analysis of placebo-controlled behavior therapy research. *Psychological Bulletin, 103*, 315–323.

Bradley, R., Greene, J., Buss, E., Deetra, L., & Westen, D. (2005). A multi-dimensional meta-analysis of psychotherapy for PTSD. *American Journal of Psychiatry, 162*, 214–227.

Cuijpers, P. (1997). Bibliotherapy in unipolar depression: A meta-analysis. *Journal of Behavior Therapy and Experimental Psychiatry, 28*, 139–147.

Glasgow, R. E., & Rosen, G. M. (1978). Behavioral bibliotherapy: A review of self-help behavior therapy manuals. *Psychological Bulletin, 85*, 1–23.

Gould, R. A. & Clum, G. A. (1993). A meta-analysis of self-help treatment approaches. *Clinical Psychology Review, 13*, 169–186.

Haaga, D. A. F. (2000). Introduction to the special section on stepped care models in psychology. *Journal of Consulting and Clinical Psychology, 68*, 547–549.

Hirai, M., & Clum, G. A. (2006). A meta-analytic study of self-help interventions for anxiety problems. *Behavior Therapy, 37*, 99–111.

Howard, K. I., Kopta, S. M., Krause, M. S., & Orlinsky, D. E. (1986). The dose effect relationship in psychotherapy. *American Psychologist, 51*, 159–164.

Howard, K. I., Lueger, R. J., Maling, M. S., & Martinovich, Z. (1993). A phase model of psychotherapy outcome: Casual motivation of change. *Journal of Consulting and Clinical Psychology, 61*, 678–685.

Lambert, M. J. (2001). Psychotherapy outcome and quality improvement: Introduction to the special section on patient-focused research. *Journal of Consulting and Clinical Psychology, 69,* 147–150.

Lambert, M. J., Hansen, N. B., & Finch, A. E. (2001). Patient focused research: Using patient outcome data to enhance treatment of fear. *Journal of Consulting and Clinical Psychology, 69,* 159–172.

Lueger, R. J., Howard, K. I., Martinovich, Z., Lutz, W., Anderson, E. E., & Grissom, G. (2001). Assessing treatment progress of individual patients using expected treatment response models. *Journal of Consulting and Clinical Psychology, 69,* 150–159.

Marrs, R. W. (1995). A meta-analysis of bibliotherapy studies. *American Journal of Community Psychology, 23,* 843–870.

Mitte, K. (2004). A meta-analysis of the efficacy of psycho- and pharmacotherapy in panic disorder with and without agoraphobia. *Journal of Affective Disorders, 88,* 127–145.

Mojica, W. A., Suttorp, M. J., Sherman, S. E., Morton, S. C., Roth, E. A., Maglione, M. A., et al. (2004). Smoking-cessation interventions by type of provider: A meta-analysis. *American Journal of Preventive Medicine, 26,* 391–401.

Newman, M. G. (2000). Recommendations for cost-offset model of psychotherapy allocation using generalized anxiety disorder as an example. *Journal of Consulting and Clinical Psychology, 69,* 549–556.

Otto, M. W., Pollack, M. H., & Maki, K. M. (2000). Empirically supported treatments for panic disorder: Costs, benefits and stepped care. *Journal of Consulting and Clinical Psychology, 69,* 556–564.

Robinson, L. A., Berman, J. S., & Neimeyer, R. A. (1990). Psychotherapy for the treatment of depression: A comprehensive review of controlled outcome research. *Psychological Bulletin, 108,* 30–49.

Roodman, A. A. (1996). *A test of the effects of assessment and feedback on individuals with panic attacks.* Unpublished master's thesis, Virginia Tech., Blacksburg, VA.

Rosen, G. M. (1987). Self-help treatment books and the commercialization of psychotherapy. *American Psychologist, 42,* 46–51.

Rosen, G. M., Barrera, M., & Glasgow, R. E. (2007). Good intentions are not enough: Reflections on past and future efforts to advance self-help. In P. L. Watkins & G. A. Clum (Eds.) *Handbook of self-help therapies* (pp. 25–39). New York: Routledge.

Rosen, G. M., Glasgow, R. E., & Barrera, M. (1976). A controlled study to assess the clinical efficacy of totally self-administered systematic desensitization. *Journal of Consulting and Clinical Psychology, 44,* 208–217.

Shapiro, D., & Shapiro, D. (1983). Comparative therapy outcome research: Methodological implications of meta-analysis. *Journal of Consulting and Clinical Psychology, 51,* 42–53.

Sobell, M. B., & Sobell, L. C. (2000). Stepped care as a heuristic approach to the treatment of alcohol problems. *Journal of Consulting and Clinical Psychology, 69,* 573–580.

van Lankveld, J. J. D. M. (1998). Bibliotherapy in the treatment of sexual dysfunctions: A meta-analysis. *Journal of Consulting and Clinical Psychology, 66,* 702–708.

Westen, D., Novotny, C. M., & Thompson-Brenner, H. (2004). The empirical status of empirically-supported therapies: Assumptions, findings, and reporting in controlled clinical trials. *Psychological Bulletin, 130*, 631–663.

Wilson, G. T., Vitousek, K. M., & Loeb, K. L. (2000). Stepped care treatment for eating disorders. *Journal of Consulting and Clinical Psychology, 69*, 564–573.

Wolf, F. M. (1986). *Meta-analysis. Quantitative methods for research synthesis.* Beverly Hills, CA: Sage.

CHAPTER 4

Self-Regulation Theory and Self-Help Therapies

GREG A. R. FEBBRARO AND GEORGE A. CLUM

Overview

Self-help treatments for emotional and physical disorders often utilize, implicitly or explicitly, principles of self-regulation that are used to produce and maximize change. An examination of these principles and the theoretical frameworks that organize them help us to understand how best to maximize change and how self-directed change comes about. Theories of self-regulation have emerged from a variety of disciplines, including psychology, sociology, physics, medicine, engineering, mathematics, and economics. This chapter first examines several prominent theories that have applied principles of self-regulation to psychological processes of change. Next examined is the empirical evidence identifying which processes are effective, especially as they relate to self-help treatments. Then, the processes that have the most promise are examined for how to best integrate these processes into self-administered treatment approaches.

Self-Regulation Theories of Human Behavior

Self-regulation refers to the psychological processes that mediate goal-directed behavior in the absence of immediate consequences (Carver & Scheier, 1986; Kanfer, 1970). Self-regulatory processes are naturally initiated when routinized activity is impeded or when goal-directedness is otherwise made salient (Karoly, 1993). However, self-regulatory processes are also initiated by prompting, as when individuals in treatment programs are prompted to engage in some behavior by the change agent. Psychologically based theories of self-regulation originate from cybernetics, the science of self-regulation (Wiener, 1948). As Watson and Tharp (2002) point out, most psychological theories of self-regulation contain several basic cybernetic principles (Bandura, 1986, 1991; Carver & Scheier, 1982, 1999; Kanfer, 1975; Kanfer & Stevenson, 1985; Miller, Galanter, & Pribram, 1960; Mithaug, 1993).

The thermostat of a home heating system has often been used as an example to illustrate the major principles and mechanisms of cybernetic theory (e.g., Endler & Kocovski, 2000; Watson & Tharp, 2002). A thermostat has four key mechanisms—a standard, sensor, comparator, and an activator. The standard (i.e., goal) identifies the temperature that is to be maintained. The sensor detects the actual temperature, while the comparator examines the current temperature against the standard. When the temperature deviates from the standard, the thermostat signals the activator, which either turns the heater on or turns it off. In this system a reasonably good balance is maintained between the actual and desired temperature.

Human behavior can be viewed as being regulated in a similar fashion. Individuals identify standards or goals, initiate a set of behaviors to attain those goals, monitor their level of accomplishment, compare their level of accomplishment to the goals, and determine whether their behaviors should be adjusted in order to meet the goals. If a discrepancy is discovered between an individual's standards and actual behaviors, attempts are made to modify the behaviors to better meet the standard (Endler & Kocovski, 2000; Watson & Tharp, 2002). This modification might take the form of increasing or decreasing the behaviors intended to help reach the goal or by identifying new strategies to help attain the objective.

Self-regulation theories vary in the extent to which they use cybernetic formulations. Carver and Scheier (e.g., 1982, 1999) base their control theory strictly on cybernetic processes, while Bandura (e.g., 1986, 1991) adds planning, judgment, and self-efficacy to these principles. Kanfer and colleagues (e.g., Kanfer, 1975; Kanfer & Schefft, 1988; Kanfer & Stevenson, 1985) have added other psychological processes, including reward, punishment, learning, and thinking to their formulation of how to maximize the change process. This chapter focuses on Carver and Scheier's, Bandura's, and Kanfer's self-regulation theories, with particular emphasis on Bandura's and Kanfer's contributions.

Carver and Scheier's control theory of self-regulation (e.g., 1982) emphasizes goal setting, feedback on efforts to reach the goal, and the individual's attempts to reduce discrepancies between the goal and performance. Goals energize and direct activities and are viewed as referencing values in feedback loops. Feedback loops include four elements: (a) an input function based on perceptions of performance, (b) a goal, (c) a comparison of performance to the goal, and (d) a continuation of or modification of the previous behavior, known as output function.

The output function is equivalent to behavior in control theory (Carver, 2004) and can be either internal or external in nature. If the comparison yields no difference between the goal and performance, the performing individual likely maintains the same behavior. If the comparison identifies a discrepancy between the goal and performance, the output function changes. Carver postulates that several responses are possible. The individual can increase the strength of the previous behavior, change strategy, or modify or abandon the goal.

Bandura's and Kanfer's theories of self-regulation have a number of principles in common and, accordingly, will be discussed together. Both Bandura and Kanfer postulate that: (a) behavior results from the interaction of various factors; (b) self-regulation proceeds through stages; (c) goals and feedback are important, as are distinctions between proximal and distal goals; (d) internal and external attributions play a role in change processes; (e) discrepancies between goals and performance motivate behavior; and (f) commitment enhances motivation. Bandura, however, also emphasizes the importance of self-efficacy, a belief in one's ability to engage in behavior that leads to goal attainment.

Both Bandura and Kanfer view behavior as resulting from a combination of factors. Bandura (1986) explains human behavior as a consequence of cognitive factors, other internal factors, and environmental events. Kanfer emphasizes the interaction among environmental, psychological, and biological events (Kanfer & Schefft, 1988). Further, Kanfer postulates that self-regulation proceeds only if a disruption in a person's system is determined to result from the person's behavioral incompetence (psychological variables) as opposed to the perception of some more basic incompetence that prevents learning new behaviors.

Kanfer views self-regulation as proceeding through three distinct stages: (a) self-monitoring (or self-observation); (b) self-evaluation (or self-reflection); and (c) self-reinforcement (or self-reaction). It should be noted that the terms in parentheses are Bandura's terms for the same stage and, therefore, both terms for each stage will be used interchangeably throughout the remainder of this chapter.

Both Bandura and Kanfer view self-monitoring as providing an individual with the information needed to establish realistic goals and for evaluating his or her progress toward those goals. Further, self-monitoring allows an individual to direct his behavior (Bandura, 1991; Kanfer & Schefft, 1988). The effectiveness of self-monitoring depends upon several factors, including: (a) whether coping behavior or the target behavior is monitored; (b) whether explicit expectations are provided by an external monitor (Kazdin, 1974; Nelson, Lipinski, & Black, 1975); (c) whether timing of the self-monitoring response is manipulated (i.e., monitoring prior to, rather than after, the occurrence of the target behavior; Bellack, Rozensky, & Schwartz, 1974; Nelson, Hay, & Hay, 1977; Romanczyk, 1974); and (d) whether the self-monitoring response itself is further specified (e.g., monitoring eating alone vs. monitoring eating as well as caloric intake of food eaten). In both Bandura's and Kanfer's theories, self-monitoring serves to increase self-awareness and possibly serves to enhance effectiveness.

In the self-evaluation stage, current behavior is compared against standards or goals. Bandura notes that monitoring performance has little meaning without comparing performance to some standard. Kanfer notes that, before comparing current behavior to a standard, a particular criterion for that behavior must be selected. Moreover, the monitored behavior must be important to the person's motivational state or current concern. "Current concern" refers to the state of the individual between the time a commitment is undertaken to pursue a particular goal and the time to either consummate the goal or abandon its pursuit and disengage from the goal. The monitored behavior attains significance in proportion to the degree that it relates to the current concern.

Kanfer's model further differentiates between short-term and long-term concerns. Short-term concerns focus on the performance of behavior relevant to the immediate situation and to specific proximal goals. Long-term concerns relate to the maintenance of enduring personal goals (i.e., distal goals), especially as they affect the person's standards for personal conduct in a wide range of situations. Long-term concerns thus relate to self-perceptions regarding personal capabilities and repertoires. In addition to the distinction between proximal and distal goals and its importance for treatment, level of goal difficulty, the individual's role in defining goals, and goals in conjunction with feedback also have important treatment implications.

Proximal goals have been noted to result in better goal-related performance than distal goals (Bandura & Schunck, 1981; Bandura & Simon, 1977). In addition, goals result in better task performance when explicit and challenging than when easy and vague (Locke, Shaw, Saari, & Latham, 1981; Masters, Furman, & Barden, 1977). Furthermore, collaborative goals have been recommended in the clinical literature (Washton & Stone-Washton, 1990). However, the goal-setting data do not clearly support an advantage of collaborative goals relative to assigned goals (Locke, 1991; Locke et al., 1981). Finally, feedback has been defined as information about performance (Kazdin, 1994) or as knowledge of results (Locke et al., 1981). In order to improve performance, both goals and feedback are necessary (Locke, 1991; Locke et al., 1981). Goals have been found to relate significantly to performance in the presence of feedback but not in its absence (Erez, 1977).

Bandura (1986) notes that feedback serves two functions: (a) it provides information regarding goal-related performance; and (b) it serves as a sign of progress, which can affect motivation through self-evaluative mechanisms. Feedback can vary along a number of dimensions, such as amount, type, specificity, timing, source, and recency (Ilgen, Fisher, & Taylor, 1979). Effectiveness of feedback in changing behavior varies depending on whether feedback is self-administered (e.g., graphing of results) or administered by another individual, such as a therapist. Self-administered feedback is usually more immediate than feedback administered by another individual and the immediacy or timing of feedback may also be a factor in behavior change.

In the self-reinforcement stage, individuals either reward or punish themselves depending on their performance (Kanfer & Hagerman, 1981; Kanfer & Schefft, 1988). Bandura (1991) notes that "people pursue courses of action that produce positive self-reactions and refrain from behaving in ways that results in self-censure" (p. 256). Self-reinforcement is most effective when the individual determines it is warranted and administers the reward (Kazdin, 1994).

Bandura's theory also specifies how an individual might react when faced with a discrepancy between performance and the goal. If the individual views the goal as important and also holds positive expectancies, goal-directed behaviors are likely increased. When the goal is met, discrepancy reduction occurs, which increases both efficacy and commitment as well as facilitates the adoption of an even more challenging goal. The new goal again may result in the creation of a new discrepancy that, in turn, motivates behavior.

Both Bandura and Kanfer view the self-regulation process as having motivational properties because goal attainment produces reinforcement (Kanfer & Schefft, 1988). Motivation is also enhanced by feedback, self-efficacy and commitment. Bandura's (1986) concept of self-efficacy determines the manner in which self-observation, self-reflection, and self-reaction components operate. For example, self-efficacy beliefs affect self-observation of various aspects of one's performance and the consequences from them. High self-efficacy can result in greater attention to information received from self-observation because of the belief in one's ability to affect one's performance. In addition, self-efficacy affects an individual's response to discrepancy between a personal standard and achievement of that standard. An individual with high self-efficacy will be motivated by a discrepancy between a goal and performance and will increase persistence toward that standard. An individual with low self-efficacy may respond to a similar situation by changing the standard or decrease persistence toward that standard (Bandura & Cervone, 1983, 1986).

Commitment is another factor affecting motivation. Commitment may be increased by having an individual sign a specific contract to work toward a goal or to contract for the assignment of penalties for failure to reach a goal. For example, Bowers, Winett, and Frederiksen (1987) effectively utilized contingent monetary contracts in decreasing smoking over a 6-month period. Factors that increase commitment and self-efficacy are likely to produce increased motivation to work toward goal attainment.

Effectiveness of Self-Regulatory Processes

A principal aim of any system of psychotherapy is to assist individuals in regulating their behavior (Endler & Kocovski, 2000). Carl Rogers (1954), for example, believed that changes within the self would occur as a result of someone becoming more aware of their emotions. Other more directive approaches to psychotherapy specify techniques that can be used to initiate and maintain changes in behavior. This is particularly the case when utilizing behavioral and cognitive–behavioral treatments. These approaches often explicitly incorporate self-regulatory strategies as part of treatment. For example, in behavior therapy, self-monitoring of target behavior, determination of realistic short- and long-term goals, and subsequent tracking of the target behavior via use of graphs (i.e., visual feedback) are key components of treatment.

Treatments based on self-regulation principles have been found generally effective with both children and adults. In children, such treatments have been found to decrease encopretic (i.e., involuntary elimination) behaviors (Grimes, 1983) and hyperactive behaviors and to increase academic performance in hyperactive boys (Varni & Henker, 1979). Self-regulatory strategies have been examined as primary interventions with adult problem behaviors. For example, adult problem behaviors successfully targeted have included smoking (e.g., Foxx & Axelroth, 1983; McFall, 1970), obsessive rumination (e.g., Mahoney, 1971), and depressive symptomatology (e.g., Harmon, Nelson, & Hayes, 1980).

While self-regulation provides a framework for understanding how self-change comes about, it remains to be determined whether and to what extent specific processes affect behavior. Armed with evidence regarding which processes are effective, one can feel secure in developing change programs that combine those strategies with the highest payoffs. We will now turn our attention to an examination of these relationships.

Meta-Analytic Review of Self-Regulation Strategies

Febbraro and Clum (1998) conducted a meta-analytic review of self-regulation strategies on adult problem behaviors to determine: (a) which strategies produce change; (b) which combination of strategies produce change; and (c) the degree of expectable change for each strategy and combination of strategies. In these analyses, various components of self-regulation were evaluated both in comparison to various types of no treatment controls and in comparison to self-monitoring alone. One question addressed in this review was whether therapist-assisted interventions were superior to self-administered interventions. A comparison of 8 studies that included therapist contact to 15 that did not support the importance of having a therapist participate in the self-regulatory process. Moreover, both individual therapist contact and mail contact produced incremental improvement over no involvement by a therapist, suggesting that only minimal amounts of contact are necessary to enhance outcomes and that unobtrusive contact may be as effective as more direct therapist contact.

When interventions that used self-regulatory processes (self-monitoring, self-evaluation, and self-reinforcement) were compared to wait-list or minimal contact controls, a small effect ($D = .25$) was found favoring the use of self-regulation techniques. Considerable variability existed among studies, however, with seven producing positive results and five producing negative results; i.e., favoring the no treatment condition (one study showed no difference). Five of the seven studies with positive results used only self-monitoring to produce change, while four of the negative studies combined self-monitoring and another self-regulatory component. The effect size when self-monitoring was compared to no treatment was small ($D = .29$), while the effect size comparing self-monitoring plus another self-regulatory component to no treatment was moderate in degree ($D = .37$). These results suggest a small advantage for adding another self-regulatory component to self-monitoring.

The next question addressed was whether self-monitoring was enhanced by using another self-regulatory process when compared to self-monitoring alone. Ten studies were found that evaluated this comparison. Adding another component produced a moderate effect ($D = .42$), again suggesting that multiple self-regulatory components produce larger effects than self-monitoring alone. Specific self-regulatory components were next examined. Adding goal-setting to self-monitoring produced a moderate effect size (D = .60), while adding feedback to self-monitoring produced a large effect (D = .80). Adding external reinforcement to self-monitoring, on the other hand, did not produce a significant increment in effect. Since internal satisfaction for accomplishing a goal can be considered a form of internal reinforcement, this latter finding seems to suggest that external rewards do not enhance the effects of feedback and self-satisfaction for reaching an identified goal.

Several studies evaluated the effects of different types of self-monitoring. Monitoring coping attempts produced a moderate effect size (D = .60), while monitoring outcome data produced a small effect size (D = .15). Studies that evaluated the effect of specific experimenter expectancies on outcome indicated that such expectancies produced an outcome effect size in the moderate range (D = .64). When explicit expectancies were not made, the overall monitoring effect was small (D = .06). Finally, instructions that indicated that specific behaviors were to be monitored produced a moderate effect size (D = .76), compared to instructions to monitor more general behaviors (D = .13). This effect was further substantiated from an analysis of studies that compared the effects of monitoring specific behaviors (D = .57) to that of monitoring change in self-report measures of target behaviors (D = .32). Overall, these findings support the contention that monitoring coping strategies has a positive effect on outcome and that monitoring specific outcomes, especially behaviors, specified by the experimenter produces more positive outcomes.

The importance of identifying specific goals was examined peripherally in the meta-analytic review. Nonetheless, identifying specific goals can be expected to have a positive effect on outcome. This question has been addressed in the literature examining the effects of abstinent versus controlled drinking as target outcomes in individuals with alcohol abuse problems. If abstinence is a more specific goal than controlled drinking, studies that evaluate these two approaches should favor the former. In fact, however, outcomes vary depending on the study. Hodgins, Leigh, Milne, and Gerrish (1997) found that choosing an abstinence goal produced better results than choosing moderate drinking. Ojehagen and Berglund (1989), on the other hand, found that individuals with an abstinence goal drank more during heavy drinking days than patients with controlled drinking goals, an outcome explainable by the abstinence violation effect.

The question of how goal-setting exerts its effects helps clarify how goal-setting should be employed in the change process. Locke and Latham (2002) specify four ways that goals influence performance, viz. via specifying direction, increasing effort and persistence, and suggesting specific strategies. Clear goals direct attention toward goal-relevant activities and away from goal-irrelevant activities. Numerous self-help books and tapes are effective expositions of the relationship of long-term goals (financial success) to short-term goals (developing previously successful stock-trading habits). Motivation to develop the identified habits is provided by numerous examples of successful people who have employed those specific habits. Breakdowns in remembering more distal goals and their relationship to proximal goals have been used to explain relapse (Baumeister & Heatherton, 1996).

Application of Self-Regulation to Self-Help Treatments

Self-help books (SH), as well as other venues for presenting SH programs, can be classified in terms of their intent. Some are designed to encourage, to provide hope for individuals who are without hope, or to raise the aspiration bar higher than previously dared. Such books often use first-person accounts of someone overcoming adversity previously thought intractable or of achieving at a level previously unimagined.

Other books seek to establish a goal as well as to provide information on how to achieve the goal. The vast majority of SH books are of this variety. The assumption of such books is that individuals provided with information will be able to use the provided information in a productive way and will accordingly attain the goal identified by the author. If the identified goal is to increase a person's net worth and a system of identifying stocks that were likely to increase in value was provided, the assumption would be that readers who share that goal and who used the information provided would become wealthier. A more sophisticated program might also provide information on when to buy the stocks and when to sell them. In either case, the program for wealth attainment remains primarily informational.

A third level of sophistication is provided by SH books that identify goals and provide information but also use self-regulation technology to increase the likelihood that the imparted information will be used at a manageable rate and that improvement will be identified and rewarded. This self-regulation technology, when provided in books, works by prescribing exercises of a graded nature as well as by identifying targets to achieve and ways of assessing progress toward those targets.

A more sophisticated self-change approach is possible but not when provided using the usual SH materials of books and tapes. This approach employs systems that evaluate the individual's progress and provides information and feedback about progress, including information regarding the skills being employed to attain the goals. In such a system, the functions of self-regulation are being assumed by the program developer.

Internet-based programs that provide the user with exercises to perform and then track progress in performing these exercises, with automatized feedback of this progress, fall into this group. Such an approach makes the entire process easier to participate in and is designed to keep the maximum number of people in the program.

The question of why people who are suffering do not identify a goal to reduce suffering and then engage in a program of change is complex. An examination of contributing factors includes: (a) the absence of a clear assessment of the problem and of reasons that the problem developed; (b) despair that the problem cannot be eliminated or even reduced; (c) the absence of a clear plan for how that change will be accomplished, along with an appreciation of the probable roadblocks that will develop along the way. This early confusion in the beginning of the change process was recognized by Prochaska (1984), who identified the stages of precontemplation and contemplation as the first two phases in the process. These stages are characterized by a failure to identify what might be wrong and why, and hence a failure to identify strategies for remedying the problem. Attempts to move problem-laden individuals to a recognition of the problem, thence to a decision to change the problem, and then into the selection and execution of a program for change are marked by strategies that increase awareness that a problem exists, awareness of the contributing factors, and the provision of specific strategies that can be used to alter the problem.

Accurate assessment of the problem itself becomes a change agent by providing individuals with a summary of their behavior and a comparison of their behavior to some normative group. Fishbein and Ajzen (1975), in their theory of reasoned action, propose that the actor's own positive and negative attitudes toward her behavior, plus subjective norms, determine her intention to perform that behavior. Assessment serves the purpose of making salient both the level of the target behavior and consequences of the behavior, as well as comparisons to some normative group's expression of that behavior. Armed with this information, the individual's attitudes to that behavior may become more positive or negative and her view of the behavior as normal may change. This reasoning underpins the administration of the Drinker Checkup (Miller, Sovereign, & Krege, 1988), which summarizes for the drinker his self-reported levels and style of drinking as well as the type and frequency of any problems associated with that drinking. Also provided are normative comparisons of these levels and problems with peers, making an evaluation of whether a problem exists easier to make. Studies have shown that participation in this assessment increases motivation to change behavior and moves the individual closer to employing agents of change.

Self-regulation principles inform the self-change process for each level described above. At level one, books that describe a person's success help individuals identify with that success and begin to hope, when previously that hope may have been absent. Such books help provide motivation toward a long-range goal, such as to be anxiety-free or to live a life without being dependent on alcohol to get through the day. Embedded within such stories are the many adversities faced by the writer that help the reader both increase his level of identification with the author and increase his hope for the possibility of change. Various individuals who study the process of psychotherapeutic change speak of "imparting hope" as the first stage of the change process.

In addition to imparting hope by effective modeling of success, a number of strategies exist to increase motivation for goal attainment. Table 4.1 provides a summary of methods used to increase motivation to persist toward a goal. In addition to assessment of the problem described above, once a problem has been identified, the individual can do a cost–benefit analysis of the likely consequences of both keeping the behavior in place or changing the behavior. Advantages and disadvantages of either decision are made by the person with the problem with the task of the person assisting in this process to remain impartial and to encourage a complete listing of the consequences. For example, an individual with a defined problem with alcohol abuse would list the benefits and costs of continuing to drink at current levels, modifying drinking levels, or becoming abstinent. SH techniques, by definition, eliminate the presence of a therapist, who exhorts the client to action. Such exhortation can be unhelpful and even counterproductive. This failure of exhortation has led to the development of Motivational Interviewing (MI; Miller et al., 1988),

Table 4.1 Strategies for Maximizing Change via Increasing Motivation for Change and Enhancing Self-Efficacy

Motivational strategies	Self-efficacy strategies
Goal-setting	Information
Public commitment	Learned coping skills
Self-monitoring	Covert practice
Recording/graphing	Focus on anticipated success
Information	Graduated imaginal rehearsal
Modeling success	Graduated in vivo practice
Assessment and feedback	Relapse prevention skills
Internal rewards	Anticipatory stress reduction
Mastery experiences	Cost–benefit analysis

a technique designed to place maximum responsibility for the decision to change in the hands of the client.

MI was designed for individuals with substance abuse problems, a group previously thought to require heavy doses of confrontation to deal with their denial. Recent research identifies MI as one of the best established treatments for substance abuse and substance dependence. Given the success of MI, SH approaches appear ideal for providing the individual with information and opportunities to evaluate reasons for and against change, an approach found efficacious in increasing motivation to change. Moreover, SH approaches are an ideal venue for exposing individuals to other individuals who have faced similar problems but who have also resolved such problems successfully. They also provide opportunities for obtaining information, illustrated with numerous examples as well as to exercises to enhance self-persuasion. An examination of the other motivation-enhancing strategies listed in Table 4.1 reveals how adaptable they are to the SH approach.

Self-regulation theory also informs the process of maintaining motivation once the change process is initiated and also for maintaining improvement once the change process is completed. Long-term goals are difficult to achieve and, accordingly, are likely to be abandoned. Maintaining motivation through the change process is accomplished by setting intermediate and short-term goals and monitoring progress toward these goals and by providing incentives and rewards for goal attainment. Motivation is also maintained by shifting focus from symptom change to process change, exemplified by focusing on the acquisition of skills requisite for producing symptom change.

Maintenance of a high level of motivation is also critical after the completion of treatment using relapse prevention methods. These methods are also designed to maintain motivation in the face of inevitable setbacks experienced subsequent to the intervention. In this approach, setbacks are anticipated and prepared for, with strategies designed to anticipate circumstances that will trigger a lapse or short-lived symptom recurrence. Critical to the planning is the development of an attitude that predicts and accepts the likelihood that a lapse will occur, but that strategies can be practiced that help the individual deal with the lapse. Relapse prevention strategies have been used mostly in the treatment of substance abuse (e.g., Marlatt & Gordon, 1985) but have also been used effectively in the treatment of anxiety disorders using self-administered treatments (Wright, Clum, Roodman, & Febbraro, 2000).

Monitoring and Recording

In order to change behavior, both distal and proximate goals must be identified. Moreover, self-observation of progress toward the goal increases awareness and helps direct progress toward the goal. Self-change programs that identify strategies for achieving the goal and make it easier for the client to monitor progress with regard to both the target behaviors and strategies employed to achieve the target increase the likelihood that the strategies will be executed and progress toward the goal achieved. Monitoring successes increases desired behavior and progress toward the goal, while monitoring failures produces little change in performance. Since self-monitoring is a device for increasing awareness, information about what works and what makes it work is more likely to produce behavior change than is information about what does not work. Moreover, information that is temporally proximate to the behavior is more likely to produce change than is information distal to the performed behavior. If an individual wants to learn that he was successful in resisting an urge to devour a favorite dessert, he would do best to examine events, both external and internal, that precede, accompany, and follow his resistance of temptation.

Accordingly, while modest, self-monitoring of strategies for changing behavior and progress toward the goal exerts an overall positive effect on goal attainment. SH programs that assist in this process, by specifying what to monitor, directing the individual to monitor, and providing easily understood and easily utilized forms to assist in the monitoring and recording process are most likely to lead to goal attainment. Programs that also provide homework assignments that prescribe learning and practicing specific coping skills in gradually more challenging situations are examples of monitoring and recording the development of skills necessary to achieve change.

Reacting positively to the performance of these observed behaviors is another aspect of learning to engage in these behaviors. Positive reactions in the form of self-satisfaction or in terms of social or self-administered rewards increase the likelihood that such behaviors will be repeated. Using highly desired or high-frequency behaviors as a reward for behaviors that are performed grudgingly has long been a recognized means for increasing behavior change.

Bandura's (1991) construct of self-efficacy plays an important role in SH treatments. An individual's motivation to attain a goal will be largely determined by her belief in her ability to engage in behaviors she thinks are related to the goal. If she possesses a strong self-efficacy in her ability, she will continue to engage in this behavior even when progress is slow and the goal is not being attained. If she does not possess the requisite skills but believes that the skills can be acquired, she will engage in behaviors necessary to acquire the skills and apply them in appropriate settings. For self-administered treatment programs, this self-regulation principle can be translated in terms of teaching skills that are requisite to attain the goal and prescribing graded exercises for practicing these skills in increasingly challenging situations. Table 4.1 provides a partial list of techniques for increasing self-efficacy in the performance of coping skills. Effective practice exercises often include imaginal exercises in which the individual visualizes performing these skills in demanding situations. Once performed imaginally in a satisfactory fashion, the individual approaches a graded series of challenging situations in the real environment. In each practice series, the level of difficulty is ratcheted up as the individual successfully employs the skill in specified situations. Success in these exercises is defined as performance of the activity or skill, not in the experience of symptom reduction, though the latter is an expected consequence of repeated performance of the behavior.

Summary and Conclusions

Theories of self-regulation provide a framework for developing effective self-administered treatments for a variety of problems. Aspects of self-regulation address the importance of enhancing motivation to change and strategies for enhancing motivation. Important to each of the theories are the strategies of goal-setting and feedback of success or failure provided by monitoring progress toward the goal. Change is seen as coming about by increasing motivation, specifying strategies for change, and having the motivated individual monitor whether the approach is moving him toward his goal. If it is, the strategies are continued, with new intermediate goals being set, further attention to improving on one's strategies, and adding new strategies. A variety of specific techniques were identified to increase motivation. Also identified were strategies to increase self-efficacy, a self-regulation component specific to Bandura's approach.

There are several limitations to self-regulation theories. As Watson and Tharp (2002) point out, an individual may have clear goals and standards and accurate monitoring of their behavior, but activation for change may not come about. That is, there is an assumption in cybernetic models of behavior that the individual is predetermined to deal with behavior in a self-regulatory manner. But this is not always the case. According to Watson and Tharp (2002), there are four basic limitations of cybernetic models. First, psychological and behavioral systems are much more complex than mechanical systems. When an individual discovers a discrepancy between standards and what exists, he must choose among a variety of alternatives. How those choices are made are not elaborated upon by cybernetic models. Second, in complex human behavior, standards or goals are adjusted continuously as one moves closer toward the goal and better understands the real conditions that the goal involves. Intentions, images, anticipations, and values cause the standard to continuously evolve. Third, the correct action that must be taken may not be available. We may have never learned the appropriate action to bring current behavior closer to the standard or goal. Fourth, not all human behavior is self-regulated, as some behavior is under the regulation of others or the environment and not the self. For example, children's behavior, and to some extent adults' behavior, is regulated by others. Given the above limitations, cybernetic theory still remains a clear, powerful model for understanding the change process in human behavior.

Chapter Points

- Strategies for behavior change, utilized in SH therapies, have their roots in principles developed from Self-Regulation Theory.
- Principles derived from Self-Regulation Theory include goal-setting, monitoring of progress toward goals, comparing one's performance to the goal, (re)directing behavior to meet the standard, and reinforcement if the standard is met.
- Specific factors can be identified within each self-regulation principle that further enhances the likelihood of change; e.g., dividing goals into proximal and distal, with attainment of proximal goals enhancing the likelihood of attaining distal goals.
- Therapist-involvement in the self-change process improves outcome.
- The positive effect of monitoring change is enhanced by adding elements based on other self-regulatory principles.
- Self-regulation principles can be utilized to guide the development of effective SH treatment formats.

References

Bandura, A. (1986). *Social foundations of thought and action: A social cognitive theory*. Englewood Cliffs, NJ: Prentice Hall.

Bandura, A. (1991). Social cognitive theory of self-regulation. *Organizational Behavior and Human Decision Processes, 50*, 248–287.

Bandura, A., & Cervone, D. (1983). Self-evaluative and self-efficacy mechanisms governing the motivational effects of goals systems. *Journal of Personality and Social Psychology, 45*, 1017–1028.

Bandura, A., & Cervone, D. (1986). Differential engagement of self-reactive influences in cognitive motivation. *Organizational Behavior and Human Decision Processes, 38*, 92–113.

Bandura, A., & Schunk, D. H. (1981). Cultivating competence, self-efficacy, and intrinsic interest through proximal self-motivation. *Journal of Personality and Social Psychology, 41*, 586–598.

Bandura, A., & Simon, K. M. (1977). The role of proximal intentions in self-regulation of refractory behavior. *Cognitive Therapy and Research, 1*, 177–193.

Baumeister, R. F., & Heatherton, T. F. (1996). Self-regulation failure: An overview. *Psychological Inquiry, 7*, 1–15.

Bellack, A. S., Rozensky, J. S., & Schwartz, J. (1974). A comparison of two forms of self-monitoring in a behavioral weight reduction program. *Behavior Therapy, 5*, 523–530.

Bowers, T. G., Winett, R. A., & Frederiksen, L. W. (1987). Nicotine fading, behavioral contracting, and extended treatment: Effects on smoking cessation. *Addictive Behaviors, 12*, 181–184.

Carver, C. S. (2004). Self-regulation of action and affect. In R. F. Baumeister & K. D. Vohs (Eds.), *Handbook of self-regulation: Research, theory, and applications* (pp. 13–39). New York: Guilford Press.

Carver, C. S., & Scheier, M. F. (1982). Control theory: A useful conceptual framework for personality—Social, clinical, and health psychology. *Psychological Bulletin, 92*, 111–135.

Carver, C. S., & Scheier, M. F. (1986). Analyzing shyness: A specific application of broader self-regulatory principles. In W. H. Jones, J. M. Cheek, & S. R. Briggs (Eds.), *Shyness: Perspectives on research and treatment* (pp. 173–185). New York: Plenum.

Carver, C.S., & Scheier, M.F. (1999). Themes and issues in the self-regulation of behavior . In R. S. Weyer, Jr. (Ed.), *Perspectives on behavioral self-regulation: Advances in social cognition* (Vol. 12, pp. 1–105). Mahwah, NJ: Lawrence Erlbaum.

Endler, N. S., & Kocovski, N. L. (2000). Self-regulation and distress in clinical psychology. In M. Boekaerts, P. R. Pintrich, & M. Zeidner (Eds.), *Handbook of self-regulation* (pp. 569–599). San Diego: Academic Press.

Erez, M. (1977). Feedback: A necessary condition for the goal setting-performance relationship. *Journal of Applied Psychology, 62*, 624–627.

Febbraro, G. A. R., & Clum, G. A. (1998). Meta-analytic investigation of the effectiveness of self-regulatory components in the treatment of adult problem behaviors. *Clinical Psychology Review, 18*, 143–161.

Fishbein, M., & Ajzen, I. (1975). *Belief, attitude, intention, and behavior: An introduction to theory and research*. Reading, MA: Addison-Wesley.

Foxx, R. M., & Axelroth, E. (1983). Nicotine fading, self-monitoring and cigarette fading to produce cigarette abstinence or controlled smoking. *Behaviour Research and Therapy, 21*, 17–27.

Grimes, L. (1983). Application of the self-regulatory model in dealing with encopresis. *School Psychology Review, 12*, 82–87.

Harmon, T. M., Nelson, R. O., & Hayes, S. C. (1980). Self-monitoring of mood versus activity by depressed clients. *Journal of Consulting and Clinical Psychology, 48*, 30–38.

Hodgins, D.C., Leigh, G., Milne, R., & Gerrish, R. (1997). Drinking goal selection in behavioral self-management treatment of chronic alcoholics. *Addictive Behaviors, 22*, 247–255.

Ilgen, D. R., Fisher, G. D., & Taylor, M. S. (1979). Consequences of individual feedback on behavior in organizations. *Journal of Applied Psychology, 64*, 349–371.

Kanfer, F. H. (1970). Self-regulation: Research, issues and speculations. In C. Neuringer & L. Michael (Eds.), *Behavior modification in clinical psychology* (pp. 178–220). New York: Appleton-Century-Crofts.

Kanfer, F. H. (1975). Self-management methods. In F. H. Kanfer & A. P. Goldstein (Eds.), *Helping people change: A textbook of methods* (pp. 334–389). New York: Pergamon.

Kanfer, F. H., & Hagerman, S. (1981). The role of self-regulation. In L. P. Rehm (Ed.), *Behavior therapy for depression: Present status and future directions* (pp. 143–179). New York: Academic.

Kanfer, F. H., & Schefft, B. K. (1988). *Guiding the process of therapeutic change.* Champaign, IL: Research Press.

Kanfer, F. H., & Stevenson, H. (1985). The effects of self-regulation on concurrent cognitive processing. *Cognitive Therapy and Research, 9*, 667–684.

Karoly, P. (1993). Mechanisms in self-regulation: A systems view. *Annual Review of Psychology, 44*, 23–51.

Kazdin, A. E. (1974). Self-monitoring and behavior change. In M. J. Mahoney & C. E. Thoresen (Eds.), *Self-control: Power to the person* (pp. 218–246). Monterey, CA: Brooks/Cole.

Kazdin, A. E. (1994). *Behavior modification in applied settings* (5th ed.). Pacific Grove, CA: Brooks/Cole.

Locke, E. A. (1991). Goal theory vs. control theory: Contrasting approaches to understand work motivation. *Motivation and Emotion, 15*, 9–28.

Locke, E. A., & Latham, G. P. (2002). Building a practically useful theory of goal setting and task motivation. *American Psychologist, 57*, 705–717.

Locke, E. A., Shaw, K. N., Saari, L. M., & Latham, G. P. (1981). Goal setting and task performance: 1969–1980. *Psychological Bulletin, 90*, 125–152.

Mahoney, M. J. (1971). The self-management of covert behavior: A case study. *Behavior Therapy, 2*, 575–578.

Marlatt, G. A., & Gordon, J. R. (1985). *Relapse prevention: Maintenance strategies in the treatment of additive behaviors.* New York: Guilford.

Masters, J. C., Furman, W., & Barden, R. C. (1977). Effects of achievement standards, tangible rewards, and self-dispensed achievement evaluations on children's task mastery. *Child Development, 48*, 217–224.

McFall, R. M. (1970). Effects of self-monitoring on normal smoking behavior. *Journal of Consulting and Clinical Psychology, 35*, 135–142.

Miller, G. A., Galanter, E., & Pribram, K. H. (1960). *Plans and the structure of behavior.* New York: Holt, Rinehart, & Winston.

Miller, W. R., Sovereign, R. G., & Krege, B. (1988). Motivational interviewing with problem drinkers: II. The Drinker's Check-up as a preventive intervention. *Behavioural Psychotherapy, 16*, 251–268.

Mithaug, D. E. (1993). *Self-regulation theory: How optimal adjustment maximizes gain.* Westport, CT: Praeger Publishers.

Nelson, R. O., Hay, L. R., & Hay, W. M. (1977). Cue versus consequence functions of high probability behaviors in the modification of self-monitored study coverants and study time. *Psychological Record, 3,* 589–599.

Nelson, R. O., Lipinski, D. P., & Black, J. L. (1975). The effects of expectancy on the reactivity of self-recording. *Behavior Therapy, 6,* 337–349.

Ojehagen, A., & Berglund, M. (1989). Changes of drinking goals in a two-year out-patient alcoholic treatment program. *Addictive Behaviors, 14,* 1–9.

Prochaska, J. O. (1984). *Systems of psychotherapy: A transtheoretical analysis.* Homewood, IL: Dorsey Press.

Rogers, C. R. (1954). Changes in the maturity of behavior as related to therapy. In C. R. Rogers & R. F. Dymond (Eds.), *Psychotherapy and personality change* (pp. 215–237). Chicago: University of Chicago Press.

Romanczyk, R. G. (1974). Self-monitoring in the treatment of obesity: parameters of reactivity. *Behavior Therapy, 5,* 531–540.

Varni, J. W., & Henker, B. (1979). A self-regulation approach to the treatment of three hyperactive boys. *Child Behavior Therapy, 1,* 171–192.

Washton, A. M., & Stone-Washton, N. (1989). Abstinence and relapse in outpatient cocaine addicts. *Journal of Psychoactive Drugs, 22,* 135–147.

Watson, D. L., & Tharp, R. G. (2002). *Self-directed behavior: Self-modification for personal adjustment.* Belmont, CA: Wadsworth Publishing.

Wiener, N. (1948). *Cybernetics: Control and communication in the animal and the machine.* Cambridge, MA: MIT Press.

Wright, J. H., Clum, G. A., Roodman, A. A., & Febbraro, G. A. (2000). A bibliotherapy approach to relapse prevention in individuals with panic attacks. *Journal of Anxiety Disorders, 14,* 483–499.

CHAPTER 5

Self-Help Therapies for Anxiety Disorders

MICHIYO HIRAI AND GEORGE A. CLUM

In the United States, approximately 18% of the population suffers from anxiety disorders, which are the most prevalent group of mental disorders (Kessler, Chiu, Demler, & Walters, 2005). According to Greenberg et al. (1999), anxiety disorders are costly, accounting for 31.5% of all mental health expenditures, based on data from the National Comorbidity Study (Kessler et al., 1994). These authors reported that the annual cost of anxiety disorders was approximately $42.3 billion in 1990, or $1,542 for each anxiety-disordered individual. While cognitive–behavioral treatments are among the most effective strategies, they are also costly, with the per session estimate of therapist-directed sessions ranging from $40 to $90 (Gould, Otto, & Pollack, 1995). Self-administered treatments have been proposed as a cost-effective approach for treating anxiety, as well as other disorders, in the last three decades. Two meta-analytic studies of self-administered treatments of psychological disorders (Gould & Clum, 1993; Marrs, 1995) and one general review of self-help (SH) interventions for anxiety disorders (Newman, Erickson, Przeworski, & Dzus, 2003) suggested that some types of anxiety disorders are treatable using SH approaches.

SH materials for anxiety problems have largely focused on written materials. According to Carlbring, Westling, and Andersson (2000), there are at least 14 published SH books for panic attacks or general fear that provide cognitive–behavioral strategies, though few were empirically validated. Written materials have several advantages: (a) they are readily accessible and, to date, are paramount in the consumer's mind as a means for obtaining information; (b) they can be accessed whenever and however the individual user wants; and (c) they can provide information, case studies, and even extractable forms to chart progress. Audiotapes, on the other hand, have the primary advantage of accessibility while the individual is otherwise occupied, such as while driving. To date, commercially available audiotapes for anxiety disorders have focused on specific strategies such as relaxation and desensitization and have not provided more comprehensive treatments.

Increasingly, studies have investigated computerized or Internet-based self-administered interventions for anxiety problems. While still in their infancy in terms of their potential, such programs offer such advantages as online assessment and feedback, tracking progress on a daily basis, and interactive treatment modules. Over 20 studies published after 1990 evaluated programs that utilized computerized/Internet-based SH interventions for anxiety disorders (Bachofen et al., 1999; Buglione, DeVito, & Mulloy, 1990; Carlbring, Ekselius, & Andersson, 2003; Carlbring et al., 2005; Carlbring, Westling, Ljungstrand, Ekselius & Andersson, 2001; Clark, Kirkby, Daniels, & Marks, 1998; Fraser, Kirkby, Daniels, Gilroy, & Montgomery, 2001; Gilroy, Kirkby, Daniels, Menzies, & Montgomery, 2000; Greist et al. 2002; Harcourt, Kirkby, Daniels, & Montgomery, 1998; Heading et al. 2001; Kenardy, McCafferty, & Rosa, 2003; Kenwright, Liness, & Marks, 2001; Kenwright & Marks, 2004; Kenwright, Marks, Graham, Franses, & Mataix-Cols, 2005; Kirkby et al., 2000; Klein & Richards, 2001; Marks et al., 1998; Newman, Kenardy, Herman, & Taylor, 1997; Schneider, Mataix-Cols, Marks, & Bachofen, 2005; Smith, Kirkby, Montgomery, & Daniels, 1997; White, Jones, & McGarry, 2000), while only four such studies (Biglan, Villwock, & Wick, 1979; Carr, Ghosh, & Marks, 1988; Ghosh & Marks, 1987; Ghosh, Marks, & Carr, 1988) had been conducted before 1990. Given that approximately 54% of the population in the United States was using the Internet, with an increase of 26 million in a period of 13 months (U.S. Department of Commerce, 2002), computers and the Internet have considerable potential to become major SH treatment modalities in the near future.

Effective Treatment Approaches

Self-administered treatments are often modeled after programs of demonstrated effectiveness, designed to be administered by trained therapists. Standards have been specified (e.g., Chambless & Hollon, 1998) to help identify empirically validated treatments (EVTs), and many of the components of these treatments are included in SH treatment programs. Many of the EVTs that have been identified for anxiety disorders utilize the cognitive–behavioral therapy (CBT) approach, with treatment components reflective of this approach. In CBT, specific aspects of the disorder are identified and specific treatments are designed for each aspect of the disorder. For anxiety disorders, the specific targets include such aspects as physiological arousal, muscle tension, cognitive worries, and avoidance behavior, among others. Treatment modules are then developed to deal with each of these target behaviors, including relaxation training, breathing retraining, identification and labeling of cognitive errors, strategies to change cognitive errors, and exposure to feared situations. Strategies have also been developed for combining these components; for example, practicing cognitive strategies while entering anxiety-producing situations. These approaches to developing and using these strategies are often ordered to increase the likelihood of success. Then they are applied to situations of increasing difficulty to provide the individual with experience in dealing with previously avoided situations. Additional strategies often include identifying specific goals, charting progress toward these goals, and providing rewards for achieving these goals.

Each of these treatment components has been embedded in various self-administered treatment programs. Given that each component reflects a skill and that each skill can be described and demonstrated, the potential of teaching these skills via books, tapes, and the Internet are considerable.

Effectiveness of Self-Help Treatments

In the last three decades, over 60 SH studies, including 43 randomized controlled studies and 11 field trials, have examined the effectiveness of various forms of SH interventions for anxiety disorders and fear-related problems. This chapter focuses on SH programs that utilized books, tapes, or computer/Internet-based materials and that were the primary treatment employed. Studies that targeted diagnosable anxiety disorders and subclinical levels of anxiety were examined. Targeted disorders included panic disorder (PD), specific phobia (SP), social phobia (SoP), generalized anxiety disorder (GAD), obsessive–compulsive disorder (OCD), posttraumatic stress disorder (PTSD), and subclinical problems such as test anxiety and interpersonal anxiety.

Three questions were addressed for each targeted problem: (a) Are SH interventions effective when compared to wait-list or placebos? (b) How do SH programs compare to therapist-directed interventions (TDIs)? and (c) Do the treatment effects last? Also examined were treatment factors that affect outcome, including the venue of presenting SH materials (e.g., book, tape, computer), duration of the intervention, and amount of personal contact. Unlike how individuals access SH materials in the real world, formal studies of the effectiveness of such materials often include intermittent contact with a therapist. To approximate the reality of how SH materials are typically used, only studies that limited therapist contact to activities other than applying treatment strategies were included. Such activities included monitoring progress, clarifying procedures, answering general questions, or providing encouragement. In research designed to evaluate such programs, potential participants are screened according to some criteria, assessed, and assigned randomly to a treatment. To enter the study, individuals advance through a series of successive hurdles, ensuring that most participants are highly motivated, possess the target problem, and are confident that they will be treated professionally. In contrast, most individuals who purchase SH books or tapes have not undergone formal assessment, access the materials at their convenience, and, unless assigned the SH book/tape by their therapist, have no contact with a professional. Accordingly, research that bears on the question of the effects of therapist contact is important to determine whether self-administered treatments can be effective with little or no therapist contact.

Outcome research presented in this chapter relies heavily on a meta-analytic investigation conducted by the authors (Hirai & Clum, 2006). Data from this meta-analytic review are summarized in this chapter as having no effect (effect size (ES) < .12), small effect (ES .12–.49), moderate effect (ES .50–.79), and large effect (ES ≥ .80).

Panic Disorders

PDs are diagnosed when a person experiences repeated panic attacks that come on suddenly and, at least in some instances, are unconnected to any identifiable stimulus. Panic disorders are usually accompanied by avoidance of situations associated with the attacks, a condition known as agoraphobia. Psychological treatments for PD have emphasized the development of skills to reduce panic attacks, including relaxation, cognitive restructuring, and exposure to both panic symptoms and the avoided situations associated with experiencing panic attacks. Self-administered treatments that have been evaluated typically include some or all of these treatment components, along with case examples and instructions in how to apply these strategies.

PDs have been one of the most frequently examined anxiety disorders using SH treatments. Thirteen randomized, controlled, SH intervention studies, comparing SH interventions to therapist-directed treatment or wait-list control conditions, published in the last three decades were identified. Written materials were the most tested SH venue (Febbraro, 2005; Febbraro, Clum, Roodman, & Wright, 1999; Ghosh & Marks, 1987; Gould & Clum, 1995; Gould, Clum, & Shapiro, 1993; Hecker, Losee, Fritzler,

& Fink, 1996; Lidren et al., 1994; Parry & Killick, 1998; Wright, Clum, Roodman, & Febbraro, 2000) followed by computerized/Internet-based self-administered programs (Carlbring et al., 2005, 2001; Ghosh & Marks, 1987; Klein & Richards, 2001). Of the 13 studies, 6 (Febbraro, 2005; Febbraro et al., 1999; Gould & Clum, 1995; Gould et al., 1993; Lidren et al., 1994; Wright et al., 2000) evaluated *Coping With Panic* (Clum, 1990). Ghosh and Marks (1987) evaluated *Living With Fear* (Marks, 1978), and Hecker et al. (1996) tested *Mastery of Your Anxiety and Panic* (Barlow & Craske, 1989). Carlbring et al. (2001) developed a program on the Internet based on three SH books, including *An End to Panic: Breakthrough Techniques for Overcoming Panic Disorder* (Zuercher-White, 1998), *Mastery of Your Anxiety and Panic II* (Barlow & Craske, 1994), and *Overcoming Panic: A Complete Nine-Week Home-Based Treatment Program for Panic Disorder* (Franklin, 1996). Carlbring and his colleagues (2001, 2005) then evaluated this program. The two remaining studies (Kline & Richards, 2001; Parry & Killick, 1998) developed original materials for their SH interventions. All of the books and protocols were cognitive–behavioral, cognitive, or behaviorally oriented. Duration of SH treatment varied across the studies, ranging from less than two weeks (Klein & Richards, 2001) to 25.8 weeks (Wright et al., 2000), with an average of 8.4 weeks. The average number of study completers was 34. The average dropout rate across the SH groups was 16.8% and ranged from 0 to 38%. Follow-up periods varied, ranging from 6 weeks to 12 months.

Participants across the 10 studies were predominantly female (75.3%), which reflects the sex ratio of individuals diagnosed with PD with agoraphobia (DSM-IV, 1994), with an average age of 38.7 (*SD* = 4.47). Eight of the 10 studies used only individuals diagnosed with PD while the remaining two studies reported that more than 75% of the participants met criteria for PD (Febbraro et al., 1999; Wright et al., 2000).

Effectiveness of Self-Help Treatments

Each of the 13 studies examined posttreatment effectiveness, with 6 (Carlbring et al., 2005; Ghosh & Marks, 1987; Gould & Clum, 1995; Hecker et al., 1996; Lidren et al., 1994; Parry & Killick, 1998) also reporting follow-up data. Overall, the average treatment effect was in the moderate range, indicating that SH approaches reduce a variety of panic symptoms more than wait-list or self-monitoring conditions. All of the 10 studies reported reductions in physical as well as cognitive panic symptoms and associated symptoms such as depressed mood. Also improved were coping skills, coping self-efficacy, and work and social adjustment. Gould and Clum (1995) found that reading *Coping With Panic* plus minimal therapist contact for 4 weeks significantly reduced the average frequency of panic attacks. Gould et al. (1993) evaluated *Coping With Panic* plus minimal therapist contact, as did Lidren et al. (1994). The percentage of individuals with zero panic attacks after treatment was 73 and 83%, respectively, in the two studies.

Maintenance of treatment improvement was demonstrated over brief periods in each of these studies. Gould and Clum (1995) and Parry and Killick (1998) reported follow-up data obtained 6–8 weeks after the treatment periods; Hecker et al. (1996), Lidren et al. (1994), and Gosh and Marks (1987) provided 6-month follow-up data; while Carlbring et al. (2005) followed participants for one year. All of these studies found that treatment effects were maintained at the follow-up periods. However, because one year was the longest follow-up assessment point, it is unclear whether durable treatment gains would be found using longer follow-up periods.

Comparisons to Therapist-Directed Interventions

Comparisons of SH treatments to TDIs for PD have yielded encouraging results for SH. Of the five studies (Carlbring et al., 2005; Ghosh & Marks, 1987; Gould et al., 1993; Hecker et al., 1996; Lidren et al., 1994) that compared SH interventions to TDIs, four (Carlbring et al., 2005; Gould et al., 1993; Hecker et al., 1996; Lidren et al., 1994) found comparable levels of effectiveness, while one (Ghosh & Marks, 1987) did not. Gould et al. (1993) reported that bibliotherapy plus minimal therapist contact produced improvements significantly superior to TDI. Similarly, Lidren et al. (1994) reported that bibliotherapy plus minimal therapist contact was superior to a group therapy condition. Hecker et al. (1996) reported that bibliotherapy plus therapist contact produced comparable symptom reductions to TDI. Carlbring et al. (2005) demonstrated comparable results for the online SH group and TDI, with a small between-treatment ES at posttreatment ($d = .16$), which favored the TDI. Each of these four studies evaluated books or an online program specifically designed to target PD. In contrast, Ghosh and Marks (1987) reported less effectiveness for both an 8-week SH computerized program without therapist contact and a book-based intervention with minimal therapist contact when compared to individual treatment. The fact that only five studies compared TDIs to SH programs limits the confidence one can have in concluding that self-administered interventions are comparable to TDIs. Nevertheless, the finding that four of five studies found equivalent or superior results is encouraging.

Factors That Impact Effectiveness

Several factors have been examined for their impact on the effectiveness of SH interventions for PD. Whether therapist contact is necessary to enhance the effectiveness of SH treatments remains a question, given the limited number of studies directly examining this variable. For example, Febbraro (2005) demonstrated that individuals in the bibliotherapy plus brief phone contact group did better than those in the bibliotherapy only group but only on several dependent measures. However, Hirai and Clum (2006) reported that studies comparing SH plus therapist contact to a wait-list control group found large ESs, not only for panic symptoms but also for coping self-efficacy, depression, or quality of life (e.g., Gould et al., 1993; Lidren et al., 1994), while studies providing no therapist contact produced relatively small ESs when compared to a wait-list control group (e.g., Febbraro et al., 1999; Gould & Clum, 1995).

Little evidence exists indicating that one type of SH venue is superior to another in treating panic. For example, three studies that produced large ESs when compared to wait-list control groups used a book (Gould et al., 1993; Lidren et al., 1994; Wright et al., 2000). Carlbring et al.'s study (2001) found a large ES when comparing a computerized program to a wait-list condition. Only one study (Parry & Killick, 1998) directly compared the same SH information provided by two different SH venues. These researchers reported that both a book and video reduced symptoms significantly, with the better effect found in the video group. Clearly, more direct comparisons, of the type provided by Parry and Killick (1998) are needed to answer this question. At this point, however, SH interventions for PD provided via several different treatments appear to yield comparable results.

Duration of SH treatment does not appear to affect strength of treatment effects. Comparisons between studies providing less than 8 weeks of exposure to SH materials and those providing 8 weeks or more of exposure yielded no ES differences (Hirai & Clum, 2006). Several studies illustrate this conclusion. Gould et al. (1993) and Lidren et al. (1994) evaluated the same SH book using similar research designs but different treatment durations. Individuals in Lidren et al.'s study spent 8 weeks completing the SH program, while individuals in Gould et al.'s study (1993) spent 4 weeks. Both studies produced significant improvement on panic symptoms and coping self-efficacy. Their ESs, when compared to the wait-list control conditions, were equivalent (Hirai & Clum, 2006). Even a one-week computerized SH intervention without therapist contact (Klein & Richards, 2001) significantly improved panic symptoms, compared to a self-monitoring condition. The ESs compared to the monitoring condition in this study were in the moderate range (Hirai & Clum, 2006). It is unclear whether the lesser effect in this latter study was due to the shorter duration of treatment or the absence of therapist contact. At present, however, no treatment gain has been demonstrated for longer treatment periods.

Summary

SH interventions based on therapist-administered treatment programs of proven effectiveness for PD have been shown to be effective when compared to wait-list or self-monitoring conditions. The effectiveness of SH programs for panic may be enhanced by interventions specifically designed to target panic. The evidence for this conclusion is most apparent when SH treatments are compared to TDIs. As mentioned, four of five studies that compared panic-specific SH interventions to TDIs found comparable effects (Carlbring et al., 2005; Gould et al., 1993; Hecker et al., 1996; Lidren et al., 1994), while Ghosh & Marks (1987) found no comparable effect using a manual targeting general fears. However, these treatments have been delivered in the context of treatment outcome studies in which individuals are recruited, interviewed, assessed, and provided a rationale for expecting improvement. No information exists on the effectiveness of SH treatments for PD without this context. Yet SH approaches can be considered as a viable, cost-effective treatment option for people who experience panic attacks but lack access to conventional treatment.

Type of SH format and duration of treatment have not been found to predict outcome. These results support the conclusion that users may select their favorite treatment venue and apply the SH materials at their own pace without fear of diminishing effectiveness. However, some therapist contact might be important in enhancing the effectiveness of SH material, though at this point the mechanism by which this factor affects outcome is unclear.

Specific Phobia

SP is diagnosed when an individual experiences persistent and irrational fear of particular objects or situations and actively avoids contact with such objects or situations. Specific phobia is one of the most common anxiety disorders. In the United States, approximately 11% of people will suffer from SP at some point in their lives (Kessler et al., 1994). Four subtypes are specified including animal, natural environment, situational, and blood-injection-injury types. Ample evidence exists that behavioral approaches, including direct exposure to the phobic stimuli, is the preferred treatment method for a wide variety of SPs (e.g., Marks, 1988; Page, 1994; Öst, 1996; Öst, Brandberg, & Alm; 1997; Öst, Hellström, & Kåver, 1992). In behavioral therapy, individuals are instructed to gradually expose themselves to feared objects or situations. Often, cognitive components, which are designed to help individuals challenge irrational fears associated with phobic objects or situations, are implemented along with exposure.

The treatment of SP using SH interventions has also been frequently studied. Ten controlled treatment studies, including six that targeted spider phobia in clinical populations (Fraser et al., 2001; Gilroy et al., 2000; Heading et al., 2001; Hellström & Öst, 1995; Öst, Salkovskis, & Hellström, 1991; Smith et al., 1997), two that targeted snake phobia in nonclinical student populations (Clark, 1972; Rosen, Glasgow, & Barrera, 1976, 1977), one that targeted acrophobia in a nonclinical student sample (Baker, Cohen, & Saunders, 1973), and one that targeted snake plus spider phobia (Cotler, 1970) have been conducted. All of these studies tested protocols developed in a cognitive–behavioral, cognitive, or behavioral framework.

Spider phobia has been targeted by written SH materials that focused on self-directed exposure (Hellström & Öst, 1995; Öst et al., 1991) by a computer-aided self-administered vicarious exposure program named CAVE (Fraser et al,, 2001; Gilroy et al., 2000; Heading et al., 2001; Smith et al., 1997), and by relaxation audiotapes (Gilroy et al., 2000). Among the book-based SH interventions for spider phobia, Öst et al. (1991) tested an exposure manual developed specifically for spider phobia. Hellström and Öst (1995) evaluated Marks' (1987) *Living With Fear* as well as the developed protocols (Öst et al., 1991). Snake phobias have been treated utilizing written materials advocating systematic desensitization combined with a relaxation tape (Rosen et al., 1976), audiotapes describing the desensitization process and relaxation (Cotler, 1970), and a booklet (Clark, 1973) providing instructions on how to construct a desensitization hierarchy. Acrophobia has been treated using an audiotaped systematic desensitization program (Baker et al., 1972).

Across the 10 studies, the average duration of SH treatment was 5.8 weeks, ranging from one week to 11 weeks. Follow-up assessments were conducted over a range of time periods in 9 studies (Baker et al., 1972; Cotler, 1970; Fraser et al., 2001; Gilroy et al., 2000; Heading et al., 2001; Hellström & Öst, 1995; Öst et al., 1991; Rosen et al., 1976; Smith et al., 1997). The longest follow-up period was approximately 2 years (Rosen et al. 1977), while the shortest was 4 weeks (Heading et al., 2001), with an average of 56 weeks. The average number of study completers was 34. Most individuals who started treatment completed it, as the average dropout rate was 8.6% during the treatment phase. Participants across the 10 studies were predominantly female (94.2%) with an average age of 30.9 ($SD = 5.08$). All spider phobia studies were conducted on individuals who met diagnostic criteria for SP, while the remaining studies were conducted on nonclinical student samples.

Effectiveness of Self-Help Treatments

Of the six studies treating individuals with a diagnosis of spider phobia, four studies (Fraser et al., 2001; Gilroy et al. 2000; Hellström & Öst, 1995;

Smith et al., 1997) reported significant improvement on self-reported phobia symptoms, behavior, and work or social adjustment from pre- to posttreatment. Heading et al. (2001) and Öst et al. (1991), in contrast, reported limited or no significant improvement on self-reported fear, work adjustment, or behavior avoidance tests (Öst et al., 1991). The four studies that targeted subclinical levels of acrophobia or snake phobia reported significant symptom reduction and behavioral improvement after treatment. Overall, self-administered interventions produced treatment effects superior to controls, particularly for people with subclinical levels of phobias. These treatment effects were less robust when treating clinical levels of SPs. Overall, results indicate that SH strategies are an effective approach for treating SPs. The types of SPs targeted have, however, been limited. No information exists on the effectiveness of approaches for such SPs as blood-injury-injection, situational phobias such as heights, natural environments (e.g., storms), or other animals.

All nine studies that evaluated the duration of treatment gains reported sustained improvement over as much as two years. Among therapist-directed treatment outcome studies, however, relapse in spider phobics was associated with shorter exposure duration (Rachman & Lopatka, 1988), massed exposure sessions completed consecutively in a single day (Rowe & Craske, 1998a), exposure to a single spider relative to multiple spiders (Rowe & Craske, 1998b), depressed mood during exposure (Salkovskis & Mills, 1994), and differences between treatment and assessment contexts (Mineka, Mystkowski, Hladek, & Rodriguez , 1999; Mystkowski, Craske, & Echiverri, 2002). Whether these factors are also associated with relapse rates in SH studies has not been explored.

Four studies (Baker et al., 1972; Cotler, 1970; Heading et al., 2001; Rosen et al., 1976) compared SH interventions to wait-list control conditions and reported significantly greater improvement in SH groups. Magnitude of treatment effect varied across the studies. Three studies (Baker et al., 1972; Cotler, 1970; Rosen et al., 1976) that targeted subclinical populations yielded medium to large ESs, whereas a computer-guided vicarious exposure approach targeting clinical levels of spider phobia (Heading et al., 2001) produced a small treatment effect. These differences among these four studies may be due to severity of symptoms, targeted phobic objects, treatment modalities, presence or absence of therapist contact, duration of treatment, or other factors. Overall, SH programs appear more effective than no treatment when used to treat subclinical phobic reactions.

Comparisons to Therapist-Directed Interventions

The majority of studies (Gilroy et al., 2000; Heading et al., 2001; Hellström & Öst, 1995; Öst et al., 1991; Rosen et al., 1976) that compared

SH treatments to TDIs found superior outcomes for TDIs. The level of added benefit for using a TDI was typically moderate in degree. Öst et al. (1991) found that few individuals improved with self-directed exposure. In a later paper, Hellström and Öst (1995) offered an explanation that avoidance tendencies were responsible for these low success rates. To counteract such avoidance, Hellström and Öst required individuals in one condition of self-directed therapy to perform exposure at the clinic. Hellström and Öst also compared two book-guided self-exposure protocols, one specifically tailored for spider fear and the other a more general book, Marks' *Living with Fear* (1987). Participants were assigned to one of five treatment conditions: (a) a one-session therapist-directed exposure (maximum of 3 hours); (b) specific manual-based treatment in the home; (c) specific manual-based treatment at the clinic; (d) general manual-based treatment in the home; or (e) general manual-based treatment at the clinic.

The TDI was more effective than three of the manual-based treatments. Ninety percent of individuals in this group held a spider at posttreatment, compared to 50% in the tailored book condition when read in the clinic and 10% in the general SH condition or in the tailored SH condition when the book was read at home. The specific manual at the clinic was more effective than the other manual-based treatments, with 63% of participants improving. However, at follow-up, the percentage of people who were able to hold a spider increased to 88% in the tailored SH/clinic condition, while it held steady in the therapist-directed group. Apparently, the context in which SH interventions are provided can influence outcome.

The therapeutic advantage for having a therapist administer exposure cannot be explained by the motivating effects of the therapist. Öst et al. (1991) and Hellström and Öst (1995) administered an SH book that instructed individuals to expose themselves to live spiders. Though individuals in these groups spent twice as much time exposing themselves to spiders as did individuals in the therapist-directed conditions, the extent of the advantage for having a therapist direct treatment was large.

Several other explanations have been offered for the superiority of individual therapy for SPs. Öst et al. (1991) attributed this superiority to the presence of cognitive components in their treatment protocols, which were not included in the self-exposure protocols. This explanation is problematic, as it reflects a flaw in the design of the studies as opposed to a real difference. Heading et al. (2001) pointed out that computerized spider images may be low-impact stimuli that do not adequately tap fear schemas, a necessary prelude to effective treatment. When exposure to feared images is the principal treatment strategy, TDIs may have an advantage, owing to therapists' ability to detect and reduce avoidance or in other ways reduce sufferers' attempts to reduce the impact of the stimuli.

In studies targeting other phobic objects in subclinical samples, the difference between SH interventions and TDIs was less remarkable. For example, Rosen et al. (1976) examined a self-administered desensitization treatment with an audio relaxation tape targeting subclinical snake fear. Treated individuals spent up to 8 weeks learning the material with or without therapist contact, while the therapist-directed group met twice a week for desensitization. These researchers reported no significant difference on any measure between the SH groups and the therapist-directed desensitization group. The ES comparing the SH groups to the therapist-directed group in this study was negative but small (Hirai & Clum, 2006), reflecting a negligible superiority for the TDI.

Overall, therapist-directed exposure treatments offer a distinct advantage in treating diagnosed SPs compared to self-administered treatments, which in turn are more effective than no treatment. The superiority of TDIs is especially clear when the outcome measure involves phobic individuals being able to engage in direct contact with the phobic object. Confidence in these results is strongest for the spider phobia studies in which all participants met criteria for SP.

Factors That Impact Effectiveness

Low variability among studies with regard to various treatment parameters makes it difficult to compare different approaches. Among the studies targeting diagnosed phobias, neither treatment modality (book or computer) nor treatment duration (2 to 8 weeks) had an impact on program effectiveness. Only two studies evaluated computer-guided vicarious exposure and no direct comparisons were made between different venues. As discussed earlier, however, Hellström and Öst (1995) found that bibliotherapy in a clinic conferred significant treatment benefits beyond bibliotherapy conducted at home. Treatment duration varied between one and 6 weeks, with no discernible effect on outcome. Further, Frasier et al. (2001) reported that a six-session, computerized exposure intervention produced similar results to a three-session program, and that treatment effects leveled off by the third session. Therapist contact could not be examined for this set of studies because no study targeting spider phobia examined the effects of this variable. When therapist contact was evaluated in subclinical samples (Clark, 1973; Rosen et al., 1976), no benefit was found. As Hellström and Öst (1995) and Öst et al.'s studies (1991) suggested, SH materials for spider phobia may need to expand the number of strategies offered, including such additions as target-specific exposure instructions and cognitive components.

Summary

Exposure-based SH interventions are moderately effective in reducing phobic symptoms and avoidance behavior in individuals with diagnosable and subclinical SPs. Both book-based and computerized exposure programs were found to be effective treatment modalities. These conclusions do not apply to all types of SPs, however, as only several types of SPs have been studied. Among the targeted objects, both spider and snake phobias appear treatable using self-administered exposure. Therapist-directed exposure offers clear advantages over self-administered exposure for this group of phobias.

No treatment factors clearly enhance the efficacy of SH interventions for SPs. SH interventions as brief as one week have been found equally effective when compared to longer interventions. These results suggest that brief SH interventions are a low-cost treatment option that can produce results fairly quickly, as would therapist-directed, single-session exposure treatments for spider phobia (e.g., Götestam, 2002; Öst et al., 1992). However, it is not known whether short-term exposure is also applicable to other types of SPs.

Future research should address SH treatments for additional types of SP using clinical samples. Given the advantage of TDIs, future studies might examine the effects of adding minimal therapist contact, a factor found to enhance outcome with other anxiety disorders. In addition, computerized programs have an impressive potential for enhancing treatment effects, especially within the anxiety disorders.

Social Phobia/Social Anxiety

SoP refers to a fear of social situations that leads to avoidance of those situations or that, when entered into, is accompanied by intense anxiety. When the situations producing the fear are avoided to the extent that the avoidance interferes with social or occupational functioning, the problem merits a diagnosis of SoP. Because of the nature of the disorder, treatments have often included exposure to social situations, either by being conducted in a group context, or by contriving exposures to the feared social situations. As with other anxiety disorders, the skills are readily adaptable to an SH format. The problem in using SH interventions has been in prescribing exposure to social situations in which the client can practice the requisite skills.

Nine randomized, controlled studies, including two studies in one publication, were identified (Abbott, Rapee, & Gaston, 2002; Ayres et al., 1993; Grossman, McNamara, & Dudley, 1991; Kirsh & Henry, 1979; Marshall, Presse, & Andrews, 1975; Schelver & Gutsch, 1983; Vestre &

Judge, 1989; Walker, Cox, Frankel, & Torgrud, 2001). Two studies (Abbot et al., 2002; Walker et al., 2001) targeted individuals with SoP and the rest used subclinical, socially anxious individuals. Within the studies conducted in subclinical populations, targets included fears related to social evaluations within the context of public speaking, dating, or interpersonal relationships.

Of the nine studies, seven used written manuals and two evaluated a videotaped SH program. Among the seven studies using written manuals, six used published SH books. *A Guide to Rational Living* and *A New Guide to Rational Living* (Ellis & Harper, 1962, 1975) emphasized cognitive strategies and were examined by two studies (Schelver & Gutsch, 1983; Vestre & Judge, 1989). *A Manual for Self-Management of Public Speaking Anxiety* (Marshall & Andrew, 1973) described relaxation and desensitization strategies and was tested in two studies (Kirsh & Henry, 1979; Marshall et al., 1976). *Dying of Embarrassment* (Markway, Carmin, Pollard, & Flynn, 1992) described cognitive–behavioral approaches for social anxiety and, along with a commercially available audiotape, *Letting Go of Stress*, was used to treat people who received a SoP diagnosis (Walker et al., 2001). *Overcoming Shyness and Social Phobia: A Step-by-Step Guide* (Rapee, 1998) is a cognitive–behavioral SH book that was evaluated in individuals with SoP (Abbott et al., 2002). The remaining study (Grossman et al., 1991) used a book that included information about dating anxiety, relaxation, cognitive restructuring, and conversation skills, as well as tests for determining the level of attained understanding. Ayres et al.'s study (1993) employed a videotape-based program emphasizing systematic desensitization and speech skills. Duration of the treatments varied, averaging 5.6 weeks and ranging from one to 12 weeks. The average number of study completers in total was 38. The average dropout rate in SH groups was 12.6%, ranging from 0 to 45.6%. Follow-up was conducted from 12 weeks (Abbott et al., 2002) to 4 to 5 months (Vestre & Judge, 1989).

Effectiveness of Self-Help Treatments

SH treatments appear effective for reducing SoP as well as social anxiety. When compared to no treatment or placebo controls, nine studies supported the effectiveness of SH interventions. Walker et al. (2001) had socially phobic individuals read *Dying of Embarrassment* for 13 weeks. These individuals reported reductions in SoP symptoms significantly more than individuals in the wait-list condition. Marshall et al. (1976) reported that three groups, all of whom read *A Manual for Self-Management of Public Speaking Anxiety*, had better treatment outcomes than wait-list controls and an expectation/placebo group. Vestre and Judge (1989) found that their two SH groups that read *A New Guide to Rational Living* to target interpersonal anxiety were superior to a no treatment group on self-reported anxiety symptoms, mood, fear of evaluation, social avoidance and distress, and general irrational beliefs. Ayres et al. (1993) evaluated the effectiveness of a videotape of an SH treatment for public speaking by comparing it to both a nontherapeutic videotape and wait-list conditions. In both studies, individuals watching the therapeutic video had reduced state anxiety and negative thoughts associated with public speaking when compared to individuals in either control condition.

Only two studies (Abbott et al., 2002; Vestre & Judge, 1989) examined long-term treatment effects in individuals with public-speaking anxiety or SoP, respectively. In Vestre and Judge's study, no effects for type of treatment were found, though all groups maintained improvement through the follow-up. In Abbott's study, individuals in the book-only group maintained therapeutic gains on some symptom dimensions, including clinician-rated severity, though they relapsed on other dimensions such as self-reported social anxiety and depression. However, given that only two studies provided follow-up data, no conclusions regarding long-term maintenance of treatment effects can be made.

Comparisons to Therapist-Directed Interventions

The limited data available indicate that SH interventions are as effective as TDIs when applied to subclinical social anxiety but not for individuals with diagnosable SoPs. Marshall et al. (1976) demonstrated that three SH groups were as effective in treating public-speaking anxiety as was the therapist-administered desensitization to reduce fear, when measured during an actual speech. The TDI, however, was better than the SH group when assessed by subjective measures of distress rated for hypothetical situations. Similarly, Vestre and Judge (1989) reported comparable effects of self-administered treatments to the therapist-administered treatment on self-reported interpersonal anxiety symptoms, the principal outcome measure in their study.

In contrast, individuals with diagnosed SoPs are more effectively treated by TDIs. A recent study by Abbott et al. (2002) found that bibliotherapy produced moderate reductions in phobia symptoms, while the TDI produced greater levels of symptom improvement. Specifically, the TDI produced 50–100% greater reductions on clinician-rated symptom severity at posttreatment than did the bibliotherapy treatment. Many individuals in both treatment groups continued to meet criteria for SoP at posttreatment. In the only other study that examined the effects of SH on SoP, Walker et al. (2001) reported comparable reductions to the TDIs on several dimensions of SoP but less improvement when symptoms were assessed by independent interviewers.

When Hirai and Clum (2006) evaluated the magnitude of therapeutic effects for social anxieties and phobias, TDIs were clearly superior to self-administered treatments. The nature of social anxiety and the importance of exposing sufferers to fear-producing social situations likely confers an advantage to TDIs. Most TDIs utilize exposure to social situations, while self-directed treatments can only direct sufferers to expose themselves to social situations.

Factors That Impact Effectiveness

Minimal therapist contact and amount of exposure to the SH treatment were the only treatment variables systematically examined in studies targeting social anxiety. Two studies (Marshall et al., 1976; Vestre and Judge, 1989) directly investigated therapist contact, with each study yielding different results. Vestre and Judge (1989) found that therapist contact enhanced the efficacy of the SH intervention, while Marshall et al. (1975) did not find such an effect. In the only other test of specific treatment variables, Abbott et al. (2002) reported that symptom reduction was related to the amount the SH book was read.

Summary

Overall, self-administered treatments reduce some anxiety symptoms in both subclinical social anxiety and SoP, though less information is available about the effectiveness of SH interventions for diagnosed individuals. Improvement in these studies has been found on measures of perceived social anxiety as well as on anxiety in social interactions. Behavior manifestations of anxiety as observed by others have not, however, been affected by these approaches. This conclusion is tempered somewhat by the finding that TDIs also did not produce changes on observer-rated anxiety. Given that TDIs were reported to produce better outcomes than SH interventions for clinical-level symptoms, incorporating actual social interactions as part of exposure exercises may be requisite to increase the efficacy of SH interventions.

Posttraumatic Stress Disorder

Experiencing or witnessing a life-threatening event significantly impacts individuals' emotions and behavior and may impair their daily functioning. People who suffer with PTSD experience flashbacks and nightmares, avoid memories and situations that are associated with the event, and experience general increases in physiological arousal. According to several recent surveys after the 9/11 attack on the World Trade Center, 11.2% of the residents in New York City developed PTSD (Schlenger et al., 2002) and 20%

of those who lived close to the WTC received such a diagnosis (Galea et al., 2002). Given the rate at which individuals experience traumatic events (Kessler, Sonnega, Bromet, & Hughes, 1995), PTSD might be one of the disorders for which cost-effective treatment options have the most potential. Research has shown that cognitive–behavioral treatments, particularly those emphasizing exposure to memories of the traumatic event, are the choice for PTSD (e.g., Foa et al, 1999; Resick, Nishith, Weaver, Astin, & Feuer, 2002; Richards, Lovell, & Marks, 1994).

Few studies exist that examined the effectiveness of SH interventions for people with a diagnosis of PTSD. One recent study (Ehlers et al, 2003) compared an SH booklet, cognitive therapy, and repeated assessments in people with PTSD after a motor vehicle accident. Comparisons based on self-report measures as well as clinician-rating scales were made at 12-weeks posttreatment and 6 months after the conclusion of treatment. Although the SH treatment reduced some symptoms, the therapist-directed cognitive therapy was clearly superior to the SH booklet. In addition, treatment using the SH booklet was only slightly more effective than the assessment group at posttreatment and slightly less effective than the assessment group at follow-up. In contrast to these relatively small therapeutic effects, Hirai and Clum (2005) reported significant improvement on symptoms produced by an online SH treatment. These authors developed an 8-week online SH program for trauma victims that consisted of four cognitive–behavioral modules, including information, relaxation-training, cognitive restructuring, and writing exposure. The program provided a mastery approach wherein individuals progressed from the least anxiety-provoking component to the most anxiety-generating component (i.e., exposure). Mastery of the material was tested by online questionnaires before allowing participants to proceed to the next module. Therapist contacts were conducted by e-mail, but only when technical problems were reported or scheduled assessments were not completed by the participant. The SH treatment decreased avoidance behavior, intrusive symptoms, state anxiety, and depressive symptoms and increased coping skills and coping self-efficacy compared to a wait-list control group at posttreatment. However, this study had a small sample size and used a nonclinical sample, leaving in question whether the results are generalizable to clinical populations.

Two online treatment studies for trauma victims (Lange et al, 2003; Lange, van de Ven, Schrieken, & Emmelkamp, 2001) have been conducted using basically the same treatment program. This program instructs trauma victims to write about their traumatic events and to employ positive cognitive reappraisal of the events. Therapist feedback was provided frequently during the 5-week treatment period, making this treatment a therapist-assisted SH program. Assessment on self-report measures demonstrated that the online program significantly reduced trauma-related symptoms and depression after 6 weeks of treatment. These results, in combination with Hirai and Clum's study (2005) indicate the possibility of using the Internet as a SH treatment modality for treating trauma victims.

Because of the limited number of studies targeting trauma consequences, no comparisons have been made between self-directed treatments and TDIs. Similarly, no information is available on what treatment components are the most helpful or how they are best delivered. While writing exposure has been the only type of exposure used in SH treatments for trauma victims, that choice is likely related to its ease of application. As more sophisticated systems are developed for idiosyncratic trauma stimuli, exposure strategies will incorporate these methods with current approaches.

Obsessive–Compulsive Disorder

OCD is characterized by unwanted, repetitive, anxiety-generating thoughts, images, ideas, or urges that seem impossible to control. Often, the person with obsessions believes that catastrophic consequences are presaged by the obsessions. Compulsions, on the other hand, are repetitive behaviors or mental acts, intended to reduce anxiety associated with obsessions. Effective psychological treatments have focused on repetitive and prolonged exposure of the obsessional material, intended to reduce the negative affect associated with and believed to sustain the obsessions. Treatment of compulsions has focused on preventing the expression of the compulsive behaviors (response prevention) in the face of the negative affect associated with the obsessions, a strategy intended to break the association between the obsessions and compulsions (e.g., Foa & Franklin, 2001). Extrapolation of these strategies to the SH venue was thought difficult, given the clinical resistance often encountered by therapists when exposing OCD sufferers to the obsessional material and to the difficulty decoupling the association between obsessions and compulsions.

Although two controlled studies for OCD (Fritzler, Hecker, & Losee, 1997; Greist et al., 2002) compared SH interventions to other venues, only one (Greist et al., 2002) reported group comparison data. Greist et al. (2002) compared computer-guided, telephone-based, behavior therapy (BT STEPS), therapist-directed behavior therapy, and book- and audiotape-guided relaxation training among individuals who received a diagnosis of OCD. The program consisted of three steps for education and assessment and six treatment steps for practicing self-exposure and ritual prevention. Individuals in all groups had 10 weeks to complete their treatment. All study participants improved at posttreatment, but the magnitude of symptom improvement assessed by self-administered and clinician-rated questionnaires was largest in the therapist-assisted treatment followed by the BT STEPS group. Individuals receiving BT STEPS had outcomes similar to individuals receiving the TDI on several measures, including time spent on rituals and obsessions, level of depression, and work and social adjustment. The self-administered relaxation treatment produced the least improvement on OCD symptoms, time spent on rituals and obsessions, and work and social adjustment, indicating that specific treatment ingredients of proven effectiveness must form the treatment content in SH materials for OCD. The possibility of using computer-guided, self-exposure interventions for treating OCD patients was examined in one controlled study comparing two SH groups (Kenwright et al., 2005) and in three open-field trials (Bachofen et al., 1999; Clark et al., 1998; Marks et al., 1998). Kenwright et al. (2005) evaluated BT STEPS over 17 weeks on the effect of phone support provided by a therapist. Treatment-resistant patients were assigned either to a group receiving nine scheduled support calls, totaling 1.25 hours, or to a group allowed to call the therapist requesting support. During calls, the therapist reviewed patient's progress and provided encouragement briefly. Results demonstrated the effectiveness of BT STEPS with therapist assistance after 16 weeks of treatment. Positive effects of scheduled contact on decreasing dropout rates and improving symptoms were also reported. The fact that individuals who did not receive scheduled contact but were allowed to request support had less improvement may suggest the importance of therapist-initiated contact.

Clark et al. (1998) developed a computerized, vicarious exposure and ritual prevention program where individuals manipulate a figure on the computer display to touch anxiety-provoking objects (e.g., dirt) and are instructed to refrain from washing the figure's hands. Individuals were treated by three SH sessions within a 5- to 7-day treatment interval. The other two used BT STEPS, described above. All three studies showed improved functioning on OCD symptoms. Bachofen et al. (1999) reported improvements based on patients' self-report comparable to those typically produced by selective serotonin reuptake inhibitors, a class of antidepressants approved for treating OCD. To date, all of the SH studies for OCD that met criteria for the current review utilized computer-based treatment programs. No SH study for OCD employed written materials, the most common SH venue for other anxiety disorders. Clearly, additional controlled studies are needed to test the effectiveness of different types of SH interventions for people with OCD and to investigate factors impacting effectiveness.

Generalized Anxiety Disorder

GAD is characterized by persistent and excessive levels of anxiety and worry that are not triggered by any external situation or object. The central feature of GAD is chronic worry that is out of proportion to the individual's circumstances. Cognitive–behavioral treatment of GAD has focused on the acquisition of several skills, including applied relaxation skills, awareness skills, cognitive restructuring skills, and desensitization skills (Brown, O'Leary, & Barlow, 2001), all of which can be learned in an SH format.

Only one controlled study examined the effectiveness of self-administered treatments for GAD. Bowman, Scogin, Floyd, Patton, and Gist (1997) examined the efficacy of a cognitive-based SH protocol called Self-Examination Therapy (SET) (Bowman, 1995), whose effectiveness had been previously demonstrated among individuals with depression (Bowman, Scogin, & Lyrene, 1995). According to these authors, individuals learned to "determine what matters to them, think less negatively about things that do not matter to them, invest their energy in things that are important to them, and accept situations they cannot change" (p. 268). Participants in the SET group had 4 weeks to complete the protocol. These individuals received weekly 5-minute calls that assessed their need for referral to a mental health professional. Individuals receiving the SH treatment experienced reduced anxiety symptoms and general psychopathology rated by both patients and clinicians, when compared to the delayed-treatment control group. The ES obtained by comparing the SH group to the delayed treatment group was large. No other studies have tested the effectiveness of SH interventions. While the results of this study are promising, the fact that this is the only controlled study that targeted GAD renders any conclusions about the general effectiveness of self-administered interventions tentative. Also unknown is whether self-administered treatments are as effective as TDIs.

Test Anxiety

Test anxiety is a nondiagnosable anxiety problem that is often associated with a variety of other, diagnosable anxiety disorders. It refers specifically to the experience of high levels of anxiety prior to and during test-taking that can interfere with a person's ability to concentrate and to perform successfully. Test anxiety can include fear of external evaluation (social anxiety), panic attacks during the testing experience (PD), and excessive worry about the consequences of failing a test (GAD). Psychological treatments for test anxiety have included relaxation training, desensitization, cognitive restructuring, and education about studying and test-taking strategies.

Three controlled studies have examined the effectiveness of self-administered treatments for test anxiety in nondiagnosed student samples (Buglione et al., 1990; Donner & Guerney, 1969; Register, Beckham, May, & Gustafson, 1991). The average duration of the SH interventions was 6 weeks, with a range from 4 to 8 weeks. The average dropout rate in these studies was 23.7%. Two of these studies (Donner & Guerney, 1969; Register, et al., 1991) conducted follow-up evaluations.

These three studies differ in several ways. Buglione et al., (1990) compared a 6-week computerized cognitive–behavioral program to group therapy. The computerized program was called *Coping with Tests* (Thoresen, Insel, Roth, Ross, & Seyler, 1986), whose main modules included systematic desensitization to anxiety-provoking scenes and audiotaped relaxation. In this study, the computerized program group was compared to a therapist-directed group condition where participants learned systematic desensitization and cognitive restructuring strategies with homework assignments prescribing use of the relaxation audiotape at home. Donner and Guerney (1969) used an audiotaped desensitization program, visualizing fear-provoking situations and engaging in relaxation training, over an 8-week treatment period. This program was administered in a group setting where participants had no verbal communications with each other and was compared to a therapist-directed group treatment that also provided systematic desensitization instructions. Register et al. (1991) examined a book-based stress inoculation program both with and without minimal therapist contact compared to wait-list control conditions with and without contact. The book consisted of education about anxiety, relaxation, coping strategies (e.g., distraction, imaging pleasant events) and imaginal exposure, and positive-self talk components. Phone calls were provided to individuals in one SH group once a week.

Each of these SH interventions successfully decreased self-reported test anxiety. Short-term follow-up data (Donner & Guerney, 1969; Register et al., 1991) revealed maintenance of therapeutic gain. However, reports on actual improvement in school performance were not consistent across the studies. Donner and Guerney (1969) reported somewhat improved grades in the SH group. Buglione et al. (1990) reported improved grades for males but not females, while Register et al. (1991) reported no relationship between grades and treatment. Given that decreased anxiety levels are not the only factor related to school performance, improving test anxiety may not always result in such improvement.

SH interventions were effective when compared to no treatment controls. However, given the small number of studies and the presence of dissimilarities in study designs and variables across these studies, clear conclusions cannot be made in terms of whether SH interventions are comparable to TDIs for test anxiety. For example, Buglione et al. (1990) reported comparable effects of a self-administered computerized treatment program to therapist-directed group therapy, whereas Donner and Guerney (1969) reported the superiority of therapist-administered desensitization in a group format. The effect of minimal therapist contact was examined in only one study (Register et al., 1991), which reported no effect of adding such contact.

Because test anxiety is prominent among students, Internet-based SH information for test anxiety, as well as instructions for enhancing study and test-taking skills, is available on many university and college Web sites. Nonetheless, additional controlled research that examines online SH programs is essential to provide empirically validated treatment programs for test-anxious students.

Summary and Conclusions

Anxiety problems have been favorite targets of individuals studying self-administered interventions. One reason for this popularity may be the ease with which specific strategies used to treat these problems are adaptable to SH venues. While a variety of anxiety problems appear treatable using self-administered techniques, considerable variability exists in the frequency with which these problems have been addressed. Moreover, the success that self-administered treatments have had varies markedly depending on the disorder targeted. Based on the available studies, symptoms associated with PDs/agoraphobia decreased with the application of SH treatments. Furthermore, these improvements were stable over short follow-up periods and, to date, were found equivalent to therapist-directed individual, as well as group, treatments. SPs also show stable improvement using self-administered interventions, though they are not equivalent to TDIs.

One reason SH programs for panic are comparable to TDIs, while such is not the case for SPs, may have to do with the type of treatment offered for each disorder. For PDs, treatments have focused on the identification and practice of specific skills; e.g., relaxation, challenging cognitions, and exposure. These skills are not actually applied by a therapist so much as taught to the client, with the therapist supervising the client's application. Such skill building may be well suited to an SH format. Early studies that evaluated SH treatments for SPs utilized systematic desensitization, whereas later studies used directed exposure. Whereas self-administered systematic desensitization produced outcomes comparable to TDIs, directed exposure did not. Systematic differences between types of individuals treated may account for the difference. Systematic desensitization was typically evaluated in student samples, while directed exposure was evaluated in clinical samples. More important, self-exposure, when not accompanied by other coping skills, may be difficult to administer. SH approaches to social anxiety may be similarly limited, when the socially anxious individual has no readily available venue to practice his skills, such as would be the case if the client were in group therapy or had a therapist directing him to enter social situations.

Although therapist-assisted interventions in general appear more effective than self-administered interventions, SH approaches produce reasonable improvement on target symptoms as well as on coping strategies and in daily function. Those SH interventions that have demonstrated comparable effectiveness to TDIs might be considered as stand-alone interventions. Those that have not demonstrated that type of equivalence might better be considered the first step in a stepped-care intervention program.

Few researchers in the SH arena have attempted to identify factors that enhance the effectiveness of these approaches. One factor that has been examined with some regularity, and that has been found to make a difference, is contact with the client. Most often, researchers have sought to limit the amount of contact, perhaps in hopes of determining whether SH programs alone can produce change in the target problems. Others, expecting that some contact might enhance treatment outcome or even be necessary for treatment to be effective, have contrived comparisons to directly test the importance of such contact. For the most part, such contact has been found to contribute to treatment response. Only one study has examined an SH treatment for anxiety (Febbraro et al., 1999) in which no direct therapist contact was present prior to or during the intervention. In their study, Febbraro et al. found that a program based on the book *Coping With Panic* did not produce the expected treatment effect when no therapist contact, whether for diagnosis, assessment, or to encourage participation, was available. The conclusions of the Febbraro et al. study, along with the failure of other studies to examine the effectiveness of SH approaches under conditions of no therapist contact whatsoever make it impossible to determine whether SH programs, such as those purchased at the local book store, have any effect. It may be that, to be effective, SH treatment programs for anxiety problems will have to include access to accurate diagnosis, assessment, and periodic contact by a program representative. Another factor that may enhance the effectiveness of SH interventions for anxiety disorders is treatment content specifically developed for the target problem. The reviewed literature revealed that PD and snake phobia were more effectively treated by specific manuals than by general anxiety workbooks. Long-term therapeutic gains were demonstrated from 6 months to 2 years. Given that factors associated with relapse have been found using TDIs for phobias, research in relapse using SH treatments is necessary to enhance long-term gains.

The future of self-administered programs in the treatment of anxiety problems lies in the use of advanced communication technology. Such programs offer the types of advantages available for users of videos or books that come only when an effort is made to conduct a study of their effectiveness. Computerized SH programs on the Internet, on the other hand, can provide the formal treatment material, pre-, during, and post-program assessment, as well as regular contact via e-mail. Such programs can also provide interactive and programmable functions, including tailoring the programs to specific needs of the clients, providing immediate assessment feedback, and augmenting the treatment experience using audio and visual displays. Future consumers of SH interventions await the development and evaluation of such approaches.

Chapter Points

- Self-help treatments for anxiety disorders have been modeled after cognitive–behavioral treatments of demonstrated effectiveness.
- Self-help treatments for PD are more effective than no treatment and as effective as therapist-administered interventions, for up to one year posttreatment.
- Minimal therapist involvement enhances treatment effectiveness, whereas type of treatment venue or treatment duration does not.
- SH treatments for SPs are more effective than no treatment, especially when administered in clinic settings, but are less effective than therapist-administered interventions.
- SH treatments for SoP are more effective than no treatment and are as effective as TDIs for subclinical social anxiety but are less effective than TDIs for diagnosed SoPs.
- Three SH studies that utilized written exposure were effective in reducing symptoms of PTSD, whereas one study not using exposure was not effective.
- Computer-based CBT treatments have been found effective in treating OCD, GAD, and test anxiety.

References

Abbott, M. J., Rapee, R. M., & Gaston, J. (2002, March). *Treatment of social phobia using bibliotherapy.* Poster session presented at the 22nd national conference of the Anxiety Disorders Association of America, Austin, TX.

American Psychiatric Association. (1994). *Diagnostic and statistical manual of mental disorders* (4th ed.). Washington, DC: Author.

Ayres, J., Ayres, F. E., Baker, A. L., Colby, N., De Blasi, C., Dimke, D., et al. (1993). Two empirical tests of a videotape designed to reduce public speaking anxiety. *Journal of Applied Communication Research, 21*, 132–147.

Bachofen, M., Nakagawa, A., Marks, I. M., Park, J. M., Greist, J. H., Baer, L., et al. (1999). Home self-assessment and self-treatment of obsessive-compulsive disorders using a manual and a computer-conducted telephone interview: Replication of a U.K.-U.S. study. *Journal of Clinical Psychiatry, 60*, 545–549.

Baker, B. L., Cohen, D. C., & Saunders, J. T. (1972). Self-directed desensitization for acrophobia. *Behaviour Research and Therapy, 11*, 79–89.

Barlow, D. H., & Craske, M. G. (1989). *Mastery of your anxiety and panic*. San Antonio, TX: The Psychological Corporation.

Barlow, D. H., & Craske, M. G. (1994). *Mastery of your anxiety and panic II*. San Antonio, TX: The Psychological Corporation.

Biglan, A., Villwock, C., & Wick, S. (1979). The feasibility of a computer controlled program for the treatment of test anxiety. *Journal of Behavior Therapy and Experimental Psychiatry, 10*, 47–49.

Bowman, D. (1995). Self-examination therapy: Treatment for anxiety and depression. In L. Vandecreek, S. Knapp, & T. Jackson (Eds.), *Innovations in clinical practice: A source book, 14*, 195–206. Sarasota, FL: Professional Resource Press.

Bowman, D., Scogin, F., Floyd, M., Patton, E., & Gist, L. (1997). Efficacy of self-examination therapy in the treatment of generalized anxiety disorder. *Journal of Counseling Psychology, 44*, 267–273.

Bowman, D., Scogin, F., & Lyrene, B. (1995). The efficacy of self-examination therapy and cognitive bibliotherapy in the treatment of mild to moderate depression. *Psychotherapy Research, 5*, 131–140.

Brown, T. A., O'Leary, T. A., & Barlow, D. H. (2001). Generalized anxiety disorder. In D. H. Barlow (Ed.), *Clinical handbook of psychological disorders. Step-by-step treatment manual* (pp. 154–208). New York: Guilford.

Buglione, S. A., DeVito, A. J., & Mulloy, J. M. (1990). Traditional group therapy and computer-administered treatment for test anxiety. *Anxiety Research, 3*, 33–39.

Carlbring, P., Ekselius, L., & Andersson, G. (2003). Treatment of panic disorder via the Internet: A randomized trial of CBT vs. applied relaxation. *Journal of Behavior Therapy and Experimental Psychiatry, 34*, 129–140.

Carlbring, P., Nilsson-Ihrfelt, E., Waara, J., Kollenstam, C., Buhrman, M., Kaldo, V., et al. (2005). Treatment of panic disorder: Live therapy vs. self-help via the Internet. *Behaviour Research and Therapy, 43*, 1321–1333.

Carlbring, P., Westling, B. E., & Andersson, G. (2000). A review of published self-help books for panic disorder. *Scandinavian Journal of Behaviour Therapy, 29*, 5–13.

Carlbring, P., Westling, B.E., Ljungstrand, P., Ekselius, L., & Andersson, G. (2001). Treatment of panic disorder via the Internet: A randomized trial of a self-help program. *Behavior Therapy, 32*, 751–764.

Carr, A.C., Ghosh, A., & Marks, I. M. (1988). Computer-supervised exposure treatment for phobias. *Canadian Journal of Psychiatry, 33*, 112–117.

Chambless, D. L., & Hollon, S. D. (1998). Defining empirically supported therapies. *Journal of Consulting and Clinical Psychology, 66*, 7–18.

Clark, A., Kirkby, K. C., Daniels, B. A., & Marks, I. M. (1998). A pilot study of computer-aided vicarious exposure for obsessive-compulsive disorder. *Australian and New Zealand Journal of Psychiatry, 32,* 268–275.

Clark, F. (1973). Self-administered desensitization. *Behavior Research and Therapy, 11,* 335–338.

Clum, G. A. (1990). *Coping with panic.* Pacific Grove, CA: Brooks/Cole.

Cotler, S. B. (1970). Sex differences and generalization of anxiety reduction with automated desensitization and minimal therapist interaction. *Behaviour Research & Therapy, 8,* 273–285.

Donner, L., & Guerney, B. G., Jr. (1969). Automated group desensitization for test anxiety. *Behavior Research and Therapy, 7,* 1–13.

Ehlers, A., Clark, D. M., Hackmann, A., McManus, F., Fennell, M., Herbert, C., et al. (2003). A randomized controlled trial of cognitive therapy, a self-help booklet, and repeated assessments as early interventions for posttraumatic stress disorder. *Archives of General Psychiatry, 60,* 1024–1032.

Ellis, A., & Harper, R. A. (1961). *A guide to rational living.* Englewood Cliffs, NJ: Prentice Hall.

Ellis, A., & Harper, R. A. (1975). *A new guide to rational living.* North Hollywood, CA: Wilshire Books.

Febbraro, G. A. R. (2005). An investigation into the effectiveness of bibliotherapy and minimal contact interventions in the treatment of panic attacks. *Journal of Clinical Psychology, 61,* 763–779.

Febbraro, G. A. R., Clum, G. A., Roodman, A. A., & Wright, J. H. (1999). The limits of bibliotherapy: A study of the differential effectiveness of self-administered interventions in individuals with panic attacks. *Behavior Therapy, 30,* 209–222.

Foa, E. B., Dancu, C. V., Hembree, E. A., Jaycox, L. H., Meadows, E. A., & Street, G. P. (1999). A comparison of exposure therapy, stress inoculation training, and their combination for reducing posttraumatic stress disorder in female assault victims. *Journal of Consulting and Clinical Psychology, 67,* 194–200.

Foa, E. B., & Franklin, M. E. (2001). Obsessive-compulsive disorder. In D. H. Barlow (Ed.), *Clinical handbook of psychological disorders* (3rd ed., pp. 209–263). New York: Guilford.

Franklin, J. A. (1996). *Overcoming panic: A complete nine-week home-based treatment program for panic disorder.* Carlton, Australia: Australian Psychological Society Ltd.

Fraser, J., Kirkby, K. C., Daniels, B., Gilroy, L., & Montgomery, I. M. (2001). Three versus six sessions of computer-aided vicarious exposure treatment for spider phobia. *Behaviour Change, 18,* 213–223.

Fritzler, B. K., Hecker, J. E., & Losee, M. C. (1997). Self-directed treatment with minimal therapist contact: Preliminary findings for obsessive-compulsive disorder. *Behaviour Research and Therapy, 35,* 627–631.

Galea, S., Ahern, J., Resnick, H., Kilpatrick, D., Bucuvalas, M., Gold, J., et al. (2002). Psychological sequelae of the September 11 terrorist attacks in New York City. *New England Journal of Medicine, 346,* 982–987.

Ghosh, A., & Marks, I. M. (1987). Self-treatment of agoraphobia by exposure. *Behavior Therapy, 18,* 3–16.

Ghosh, A., Marks, I. M., & Carr, A. C. (1988). Therapist contact and outcome of self-exposure treatment for phobias. *British Journal of Psychiatry, 152,* 234–238.

Gilroy, L. J., Kirkby, K. C., Daniels, B. A., Menzies, R. G., & Montgomery, I. M. (2000). Controlled comparison of computer-aided vicarious exposure versus live exposure in the treatment of spider phobia. *Behavior Therapy, 31,* 733–744.

Götestam, K. G. (2002). One session group treatment of spider phobia by direct or modelled exposure. *Cognitive Behaviour Therapy, 31,* 18–24.

Gould, R. A., & Clum, G. A. (1993). A meta-analysis of self-help treatment approaches. *Clinical Psychology Review, 13,* 169–186.

Gould, R. A., & Clum, G. A. (1995). Self-help plus minimal therapist contact in the treatment of panic disorder: A replication and extension. *Behavior Therapy, 26,* 533–546.

Gould, R. A., Glum, G. A., & Shapiro, D. (1993). The use of bibliotherapy in the treatment of panic: A preliminary investigation. *Behavior Therapy, 24,* 241–252.

Gould, R. A., Otto, M. W., & Pollack, M. H. (1995). A meta-analysis of treatment outcome for panic disorder. *Clinical Psychology Review, 15,* 819–844.

Greenberg, P. E., Sisitsky, T., Kessler, R. C., Finkelstein, S. N., Berndt, E. R., Davidson, J. R. T., et al. (1999). The economic burden of anxiety disorders in the 1990s. *Journal of Clinical Psychiatry, 60,* 427–435.

Greist, J. H., Marks, I. M., Baer, L., Kobak, K. A., Wenzel, K. W., Hirsch, M. J., et al. (2002). Behavior therapy for obsessive-compulsive disorder guided by a computer or by a clinician compared with relaxation as a control. *Journal of Clinical Psychiatry, 63,* 138–145.

Grossman, K. S., McNamara, J. R., & Dudley, K. (1991). Treatment effectiveness of a self-help manual for dating anxiety. *Journal of College Student Psychotherapy, 6,* 85–106.

Harcourt, L., Kirkby, K., Daniels, B., & Montgomery, I. (1998). The differential effect of personality on computer-based treatment of agoraphobia. *Comprehensive Psychiatry, 39,* 303–307.

Heading, K., Kirkby, K. C., Martin, F., Daniels, B. A., Gilroy, L. J., & Menzies, R. G. (2001). Controlled comparison of single-session treatments for spider phobia: Live graded exposure alone versus computer-aided vicarious exposure. *Behaviour Change, 18,* 103–113.

Hecker, J. E., Losee, M. C., Fritzler, B. K., & Fink, C. M. (1996). Self-directed versus therapist-directed cognitive behavioral treatment for panic disorder. *Journal of Anxiety Disorder, 10,* 253–265.

Hellström, K., & Öst, L. G. (1995). One-session exposure directed exposure vs. two forms of manual directed self-exposure in the treatment of spider phobia. *Behavior Research and Therapy, 33,* 959–965.

Hirai, M., & Clum, G. (2005). An Internet-based self-change program for traumatic event related fear, distress, and maladaptive coping. *Journal of Traumatic Stress, 18,* 631–636.

Hirai, M., & Clum, G. (2006). A meta-analytic study of self-help interventions for anxiety disorders. *Behavior Therapy, 37,* 99–111.

Hoffman, H. G., Garcia-Palacios, A., Carlin, A., Furness, T. A., III, & Botella-Arbona, C. (2003). Interfaces that heal: Coupling real and virtual objects to treat spider phobia. *International Journal of Human-Computer Interaction, 16,* 283–300.

Kenardy, J., McCafferty, K., & Rosa, V. (2003). Internet-deliverered indicated prevention for anxiety disorders: A randomized controlled trial. *Behavioural and Cognitive Psychotherapy, 31,* 279–289.

Kenwright, M., Liness, S., & Marks, I. (2001) Reducing demands on clinicians by offering computer-aided self-help for phobia/panic: Feasibility study. *British Journal of Psychiatry, 179,* 456–459.

Kenwright, M., Marks, I. M. (2004). Computer-aided self-help for phobia/panic via Internet at home: A pilot study. *British Journal of Psychiatry, 184,* 448–449.

Kenwright, M., Marks, I., Graham, C., Franses, A., & Mataix-Cols, D. (2005). Brief scheduled phone support from a clinician to enhance computer-aided sell-help for obsessive-compulsive disorder: Randomized controlled trial. *Journal of Clinical Psychology, 61,* 1499–1508.

Kessler, R. C., Chiu, W. T., Demler, O., & Walters, E. E. (2005). Prevalence, severity, and comorbidity of 12-month DSM-IV disorders in the national comorbidity survey replication. *Archives of General Psychiatry, 62,* 617–627.

Kessler, R. C., McGonagle, K. A., Zhao, S., Nelson, C. B., Hughes, M., Eshleman, S., et al. (1994). Lifetime and 12-month prevalence of DSM-III-R psychiatric disorders in the United States: Results from the National Comorbidity Survey. *Archives of General Psychiatry, 51,* 8–19.

Kessler, R. C., Sonnega, A., Bromet, E., & Hughes, M. (1995). Posttraumatic stress disorder in the national comorbidity survey. *Archives of General Psychiatry, 52,* 1048–1060.

Kirkby, K. C., Berrios, G. E., Daniels, B. A., Menzies, R. G., Clark, A., & Romano, A. (2000). Process-outcome analysis in computer-aided treatment of obsessive-compulsive disorder. *Comprehensive Psychiatry, 41,* 259–265.

Kirsch, I., & Henry, D. (1979). Self-desensitization and meditation in the reduction of public speaking anxiety. *Journal of Consulting and Clinical Psychology, 47,* 536–541.

Klein, B., & Richards, J. C. (2001) A brief Internet-based treatment for panic disorder. *Behavioural & Cognitive Psychotherapy, 29,* 113–117.

Lange, A., Rietdijk, D., Hudcovicova, M., van den Ven, J. P., Schrieken, B., & Emmelkamp, P. M. G. (2003). Interapy: A controlled randomized trial of the standardized treatment of posttraumatic stress through the Internet. *Journal of Consulting & Clinical Psychology, 71,* 901–909.

Lange, A., van de Ven, J. P., Schrieken, B., & Emmelkamp, P. M. G. (2001). Interapy. Treatment of posttraumatic stress through the Internet: A controlled trial. *Journal of Behavior Therapy & Experimental Psychiatry, 32,* 73–90.

Lidren, D. M., Watkins, P. L., Gould, R. A., Clum, G. A., Asterino, M. A., & Tulloch, H. L. (1994). A comparison of bibliotherapy and group therapy in the treatment of panic disorder. *Journal of Consulting and Clinical Psychology, 62,* 865–869.

Marks, I. M., (1978). *Living with fear.* New York: McGraw-Hill.

Marks, I. M. (1988). Blood-injury phobia: A review. *American Journal of Psychiatry, 145,* 1207–1213.

Marks, I. M., Baer, L., Greist, J. H., Park, J., Bachofen, M., Nakagawa, A., et al. (1998). Home self-assessment of obsessive-compulsive disorder: Use of a manual and a computer-conducted telephone interview: two U.K., U.S. studies. *British Journal of Psychiatry, 172,* 406–412.

Markway, B., Carmin, C. N., Pollard, C. A., & Flynn, T. (1992). *Dying of embarrassment: Help for social anxiety & phobia.* Oakland, CA: New Harbinger.

Marrs, R. W. (1995). A meta-analysis of bibliotherapy studies. *American Journal of Community Psychology, 23,* 843–870.

Marshall, W. L., & Andrew, W. R. (1973). *A manual for the self-management of public speaking anxiety.* Kingston, Ontario: McArthur College Press.

Marshall, W. L., Presse, L., & Andrews, W. R. (1976). A self-administered program for public speaking anxiety. *Behaviour Research and Therapy, 14,* 33–39.

Mineka, S., Mystkowski, J., Hladek, D., & Rodriguez, B. I. (1999). The effects of changing contexts on return of fear following exposure therapy for spider fear. *Journal of Consulting and Clinical Psychology, 67,* 599–604.

Mystkowski, J., Craske, M. G., & Echiverri, A. M. (2002). Treatment context and return of fear in spider phobia. *Behavior Therapy, 33,* 399–416.

Newman, M. G., Erickson, T., Przeworski, A., & Dzus, E. (2003). Self-help and minimal-contact therapies for anxiety disorders: Is human contact necessary for therapeutic efficacy? *Journal of Clinical Psychology, 59,* 251–274.

Newman, M. G., Kenardy, J., Herman, S., & Taylor, C. B. (1997). Comparison of palmtop-computer-assisted brief cognitive-behavioral treatment to cognitive-behavioral treatment for panic disorder. *Journal of Consulting and Clinical Psychology, 65,* 178–183.

Öst, L. G. (1996). One-session group treatment of spider phobia. *Behaviour Research and Therapy, 34,* 707–715.

Öst, L. G., Brandberg, M., & Alm, T. (1997). One versus five sessions of exposure in the treatment of flying phobia. *Behaviour Research and Therapy, 35,* 987–996.

Öst, L. G., Hellström, K., & Kåver, A. (1992). One versus five session of exposure in the treatment of injection phobia. *Behavior Therapy, 23,* 263–282.

Öst, L. G., Salkovskis, P. M., & Hellström, K. (1991). One-session therapist-directed exposure vs. self-exposure in the treatment of spider phobia. *Behavior Therapy, 22,* 407–422.

Page, A. C. (1994). Blood-injury phobia. *Clinical Psychology Review, 14,* 443–461.

Parry, R., & Killick, S. (1998). An evaluation of the impact of an individually administered videotape for people with panic disorder. *Behavioural and Cognitive Psychotherapy, 26,* 153–161.

Rachman, S. J., & Lopatka, C. (1988). Return of fear: underlearning and overlearning. *Behaviour Research and Therapy, 26,* 99–104.

Rapee, R. M. (1998). *Overcoming shyness and social phobia: A step-by-step guide.* Lanham, MD: Jason Aronson.

Register, A. C., Beckham, J. C., May, J. G., & Gustafson, D. J. (1991). Stress inoculation bibliotherapy in the treatment of test anxiety. *Journal of Counseling Psychology, 38,* 115–119.

Resick, P. A., Nishith, P., Weaver, T. L., Astin, M. C., & Feuer, C. A. (2002). A comparison of cognitive-processing therapy with prolonged exposure and a waiting condition for the treatment of chronic posttraumatic stress disorder in female rape victims. *Journal of Consulting and Clinical Psychology, 70,* 867–879.

Richards, D. A., Lovell, K., & Marks, I. M. (1994). Post-traumatic stress disorder: Evaluation of a behavioral treatment program. *Journal of Traumatic Stress, 7,* 669–680.

Rosen, G. M., Glasgow, R. E., & Barrera M., Jr. (1976). A controlled study to assess the clinical efficacy of totally self-administered systematic desensitization. *Journal of Consulting and Clinical Psychology, 44,* 208–217.

Rosen, G. M., Glasgow, R.E., Barrera, M., Jr. (1977). A two-year follow-up on systematic desensitization with data pertaining to the external validity of laboratory fear assessment. *Journal of Consulting and Clinical Psychology, 45,* 1188–1189.

Rowe, M. K., & Craske, M. G. (1998a). Effects of an expanding-spaced vs. massed exposure schedule on fear reduction and return of fear. *Behaviour Research and Therapy, 36,* 701–717.

Rowe, M. K., & Craske, M. G. (1998b). Effects of varied-stimulus exposure training on fear reduction and return of fear. *Behaviour Research and Therapy, 36,* 719–734.

Salkovskis, P., & Mills, I. (1994). Induced mood, phobic responding and the return of fear. *Behaviour Research and Therapy, 32,* 439–445.

Schlenger, W. E., Caddell, J. M., Ebert, L., Jordan, B. K., Rourke, K. M., Wilson, D., et al. (2002). Psychological reactions to terrorist attacks: Findings from the national study of Americans' reactions to September 11. *JAMA: Journal of the American Medical Association, 288,* 581–588.

Schneider, A. J., Mataix-Cols, D., Marks, I. M., & Bachofen, M. (2005). Internet-guided self-help with or without exposure therapy for phobic and panic disorders. *Psychotherapy and Psychosomatics, 74,* 154–164.

Schelver, S. R., & Gutsch, K. U. (1983). The effects of self-administered cognitive therapy on social-evaluative anxiety. *Journal of Clinical Psychology, 39,* 658–666.

Smith, K. L., Kirkby, K. C., Montgomery, I. M., & Daniels, B. A. (1997). Computer-delivered modeling of exposure for spider phobia: Relevant versus irrelevant exposure. *Journal of Anxiety Disorders, 11,* 489–497.

Thorensen, C. E., Insel, P. M., Roth, W. T., Ross, D., & Seyler, M. F. (1986). *Coping with tests.* Palo Alto, CA: Counseling Psychologists Press.

U.S. Department of Commerce. (2002). *A nation online: How Americans are expanding their use of the Internet.* Washington, DC: Government Printing Office.

Vestre, N. D., & Judge, T. J. (1989). Evaluation of self-administered rational emotive therapy programs for interpersonal anxiety. *Journal of Rational-Emotive & Cognitive-Behavioral Therapy, 7,* 141–154.

Walker, J. R., Cox, B. J., Frankel, S., & Torgrud, L. J. (2001, July). *Evaluating two cognitive-behavioral self-help approaches for generalized social phobia.* Paper presented at the World Congress of Behavioral and Cognitive Therapies, Vancouver, B.C.

White, J., Jones, R., & McGarry, E. (2000). Cognitive behavioural computer therapy for the anxiety disorders: a pilot study. *Journal of Mental Health (UK), 9,* 505–516.

Wright, J., Clum, G. A., Roodman, A. A., & Febbraro, G. A. R. (2000). A bibliotherapy approach to relapse prevention in individuals with panic attacks. *Journal of Anxiety Disorders, 14,* 483–499.

Zuercher-White, E. (1998). *An end to panic: Breakthrough techniques for overcoming panic disorder.* Oakland, CA: New Harbinger Publications, Inc.

CHAPTER 6

Self-Help Therapies for Depression

JENNIFER A. KARPE AND FORREST R. SCOGIN

What is meant by the term self-administered treatment? According to Glasgow and Rosen (1978), there are four degrees of therapist/patient contact: self-administered therapy, which may include contact for assessment only; predominantly self-help treatment including check-ins and an initial introduction to the materials; minimal contact therapy with some active involvement of a therapist; and therapist-administered treatments. The first three degrees of therapist/patient contact can all be viewed as different levels of self-administered treatment varying in amount of contact between therapist and client. Although most real-world self-help use most closely resembles the category self-administered therapy, the majority of research conditions in the self-help literature more often approximate predominantly self-help and minimal contact paradigms. Some self-administered treatments require a moderate level of continuing interaction with a clinician while others require none at all. The varying degrees of contact with the patient can be manipulated when identifying a course of self-administered treatment that is the best fit for a given individual.

This chapter focuses on the extant research on self-administered treatments for depression including their effectiveness when integrated with therapist contact, antidepressants, or implemented alone. One application of self-administered treatments is as a first line in a stepped-care model of depression intervention (Scogin, Hanson, & Welsh, 2003). In such a model, the first line of intervention should be the least intrusive, most basic option available. When a lower level treatment fails to be effective for an individual, the following step becomes more intense as needed until an appropriate treatment response is obtained. Stepped-care models allow individuals to be treated by the simplest, most cost-effective method that is acceptable and works for them.

Self-administered treatments can be considered a possible first step in mild to moderate cases of depression. Using self-administered treatments first may save some individuals the money and time usually spent on more rigorous treatment courses. In more complex or severe cases, bibliotherapy could still be applied as an adjunct to more traditional treatment in an effort to maximize treatment gains. Bibliotherapy is one form of self-administered treatment that has been researched as both the first step in intervention and as a stand-alone treatment for depression. Studies looking at the efficacy of bibliotherapy treatments for depression have compared bibliotherapy to a host of other treatments, including standard cognitive–behavioral therapy (CBT), interpersonal therapy (IPT), and antidepressant medications.

Self-administered treatment for depression can also be other forms of media, including computer programs, automated telephone systems, audiotapes, and videotapes in addition to books. Such programs may require work to be done at home or in a clinic setting under supervision. There is a high degree of variability among self-administered treatments for depression in the amount of multimedia access they provide. While some self-help materials consist of a single book, such as *Feeling Good* (Burns, 1980) and *Control Your Depression* (Lewinsohn, Munoz, Youngren, & Zeiss, 1986), more elaborate treatment packages exist such as the *Feeling Good* program, which includes multiple books, a workbook, audiotapes, and a video to provide a multimedia approach to teaching cognitive behavioral techniques.

Although this chapter provides an overview of the most common self-administered treatments for depression currently in use, it will not address the efficacy of such therapies as self-help groups, cinematherapy, or inspirational bibliotherapy. Instead, this chapter will focus wholly on two types of self-administered treatments for depression: bibliotherapy and computer-administered therapy. Both bibliotherapy and computer-based treatment have shown promise for depression in the absence or minimization of therapist contact. Computer-based treatments are being explored due to the rise in home computer use, and several forms of bibliotherapy have already proven effective in the treatment of depression (Mains & Scogin, 2003). Following a review of the empirical research examining the effectiveness of these modalities, we will provide practice-friendly suggestions for using self-administered treatment in clinical settings. For instance, we will address considerations such as with whom self-help programs might be most effective and how therapists might present self-help interventions in a way that makes them most palatable to clients.

Bibliotherapy

Overview

The most common self-administered treatments for depression are bibliotherapies, or self-help techniques presented in the written format of a book or tract. This self-help modality already has a place in depression treatment as an adjunct to therapist-led interventions. One survey indicated that 60 to 97% of psychologists use bibliotherapy as part of their treatment for at least some of their clients (Starker, 1988). Of the available types of bibliotherapy for depression, the majority are those that use either cognitive therapy or behavioral therapy techniques; some use a combination approach. Cognitive bibliotherapy involves helping depressed individuals identify their negative and distorted thought patterns. After an individual's thought patterns are identified, she is encouraged to evaluate their adaptiveness and redefine her cognitions in more functional ways (Beck, Rush, Shaw, & Emery, 1979). Behavioral therapy targets specific responses that are known to be problematic for depressed individuals. As such, this intervention might address the adequacy of clients' social skills, their ability to engage in pleasant activities, and their ability to achieve relaxation (Scogin et al., 2003).

To date, few bibliotherapy materials for depression have received empirical support. *Feeling Good* (Burns, 1980) and *Control Your Depression* (Lewinsohn, et al., 1986) are two bibliotherapy programs that are supported by research. *Feeling Good* is a self-help book that disseminates cognitive therapy techniques, and *Control Your Depression* is a self-help book that disseminates behavioral therapy strategies. One study has been conducted using *Mind Over Mood* (Greenberger & Padesky, 1995) that found improvement in depression; however, the small sample size urges caution in viewing this book as empirically supported (Rohen, 2002). Lewinsohn's audiocassette tapes, *Combating Depression: Practical Techniques,* were also evaluated in a small sample ($N = 12$), resulting in treatment gains despite several limitations (Neumann, 1981). In part, the reason only the two aforementioned books are considered efficacious is not because other bibliotherapy treatments for depression have been proven ineffective, but rather because such a large majority of the available self-help books for depression have not been empirically researched at all. One can locate a vast array of books for mood disturbances in the self-help section of any major bookstore; however, the great majority of these have not been tested for efficacy.

A major limitation of the current research on bibliotherapy is that most bibliotherapy studies investigating the efficacy of self-help treatment for depression have consisted of predominantly Caucasian samples; this is true of studies looking at efficacy in adolescents, adults, and older adults. Please note that the generalizability of such findings, particularly with respect to ethnic and cultural minorities, is limited due to the homogeneity of research samples.

General Adult Population

Studies investigating the efficacy of self-help treatment for depression in adults typically use samples ranging in age from 18 to 60; the studies reviewed below all used mixed gender samples that typically consisted of more women than men. Although there has been some diversity in demographic characteristics of samples, generally speaking the participants have been Caucasian individuals with a high school education or better who mostly fall within the socioeconomic status middle class. It may be the case that minorities and less educated individuals may not experience the same treatment gains when using bibliotherapy.

Schmidt and Miller (1983) conducted one of the earliest studies on the efficacy of bibliotherapy for depression as compared to a wait-list control group, group therapy in a small group, group therapy in a large group, and individual therapy. The authors created a multidimensional program that consisted of cognitive restructuring, assertiveness training, and behavior management. Results indicated that participants in all treatment conditions improved significantly on all depression measures, and gains were maintained at an 18-week follow-up. There were no differences across treatment groups. However, none of the therapists in the study were professionals, which may affect the generalizability of the results.

Another early study conducted by Brown and Lewinsohn (1984) compared four versions of Lewinsohn's then-preliminary program *Control Your Depression*, including a class, individual tutoring, phone contact, and delayed treatment; the bibliotherapy version of *Control Your Depression* was published two years later (Lewinsohn, et al., 1986). Like the bibliotherapy version of *Control Your Depression*, these treatments all targeted problematic behaviors for individuals who are depressed. There was improvement in depressive symptomology for all groups with no significant differences among them, indicating that one modality was not more helpful than any other.

In the early 1990s, Wollersheim and Wilson (1991) compared bibliotherapy based on CBT to a cognitive–behavioral group therapy, a supportive group therapy, and a delayed treatment condition. Again, participants in all conditions evidenced improvements on depression ratings over time.

Depression ratings completed by someone who knew the participant well were the only measures that indicated group treatment was more effective than bibliotherapy.

More recently, Bowman, Scogin, and Lyrene (1995) conducted a study comparing cognitive bibliotherapy to self-examination therapy and a wait-list control group. Self-examination therapy entails having individuals use a flowchart to determine what matters to them, to think less negatively about things that are not important, to accept situations they cannot change, and to invest energy in things that do matter and can be changed. Individuals in the bibliotherapy and self-examination therapy groups evidenced greater reductions in depressive symptoms than those in the wait-list control group.

This same year, Jamison and Scogin (1995) compared cognitive bibliotherapy to a wait-list control group. Cognitive bibliotherapy significantly decreased depressive symptoms, automatic negative thoughts, and dysfunctional attitudes. This research indicates that cognitive bibliotherapy produces more treatment gains for depressed individuals receiving it as compared to depressed individuals in a wait-list control group.

A study evaluating both cognitive and behavioral bibliotherapy for depression as compared to a delayed control treatment group found the cognitive bibliotherapy group was superior to the control group on measures of depressive symptoms and severity. There was no difference in outcome between the cognitive and behavioral treatment groups. Both groups maintained treatment gains at a 3-month follow-up (McKendree-Smith, 1998).

Based on the findings described above, bibliotherapy results in significant improvement on measures of depression. From the research available, it appears that both cognitive bibliotherapy and behavioral bibliotherapy are useful tools in the treatment of depression. The majority of studies on bibliotherapy have compared it to wait-list controls; bibliotherapy is indeed better than receiving no treatment. In the studies that compared bibliotherapy to group and individual therapy treatments, individual and group therapies did not perform significantly better than bibliotherapy, supporting its use as a stand-alone treatment. However, it is important to note that the treatment gains are indicative of the efficacy of the bibliotherapy materials used in these studies and not of all bibliotherapy materials.

Older Adults and Adolescents

In addition to being efficacious among the general adult population, bibliotherapy might also be of value among more diverse age groups. Several studies have evaluated various bibliotherapy programs among samples of older adults.

In the late 1980s, Scogin, Hamblin, and Beutler (1987) evaluated the efficacy of bibliotherapy with depressed older adults, comparing cognitive bibliotherapy based on *Feeling Good* (Burns, 1980) to a wait-list control and an attention control condition in which participants read *Man's Search for Meaning* (Frankl, 1959). The latter text represents inspirational rather than technique-based bibilotherapy. Participants in the cognitive bibliotherapy condition had significantly greater improvement on depression measures than participants in both the wait-list control and the attention control conditions. In an extension of this work, Scogin, Jamison, and Gochneaur (1989) conducted a study comparing cognitive bibliotherapy based on *Feeling Good* to behavioral bibliotherapy based on *Control Your Depression* and a wait-list control. The results indicated no difference between cognitive and behavioral bibliotherapy, with both groups significantly improving on measures of depressive symptomology as compared to the control group.

Another study investigated the efficacy of cognitive bibliotherapy based on *Feeling Good* among depressed older adults with physical disabilities, defined as one or more disabilities in activities of daily living (Landreville & Bissonnette, 1997). Participants were randomly assigned to either bibliotherapy treatment or a 4-week delayed treatment condition. There was a significant improvement in symptoms for individuals receiving treatment, but posttreatment scores were still classified in the mildly depressed range. Participants who received the treatment were only slightly more improved than untreated participants. According to the authors, the findings may be due in part to the older adults' disabilities, which could be linked to more resistant depression.

Most recently, a study comparing individual CBT to *Feeling Good* (Burns, 1980) for depressed older adults found that both treatments were better than a delayed treatment control. At posttreatment, individual psychotherapy resulted in significantly more improvement than bibliotherapy on self-reported depression, but there was no difference between treatment groups on clinician-rated depression. There were no differences between treatment groups at a 3-month follow-up on self-reported and clinician-rated depression (Floyd, Scogin, & McKendree-Smith, 2004).

At the other end of the age spectrum, Ackerson, Scogin, McKendree-Smith, and Lyman (1998) tested the efficacy of the cognitive therapy–based book, *Feeling Good* (Burns, 1980), among 13- to 18-year-old adolescents. They found that the adolescents in the bibliotherapy group significantly improved on measures of depression severity and dysfunctional attitudes as compared to those in a delayed treatment control group. These findings indicate that self-administered treatment for depression may be appropriate across the age range. However, much like the research with adult populations, studies conducted with older adults and adolescents have included predominantly

Caucasian samples; until further research is conducted with more diverse samples, it is unclear whether we can expect the same results across race and ethnicity.

Primary Care Patients

Two studies have examined the use of bibliotherapy in addition to pharmacotherapy for primary care patients to investigate whether an additive effect can be achieved. The self-administered treatment in the first study was a self-help guide developed by the researchers that gave instructions to identify and change thoughts, feelings, and behaviors that were causing distress (Holdsworth, Paxton, Seidel, Thomson, & Shrubb, 1996). Participants between the ages of 16 and 65 were recruited from a primary care setting and were experiencing anxiety, depression, or comorbid anxiety and depression ($N = 62$). The sample was mixed gender, but no information was provided regarding the proportion of the sample that was male versus female. Individuals' medication use was monitored for the duration of the study; type of medication varied as a function of practitioner recommendation, and results were not analyzed based on type of medication received. The study found no significant effects for bibliotherapy when utilized in conjunction with pharmacotherapy over and above the effect of pharmacotherapy alone. Additionally, no significant reduction in medication use following the use of the bibliotherapy guide was found.

A study comparing multifaceted care for depression with usual care found that individuals with major depression, but not minor depression, fared better than those receiving usual care and were more satisfied with the care they received (Katon et al., 1995). The average age of the 217 participants was 48, and 75% of the sample was female. Individuals in the treatment condition received alternating weekly visits with a psychiatrist and primary care physician during the first 4–6 weeks of the intervention along with more rigorous medication monitoring and patient education. Patient education included a behavioral health booklet, medication booklet, and video as well as alternating visits between a primary care physician and a psychiatrist. The self-administered treatment group was compared to a treatment-as-usual group, which consisted of treatment administered by the primary care physician at his or her discretion. In general, visits were shorter, less frequent, and patient education was not provided. Despite the significant finding only for major depression, 75% of all participants reported that they read the bibliotherapy materials provided and 80% reported finding them helpful (Robinson et al., 1997). In a follow-up to this study, the participants who received a combination of bibliotherapy and pharmacotherapy during the acute phase of their depression were comparable to those who had received only pharmacotherapy on measures of depressive symptomology at 19 months posttreatment (Lin et al., 1999). The initial effect of bibliotherapy in combination with pharmacotherapy in individuals with severe depression was not maintained over time.

According to the available literature, we cannot expect a greater reduction in depressive symptomology by combining bibliotherapy with pharmacotherapy. However, the available literature consists largely of bibliotherapy treatments that have used materials designed especially for the study that did not undergo empirical testing. It is possible that empirically supported materials such as *Feeling Good* (Burns, 1980) and *Control Your Depression* (Lewinsohn et al., 1986), or as-yet untested bibliotherapy materials, might yield more promising results and additive effects when used in combination with pharmacotherapy.

Meta-Analytic Studies

In a meta-analysis of seven studies investigating bibliotherapy for depression, an overall effect size of .83 was found, indicating efficacy of bibliotherapy (Cuijpers, 1997). Included in this meta-analysis were the three studies that made up the earlier Gould and Clum (1993) meta-analytic study of bibliotherapy for the treatment of depression, which also revealed a strong effect size of .74. The overall effect size in both of these meta-analytic reviews is comparable to the effect size of .73 for bibliotherapy found in a review of psychotherapies for depression (Robinson, Berman, & Neimeyer, 1990). These findings are indicative of a reliable, robust effect for bibliotherapy that rivals that of other more traditional treatment modalities for depression. These findings are based on studies that included adolescents, adults, and older adults.

Follow-Up Studies

Several studies have specifically examined whether the effects of bibliotherapy treatment are sustained over time. Although, as reviewed thus far, there is considerable support for the efficacy of bibliotherapy, we know less about maintenance of treatment gains. Researchers have speculated that improvements should persist, in part because individuals can refer to the bibliotherapy materials whenever they experience relapse or residual depressive symptoms. Thus far, two studies have provided an empirical answer to the question of maintenance.

As a follow-up to Jamison and Scogin's study of cognitive bibliotherapy in the general adult population, improvement in the form of decreased depressive symptoms, automatic negative thoughts, and dysfunctional attitudes were maintained at a 3-year follow-up, lending support to the idea that treatment gains attributable to bibliotherapy are maintained over time (Smith, Floyd, Scogin, & Jamison, 1997). Subsequent to Scogin et al.'s (1989) investigation of bibliotherapy among older adults, 6-month and 2-year follow-ups were conducted to determine whether treatment gains were maintained for cognitive bibliotherapy and behavioral bibliotherapy treatment completers. The results of this follow-up study also indicated that treatment gains could be maintained. In this case, both bibliotherapy groups remained improved at 6 months as well as 2 years (Scogin, Jamison, & Davis, 1990).

Supplemented Bibliotherapy

One study evaluated a version of self-help in which bibliotherapy was supplemented with a videotape and periodic telephone contact (Osgood-Hynes, Greist, & Marks, 1998). This 12-week treatment, known as COPE™, was used in an uncontrolled open trial with a general adult population. COPE contains three modules: Pleasant Activities, Assertive Communication, and Constructive Thinking, thus reflecting a cognitive–behavioral approach. The 13-minute video described common symptoms of depression, reviewed self-help treatment options, and introduced the COPE components. Participants received booklets that introduced skills revolving around these three modules. The booklets also provided instructions regarding when participants were to make phone calls to the interactive voice response (IVR) system; participants were required to make 11 such phone calls throughout the 12 weeks. During the calls, participants completed self-assessments and were directed in role-play activities corresponding with the material they read prior to the call. Following the assessment and activities, prerecorded voice files were played back to participants; the content of these files was based on the participants' individualized answers to the assessments. Participants could choose whether to engage in the role-play activities on the phone system and how long to engage in them, so they had control over the amount of time they spent on each call. The mean call length across the study was 14 minutes. Participants could also leave messages on the system up to three times during treatment if they had questions about the materials; those questions would result in recorded responses from research team members that would play at the beginning of the participant's next phone call. Participants significantly improved in work and social functioning as well as degree of depressive symptomology. Importantly, treatment gains correlated with the time individuals spent using the phone system with greater treatment gains being associated with more individual use of the phone system.

Computer-Administered Therapy

Computer-based treatments for various forms of psychological distress have begun to emerge given the rise in home computer use. In a review of computer-assisted psychotherapy programs, Wright and Wright (1997) asserted that computer use in conjunction with psychotherapy "includes the possibility that therapeutic software could improve the efficiency of treatment and provide access for greater numbers of patients" (p. 76). To date, only a few studies have investigated computer-administered treatment for depression. Those that have are reviewed in the following paragraphs. Thus far, this literature again includes participants that consist mainly of young, educated Caucasians, the majority of whom have computer experience and own home computers.

In a small study ($N = 36$) comparing a six-session, computer-administered CBT program, six sessions of CBT with a therapist, and a wait-list control group, participants in both treatment conditions evidenced significant improvement on the Beck Depression Inventory (BDI; Beck et al., 1961), Hamilton Rating Scale for Depression (HRSD; Hamilton, 1960), and Automatic Thoughts Questionnaire (Selmi, Klein, Greist, Sorrell, & Erdman, 1990). Sixty-four percent of participants were female, and all of them had completed at least some college. The content of the computer-administered sessions and therapist-administered sessions was identical. The computer sessions were completed in an office with an experimenter present, and the computer program presented key therapy concepts and assigned homework based on the participants' progress. There were no significant differences between the two treatment groups.

In an uncontrolled study of both inpatients and outpatients with diagnoses of depression or anxiety spectrum disorders, Wright et al. (2002) tested a multimedia program providing computer-assisted cognitive therapy. This six-module program, which provides clinicians with progress reports based on participant responses, was developed to serve as an adjunct to therapist-implemented cognitive therapy. The program includes an interactive video format to provide examples of cognitive therapy strategies being applied appropriately. In theory, by using this program to teach basic cognitive concepts and reinforce self-help exercises, a clinician could focus on interventions demanding the expertise of a live therapist. Participants continued with treatment as usual while using the computer program at their own pace. Treatment as usual varied depending upon participant but included individual psychotherapy, medication management, and no additional treatment. Program use was not monitored; however, 94% of participants reported completing at least the first three modules. In general, participants reported high satisfaction with the software, and measures of anxiety, depression, and automatic thoughts indicated improvement during the use of the program.

Most recently, Marks, Mataix-Cols, and Kenwright (2003) researched a free primary-care clinic's implementation of computer-aided self-help systems for depression, generalized anxiety, obsessive–compulsive disorder, and panic/phobia. The clinic's goal in using computerized treatment was to substitute a self-help approach for some one-on-one therapy time in an effort to offset the per patient cost of treatment. Of the 266 patients screened, 108 completed the treatment protocol consisting of an average of one hour with a therapist over 12 weeks, together with ongoing use of the computer program. The depressed individuals ($n = 33$) completing the course of combination treatment via computer used the computer program COPE (Osgood-Hynes et al., 1998) and evidenced significantly improved scores on the BDI and HRSD. Participants reported being "fairly satisfied" with their progress.

The literature on computer-administered treatment illustrates that it can serve as a complement to therapist-administered intervention and could improve the efficiency and cost-effectiveness of depression treatment. Computer-aided self-help could appropriately be used to cut down the per client cost of CBT through minimizing therapist contact hours (Marks et al., 2003). Limitations in generalizing the effectiveness of computer-administered treatment to the general population should be carefully considered. Several of the studies above consisted of very small samples; additionally, the majority of these studies included primarily participants who were young, educated Caucasians. Many of the participants had prior experience with computers and had computers in their home. Therefore, the appropriateness of computer-administered treatment for older individuals, less educated individuals, minorities, and individuals with little or no computer experience is unknown.

Clinical Considerations

Individual characteristics as well as the manner in which self-help materials are introduced and administered to clients may influence the effectiveness of this form of therapy. Selecting appropriate self-help materials is also important in determining treatment outcome.

Client Characteristics

Despite a generally supportive research literature, empirical research on self-administered treatment has not adequately investigated what role client characteristics play in determining the appropriateness and usefulness of such treatment. In part, the lack of empirical evidence identifying significant client characteristics is due to the small literature base on the use of self-administered treatment for depression and the small sample sizes typically used. However, several client characteristics have been significantly related to outcome in the literature.

Several studies of self-help for depression have examined variables that may moderate treatment outcome. In a study conducted by Landreville and Bissonnette (1997), cognitive bibliotherapy was administered to older adults with a disability. Although the other studies of bibliotherapy with older adults indicated significant treatment gains over wait-list control, improvements for depressed older adults using bibliotherapy in this study were only slightly greater than for individuals in the wait-list control group. Landreville and Bissonnette speculate that this may be due to chronic disabilities and related limitations in daily living that create a more resistant, harder to treat depression.

McKendree-Smith (1998) investigated potential mediators and moderators of change following cognitive and behavioral bibliotherapy for depression and found that two variables correlated with outcome. For the behavioral bibliotherapy group, initial depression level and expectations about the helpfulness of treatment were correlated with treatment outcome such that lower initial level of depression and more positive expectations about treatment were related to more positive treatment outcome.

A study attempting to identify mediating variables for treatment outcome was unsuccessful in supporting the hypothesis that hopelessness and learned resourcefulness play mediating roles in outcome (Rohen, 2002). Evidence for mediation in the case of both of these variables was not found, despite the fact that the treatment resulted in significant treatment gains. Although hopelessness and learned resourcefulness were not mediators in this study, they were moderately related to change in depression.

Although several studies have researched individual characteristics such as external locus of control, learned resourcefulness, symptom severity and complexity, and resistance potential, none of these characteristics have proven reliable in distinguishing positive or negative outcomes. Despite the lack of empirical evidence for some client characteristics, we believe a number of factors should be considered when determining whether self-administered treatment may be appropriate for a given individual. The following considerations are offered as tentative characteristics we expect can play a role in treatment effectiveness. Motivation and concentration are both relevant when deciding whether to prescribe self-help. A depressed individual experiencing significant problems with motivation and concentration may be unable to work through techniques introduced in self-administered treatment. Preliminary research being done on the role of concentration in predicting bibliotherapy outcome has indicated that, for older adults, the person's self-reported concentration problems are linked to the amount of improvement in depressive symptomology following the use of bibliotherapy materials (Floyd, personal communication, June 23, 2004).

Other individual factors that can moderate self-administered treatment gains or even make this modality inappropriate for a given individual include resistance to treatment, a preference for more traditional treatment, impairments that make reading difficult, severity of depression, suicidality, and comorbidity with an Axis II disorder or other psychological issue. It is reasonable to expect that individuals who have negative attitudes or beliefs regarding self-help treatment will not be ideal candidates and, for obvious reasons, individuals who have impairments that make reading problematic are not likely to receive maximum benefit from written self-administered treatments.

McKendree-Smith's (1998) study revealing that higher levels of depression are correlated to less improvement is evidence that depression severity should be considered. Suicidality and comorbidity with other disorders are often other indicants of severity and complexity of problems; for this reason, we believe such characteristics can inhibit the effectiveness of self-administered treatment or even render it inappropriate. Empirical findings to date do not consistently support the role of these factors in self-administered treatment outcome, but it is commonly accepted that more severe or complicated mental health issues are best addressed with more rigorous treatment.

In summary, there is empirical evidence that both initial depression level and expectations of the helpfulness of treatment are client characteristics related to self-administered treatment outcome. Additionally, disability in older adults may moderate outcome such that disability is predictive of poorer outcome. Although there is little research identifying other client characteristics predictive of outcome, we believe that suicidality, comorbidity, treatment resistance, preference for more traditional treatment, motivation, and concentration are all additional client characteristics that should be considered when considering self-administered treatment.

Administration of Self-Help Programs

Regardless of individual characteristics, each client's progress with self-administered materials should be carefully monitored, particularly at the beginning of treatment (Scogin et al., 2003). Collecting information regarding a client's progress, such as administering a measure of depression severity regularly, helps monitor an individual to ensure that he or she is not worsening over time. Having an objective measure of a client's progress, or lack thereof, can be useful in determining whether more intensive treatment is required. Using a measure such as the Beck Depression Inventory (BDI-II; Beck, 1996) for adults or Geriatric Depression Scale (GDS;

Yesavage, 1983) for older adults on a weekly or biweekly basis provides a much better measure of progress than client report.

Additionally, consideration should be given to how treatment integrity will be maintained. Making sure that the clients read the books and follow the homework assignments is as important as monitoring client progress. In McKendree-Smith (1998), percentage of pages read was correlated with outcome for adults using cognitive bibliotherapy but no client variables were significantly correlated with outcome, indicating receipt of treatment is a better predictor of outcome than any client variable measured. Ensuring treatment receipt is tantamount to monitoring changes in depression severity for depressed individuals using self-administered treatment. In fact, treatment receipt may be a factor in studies finding an unexpected lack of effectiveness in some cases.

Mental health practitioners recommending self-administered treatments to their depressed patients are encouraged to explain the reasoning behind their recommendations: the self-administered treatment is being used because of its cost-effectiveness, convenience, and empirical support. Regarding the last point, caution should be exercised when implementing a self-administered treatment that has not been researched. Prior to recommending self-administered treatment, mental health professionals are encouraged to engage in an active discussion with their clients regarding treatment options.

Depressed individuals may prefer self-administered treatments to more conventional treatment for a number of reasons, including cost, problems with transportation, time constraints, not wanting to take medication, or a fear of the stigma or process of therapy. For example, individuals high in reactance, the tendency to desire more behavioral freedoms if they become denied, are more likely to benefit from less directive therapists and from self-administered treatments, perhaps because they have more control over their own treatment (Beutler et al., 1991). However, some individuals will prefer pharmacotherapy or psychotherapy to self-administered treatments, feeling that traditional professionally administered treatments would be more effective. Although some individuals may express an interest in psychotherapy or self-help treatment alone, both modalities can be used together. For example, bibliotherapy is often suggested as a homework assignment in several forms of psychotherapy. Combining these two treatments may speed up progress for depressed individuals. Client expectations for change should also be addressed. Discussing realistic expectations for improvement should include addressing how soon therapy will work and how long the effects can be expected to last. Setting goals with the client prior to treatment can also help ensure the client's expectations are reasonable. In addition, it is wise to explicitly discuss that clients may experience relapses or reemergence of depressive symptoms and that part of the appeal of self-help materials is that the client can reaccess them at will during such times.

Although research indicates bibliotherapy has shown efficacy as a treatment for depression, its effects may not be as immediate as those of psychotherapy. One study revealed that psychotherapy led to greater improvement posttreatment than bibliotherapy in a comparison study of older adults (Floyd, Scogin, McKendree-Smith, Floyd, & Rokke, 2001). However, at 3 months posttreatment, the depressive symptomology of individuals using bibliotherapy was not significantly different from those in individual psychotherapy, because individuals receiving bibliotherapy continued to evidence gains subsequent to the end of treatment. This may be a result of the individual's ability to continually re-reference the material learned through bibliotherapy if needed. Some individuals, such as older adults with disabilities or individuals with cognitive impairments, may benefit from the additional guidance provided by psychotherapy.

Future Directions

Further research identifying predictors of outcome would be especially useful in helping practitioners make decisions about the appropriateness of self-administered treatment for a given candidate. Finding reliable ways to measure an individual's fit with self-administered depression treatment would prove invaluable when identifying the most cost-effective, least intrusive treatment modality that will still effect change.

In addition to identifying potential predictors, the literature is lacking in empirical research for most of the self-help materials for depression available in the commercial market. Many practitioners recommend books for their clients that have not been rigorously researched. Until we know more about the books consumers can buy, it is difficult to make a good clinical judgment about whether a given self-administered treatment is appropriate for a particular individual. By broadening the research base to include some of the more commonly used or recommended self-administered treatments for depression, clinicians can be better informed about the best treatment options for clients interested in bibliotherapy.

Because preliminary research has highlighted the utility of computer-aided therapy as both a time-saver for therapists and a money-saver for clients, research devoted to creating and testing such programs could result in the refinement of computer-aided tools that would be instrumental in cost-effective depression treatment. Computer-aided therapy could potentially take some of the load off the therapist without diminishing the quality of care received by depressed individuals, provided the software meets the needs of the clients and can convey the therapy content to the client effectively. However, until further research is done in this area, we cannot be confident in the efficacy of computer-aided therapy.

Future directions also include incorporating self-administered treatments in both stepped-care and collaborative care models. In stepped-care models, self-administered treatments can serve as a first line of treatment for mild to moderately depressed individuals. Due to the lack of invasiveness and cost-effectiveness, this modality is a good fit as a first approach to treatment. Additionally, research on self-administered treatments such as bibliotherapy and computer-assisted therapy used in conjunction with pharmacotherapy has not shown enhanced treatment outcome as compared to pharmacotherapy alone; however, the existing literature has used self-help materials of unknown effectiveness. We expect that empirically supported bibliotherapy and computer-assisted therapy used together with pharmacotherapy or psychotherapy would be beneficial, and we believe this modality should be incorporated into collaborate models of depression treatment. For individuals taking antidepressants but not receiving therapy, self-administered treatment could potentially enhance treatment outcome without significant cost.

Practice Recommendations

We have attempted to briefly summarize the research evidence of the effectiveness of self-administered treatments for depression. We now present practice recommendations for using self-help treatments with depressed individuals.

- Be sure to address a depressed individual's treatment preferences and attitude about self-administered treatment prior to recommending this modality to the individual. Additionally, make a point to explain the rationale behind self-administered treatment including the cost-effectiveness and empirical support for self-administered treatment.
- Take individual characteristics into account. Individuals with other comorbid psychological issues, suicidality, severe symptomology, cognitive impairments, or concentration problems are better served through more intensive treatment courses.
- Exercise caution when recommending a self-administered treatment that has not been empirically researched.

- Monitor the depressed individual's progress in treatment, beginning immediately. Response to treatment should be monitored for any changes in severity or symptomology that may require the implementation of a more intensive treatment.
- If the individual's depression improves, a maintenance program should be created to help adjust the program to meet his or her current needs.

Generally speaking, self-administered treatments that involve at least a minimal level of therapist contact and client accountability work better than self-administered treatments where the individual has no contact with a mental health professional.

The research indicates that depression can be successfully treated with a variety of self-administered treatments including both bibliotherapy and computer-aided self-administered treatment. These programs can be used as stand-alone treatment or integrated with traditional treatments such as psychotherapy and pharmacotherapy. Although COPE is available to individuals, to our knowledge there are currently no empirically tested computer programs for clinicians on the market.

Although many self-help books for depression are widely available, few have been tested for efficacy. Those that have received empirical support include *Feeling Good* (Burns, 1980), *Mind Over Mood* (Greenberger & Padesky, 1995), and *Control Your Depression* (Lewinsohn et. al, 1986).

Chapter Points

- Cognitive therapy and behavior therapy approaches, presented via books or computers, have been validated in the treatment of depression.
- Cognitive therapy and behavior therapy, delivered via bibliotherapy, are equivalent to therapist-administered treatments in adults, adolescents, and the elderly suffering from mild and moderate levels of depression.
- Treatment effects are maintained over time for bibliotherapy-delivered cognitive and behavioral treatments.
- Computer-assisted treatments for depression have so far been limited to being evaluated within a treatment-as-usual approach.
- Little information exists indicating who profits from self-help treatments, but higher levels of depression, negative expectation for outcome using self-help approaches, as well as reading level and ability to concentrate may all predict outcome and attitude toward self-help treatments.

References

Ackerson, J., Scogin, F., McKendree-Smith, N., & Lyman, R. D. (1998). Cognitive bibliotherapy for mild and moderate adolescent depressive symptomatology. *Journal of Consulting and Clinical Psychology, 66*, 685–690.

Beck, A. T. (1996). *Beck Depression Inventory* (2nd ed.). San Antonio, TX: The Psychological Corporation.

Beck, A. T., Rush, J., Shaw, B., & Emery, G. (1979). *Cognitive therapy of depression*. New York: Guilford.

Beck, A. T., Ward, C. H., Mendelson, M., Mock, J. E., Erbaugh, J. (1961). An inventory for measuring depression. *Archives of General Psychiatry, 4*, 561–571.

Beutler, L. E., Engle, D., Mohr, D., Daldrup, R. J., Bergan, J., Meredith, K., et al. (1991). Predictors of differential response to cognitive, experiental, and self-directed psychotherapeutic procedures. *Journal of Consulting and Clinical Psychology, 59*, 333–340.

Bowman, D., Scogin, F., & Lyrene, B. (1995). The efficacy of self-examination therapy and cognitive bibliotherapy in the treatment of mild to moderate depression. *Psychotherapy Research, 5*, 131–140.

Brown, R. A., & Lewinsohn, P. M. (1984). A psychoeducational approach to the treatment of depression: Comparison of group, individual, and minimal contact procedures. *Journal of Consulting and Clinical Psychology, 52*, 774–783.

Burns, D. D. (1980). *Feeling good: The new mood therapy*. New York: New American Library.

Cuijpers, P. (1997). Bibliotherapy in unipolar depression: A meta-analysis. *Journal of Behavior Therapy and Experimental Psychiatry, 28*, 139–147.

Floyd, M., Scogin, F., McKendree-Smith, N., Floyd, D., & Rokke, P. D. (2004). Cognitive therapy for depression: A comparison of individual psychotherapy and bibliotherapy for depressed older adults. *Behavior Modification, 28*, 297–318.

Frankl, V. (1959). *Man's search for meaning*. New York: Pocket Books.

Glasgow, R. E., & Rosen, G. M. (1978). Behavioral biblioherapy: A review of self-help behavior therapy manuals. *Psychological Bulletin, 85*, 1–23.

Gould, R., & Clum, G. (1993). A meta-analysis of self-help treatment approaches. *Clinical Psychology Review, 13*, 169–186.

Greenberger, D., & Padesky, C. A. (1995). *Mind over mood*. New York: Guilford.

Hamilton, M. (1960). A rating scale for depression. *Journal of Neurology, Neurosurgery and Psychiatry, 23*, 56–61.

Holdsworth, N., Paxton, R., Seidel, S., Thomson, D., & Shrubb, S. (1996). Parallel evaluations of new guidance materials for anxiety and depression in primary care. *Journal of Mental Health, 5*, 195–207.

Jamison, C. S., & Scogin, F. (1995). Outcome of cognitive bibliotherapy with depressed adults. *Journal of Consulting and Clinical Psychology, 63*, 644–650.

Katon, W., Von Korff, M., Lin, E., Walker, E., Simon, G. E., Bush, T., et al. (1995). Collaborative management to achieve treatment guidelines: Impact on depression in primary care. *Journal of the American Medical Association, 273*, 1026–1031.

Landreville, P., & Bissonnette, L. (1997). Effects of cognitive bibliotherapy for depressed older adults with a disability. *Clinical Gerontologist, 17*, 35–55.

Lewinsohn, P., Munoz, R., Youngren, M., & Zeiss, A. (1986). *Control your depression.* New York: Simon & Schuster.

Lin, E. H. B., Simon, G. E., Katon, W. J., Russo, J. E., Von Korff, M., Bush, T. M., et al. (1999). Can enhanced acute-phase treatment of depression improve long-term outcomes? A report of randomized trials in primary care. *American Journal of Psychiatry, 156,* 643–645.

Mains, J. A., & Scogin, F. R. (2003). The effectiveness of self-administered treatments: A practice-friendly review of the research. *Journal of Clinical Psychology, 59,* 237–246.

Marks, I. M., Mataix-Cols, D., & Kenwright, M. (2003). Pragmatic evaluation of computer-aided self-help for anxiety and depression. *British Journal of Psychiatry, 183,* 57–65.

McKendree-Smith, N. (1998). *Cognitive and behavioral bibliotherapy for depression: An examination of efficacy and mediators and moderators of change.* Unpublished doctoral dissertation, University of Alabama, Tuscaloosa.

Neumann, J. K. (1981). Self-help depression treatment: an evaluation of an audio cassette program with hospitalized residents. *Behavior Therapist, 4,* 15–16.

Osgood-Hynes, D. J., Greist, J. H., & Marks, I. M. (1998). Self-administered psychotherapy for depression using a telephone-accessed computer system plus booklets: An open U.S.-U.K. study. *Journal of Clinical Psychiatry, 59,* 358–365.

Robinson, L. A., Berman, J. S., & Neimeyer, R. A. (1990). Psychotherapy for the treatment of depression: A comprehensive review of controlled outcome research. *Psychological Bulletin, 108,* 30–49.

Robinson, P., Katon, W., Von Korff, M., Bush, T., Simon, G., Lin, E., et al. (1997). The education of depressed primary care patients: What do patients think of interactive booklets and a video? *Journal of Family Practice, 44,* 562–571.

Rohen, N. (2002). *Analysis of efficacy and mediators of outcome in minimal-contact cognitive bibliotherapy used in the treatment of depressive symptoms.* Unpublished doctoral dissertation, University of Alabama, Tuscaloosa.

Schmidt, M., & Miller, W. (1983). Amount of therapist contact and outcome in a multidimensional depression treatment program. *Acta Psychiatrica Scandinavica, 67,* 319–332.

Scogin, F., Hamblin, D., & Beutler, L. (1987). Bibliotherapy for depressed older adults: A self-help alternative. *The Gerontologist, 27,* 383–387.

Scogin, F., Hanson, A., & Welsh, D. (2003). Self-administered treatment in stepped-care models of depression treatment. *Journal of Clinical Psychology, 59,* 341–349.

Scogin, F., Jamison, C., & Davis, N. (1990). Two-year follow-up of bibliotherapy for depression in older adults. *Journal of Consulting and Clinical Psychology, 58,* 665–667.

Scogin, F., Jamison, C., & Gochneaur, K. (1989). Comparative efficacy of cognitive and behavioral bibliotherapy for mildly and moderately depressed older adults. *Journal of Consulting and Clinical Psychology, 57,* 403–407.

Selmi, P. M., Klein, M. H., Greist, J. H., Sorrell, S. P., & Erdman, H. P. (1990). Computer-administered cognitive-behavioural therapy for depression. *American Journal of Psychiatry, 147,* 51–56.

Smith, N. M., Floyd, M. R., Scogin, F., & Jamison, C. S. (1997). Three-year follow-up of bibliotherapy for depression. *Journal of Consulting and Clinical Psychology, 65*, 324–327.

Starker, S. (1988). Do-it-yourself therapy: The prescription of self-help books by psychologists. *Psychotherapy, 25*, 142–146.

Wollersheim, J. P., & Wilson, G. L. (1991). Group treatment of unipolar depression: A comparison of coping, supportive, bibliotherapy, and delayed treatment groups. *Professional Psychology: Research and Practice, 22*, 496–502.

Wright, J. H., & Wright, A. S. (1997). Computer-assisted psychotherapy. *Journal of Psychotherapy Practice and Research, 6*, 315–329.

Wright, J. H., Wright, A. S., Salmon, P., Beck, A. T., Kuykendall, F., Goldsmith, L. J., et al. (2002). Development and initial testing of a multimedia program for computer-assisted cognitive therapy. *American Journal of Psychotherapy, 56*, 76–86.

Yesavage, J. A. (1983). Development and validation of a geriatric depression screening scale: A preliminary report. *Journal of Psychiatric Research, 17*, 37–49.

CHAPTER 7

Self-Help Therapies for Childhood Disorders

FRANK J. ELGAR AND PATRICK J. MCGRATH

The past decade has seen an astonishing proliferation of self-help material for pediatric mental health and physical health conditions through books, videos, and the Internet. More than at any point in history, self-help (or self-administered) interventions are now aggressively promoted to consumers for a broad range of health conditions and disorders. There is good reason for optimism that this trend will benefit children. Self-help circumvents barriers to traditional delivery models of health care. Self-help is convenient and inexpensive to families at a time that health care treatments are punitively costly. Moreover, self-help may work as effectively as therapist-based care to treat some childhood disorders.

In a review of the research on self- and parent-facilitated self-help treatments for childhood disorders (Elgar & McGrath, 2003), we concluded that a small but robust evidence base exists in support of manual and multimedia-based treatments but very few empirical studies support the use of inspirational literature and support groups. Today, large gaps still exist in the evidence for self-help. These gaps present unique challenges for health care providers who wish to share self-help treatments with children and parents, but they also offer fruitful opportunities for further research and development.

In this chapter, we update and summarize our findings regarding three, not necessarily exclusive, forms of self-help for children and parents: bibliotherapy, including fictional books and other inspirational literature and manual-based treatments; instructional multimedia; and social support treatments. Our review is generally limited to treatments involving minimal or no therapist contact, although treatments and research involving stepped-care approaches to gradually increasing or decreasing therapist contact are also addressed. We explore some of the practical concerns that parents may have about these treatments and the ethical and legal issues facing health practitioners when deciding to share self-help materials with families. We also highlight important new directions for future research. We begin the discussion by exploring the problem of access to psychosocial interventions.

The Problem of Access

In both developed and underdeveloped countries, behavioral and emotional disorders are among the most common chronic health problems among children. Epidemiological studies that have been conducted around the world indicate that approximately 15–25% of children in the general population could be diagnosed with a psychological disorder (e.g., Breton et al., 1999; Offord et al., 1987; Rutter, Cox, Tupling, Berger, & Yule, 1975; Zubrick, Silburn, Burton, & Blair, 1995). Many other children need psychosocial treatments for a range of behavioral health problems. Enuresis afflicts 9–13% of 5-year-olds and 9–22% of 7-year-olds (Butler, 1998). Frequent, recurrent pain afflicts at least 12–15% of adolescents (Goodman & McGrath, 1991). As well, many childhood disorders that are presented to pediatricians and family physicians have substantial behavioral components for which prevention, intervention, or rehabilitation services by psychologists could improve child health outcomes (American Psychological Association, 2001).

Childhood disorders have negative and lasting consequences for the psychological well-being and social functioning of afflicted children and cause a significant burden on children, families, and communities (Cappelli et al., 1989; Silver, Stein, & Bauman, 1999). Without treatment, the prognosis for many of these problems is usually poor. Left untreated, disruptive and aggressive behavior in childhood tends to persist and evolve to more sociopathic behaviors in adulthood (McMahon & Wells, 1998). Internalizing problems such as depressive and anxiety disorders places individuals at risk of relapse of these disorders throughout the life span (Hofstra, Van der Ende, & Verhulst, 2000). Other developmental problems may also impinge on children's self-esteem and cause frustration and stress for the entire family (Schulpen, 1997).

The good news is that effective treatments exist for many of these health conditions (Carr, 2000; Weisz, Weiss, Han, Granger, & Morton, 1995). The bad news is that only a small minority of children who need these treatments are able to access them. The tragic reality is that most children's access to health treatments is complicated or impeded by the very systems that deliver these treatments. This rift between the care needs of children in the population and the delivery of health care services is even found in countries that have established public health care systems. In Canada, for example, the Ontario Child Health Study found that fewer than one in five children who showed symptoms of a diagnosable psychological disorder had any contact with a mental health service provider in the previous 6 months (Offord et al., 1987).

The interface between the delivery of behavioral health care and the needs of children has now come under scrutiny in many countries. Access, however, is just part of a larger problem in the delivery of health care to children. Many children who manage to have some contact with a health care provider will not actually receive treatment. An impressive body of research has exposed barriers to care that include the stigma associated with seeking treatment, the time and expense involved in traveling regularly with a child to a mental health clinic, and motivation and willingness of the parents to follow therapists' guidelines in carrying out a care plan at home. Not surprisingly, it is the children from low-income families or from rural communities who are less likely to receive psychological treatments than their more affluent and urban counterparts (Hunsley, Aubry, & Lee, 1997) and it is the children of depressed or distressed parents who are less likely than children of healthy parents to regularly attend therapy sessions (Calam, Bolton, & Roberts, 2002).

Too often, the obstacles to accessing specialist care lead many families to rely exclusively on primary care physicians who are not usually well prepared to recognize and treat psychological problems (Higgins, 1994) or to a de facto mental health system of ministers, school teachers, extended family members, and friends (Fox, Merwin, & Blank, 1995). These are important components of total care but are unlikely to be comprehensive or adequate. It is not surprising then that so many children and families are seeking a self-help alternative.

The Self-Help Alternative

Self-help interventions have the potential to circumvent, at least in part, common barriers to psychosocial treatments for childhood disorders. Self-help cannot replace care for serious mental or physical illness but it does offer a viable alternative to treatment that is normally delivered by clinicians in urban-based health facilities. Examples of self-help treatments include the use of parent training videos for managing disruptive behavior disorders (Webster-Stratton, 1990), cognitive bibliotherapy for adolescent depression (Ackerson, Scogin, McKendree-Smith, & Lyman, 1998), and booklets and audiotapes for recurrent pain (McGrath et al.,

1992). Treatments such as these are inexpensive, easily accessible, and convenient for families and do not carry the stigma associated with traditional mental health services. More importantly, there is now good evidence that self-help psychosocial treatments for children are often as effective as traditional treatments (Scogin, Bynum, Stephens, & Calhoon, 1990).

Self-help does not necessarily imply that families are isolated from their health care providers. Psychologists, educators, family physicians, or health paraprofessionals can all help facilitate self-help for children. There is a continuum from entirely self-administered to entirely therapist-administered treatments; some self-administered interventions exist outside the health care system, whereas others are an integral part of a stepped-care system. However, the involvement of health care professionals may be minimal, such as a recommendation to a family who seeks to contact a self-help group, or may entail involvement in the development, provision, and monitoring of the intervention. In practice, varying the degree of therapist contact facilitates stepped-care models of increasing treatment complexity (e.g., from psychoeducation to inpatient care; Davison, 2000). Gradually reducing the amount of therapist contact can foster independence and self-care by the child and family.

The advantages of self-help are many. Self-help is certainly not a panacea for eliminating all barriers to health care, but it can allow greater flexibility for psychologists to bring treatments closer to the child's natural environment and to allow the child and the family to assume the responsibility for behavior change. When used in conjunction with traditionally delivered treatments, there are important opportunities for continuity of care from the artificial setting of a therapist's office to the home and school.

Most forms of psychosocial treatment, regardless of how they are delivered, share at least three objectives: (a) to teach self-management skills to the child and family (e.g., teaching relaxation techniques or cognitive restructuring, modeling behavior modification techniques to parents); (b) to provide information to the child and family about the nature of the condition, including its typical etiology, course, and available treatments; and (c) to augment social support networks to enable the child and family to learn from others, cope with their problems, and feel comfort in knowing that their condition is not unique. Self-help can serve all three functions when used either as a complement to face-to-face treatment or as a stand-alone treatment.

Does Self-Help Work for Children?

Discussing the advantages and limitations of alternative forms of health care is moot if these modalities are ineffectual. Self-help for childhood disorders has a somewhat weak evidence base. For some formats and some health conditions, the data are very encouraging. But for other combinations of formats and health conditions, few if any data are available to indicate that effects are anything more than placebo. We now turn to the state of the evidence for self-help interventions for children and parents. Below we have attempted to consolidate and summarize a diverse patchwork of studies on bibliotherapy, telehealth, and social support groups and have provided details about these studies in Table 7.1 to Table 7.3.

Bibliotherapy

Bibliotherapy involves the use of literature, poetry, plays, and movies that provide inspiration, support, or guidance to help children learn ways to manage an illness or personal problem (Ouzts, 1991). There are two general types of bibliotherapy—inspirational self-help and instructional self-help. The function of inspirational bibliotherapy is to offer support and oftentimes to model solutions to problems. In either fiction or nonfiction works or biographies, typically, a protagonist faces a problem similar to what the child is experiencing and offers hope that the child can overcome these difficulties. Self-management skills and information about the condition are not usually taught directly but may be provided indirectly within a story. Some inspirational books offer general advice to the child or family to help boost self-esteem and develop the skills needed to cope with a particular problem. Instructional manuals, on the other hand, have been developed and sometimes tested by authors, who may be health professionals, for the specific purpose of managing a health condition. These materials may include health information, illustrative examples, testimonials, assignments, and symptom checklists to monitor progress through a self-administered care plan.

Inspirational Bibliotherapy   Many retail bookstores stock a multitude of inspirational bibliotherapy products that are designed to help children manage a wide array of problem areas (Hipple, Comer, & Boren, 1997; Norcross et al., 2000). John Pardeck, an advocate of bibliotherapy, has written extensively to promote the use of literature to help children cope with such personal and social issues as adoption (Pardeck, 1989, 1994; Pardeck & Pardeck, 1997), divorce (Pardeck, 1996), substance abuse (Pardeck, 1991), chronic illness and special developmental needs (Pardeck, 1992, 1993), and physical or sexual abuse (Pardeck, 1990a, 1990b). Most of the self-help material that is available in bookstores is intended for mass audiences rather than clinical populations, and the self-help industry (e.g., publishers and lay self-help associations) has not benefited from outcome-based evaluation. Market forces drive self-help publishing and the aim is to publish products that are profitable. The result is a barrage of self-help literature with little empirical evidence to support its use (Adams & Pitre, 2000; Riordan & Wilson, 1989; Stevens & Pfost, 1982).

Table 7.1 Research on Bibliotherapy (Instructional Manuals) for Childhood Disorders

Study	Type	Problem area	Sample	Methods	Results	Implications
Ackerson et al., 1998	C	Depression	22 children aged 11–16 years	Randomized trial (bibliotherapy vs. wait-list control). Treatment consisted of reading *Feeling Good* (Burns, 1980) over 4 weeks	Improvements in self-reported symptoms post-intervention and one-month follow-up	Bibliotherapy may be an effective treatment for childhood depression
Burke et al., 2004	C	Bedtime resistance and night waking	4 families with children aged 2–7 years	Single-subject design. Parents read Peterson & Peterson's (2003) *The Sleep Fairy* to their children at bedtime	78% decrease in frequency of disruptive bedtime behaviors from baseline with another 7% decrease at 3-month follow-up	A potentially effective application of bibliotherapy to help children achieve more restful sleep
Cedar & Levant, 1990	P	Parenting skills	Meta-analysis	Literature search (pre-1990) yielded 26 outcome evaluation studies	*Parent Effectiveness Training* (PET; Gordon, 1975) showed overall effect size of .33 on parents' knowledge, attitudes, and behavior and on children's self-esteem. These effects were shown to last up to 26 weeks	PET is an inexpensive and effective resource for teaching basic parenting skills

Study	Type	Disorder	Sample	Design	Results	Comments
Chambers et al., 1997	P	Postoperative pain	82 families with children aged 2–12 years	Randomized trial (parent-administered, manual-assisted education vs. pain control vs. no pain control)	Parents who read *Pain, Pain Go Away* (McGrath et al., 1994) expressed more positive attitudes towards medication at one-week postoperative; no group differences in pain assessment or medicine administration	*Pain, Pain Go Away* offers support and information to parents about managing child pain but more targeted intervention may be needed to change parents' behaviors
Evans et al., 1999	C	Self-harming behavior	34 adolescents and adults aged 16–50 years	Randomized trial (manual-based self-help vs. usual care)	Self-help group showed fewer suicidal acts and depressive symptoms than patients who received usual care	Sample included adolescents and adults so findings cannot be generalized to adolescents alone
Gienbenhain & O'Dell, 1984	P	Fear of the dark	Six families of children aged 3–11 years	Clinical series; parents were given a manual for reducing children's fear of the dark	With 2 weeks of treatment, children slept with low levels of light; improvement was maintained at 12-month follow-up	Parent manuals may help specific anxiety in children
Griffiths & Martin, 1996	C	Chronic headache	51 children aged 10–12 years	Randomized trial (distance treatment from therapist plus self-help manuals vs. clinic-based treatment)	Both treatment conditions were equally effective in reducing headaches but the self-help format was twice as cost-effective as the clinic-based format	Chronic headache may be effectively self-managed with minimal contact with a therapist

Note. Type C = *self-administered by the child; P = parent-administered.*

(continued)

Table 7.1 (*continued*)

Study	Type	Problem area	Sample	Methods	Results	Implications
Heifetz, 1977	P	Disruptive behavior	160 parents of mentally retarded children aged 2–14 years	Families were randomly assigned to five groups: (a) manuals only; (b) manuals and telephone contact with therapist; (c) manuals and group meetings; (c) manuals, group meetings, and face-to-face contact with therapist; and (d) no treatment control	After 20 weeks of treatment, the manuals-only condition was as effective as more expensive formats in reducing behavioral problems and teaching self-help skills	Parent manuals provided effective and inexpensive self-help for parents of children with learning disabilities
Long et al., 1993	P	Inattention and Hyperactivity	32 families with children diagnosed with attention deficit–hyperactivity disorder (ADHD) aged 6–11 years	Randomized trial (manual-based parent-administered behavior modification vs. stimulant medication alone)	Self-help group showed more improvement in intensity of ADHD symptoms, parents' knowledge of behaviour management principles and teacher ratings of behavior. No difference between groups in symptom frequency	Parent manuals may be an inexpensive adjunct to stimulant medication but small sample precludes strong conclusions

McGrath et al., 1992	C	Migraine headache	87 children (11–18 years)	Randomized trial (manual-based self-help plus therapist contact vs. therapist contact vs. control treatment)	Self-help and clinic treatment were both effective up to 1-year posttreatment and superior to control treatment. Self-help was more cost-effective than therapist-based care	Migraine headaches may be effectively self-managed by children
Montgomery & Stores, 2000	P	Sleep problems	77 families of children with learning disabilities	Double-blind randomized trial (parent-administered manual-based behavioral treatment plus methylphenidate vs. methylphenidate with standard care from therapist vs. wait-list control)	Both treatments showed similar improvement in frequency and duration of night waking and in settling problems	Parent manuals were as effective as therapist-based treatment in improving sleep problems in learning disabled children
Salehpour, 1996	P	Disruptive behavior	24 parents	Randomized trial; parents were assigned to either 1-2-3 Magic instruction with group discussion, 1-2-3 Magic instruction without group discussion, or no 1-2-3 Magic instruction	Both groups who received instruction on 1-2-3 Magic reported greater competence in disciplining their children compared to parents in the control group	Phelan's (1996) 1-2-3 Magic improved parents' sense of competence in using "time out," a simple discipline technique
Seymour et al., 1989	P	Sleep problems	45 families of children with sleep difficulties aged 9 months to 5 years	Randomized trial (parent manuals vs. parent manuals plus daily phone calls to a therapist vs. wait-list control)	Both treatment groups showed similar improvement in frequency and duration of night waking	Telephone contact with a therapist had no additional benefits for sleep problems

Note. Type C = self-administered by the child; P = parent-administered.

(continued)

Table 7.1 (continued)

Study	Type	Problem area	Sample	Methods	Results	Implications
Shechtman, 2000; Shechtman & Ben-David, 1999	C	Aggression	20 children with aggressive behaviors aged 8 years	Case study design; 10 children received bibliotherapy and group therapy, 10 received interpersonal therapy	Both treatment groups showed reduction in aggression	Effect of self-help manuals alone are unknown due to study design; lack of follow-up assessments precluded determination of economic benefits of self-help (see Dodge, 1999)
van Londen et al., 1993	P	Nocturnal enuresis	127 families of children aged 6–12 years (110 primary enuresis, 17 secondary enuresis)	Randomized trial (parent-administered manual-based arousal training plus urine alarm device and conditioning with stickers and praise vs. urine alarm and standard conditioning	After 20 weeks, 97 vs. 33 vs. 26% were dry at night for 2 consecutive weeks. Parents who taught arousal training to children using manuals responded better to bed-wetting episodes than parents in other groups	Parent manuals on arousal training are effective for managing enuresis
van Londen et al., 1995	P	Nocturnal enuresis	127 families of children aged 6–12 years (110 primary enuresis, 17 secondary enuresis)	2½-year follow-up of families from van Londen et al. (1993)	30 months posttreatment, 92 vs. 77 vs. 72% were dry at night for 2 consecutive weeks	Parent manuals on arousal training may have long-term benefits for enuretic children

Note. Type C = self-administered by the child; P = parent-administered.

Table 7.2 Research on Electronic Self-Help Treatments for Childhood Disorders

Study	Type	Problem area	Sample	Methods	Results	Implications
Davis et al., 2004	C	Cystic fibrosis	47 children aged 7–17 years	Randomized trial (*STARBRIGHT™ Fitting Cystic Fibrosis in Your Life Everyday* CD-ROM vs. wait-list control)	Disease-related knowledge and coping strategies improved as a result of using the CD-ROM	A promising educational intervention for children that is inexpensive and portable
Hicks et al., 2006	C	Recurrent pain	47 children aged 9–16 years	Randomized trial (Internet-based manual for children and parents plus weekly therapist contact by telephone or email vs. wait-list control group)	72% of the treatment group achieved improvement in pain at 3-months follow-up compared to 14% of the control group	Telehealth self-help can make effective treatments for recurrent pain more accessible at less cost
Houts et al., 1987	C/P	Enuresis	40 families (Study 1) and 15 families (Study 2) of children aged 5–15 years	Randomized trial (live vs. videotaped behavioral treatment)	Superior outcomes with the live delivery in both studies. Film delivery resulted in higher confidence of children in their parents but lower confidence of parents in their children	Parents and children may respond differently to the same multimedia intervention

Note. Type C = self-administered by the child; P = parent-administered.

(continued)

Table 7.2 (*continued*)

Study	Type	Problem area	Sample	Methods	Results	Implications
Krishna et al., 2003	C	Asthma	228 children, 113 between 0 and 6 years of age and 115 between 7 to 17 years of age	Randomized trial (multimedia self-help materials and usual care vs. usual care alone)	Self-help materials improved knowledge and reduced asthma symptoms, hospital visits, and medication use	Supplementing conventional care with interactive multimedia education can significantly improve self-management
Larsson et al., 1990	C	Conduct disorder	114 families of children aged 3–8 years	Randomized trial (self-administered modeling vs. videotape modeling plus group discussion vs. videotape modeling plus group discussion and one-on-one therapist sessions vs. wait-list control)	Parental reports and behavior ratings at home and at school showed improvement in both treatment groups. Adding group discussion to videotape modeling improved outcomes on some measures	Group discussions with other parents may enhance the effectiveness of videotapes
Ritterband et al., 2003	C	Encopresis	24 children, average age 8.5 (SD = 1.8) years	Randomized trial (Internet-based enhanced toilet training vs. no Internet training)	Internet training reduced fecal soiling, increased defecation in the toilet, and increased unprompted trips to the toilet	Internet interventions may be an effective way of delivering sophisticated interventions to a large and dispersed population

Study	Type	Disorder	Sample	Design	Outcome	Conclusion
Rubin et al., 1986	C	Asthma	54 children age 7–17 years	Randomised trial (*Asthma Command* educational video game vs. routine computer games)	Playing the educational video improved knowledge about asthma and self-management of asthma symptoms	An illness-specific computer game can affect knowledge and behavior in children
Webster-Stratton et al., 1989	P	Conduct disorder	94 families from Webster-Stratton et al. (1988); families from wait-list control group were randomly reallocated	Randomized trial (one-year follow-up of Webster-Stratton et al. [1988])	Parental reports and independent behavior ratings at home and school; replicated findings from Webster-Stratton et al. (1988)	There is converging evidence of effectiveness of video-based, parent-facilitated treatments for ADHD in children
Webster-Stratton, 1990	P	Conduct disorder	43 families of children aged 3–8 years	Randomized trial (self-administered videotape modeling vs. self-administered videotape modeling with 2-hour therapist consultation vs. wait-list control)	Both treatment groups reported fewer behavior problems, less stress, and less spanking. There were few differences between treatment groups, but children of parents assigned to videotape modeling plus therapist contact showed more improvement on independent ratings than children of parents who had no therapist contact	Parents are capable of effectively using behavior management techniques modeled on videotapes. Minimal contact with a therapist may enhance effectiveness of videotapes

Note. Type C = self-administered by the child; P = parent-administered.

Table 7.3 Research on Social Support Self-Help Treatments for Childhood Disorders

Study	Type	Problem area	Sample	Methods	Results	Implications
Baum, 2004	P	Chronic physical illness	114 parents (age of children not reported)	Descriptive study using an Internet-based parent survey	Parents reported to have received more support and information than expected	Internet-based support groups for parents many be an effective adjunct to home care for chronic pediatric illness
Dunham et al., 1998	C	Not applicable	42 pregnant teenagers aged 15–20 years	Evaluation of a computer-mediated social support network after 6 months	98% of messages exchanged provided positive support. Those who participated regularly in the network reported a reduction in stress following the intervention. Qualitative data suggested that a supportive on-line community was developed	On-line exchange of information and emotional support may reduce pregnancy-related stress
Han & Belcher, 2001	P	Cancer	73 parents (age of children not reported)	Descriptive study using a parent survey	Parents found the on-line group helpful in exchanging information and social support but disliked large volumes of e-mail and the lack of physical proximity	While more common among higher income earners, on-line support communities may be helpful to parents with special care needs

Study	Type	Condition	Sample	Study design	Results	Conclusions
Johnson et al., 2001	C	Cystic fibrosis	37 children aged 13–18 years	Evaluation of a computer-mediated social support after 5 months	77% of the sample reported to maintain e-mail contact. Children also reported that they had more friends who they could relate to than they did at the beginning of the study	Computer-based social support groups may be an inexpensive and effective way to help meet the psychosocial needs of pediatric patients
Scharer, 2005	P	Various psychiatric conditions	6 mothers of children aged 5–12 years	Pilot study	Over 13.8 weeks of participation (on average), mothers sent an average of 5.2 messages to the bulletin board	While the study findings cannot be generalized, these results suggest that parents will use electronic discussion boards
Tetzlaff, 1997	P	Cancer	101 parents (age of children not reported)	Descriptive study using a mail-in survey	Parents sought information and emotional support. Responses were positive about computer technology to support home care. Live interaction was preferred to on-line video, which was preferred to text-only content	Parents of children with specific home care needs were positive toward an Internet-based social support

Note. Type C = self-administered by the child; P = parent-administered.

However, some texts have gained popularity among psychologists and lay audiences and are worthy of mention even though they have not been evaluated as interventions. Seligman's (2006) *Learned Optimism*, Canfield's *Chicken Soup for the Soul* series (Canfield, Hansen, Hansen, Dunlap, & Thompson, 2000; Canfield, Hansen, & Kirberger, 1997), and Covey's (1998) *7 Habits of Highly Effective Teens* have all been rated highly by psychologists (Norcross et al., 2000) but they have yet to be tested as treatments for specific disorders or problems. Nonetheless, despite the lack of evidence for the effectiveness of inspirational bibliotherapy, its widespread use suggests it meets an important need for many.

Unlike inspirational bibliotherapy, there is sound evidence for the use of instructional manuals for treating some specific problem areas. These interventions are either self-administered by children or parent-administered and have been used effectively both as stand-alone treatments and as complementary interventions to pharmacological or therapist-based treatments. Some of these are also quite popular and available in many bookstores. A detailed summary of research on manual-based self-help treatments for children and parents is provided in Table 7.1.

Instructional Manuals for Children There are currently two popular instructional manuals that have been evaluated on children. The first, *Feeling Good* (Burns, 1999), first published in 1980, remains the only mass-market text to have been tested as a self-help intervention for childhood depression. A randomized trial found this cognitive–behavioral approach to the treatment of depression led to long-term reductions in depressive symptoms (Ackerson et al., 1998). The second book is designed to help children's disruptive bedtime behavior and frequent night waking. A pilot study found that parents' reading Peterson and Peterson's (2003) *The Sleep Fairy* to their children at the end of their bedtime routine helped achieve more restful sleep (Burke, Kuhn, & Peterson, 2004). This book sets out parental expectations for appropriate bedtime behavior and rewards for meeting those expectations.

Other books are widely available but unlikely to have been evaluated with children. One example is the book *Control Your Depression* (Lewinsohn, Munoz, Youngren, & Zeiss, 1996), which has been shown to effectively treat depression in adults (Cuijpers, 1998), but its suitability for children is unknown. Given their widespread use and the potential of cost-effective intervention, we hope to see popular texts such as this evaluated with children.

Less widely available manuals have been shown to effectively treat chronic and migraine headaches in children. Randomized trials have shown that self-help manuals work as effectively as clinic-based treatment for chronic headache (Griffiths & Martin, 1996) and migraine headache

(McGrath et al., 1992) and that self-help is much more cost-effective and convenient than therapist-based care.

There are few studies that tested the self-help manuals for children as an intervention for disruptive behavioral problems. Shechtman and Ben-David (Shechtman, 2000; Shechtman & Ben-David, 1999) reported that the combination of bibliotherapy and group therapy was as effective (and therefore more cost-effective) as individual therapy in reducing aggressive behavior. However, their single case study design and the fact that bibliotherapy was primarily facilitated by a therapist diminished the evidence for the generalizability of this approach as self-help. Evans et al. (1999) also used self-help manuals to treat self-harming behavior in a sample of children and adults. Compared to a group that received usual care, the self-treated group showed fewer suicidal acts and less depressive symptoms. Because their sample included both children and adults, their findings cannot be generalized to children alone. There appears to be more support for the use of parent manuals for treating behavioral problems such as these.

Instructional Manuals for Parents Instructional manuals have also been used successfully with parents, but many of these are not widely available. For parents managing difficult behavior in their children, Gordon's (1975) *Parent Effectiveness Training: The Tested Way to Raise Responsible Children*, has been shown to be effective in several outcome studies. In a meta-analysis of 26 such studies, Cedar and Levant (1990) found a moderate effect size of .33 attributed to Gordon's program on parents' knowledge, attitudes, and self-reported behavior and on children's self-esteem. A revised edition of this book was published in 2000.

Phelan's (2004) *1-2-3 Magic: Effective Discipline for Children 2–12*, first published in 1996, has also been used successfully to teach parents to use "time out" with their children. In a study by Salehpour (1996), parents who learned *1-2-3 Magic* using a book and video demonstrated higher competence in disciplining their children than parents who did not learn this technique.

Gordon's and Phelan's books are popular and there are other lesser known (and perhaps less available) manuals that have been tested as well. Heifetz (1977) used parent manuals to treat disruptive behavior problems in mentally retarded children and found that this method was as effective as the combination of manuals and face-to-face contact with a therapist in reducing disruptive behaviors and teaching self-help skills in children. Long, Rickert, and Ashcraft (1993) used parent manuals in addition to stimulant medication in treating attention deficit–hyperactivity disorder in children. They found less intense behavior problems and more parental knowledge of behavioral principles among families who received manuals and medication compared to families who received medication alone.

Parent manuals have also been shown to help children with specific health problems. To treat nocturnal enuresis, van Londen, van Londen-Barentsen, van Son, and Mulder (1993) used self-administered arousal training in addition to urine alarms. Compared to families who used only the alarm with a simple reward system involving praise and stickers, the group that also used parent manuals showed higher success rates after treatment and at 30-months follow-up (van Londen, van Londen-Barentsen, van Son, & Mulder, 1995). Seymour, Brock, During, and Poole (1989) found that the use of parent manuals was effective in treating sleeping difficulties in young children and that the addition of regular telephone contact with a therapist had no additional benefit. Montgomery and Stores (2000) achieved similar results from the use of parent manuals in treating sleep problems among mentally retarded children. Gienbenhain and O'Dell (1984) found parent manuals helped children who were afraid of the dark achieve more restful sleep after just 2 weeks of treatment. In another study, Chambers and her colleagues provided parents of children suffering from postoperative pain with an education manual, *Pain, Pain, Go Away: Helping Children with Pain* (McGrath, Finley, & Ritchie, 1994). The manual improved parents' attitudes toward managing pain in their children but did not affect their behavior (e.g., administering medication) or the severity of their children's pain (Chambers, Reid, McGrath, Finley, & Ellerton, 1997).

When used for an appropriate problem area, parent manuals can help children and families self-manage symptoms and provide useful resources to families that want to learn more about the nature of the problem they are dealing with. These manuals mostly teach self-management skills but also provide health information and include case studies and testimonials that help families realize that the problems they face are common and manageable. Their therapeutic orientation is typically behavioral or cognitive–behavioral, as these are the most tried and tested approaches to treating many childhood disorders (see Weisz, Weiss et al., 1995).

The primary advantage of manual-based bibliotherapy is that it is inexpensive and convenient, although access is obviously constrained by literacy problems and families' acceptance of self-help as a viable treatment option. Moreover, as discussed in greater depth later in this chapter, manuals have been created and validated for only a few problem areas and the studies evaluating these manuals have tended to be small and not always of the highest quality.

Electronic Media

Parents of children with specific care needs often need health information and instruction that is not well suited to books and manuals. In such cases it may be advantageous for information and instructions to be delivered by way of electronic media, including audiotapes, computer CD-ROMs, videos, DVDs, and the Internet. Today, electronic media are integral to self-help interventions for childhood disorders. To illustrate why this is, imagine a mother who has difficulty managing her overly aggressive teenage son. She has been advised by her family doctor to see a psychologist and to learn some behavioral techniques that will help tame her teenager and alleviate some of the stress that she has been experiencing. She quietly accepts the referral but knows that attending therapy sessions with a psychologist is simply impossible because of the time, travel, and costs involved. So this parent visits a local bookstore and finds a book that discusses behavioral interventions for conduct disorder, including how to identify target behaviors, how to reinforce positive behaviors, how to ignore targeted aggressive behaviors, how to implement a point reward system, and so on. Overwhelmed with the details and unable to grasp these concepts, she puts the book aside and, like millions of other parents, turns to the Internet for help.

Given the popularity of online health information, it is somewhat surprising that few self-help telehealth products have been developed and evaluated for childhood disorders (Table 7.2). Still, there are some encouraging and highly innovative approaches to electronic self-help for children and parents that are worth recognition.

Electronic Self-Help for Children   Audiobooks and Internet podcasting have recently become popular in self-help tools for adults but our literature search yielded only two studies involving audio products for children. Both of these studies used audiotapes as part of a manual-based self-help relaxation training program for children with chronic headache (Larsson, Melin, & Doberl, 1990) and migraine headache (McGrath et al., 1992). Both studies found that audiotaped relaxation training reduced the severity of headaches and that these effects persisted in follow-up assessments.

With regard to computers and the Internet, there are several new and emerging products for children that are worth noting. Davies and colleagues recently evaluated the STARBRIGHT™ *Fitting Cystic Fibrosis Into Your Life Everyday* CD-ROM as a means to deliver illness-related information to children with cystic fibrosis (Davis, Quittner, Stack, & Yang, 2004).[1] Findings showed significant increases in both knowledge and coping competency

---

[1] At the time of going to press, this CD-ROM was available free of charge from the STARBRIGHT™ Foundation at http://www.starbright.org/projects/hes. Incidentally, we look forward to any forthcoming studies on the STARBRIGHT™ Sickle Cell Slime-O-Rama™ Game, also available to order from this Web site.

after only 30 minutes' exposure to the computer-based materials. Another educational interactive CD-ROM was evaluated with a group of child asthma patients at the University of Missouri (Krishna et al., 2003). The data showed that giving children a CD-ROM in addition to usual clinic-based care led to a greater reduction in asthma symptoms, improvement in self-management knowledge, and fewer hospital visits as compared to a control group that received usual care. In both of these studies, computers were provided to families that did not own one.

Electronic self-help can also be used to supplement bibliotherapy interventions or telephone contact with a therapist. In Nova Scotia, the Family Help Project (www.bringinghealthhome.com) is currently evaluating self-help treatments of five health conditions: attention deficit–hyperactivity disorder, disruptive behavior disorder, anxiety, enuresis, and pain. Preliminary outcome data from Family Help look very encouraging (Hicks, von Baeyer, & McGrath, 2006; Lingley-Pottie, Watters, McGrath, & Janz, 2005). Family Help uses online manuals for parents and children supplemented with regular telephone or e-mail contact with a therapist. An evaluation of the Family Help pain module showed that many more children who received the self-help intervention reported clinically significant reductions in pain scores at 3-months follow-up compared to a wait-list control group that received standard care (72% vs. 14%; Hicks et al., 2006).

Ritterband and colleagues reported findings from an Internet-based family intervention for pediatric encopresis, which demonstrated reductions in soiling accompanied by increased unprompted trips to the toilet and defecation in the toilet relative to a standard-care comparison group (Ritterband et al., 2003). Similar to the Davis et al.'s (2004) intervention, the encopresis Web site was self-guided and involved minimal additional input from health care professionals. The intervention was home based and required an investment of approximately 6 hours of the caregiver's and child's time over a period of several weeks. Unlike the educational games but like Family Help, the "U-Can-Poop-Too" Web site constructed an individualized behavioral contract for each child based on information gathered from the family.

Electronic Self-Help for Parents The distinction between electronic self-help for children and for parents is not always clear-cut. Several of the Internet-based self-help treatments for children also involve parent modules (e.g., Hicks et al., 2006; Lingley-Pottie et al., 2005; Ritterband et al., 2003). However, some products are used exclusively by parents. This is most appropriate for management of disruptive behavioral problems in their children. One of the best known applications of video for managing behavior disorders comes from Webster-Stratton and colleagues at the University of Washington. This group developed training videos for parents to teach behavior management techniques for treating disruptive behavior disorder in their children (Webster-Stratton, Kolpacoff, & Hollinsworth, 1988). Their results showed that parent training videos were as effective as face-to-face therapist contact in helping parents learn and use these techniques and these effects were durable over one year (Webster-Stratton, Hollinsworth, & Kolpacoff, 1989). In other research, they demonstrated that the benefits of parent training videos could be enhanced with group sessions (Webster-Stratton et al., 1988) or occasional contact with a therapist (Webster-Stratton, 1990). This group is now evaluating CD-ROM and Internet versions of the Webster-Stratton's Parenting Program.

Video is also an effective medium for providing information to families. Borgschatz, Frankenberger, and Eder (1999) used videos to present scientific information to parents on stimulant medications for ADHD and found that these videos helped parents to make more informed decisions about treatments for their children. But not all the video-based self-help interventions have shown positive results. One study of live versus videotaped home training for treating enuresis found better outcomes in families who received live training (Houts, Whelan, & Peterson, 1987).

There are other videos and DVDs available on the market that can be used to supplement manuals that are known to be effective. In child welfare settings, for example, the video *1-2-3 Magic: Effective Discipline for Children 2–12* (Phelan & Miller, 1990) is a popular supplement to the book (Phelan, 2004) in teaching a simple behavioral technique to parents who may not otherwise benefit from the book alone.

Electronic self-help is noninvasive, convenient, and inexpensive but, unlike bibliotherapy, reading difficulties do not necessarily preclude access. One disadvantage is that prototypical situations depicted in multimedia products are unlikely to resemble individual cases and family members would have to consult a professional if they have questions about their specific situation. Still, electronic self-help products for children and parents present unique opportunities to devise more interactive treatments that might capture children's attention in ways that manuals do not (Carrol, Bain, & Houghton, 1994; Favelle, 1994; Resnick & Sherer, 1994).

Support Groups

Child disorders isolate families. While it may be helpful to families to read or view testimonials included in books or videos, live interaction with others who encounter similar problems can be an invaluable source of support. The social and expressive aspects of support groups are well recognized as beneficial to children and parents living with a chronic illness.

Support groups vary in the degree of being moderated and organized by a health care provider but their main objective is to provide the opportunity to learn skills from peers, to feel cared for, and to normalize the participant's condition.

Support groups enable children to share information, to express themselves, and to exchange experiences and coping strategies. Most importantly, they reduce feelings of isolation by demonstrating to children and parents that they are not alone in the challenges that are posed to them. But there are limitations to support groups. Vast geographic distances separating children with rare conditions may make meetings unfeasible for some families, and the intention to help children achieve greater independence over their health problem may run counter to their dependence on parents for travel to meetings (Johnson, Ravert, & Everton, 2001).

The growth of the Internet has brought with it a rapid transformation in the delivery and function of support groups. More than a thousand national and international support groups can now be accessed online (White & Madara, 2000) and children and parents are increasingly going online to access health information and to reach out to one another. Internet-based support groups may be particularly beneficial to children living with chronic health problems or difficult personal issues. Many of the telehealth self-help products described in this chapter include support group functions. Examples include the STARBRIGHT™ Family Room™ for parents (www.starbright.org) and Family Help Internet chat room (www.bringinghealthhome.com).

Evaluation data on Internet support groups are scarcely reported because these groups normally are a part of a more comprehensive electronic product. Some data are available. In an evaluation of an Internet support group for children with cystic fibrosis, it was found that most participants continued to e-mail each other regularly after the study and believed that they had more friends who they could relate to than they did at the beginning of the study (Johnson et al., 2001). Another study of an Internet support network provided to pregnant adolescents found that after 6 months of participation in the network, participants reported a reduction in pregnancy-related stress (Dunham et al., 1998).

Parents, too, have shown a willingness to use the Internet for support. Scharer (2005) reported on a pilot study of parents of children with emotional and behavioral problems who exchanged supportive messages through an Internet bulletin board. Other research has been carried out on Internet support groups for parents of children with cancer, all finding that the majority of parents who use these groups benefit from the exchange of information and social support (Baum, 2004; Han & Belcher, 2001; Tetzlaff, 1997).

These descriptive studies are suggestive of positive effect, but evaluation studies are needed to ascertain a causal therapeutic effect of Internet-based social support. These groups are inexpensive, available 24 hours a day, and accessible to children who are homebound and families that live in rural areas and could not otherwise participate in a support group. They also enable rapid dissemination of information, an advantage that can also become a problem when misleading information spreads to families who may form opinions before having a chance to talk to their health providers (Culver, Gerr, & Frumkin, 1997). Another shortcoming is that Internet access in the home is social class dependent. Poor families often do not have access at home, and for most families, using the Internet at work or from public access sites is not a viable alternative. Also, the Internet usage may actually increase feelings of loneliness and decrease perceptions of social support. Scherlis (1998) attributed this to the notion that on-line friendships can be less reliable than in-person ones. Furthermore, as Johnson and colleagues (2001) pointed out, "Although adolescents tend to be more facile with computer technology than many adults, this skill may be offset by their needs as adolescents who, as a group, tend to be highly impressionable, risk-seeking, and, at times, overly independent" (p. e24).

Opportunities for Further Research

Self-help for children and parents should be evaluated more rigorously given their widespread use and the potential of very cost-effective intervention. As Rosen (1987) noted, the growing proliferation of self-help treatments necessitates better research on their effectiveness. The development and integration of alternative, testable approaches to mental health care that engage families and communities have been recognized as a key area of future research in the area of child mental health services (Surgeon General, 1999). There are several areas in which researchers have a role to play in developing the evidence base for self-help for childhood disorders.

First, there is evidence to support the use of some treatments for some problems, but too few rigorous evaluations have been conducted to endorse their widespread implementation. More randomized trials involving a variety of problem areas, populations, and media are needed to discern the efficacy of text- and electronic-based interventions in treating a range of health problems.

Second, the role of therapist assistance in self-help treatments needs to be delineated. Therapist assistance increases the cost and decreases ease of access but may boost persistence in the intervention and effectiveness of treatment. More studies are needed to examine the circumstances in which therapist facilitation is useful and to determine the optimal amount of therapist assistance (e.g., Baker et al., 1997).

Third, treatment acceptability is recognized as a prerequisite to successful intervention (Cross Calvert & Johnston, 1990), but little is known about children's and parents' pretreatment attitudes toward self-administered versus traditional treatments. Such research is needed for clinicians to be able to predict families' potential to benefit from self-help treatments. It is apparent that personal and sociodemographic factors influence families' choices of self-help alternatives to traditional treatments (e.g., literacy problems, computer access, geographic distances to support group meetings). This area of research remains relatively untapped.

Fourth, there is a need to evaluate the long-term benefits of self-administered treatments. Debate over the decay of treatment effects over time precludes definitive conclusions about their long-term health and economic benefits (e.g., Dodge, 1999; Mohr, 1995; Scogin et al., 1996).

Fifth, while well-controlled, university-based efficacy studies show success with some self-administered treatments, there have been few naturalistic effectiveness studies in which these models have been integrated into the health care system. Essentially, all trials have been on single elements or single disorders. The challenges in conducting systematic outcome-based evaluation studies in naturalistic settings have been clearly described (Weisz, Donenberg, Han, & Weiss, 1995) but effectiveness studies—not just efficacy trials—and cost analyses are needed to ascertain the place of self-help treatments in health care systems.

Advances in each of these areas will benefit in helping bring self-help treatments that work to families who need them. A stronger evidence base also will facilitate advocacy for the continued development of self-help books and telehealth products for children and parents.

Issues for Clinicians

Self-help for children is effective for some types of problems, although whether or not its therapeutic benefits meet or exceed that of traditional face-to-face therapy is not yet clear. A similar conclusion was drawn in a recent Cochrane Library systematic review of media-based treatments for child behavior problems (Montgomery, 2001). So, when introducing self-help treatments to families, clinicians should be aware of the gaps in the evidence base and recommend only treatments for appropriate problem areas. For example, parent training videos for treating anxiety disorders in children or self-help bibliotherapy for children exhibiting conduct disordered behavior are not evidence-based options at this time.

Caution also is prudent in preparing families for any deviation in treatment from what is expected. A child who is expecting to receive interpersonal therapy from a therapist and is instead given a book to read or a CD-ROM to use at home may feel confused or disparaged. These feelings could thereby compromise any therapeutic benefits that self-help might have reaped (Scogin et al., 1996). The onus is on clinicians to decide whether a self-help intervention might be seen as acceptable to the family. Offering a parent training video to help a family manage an aggressive child is futile if parents are not willing to accept the responsibility to carry out a behavior management plan with little or no support from a therapist.

Internet-based treatments and support groups present unique challenges to clinicians. There is a burgeoning literature on the ethics of online interventions (Fisher & Fried, 2003; Ragusea & VandeCreek, 2003). If clinicians are going to use e-mail or interactive chat, then they will need to familiarize themselves with the nuances of communicating electronically and the limitations of these media with clients who have limited written communication skills (Maheu, 2003; Ragusea & VandeCreek, 2003). Even experienced telehealth providers will be confronted with newly emerging security threats such as computer hackers and viruses. Thus, the competent practice of electronic self-help requires technical expertise and the ability to continuously learn and adapt.

Self-help treatments that are offered or supervised by clinicians pose new problems of jurisdiction. If a psychologist in Nova Scotia is treating a patient in Ontario or in California, which regulatory body credentials the psychologist and oversees his professional behavior? What security should be implemented to ensure confidentiality? For clinicians to embrace the use of self-administered treatments, looming questions about such issues require innovative, definitive solutions. Self-help also raises legal liability questions about the standardization and quality assurance of these materials. Does the delivery of treatments with professional fees invoke a different standard of care than the sale of a self-help book? Who protects the public if professionals are not delivering treatment? Should professional regulatory bodies establish standards for treatments that are promoted by professionals? Is consumer protection legislation required? Do consumers need or want evidence-based reviews of the efficacy of self-help products? And should professional associations formally recognize those products that show evidence of efficacy?

In addition, the growing popularity of self-help will inevitably influence the face of professional psychology. Clinicians who endorse these treatments may find themselves adapting to new roles and delivering treatments outside traditional environments. Training programs for clinicians must respond to these changes.

Conclusion

Self-help treatments for childhood disorders tend to lack empirical evaluation and, with notable exceptions, lack randomized trials showing efficacy. The challenge for clinicians and families in assessing the viability of self-help lies in making sense of this piecemeal evidence base. The public increasingly recognizes the importance of psychosocial interventions that are readily accessible, suitable to presenting symptoms, adaptable to new technology, and inexpensive (Black, 2000). Self-help is a promising avenue to improve the accessibility and availability of psychosocial interventions to children, but more research and clearer guidelines are needed to ensure that they actually help families. From a public health perspective, there is great potential in self-help treatments to improve the health of the many children who suffer from chronic physical and psychological illness but are unable to access services.

While many of the self-help treatments described here involve cutting-edge technology, it is worth noting that self-help for children actually has a long history. When faced with a serious health condition, families normally respond by self-managing the symptoms, learning about the nature of the condition, and seeking support from others. Self-help is neither a passing fad nor a novel approach to health care, so it is essential to continue to develop, evaluate, and disseminate self-help treatments that work. These treatments have great promise to help reduce suffering from childhood illnesses that are too often left untreated.

Chapter Points

- Though 15–25% of children suffer from psychological problems, fewer than one in five who show such symptoms had contact with a health professional in the most recent 6 months.
- Barriers to effective health care for children include the stigma associated with seeking treatment, the time and expense of traveling to a health care provider, and the motivation to implement treatment.
- Self-help approaches produce change by providing information, teaching skills, and providing social support.
- Inspirational texts are both widely used and highly valued, despite the lack of evidence to support their efficacy.
- Popular books on depression (*Feeling Good*) and disruptive bedtime behavior (*The Sleep Fairy*) are the only widely disseminated books to have been empirically validated.
- Effective self-help programs for children have targeted tension and migraine headaches and suicidal behaviors.

- Effective self-help programs for parents have been found to reduce behavioral problems in normal and mentally retarded children, reduce enuresis and sleep difficulties, and improve parental attitudes in dealing with their children's postoperative pain.
- Electronic self-help programs have been used to help children deal with the stress of cystic fibrosis and improve coping with asthma.
- Online support groups provide the opportunity to learn coping skills from peers, reduce isolation, and increase feelings of being cared for and normalize the child's condition.
- Over 1000 online support groups exist on the Internet, with several studies demonstrating a positive effect for children and their parents, but no controlled studies are yet available.

References

Ackerson, J., Scogin, F., McKendree-Smith, N., & Lyman, R. D. (1998). Cognitive bibliotherapy for mild and moderate adolescent depressive symptomatology. *Journal of Consulting and Clinical Psychology, 66*, 685–690.

Adams, S. J., & Pitre, N. L. (2000). Who uses bibliotherapy and why? A survey from an underserviced area. *Canadian Journal of Psychiatry, 45*, 645–649.

American Psychological Association. (2001, February). *Psychology: Promoting health and wellbeing through high quality, cost-effective treatment.* Retrieved December 10, 2001, from the American Psychological Association Web site: http://www.apa.org/practice/psych.html

Baker, B. L., Brightman, A. J., Blacher, J. B., Heifetz, L. J., Hinshaw, S. P., & Murphy, D. M. (1997). *Steps to independence: Teaching everyday skills to children with special needs* (3rd ed.). Baltimore: Brooks.

Baum, L. S. (2004). Internet parent support groups for primary caregivers of a child with special health care needs. *Pediatric Nursing, 30*, 381–390.

Black, D. A. (2000, September). *Improving population health through self-administered health education interventions.* Paper presented at the Inaugural Scientific Meeting of the American Academy of Health Behavior, Santa Fe, NM.

Borgschatz, H., Frankenberger, W., & Eder, R. (1999). Effects of information on perceptions of stimulant medication efficacy for treatment of attention-deficit hyperactivity disorder. *Psychology in the Schools, 36*, 515–522.

Breton, J. J., Bergeron, L., Valla, J. P., Berthiaume, C., Gaudet, N., & Lambert, J. (1999). Quebec child mental health survey: Prevalence of DSM-III-R mental health disorders. *Journal of Child Psychology and Psychiatry and Allied Disciplines, 40*, 375–384.

Burke, R. V., Kuhn, B. R., & Peterson, J. L. (2004). A "storybook" ending to children's bedtime problems: The use of a rewarding social story to reduce bedtime resistence and frequent night waking. *Journal of Pediatric Psychology, 29*, 389–396.

Burns, D. (1999). *Feeling good: The new mood therapy.* New York: Avon.

Butler, R. J. (1998). Annotation: Night wetting in children: Psychological aspects. *Journal of Child Psychology and Psychiatry and Allied Disciplines, 39,* 453–463.

Calam, R., Bolton, C., & Roberts, J. (2002). Maternal expressed emotion, attributions and depression and entry into therapy for children with behaviour problems. *British Journal of Clinical Psychology, 41,* 213–216.

Canfield, J., Hansen, M. V., Hansen, P., Dunlap, D., & Thompson, K. (2000). *Chicken soup for the preteen soul: 101 stories of changes, choices and growing up for kids (ages 10–13).* Deerfield Beach, FL: Health Communications.

Canfield, J., Hansen, M. V., & Kirberger, K. (1997). *Chicken soup for the teenage soul: 101 stories of love, life and learning.* Deerfield Beach, FL: Health Communications.

Cappelli, M., McGrath, P. J., Heick, C. E., MacDonald, N. E., Feldman, W., & Rowe, P. (1989). Chronic disease and its impact: The adolescent's perspective. *Journal of Adolescent Health Care, 10,* 283–288.

Carr, A. (2000). *What works with children and adolescents? A critical review of psychological interventions with children, adolescents and their families.* New York: Routledge.

Carrol, A., Bain, A., & Houghton, S. (1994). The effects of interactive versus linear video on the levels of attention and comprehension of social behavior by children with attention disorders. *School Psychology Review, 23,* 29–43.

Cedar, B., & Levant, R. F. (1990). A meta-analysis of the effects of parent effectiveness training. *American Journal of Family Therapy, 18,* 373–384.

Chambers, C. T., Reid, G. J., McGrath, P. J., Finley, A. G., & Ellerton, M. L. (1997). A randomized trial of a pain education booklet: Effects on parents' attitudes and postoperative pain management. *Children's Health Care, 26,* 1–13.

Covey, S. (1998). *The 7 habits of highly effective teens: The ultimate teenage success guide.* New York: Simon & Schuster.

Cross Calvert, S., & Johnston, C. (1990). Acceptability of treatments for child behavior problems: Issues and implications for future research. Journal of *Clinical Child Psychology, 19,* 61–74.

Cuijpers, P. (1998). A psychoeducational approach to the treatment of depression: A meta-analysis of Lewinsohn's "Coping with Depression" course. *Behavior Therapy, 29,* 521–533.

Culver, J. D., Gerr, F., & Frumkin, H. (1997). Medical information on the Internet: A study of an electronic bulletin board. *Journal of General Internal Medicine, 12,* 466–470.

Davis, M. A., Quittner, A. L., Stack, C. M., & Yang, M. C. K. (2004). Controlled evaluation of the STARBRIGHT CD-ROM program for children and adolescents with cystic fibrosis. *Journal of Pediatric Psychology, 29,* 259–267.

Davison, G. C. (2000). Stepped care: Doing more with less? *Journal of Consulting and Clinical Psychology, 68,* 580–585.

Dodge, K. A. (1999). Cost effectiveness of psychotherapy for child aggression: First, is there cost effectiveness? *Group Dynamics, 3,* 275–278.

Dunham, P. J., Hurshman, A., Litwan, E., Gusella, J., Ellsworth, C., & Dodd, P. W. D. (1998). Computer mediated social support: Single young mothers as a model system. *American Journal of Community Psychology, 26,* 281–306.

Elgar, F. J., & McGrath, P. J. (2003). Self-administered psychosocial treatments for children and families. *Journal of Clinical Psychology, 59,* 321–339.

Evans, K., Tyrer, P., Catalan, J., Schmidt, U., Davidson, K., Dent, J., et al. (1999). Manual-assisted cognitive-behavior therapy (MACT): A randomized controlled trial of a brief intervention with bibliotherapy in the treatment of recurrent deliberate self-harm. *Psychological Medicine, 29*, 19–25.

Favelle, G. K. (1994). Therapeutic applications of commercially available computer software. *Computers in Human Services, 11*, 151–158.

Fisher, C. B., & Fried, A. L. (2003). Internet-mediated psychological services and the American Psychological Association Ethics Code. *Psychotherapy: Theory, Research, Practice, Training, 40*, 103–111.

Fox, J., Merwin, E., & Blank, M. (1995). De facto mental health services in the rural south. *Journal of Health Care for the Poor and Underserved, 6*, 434–468.

Gienbenhain, J. E., & O'Dell, S. L. (1984). Evaluation of a parent-training manual for reducing children's fear of the dark. *Journal of Applied Behavior Analysis, 17*, 121–125.

Goodman, J. E., & McGrath, P. J. (1991). The epidemiology of pain in children and adolescents: A review. *Pain, 46*, 247–264.

Gordon, T. (1975). *Parent effectiveness training: The tested way to raise responsible children*. New York: Wyden.

Gordon, T. (2000). *Parent effectiveness training: The tested way to raise responsible children*. New York: Three Rivers Press.

Griffiths, J. D., & Martin, P. R. (1996). Clinical-versus home-based treatment formats for children with chronic headache. *British Journal of Health Psychology, 1*, 151–166.

Han, H. R., & Belcher, A. E. (2001). Computer-mediated support group use among parents of children with cancer: An exploratory study. *Computers in Nursing, 79*, 27–33.

Heifetz, L. (1977). Behavioral training for parents of retarded children: Formats based on instructional manuals. *American Journal of Mental Deficiency, 82*, 194–203.

Hicks, C. L., von Baeyer, C. L., & McGrath, P. J. (2006). Online psychological treatment for pediatric recurrent pain: A randomized evaluation. *Journal of Pediatric Psychology, 31*, 724–736.

Higgins, E. S. (1994). A review of unrecognized mental illness in primary care. *Archives of Family Medicine, 3*, 908–917.

Hipple, T. C., Comer, M., & Boren, D. (1997). Twenty recent novels (and more) about adolescents for bibliotherapy. *School Counseling, 1*, 65–67.

Hofstra, M. B., Van der Ende, J., & Verhulst, F. C. (2000). Continuity and change of psychopathology from childhood into adulthood: A 14-year follow-up study. *Journal of the American Academy of Child and Adolescent Psychiatry, 39*, 850–858.

Houts, A. C., Whelan, J. P., & Peterson, J. K. (1987). Filmed versus live delivery of full-spectrum home training for primary enuresis: Presenting the information is not enough. *Journal of Consulting and Clinical Psychology, 55*, 902–906.

Hunsley, J., Aubry, T., & Lee, C. (1997). *A profile of Canadian consumers of psychological services*. Ottawa: Canadian Psychological Association.

Johnson, K. B., Ravert, R. D., & Everton, A. (2001). Hopkins teen central: Assessment of an Internet-based support system for children with cystic fibrosis. *Pediatrics, 107*, e24.

Krishna, S., Francisco, B. D., Balas, E. A., König, P., Graff, G. R., & Madsen, R. W. (2003). Internet-enabled interactive multimedia asthma education program: A randomized trial. *Pediatrics, 111*, 503–510.

Larsson, B. S., Melin, L., & Doberl, A. (1990). Recurrent tension headache in adolescents treated with self-help relaxation training and a muscle relaxant drug. *Headache, 30*, 665–671.

Lewinsohn, P., Munoz, R., Youngren, M. A., & Zeiss, A. (1996). *Control your depression*. Englewood Cliffs, NJ: Prentice Hall.

Lingley-Pottie, P., Watters, C., McGrath, P. J., & Janz, T. (2005). *Providing family help at home*. Paper presented at the 38th Annual Hawaii International Conference on System Sciences, Hawaii.

Long, N., Rickert, V. I., & Ashcraft, E. W. (1993). Bibliotherapy as an adjunct to stimulant medication in the treatment of attention-deficit hyperactivity disorder. *Journal of Pediatric Health Care, 7*, 82–88.

Maheu, M. (2003). The online clinical practice management model. *Psychotherapy: Theory, Research, Practice, Training, 40*, 20–32.

McGrath, P. J., Finley, G. A., & Ritchie, J. (1994). *Pain, pain, go away: Helping children with pain*. Bethesda, MD: Association for the Care of Children's Health.

McGrath, P. J., Humphreys, P., Keene, D., Goodman, J. T., Lascelles, M. A., Cunningham, S.J., et al. (1992). The efficacy and efficiency of a self-administered treatment for adolescent migraine. *Pain, 49*, 321–324.

McMahon, R. J., & Wells, K. C. (1998). Conduct problems. In E. J. Mash & R. A. Barkley, (Eds.), *Treatment of childhood disorders* (2nd ed., pp. 111–207). New York: Guilford.

Mohr, D. C. (1995). Negative outcome in psychotherapy: A critical review. *Clinical Psychology: Science and Practice, 2*, 1–27.

Montgomery, P. (2001). *Media-based behavioral treatments for behavioural disorders in children*. In *The Cochrane Library, Issue 1*. Oxford: Update Software.

Montgomery, P., & Stores, G. (2000). Behavioral treatment of severe sleep disorders in children with learning disability (mental retardation): A randomized controlled trial of treatment delivery methods. *Journal of Sleep Research, 9*, 269.

Norcross, J. C., Santrock, J. W., Campbell, L. F., Smith, T. P., Sommer, R., & Zuckerman, E. L. (2000). *Authoritative guide to self-help resources in mental health*. New York: Guilford.

Offord, D. R., Boyle, M. H., Szatmari, P., Rae-Grant, N. I., Links, P. S., Cadman, D. T., et al. (1987). Six-month prevalence of disorder and rates of service utilization. *Archives of General Psychiatry, 44*, 832–836.

Ouzts, D. T. (1991). The emergence of bibliotherapy as a discipline. *Reading Horizons, 31*, 199–206.

Pardeck, J. T. (1989). Children's literature and adoption. *Child Psychiatry Quarterly, 22*, 115–123.

Pardeck, J. T. (1990a). Bibliotherapy with abused children. *Families in Society, 71*, 229–235.

Pardeck, J. T. (1990b). Children's literature and child abuse. *Child Welfare, 69*, 83–88.

Pardeck, J. T. (1991). Using books to prevent and treat adolescent chemical dependency. *Adolescence, 26*, 201–208.

Pardeck, J. T. (1992). Bibliotherapy and cancer patients. *Family Therapy, 19*, 223–232.

Pardeck, J. T. (1993). Literature and adoptive children with disabilities. *Early Child Development and Care, 91*, 33–39.

Pardeck, J. T. (1994). Using literature to help adolescents cope with problems. *Adolescence, 29*, 421–427.

Pardeck, J. T. (1996). Recommended self-help books for families experiencing divorce: A specialized form of bibliotherapy. *Psychotherapy in Private Practice, 15*, 45–58.

Pardeck, J. T., & Pardeck, J. A. (1997). Recommended books for helping young children deal with social and development problems. *Early Child Development and Care, 136*, 57–63.

Peterson, J. L., & Peterson, M. (2003). *The sleep fairy.* Omaha, NE: Behave'n Kids Press.

Phelan, T. W. (1996). *1-2-3 Magic: Effective discipline for children 2–12* (2nd ed.). Glen Ellyn, IL: Child Management Inc.

Phelan, T. W. (2004). *1-2-3 Magic: Effective discipline for children 2–12* (3rd ed.). Glen Ellyn, IL: Parentmagic.

Phelan, T. W. (Producer), & Miller, N. (Director). (1990). *1-2-3 Magic: Effective discipline for children 2–12* [Motion picture]. (Available from Child Management Inc., 800 Roosevelt Road, Glen Ellyn, IL 60137)

Ragusea, A., & VandeCreek, L. (2003). Suggestions for the ethical practice of online psychotherapy. *Psychotherapy: Theory, Research, Practice, Training, 40*, 94–102.

Resnick, H., & Sherer, M. (1994). Computer games in the human services: A review. *Computers in Human Services, 11*, 17–29.

Riordan, R. J., & Wilson, L. S. (1989). Bibliotherapy: Does it work? *Journal of Counseling and Development, 67*, 506–508.

Ritterband, L. M., Cox, D. J., Walker, L. S., Kovatchev, B., McKnight, L., Patel, K., et al. (2003). An Internet intervention as adjunctive therapy for pediatric encopresis. *Journal of Consulting and Clinical Psychology, 71*, 910–917.

Rosen, G. M. (1987). Self-help treatment books and the commercialization of psychotherapy. *American Psychologist, 42*, 46–51.

Rubin, D. H. Leventhal, J. M., Sadock, R. T., Letovsky, E., Schottland, P., Clemente, I., et al. (1986). Educational intervention by computer in childhood asthma: A randomized clinical trial testing the use of a new teaching intervention in childhood asthma. *Pediatrics, 77*, 1–10.

Rutter, M., Cox, A., Tupling, C., Berger, M., & Yule, W. (1975). Attainment and adjustment in two geographical areas: I. The prevalence of psychiatric disorder. *British Journal of Psychiatry, 126*, 493–509.

Salehpour, Y. (1996). *1-2-3 Magic: Part I. Its effectiveness on parental function in child discipline with preschool children.* Unpublished doctoral dissertation, Indiana University, Bloomington.

Scharer, K. (2005). An Internet discussion board for parents of mentally ill young children. *Journal of Child and Adolescent Psychiatric Nursing, 18*, 17–25.

Scherlis, W. (1998). Internet paradox: A social technology that reduces social involvement and psychological well-being? *American Psychologist, 52*, 1017–1031.

Schulpen, T. W. (1997). The burden of nocturnal enuresis. *Acta Paediatrica, 86*, 981–984.

Scogin, F., Bynum, J., Stephens, G., & Calhoon, S. (1990). Efficacy of self-administered treatment programs: A meta-analytic review. *Professional Psychology: Research and Practice, 21*, 42–47.

Scogin, F., Floyd, M., Jamison, C., Ackerson, J., Landreville, P., & Bissonnette, L. (1996). Negative outcomes: What is the evidence on self-administered treatments? *Journal of Consulting and Clinical Psychology, 64,* 1086–1089.

Seligman, M. (2006). *Learned optimism: How to change your mind and your life* (2nd ed.). New York: Pocket Books.

Seymour, F. W., Brock, P., During, M., & Poole, G. (1989). Reducing sleep disruptions in young children: Evaluations of therapist guided and written information approaches: A brief report. *Journal of Child Psychology and Psychiatry, 30,* 913–918.

Shechtman, Z. (2000). Bibliotherapy: An indirect approach to treatment of childhood aggression. *Child Psychiatry Human Development, 30,* 39–53.

Shechtman, Z., & Ben-David, M. (1999). Individual and group psychotherapy of childhood aggression: A comparison of outcomes and processes. *Group Dynamics, 3,* 263–274.

Silver, E. J., Stein, R. E., & Bauman, L. J. (1999). Sociodemographic and condition-related characteristics associated with conduct problems in school-aged children with chronic health conditions. *Archives of Pediatric and Adolescent Medicine, 153,* 815–820.

Stevens, M. J., & Pfost, K. S. (1982). Bibliotherapy: Medicine for the soul? *Psychology: A Quarterly Journal of Human Behavior, 19,* 21–25.

Surgeon General. (1999). Report of the Surgeon General's Conference on Children's Mental Health: A National Action Agenda. Washington, DC: Department of Health and Human Services.

Tetzlaff, L. (1997). Consumer informatics in chronic illness. *Journal of the American Medical Informatics Association, 4,* 285–300.

van Londen, A., van Londen-Barentsen, M. W., van Son, M. J., & Mulder, G. A. (1993). Arousal training for children suffering from nocturnal enuresis. *Behavioral Research and Therapy, 31,* 613–615.

van Londen, A., van Londen-Barentsen, M. W., van Son, M. J., & Mulder, G. A. (1995). Relapse rate and subsequent parental reaction after successful treatment of children suffering from nocturnal enuresis: A 2½-year follow-up of bibliotherapy. *Behavioral Research and Therapy, 33,* 309–311.

Webster-Stratton, C. (1990). Enhancing the effectiveness of self-administered videotape parent training for families with conduct-problem children. *Journal of Abnormal Child Psychology, 18,* 479–492.

Webster-Stratton, C., Hollinsworth, T., & Kolpacoff, M. (1989). The long-term effectiveness and clinical significance of three cost-effective training programs for families with conduct problem children. *Journal of Consulting and Clinical Psychology, 57,* 550–553.

Webster-Stratton, C., Kolpacoff, M., & Hollinsworth, T. (1988). Self-administered videotape therapy for families with conduct-problem children: Comparison with two cost effective treatments and a control group. *Journal of Consulting and Clinical Psychology, 56,* 558–566.

Weisz, J. R., Donenberg, G. R., Han, S. S., & Weiss, B. (1995). Bridging the gap between laboratory and clinic in child and adolescent psychotherapy. *Journal of Consulting and Clinical Psychology, 63,* 688–701.

Weisz, J. R., Weiss, B., Han, S. S., Granger, D. A., & Morton, T. (1995). Effects of psychotherapy with children and adolescents revisited: A meta-analysis of treatment outcome studies. *Psychological Bulletin, 117,* 450–468.

White, B. J., & Madara, E. J. (2000). Online mutual support groups: Identifying and tapping new I & R resources. *Information & Referral: The Journal of the Alliance of Information and Referral Systems, 22*, 63–82.

Zubrick, S. R., Silburn, S. R., Burton, P., & Blair, E. (1995). Mental health disorders in children and young people: Scope, cause and prevention. *Australian and New Zealand Journal of Psychiatry, 34*, 570–578.

CHAPTER 8

Self-Help Therapies for Eating Disorders

ANDREW WINZELBERG, KRISTINE H. LUCE
AND C. BARR TAYLOR

In this chapter, we present an overview of self-help approaches used in the treatment of eating disorders. We describe the types of self-help approaches currently available, outline the advantages and limitations of these approaches, and review what is known about the effectiveness of these approaches. This chapter concludes with recommendations for clinicians and a discussion of future directions for self-help treatments for eating disorders.

Eating disorders, including subclinical disorders and disordered eating, are common psychiatric problems in women (Fairburn, Cooper, Doll, Norman, & O'Connor, 2000; Lewinsohn, Streigel-Moore, & Seeley, 2000). For example, between 1 and 2% of the young adult female population suffers from full syndrome bulimia nervosa (BN; Fairburn & Beglin, 1990; Kjelsas, Bjornstrom, & Gotestam, 2004) and, depending on the diagnostic criteria used, between 1% and 14% meet criteria for an eating disorder not otherwise specified (EDNOS) or subclinical eating disorders (Fairburn & Beglin, 1990; Kjelsas, Bjornstrom, & Gotestam, 2004). Excessive weight concerns, body image dissatisfaction, and disordered eating behaviors are common among female college students, and although they may not meet strict diagnostic criteria, they result in clinically significant distress and impairment in multiple areas of functioning (Bushnell, Wells, Hornblow, Oakley-Brown, & Joyce, 1990; Drewnowski, Yee, Kurth, & Krahn, 1994).

Only a few studies examined the number of women with eating disorders who initiate professional treatment and the results are inconsistent. The largest sample ($N = 641$) studied found that the majority of women who had eating disorders initiated professional treatment (61–93%; Yager, Landsverk, & Edelstein, 1989). More recent studies with smaller samples paint a different picture. These studies indicate that although the majority of women reported that they wanted treatment, many fewer obtained treatment (17–57% sought treatment; Becker, Thomas, Franko, & Herzog, 2005; Cachelin, Rebeck, Veisel, & Striegel-Moore, 2001; Cachelin & Striegel-Moore, 2005; Fairburn et al., 2000). Women from ethnic minority groups were less likely to seek and obtain treatment.

More is known about the effectiveness of treatment. A recent meta-analysis of studies completed between 1980 and 2000 on the treatment of BN found that 40% recovered completely and the remaining 60% maintained clinically significant symptoms (Thompson-Brenner, Glass, & Western, 2003). Longitudinal studies with between 5 and 11 years' follow-up indicate 50–70% full remission rates (Keel & Mitchell, 1997; Keel, Mitchell, Miller, Davis, & Crow, 1999). Evidence suggests that cognitive–behavioral treatments (CBT) are superior to other treatments, although dropout rates tend to be high for all treatments: 25–45% for CBT, 40% for pharmacological treatments, and 11–37% for interpersonal psychotherapy (Agras, Walsh, Fairburn, Wilson, & Kramer, 2000; Bacaltchuk, Trefiglio, Oliveria, Lima, & Mari, 1999).

Types of Self-Help Programs

Self-help programs for eating disorders are offered in a variety of formats. The most common format is bibliotherapy. Hundreds of self-help books on eating disorders have been published. The approaches range from empirically validated CBT (e.g., *Overcoming Binge Eating*; Fairburn, 1995) to religiously oriented (e.g., *Loving Your Body: Embracing Your True Beauty in Christ*; Newman, 2002) to those using the popular *For Dummies* series format (*Anorexia & Bulimia for Dummies*; Beck, 2004). Didactic interventions that provide general information and education are routinely published in magazines and also are available on numerous Web sites. Williams (2003) reported finding approximately 218,000 "hits" for self-help and eating disorders in August 2002.

Self-help in the form of support groups is widely available for women with eating concerns. Many support groups are delivered using Internet technology and target general eating concerns or specific issues (e.g., alopecia universalis). Facilitation of support groups can be accomplished with professional, paraprofessional, or peer leaders. Unfortunately, detailed discussion of group interventions is beyond the scope of this chapter.

A hybrid form of self-help with limited professional guidance also is available. This format typically follows a structured format that unfolds over time. The majority of structured self-help programs take a socio-cognitive or CBT approach; that is, they instruct the participant to identify one or a small number of specific, time-limited goals or treatment targets; help the participant better understand related environmental conditions, antecedents, reinforcement contingencies, and cognitions; and outline specific steps for change. Specific treatment topics typically address meal planning, normalization of meal pattern, behavioral strategies to avoid triggers for binge eating and purging, cognitive restructuring, body image concerns, and prevention of relapse. The participant usually is responsible for maintaining his or her own motivation and adherence to the program protocol.

Advantages and Disadvantages of Self-Help Programs for Eating Disorders

Self-help interventions may be particularly beneficial for individuals who work nonstandard hours (e.g., high-risk groups such as athletes and dancers) or who are physically unable or psychologically reluctant to seek help (e.g., shame or fear of stigmatization). In particular, adolescents and young adults with academic commitments and limited access to transportation may find the accessibility of self-help interventions appealing.

Self-help approaches are not a panacea, however. Text-based interventions may require high levels of literacy. Credibility of content and credentials is difficult to determine on many commercial Web sites. Most structured programs for eating disorders require extensive self-monitoring and the ability to generalize self-monitoring data to multiple contexts in daily life can be difficult for people with limited psychological sophistication or motivation.

Self-help approaches, as the initial treatment approach in stepped care models for eating disorders, are recommended by several experts who practice in the specialty area of eating disorders (Fairburn & Peveler, 1990; Garner & Needleman, 1996; National Collaborating Centre for Mental Health, 2004; Williams, 2003; Wilson, Vitousek, & Loeb, 2000).

Self-Help Bibliotherapy for Eating Disorders

Reading self-help books is commonly reported by women with eating disorders. Rorty, Yager, and Rossotto (1993) found that almost half (43%) of women with eating disorders reported reading self-help books. The majority reported high levels of satisfaction with this approach. Although a number of studies examined self-help workbooks with modest therapist contact, to our knowledge there have been no studies that examine the efficacy of self-help books without additional intervention.

In 1993, Schmidt, Tiller, and Treasure evaluated a CBT-based self-help handbook with women with BN. Participants were assessed 4–6 weeks after the onset of treatment. The intervention was found to be effective in reducing bulimic symptoms and increasing nutritional knowledge. Participants significantly reduced binge eating and purging behavior but their weight and shape attitudes did not change significantly during treatment.

Carter and colleagues (2003) extended the findings of previous studies by comparing the self-help treatment condition to two control conditions, an attention-placebo control and a standard wait-list control (WL). Women who met criteria for BN were randomly assigned to one of three conditions for 8 weeks: (a) unguided CBT self-help; (b) attention-placebo control; or (c) wait-list control. The duration of the self-help treatment was 2 months. Women in the CBT self-help condition received *Overcoming Binge Eating* (Fairburn, 1995). The attention-placebo group was designed to provide nonspecific self-help and control for nonspecific treatment factors. Women in the attention-placebo condition received the self-help manual *Self-Assertion for Women* (Butler, 1992). Women in both self-help conditions were instructed to read the manuals and follow the advice to the best of their ability. Although no significant treatment by time effects were found, significant decreases in binge eating and purge frequency were observed in both self-help conditions but not in the WL group. Approximately 54% in the CBT self-help group and 50% in the attention-placebo control group reported at least a 50% reduction in binge eating or purging, compared to 31% for the WL group.

Assisted Self-Help Treatment for Eating Disorders

Assisted self-help programs include any combination of features available in standard self-help programs combined with some level of therapist/ facilitator contact. Contact varies from minimal to fairly active and can be provided in many ways, including: (a) moderation of a psychoeducation, support, or therapy group; (b) brief contact for the purpose of setting goals, reviewing journal entries, exploring setbacks and obstacles, and reviewing progress of intervention goal attainment; and (c) provision of guidance or support offered by a professional.

Several treatment studies examined the feasibility and effectiveness of guided self-help programs for the bulimic spectrum eating disorders, namely BN, binge eating disorder (BED), and EDNOS, with binge eating identified as the key feature but occurring at a subthreshold level. In the following sections, we review findings from these studies. See Table 8.1 for a summary of structured self-help interventions for the treatment of eating disorders.

Table 8.1 Summary of Structured Self-Help Interventions for Bulimia Nervosa and Binge Eating Disorder

Study	Participants	Design	Outcome	Comments
Huon, 1985	90 females with BN	Randomized to 3 groups, but no control group; SH with 7 monthly reading; SH + support from improved bulimic; SH + support from cured bulimic	19% stopped binge/purging at post and 32% stopped binge/purging at follow-up. 68% reported improvement	No dropouts reported. Those who received both the SH manual and either form of support were most successful. No control group
Schmidt et al., 1993	28 females with BN	Uncontrolled. SH CBT handbook	On clinical-rated global improvement, 43% much improved and 29% improved. 43% stopped bingeing and purging	Dropout rate 7%. 57% of bingers reported a significant reduction in binge episodes
Cooper et al., 1994	18 females with BN	Uncontrolled. SH manual plus meetings with 20–30 minute consultation with social worker	50% of the participants had stopped bingeing/vomiting at follow-up, binge rates decreased by 85%, vomiting decreased by 88%	No dropout rate reported. The ratio between self-help and social work session is not noted by the authors
Treasure et al., 1994	81 participants with BN and mixed ED	Randomized to three groups: SH (to be completed over 8 weeks), CBT (16 sessions), or WL	22% SH, 24% CBT, 11% WLC in "full remission" at 8 weeks	No dropout rate reported. Authors conclude that SH can be a useful first step in treatment. No significant differences between CBT and SH. Participants in CBT condition were evaluated at 8 weeks for equal comparison with SH

Note. SH = *self help,* WL = *wait-list,* BN = *bulimia nervosa,* BED = *binge eating disorder,* EDNOS = *eating disorders not otherwise specified,* BF = *binge frequency,* CBT = *cognitive-behavior therapy.*

(continued)

Table 8.1 (*continued*)

Study	Participants	Design	Outcome	Comments
Cooper et al., 1996	82 females with BN	Uncontrolled. BN manual supervised by a social worker	Excluding dropouts, 45% ceased vomiting, 51% ceased purging, and 33% had "full remission." 80% reduction bulimic episodes, 70% reduction in vomiting	Dropout rate 18%. Modal number of social worker sessions (20–30 minutes) was 8 (range 4–13) over 4–6 months
Dalle Grave, 1997	17 females with BN	Uncontrolled. SH with 8 20-minute sessions with therapist	35% full remission; 59% reported at least 50% reduction in bingeing/purging	Dropout rate 41%.
Wells et al., 1997	9 females with BED	Uncontrolled SH using *Overcoming Binge Eating* and 30-minute phone sessions	Of the seven participants who completed post-measures, 3 reported cessation of binge eating and 2 reported significant reduction in binge frequency	Dropout rate 11%. Compliance rates reported for each of the six steps of the program
Carter & Fairburn, 1998	72 females with BED	Randomized to three groups: WL; SH using *Overcoming Binge Eating* (12 weeks); SH plus six to eight 23-minute sessions with lay facilitator	Binge frequency decreases = WL 38%, SH 53%, and SH plus lay session 78%	Dropout rate12% (1 from WL, 8 from SH): Both SH and SH with guidance reduced binge eating

Thiels et al., 1998	62 participants with BN	Randomized to SH + 8 weeks of therapy or 16 weeks group CBT	At follow-up (41 weeks post), 61% of the SH group, and 71% of CBT were in remission	Dropout rate was 29% SH and 13% CBT. There were no significant differences between the two treatments. No control group
Loeb et al., 2000	40 females with binge eating (83% with BED)	Randomized to SH only or SH + six therapy sessions SH over 20 weeks	SH reduced binge eating episodes by 55%, SH + reduced binge eating episodes by 68%	Dropout rates: 33% at post and 45% at 6 month follow-up. Authors argue that guided self-help was notably better, but there were no significant differences between the groups. No control group
Bell & Hodder, 2001	40 females with BN or BED, EDNOS (only 21 used in data analysis)	Uncontrolled evaluation of SH Getting Better Bit(e) by Bit(e) with 30-minute weekly sessions with a mental health professional	"Significant" decreases in disordered eating symptoms	Dropout rate of 25%. No measure of ED symptoms tied to diagnostic criteria for specific eating disorders
Mitchell et al., 2001	91 females with BN	Randomized to four conditions: placebo only; fluoxetine only; SH + placebo; SH + fluoxetine	Percent reduction in vomiting: (1) placebo only = 22%; (2) fluoxetine only = 43%; (3) SH plus placebo =35%; (4) SH plus fluoxetine = 62%	Dropout rate 3% at 4 weeks. No endpoint drop out rate reported. Weekly monitoring first month then biweekly monitoring for 12 weeks. No control group
Palmer et al., 2002	121 patients with BN, BED, or EDNOS	Randomized to four groups: WL; SH only; SH + telephone; SH + face-to-face	At 4 months "Importantly improved" (dropouts included); WL = 6.6%; SH only = 13%; SH + phone = 21%; SH + face-to face = 27%	Dropout rate 22–29%. Authors conclude that self-help materials require some guidance. No control group

Note. SH = self help, WL = wait-list, BN = bulimia nervosa, BED = binge eating disorder, EDNOS = eating disorders not otherwise specified, BF = binge frequency, CBT = cognitive-behavior therapy.

(continued)

Table 8.1 (*continued*)

Study	Participants	Design	Outcome	Comments
Carter et al., 2003	82 females with BN	Randomized to 3 groups: WL; SH CBT; AP: Attention-placebo control (assertiveness training)	No statistically significant overall treatment by time effects. SH CBT = 53% had 50% reduction in binge eating or purging; AP = 50% had 50% reduction in binge eating or purging	Dropout rate 26%. 78% compliance with SH CBT manual vs. 59% compliance with AP manual
Durand & King, 2003	68 females with BN	Randomized to two groups: SH with MD support or psychotherapy	Significant decreases in BITE and EDE scores pre-post. No group differences	Dropout rate 26% at post. No control group. SH has mean of 4.9 MD visits, psychotherapy 1.9 MD visits and 4.8 psychotherapy visits
Ghaderi & Scott, 2003	31 participants with BN, BED, or EDNOS	Randomized to SH using *Overcoming Binge Eating* or guided SH (6–8 sessions with lay facilitators)	Objective binges decreased 33% for both groups; purging decreased 28% for pure and 25% for guided self-help	Dropout rate 40% SH and 44% guided SH. No control group
Bailer et al., 2004	81 females with BN	Randomized to guided self-help SH or CBT group. Each treatment was 18 sessions	No significant differences between treatment format: Remission rate 40% SH and 29% for CBT	Dropout rate 25% SH and 37% CBT. Unclear if group CBT is as effective as individual CBT for BN. No control group

Bara-Carril et al., 2004	45 participants with BN or EDNOS (94% female)	Uncontrolled study. Eight 45-minute sessions of a CD-ROM CBT self-help treatment without therapist input	Significant decreases in bingeing and vomiting. Percent vomiting at least once per week decreased by 78 to 54%; percent bingeing at least once per week dropped from 93 to 87%	Dropout rate 13%. The study provides preliminary evidence for the efficacy of a computer delivered intervention in the tx of BN. 47% completed 6 or more sessions
Walsh et al., 2004	91 females with BN	Randomized to four cognitions: placebo only; fluoxetine only; SH + placebo; SH + fluoxetine. SH group had six to eight 30-minute sessions with nurse who encouraged use of SH manual	Fluoxetine group found to significantly decrease bingeing by 23% and purging by 21%. No significant benefits found from guided SH	Dropout rate of 70%; 33% of dropouts indicated the tx offered was either too demanding or not intense enough

Note. SH = self-help, WL = wait-list, BN = bulimia nervosa, BED = binge eating disorder, EDNOS = eating disorders not otherwise specified, CBT = cognitive-behavior therapy.

Professionally Assisted Self-Help Treatment for Bulimia Nervosa

A number of studies evaluated professionally assisted self-help treatments for BN. The earliest study of combined bibliotherapy and support intervention for women with BN was completed by Huon in 1985. This study evaluated three versions of a self-administered intervention that included seven monthly readings containing information and specific suggestions about food, body image, self-concept and emotional support. The first version received information alone, the second received support from a woman with BN who was "improved," and the final version received support from a woman with BN who was "cured." Women were randomly assigned to one of the three interventions and an additional 30 women agreed to be in a comparison group. For the entire sample, 19% of subjects were abstinent at the end of the 7-month treatment, and an additional 68% were improved; at 6-month follow-up, abstinence rates increased to 32%. Those who received both the mailing and either form of contact were most successful.

Using a similar approach, Cooper and colleagues (Cooper, Coker, & Fleming; 1994) conducted an uncontrolled study to evaluate the effectiveness of a supervised CBT-based self-help manual for women with BN. For 4–6 months, participants completed the CBT manual, *Bulimia Nervosa and Binge Eating: A Guide to Recovery* (Cooper, 1993) and received guidance from a social worker with no previous specialist training in the treatment of eating disorders. Guidance included 20- to 30-minute sessions for support and encouragement to continue applying the strategies in the self-help manual. At post-assessment, half of the participants had discontinued binge eating and self-induced vomiting. On average, the frequency of binge eating decreased by 85% and self-induced vomiting was reduced by 88%. Improvement on other key features including body shape and weight dissatisfaction and dietary restraint were also noted.

In 1996, Cooper, Coker, and Fleming reported similar results using their structured CBT-based self-help manual in an open clinical trial with individuals with BN. The authors reported an 80% decrease in binge eating episodes and a 79% decrease in self-induced vomiting. Poor treatment responders or dropouts were more likely to have had a previous diagnosis of anorexia and were somewhat more likely to meet diagnosis for a personality disorder. After one year, almost two thirds of those who completed the follow-up assessment reported complete cessation of both binge eating and self-induced vomiting.

Treasure and colleagues (1994) compared a CBT-based self-help manual against standard individual CBT for BN with participants who were randomly assigned to one of three conditions: (a) self-help; (b) individual CBT; or (c) wait-list control. Participants in the self-help condition received the manual and were instructed to complete the exercises and practice the strategies in the manual during the following 8 weeks. CBT participants were assigned to a therapist for 16 sessions of psychotherapy. Participants in both treatment conditions showed significant improvements in eating disorder symptoms compared to WL. Participants in both interventions showed significant reductions in the frequency of binge eating and other weight control behaviors. Twenty-four percent of CBT participants, 22% of self-help participants, and 11% of WL participants reported full remission of symptoms.

In Italy, Dalle Grave (1997) evaluated a translated version of Fairburn's *Overcoming Binge Eating* (1995) in an uncontrolled study. In addition to reading the book, participants completed eight 20-minute sessions with a therapist spaced 2 weeks apart. Overall, 59% of participants improved and 35% discontinued binge eating and self-induced vomiting. In Germany, Thiels, Schmidt, Treasure, Garthe, and Troop (1998) evaluated a guided self-help program against standard individual CBT for BN. Participants were randomly assigned to one of two treatment conditions: guided self-help (GSH) or individual CBT. The GSH participants received the treatment manual and eight 50- to 60-minute, face-to-face sessions with a therapist every other week. The primary role of the therapist was to encourage use of the manual and manage acute crises. Participants in the CBT condition received weekly 50- to 60-minute sessions of standard CBT-based individual psychotherapy. Significant improvements were observed for both treatment groups in overeating, self-induced vomiting, dietary restraint, and shape and weight concerns. Improvements were maintained at follow-up.

Upon further examination of outcome predictor variables (Thiels, Schmidt, Troop, Treasure, & Garthe, 2000), the investigators found that, in the GSH condition, lower pretreatment frequency of binge eating predicted better outcome. In the CBT condition, the absence of pretreatment depression and baseline psychiatric comorbidity and a positive history of psychiatric illness predicted good outcome. In a 4-year follow-up, Thiels and colleagues (Thiels, Schmidt, Treasure, & Garthe, 2003) assessed 45% of the original study participants. The authors reported that significant improvements for both groups were attained or preserved on eating disorder symptom measures including overeating, self-induced vomiting, dietary restraint, and shape and weight concerns.

In an innovative study, Mitchell and colleagues (2001) compared fluoxetine (Prozac) and a CBT-based self-help manual for the treatment of BN. Participants were randomly assigned to one of four conditions: (a) placebo only; (b) fluoxetine only; (c) placebo plus CBT self-help manual only; and (d) fluoxetine plus CBT self-help manual. Participants were seen by a research assistant weekly for the first 4 weeks and every other week for the remaining 12 weeks of the study. Participants also were seen every other week by a study investigator. The self-help manual was comprised of standard CBT for BN. Participants were instructed to spend approximately one hour each evening completing readings and assignments. Participants who received the self-help or medication improved significantly compared to the WL. Participants in the fluoxetine plus self-help manual group reported the greatest improvement in self-induced vomiting and binge eating episodes. However, abstinence rates in the active treatment conditions were not found to be significantly different (i.e., fluoxetine, 16%; manual plus placebo, 24%; and manual plus fluoxetine, 26%).

In a randomized controlled trial, Durand and King (2003) assigned participants diagnosed by their general medical practitioner and referred for specialist eating disorder treatment to one of two conditions: (a) self-help plus regular general medical practitioner contact for support; and (b) standard individual CBT. General medical practitioners received a training manual to assist participants with the self-help treatment. Participants in the self-help condition received a CBT-based self-help manual. Participants in both groups decreased their bulimic symptoms and no significant differences were observed between the groups. Approximately 20% of participants in both treatment arms prefered a self-help treatment and 38% (self-help) and 27% (CBT) had no treatment preference.

Embracing the potential for computer software programs to provide cost-effective self-help interventions, Bara-Carril and colleagues (2004), in an uncontrolled study, evaluated an eight-module CD-ROM–based CBT intervention for BN. Participants reported significant decreases in binge eating and self-induced vomiting. The percent of participants vomiting and binge eating at least once per week decreased from 78 to 54% and from 93 to 87%, respectively. Bara-Carril et al. (2004) reported that approximately 4 in 5 patients accepted the offer to complete the CD-ROM intervention, a rate similar to the acceptance rate received for therapist-aided treatment. However, patients with more severe eating disorder symptoms were less likely to accept the self-help treatment.

Lastly, Bailer and colleagues (2004) compared guided self-help (GSH) to CBT-based group therapy (CBT) with an Austrian sample. Participants diagnosed with BN were randomly assigned to either GSH or CBT group. The GSH group received a self-help manual and a maximum of 18 brief weekly visits. The CBT group met for 18 weekly 1.5-hour sessions. Bailer et al. (2004) found significant decreases in the frequency of binge eating episodes and self-induced vomiting in both treatment groups. These improvements were maintained after one year. Analysis of treatment completers at follow-up showed that remission rates in the GSH condition (74%) were superior to the CBT group condition (44%).

In summary, studies from North America and Europe found assisted self-help interventions for the treatment of BN to be effective. The interventions used structured CBT-based manuals that unfold over time (range 8–20 weeks). Although improvement rates vary widely (ranging from 22 to 88%), all studies report that self-help is helpful. Differences may result from different measures and criteria used to define improvement, the amount of outside "assistance," and the frequency of contact with the researchers. Durand and King (2003) confirm that many women with eating disorders prefer a self-help treatment approach and Bara-Carril and colleagues (2004) found that 80% of patients accepted a referral to self-help computer-delivered treatment.

Professionally Assisted Self-Help Treatment for Binge Eating Disorder (Primary Focus)

To our knowledge, the most frequently evaluated self-help program for the treatment of BED has been Fairburn's *Overcoming Binge Eating* (Fairburn, 1995). In 1997, Wells, Garvin, Dohm, and Striegel-Moore conducted an uncontrolled study to evaluate the feasibility of providing a self-help plus telephone guidance program for BED. The duration of the program was 3 months. For the self-help component, all women received *Overcoming Binge Eating*. Participants were instructed to complete daily self-monitoring logs. For the telephone guidance component, participants received 30-minute telephone sessions weekly for the first month and every other week for the following 2 months. Telephone sessions, conducted by a psychology graduate student, focused on the participants' progress with the self-help program. Reductions were observed on the Eating Disorder Examination Questionnaire (Beglin & Fairburn, 1992) total score and in the frequency of binge eating. Compliance with the program sessions varied between participants.

Carter and Fairburn (1998) conducted a controlled effectiveness study to compare pure and GSH programs for BED. Women diagnosed with BED were randomized to one of three conditions and followed for 6 months: (a) pure self-help; (b) guided self-help (GSH); and (c) wait-list control. Treatment duration was 12 weeks. Participants in the active treatments received *Overcoming Binge Eating* (Fairburn, 1995). Participants assigned to the pure self-help condition were instructed to follow the program over the 12 treatment weeks. They received no additional contact. Participants assigned to GSH met with one of three lay facilitators for six to eight 25-minute sessions to support the participants' use of the program. Results indicated that the mean frequency of binge eating at post-treatment was significantly lower and cessation of binge eating was significantly higher for both treatment groups than WL. Reductions in binge eating were maintained at follow-up.

Loeb, Wilson, Gilbert, and Labouvie (2000) compared pure self-help and therapist GSH for women who engage in binge eating in a randomized trial. Eighty-three percent met the diagnostic criteria for BED. All participants received a copy of *Overcoming Binge Eating* (Fairburn, 1995). Both treatment conditions resulted in improvements in eating behavior, elimination of inappropriate compensatory behaviors, reductions in weight and shape concerns, and reductions in other eating symptomatology. The GSH condition was most successful in reducing binge eating episodes.

In a randomized, controlled treatment trial, Palmer, Birchall, McGrain, and Sullivan (2002) compared three formats of self-help for individuals diagnosed with BN, BED, and EDNOS. Participants were randomly assigned to one of four conditions: (a) self-help with minimal guidance; (b) self-help with face-to-face guidance; (c) self-help with telephone guidance; and (d) WL. The duration of the treatment was 4 months. All participants received a copy of *Overcoming Binge Eating* (Fairburn, 1995) and a brief description by a therapist of how to use the program. In the self-help with face-to-face guidance condition, participants were invited to attend four 30-minute outpatient guidance sessions. In the self-help with telephone guidance condition, guidance was delivered over 30-minute telephone sessions. Guidance was provided by nurse therapists who help participants organize their use of the self-help program. The greatest improvements were observed in participants who received face-to-face guidance (50%) and telephone guidance (36%) conditions followed by self-help with minimal guidance (25%) and WL (19%).

In a Swedish study, investigators (Ghaderi & Scott, 2003) compared pure and GSH for participants diagnosed with BN, BED, and EDNOS with binge eating as the primary problem. Participants were randomly assigned to either pure or GSH conditions. The duration of treatment was 16 weeks. All participants received a copy of *Overcoming Binge Eating* (Fairburn, 1995), 16 copies of a symptom list, and prepaid envelopes in which to return the symptom lists each week. No other advice or information was provided. Participants in the GSH condition met individually with an undergraduate psychology student for six to eight 25-minute sessions. The psychology students were trained to provide support and review the self-help program according to the guidelines in Fairburn's (1998) *Guided Self-Help for Bulimia Nervosa. Therapist's Manual for use in Conjunction with Overcoming Binge Eating.* There were no significant differences between the pure and GSH conditions. Mean percentage reductions in objective binges was 33% for both groups. Mean percentage reductions in purging were 28% for pure and 25% for GSH. Treatment gains were maintained at 6-month follow-up.

Lastly, in an uncontrolled study, Bell and Hodder (2001) evaluated a supervised self-help program for BN and binge eating that combines CBT with motivational enhancement (MET), *Getting Better Bit(e) by Bit(e): A Survival Kit for Sufferers of Bulimia Nervosa and Binge Eating Disorders* (Schmidt & Treasure, 1996). Participants received GSH using the *Getting Better Bit(e) by Bit(e)* CBT plus MET manual. Participants were provided 30-minute weekly sessions with a mental health professional. Significant differences were found on pre and post scores of eating disorder symptoms and severity.

As with assisted self-help interventions for BN, interventions for BED effectively reduced binge eating symptoms. Improvement rates ranged from 13 to 74% depending on the criteria used. Sufficient evidence exists to recommend Fairburn's (1995) *Overcoming Binge Eating* book for the treatment of BED. No ideal or necessary treatment length has been identified, but most studies require a minimum of eight sessions. Effective "assistance" has been provided by clinicians, undergraduate psychology students, and nurses.

Preventing Eating Disorders

Self-help interventions also have been applied to the prevention of eating disorders primarily with female adolescents and young adults. A number of studies evaluated these interventions using individual and group formats (Kaminski & McNamara, 1996; Zabinski, Wilfley, Calfas, Winzelberg, & Taylor, 2004; Zabinski, Wilfley et al., 2001). An exemplar of prevention programs can be seen in the work developed at the Stanford University Behavioral Medicine Media Laboratory. Named *Student Bodies*, the program targets young women with weight and shape concerns, as well as unhealthy eating attitudes and behaviors. *Student Bodies* has three central components and is divided into eight sessions. The components are psychoeducational readings, an Internet-based body image journal, and a moderated asynchronous electronic discussion group. The readings were selected to educate women about body image, healthy dietary and physical activity practices, and eating disorders. The body image journal allows participants to monitor events that trigger body image dissatisfaction as well as ensuing thoughts and feelings about their bodies. The asynchronous electronic discussion group is moderated and gives participants a place to post their reactions to the group content and to receive and provide emotional support to other group members. The discussion group is not designed to be a form of psychotherapy nor is it intended to replace psychotherapy, and this is clearly disclosed to participants at the onset. The discussion group moderator facilitates the group discussion, helps the group members stay on target, redirects the group discussion if it leads into nonproductive discourse, and generally oversees group interactions. Each session's psychoeducational content is made available to participants at the beginning of the corresponding session week. Once a session is available, participants have access to previous session content but they do not have access to subsequent content and therefore cannot proceed ahead. Posting to the discussion group is always available to participants.

Since the creation of the *Student Bodies* program, five iterations have been developed and evaluated with female college students (Celio et al., 2000; Taylor et al., 2006; Winzelberg et al., 2000, 1998; Zabinski, Pung, et al., 2001). Each new version of the program has been revised to incorporate research findings and feedback from participants. Overall, participants completing *Student Bodies* reported significant improvements in weight and shape concerns and healthier eating attitudes and behaviors. Recently, Low and colleagues (Low et al., 2006) evaluated the importance of discussion group in the *Student Bodies* intervention. In this study, participants were randomly assigned to one of four conditions: (a) clinically moderated discussion group; (b) unmoderated discussion group; (c) no discussion group; and (d) WL group. Low et al. (2006) found that participants using the *Student Bodies* program without a moderator fared best and had significantly lower eating and body image concerns at long-term follow-up compared to controls. The most recent evaluation of *Student Bodies* tracked 481 female undergraduate students for up to 3 years post-intervention (Taylor et al., 2006). Investigators found a significant reduction in weight and shape concerns in the intervention group compared to the control group during the first 2 years of follow-up. Improvement was sustained through the 3rd year of follow-up. The *Student Bodies* intervention significantly reduced the time to onset of eating disorders in students who were overweight and/ or had low-level compensatory behaviors at baseline. This is one of the few studies to show that a clinical disorder can be prevented.

Student Bodies also has been evaluated in high school age female samples (Abascal, Bruning, Winzelberg, Dev, & Taylor, 2004; Bruning-Brown, Winzelberg, Abascal, & Taylor, 2004). Bruning-Brown and colleagues (2004) compared 10th-grade females who completed the psychoeducation course combined with a moderated group with a comparison group of students. Students using the program reported significantly reduced eating restraint and had significantly greater increases in knowledge than did students in the comparison group. However, there were no significant differences at follow-up.

Abascal and colleagues (2004) used the *Student Bodies* intervention to simultaneously provide a universal and a targeted intervention in two studies with over 250 students. Abascal stratified students by their level of risk for developing an eating disorder and motivation to improve their bodies. Students in the same classroom were then assigned to universal and targeted curriculums without the participants' awareness of being assigned to different groups. At the post-intervention assessment, participants who were identified as being higher risk reported significant improvements on measures of weight and shape concerns.

Conclusion and Recommendations

The research to date suggests that self-help approaches for women with eating disorders and those at risk for developing an eating disorder are widely used, feasible to deliver, and effective. Studies conducted in Europe, Canada, and the United States contribute to the generalizability of findings. However, the majority of studies sampled young, white women and recent research shows that eating disorders and body image issues occur across a broader age range and among more ethically diverse groups than once assumed. As noted earlier, most of the studies evaluating self-help approaches employed structured interventions with assistance from either a professional or lay helper. Consequently, our knowledge of the effectiveness of self-help approaches is best defined in terms of assisted self-help. That said, most studies found improvement rates in the range from 20 to 50%. In particular, there is significant empirical evidence that self-help approaches are effective in the treatment of BED.

Because of the lack of standardized outcome measures, we did not calculate effect sizes to compare differences between specific interventions, but the rates of improvement appear to be clinically meaningful. Similarly, there does not appear to be a standardized treatment dosage provided, with ranges between six weekly sessions to 7 months. To date, no studies have examined self-help approaches for the treatment of anorexia nervosa although the seriousness of the disorder may preclude it from being a suitable candidate for self-help treatments. Self-help interventions designed to prevent eating disorders also appear to be beneficial. However, these studies measured disordered eating symptoms and did not follow participants long enough to determine whether they prevent the onset of full syndrome eating disorders.

Dropout rates from eating disorder self-help programs range from 3 (Mitchell et al., 2001) to 70% (Walsh, Fairburn, Mickley, Sysko, & Parides, 2004). One explanation for the wide range in dropout rates is the amount of participant contact with the researchers and treatment assistants. In Mitchell and colleagues' study (2001), for example, participants initially had weekly contact with the treating physician, potentially enhancing compliance. It is unclear, however, how dropout rates reflect compliance with the self-help treatment and compliance rates were rarely reported by researchers in these studies.

To put these finding in perspective, it may be helpful to compare results of self-help interventions with professionally delivered treatments. Professionally delivered interventions, as noted in the introduction, produce a 40–70% recovery rate over the long term. While these rates are similar to those found in short-term self-help interventions, the long-term effects of self-help interventions have not been evaluated. The dropout rates of self-help interventions appear to be comparable to the 11–45% found in professional interventions although there is a wider range of dropout rates reported for self-help interventions.

How should the clinician interpret these findings? The clinician may feel confident recommending these self-help interventions in the first step of a stepped-care approach to treating eating disorders. Some of the self-help interventions, such as Fairburn's (1995) book *Overcoming Binge Eating* are easily accessible. It is important that the clinician maintain some oversight over the patient's treatment, however, to ensure adherence to the self-help protocol and advancement to a more intensive treatment if the self-help approach is not effective. Given the brief nature of most structured interventions, it is likely that follow-up in 2 months is sufficient to determine whether the intervention is helpful. Although unstructured and unmoderated self-help groups for eating disorders are widely available and widely used by women with eating disorders, there does not appear to be sufficient empirical evidence from controlled studies of the effectiveness of these groups to warrant unqualified referral to this treatment. Consequently, the clinician should exercise some caution before referring patients to support groups whether they are delivered face to face or online. It must be noted, however, that there is no evidence that self-help support groups are not effective or potentially harmful but rather that researchers have not addressed this treatment format with significant vigor.

Many important research questions regarding self-help approaches to eating disorders remain unanswered. Most studies employed modest or minimal professional contact and few studies examined pure self-directed psychoeducational interventions or the use of a lay person as a group leader in eating disorder support groups. It is unclear what role professional contact serves as a treatment mediator. Future studies should examine this variable as well as self-help approaches that are more widely available to patients, including the delivery of structured interventions in the format of books, videos, and computer-assisted intervention. The potential for computer-assisted treatments is particularly exciting as preliminary evidence from Bara-Carril and colleagues (2004) suggest that a stand-alone program for the treatment of BN is effective. Work by Zabinski and colleagues

(2001, 2004) and the Stanford University Multi-Media Laboratory indicate that Internet-delivered interventions are readily accepted by women at risk for developing eating disorders and, as noted above, are effective in reducing a range of disordered eating symptoms.

Little is known about the pattern of use of such programs; for example, when and how often participants read the intervention material. Studies that dismantle the intervention components are needed to determine which features are most important. Maintaining the participant's motivation is important to the success of self-help approaches, yet few studies examined factors that might enhance adherence. As a number of researchers note, we need to discover how self-contained and self-directed approaches can maintain motivation and enhance adherence to the intervention protocol and how failure while using a self-help program affects a participant's willingness to seek other assistance. If self-help interventions are going to be useful in a stepped-care approach to care, it is important that program failure does not discourage participants from seeking additional assistance.

Finally, the rapid rise of the Internet in the last decade has created an opportunity for the use of this communication technology in mental health services. How to best use this technology in the treatment of eating disorders, as well as other mental health concerns, remains largely unexamined despite the wide acceptance of this delivery method by patients.

Chapter Points

- Many women have clinical and subclinical levels of eating disorders, but research indicates a large portion of women who want treatment never seek treatment.
- Many women who seek treatment drop out and the number of treated women with clinically significant symptoms is high.
- While many women with eating disorders read self-help books and report high satisfaction, no study has evaluated the effectiveness of such an approach without therapist contact.
- Self-help interventions with some therapist contact have produced consistent improvements in binge eating and purging and less frequent improvements in self-attitudes toward weight and shape.
- Severity of eating problems is related to both selection of therapies other than self-help treatments and poorer outcome.
- Most women with eating disorders are open to various self-administered treatments.
- Therapist-assisted self-help programs are superior to pure self-help for binge-eating disorder.
- Prevention programs are successful for reducing target problems for women at risk for developing eating disorders.

References

Abascal, L., Bruning, J., Winzelberg, A. J., Dev, P., & Taylor, C. B. (2004). Combining universal and targeted prevention for school based eating disorder programs. *International Journal of Eating Disorders, 35*, 1–9.

Agras, S. W., Walsh, B. T., Fairburn, C. G, Wilson, G. T., & Kramer, H. C. (2000). A multicenter comparison of cognitive-behavioral therapy and interpersonal psychotherapy for bulimia nervosa. *Archives of General Psychiatry, 57*, 459–466.

Bacaltchuk, J., Trefiglio, R. P., Oliveira, I. R., Lima, M. S., & Mari, J. J. (1999). Antidepressants versus psychotherapy for bulimia nervosa: A systematic review. *Journal of Clinical Pharmacy and Therapeutics, 24*, 23–31.

Bailer, U., de Zwaan, M., Leisch, F., Strnad, A., Lennkh-Wolfsberg, C., El-Giamal, N., et al. (2004). Guided self-help versus cognitive-behavioral group therapy in the treatment of bulimia nervosa. *International Journal of Eating Disorders, 35*, 522–537.

Bara-Carril, N., Williams, C. J., Pombo-Carril, M. G., Reid, Y., Murray, K., Aubin, S., et al. (2004). A preliminary investigation into the feasibility and efficacy of a CD-ROM-based cognitive-behavioral self-help intervention for bulimia nervosa. *International Journal of Eating Disorders, 35*, 538–548.

Beck, C. (2004). *Anorexia and bulimia for dummies.* Indianapolis, IN: John Wiley and Sons.

Becker, A. E., Thomas, J. J., Franko, D. L., & Herzog, D. B. (2005). Disclosure patterns of eating and weight concerns to clinicians, educational professionals, family, and peers. *International Journal of Eating Disorders, 38*, 18–23.

Beglin, S. J., & Fairburn, C. G. (1992). Evaluation of a new instrument for the detection of eating disorders in community samples. *Psychiatry Research, 44*, 191–201.

Bell, L., & Hodder, L. (2001). An evaluation of a supervised self-help programme for bulimic disorders. *Clinical Psychology and Psychotherapy, 8*, 252–262.

Bruning-Brown, J., Winzelberg, A., Abascal, L., & Taylor, C. B. (2004). An evaluation of an Internet-delivered eating disorder prevention program for adolescents and their parents. *Journal of Adolescent Health, 35*, 290–296.

Bushnell J. A., Wells J. E., Hornblow, A. R., Oakley-Browne, M. A., & Joyce, P. (1990). Prevalence of three bulimia syndromes in the general population. *Psychological Medicine, 20*, 671–680.

Butler, P. E. (1992). *Self-assertion for women.* New York: HarperCollins.

Cachelin, F. M., Rebeck, R., Veisel, C., & Striegel-Moore, R. H. (2001). Barriers to treatment for eating disorders among ethnically diverse women. *International Journal of Eating Disorders, 30*, 269–278.

Cachelin, F. M., & Striegel-Moore, R. H. (2005). Help seeking and barriers to treatment in a community sample of Mexican American and European American women with eating disorders. *International Journal of Eating Disorders, 39*, 154–161.

Carter, J. C., & Fairburn, C. G. (1998). Cognitive-behavioral self-help for binge eating disorder: A controlled effectiveness study. *Journal of Consulting and Clinical Psychology, 66*, 616–623.

Carter, J. C., Olmsted, M. P., Kaplan, A. S., McCabe, R. E., Milles, J. S., & Aime, A. (2003). Self-help for bulimia nervosa: A randomized controlled trial. *American Journal of Psychiatry, 160*, 973–978.

Celio, A., Winzelberg, A., Wilfley, D., Eppstein-Harald, D., Springer, E., Dev, P., et al. (2000). Reducing risk factors for eating disorders: Comparison of an Internet- and a classroom-delivered psychoeducation program. *Journal of Clinical and Consulting Psychology, 68*, 650–657.

Cooper, P. (1995). *Bulimia nervosa and binge eating. A guide to recovery.* London: Robinson.

Cooper, P. J., Coker, S., & Fleming, C. (1994). Self-help for bulimia nervosa: A preliminary report. *International Journal of Eating Disorders, 16*, 401–404.

Cooper, P. J., Coker, S., & Fleming, C. (1996). An evaluation of the efficacy of supervised cognitive behavioral self-help bulimia nervosa. *Journal of Psychosomatic Research, 40*, 281–287.

Dalle Grave, R. (1997). Guided self-help of bulimia nervosa in a specialist setting: A pilot study. *Eating and Weight Disorders, 2*, 169–172.

Drewnowski, A., Yee, D. K., Kurth, C. L., & Krahn, D. D. (1994). Eating pathology and DSM-III-R bulimia nervosa: A continuum of behavior. *American Journal Psychiatry, 151*, 1217–1219.

Durand, M. A., & King, M. (2003). Specialist treatment versus self-help for bulimia nervosa: A randomised controlled trial in general practice. *British Journal of General Practice, 53*, 371–377.

Fairburn, C. G. (1995). *Overcoming binge eating.* New York: Guilford.

Fairburn, C. G. (1998). *Guided self-help for bulimia nervosa. Therapist's manual for use in conjunction with Overcoming Binge Eating.* Unpublished manuscript.

Fairburn, C. G., & Beglin, S. J. (1990). Studies of the epidemiology of bulimia nervosa. *American Journal Psychiatry, 147*, 401–408.

Fairburn, C. G., Cooper, Z., Doll, H. A., Norman, P., & O'Connor, M. (2000). The natural course of bulimia nervosa and binge eating disorder in young women. *Archives of General Psychiatry, 57*, 659–665.

Fairburn, C. G., & Peveler, R. C. (1990). Bulimia nervosa and a stepped care approach to management. *Gut, 31*, 1220–1222.

Garner, D. M., & Needleman, L. D. (1996). Stepped-care and decision-tree models for treating eating disorders. In J. K. Thompson (Ed.), *Body image, eating disorders, and obesity: An integrative guide for assessment and treatment* (pp. 225–252). Washington, DC: American Psychological Association.

Ghaderi, A., & Scott, B. (2003). Pure and guided self-help for full and subthreshold bulimia nervosa and binge eating disorder. *British Journal of Clinical Psychology, 42*, 257–269.

Huon, G. F. (1985). An initial validation of a self-help program for bulimia. *International Journal of Eating Disorders, 4*, 573–588.

Kaminski, P., & McNamara, K. (1996). A treatment for college women at risk for bulimia: A controlled evaluation. *Journal of Counseling and Development, 74*, 288–294.

Keel P. M., & Mitchell, J. E. (1997). Outcome in bulimia nervosa. *American Journal of Psychiatry, 154*, 313–321.

Keel, P. K., Mitchell, J. E., Miller, K. B., Davis, T. L., & Crow, S. J. (1999). Long-term outcome of bulimia nervosa. *Archives of General Psychiatry, 56*, 63–69.

Kjelsas, E., Bjornstrom, C., & Gotestam, K. G. (2004). Prevalence of eating disorders in female and male adolescents (14–15 years). *Eating Behaviors, 5*, 13–25.

Lewinsohn, P. M., Striegel-Moore, R. H., & Seeley, J. R. (2000). Epidemiology and natural course of eating disorders in young women from adolescence to young adulthood. *Journal of the American Academy of Child and Adolescent Psychiatry, 39*, 1284–1292.

Loeb, K. L., Wilson, G. T., Gilbert, J. S., & Labouvie, E. (2000). Guided and unguided self-help for binge eating. *Behavior Research and Therapy, 38*, 259–272.

Low, K. G., Charanasomboon, S., Jones, H., Lesser, J., Reinhalter, K., Martin, R., et al. (2006). Effectiveness of a computer-based interactive eating disorders prevention program at long-term follow-up. *Eating Disorders, 14*, 17–30.

Mitchell, J. E., Fletcher, L., Hanson, K., Mussell, M. P., Seim, H., Crosby, R., et al. (2001). The relative efficacy of fluoxetine and manual-based self-help in the treatment of outpatients with bulimia nervosa. *Journal of Clinical Psychopharmacology, 21*, 298–304.

National Collaborating Centre for Mental Health. (2004). *National clinical practice guideline* (No. CG9). London: The British Psychological Society and the Royal College of Psychiatrists.

Newman, D. (2002). *Loving your body: Embracing your true beauty in Christ.* Carol Stream, IL: Tyndale House Publishers.

Palmer, R. L., Birchall, H., McGrain, L., & Sullivan, V. (2002). Self-help for bulimic disorders: A randomized controlled trial comparing minimal guidance with face-to-face or telephone guidance. *British Journal of Psychiatry, 181*, 230–235.

Rorty, M., Yager, J., & Rossotto, E. (1993). Why and how do women recover from bulimia nervosa: The subjective appraisal of forty women recovered for a year or more. *International Journal of Eating Disorders, 14*, 249–260.

Schmidt, U., Tiller, J., & Treasure, J. (1993). Self-treatment of bulimia nervosa: A pilot study. *International Journal of Eating Disorders, 13*, 273–277.

Schmidt, U., & Treasure, J. (1996). *Getting better bit(e) by bit(e): A survival kit for sufferers of bulimia nervosa and binge eating disorders.* Hove, United Kingdom: Psychology Press.

Taylor, C. B., Bryson, S. W., Luce, K. H., Cunning, D., Celio, A., Abascal, L., et al. (2006). Prevention of eating disorders in at-risk college-age women. *Archives of General Psychiatry, 63*, 881–888.

Thiels, C., Schmidt, U., Treasure, J., & Garthe, R. (2003). Four-year follow-up of guided self-change for bulimia nervosa. *Eating and Weight Disorders, 8*, 212–217.

Thiels, C., Schmidt, U., Treasure, J., Garthe, R., & Troop, M. (1998). Guided self-change for Bulimia Nervosa incorporating use of a self-care manual. *The American Journal of Psychiatry, 155*, 947–953.

Thiels, C., Schmidt, U., Troop, N., Treasure, J., & Garthe, R. (2000). Binge frequency predicts outcome in guided self-care treatment of bulimia nervosa. *European Eating Disorders Review, 8*, 272–278.

Thompson-Brenner, H., Glass, S., & Western, D. (2003). A multidimensional meta-analysis of psychotherapy for bulimia nervosa. *Clinical Psychology: Science and Practice, 10*, 269–287.

Treasure, J., Schmidt, U., Troop, N., Tiller, J., Todd, G., Keilen, M., et al. (1994). First step in managing bulimia nervosa: Controlled trial of therapeutic manual. *BMJ Publishing Group, 308*, 686–689.

Walsh, T. B., Fairburn, D. G., Mickley, D., Sysko, R., & Parides, M. K. (2004). Treatment of bulimia nervosa in a primary care setting. *American Journal Psychiatry, 161,* 556–561.

Wells, A. M., Garvin, V., Dohm, F. A., & Striegel-Moore, R. H. (1997). Telephone-based guided self-help for binge eating disorder: A feasibility study. *International Journal of Eating Disorders, 21,* 341–346.

Williams, C. (2003). New technologies in self-help: Another effective way to get better? *European Eating Disorders Review, 11,* 170–182.

Wilson, G. T., Vitousek, K. M., & Loeb, K. L. (2000). Stepped care treatment for eating disorders. *Journal of Consulting and Clinical Psychology, 68,* 564–572.

Winzelberg, A., Epstein, D., Eldredge, K., Wilfley, D., Dasmahapatra, R., Dev, P., et al. (2000). Effectiveness of an Internet-based program for reducing risk factors for eating disorders. *Journal of Consulting and Clinical Psychology, 68,* 346–350.

Winzelberg, A., Taylor, C. B., Altman, T., Eldredge, K., Dev, P., & Constantinou, P. (1998). Evaluation of a computer-mediated eating disorder prevention program. *International Journal of Eating Disorders, 24,* 339–350.

Yager, J., Landsverk, J., & Edelstein, C. K. (1989). Help seeking and satisfaction with care in 641 women with eating disorders. I. Patterns of utilization, attributed change, and perceived efficacy of treatment. *Journal of Nervous and Mental Disorders, 177,* 632–637.

Zabinski, M., Wilfley, D., Calfas, K., Winzelberg, A., & Taylor, C. B. (2004). An interactive psychological intervention for women at risk of developing an eating disorder. *Journal of Clinical and Consulting Psychology, 72,* 914–919.

Zabinski, M. F., Pung, M. P., Wilfley, D. E., Eppstein, D. L., Winzelberg, A. J., Celio, A., et al. (2001). Reducing risk factors for eating disorders: Targeting at-risk women with a computerized psychoeducational program. *International Journal of Eating Disorders, 29,* 401–408.

Zabinski, M. F., Wilfley, D. E., Fernandez, S., Calfas, K. J., Winzelberg, A. J., & Taylor, C. B. (May 2001). *A synchronous, computerized intervention to reduce body image and disturbed eating concerns among college-aged women: A pilot study.* Paper presented at the annual conference of the Academy for Eating Disorders, Vancouver, Canada.

CHAPTER 9

Self-Help Therapies for Sexual Dysfunctions

JACQUES VAN LANKVELD

Overt sexual behavior of humans is not observable in public as it is in other mammals. Although the promotion and depiction of sexuality by the media has raised general awareness, sexual behavior in the strict sense of genital contact is likely to be covert. Moreover, public displays of sexual behavior often elicit censure, as the example of legal consequences for exhibitionism demonstrates. Similarly, men and women with sexual problems commonly keep them hidden from others. Not only are sexual problems viewed as limiting the opportunity to find and bond with a suitable sexual partner; people who experience such difficulties also fear exposure and humiliation. This fear of exposure generalizes to help-seeking from professional health care workers, to whom sexual problems are revealed in a by-the-way or door-in-hand fashion. Professionals who inquire directly about sexual problems, therefore, are more likely to learn of them than are those who rely on their clients taking the initiative (Bachmann, Leiblum, & Grill, 1989; van Lankveld & van Koeveringe, 2003). This general reluctance of sufferers to openly discuss sexual problems may recommend the use of self-help approaches, as such approaches fit well with privacy concerns. Whether self-help interventions will be accepted by and found helpful to those with sexual dysfunctions, however, will ultimately determine the extent to which they will be adopted.

Although they are not easily revealed, sexual problems appear to be very prevalent in men and women in the community, as prevalence studies have repeatedly shown. The scientific literature on prevalence varies depending on whether one is referring to clinically diagnosable sexual dysfunctions or to sexual problems in general (Heiman, 2002). Defining sexual problems in broad terms typically yields high prevalence rates in the general population (Feldman, Goldstein, Hatzichristou, Krane, & McKinlay, 1994; Laumann, Paik, & Rosen, 1999), while limiting the definition of sexual problems to diagnosable disorders, as defined by the Diagnostic and Statistical Manual of Mental Disorders (DSM-IV-TR) (APA, 2000) or the International Classification of Diseases (ICD-10) (WHO, 2007) yields considerably lower prevalence rates. The diagnoses from the DSM and ICD classification systems typically require the report of distress, associated with a sexual problem, of the sufferer or his or her partner. In a similar vein, studies that limit the prevalence of sexual problems to those sufferers who seek help yield lower estimates than studies that only require the presence of a problem as such. Whereas, for example, Laumann et al. (1999) found lack of interest in sex among men to vary—dependent on age—between 13 and 17% of the population, male hypoactive sexual desire disorder meeting DSM criteria was found to range from 0 to 3% in Simons and Carey's (2001) review. Likewise, trouble maintaining or achieving an erection ranged from 7 to 18% in the Laumann et al. (1999) study but from 0 to 5% in Simons and Carey (2001), who used DSM criteria for erectile disorder. In women, inability to reach orgasm was estimated to range from 22 to 28% in the general population (Laumann et al., 1999), but female orgasmic disorder ranged from 7 to 10% in the Simons and Carey (2001) review.

Advantages and Disadvantages of the Self-Help Approach

As with many other physical and mental problems, self-help approaches for sexual dysfunctions have been pursued throughout human history. Examples include herbal and animal medicines that have been passed on through generations and were believed to enhance male potency and female erotic responsiveness, to delay male ejaculation, or to relieve sexual pain. General models of help-seeking behavior (Dean, 1989; Wills & DePaulo, 1991) have been applied to sexual dysfunctions (Catania et al., 1990). Catania et al. (1990) found a common sequence that individuals used for seeking help for sexual problems in a sample of community respondents. Individuals first utilized self-help approaches, then help from other persons in their informal network, and finally professional help. Across age groups, self-help remedies currently in use include many different types of media resources, such as books, almanacs, and journals.

Such materials were employed by 50–61% of the individuals who reported having sexual problems. Including other, unspecified, self-help methods, 72% of all individuals with sexual problems had tried some form of self-help. Most respondents (80%) who sought help from partners, friends, relatives, clergy, or other informal sources for their sexual problem, and the large majority (88%) of respondents who sought professional help, had employed some type of self-help before moving to remedies typical of later stages in the help-seeking process.

All self-help interventions share potential advantages. Privacy maintenance is more easily secured using self-help approaches. Moreover, improvements in problem status after self-help interventions are more easily attributed to the self-helper's own competence, with a concomitant increase in self-esteem. Autonomy is more easily preserved than in face-to-face therapy, as there is less dependence on a therapist. Moreover, because therapy is delivered in the natural environment, the failure of strategies and their effects to generalize to real-life sexual situations is seldom encountered.

The economic and societal advantages of successful self-help are obvious. "Care made to measure" converges with the governmental health care goal to decrease public health costs as much as possible. All other things remaining equal, successful evidence-based (assisted) self-help strategies would leave more time available for professionals to deliver face-to-face treatment to sufferers of more complex sexual problems.

The potential of self-help treatments for reducing shame and embarrassment attached to revealing sexual problems to a health expert is a major advantage. First, there is the common reluctance of many people to disclose details of their sexual life. Beyond that, individuals who suffer from sexual phobia, or of sexual problems that are associated with feelings of shame or guilt, may find the disclosure of such problems an insurmountable obstacle to seeking out effective professional help.

Possible disadvantages of self-help approaches should also be recognized and understood. Unsuccessful application of self-help strategies may lower the help-seeker's belief in the potential helpfulness of professional sex therapy, even when such approaches have a high effectiveness rate. Incorrect self-diagnosis of problem type may lead the help-seeker to embark on a mission impossible. A man who believes that his erectile problem is fully caused by being out of shape may start a self-help program of fitness training in vain.

It has long been recognized that therapy for sexual problems does not always require major psychotherapy. As early as 1974, Jack Annon launched his PLISSIT model for accessing professional help for sexual problems, which sequences interventions in terms of their comprehensiveness and cost (Annon, 1974). The term is an acronym for P(ermission), L(imited) I(nformation), S(pecific) S(uggestions), and I(intensive) T(reatment). This model advocates matching the type of help provided to the demands of the help-seeker and his or her problem. Increasingly complex and demanding sexual problems are matched with increasingly extensive treatment programs. Many sexual problems, especially when presented for treatment during their early stages, are little more than sexual health concerns and can often be solved with minimal intervention. For instance, giving a woman who is experiencing difficulty having an orgasm permission to masturbate often solves the problem. Other problems require education on sexual anatomy and physiology, on normal ranges of sexual experiences, etc. The next step in the intervention hierarchy involves giving specific suggestions, such as how to employ masturbation techniques, the use of lubricants, specific intercourse positions, or the squeeze technique for premature ejaculation (Masters & Johnson, 1970). Few problems are likely to require prolonged professional help in the form of in-depth analysis of sexual history, processing of childhood experiences, or cognitive restructuring.

Elements in Therapist-Administered Treatments

Modern self-help formats for sexual dysfunctions are typically based on the standard face-to-face therapies for sexual dysfunctions that began with Masters and Johnson's *Human Sexual Inadequacy* (1970). An important aspect of the treatment format they described is called *sensate focus therapy*. Elements include: (a) a relational frame or reference in which sexual problems are diagnosed and treated; (b) a ban on intercourse; (c) a series of sensate focus exercises, used to produce a safe atmosphere, in which partners touch each others' bodies without imposing demands for sexual performance; and (d) a framework of communication between partners who mutually disclose their desires, anxieties, and wishes concerning their sexual interaction. The sensate focus exercises are considered the essential ingredients of this treatment. They enable the couple to create new, positive experiences with sensual touching, enhanced by the nondemanding sensation-focused nature of the exercises. Following are instructions for the nongenital pleasuring exercise that is often given as a first homework assignment (van Lankveld, 2004).

> You can both lie on a soft surface, in the nude if possible. One of you, decide in advance who will be the first in the more active or the more receptive role during this exercise, lies down, backside up. When you take this role of just lying down, you don't have to perform in any sense. It is neither necessary nor required that you experience any

sexual excitement or arousal, or that you come to feel like going on with any sexual behavior. If you do become sexually excited, nevertheless, you do not act upon it in this stage of therapy. It is your privilege now to enjoy receiving your partner's pleasurable touches. If you find anything unpleasant that your partner does, do not hesitate to express this. Try to be both clear and specific, and gentle in your comment. The comment "I find it painful when you knead my shoulders so hard" is better than "can't you watch out what you're doing?" Don't give very specific suggestions to your partner about what you think that you would find most pleasurable at this point. Give your partner a fair opportunity to explore your body and his/her skills in giving you pleasure.

The other partner's task now is to give pleasure. During a certain time—you may start with 5 minutes; you can both keep an eye on time—you touch and caress the backside of your partner's body.

Very important: do not touch the erogenous zones (penis, breasts, vagina, anus)! You should both feel secure that none of you will do so in the course of this exercise.

Touching may be done in different ways. You can stroke very lightly, hardly touching the skin. You can make long, slow strokes, descending in a gentle tempo from the head, via the neck, the shoulders, the back and the buttocks to legs and feet and return to the head again in the opposite sequence. You might jump from one part of the body to another, skipping certain parts. You can touch in a massaging way. You can vary the tempo, from flashing to slow and languid. Search your entire behavioral repertoire. Don't hesitate to touch your partner's body in ways that you have never tried before. If a certain way of touching is not pleasurable, it is the receiving partner's responsibility to signal this. The exercise is not intended to make your partner sexually aroused or to give an orgasm.

Try to shape a clear sensual map of your partner's body in your head in the course of doing this exercise several times.

Besides your hands you can use your lips, your nose, your cheeks or your hair to touch and caress.

When the agreed upon time has passed, you change roles and places. The recipient now becomes the active participant; the active one may now receive. The tasks in both roles remain the same in this second part of the exercise.

After finishing the second part, you may repeat the exercise, now while lying on your back, so that your partner may caress the front side of your body. Keep to the same duration of the phases, and remember: no touching of the erogenous zones! (pp. 94–95)

Some treatment elements of self-help approaches for sexual dysfunctions are based on cognitive–behavioral therapy. The effectiveness of cognitive–behavioral therapies has been established for several types of sexual dysfunctions in controlled trials. Using the criteria of the American Psychological Association's Task Force (1995) for determining *well-established* and *probably efficacious* treatments for sexual dysfunctions, Heiman and Meston (1997) and Heiman (2002) argued that "well-established" treatments were shown to exist for primary anorgasmia in women (directed masturbation exercises), erectile dysfunction (systematic desensitization), and premature ejaculation (gradual approximation of ejaculatory delay using stop–start exercises or the squeeze technique). In addition, a combination of psychoeducation, sex therapy including sexual skills training and communication between partners, and directed masturbation training was suggested to be a "probably efficacious" treatment for secondary female anorgasmia. For other sexual dysfunctions, including vaginismus, dyspareunia, delayed male orgasm, and the sexual desire disorders, empirical support for cognitive–behavioral therapy (CBT) approaches was insufficient or poor (Heiman & Meston, 1997). Trudel and coworkers (Trudel et al., 2001) only recently published the first evidence for the efficacy of CBT for sexual desire disorder in women. Couples attended a group program of 12 weekly, two-hour sessions with four to six couples per group with male and female therapist teams to guide the groups. Participants were asked to complete homework assignments and to read a treatment manual. The interventions comprised cognitive restructuring and graded exercises of mutual pleasurable touching by partners. From 1998 onward, a new impetus to the treatment of male erectile dysfunction was given by the introduction of phosphodiesterase-5 inhibitors such as sildenafil citrate (Goldstein et al., 1998) and dopamine agonists such as apomorphine (Heaton, 2000).

Therapist-administered sex therapy has, to a considerable extent, relied on self-help strategies since its emergence in the 1970s. In contrast to the treatment of other psychological disorders and couples problems, the core elements of therapeutic change in sex therapy have usually been performed in the privacy of the couples' homes. Unlike treatment procedures for these problems that could be performed in the therapist's office or together with the therapist in a natural setting, many of the behavioral prescriptions for sexual dysfunctions have never been performed in the therapist's office. The exception to this rule was the doctor-sexologist or gynecologist who assisted the female patient in the treatment of vaginismus through the vaginal insertion of dilators. The use of professionals within the sexual setting was more commonly practiced during the first decade after Masters and Johnson's (1970) pioneering work. The current practice of relying on the client to perform homework assignments, unmonitored by a therapist, limits the therapist's ability to observe how the exercises are performed. To a large extent, sex therapists rely on self-report from patients and their partners as to what goes on in the privacy of their home. Moreover, the therapist's provision of feedback and reinforcement is necessarily noncontingent, and self-reinforcement plays a far larger role than when behavioral or emotional problems are the intervention target.

Little is know regarding the differential contribution of therapist and client variables to the outcome of face-to-face therapies for sexual dysfunctions. Some dismantling studies were conducted in which the contributions of nonspecific treatment factors were examined (for reviews, see Hawton, 1995; Heiman & Meston, 1997; Rosen & Leiblum, 1995). In fact, some light was shed on the contribution of therapists' efforts and characteristics and of the working alliance between therapist and client in studies of the treatment of sexual dysfunctions comparing standard therapist-delivered treatment with self-help therapy formats. For instance, no differences were found between a bibliotherapy and a group therapy format in the treatment of women with lifelong anorgasmia (Mathews et al., 1976) or between teams of female and male cotherapists or a single therapist (see Hawton, 1995).

Types of Self-Help for Sexual Dysfunctions

Self-help interventions for sexual dysfunctions can be grouped by type of venue and further examined by amount of therapist contact. Bibliotherapy, video therapy, and computer-assisted sex therapy can be conducted with little or no therapist involvement using a program installed on a home computer. Telephone therapy, conducted by itself or as an adjuvant to bibliotherapy or video therapy, and Internet therapy using e-mail communication, requires some therapist involvement. These different venues for delivering self-help treatments are described in the following paragraphs and their effectiveness is evaluated from the available empirical research. Table 9.1 presents an overview of various studies.

Bibliotherapy

Bibliotherapy refers to the self-help approach in which written material is used to present information or describe and prescribe change techniques that resemble those used in face-to-face therapy. The written material used in bibliotherapy for sexual dysfunctions is based on methods developed by Masters and Johnson (1970) and Maultsby (1975; see also Hawton, 1995; Leiblum & Rosen, 2000, for reviews). Self-help manuals in this field, commercially available in the English language, were written by Barbach (1974),

Table 9.1 Overview of Outcome Studies of Bibliotherapy for Sexual Dysfunction

Study	N	Type of sexual dysfunction	Subject characteristics	Bibliotherapy characteristics	Comparison conditions	Outcome
Lowe & M Mikulas, 1975	10	Premature ejaculation	Mixed sample	Manual + twice-weekly telephone support: sensate focus therapy, squeeze technique	1. Minimal-contact BT 2. WL	Increase in ejaculation latency in minimal-contact BT; no increase in WL group
Mathews et al., 1976	36	Various dysfunctions	Outpatients	Manual: sensate focus therapy	1. Systematic desensitization 2. Standard sex therapy 3. Minimal-contact BT	All groups increased in general and sexual satisfaction and sexual adjustment; no difference between treatments found
Heinrich, 1976	44	Preorgasmia	Mixed sample	Manual + one session: directed masturbation training	1. BT 2. Group therapy 3. WL	All group participants became orgasmic; more than half of BT participants became orgasmic; BT not significantly better than WL
Zeiss & Zeiss, 1978	18	Premature ejaculation	Mixed sample	Manual: sensate focus therapy, squeeze- and pause-technique	1. No-contact BT 2. Minimal-contact BT 3. Standard couples sex therapy	Increase in ejaculation latency in standard therapy and minimal-contact BT; no increase in no-contact BT

Study	N	Dysfunction	Sample	Intervention	Conditions	Results
McMullen & Rosen, 1979	60	Preorgasmia	Recruited participants	Video: behavioral modeling; mastery learning manual: instructions equivalent with videotape content	1. Videotape modeling 2. BT 3. WL	60% of treated participants became orgasmic; no difference between videotape modeling and BT
Dodge et al., 1982	13	Orgasmic dysfunction	Recruited participants	Manual: directed masturbation training	1. Minimal-contact BT 2. WL	Increase in orgasm during intercourse but not masturbation in treated group; no change in control group; results maintained at 6-week follow-up
Hahn, 1982	60	Orgasmic dysfunction	Mixed sample	Manual: directed masturbation training	1. Minimal-contact BT 2. Minimal-contact BT + film 3. Minimal-contact BT + film + vicarious learning 4. Standard sex therapy	No difference in percentage orgasmic during masturbation between conditions at posttreatment
Dow, 1983	48	Various dysfunctions	Outpatients	Manual + weekly telephone support: sensate focus therapy	1. BT 2. Standard couples sex therapy	Frequency of pleasurable intercourse higher after BT, compared with standard sex therapy

Note. *Mixed sample:* Includes outpatients and recruited participants; BT = bibliotherapy; WL = waiting list.

(continued)

Table 9.1 (continued)

Study	N	Type of sexual dysfunction	Subject characteristics	Bibliotherapy characteristics	Comparison conditions	Outcome
Libman et al., 1984	23	Secondary orgasmic dysfunction	Recruited participants	Manual: directed masturbation training	1. Minimal-contact BT 2. Standard couples sex therapy 3. Group format sex therapy	All participants increased in orgasmic capacity during masturbation (65% posttreatment; 77% follow-up) and manual and oral partner stimulation (33% posttreatment; 27% follow-up); couples therapy and BT superior to group therapy in percentage orgasmic by manual partner stimulation
Morokoff & LoPiccolo, 1986	43	Preorgasmia	Outpatients	Manual + 4 therapy sessions: directed masturbation training	1. 4-Session minimal-contact BT 2. 15-Session standard couples sex therapy	75% of BT participants orgasmic at posttreatment; 43% of standard therapy participants orgasmic at posttreatment; no loss of gains at 3-month follow-up
Trudel & Proulx, 1987	25	Premature ejaculation	Recruited participants	Manual + weekly telephone contact in minimal-contact BT: sensate focus therapy, squeeze-and-pause technique	1. No contact BT 2. Minimal-contact BT 3. Standard couples sex therapy 4. WL	All treated groups showed increase in ejaculation latency; no change noted in control group; no decrease at follow-up was found

Trudel & Laurin, 1988	17	Orgasmic dysfunction	Recruited participants	Manual + weekly telephone support: directed masturbation training	1. BT 2. WL	No change in orgasmic response; BT > increase of sexual arousability, sexual satisfaction, and sexual repertoire
van Lankveld et al., 2001	199	Various dysfunctions	Mixed sample	Manual + two weekly telephone support: sensate focus therapy + cognitive restructuring	1. Minimal-contact BT 2. WL	Compared to WL, treated participants had lower complaints of low frequency of sexual interaction, general improvement of sexual problem, lower male posttreatment ratings of problem-associated distress. Less vaginistic symptoms in women with vaginismus; increased vaginistic symptoms in women with dyspareunia

Note. Mixed sample: Includes outpatients and recruited participants; BT = bibliotherapy; WL = waiting list.

Heiman, LoPiccolo, and LoPiccolo (1976), and Zeiss and Zeiss (1978). Slob and Vink (2002), Hengeveld (1994), and van Lankveld (1993, 2004) have written similar manuals in the Dutch language. Bibliotherapy is often applied within self-help formats with minimal or no therapist contact but has also been applied as an adjuvant to therapist-administered treatments (Gillan, Golombok, & Becker, 1980; Halvorsen & Metz, 1992; McCarthy, 1984, 1989). Although these manuals vary in several respects, all share an emphasis on behavioral strategies that agree with the Masters and Johnson (1970) approach of the couple-based directed practice. When the sexual problems are experienced by men and women who are in a steady relationship, the focus of change is on the couple, with the exception of the directed masturbation practice for anorgasmia. The treatment is learning oriented and stipulates gradual exposure to problematic aspects of sexual functioning. In the more recent manuals, a stronger emphasis is placed on the cognitive restructuring of negative and sexually dysfunctional beliefs and cognitions.

The effectiveness of bibliotherapy treatments for sexual dysfunctions has been evaluated in controlled treatment studies. Gould and Clum (1993) conducted a meta-analysis of 40 self-help studies for a variety of emotional problems. They reported that bibliotherapy for sexual dysfunctions had one of the largest mean effect sizes (ES = 1.86), compared with an average ES of .76 for all target problems. This finding, however, rested on a single study (Dodge, Glasgow, & O'Neill, 1982). The authors noted that published studies on bibliotherapy for sexual dysfunctions generally failed to include adequate numbers of participants, to control for threats to internal validity by incorporating some form of control condition, and to assign participants randomly to treatment and control groups. Researchers also failed to employ valid assessment measures, to collect adequate follow-up data, or to elaborate on statistical analyses. Bibliotherapy for sexual dysfunctions also produced the highest effect size (ES = 1.28) of all targeted problems in Marr's (1995) meta-analysis of self-help interventions. This ES was based on 4 studies, all of which were published in major journals and compares to an average ES of 0.565 for all 70 studies evaluated in Marr's review. A more recent and thorough meta-analysis by van Lankveld (1998) examined 12 controlled bibliotherapy studies aimed specifically at the treatment of sexual dysfunctions. This review reported a mean ES of 0.68 at posttreatment (0.50 when weighted for sample size), which is considerably smaller than prior estimates. Furthermore, the posttreatment effect had largely eroded at follow-up. The included studies were largely limited to treatments for orgasmic disorders, both in men and women. It is remarkable that the more recent meta-analyses found lower average effect sizes of the effects of bibliotherapy for sexual dysfunctions as they included increasingly larger numbers of studies. Also, studies using fewer individuals tended to show larger mean ESs (van Lankveld, 1998) than those examining larger numbers of individuals. If more confidence can be put in larger studies, then the treatment effect from bibliotherapy interventions is likely lower than initially thought.

More recently, a large study in this field was conducted in The Netherlands (van Lankveld, Everaerd, & Grotjohann, 2001). In a randomized controlled clinical trial, CBT, based on sensate focus therapy and rational-emotive therapy, was compared to a wait-list control in a sample of 199 heterosexual couples. Participants in the treatment group received a manual (van Lankveld, 1993) and limited therapeutic assistance by telephone. After a 10-week treatment period, participants reported improvement in frequency of sexual interaction, general improvement of their sexual problem, and lower posttreatment ratings of problem-associated distress (males only). Gains with respect to the frequency of sex and problem-associated distress had mostly eroded at follow-up. Female participants with vaginismus reported fewer complaints posttreatment and at follow-up. However, female participants with dyspareunia reported more complaints at the termination of treatment, an effect that continued through follow-up. Compliance varied widely. Estimated time reading the manual varied from 0 to 40 (M = 5.4) hours for male and from 0 to 30 hours (M = 6.1) for female participants. The number of completed rational-emotive self-analyses ranged from 0 to 35 (M = 1.2) for male and 0 to 20 (M = 1.1) for female participants. The number of different sensate focus exercises used during treatment ranged from 0 to 6 (M = 1) for male and 0 to 6 (M = 1.2) for female participants. The total number of times individuals performed these exercises ranged from 0 to 40 (M = 5.1) for male participants and from 0 to 40 (M = 4.3) for female participants. Treatment compliance as perceived by both partners was positively associated with outcome at posttreatment and follow-up. Male participants making more efforts to solve the sexual problem, as rated by their partner, showed stronger posttreatment effects. Female participants also showed stronger posttreatment effects with better compliance. Women whose partners rated their effort as more substantial, who completed more rational-emotive self-analyses, and who initiated therapist support by telephone more often were found to have made larger gains at posttreatment. These factors, however, did not predict women's treatment response at follow-up assessment. In sum, results of this study were that bibliotherapy resulted in improvement of self-reported sexual functioning in men and women with various sexual dysfunctions that diminished, however, at follow-up assessment.

The efficacy of bibliotherapy has been evaluated by comparing individuals who receive treatment with those who either do not receive treatment or who receive a psychological placebo. Dodge et al. (1982), for example, compared a minimal-contact bibliotherapy condition with a delayed-treatment information control condition in women with either primary or secondary anorgasmia. Treated women were significantly more often orgasmic during sexual intercourse after treatment than controls. The gains were found sustained at follow-up assessment.

Several studies were found that compared bibliotherapy plus support via contact with a psychotherapist to bibliotherapy alone. When data from these studies were combined in a meta-analysis (van Lankveld, 1998), bibliotherapy with minimal therapist support appeared to do better than totally self-administered bibliotherapy, but this difference reached only borderline statistical significance.

The issue of whether self-administered treatments are cost-effective can be addressed by comparing self-help approaches with standard therapist-directed treatments. If both treatment types are equally effective, self-administered treatments are more cost-effective as they incur lower costs for individuals compared with therapist-delivered treatment. Several studies of this type exist for the treatment of sexual dysfunctions. One such study was conducted by Mathews et al. (1976). This study evaluated the contributions to treatment outcome of the directed practice and counseling elements of Masters and Johnson's (1970) therapy model for sexual dysfunctions. The directed practice element in this model specifies the behavior that individuals are supposed to engage in to improve their sexual functioning. Specific and detailed suggestions are provided for behavioral exercises; for instance, to enhance clitoral stimulation for women with anorgasmia or the stop–start exercises for men with premature ejaculation. The counseling element refers to the face-to-face situation of clients and therapists in which sexual history-taking and discussion and evaluation of behavioral assignments takes place. Thirty-six couples entered the study with various sexual difficulties. With the gender of the main complainant balanced across treatments and therapists, couples were randomly assigned to three treatment formats—systematic desensitization plus counseling, directed practice plus counseling, or directed practice with minimal therapist contact. Treatment consisted of 10 weekly therapy sessions, except for the minimal contact condition. This latter condition consisted of weekly exchange of letters plus four contacts at the start, a mid-treatment session, and a concluding session. No significant differences emerged between treatment formats on any of the outcome ratings. The results imply, among others, that the face-to-face counseling element is not superior to a minimal-contact self-help treatment, and that the self-help format is to be recommended because of its better cost-effectiveness ratio.

The question of whether self-help treatments are equivalent to therapist-directed treatments was addressed in a recent meta-analytic review (van Lankveld, Wylie, & Hunot, in press). Seven studies were identified that compared self-help treatments to therapist-directed treatments. For men with premature ejaculation, no difference on any outcome measures was found between minimal-contact bibliotherapy and standard sex therapy. In women with orgasmic disorder, the percentage of preorgasmic female participants having become orgasmic after treatment, unspecified for situation (with partner or during masturbation), was smaller in minimal-contact bibliotherapy when compared to standard sex therapy (Hahn, 1981; Heinrich, 1976). However, Morokoff and LoPiccolo (1986) examined the ability of women to have orgasms after treatment in several different sexual stimulus situations. These authors reported that a higher percentage of participants became orgasmic with minimal-contact bibliotherapy than with standard sex therapy while masturbating, while masturbating with a vibrator, when with a partner during intercourse, and when with a partner while using a vibrator. Self-reported physical sensations consistent with orgasm were greater after minimal-contact bibliotherapy than after standard sex therapy (Hahn, 1981). No difference was found with regard to orgasmic capacity with noncoital partner contact. Sexual attitudes and beliefs were also not significantly different before and after treatment when minimal-contact bibliotherapy and standard sex therapy were compared.

In a mixed sample of men and women with various sexual dysfunctions, Mathews et al. (1976) reported that frequency of intercourse was lower after minimal-contact bibliotherapy as compared to standard sex therapy. However, in another sample of men and women with various sexual dysfunctions (Dow, 1983), frequency of pleasurable intercourse was higher after minimal-contact bibliotherapy, compared with standard sex therapy. Seventeen other outcome measures in these and other samples and studies were not significantly different between minimal-contact bibliotherapy and standard sex therapy.

When these comparisons of bibliotherapy and standard sex therapy were aggregated across studies, neither approach emerged as consistently superior to the other. Rather, bibliotherapy was superior to standard therapy with some types of sexual dysfunction, whereas standard treatment was superior with other types. With some sexual dysfunctions, therefore, bibliotherapy seems warranted as the treatment of first choice in a stepped-care model. Intensive treatment may be pursued after self-help is found to yield insufficient progress.

In sum, a number of comparative studies have been published that assess the efficacy of several variants of bibliotherapy for male and female sexual dysfunctions. Although studies in the first decades of research in this area mainly focused on orgasmic disorders, more recent investigations included other dysfunction types as well. The efficacy of bibliotherapy in this field generally compares favorably with no treatment comparison groups when assessed immediately after the treatment/study period. Loss of gains after treatment termination is reported in many cases when follow-up data are considered. Bibliotherapy with some support by a therapist, even if modest, appears to yield better results than fully unassisted self-help. Such support can be provided by telephone, by mail, or in face-to-face contact. The impact of assessment-related bias on these results remains to be examined in future research designs. The outcome data as described warrant the use of a number of self-help manuals for sexual dysfunction that are commercially available in the English language (Barbach, 1974; Heiman et al., 1976; Zeiss & Zeiss, 1978) and in Dutch (van Lankveld, 2004).

Video Therapy

When compared with bibliotherapy, video therapy relies more heavily on the principles of observational or "vicarious" learning. Using videos, the sexually dysfunctional individual or couple watches, for instance, another individual or couple perform sensate focus exercises or directed masturbation for orgasmic disorder. Although spoken information on the video usually covers the same topics as in bibliotherapy or in face-to-face treatment, the emphasis in video therapy is on observing the visual behavioral example first and then reproducing it in the participants' personal situation afterwards.

Video therapy for sexual dysfunctions has, in most cases, consisted of demonstrating the process of sensate focus therapy. In addition, the tapes often provide psychoeducational information on human sexuality (Hahn, 1981; Jankovich & Miller, 1978), as well as elements of cognitive therapy. Typical of such videos is a Dutch-language series made in the early 1990s, in which female and male sex therapists provided information on different aspects of sexual functioning (Liekens & Drenth, 1990), accompanied by a discussion of myths and erroneous beliefs surrounding that aspect of sexual life. Discussions of the rational and irrational aspects of those cognitions and suggestions of alternative beliefs and the use of self-instructions stimulated cognitive restructuring. Further behavioral exercises from sensate focus therapy could then be approached with the aid of more helpful beliefs.

Four studies examining the effectiveness of video therapy were found (Hahn, 1981; Jankovich & Miller, 1978; McMullen & Rosen, 1979; Wincze & Caird, 1976). McMullen & Rosen (1979) compared written instructions and videotape modeling to a wait-list control condition in a study of 60 preorgasmic women using a minimal therapist contact format. Subjects in the videotape condition received a series of 20-minute videotape sequences in which a coping model was utilized. An actress portrayed a preorgasmic woman who learns to stimulate herself to orgasm and to transfer this newly acquired ability to sexual interaction with a partner. The bibliotherapy condition contained written excerpts of the videotaped sequences with an equivalent content. Treatment duration was 6 weeks, during which participants in both conditions paid weekly visits to the treatment center, where the video was shown and the written material was read outside the presence of a therapist. Subjects in both conditions were supplied with a vibrator during the 4th week of treatment. Contact time with a therapist in both conditions was limited to the initial screening session. During the treatment program, 24 of 40 women in the treatment groups became orgasmic, as assessed by questionnaires and structured clinical interviews. None of the women in the control group became orgasmic. No difference was found between the video modeling and bibliotherapy conditions, in spite of the additional benefit of observational learning through the videotape model. Closer examination of responders and nonresponders revealed that responders had spent more time doing homework and reported a larger repertory of sexual behaviors prior to treatment. At one-year follow-up four more married women in the treatment conditions had become orgasmic and no relapse or worsening of problems was reported.

In an uncontrolled study by Jankovich and Miller (1978), 7 of 17 women (19 to 38 years of age) with primary orgasmic dysfunction achieved orgasm within a week after viewing an audiovisual sex education program, while no other interventions (educational, behavioral, or psychotherapeutic) were included.

Hahn (1981) reported a randomized controlled trial with 60 female patients (M = 35 years) with primary or secondary orgasmic dysfunction. Participants, who were recruited through advertisements in local newspapers, were randomly allocated to one of four treatments: (a) direct treatment in a therapist-administered format, including the use of a treatment manual and a modeling video (standard sex therapy + video); (b) vicarious treatment, with no direct interventions by a therapist—interventions were shown by means of videotaped sessions of the first treatment condition, a modeling video, and treatment manual (minimal-contact bibliotherapy + vicarious learning using video recordings); (c) a variation on (b) with repeated presentation of the modeling video but not the videotaped sessions of the first treatment condition (video therapy only); and (d) self-administered video/bibliotherapy without direct therapist interventions, including use of a treatment manual and a modeling video. Each treatment group met for 1 to 1½ hours once a week. Duration of the treatment was 5 weeks. Outcome was measured by percentage of women orgasmic at posttreatment, scores on the Sexual Attitudes and Beliefs scale, and on a Physiological Response Inventory. Compared with standard sex therapy combined with videotape modeling, minimal contact bibliotherapy combined with videotape modeling resulted in a greater increase of the sensations of genital sexual arousal. Most participants in both treatments had become orgasmic by the end of treatment, but no difference was found with respect to percentage of participants becoming orgasmic between treatments.

Wincze and Caird (1976) treated 21 women complaining of essential sexual dysfunction using either systematic or video desensitization. In a crossover design, seven women experienced a no treatment control phase before receiving therapy. Video therapy was more effective than systematic desensitization, and both desensitization procedures resulted in significant reductions in heterosexual anxiety compared to participants in the no treatment control group. Approximately 25% of the nonorgasmic women were orgasmic at the conclusion of the study.

Video therapy, in sum, has only been investigated in the treatment of female orgasmic disorder and appears to yield positive results. Comparison with other self-help methods (bibliotherapy) produced no advantages of one over the other (Hahn, 1981). Video methods that cover a broader range of sexual dysfunctions (e.g., Liekens & Drenth, 1990) have not been empirically tested. To date there have been no research efforts to identify client characteristics that predict who responds to different self-help therapy formats.

Computer-Assisted Sex Therapy

This type of self-help for sexual disorders represents the low extreme of the therapist involvement dimension of sex therapy. No or very little contact with a human therapist is required for the administration of inventions through a computerized system. Limited contact is needed when such a system is made available within a standard health care context in order to match the type of help required with the available computerized services. No contact at all may be needed when computerized sex therapy is made available through the Internet. Although it has not been introduced yet, it is conceivable that help-seekers access such systems through the Internet, make use of it, and terminate their participation without any interference by a human health care provider.

Binik, Servan-Schreiber, Freiwald and Hall (1988) developed a rule-based expert system, *Sexpert*, for computerized psychotherapy that could assess and treat female and male orgasmic dysfunction. They based their system on developments in the areas of artificial intelligence, intelligent tutoring systems, and cognitive therapy in the early 1980s. This approach combined the capacity for intelligent therapeutic dialogue with the presentation of individualized therapeutic interventions. The authors describe *Sexpert* as follows:

Like a sex therapist, *Sexpert* prefers dealing with couples although it will interact with individuals. Both members of the couple are seated in front of a microcomputer and answer multiple-choice, yes/no, and quantitative questions that are addressed to one or the other. The first session lasts approximately 1 hour and focuses on potential problem areas of their sexual, marital, and general functioning. The program attempts to identify sexual dysfunctions and informs the couple about what it has found. When dysfunctions are present, the session continues with an attempt to place the dysfunctions in their proper context. Possible causes or maintaining factors are sought and the influence of the dysfunction on sexual and on nonsexual aspects of the relationship are investigated and discussed with the couple. At the end of this session, *Sexpert* may recommend an individualized treatment program, which the couple is free to accept, to refuse, or, in some cases, to modify. (p. 391)

In the diagnostic module, the first step is "the identification of a problem or misconception from a set of questions asked of the partners" (Servan-Schreiber & Binik, 1989, p. 245; see also Binik et al., 1998). The second step involves the identification of what are called *bugs* or underlying cognitive misconceptions. This is accomplished by asking the couple to endorse their agreement with a large set of propositions representing misconceptions about sexuality, collected by the authors from both the literature and clinical experts. These propositions were grouped into categories of misinformation, poor cognitive strategies, and mislabeling or false expectations. *Sexpert* is able to integrate the endorsement of specific types of misinformation into more abstract misconceptions.

In the dialogue driver, therapeutic dialogues are simulated based on dialogue plans that follow the common logic of therapist–client conversations about particular topics ranging from general specifications of the structure of a session, to very detailed ordering of particular questions about sexual attitudes.

These dialogue plans are grouped in hierarchies in which each level successively refines the actions of the system. Only abstract specifications of the topic to be discussed are implemented at the top level, while an intermediate level specifies the issues to be raised and their order, while the lowest level determines the exact order and content of questions or explanations to be presented for each issue. (Servan-Schreiber & Binik, 1989, p. 248).

In the coaching-treatment module, *Sexpert* may recommend treatment once a sexual dysfunction is identified. The treatment plans are based on standard sex therapy, but the homework to be done and the choices of which treatment plan to offer are individually determined by the program. We quote from the article of Binik et al. (1988):

> This is possible because a wealth of information is already available at the first stage of therapy based on the assessment, and new information is accumulated and integrated at each stage of therapy. For example, a woman who can reach orgasm regularly during masturbation but is having difficulty experiencing orgasm frequently with her partner would not be asked to carry out individual assignments. In order to determine the exact nature of their couple assignment, *Sexpert* attempts to integrate information it had already collected concerning the couple's sexual communication, repertoire, and overall relationship. Perhaps even more important is that *Sexpert* will attempt to monitor treatment progress and tries to infer the reasons for a couple's failure to complete or succeed at an exercise. (pp. 255–256)

Consider the following dialogue (Binik et al., 1988):

Sexpert: Were you able to carry out the touching exercises (sensate focus) at least three times since I last saw you?
Client: No.
Sexpert: How many times were you able to carry them out?
Client: 0.
Sexpert: I see. I hope this was an unusual week. Let me try to pin down some of the difficulties you might have had. Was the assignment clear?
Client: Yes.
Sexpert: Were there any particular parts of the assignment that either or both of you found difficult?
Client: Yes.
Sexpert: Did it have to do with initiating the exercise?
Client: Yes.
Sexpert: Was the problem
a. who should initiate
b. the manner of initiating
c. both
d. neither.
Client: b.
Sexpert: I'm a little surprised to hear this since you hadn't mentioned initiation difficulties before starting treatment. Perhaps the homework assignment is very different for you than regular sex. Let me try to give you some ideas on how to get going... (pp. 255–256)

Sexpert also has a built-in stopping device. If it fails to discover the reason for a couple's lack of progress, the program will admit that it does not know how to proceed and then encourage the couple to go on a trouble-shooting expedition by themselves or to seek professional help.

A pilot study to investigate user acceptance involved 15 patient and non-patient couples. All participants viewed the dialogue with *Sexpert* to be logical, appropriate, and intelligent. Participants did not have complaints regarding the length of the session or the amount of text to be read. In a follow-up experimental study (Binik, Westbury, & Servan-Schreiber, 1989), individuals interacting with *Sexpert* for 20 minutes showed positive shifts in their attitudes toward computerized sex therapy, compared with subjects receiving identical assessment but who interacted with a non-sex–related computer program and who completed a sex-related questionnaire with questions almost identical to those asked by *Sexpert*.

Although the preliminary results of this intelligent tutoring system appeared very promising, its development was halted. An important factor may have been the proliferation of the computer program that was launched before the era of Internet had started (Y. M. Binik, personal communication, June 16, 2003). A new effort to implement and research such computer-based self-help methods, given the opportunities provided by the widespread availability of Internet, might well prove successful. In addition to written text, educational videos might be included.

Sex Therapy Through the Internet

Although not a pure self-help method, therapist-administered sex therapy, delivered through the Internet, shares many features with other self-help formats. Like bibliotherapy and video therapy, the client and therapist are not in face-to-face contact. It also requires limited time investment of both help-seeker and therapist and eliminates transportation time and costs.

Interactive Internet sex therapy may be delivered in a synchronous manner by establishing on-line contact through some Web-based communication system or in an asynchronous manner by relying on e-mail contact.

Many sex therapists have built their own Internet Web sites. These sites are easily tracked with the help of a Web search engine. The service they provide is often limited to a therapist responding to questions posted by clients. In principle, however, a longer lasting therapeutic contact with repeated exchanges of messages could be established, with all the advantages of wide spatial availability and the possibility of temporal asynchronicity. Hall (2004) published the first account of on-line sex therapy. The article describes her experiences with 9 clients who participated in a pilot study of an on-line task-based approach. Hall concluded that on-line work was a viable alternative to face-to-face therapy and stressed that the anonymity provided made on-line therapy a preferable option. Of 12 individuals who contacted the site, 9 were male and 3 were female. Six of 7 individuals who were sent a sexual history form completed the assessment. Of the participants who were allowed to choose between e-mail and real-time chat contact, 6 chose e-mail and one chose chat contact. Eight participants received sex therapy through the Internet. Five participants who finished the on-line therapy completed evaluation questionnaires. Of 8 treated participants who were asked about the resolution of their specific sexual problem, 2 said it was significantly improved, 3 said it was much improved, 2 said it had slightly improved, and one person reported no change. All participants reported improvement in other areas.

van Lankveld, Leusink, van Diest, Slob, and Gijs (2004) recently conducted a pilot study to gauge the possible efficacy of sex therapy through the Internet for heterosexual men with sexual dysfunctions. A relatively homogeneous sample was investigated, from which men with hypersexuality and problems with gender identity or sexual orientation were excluded, as were men with depressive symptoms, psychotic comorbidity, substance abuse disorder, and major marital problems. The study had a pre-post participants-as-own-control design. After completing a Web-based questionnaire, participants were offered 3 months of sex therapy with e-mail contact only. Three experienced therapists provided treatment. Treatment followed a cognitive–behavioral approach and included sensate focus exercises and cognitive restructuring. Of 81 applicants, 39 were enrolled in treatment. Of this group, 8 men never started therapeutic contacts, 10 started therapy until they or the therapist considered treatment completed but did not answer the posttreatment Web-based questionnaire, 21 men completed posttreatment measures, and 15 of them responded to the follow-up assessment one month after treatment termination. About half of the participants had erectile dysfunction, 25% had premature ejaculation, and the remaining participants had various problems such as sexual phobia, anorgasmia, etc. At posttreatment, 66% of the participants indicated that their sexual problem was improved or much improved, 30% reported that it had stayed the same, and the problem of one participant had become worse. At follow-up, 7 of 15 participants indicated that their sexual problem was improved or much improved after treatment termination, while 8 reported it had remained the same. These global evaluations of treatment outcome were corroborated by changes between pre- and posttreatment scores on three psychometrically validated measures of sexual and marital functioning.

Interesting questions are whether sex therapy through the Internet leads to the development of some form of working alliance between client and therapist and whether development of a working alliance mediates therapy outcome. When asked in an open-ended e-mail, 12 of 13 participants reported that they had a sense of confidentiality and that the therapist was highly empathic. All reported that they felt free to pose any questions or discuss any topic that arose in the course of therapy. The average therapist time spent per treated participant was approximately 4 hours.

Although controlled research is still lacking of the effectiveness of Internet-based sex therapy, preliminary data suggests that such treatment is a viable and possibly efficacious approach. Most of the sexually dysfunctional individuals treated thus far were males. It remains to be seen whether this reflects a gender difference regarding the willingness to reveal intimate details of sexual life to an anonymous therapist.

Conclusion

The self-help approach to sexual problems has been the subject of a considerable number of empirical investigations. Bibliotherapy, video therapy, computerized sex therapy, and individualized sex therapy through the Internet were documented. The evidence needed to warrant broad applications of these approaches, however, is still scarce and fragmented. Bibliotherapy in various formats has been the venue most thoroughly researched. The results of bibliotherapy compared favorably with no treatment alternatives, although gains that were reported immediately after treatment tended to diminish at follow-up. Differences between bibliotherapy and standard forms of face-to-face sex therapy have been small or absent. The outcomes of video therapy have been encouraging, but the number of controlled studies to date is insufficient to judge the robustness of these effects. Individualized sex therapy through online chat contact or through e-mail contact, which shares certain advantages with other self-help formats, has only recently begun to be explored but appears to show good prospects. Further testing in methodologically sound trials is of course required. The promising rise of sex therapy within the context of artificial intelligence based systems that started in the 1980s has subsided, but a revival of this type of self-help for sexual problems, now delivered through the Internet or through home-based computer programs, may be a viable approach.

Chapter Points

- Diagnosable sexual dysfunctions are much less frequent than subclinical dysfunctions, which are prevalent in both men and women.
- Various self-administered remedies for sexual problems have been tried through the ages, with more than half of current sufferers accessing some type of self-help remedy.

- Self-help interventions range from simple informational solutions to instructional information on specific techniques to more complex, sequenced interventions.
- Empirically supported treatments, administered by a therapist, have been established for some sexual dysfunctions (e.g., premature ejaculation) but not others (e.g., vaginismus).
- Overall effectiveness using bibliotherapy for sexual dysfunctions, based on a meta-analysis of 12 studies, was moderate in degree (ES = .68), an effect that had been largely eroded at follow-up.
- In a large study targeting a variety of sexual problems, posttreatment and follow-up outcomes varied by type of problem, with treatment compliance related to success.
- Therapist-assisted self-help treatments are marginally more effective than self-help-only treatments.
- Therapist-directed treatments confer some advantage over therapist-asisted self-help for some sexual dysfunctions but not others.
- Videotherapy has been found effective for female orgasmic problems but confers no advantage over other self-help methods.
- Internet-based therapy has promise, as indicated by some preliminary studies, but has not been evaluated in controlled studies.

References

American Psychiatric Association (2000). *Diagnostic and statistical manual of mental disorders*, 4th edition (text revision). Washington, DC: Author.

American Psychological Association (1995). *Template for developing guidelines: Intervention for marital disorders and psychosocial aspects of physical disorders.* Washington, DC: Author.

Annon, J. S. (1974). *The behavioral treatment of sexual problems.* Vol. 1. Brief *therapy.* Honolulu: Enabling Systems.

Bachmann, G. A., Leiblum, S. R., & Grill, J. (1989). Brief sexual inquiry in gynecologic practice. *Obstetrics and Gynecology, 73*, 425–427.

Barbach, L. G. (1974). *For yourself: The fulfillment of female sexuality.* New York: Doubleday.

Binik, Y. M., Servan-Schreiber, D., Freiwald, S., & Hall, K. S. (1988). Intelligent computer-based assessment and psychotherapy. An expert system for sexual dysfunction. *The Journal of Nervous and Mental Disease, 176*, 387–400.

Binik, Y. M., Westbury, C. F., & Servan-Schreiber, D. (1989). Interaction with a "sex-expert" system enhances attitudes towards computerized sex therapy. *Behaviour Research and Therapy, 27*, 303–306.

Catania, J. A., Pollack, L., McDermott, L. J., Qualls, S. H., Cole, L. (1990). Help-seeking behaviors of people with sexual problems. *Archives of Sexual Behavior, 19*, 235–250.

Dean, K. (1989). Conceptual, theoretical and methodological issues in self-care research. *Social Science and Medicine, 29,* 117–123.

Dodge, L. J., Glasgow, R. E., & O'Neill, H. K. (1982). Bibliotherapy in the treatment of female orgasmic dysfunction. *Journal of Consulting and Clinical Psychology, 50,* 442–443.

Dow, M. G. T. (1983). *A controlled comparative evaluation of conjoint counselling and self-help behavioural treatment for sexual dysfunction.* Unpublished dissertation, University of Glasgow, Scotland.

Feldman, H. A., Goldstein, I., Hatzichristou, D. G., Krane, R. J., & McKinlay, J. B. (1994). Impotence and its medical and psychosocial correlates: Results of the Massachusetts Male Aging Study. *Journal of Urology, 151,* 54–61.

Gillan, P., Golombok, S., & Becker, P. (1980). NHS sex therapy groups for women. *British Journal of Sexual Medicine, 7,* 44–47.

Goldstein, I., Lue, T. F., Padma-Nathan, H., Rosen, R. C., Steers, W. D., & Wicker, P. A. (1998). Oral sildenafil in the treatment of erectile dysfunction. *New England Journal of Medicine, 338,* 1397–1404.

Gould, R. A., & Clum, G. A. (1993). A meta-analysis of self-help treatment approaches. *Clinical Psychology Review, 13,* 169–186.

Hahn, M. J. (1982). *The vicarious treatment of primary sexual dysfunction.* Dissertation Abstracts International, 43(1–B), 249. Pennsylvania State University, State College, PA.

Hall, P. (2004). Online psychosexual therapy: A summary of pilot study findings. *Sexual and Relationship Therapy, 19,* 167–178.

Halvorsen, J. G., & Metz, M. E. (1992). Sexual dysfunction, Part II: Diagnosis, management, and prognosis. *Journal of the American Board of Family Practitioners, 5,* 177–192.

Hawton, K. (1995). Treatment of sexual dysfunctions by sex therapy and other approaches. *The British Journal of Psychiatry, 167,* 307–314.

Heaton, J. P. (2000). Central neuropharmacological agents and mechanisms in erectile dysfunction: The role of dopamine. *Neuroscience and Biobehavioral Reviews, 24,* 561–569.

Heiman, J. R. (2002). Sexual dysfunction: Overview of prevalence, etiological factors, and treatments. *Journal of Sex Research, 39,* 73–78.

Heiman, J. R., LoPiccolo, L., & LoPiccolo, J. (1976). *Becoming orgasmic: A sexual growth program for women.* Englewood Cliffs, NJ: Prentice Hall.

Heiman, J. R., & Meston, C. M. (1997). Empirically validated treatment for sexual dysfunction. *Annual Review of Sex Research, 8,* 148–194.

Heinrich, A. G. (1976). *The effect of group- and self-directed behavioral-educational treatment of primary orgasmic dysfunction in females treated without their partners.* Unpublished dissertation, University of Colorado, Boulder.

Hengeveld, M. W. (1994). *Willen maar niet kunnen: Zelfhulp en behandeling bij erectiestoornissen.* Utrecht: Kosmos-Z&K.

Jankovich, R., & Miller, P. R. (1978). Response of women with primary orgasmic dysfunction to audiovisual education. *Journal of Sex and Marital Therapy, 4,* 16–19.

Laumann, E. O., Paik, A., & Rosen, R. C. (1999). Sexual dysfunction in the United States: Prevalence and predictors. *Journal of the American Medical Association, 281,* 537–544.

Leiblum, S. R., & Rosen, R. C. (2000). *Principles and practice of sex therapy* (3rd ed.). New York: Guilford.

Libman, E., Fichten, C. S., Brender, W., et al. (1984). A comparison of three therapeutic formats in the treatment of secondary orgasmic dysfunction. *Journal of Sex and Marital Therapy, 10,* 147–159.

Liekens, G., & Drenth, J. J. (1990). *Seks je lust en je leven* [Self-help video]. Amsterdam: Universal Pictures.

Lowe, J. C., & Mikulus, W. L. (1975). Use of written material in learning self-control of premature ejaculation. *Psychological Reports, 37,* 295–298.

Marrs, R. W. (1995). A meta-analysis of bibliotherapy studies. *American Journal of Community Psychology, 23,* 843–870.

Masters, W. H., & Johnson, V. E. (1970). *Human sexual inadequacy.* Boston: Little, Brown.

Mathews, A., Bancroft, J., Whitehead, A., Hackmann, A., Julier, D., Bancroft, J., et al. (1976). The behavioural treatment of sexual inadequacy: A comparative study. *Behaviour Research and Therapy, 14,* 427–436.

Maultsby, M. C. (1975). *Help yourself to happiness through rational self-counselling.* Boston: Esplanada.

McCarthy, B. W. (1984). Strategies and techniques for the treatment of inhibited sexual desire. *Journal of Sex and Marital Therapy, 10,* 97–104.

McCarthy, B. W. (1989). Cognitive-behavioral strategies and techniques in the treatment of early ejaculation. In S. R. Leiblum & R.C. Rosen (Eds.), *Principles and practice of sex therapy: Update for the 1990s,* pp. 141–167. New York: Guilford.

McMullen, S., & Rosen, R. C. (1979). Self-administered masturbation training in the treatment of primary orgasmic dysfunction. *Journal of Consulting and Clinical Psychology, 47,* 912–918.

Morokoff, P. J., & LoPiccolo, J. L. (1986). A comparative evaluation of minimal therapist contact and 15 session treatment for female orgasmic dysfunction. *Journal of Consulting and Clinical Psychology, 54,* 294–300.

Rosen, R. C., & Leiblum, S. R. (1995). Treatment of sexual disorders in the 1990s: An integrated approach. *Journal of Consulting and Clinical Psychology, 63,* 877–890.

Servan-Schreiber, D., & Binik, Y. M. (1989). Extending the intelligent tutoring system paradigm: Sex therapy as intelligent tutoring. *Computers in Human Behavior, 5,* 241–259.

Simons, J. S., & Carey, M. P. (2001). Prevalence of sexual dysfunctions: Results from a decade of research. *Archives of Sexual Behavior, 30,* 177–219.

Slob, A. K., & Vink, I. (2002). *Mannen, vrouwen en vrijen.* Rijswijk, The Netherlands: Elmar.

Trudel, G., & Laurin, F. (1988). The effects of bibliotherapy on orgasmic dysfunction and couple interactions: An experimental study. *Sexual and Marital Therapy, 3,* 223–228.

Trudel, G., & Proulx, S. (1987). Treatment of premature ejaculation by bibliotherapy: An experimental study. *Sexual and Marital Therapy, 2,* 163–167.

Trudel, G., Marchand, A., Ravart, M., Aubin, S., Turgeon, L., & Fortier, P. (2001). The effect of a cognitive-behavioral group treatment program on hypoactive sexual desire in women. *Sexual and Relationship Therapy, 16,* 145–164.

van Lankveld, J. J., & van Koeveringe, G. (2003). Predictive validity of the Golombok Rust Inventory of Sexual Satisfaction (GRISS) for the presence of sexual dysfunctions within a Dutch urological population. *International Journal of Impotence Research, 15,* 110–116.

van Lankveld, J. J. D. M. (1993). *Zelf je seksuele relatie verbeteren [How to improve your sexual relationship].* Cothen, The Netherlands: Servire.

van Lankveld, J. J. D. M. (1998). Bibliotherapy in the treatment of sexual dysfunctions: A meta-analysis. *Journal of Consulting and Clinical Psychology, 66,* 702–708.

van Lankveld, J. J. D. M. (2004). Naar de 7e hemel: verbeter zelf je seksuele relatie [*Going to seventh heaven: Self-improvement of your sexual relationship*]. Haarlem, The Netherlands: Aramith.

van Lankveld, J. D. M., Everaerd, W., & Grotjohann, Y. (2001). Cognitive-behavioral bibliotherapy for sexual dysfunctions in heterosexual couples: A randomized waiting-list controlled clinical trial in The Netherlands. *The Journal of Sex Research, 38,* 51–67.

van Lankveld, J. J. D. M., Leusink, P., van Diest, S. L., Slob, A. K., & Gijs, L. (2004). Sekstherapie via Internet bij mannen met seksuele disfuncties: Een pilot-onderzoek. *Tijdschrift voor Seksuologie, 28,* 220–229.

van Lankveld, J. J. D. M., Hunot, K., & Wylie, V. (2006). Bibliotherapy for sexual dysfunction (Protocol). *Cochrane database of systematics reviews.* Issue 4. Art. No : CD006238. DOI : 10.1002/14651858: CD006238.

World Health Organization (2007). *International statistical classification of diseases and related health problems* (10th revision). Geneva: Authors.

Wills, T. A., & DePaulo, B. M. (1991). Interpersonal analysis of the help-seeking process. *See Boek, 162,* 350–375.

Wincze, J. P., & Caird, W. K. (1976). The effects of systematic desensitization and video desensitization in the treatment of essential sexual dysfunction in women. *Behavior Therapy, 7,* 335–342.

Zeiss, R. A., & Zeiss, A. M. (1978). *Prolong your pleasure.* New York: Pocket Books.

CHAPTER **10**

Self-Help Therapies for Insomnia

SHAWN R. CURRIE

Overview

This chapter provides the reader with a review of self-help approaches for sleep problems. The primary focus will be on self-help for insomnia. The first half of the chapter will overview the scope of insomnia as a problem in the general and clinical populations. This is followed by a review of current empirically supported methods of assessing and treating insomnia with implications for self-help applications. The second half of the chapter will provide readers with an overview of the empirical evidence on self-help treatment of insomnia. Limitations of this evidence will be discussed along with suggestions for future research.

History and Theoretical Basis

Prevalence of Insomnia

Sleep disturbances are very common. In the general adult population, the rate of chronic insomnia is estimated as between 9 and 20% (Ancoli-Israel & Roth, 1999; Ohayon, 2002; Partinen & Hublin, 2000). The variability in prevalence rates is due largely to the inconsistent use of strict diagnostic criteria for defining insomnia. Ohayon (2002) recently estimated the prevalence of DSM-IV–defined insomnia disorder as 6% in the general population. A further 25–30% of adults complain of occasional or transient insomnia (Ancoli-Israel & Roth, 1999; Ohayon, 2002). Insomnia was present in 27% of the 26,000 patients from 15 countries that participated in the World Health Organization (WHO) International Collaborative Study on Psychological Problems in General Health Care (Üstün et al., 1996). Patients reported a significant degree of disability in their daily activities and social roles arising from their sleep problems. Half of the patients followed up one year later still reported significant sleep problems. Prevalence rates of both chronic and transient insomnia increase with age, reaching as high as 50% in the elderly in some studies (Ohayon, 2002).

Insomnia frequently co-occurs with another medical or psychiatric disorder (Lichstein, McCrae, & Wilson, 2003; Zorick & Walsh, 2000). Fifty-two percent of insomnia cases in the WHO general health care study were diagnosed with another mental disorder (Üstün et al., 1996). In epidemiological studies the comorbidity of insomnia and psychiatric disorders occurs in between 40 and 65% of cases (Lichstein et al., 2003; Ohayon, 2002). Specific patient groups have been identified as being particularly vulnerable to sleep disturbances. For example, up to 70% of treatment-seeking chronic pain patients report significant insomnia (Moldofsky, 1990; Pilowsky, Crettenden, & Townley, 1985; Wilson, Watson, & Currie, 1998). High rates of insomnia are associated with major depression (Morawetz, 2003), anxiety disorders (McCall & Reynolds, 2000), and alcohol dependence (Brower, 2001; Currie, Clark, Rimac, & Malhotra, 2003). Historically, disturbed sleep in these populations has been considered a consequence or symptom of the primary disorder. However, insomnia often persists even after the primary disorder resolves (Currie et al., 2003; Lichstein, McCrae, et al., 2003). Furthermore, there is compelling epidemiological evidence that insomnia is a risk factor for the later development of major depression (Ford & Kamerow, 1989) and alcohol abuse (Weissman, Greenwald, Nino-Murcia, & Dement, 1997).

Significant health care costs are associated with insomnia. Medications and other sleep-promoting substances cost the United States about $1.7 billion annually. Health care costs (physician visits, sleep medicine consultations) directly attributed to insomnia are estimated at $12 billion annually (Morin, Bastien, & Savard, 2003). Indirect costs, including lost work time, reduced productivity, and fatigue-related accidents, are estimated at $30 to $35 billion per year in the United States (Chilcott & Shapiro, 1996). Despite the high prevalence and enormous cost associated with insomnia, access to treatment is extremely limited. Screening for sleep disturbances only occurs in about half of patients attending primary care (Üstün et al., 1996). Less than 1% of sleep disordered patients are referred on to sleep clinics. Furthermore, less than 15% of sleep clinics provide psychological treatment for insomnia (Ruyak, Bilsbury, & Rajda, 2004).

The majority of insomniacs attempt self-management of their condition using nonprescription sleep aids and alcohol (Ancoli-Israel & Roth,

1999). In a 1995 Gallup Survey of sleep problems in America, only 28% of respondents felt they knew the available treatments for insomnia very well or well. The large majority (72%) reported they did not understand current treatments available (Ancoli-Israel & Roth, 1999). These findings suggest there is both the opportunity and need for self-help interventions for sleep problems.

Other Sleep Disorders

Insomnia is by far the most prevalent of all sleep disorders. Sleep apnea, characterized by the cessation of airflow through the mouth and nose during the sleep period, affects about 2% of adult women and 4% of adult males (Flemons, 1999; Partinen & Hublin, 2000). Because people with apnea breathe normally during the day, this potentially fatal disorder can go undetected for many years. Restless legs syndrome and periodic limb movement appear with approximately the same frequency as sleep apnea, although the majority of cases are considered mild with little functional impairment (Montplaisir, Nicolas, Godbout, & Walters, 2000). The International Classification of Sleep Disorders—Revised (ICSD-R; American Sleep Disorders Association, 1997) lists dozens of other sleep disorders, most of which are extremely rare (e.g., narcolepsy) or occur exclusively in children (Partinen & Hublin, 2000). The non-insomnia sleep disorders usually require medical interventions. As such, self-help treatment for sleep apnea and other non-insomnia disorders would be inappropriate. There is an abundance of educational material available to the general public on these disorders. Much of the educational focus for sleep apnea has been on identifying the disorder and encouraging individuals to seek medical treatment. There are also support groups for the more common sleep disorders (e.g., A.W.A.K.E. network for persons affected by sleep apnea; Restless Legs Syndrome Foundation support network). The impact of these support groups on the course and severity of these sleep disorders has not been evaluated. Similarly, there is no research on the impact of patient-oriented educational material on the identification, course, or severity of non-insomnia disorders. Therefore, the remainder of this chapter will focus on self-help treatments for the insomnia-spectrum disorders.

Diagnosis of Insomnia

A basic tenet of the self-help approach is that individuals are able to diagnose themselves. Nevertheless, a concern is that consumers will misdiagnose themselves, apply the wrong intervention, and possibly exacerbate the problem. If the insomnia is the direct result of another medical or psychiatric condition, it is critical to identify the condition to ensure it also receives proper attention and treatment. Furthermore, other sleep disorders can have similar nocturnal and daytime characteristics as insomnia. For example, unrefreshing sleep and daytime fatigue are symptoms of both insomnia and sleep apnea. An individual with undiagnosed sleep apnea attempting to apply behavioral techniques developed for managing insomnia would likely experience little benefit. Most self-help books for insomnia include a section on other sleep disorders with the intention of helping readers to detect and seek treatment for conditions other than insomnia.

Two parallel classification schemes exist for diagnosing sleep disorders. The DSM-IV system (American Psychiatric Association, 1994) is the most widely known but generally not preferred by sleep experts because the criteria do not include any specification for frequency or severity of insomnia symptoms. The DSM-IV criteria for primary insomnia specify a minimum duration of one month of difficulty initiating or maintaining sleep or nonrestorative sleep. The sleep problem must interfere with the individual's ability to function during the day or cause clinically significant distress. The ICSD-R definition of psychophysiological insomnia is comparable to the DSM system in terms of the duration and functional impairment criteria. The ICSD-R is similarly vague in the specification for frequency of symptoms (the sleep problem must occur "almost nightly"). Neither system provides specific quantitative criteria for distinguishing normal from abnormal sleep. For many years, researchers have adopted the following quantitative criteria to identify insomniacs: the individual must have a sleep onset latency (SOL) or time awake after sleep onset (WASO) greater than 30 minutes for a minimum of 3 nights per week. In a rigorous sensitivity–specificity analysis, Lichstein, Durrence, Taylor, Bush, and Riedel (2003) provided empirical support for these criteria in identifying "research-grade" insomnia. They also found that a duration specifier of at least 6 months rather than one month is a more defensible criterion for identifying a chronic sleep problem.

Research studies that evaluate self-help materials have generally screened participants in person using recognized diagnostic instruments such as structured interviews, sleep diaries, and questionnaires (Pittsburgh Sleep Quality Index; Buysse, Reynolds, Monk, Berman, & Kupfer, 1989; and Sleep Impairment Index; Morin, 1993, are two popular insomnia questionnaires). Consumers of self-help books do not usually have the luxury of a professional consultation. Some self-help books include a self-diagnostic test to identify insomnia. Table 10.1 contains the brief assessment tool from my own book :60 Second Sleep Ease (Currie & Wilson, 2002). The items and scoring for this tool are taken directly from the DSM-IV criteria for primary insomnia. Unfortunately, there is no evidence that consumers can reliably and accurately self-diagnose insomnia using such

Table 10.1 Example of a Self-Diagnostic Test for Insomnia

1. a. In a typical week, do you have nights when it takes you more than 30 minutes to fall asleep? _____Yes _____No

   b. If you answered yes, how many nights in a typical week does this happen?
      _____Once
      _____Twice
      _____Three times or more

2. a. In a typical week, do you have nights when wake up through the night and have a problem getting back to sleep? _____Yes _____No

   b. If you answered yes, how many nights in a typical week does this happen?
      _____Once
      _____Twice
      _____Three times or more

3. a. In a typical week, do you have mornings when you wake up earlier than you wanted to and have a problem getting back to sleep? _____Yes _____No

   b. If you answered yes, how many nights in a typical week does this happen?
      _____Once
      _____Twice
      _____Three times or more

4. a. In a typical week, do you wake up feeling like your sleep was not restful? _____Yes _____No

   b. If you answered yes, how many nights in a typical week does this happen?
      _____Once
      _____Twice
      _____Three times or more

5. Do you feel your sleep problem is a direct cause of:
   _____significant distress for you
   _____missing time at work
   _____not doing your job well when at work
   _____missing social functions
   _____problems getting along with friends, family, or coworkers

6. Have your sleep difficulties been going on for more than one month? _____Yes _____No

   If you answered yes to questions 1, 2, 3, or 4 and indicated that the sleep problem happens three times per week or more for at least one of these questions, then you do indeed have some significant symptoms of insomnia. If you checked off at least one of the problems listed in question 5 and indicated on question 6 that this has been going on for more than one month, then there is a good chance you have an insomnia disorder. A disorder means that the insomnia symptoms are severe enough to cause problems in your life.

Note: From *60 Second Sleep Ease: Quick Tips to Get a Good Night's Rest*, by S. R. Currie and K. G. Wilson, 2002, 16–17. Far Hills, NJ: New Horizon Press. Reprinted with permission a test. It should also be noted that many books include no self-diagnostic tests for sleep problems.

Treatment of Insomnia

Until about 20 years ago, the only treatment available for insomnia was medication. At present, medication remains the most commonly used form of treatment for insomnia and related sleep disorders. A contributing factor is the paucity of health professionals trained in psychological methods for improving sleep, combined with the difficulty patients often experience in accessing such professionals (Morin et al., 2003). As noted, even sleep clinics provide relatively little treatment for insomnia (Ruyak et al., 2004). The services of a psychologist or sleep medicine specialist are not always covered by health insurance plans. In contrast, sleep medication is widely available and relatively inexpensive. These facts provide further justification for developing and testing self-help interventions for insomnia to give patients more accessible and affordable alternatives to drug therapy.

The most common medications for sleep are the benzodiazepine receptor agents, which include the traditional benzodiazepines (e.g., oxazepam, triazolam) and several newer hypnotics that are not labeled benzodiazepines (e.g., zolpidem, zopiclone) but act on the same neuroreceptor. Sedating antidepressants (e.g., trazodone, amitriptyline) are also used as sleep aids primarily among depressed patients. The majority of over-the-counter sleep medications contain diphenhydramine as the active ingredient. Empirical support for the benzodiazepine receptor agents as short-term sleep aids is very good (Smith et al., 2002). Older medications suppress slow-wave sleep, which can decrease sleep quality and increase daytime fatigue. The newer hypnotics and the sedating antidepressants seem to have less impact on slow-wave sleep (Roehrs & Roth, 1997). Evidence of long-term efficacy is lacking with all the sleeping pills (Smith, Smith, Nowakowski, & Perlis, 2003). Over time, individuals can develop a tolerance to the hypnotic effects. There is also the risk of drug dependence and daytime impairment (drowsiness, memory problems, dizziness, etc.). Sleep medications are recommended for short-term (<4 weeks) use only and are contraindicated as a monotherapy in the treatment of chronic insomnia (Morin et al., 2003).

Psychological management techniques have been available for many years but only recently have come into the forefront as the preferred treatment for chronic insomnia. Cognitive–behavioral treatment (CBT) of insomnia has been well researched in the last 15 years (Morin, Hauri, et al., 1999) with recent studies published in high-profile, non-sleep journals such as the *Journal of the American Medical Association* (Edinger,

Wohlgemuth, Radtke, Marsh, & Quillian, 2001; Morin, Colecchi, Stone, Sood, & Brink, 1999), *Journal of Consulting & Clinical Psychology* (Currie, Wilson, Pontefract, & deLaplante, 2000; Mimeault, & Morin, 1999), and *American Journal of Psychiatry* (Smith et al., 2002). More than 50 clinical trials (involving over 2000 patients) have been conducted that demonstrate the efficacy of CBT approaches to managing insomnia. Robust changes in sleep onset latency, nocturnal wakefulness, and sleep quality ratings have been reported. The results of two meta-analyses (Morin, Culbert, & Schwartz, 1994; Murtagh & Greenwood, 1995) revealed changes in sleep parameters with large effect sizes. Approximately 75% of insomnia patients benefit from CBT, with an average decrease in time to fall asleep and wake time after sleep onset of 50% (Currie, Wilson, & Curran, 2002; Morin et al., 2003). Posttreatment and follow-up values for sleep latency and wake after sleep onset are generally below or near the 30-minute cutoff criterion used to distinguish normal from problematic sleep. The rate of clinically significant change, defined as achieving normal sleep according to the current criteria, ranges from 18 to 50% with lower rates for persons with comorbid conditions (Morin et al., 2003). Furthermore, CBT can be effective in getting 50–84% of patients to wean off hypnotics (Currie, Clark, Hodgins, & el-Guebaly, 2004; Currie et al., 2000; Espie, Inglis, & Harvey, 2001; Gustafson, 1992; Jacobs, Benson, & Friedman, 1996). There is sufficient empirical evidence to support the classification of CBT for insomnia as a well-established treatment according to the American Psychological Association's task force criteria for Empirically Supported Therapies (Morin et al., 2003).

Psychological treatment for insomnia has its origins in cognitive–behavior therapy with four key interventions that continue to dominate treatment approaches: stimulus control, sleep restriction, relaxation training, and cognitive restructuring. All the self-help materials used in research applications include one or more of these key interventions. Many of the untested materials include variations of these interventions, often in a diluted or more generic form. For example, the stimulus control principles are sometimes summarized as "good sleep habits." Unfortunately, many self-help books integrate stimulus control with a great deal of untested advice.

Stimulus control and sleep restriction are intended to reestablish the bed as the dominant cue for sleep, regulate sleep–wake schedules, and consolidate sleep over a shorter period of time. Stimulus control consists of directing patients to avoid napping, to go to bed only when sleepy, to use the bedroom only for sleep and sex, to establish a presleep routine to be used every night, and to get out of bed when unable to fall asleep within 20 minutes. Although these rules appear simple, adherence and regular nighttime application can be a challenge for insomniacs (Morin et al., 2003). For example, the rule concerning getting out of bed when not sleeping should be practiced throughout the night, which may require the individual to leave her bed 3 or 4 times during a particularly bad night of sleeplessness. Noncompliance with the stimulus control guidelines is associated with poor outcome (Riedel & Lichstein, 2001).

With sleep restriction, participants are directed to reduce their time in bed to the total sleep time recorded during the baseline self-monitoring period. The "sleep window," never less than 5 hours, is increased in 15- to 30-minute increments in subsequent weeks, with the goal of achieving 85% sleep efficiency within 3 to 4 weeks. The purpose of sleep restriction is to help the individual concentrate his or her sleep into a shorter period of time spent in bed. A variation of sleep restriction has the patient gradually decrease time in bed over several nights rather than all at once. This approach may be more palatable to severe insomniacs, but there is greater risk of noncompliance. With proper application, sleep restriction reduces sleep fragmentation and increases sleep quality. Total sleep time may also show a small gain of 25 to 30 minutes with consistent application of both stimulus control and sleep restriction (Morin, Hauri, et al. 1999). However, patients are told not to expect a large increase in total sleep duration. Behavioral management of insomnia generally aims to increase the quality but not necessarily quantity of sleep time.

Relaxation techniques are used as a form of counterconditionining to reduce physiological arousal in the sleep setting. The rationale for relaxation therapy is based on the strong evidence of hyperarousal in insomniacs both at night and during the daytime. Compared to good sleepers, insomniacs show higher metabolic rates, muscle tension, cardiovascular activity, and cortical activation (Bonnet & Arand, 1997; Morin, 1993). Cognitive arousal is strongly implicated in the etiology of poor sleep. Compared to good sleepers, insomniacs demonstrate overactive cognitive activity (e.g., racing thoughts, instrusive cognitions) during the presleep period (Harvey, 2002). Moreover, the content of their thoughts is typically negative, often filled with excessive worries about lack of sleep and related consequences. Cognitive hyperarousal contributes to heightened physiological arousal that can disrupt the normal transition from awake to sleep. Over time, the arousal becomes associated with the bedroom environment. Conditioned arousal is the primary rationale underlying stimulus control, which aims to break the association between the bedroom and sleeplessness.

Several methods of relaxation are available: progressive muscle relaxation (PMR), imagery training, meditation, and hypnosis are the most common. All have the same goal of reducing arousal before bedtime and faciliating sleep onset. The most researched method is progressive muscle relaxation, a technique involving the systematic tensing and relaxing of muscles in the body. Studies comparing the relative efficacy of relaxation methods have produced largely equivocal results. Imagery-based relaxation may have an advantage over PMR in addressing cognitive arousal in insomniacs, although apart from a single study (Woolfolk & McNulty, 1983) there is no strong evidence of superior outcomes. The basic premise of relaxation for sleep induction has strong face validity among insomniacs (in contrast to sleep restriction, which many insomniacs find counterintuitive). The instructions are simple and easily presentable in a written format. Consequently, the majority of self-help books for insomnia include a relaxation script. Readers are often encouraged to read the relaxation instructions into a tape recorder to produce their own relaxation tape. Commercial audiotapes of relaxation exercises are also widely available.

Cognitive restructuring interventions, adapted from Aaron Beck's work in the treatment of depression, were added to insomnia treatment based on the work of Charles Morin at Laval University and recently expanded upon by Alison Harvey at Oxford University (Harvey, 2002). Compared to imagery relaxation, which indirectly targets the problem of excessive cognitive arousal in insomniacs, restructuring methods help patients to modify the content of negative thoughts contributing to sleeplessness. Many insomniacs have maladaptive beliefs about sleep and the consequences of insomnia (Morin, 1993). Erroneous thoughts about sleep and insomnia can increase the level of sleep-related performance anxiety and promote adoption of counterproductive compensatory behaviors (Smith et al., 2003). For example, an insomniac may cope with a bad night of sleep by napping during the day or going to bed earlier in an attempt to recover lost sleep. Insomniacs can also use the bedroom as a "worry zone," often lying in bed at night ruminating about negative life events and personal problems. Cognitive interventions for insomnia focus on decatastrophizing insomniacs' thoughts about sleep and the consequences of insomnia. Basic education on the nature of sleep, the individuality of sleep needs, and importance of sleep quality over sleep quantity can be helpful in getting patients to challenge some of their beliefs about sleep. Nevertheless, cognitive interventions can be difficult to translate into a self-help format.

Assessing Outcome

Methods for assessing change following treatment tend to be different in clinical and research applications. In clinical settings, changes in sleep are most often assessed on the basis of global, retrospective evaluations. The use of standardized, prospective measures is usually rare in clinical settings. Global evaluations are not necessarily inaccurate but lack the depth of information that can be indispensable for properly diagnosing and assessing treatment response. The main dimensions of insomnia to be assessed include:

- Number of minutes it takes the patient to fall asleep, referred to as *sleep onset latency* (SOL);
- Number of minutes the patient spends awake throughout the night, known as *wake after sleep onset* (WASO);
- How often the patient wakes up, known as *number of awakenings* (AWK);
- The total length of time spent asleep, known as *total sleep time* (TST—can be expressed in minutes or hours);
- The patient's satisfaction with his or her sleep known as sleep quality (SQL; usually assessed with a numerical rating scale such as 0–10 with 0 being *extremely poor* and 10 being *extremely good*).

The ratio of hours slept to time in bed, known as sleep efficiency (SEF), is another commonly reported outcome variable. Higher values of SEF indicate less sleep fragmentation. With the exception of sleep quality, all these dimensions can be assessed via subjective (questionnaires and sleep logs) and objective sleep measures. In treatment outcome studies, sleep diaries are the primary source of data for determining response. Although subjective estimates of sleep parameters often do not agree with absolute values obtained from polysomnography (Edinger & Fins, 1995), sleep diaries provide a valid and reliable index of insomnia severity (Morin, 1993; Currie, Malhotra & Clark, 2004). In addition to being reliable, sleep diaries provide a daily record of sleep habits, which by their very nature are variable over time. Polysomnography (PSG) is considered the gold standard for sleep measures. However, its utility in assessing insomnia is limited. Several nights of PSG data are needed to properly assess insomnia (Bootzin et al., 1995; Wohlgemuth, Edinger, Fins, & Sullivan, 1999), but it is expensive and inconvenient for patients to spend multiple nights in a sleep lab. Furthermore, estimates of sleep from PSG and self-report often disagree. Nevertheless, PSG remains the only way to accurately diagnose sleep disorders such as sleep apnea and periodic limb movements. Alternatives to PSG for obtaining objective sleep data have been developed in recent years. The actigraph is a popular device for supplementing the data obtained from sleep diaries (Currie, Malhotra et al., 2004; Sadeh & Acebo, 2002). When compared to the gold standard of PSG, however, the movement-based sleep estimates from the actigraph are prone to large measurement errors. Researchers generally use a combination of sleep measures to assess outcome following insomnia treatment.

Available Self-Help Materials and Target Audience

A search of the Amazon.com Web site using the keywords "self-help" and "sleep" produced over 40 hits. Included in the top-selling books were *No More Sleepless Nights* (Hauri, 1996), *Can't Sleep, Can't Stay Awake: A Woman's Guide to Sleep Disorders* (Kryger, 1999), *Say Good Night to Insomnia* (Jacobs, 1999), and *Seven Days to a Perfect Sleep* (Gordon, 2003). The majority of available materials come in book form. Audio media (tapes or compact disks) comprise the remaining commercially available titles. The latter products typically consist of audio recordings of relaxation or self-hypnotic exercises. It should be noted that these titles are ones devoted exclusively to the topic of sleep. Many self-help books on other health problems (e.g., chronic pain, depression, menopause) include abbreviated advice for enhancing sleep or combating insomnia.

Although no data have been collected, the largest consumers of self-help materials on sleep are most likely persons with primary or secondary insomnia, which account for over 90% of all persons with sleep disorders. In general, self-help books are predominantly purchased by women (Marx, Gyorky, Royalty, & Stern, 1992). Furthermore, women and older adults are 1.5 times more likely to report insomnia than men or younger adults (Smith et al., 2003). Hence, it is not unrealistic to assume that the majority of self-help books on insomnia are purchased by women. This may explain why so many titles are specifically targeted at women.

Empirical Basis

Efficacy

To date there have been nine published outcome studies of self-help treatments for sleep problems. Table 10.2 provides the details of each study, including the design used, type of self-help material, sample characteristics, outcome measures, and main findings. The majority of studies recruited insomniacs through the media. Ström, Pettersson, and Andersson (2004) also recruited persons through the Internet. Both Morawetz (2003) and Currie, Clark et al. (2004) accepted clinic referrals. Participant samples are overrepresented by women and middle-aged to elderly individuals, consistent with demographic trends in the prevalence of insomnia (Partinen & Hublin, 2000). Sample sizes ranged from 22 to 219. These studies primarily targeted persons with insomnia, although not all studies screened for other sleep disorders, and Riedel and Lichstein (1995) included non-insomniacs. Six studies employed randomized controlled designs; the remaining studies employed single group, pre-post designs. The control group employed in all RCTs was a waiting-list control; three of the six RCTs had control

Table 10.2 Studies of Self-Help Treatment of Insomnia

Investigations	Design (control)	N	Sample characteristics	Conditions	Self-help sleep materials	Main Outcome Measures	FU (months)	Outcomes
1. Alperson & Biglan, 1979	RCT (WL)	29	M age = 37 (17–80); 48% female; media recruited	Relaxation/stimulus control, young vs. old vs. self-monitoring/WL	Manual version of Benson's (1975) *The Relaxation Response* with stimulus control instructions	SOL, TST, AWK, SQL, worry scale	2	SOL reduced (66 to 41) in both self-help conditions; younger Ss showed more improved than old Ss
2. Morawetz, 1989	RCT (WL)	141	M age = 44 (23–60) yrs; media recruited; 45% on sleep medication	Self-help tape vs. group therapy (10 hrs) vs. WL	*Self-Management Techniques for Controlling Insomnia* (Tape + manual; Bootzin, 1976); written relaxation instructions (cf. Alperson & Biglan, 1979)	SOL, WASO, AWK	4	Active treatments superior to WL; self-help & group comparable for non-medication users; group superior to self-help for medication users
3. Gustafson, 1992	CRS (none)	22	M age = 42 yrs; 55% female; media recruited; 64% on sleep medication	Relaxation tape	Audio version of Jacobson's (1957) *You Must Relax*	TST, medication, global improvement rating	12	TST increased (4 to 6.5 hrs.); 86% self-rated sleep as improved; 68% reported benefit in daytime functioning; 27% felt they needed more treatment

4. Riedel & Lichstein, 1995	RCT (WL)	125	M age = 67 yrs; 66% female; media recruited; all non-medication users; non-insomniacs included	Video (15 mins × 2) vs. video + group (4 hrs) vs. WL	Sleep Education for Seniors (Video + brochure; Lichstein, 1989)	SOL, TST, WASO, SEF, SQL	2	Active treatments superior to WL; video + group superior to video alone on 4/5 sleep variables; non-insomniacs improved on 2/5 sleep variables
5. Oosterhuis & Klip, 1997	Single group pre-post	219	M age = 55 yrs; 63% female; media recruited; 55% medication users	TV & radio lessons (15 min × 8 weeks) broadcast to general public in Holland + book and audiotape	TV: education, sleep hygiene, thought-stopping, relaxation. Book: You Can Learn to Sleep (Klip, 1987)	SOL, TST, AWK, SQL, medication	4.5	Improvement in SOL, awakenings, TST, & quality at post and FU; 40% of medication users quit use at post
6. Mimeault & Morin, 1999	RCT (WL)	54	M age = 51 yrs; 59% female; media recruited; 54% medication users	Book vs. book + therapist phone support (6 calls) vs. self-monitoring/WL	Relief From Insomnia (Morin, 1996)	SOL, TST, WASO, AWK, SQL, DBAS, PSQI, BAI, BDI	3	Active treatments superior to WL; addition of therapist support did not improve outcomes at follow-up
7. Morawetz, 2003	CRS	86	M age = 42 (16–88) yrs; 54% female; clinic referred; 60% on sleep medication	Book + tape for 6–8 weeks	Sleep Better Without Drugs (Morawetz, 2003)	SOL, TST, WASO, AWK, BDI, medication	None	87% showed improvement in sleep; 70% showed improvement in depression

(continued)

Table 10.2 *(continued)*

Investigations	Design (control)	N	Sample characteristics	Conditions	Self-help sleep materials	Main Outcome Measures	FU (months)	Outcomes
8. Currie, Clark et al., 2004	RCT (WL)	60	M age = 43 (18–70) yrs; 30% female; recovering alcoholics; media recruited and clinic-referrred; 30% on sleep medication	Manual + therapist phone support (5 calls) vs. CBT individual therapy (IT; 5 hrs) vs. self-monitoring/ WL	*:60 Second Sleep-Ease: Quick Tips to Get a Good Night's Rest* (Currie & Wilson, 2002)	SOL, TST, SEF, AWK, SQL, PSQI, SII, BDI	6	Active treatments superior to WL; no difference in self-help and IT outcomes; rate of clinically significant change higher in IT condition at follow-up
9. Ström et al., 2004	RCT (WL)	109	M age = 44; 71% female; media/Internet recruited; 43% on regular sleep medication	Internet version of CBT (5 weeks) + e-mail therapist support vs. WL	Adapted version of *Relief From Insomnia* (Morin, 1996) + relaxation instructions	SOL, TST, WASO, SEF, AWK, SQL, DBAS	6–9	Treated and controls improved on SOL, AWK, WASO; treated more improved on SEF, TST, and sleep beliefs

Note: RCT = randomized controlled trial; CRS = clinical replication series; WL = waiting list control; FU = follow-up; WASO = wake time after sleep onset; SEF = sleep efficiency; SOL = sleep onset latency; TST = total sleep time; SQL = sleep quality; CBT = cognitive–behavior therapy; DBAS = Dysfunctional Beliefs about Sleep Scale; PSQI = Pittsburgh Sleep Quality Index; SII = Sleep Impairment Index; BDI = Beck Depression Inventory; BAI = Beck Anxiety Inventory.

[a] *All sleep parameters derived from sleep diary except Morawetz (2003), which used an interview.*

participants also fill out sleep diaries during the waiting period. The latter design feature is to control for changes in sleep that can occur by regular self-monitoring (Currie et al., 2000; Morin, 1993). In all but one study (Morawetz, 2003) the primary outcome measures were derived from a sleep diary, which is also the most common outcome instrument for therapist-directed studies of insomnia. Some studies used auxiliary measures such as the Pittsburgh Sleep Quality Index to assess outcomes. Two studies assessed change in domains of functioning other than sleep. Only one study to date employed an objective measure of sleep (in this case, the actigraph), although it failed to show a robust treatment effect in either the self-help or individual therapy condition (Currie, Clark et al., 2004). Overall, the use of outcome measures is comparable to those employed in face-to-face therapy trials.

A wide variety of self-help materials have been tested. Early studies employed manuals that combined the instructions for relaxation and stimulus control (Alperson & Biglan, 1979; Morawetz, 1989). Two studies made use of video for delivering sleep hygiene education and behavioral strategies for insomnia (Oosterhuis & Klip, 1997; Riedel & Lichstein 1995). A recent innovative study made use of the Internet to deliver a CBT-based insomnia intervention (Ström et al., 2004). The Internet is a promising mode for delivering sleep treatment to persons unable or unwilling to seek direct professional assistance. All studies resulted in improvements in sleep for participants. Table 10.3 displays in detail the pretreatment to posttreatment and pre to follow-up improvements in SOL, SEF, WASO, and AWK for individual studies and the overall, unweighted effects. The number of studies is too small to apply meta-analysis. The unweighted means comparing pretreatment and posttreatment sleeping status revealed average improvements ranging from 7 (TST) to 40% (WASO). In actual measurement units, sleep onset reduced an average of 14 minutes from pretreatment levels, wake after sleep onset time decreased an average of 39 minutes, and sleep duration increased an average of 24 minutes. Five studies also included daily ratings of sleep quality (Likert-type scale ranged from 1 indicating *extremely poor* to 5 or 10 indicating *extremely good*) as an outcome measure (Alperson & Biglan, 1979; Currie, Clark et al., 2004; Mimeault & Morin, 1999; Oosterhuis & Klip, 1997; Riedel & Lichstein, 1995). The average improvements in sleep quality ratings from baselines to posttreatment and baseline to follow-up were 11% each.

These improvements, although statistically significant in most studies, are inferior to the changes in the same sleep parameters reported for in-person psychological treatment for insomnia. The average reduction in sleep latency is approximately half of the 30-minute reduction reported from quantitative reviews of CBT for insomnia (Morin et al., 2003). Similarly, change in

Table 10.3 Detailed Examination of Changes in Sleep Following Self-Help Treatment

Study[a]	SOL (mins)		TST (mins)		WASO (mins)		AWK (#)		SEF (%)	
	Pre to posttest	Pre to FU	Pre to posttest	Pre to FU	Pre to posttest	Pre to FU	Pre to posttest	Pre to FU	Pre to posttest	Pre to FU
1.	−18.6 (42.8)	−24.4 (37)	17.1 (418)	23.9 (424.8)	—	—	0.3 (1.6)	0.4 (1.5)	—	—
2.	−14.0 (30)	−28.0 (26)	—	—	23.0 (26)	33.0 (16)	—	—	—	—
4.	−2.2 (37.8)	−10.8 (29.2)	25.7 (332.2)	44 (350.5)	29.0 (62.9)	43.7 (48.2)	—	—	7.2 (71.3)	12.5 (76.6)
5.	−8.7 (55.1)	−21.4 (42.4)	24.0 (391.8)	34.8 (402.6)	—	—	0.2 (1.9)	0.28 (1.8)	—	—
6.	−17.7 (35.3)	−8.6 (44.4)	33.3 (361.4)	57.7 (385.8)	33.8 (28.8)	33.8 (28.9)	—	—	10.6 (76.6)	12.6 (78.6)
8.	−18.2 (25)	−16.3 (26.9)	12.0 (390)	30.0 (408)	19.1 (40.9)	16.3 (43.3)	0.30 (2)	0.6 (1.7)	6.6 (87.1)	2.9 (83.4)
9.	−11.0 (27.3)	—	34.2 (372)	51.0 (388.8)	22.1 (34.8)	—	0.8 (1.2)	—	10.4 (79.9)	9.8 (79.3)
Unweighted mean	−14.3 (36.2)	−21.1 (34.3)	24.4 (377.6)	40.2 (393.4)	−25.4 (38.7)	−36.8 (34.1)	−0.4 (1.7)	−0.8 (1.7)	8.7 (78.7)	9.5 (79.5)
% Change	28.4	41.8	6.9	11.4	39.7	57.4	18.4	39.8	12.4	13.6

Note: Posttest or follow-up means shown in parentheses. FU = follow-up; SOL = sleep onset latency; TST = total sleep time; WASO = wake time after sleep onset; SEF = sleep efficiency; AWK = awakenings.

[a]*Studies by Gustafson (1992) and Morawetz (2003) did not report quantitative changes in sleep parameters.*

number of awakenings falls short in comparison to the average reduction of one awakening per night following face-to-face treatment of insomnia. On the other hand, the average reduction in nocturnal wake time is comparable to the 32-minute reduction reported from the same literature.

The absence of more robust changes could be attributed to a variety of factors. Fundamentally, the effect size for self-help insomnia treatment may be less than therapist-directed interventions. In other words, receiving treatment via a workbook may be less potent than receiving treatment in person. Furthermore, there could be large unexplained sources of error contributing to the smaller effect size. Only a limited number of outcome studies on self-help treatment have been completed with a much greater range of participants and treatment delivery methods (e.g., books, video, Internet) than is typically seen in therapist-led interventions. Finally, none of the published self-help studies provide detailed information on subject adherence with the treatment procedures. Mimeault and Morin (1999) collected ratings of self-reported compliance with the treatment methods but only reported that there was no difference in compliance between the book-only and book plus telephone support conditions. Success in CBT for insomnia depends on regular practice of the behavior change strategies (e.g., applying stimulus control every night). Inability to monitor treatment adherence is a noted limitation of self-guided therapy (Rosen, 1987). Future studies comparing self-help and therapist-led interventions should collect data on adherence to change strategies to better explain the differences in efficacy.

Duration of Benefits

All of the studies in Table 10.2 except one (Morawetz, 2003) conducted follow-up assessments with intervals ranging from 2 to 12 months. Generally, improvements in sleep latency and wake time after sleep onset were maintained at follow-up. In fact, these and the other sleep measures showed additional improvement at the follow-up. Sleep onset latency was on average 42% improved (reduction of 21 minutes) at follow-up compared to baseline levels. Number of awakenings decreased 40% from baseline to follow-up across studies, and total sleep time increased an average of 40 minutes. This evidence suggests that self-help treatment for insomnia leads to sustained improvement in sleep. Nevertheless, follow-up data need to be interpreted cautiously. As noted, the length of the follow-up interval varied considerably across studies. The only study to include a 12-month follow-up assessment unfortunately reported no quantitative data on change in sleep parameters (Gustafson, 1992). Studies also varied in their handling of dropouts. Most studies employed an analytic strategy in which only completers were included in the analysis. Using this approach, the data from dropouts and persons lost to follow-up are excluded from the analysis of long-term outcomes. The potential bias of this approach is that persons who felt the treatment was not beneficial are not included in the results. Unfortunately, self-help treatment studies are vulnerable to high dropout rates given that after participants receive the materials their motivation to volunteer for follow-up testing is likely to wane.

Clinically Significant Change

In recent years, researchers have been challenged to demonstrate that psychological treatments lead to meaningful changes in people's lives in addition to aggregate statistical improvements. Critical reviews of insomnia treatment research have questioned the clinical significance of individual client outcomes (National Institutes of Health Technology Assessment Panel, 1996). The usual approach to measuring clinically significant change has been to determine whether the client's level of function after treatment falls within the normal range (Jacobson, Roberts, Berns, & McGlinchey, 1999). The appeal of this method is that posttreatment data are evaluated within the context of normal functioning for the target symptom of treatment. The drawback is that sometimes even clinically valuable therapy may not result in clients functioning within the normal range; they may be improved but not necessarily recovered. Within the sleep disorders field, accepted criteria are available for defining the normative range of sleep parameters. The cutoff values for sleep onset latency (SOL) and wake time after sleep onset (WASO) are 30 minutes each (Lichstein, Durrance et al., 2003). For sleep efficiency (the ratio of time spent sleeping to time in bed) a cutoff of 85% has been proposed (i.e., the individual is asleep for 85% of the time spent in bed), with higher values indicating good sleep. Applying these criteria to the outcome data displayed in Table 10.3, we find that none of the posttreatment and follow-up means for sleep parameters fall within the normative range. The average follow-up values for SOL and WASO approach but do not exceed the 30-minute criteria. The follow-up mean for SEF falls considerably short of the 85% cutoff. Nevertheless, these data do not discount the possibility of clinically significant change in individual clients. For example, Currie, Clark et al. (2004) report that 86% of participants in the self-help treatment condition displayed SOL values below the 30-minute cutoff at posttreatment. Mimeault and Morin (1999) reported that 50% of participants who received only the self-help book met criteria for clinically significant improvement on sleep efficiency.

Comparison with In-Person Interventions

Only three studies have directly compared self-help to face-to-face therapy for insomnia. Morawetz (1989) reported differential effects of treatment modality for sleep medication users compared to non-users. For medication-free insomniacs, outcomes for patients who received treatment via a self-help tape were comparable to patients who received treatment in a group format. For regular users of sleep medication (about 45% of the sample), the self-help format produced nonsignificant changes in sleep that were indistinguishable from the control group. Morawetz (1989) concluded that sleep medication users require more intensive interventions for sleep than provided by self-help. Riedel and Lichstein (1995) reported that for elderly insomniacs self-help treatment delivered via a video led to smaller changes in sleep compared to the video plus group therapy condition. Currie, Clark et al. (2004) found that recovering alcoholics with insomnia showed the same pattern of sleep improvement whether treatment was provided individually or through a manual with periodic telephone support. However, clients who received individual CBT showed a higher rate of clinically significant change (50 vs. 7% were normal sleepers in the individual and self-help conditions, respectively) at 6 months follow-up.

Firm conclusions on the comparability of self-help and direct treatment are difficult to make because of the small number of outcomes studies in the area. Furthermore, some self-help conditions are not truly representative of a self-guided treatment—participants in Currie, Clark et al. (2004), for example, also received telephone support from a therapist. However, the limited data available suggest that self-help treatment does not produce the same degree of improvement as face-to-face therapy. This may be particularly true for difficult or vulnerable populations (e.g., the elderly, medication-reliant insomniacs) for which a high degree of comorbidity is expected. These groups of insomnia patients may be better served with face-to-face sleep treatment. On the other hand, self-help treatment has proven to be significantly more effective than no treatment.

Implementation Issues

Choice of Materials   Clinicians wanting to recommend a book for their clients are advised to choose from the materials containing empirically tested strategies. None of the top-selling books listed on the Amazon.com Web site have been directly used in a controlled trial of efficacy. However, many of these titles contain the same basic stimulus control and relaxation instructions used in the empirically tested materials. *No More Sleepless Nights* (1996) was written by a well-known sleep researcher from the Mayo Clinic Sleep Disorders Centre, Dr. Peter Hauri. The book contains all of the CBT strategies for sleep with a particular emphasis on stimulus control. Similarly, *Say Good Night to Insomnia* (Jacobs, 1999) provides very thorough and comprehensible chapters on changing negative sleep thoughts and establishing sleep-promoting habits (including stimulus control and sleep restriction). Most of *Can't Sleep, Can't Stay Awake: A Woman's Guide*

To Sleep Disorders (1999; written by Dr. Meir Kryger, who was formerly president of the American Academy of Sleep Medicine) is devoted to explaining the neurobiological process of sleep, the impact of pregnancy and menstrual functioning on sleep, and a thorough review of other sleep disorders. The CBT strategies for insomnia are summarized, in a succinct but thorough fashion, in a single chapter titled "Treating Insomnia without Pills." The book *Seven Days to a Perfect Sleep* (Gordon, 2003) is perhaps the easiest of all these books to read including, as the title describes, a 7-day sleep-promotion change program. Sleep restriction is not among the strategies suggested and the stimulus control rules are interspersed with largely untested advice concerning diet and natural sleep remedies.

Among the self-help books and audio-visual media used in the controlled studies listed in Table 10.2, the following are still commercially available:

- *The Relaxation Response*, by Herbert Benson (1975);
- *Relief From Insomnia*, by Charles Morin (1996);
- *:60 Second Sleep-Ease: Quick Tips to Get a Good Night's Rest*, by Shawn Currie & Keith Wilson (2002).

The latter two titles contain all the key CBT interventions (stimulus control, sleep restriction, relaxation, and cognitive restructuring) that have been tested in empirical research. Benson's (1975) *The Relaxation Response* focuses solely on relaxation training, although this book was never marketed as a treatment for primary insomnia. When searching for a self-help book on insomnia, clinicians should ensure the title includes most if not all of the following elements that are considered integral to the cognitive–behavioral approach for insomnia:

- a screening test or sufficiently detailed information that would allow the reader to distinguish between insomnia and a more serious sleep disorder such as sleep apnea;
- stimulus control guidelines written in sufficient detail to make the rationale and technique clear to the reader; to avoid dilution of both impact and importance, the stimulus control guidelines should be kept separate from more general sleep hygiene advice (e.g., avoiding caffeine at night, regular exercise);
- a relaxation script (progressive muscle or imagery);
- recommendations for lifestyle changes conducive to good sleep;
- a sleep diary (containing at a minimum entries for time to bed, time out of bed, SOL, TST, AWK, WASO, and sleep quality; logging medication use is also helpful) for clients to record their progress;
- information designed to correct faulty beliefs about sleep; and education on the advantages and disadvantages of sleep medications.

Using a Self-Help Book in Therapy It is common practice for clinicians to recommend self-help materials to their clients and then supervise their usage and progress in therapy. Directed reading on insomnia as an adjunct to psychotherapy for another Axis I disorder (e.g., depression or anxiety) is potentially an efficient use of a self-help sleep book. Valuable therapy time can be spent on dealing with complex interpersonal or emotional issues. In contrast, the management of insomnia has good face validity, is relatively straightforward, and behavior change oriented. Nevertheless, clinicians cannot assume that clients are actually following the strategies. It is critical for clinicians to monitor clients' adherence to the sleep behavior modifications demanded by the CBT approach.

The core intervention in CBT for insomnia is stimulus control. Success with the remaining strategies depends on regular, nightly adherence to stimulus control. The following tips may help to ensure compliance: (a) have clients self-monitor their sleep with a log and check the log every session to ensure clients are maintaining a regular rising time regardless of sleep duration or quality; (b) emphasize the need to get out of bed when unable to fall asleep; (c) ask clients if they get out of bed *every* time sleep onset is delayed and whether they leave the bedroom as directed by stimulus control; (d) problem-solve with clients around adherence to stimulus control (e.g., suggest preplanned activities to engage the client after leaving the bed); and (e) whenever possible, integrate principles of insomnia management with other CBT interventions to consolidate general learning.

Bibliotherapy for insomnia can be started at any point during treatment for another disorder. Unless clinically contraindicated, it is preferred that stimulus control and other strategies started as early as possible in the course of treatment. This allows the clinician sufficient time to monitor the client's application of the strategies from a book. Moreover, recent research suggests that targeting insomnia in treatment can alleviate depressive symptoms in the absence of any specific interventions for depression (Morawetz, 2003).

Conclusions and Future Directions

The preceding review indicates that self-help materials for insomnia are efficacious in helping individuals to reduce time to fall asleep, decrease the duration and frequency of awakenings, and increase sleep quality. The magnitude of change is not as large as in-person treatment for insomnia but posttreatment improvements are sustained at follow-up assessments. Furthermore, most sleep parameters show additional improvement over time. Self-help therapy for insomnia is also associated with clinically significant changes as reflected in two important areas of sleep functioning. First, many treated participants demonstrate sleep patterns in the normal range (Currie, Clark et al., 2004; Mimeault & Morin, 1999). Second, self-help treatment can help individuals to wean off sleep medication by providing alternative coping strategies (Currie, Clark et al., 2004; Oosterhuis & Klip, 1997). These findings suggest that self-help treatment for insomnia is a potentially cost-effective and easily disseminated method for treating persons with sleep disorders.

Most researchers concede that self-help can never fully replace the benefits of face-to-face therapy. Ideally, all insomnia patients should have unrestricted access to direct mental health care. The preferred approach to treating insomnia remains individual or group interventions conducted by professionals trained in behavioral sleep medicine. Research conducted to date suggests that elderly persons and medication-reliant patients would be better served by in-person treatment of insomnia. With direct treatment, patients can be properly assessed, closely monitored, and appropriately guided in the most effective application of behavioral methods for improving sleep. For patients with limited access to professional sleep services, self-help materials can serve as a less intensive alternative for motivated, self-directed individuals. Self-help books could also provide an important bridge in the treatment continuum. Patients waiting to see a sleep specialist or deciding whether a specialist is necessary could gain valuable insight and coping strategies from a well-written book on insomnia. After CBT for insomnia, an insomnia book can serve as a valuable resource guide to help the patient maintain progress and manage relapses in the absence of professional guidance.

Although self-help approaches for insomnia show promise, there are still important gaps in our knowledge base. More studies that directly compare self-help and face-to-face therapy are needed to properly assess the strengths and weaknesses of both modalities. Furthermore, the benefits of self-help need to be assessed as these materials are intended to be used—without the luxury of an initial professional consultation and ongoing telephone support. The Internet may be the most promising means of delivering a self-guided insomnia program, given the sophistication of the technology and the increasing numbers of people who regularly use the media to access health-related information.

There has been no cost-effective comparison of self-help and direct therapy for insomnia. Self-help for insomnia is generally assumed to be more cost-effective but studies need to be conducted to determine the actual savings in health care costs in relation to therapeutic gains. Finally, dismantling studies are needed to determine how people actually use and benefit from the material in a self-help book. The effective elements of CBT for insomnia are thought to be the behavior change strategies (stimulus control and sleep restriction). However, it is not known how well readers actually follow the recommended steps considered integral to the stimulus control approach.

Chapter Points

- Transient and chronic insomnia affects a large portion of the population, with comorbid medical and psychiatric problems occurring in 50% of insomniacs.
- While costs for insomnia, including sleep medications, physician visits, and lost productivity are in the billions of dollars, effective screening and access to psychological treatments is limited.
- Sleep-onset insomnia is defined as requiring more than 30 minutes to get to sleep at least three times/week for 6 months. Few self-help books provide diagnostic information or information to distinguish insomnia from other disorders, such as sleep apnea.
- Seventy-five percent of insomnia sufferers benefit from cognitive behavior therapy, with an average decrease in wakefulness of 50% and the number of people who recover ranging from 18 to 50%.
- Techniques used to improve sleep quality and the time asleep include stimulus control, sleep restriction, relaxation techniques, and cognitive restructuring.
- Assessment is usually based on sleep diaries that include measures of time to sleep onset, minutes awake, number of awakenings, total time asleep, sleep quality, and sleep efficiency (time asleep/time in bed).
- Six controlled studies of insomnia, with treatments advocating the above strategies, showed improvements on all outcome measures but with less effectiveness than when delivered in therapist-directed treatments.
- Six studies that evaluated whether treatment effects persisted over 2- to 12-month follow-ups found an acceleration in the effectiveness of treatments.
- Based on two studies, self-help led to clinically significant improvement in 50–86% of treated individuals.
- Self-help approaches are less effective than therapist-directed treatments, especially for those on sleep medications and the elderly.

References

Alperson, J., & Biglan, A. (1979). Self-administered treatments of sleep onset insomnia and the importance of age. *Behavior Therapy, 10,* 347–356.

American Psychiatric Association. (1994). *Diagnostic and statistical manual of mental disorders* (4th ed.). Washington, DC: Author.

American Sleep Disorders Association. (1997). *International classification of sleep disorders: diagnostic and coding manual.* Lawrence, KS: Allen Press.

Ancoli-Israel, S., & Roth, T. (1999). Characteristics of insomnia in the United States: Results of the 1991 National Sleep Foundation Survey I. *Sleep, 22*(Suppl. 2), S347–S353.

Benson, H. (1975). *The relaxation response.* New York: Harper Torch.

Bonnet, M. H., & Arand, D. L. (1997). Physiological activation in patients with sleep state misperception. *Psychosomatic Medicine, 59,* 533–540.

Bootzin, R. R. (1976). Self-management techniques for controlling insomnia. In C. M. Franks (Ed.), *Behavior therapy: Techniques, principles and patient aids* (tape). New York: Biomonitoring Applications.

Bootzin, R. R., Bell, I. R., Halbisch, R., Kuo T. F., Wyatt, J. K., Rider, S. P., et al. (1995). Night-to-night variability in measures of sleep and sleep disorders: A six night PSG study. *Sleep Research, 24,* 121.

Brower, K. J. (2001). Alcohol's effects on sleep in alcoholics. *Alcohol Health & Research World, 25,* 110–125.

Buysse, D. J., Reynolds, C. F., Monk, T. H., Berman, S. R., & Kupfer, D. J. (1989). The Pittsburgh Sleep Quality Index: A new instrument for psychiatric practice and research. *Psychiatry Research, 28,* 193–213.

Chilcott, L. A., & Shapiro, C. M. (1996). The socioeconomic impact of insomnia: An overview. *PharmacoEconomics, 10,* 1–14.

Currie, S. R., Clark, S., Hodgins, D. C., & el-Guebaly, N. (2004). Randomized controlled trial of brief cognitive-behavioural interventions for insomnia in recovering alcoholics. *Addiction, 99,* 1121–1132.

Currie, S. R., Clark, S., Rimac, S., & Malhotra, S. D. (2003). Comprehensive assessment of insomnia in recovering alcoholics using daily sleep diaries and ambulatory monitoring. *Alcoholism: Clinical and Experimental Research, 27,* 1262–1270.

Currie, S. R., Malhotra, S. D., & Clark, S. (2004). Agreement among objective, subjective, and collateral reports of poor sleep in recovering alcoholics. *Behavioral Sleep Medicine, 2,* 148–161.

Currie, S. R., & Wilson, K. G. (2002). *:60 Second sleep ease: Quick tips to get a good night's rest.* Far Hills, NJ: New Horizon Press.

Currie, S. R., Wilson, K. G., & Curran, D. (2002). Clinical significance and predictors of treatment response to cognitive-behavior therapy for insomnia secondary to chronic pain. *Journal of Behavioral Medicine, 25,* 153.

Currie, S. R., Wilson, K. G., Pontefract, A. J., & deLaplante, L. (2000). Cognitive-behavioral treatment of insomnia secondary to chronic pain. *Journal of Consulting and Clinical Psychology, 68,* 407–416.

Edinger, J. D., & Fins, A. I. (1995). The distribution and clinical significance of sleep time misperceptions among insomniacs. *Sleep, 18,* 232–239.

Edinger, J. D., Wohlgemuth, W. K., Radtke, R. A., Marsh, G. R., & Quillian, R. E. (2001). Cognitive behavioral therapy for treatment of chronic primary insomnia: a randomized controlled trial. *Journal of the American Medical Association, 285,* 1856–1864.

Espie, C. A., Inglis, S. J., & Harvey, L. (2001). Predicting clinically significant response to cognitive behavior therapy for chronic insomnia in general medical practice. *Journal of Consulting and Clinical Psychology, 69,* 58–66.

Flemons, W. W. (1999, April). Treating sleep apnea. *Canadian Journal of CME,* 105–122.

Ford, D. E., & Kamerow, D. B. (1989). Epidemiological study of sleep disturbances and psychiatric disorders. *Journal of the American Medical Association, 262,* 1479–1484.

Gordon, D. L. (2003). *Seven days to a perfect sleep.* New York: St. Martin's Paperbacks.

Gustafson, R. (1992). Treating insomnia with a self-administered muscle relaxation training program: A follow-up. *Psychological Reports, 70,* 124–126.

Harvey, A. (2002). A cognitive model of insomnia. *Behavior Research & Therapy, 40,* 869–894.

Hauri, P. J. (1996). *No more sleepless nights.* Indianapolis, IN: John Wiley & Sons.

Jacobs, G. (1999). *Say good night to insomnia.* New York: Henry Holt & Company.

Jacobs, G. D., Benson, H., & Friedman, R. (1996). Perceived benefits in behavioral-medicine insomnia program: A clinical report. *American Journal of Medicine, 100,* 212–216.

Jacobson, E. (1957). *You must relax.* New York: McGraw-Hill.

Jacobson, N. S., Roberts, L. J., Berns, S. B., & McGlinchey, J. B. (1999). Methods for defining and determining the clinical significance of treatment effects: Description, application, and alternatives. *Journal of Consulting and Clinical Psychology, 67,* 300–307.

Klip, E. C. (1987). *Slapen kun je leren* [You can learn to sleep]. Utrecht, The Netherlands: Teleac.

Kryger, M. (1999). *Can't sleep, can't stay awake: A woman's guide to sleep disorders.* New York: McGraw-Hill.

Lichstein, K. L. (writer/producer) (1989). *Sleep education for seniors* [Motion picture]. Memphis, TN: University of Memphis. Available from Dr. Kenneth Lichtstein, Sleep Research Project, Department of Psychology, University of Alabama, Box 870348, Tuscaloosa, AL 35487–0348.

Lichstein, K. L., Durrence, H. H., Taylor, D. J., Bush, A. J., & Riedel, B. W. (2003). Quantitative criteria for insomnia. *Behaviour Research and Therapy, 41,* 427–455.

Lichstein, K. L., McCrae, C. S., & Wilson, N. M. (2003). Secondary insomnia: Diagnostic issues, cognitive-behavioral treatment, and future directions. In M. L. Perlis & K. L. Lichstein (Eds.), *Treating sleep disorders: Principles and practice of behavioral sleep medicine* (1st ed., pp. 286–304). Toronto: John Wiley & Sons Canada.

Marx, J. S., Gyorky, Z. K., Royalty, G. M., & Stern, T. E. (1992). Use of self-help books in psychotherapy. *Professional Psychology: Research and Practice, 23,* 300–305.

McCall, W. V., & Reynolds, D. (2000). Psychiatric disorders and insomnia. In M. H. Kryger, T. Roth, & W. C. Dement (Eds.), *Principles and practice of sleep medicine* (3rd ed., pp. 640–646). Toronto: W. B. Saunders.

Mimeault, V., & Morin, C. M. (1999). Self-help treatment for insomnia: Bibliotherapy with and without professional guidance. *Journal of Consulting and Clinical Psychology, 67,* 511–519.

Moldofsky, H. (1990). The contribution of sleep-wake physiology to fibromyalgia. *Advances in Pain Research and Therapy, 17,* 227–240.

Montplaisir, J., Nicolas, A., Godbout, R., & Walters, A. (2000). Restless legs syndrome and periodic limb movement disorders. In M. H. Kryger, T. Roth, & W. C. Dement (Eds.), *Principles and practice of sleep medicine* (pp. 742–752). Toronto: W. B. Saunders.

Morawetz, D. (1989). Behavioral self-help treatment for insomnia: A controlled evaluation. *Behavior Therapy, 20,* 365–379.

Morawetz, D. (2003). Insomnia and depression: Which came first. *Sleep Research Online, 5,* 77–81.

Morin, C. M. (1993). *Insomnia: Psychological assessment and management.* New York: Guilford.

Morin, C. M. (1996). *Relief from insomnia.* New York: Doubleday.

Morin, C. M., Bastien, C., & Savard, J. (2003). Current status of cognitive-behavior therapy for insomnia: Evidence for treatment effectiveness and feasibility. In M. L. Perlis & K. L. Lichstein (Eds.), *Treating sleep disorders: Principles and practice of behavioral sleep medicine* (1st ed., pp. 262–285). Toronto: John Wiley & Sons Canada.

Morin, C. M., Colecchi, C., Stone, J., Sood, R., & Brink, D. (1999). Behavioral and pharmacological therapies for late-life insomnia: A randomized controlled trial. *Journal of the American Medical Association, 281,* 991–999.

Morin, C. M., Culbert, J. P., & Schwartz, S. M. (1994). Nonpharmacological interventions for insomnia: A meta-analysis of treatment efficacy. *American Journal of Psychiatry, 151,* 1172–1180.

Morin, C. M., Hauri, P. J., Espie, C. A., Spielman, A. J., Buysse, D., & Bootzin, R. R. (1999). Nonpharmacologic treatment of chronic insomnia. *Sleep, 22,* 1134–1156.

Murtagh, D. R. R., & Greenwood, K. M. (1995). Identifying effective psychological treatments for insomnia: a meta-analysis. *Journal of Consulting and Clinical Psychology, 63,* 79–89.

National Institutes of Health Technology Assessment Panel. (1996). Integration of behavioral and relaxation approaches into the treatment of chronic pain and insomnia. *Journal of the American Medical Association, 276,* 313–318.

Ohayon, M. (2002). Epidemiology of insomnia: What we know and what we still need to learn. *Sleep Medicine Reviews, 6,* 97–111.

Oosterhuis, A., & Klip, C. (1997). The treatment of insomnia through mass media: The results of a televised behavioural training programme. *Social Science and Medicine, 45,* 1223–1229.

Partinen, M., & Hublin, C. (2000). Epidemiology of sleep disorders. In M. H. Kryger, T. Roth, & W. C. Dement (Eds.), *Principles and practice of sleep medicine* (3rd ed., pp. 558–579). Toronto: W. B. Saunders.

Pilowsky, I., Crettenden, I., & Townley, M. (1985). Sleep disturbance in pain clinic patients. *Pain, 23,* 27–33.

Riedel, B. W., & Lichstein, K. L. (1995). Sleep compression and sleep education for older insomniacs: Self-help versus therapist guidance. *Psychology and Aging, 10,* 54–63.

Riedel, B. W., & Lichstein, K. L. (2001). Strategies for evaluating adherence to sleep restriction treatment for insomnia. *Behaviour Research and Therapy, 39,* 201–212.

Roehrs, T., & Roth, T. (1997). Hypnotics, alcohol, and caffeine: Relation to insomnia. In M. R. Pressman (Ed.), *Understanding sleep: The evaluation and treatment of sleep disorders. Application and practice in health psychology* (pp. 339–355). Washington, DC: American Psychological Association.

Rosen, G. M. (1987). Self-help treatment books and the commercialization of psychotherapy. *American Psychologist, 42,* 46–51.

Ruyak, P. S., Bilsbury, C. D., & Rajda, M. (2004). A survey of insomnia treatment at Canadian sleep centres: Is there a role for clinical psychologists? *Canadian Psychology, 45,* 165–173.

Sadeh, A., & Acebo, C. (2002). The role of actigraphy in sleep medicine. *Sleep Medicine Reviews, 6,* 113–124.

Smith, L. J., Smith, L. J., Nowakowski, S., & Perlis, M. L. (2003). Primary insomnia: Diagnostic issues, treatment, and future directions. In M. L. Perlis & K. L. Lichstein (Eds.), *Treating sleep disorders: Principles and practice of behavioral sleep medicine* (1st ed., pp. 214–261). Toronto: John Wiley & Sons Canada.

Smith, M. T., Perlis, M. L., Park, A., Smith, M. S., Pennington, J., Giles, D. E., et al. (2002). Comparative meta-analysis of pharmacotherapy and behavior therapy for persistent insomnia. *American Journal of Psychiatry, 159,* 5–11.

Ström, L., Pettersson, R., & Andersson, G. (2004). Internet-based treatment for insomnia: A controlled evaluation. *Journal of Consulting and Clinical Psychology, 72,* 113–120.

Üstün, T. B., Privett, M., Lecrubier, Y., Weiller, E., Simon, A., Korten, A., et al. (1996). Form, frequency, and burden of sleep problems in general health care: A report from the WHO Collaborative Study on Psychological Problems in General Health Care. *European Psychiatry, 11* (Suppl. 1), 4S–10S.

Weissman, M. M., Greenwald, S., Nino-Murcia, G., & Dement, W. C. (1997). The morbidity of insomnia uncomplicated by psychiatric disorders. *General Hospital Psychiatry, 19,* 245–250.

Wilson, K. G., Watson, S. T., & Currie, S. R. (1998). Daily diary and ambulatory activitiy monitoring of sleep in patients with insomnia secondary to chronic pain. *Pain, 75,* 75–84.

Wohlgemuth, W. K., Edinger, J. D., Fins, A. I., & Sullivan, R. J. (1999). How many nights are enough? The short-term stability of sleep parameters in elderly insomniacs and normal sleepers. *Psychophysiology, 36,* 233–244.

Woolfolk, R. L., & McNulty, T. F. (1983). Relaxation treatment for insomnia: A component analysis. *Journal of Consulting and Clinical Psychology, 51,* 495–503.

Zorick, F. J., & Walsh, J. K. (2000). Evaluation and management of insomnia: An overview. In M. H. Kryger, T. Roth, & W. C. Dement (Eds.), *Principles and practice of sleep medicine* (3rd ed., pp. 615–623). Toronto: W. B. Saunders.

CHAPTER 11

Self-Help Therapies for Problem Drinking

KYP KYPRI AND
JOHN A. CUNNINGHAM

An Overview of Alcohol and Health

Alcohol harms the user via three general mechanisms: intoxicating effects, which produce acute problems such as injury; relatively immediate toxic effects such as alcohol poisoning; and chronic disease effects, including addiction, a variety of cancers, and gastrointestinal problems (Rehm, Room, Monteiro et al., 2003). Consumption of alcohol can also harm persons other than the user, via drink driving, assault, fetal alcohol syndrome, and a variety of other second-hand effects (Langley, Kypri, & Stephenson, 2003). The social patterning and extent of alcohol-related harm depend on the pattern and context of consumption, and there is enormous cultural variation in the interpretation of what constitutes problem drinking and in the terminology used to describe it (Heath, 1998).

Approximately 2 billion people consume alcohol each year, of whom more than 76 million are diagnosed with an alcohol use disorder (World Health Organization, 2002). In 2002, 4% of the global disease burden and 3.2% of all deaths internationally were attributable to alcohol (World Health Organization, 2002). Over the past decade, alcohol has increased its share of the global burden of disease, despite relatively stable overall consumption levels in many developed countries (Babor et al., 2003).

Shifts in terminology reflect historical changes in the nature and focus of alcohol research (Grant & Litvak, 1998). An early focus on the relationship between national aggregate consumption and the incidence of disease has given way to research in which drinking patterns and the social context of alcohol consumption are examined in terms of their health and other consequences (Saunders & de Burgh, 1998). Some commonly used terms are discussed below.

Heavy drinking typically refers to high overall levels of alcohol consumption; for example, weekly or annual consumption that either exceeds a societal norm (e.g., the median consumption level for the country) or a criterion reference (e.g., medically recommended limits). Heavy drinking has also been used to refer to a large quantity of alcohol consumed on a single occasion, often called *heavy episodic drinking* or *binge drinking*. Binge drinking is operationally defined in the United States as the equivalent of 60 grams of ethanol (5 U.S. standard drinks) for males and 48 grams (4 U.S. standard drinks) for females consumed within a 2-hour period (National Institute on Alcohol Abuse and Alcoholism, 2004). In men and women of average weight, this level of consumption typically produces a blood alcohol concentration of more than 0.08 g/ml, the legal limit for driving in the United States (the limit is 0.05 g/ml or lower in most other developed countries).

Alcohol dependence and *alcohol abuse* are diagnostic categories of the *Diagnostic and Statistical Manual of Mental Disorders*, fourth edition (DSM-IV; American Psychiatric Association, 1994), the most widely used mental health classification system in North America. *Alcohol dependence* is characterized by a "cluster of cognitive, behavioral, and physiological symptoms indicating that the individual continues [drinking] despite significant [alcohol]-related problems" (p. 176). *Alcohol abuse* is defined as "a maladaptive pattern of [alcohol] use manifested by recurrent and significant adverse consequences related to the repeated use of [alcohol]" (p. 182). For each diagnosis, the drinker is required to have exhibited a certain number of specified symptoms.

Alcohol dependence syndrome and *harmful drinking* are the terms used in the *International Classification of Diseases*, tenth edition (ICD-10; World Health Organization, 1992). The ICD *alcohol dependence syndrome* is defined similarly to that in its DSM counterpart, but in contrast, the diagnosis *harmful drinking*, "a pattern of [drinking] that is causing damage to physical...or mental health" (p. 106), differs markedly from its DSM counterpart, *alcohol abuse*, which reflects more the social consequences of excessive alcohol consumption. Prevalence estimates of alcohol dependence obtained under DSM and ICD tend to be similar, whereas estimates for *alcohol abuse* tend to be higher than those for *harmful drinking* (Hasin et al., 1997; Hasin, Li, McCloud, & Endicott, 1996).

A term beginning to appear frequently is *hazardous drinking*, defined as alcohol consumption "that will probably lead to harmful consequences

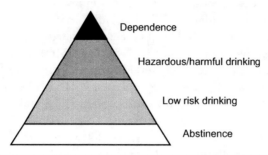

Figure 11.1 Relative proportion of dependent, hazardous, and low-risk drinkers. The size of segment indicates the approximate proportion of the population in each category. From "Hazardous Alcohol Use: Its Delineation as a Subthreshold Disorder, and Approaches to Its Diagnosis and Management," by J. B. Saunders and N. K. Lee, 2000, *Comprehensive Psychiatry*, 41(2 Suppl. 1), pp. 95–103. Reprinted with permission.

for the user" (Edwards, Arif, & Hadgson, 1981). The adoption of this term reflects empirical findings of a *spectrum* of alcohol use and related problems (see Figure 11.1), in which a small proportion of drinkers are alcohol dependent, a larger minority drink in a harmful or hazardous manner, the majority drink at low risk levels, and some are abstinent (Saunders & Lee, 2000).

For the purposes of this chapter, we use the term *problem drinking* to cover the full spectrum of alcohol use patterns that produce harm or place the drinker at high risk of experiencing harm. The harm can be acute—e.g., poisoning, injury, social embarrassment, legal sanction, damage to the fetus—or chronic; e.g., cancer, cirrhosis, addiction, depression, and family breakdown.

The Prevalence of Alcohol Consumption and Alcohol Use Disorders

There is evidence of a move toward less frequent drinking but increased quantities per drinking occasion in many countries, a pattern associated with a high social cost (Rehm, Room, Graham et al., 2003), which may also reduce some of the benefits of moderate consumption (Breslow & Smothers, 2005). For example, epidemiological data from the United States reveal a 17% increase from 1993 to 2001 in binge drinking episodes per person in the adult population (Naimi et al., 2003). Among those who consumed alcohol in 2001, 51% of 18–20 year-olds and 49% of 21–25 year-olds had consumed five or more drinks (>60g ethanol) at least once in the last 30 days (Naimi et al., 2003). Notably, 69% of such drinking episodes occurred in persons aged 26 years or older, demonstrating that the problem is not limited to adolescents and young adults.

Alcohol use disorders are among the most prevalent mental health disorders and they have a high rate of comorbidity. In the Australian National Survey of Mental Health and Well Being, conducted in 1997 (n = 10,641, 78% response), one third of persons with a DSM alcohol use disorder met criteria for one or more comorbid mental disorders in the previous 12 months (Teesson, Dietrich, Degenhardt, Lynskey, & Beard, 2002). The most common comorbid disorders were anxiety (20%) and affective disorders (24%) (Teesson, Hall, Lynskey, & Degenhardt, 2000).

In the United States, the 1999 National Household Survey on Drug Abuse (Substance Abuse and Mental Health Services Administration, 2000) showed that alcohol dependence was more common than dependence on illicit substances. Twelve-month prevalence rates of alcohol dependence were 6.5% at age 15, climbing to a peak of 11.7% at age 21 and declining to 6.6% at age 25. Rates were 3–4% for persons aged 30–49 years and around 1% for persons 50 years and older. These results are similar to those obtained in Australia, where 9.3% of persons aged 18–24 years meet criteria for dependence (Teesson et al., 2000).

The Need for Self-Help Approaches in Reducing Problem Drinking

A recent comprehensive review of evidence for policy and other interventions to address alcohol-related harm (Babor et al., 2003), concludes with a list of best practice recommendations including: increasing taxes on alcohol, a minimum purchase age of 21, reducing the density of liquor outlets, curtailing hours of sale, and a range of drink-driving countermeasures.

While the evidence for these is robust across a variety of settings and cultures, political and public support for placing greater restrictions on the availability of alcohol is currently low. In England, for example, the government recently moved to permit 24-hour liquor licenses and to substantially reduce local authority powers to restrict locations of outlets (Room, 2004). Surveys of Canadians in 2000 and 2002 reveal little support for increased alcohol taxes (20% in favor, 80% against) and opposition to the prohibition of liquor advertising on television (40% in favor, 60% against), while only 9% said there were too many liquor outlets in their communities (Giesbrecht, Ialomiteanu, & Anglin, 2005).

Although efforts should no doubt continue to bring about shifts in public sentiment and policy in order to create environments that discourage problem drinking, these findings reinforce the need for the development and widespread implementation of effective demand-side interventions. Among the interventions that may be useful as part of an overall strategy are self-help approaches.

Overview of Self-Help for Problem Drinking

In Australia, only about one third of persons diagnosable with an alcohol use disorder in the last 12 months had consulted a health professional about it (Teesson et al., 2002). This may in part be evidence of the failure to detect persons with disorder in primary health care (Denny, Serdula, Holtzman, & Nelson, 2003) and real or perceived barriers to accessing treatment. It probably also reflects the fact that many people recover from alcohol use disorders without recourse to professional help (Sobell, Wilkinson, & Sobell, 1990). Self-help approaches have the potential to bridge a gap for those in need of some assistance but unable or unwilling to access help via conventional means.

For several decades now, self-help pamphlets, manuals, and books have been used to supplement traditional treatment of alcohol use disorders (Richmond, Heather, Wodak, Kehoe, & Webster, 1995), to stimulate interest in treatment, and to encourage maintenance along with telephone follow-up (Heather, Kissoon-Singh, & Fenton, 1990). The use of these materials has been studied in clinical settings as self-standing interventions, to raise awareness about safe drinking guidelines, to help people assess their own alcohol use, and to suggest strategies for cutting down (Heather, Whitton, & Robertson, 1986).

These interventions use a variety of techniques, typically based on cognitive–behavior therapy (CBT) and/or motivational interviewing (Miller & Rollnick, 1991). For example, Sitharthan and colleagues administered a CBT treatment program by correspondence (Sitharthan, Kavanagh, & Sayer, 1996) to adults with self-professed problem drinking but without physical dependence who were seeking to cut down on their own. After initial assessment, participants received five letters over a 4-month period describing methods they could use to control their drinking. These included standard features of CBT: goal-setting, keeping record of when they exceeded their goals, problem-solving, planning approaches to avoid high-risk settings, methods to resist temptation, relapse prevention, and lifestyle change.

The FRAMES approach described by Miller and Rollnick (1991) is the foundation for many motivationally based self-help programs. FRAMES stands for generating Feedback on the basis of a detailed assessment, emphasizing the client's Responsibility for changes, providing clear Advice to a client to reduce their drinking, offering a Menu of strategies for accomplishing goals, adopting an Empathic style, and promoting Self-efficacy. Given the lack of clinician contact in self-help approaches, FRAMES is typically used selectively and within the confines of the medium of communication. Feedback is commonly used in interactive approaches, by mail or over the Internet. Cunningham and colleagues developed a self-help booklet based on these principles for use in an addiction clinic (Cunningham, Sdao-Jarvie, Koski-Jannes, & Breslin, 2001). After a clinician-administered assessment, clients were given a booklet titled "Alcohol and You," containing a summary of their consumption and alcohol-related problems, comparison of the client's drinking with others in the population, a drinking diary for regular self-monitoring, information on the effects of reducing their drinking, a decisional balance exercise, encouragement to set a goal and to seek further help, and a menu of options the client could use to affect a change. Many clients express surprise at the extent to which their drinking exceeds medically recommended limits and societal norms and report that this has a motivating influence (Kypri, 2002).

The provision of self-help materials and support by correspondence have features that make them attractive for community-level intervention for problem drinking: they minimize costly professional contact, they can be tailored to fit a person's motivational state, and they can be used to supplement more intensive intervention. These interventions have the potential to reach segments of the population not normally in contact with alcohol treatment services, thereby broadening the base of treatment (Institute of Medicine, 1990).

More recently, the efficacy of self-help materials outside health care settings has been studied, in which materials are posted to entire communities (Cunningham, Wild, & Walsh, 1999; Sobell et al., 2002). Since the mid-1980s, computers have been used to deliver self-help resources (Skinner, Allen, McIntosh, & Palmer, 1985), and interactive applications via the Internet have recently begun to proliferate (Skinner, Maley, Smith, Chirrey, & Morrison, 2001).

There is considerable community interest in self-help resources delivered by a variety of methods. In a survey of a random sample from the general population in Ontario, Canada, Cunningham and colleagues (1999) found that 45% of problem drinkers expressed interest in receiving a free self-help booklet. In a second such survey by Koski-Jannes & Cunningham (2001), current drinkers were asked about their interest in: (a) a telephone assessment with a therapist, (b) a self-help book, and (c) computerized normative feedback concerning their drinking. Interest in (a), (b), and (c) was 16, 26, and 39%, respectively.

With respect to the provision of self-help material via computers, Kypri and colleagues (Kypri, Saunders, & Gallagher, 2003) found that university students considered Web-based assessment and personalized feedback the most acceptable of a range of brief interventions for hazardous drinking. Four out of five hazardous drinkers said they would use such a resource if they felt they had a drinking problem (Kypri et al., 2003).

For the general population, Cunningham and colleagues (Cunningham, Humphreys, & Koski-Jannes, 2000) developed a service in which users provided details of their drinking and related experiences through a Web site and were given personalized, normative feedback on-line. A voluntary Web survey linked to the feedback, assessing acceptability of the materials and process, showed that feedback was generally well received by respondents. It was concluded that the Internet format is promising as a means of providing motivational feedback on alcohol use. However, significant challenges were identified with respect to evaluating the instrument's efficacy. Unlike interventions that are delivered in structured settings (e.g., primary care facilities), a free access Web site does not readily accommodate the tracking of service users over time for the purpose of evaluation. Furthermore, there is a potential that seeking to track users for follow-up, via a voluntary login, might reduce its appeal to problem drinkers who prefer to remain anonymous and thereby reduce the reach of the intervention.

These research challenges may lie behind the tendency among providers to *oversell* self-help services offered over the Internet. On the basis of an extensive search, Toll and colleagues present a description of alcohol-related Web sites, reporting that only 5 of 68 treatment-related sites (7%) provided on-line treatment. Seventy percent of treatment sites applied 12-step facilitation, and only 4% focused on motivational strategies; i.e., those for which there is strong evidence of efficacy. Few sites provided references (13%) or outcome data (7%) on the treatment that they recommended (Toll et al., 2003).

The recognition of a need for greater attention to the validation of self-help approaches is not new. In a paper motivated by the rapidly growing interest in self-help interventions in the 1970s, Glasgow and Rosen (1978) reviewed studies of interventions for a range of behaviors (not including problem drinking). They concluded that although a number of interventions were evidence based, in general, "the extent to which self-help programs have been validated remains extremely variable" (p. 16). They called for greater methodological rigor in the evaluation of efficacy, in particular: use of study samples that allow for generalizability to the population of interest, reducing loss to follow-up, longer follow-up, identification of key mediating variables in effective interventions, and efforts to quantify cost-effectiveness.

Glasgow and Rosen (1978) also called on researchers to adopt common definitions of intervention types. They defined *self-administered* programs as those in which "a written program constitutes the sole basis for treatment and clients administer materials without therapist contact" (p. 2). *Minimal contact* referred to programs "in which there is some contact with the therapist, but clients rely primarily on a written program" (p. 2). *Therapist-administered* programs involved regular contact with a therapist, where meetings supplement the written material. This three-way classification still usefully reflects the heterogeneity in the application of self-help methods for behavioral change. Given the advances in electronic communication, the classification could be expanded to include a specification of the medium through which the approach operates.

Effectiveness of Self-Help Interventions

The media through which self-help has been delivered include books, pamphlets, the telephone, and computers. In a recent paper, Apodaca and Miller (2003) reported on a meta-analytic review of the efficacy of bibliotherapy for alcohol problems. Bibliotherapy was operationally defined as "any therapeutic intervention that was presented in a written format, designed to be read and implemented by the client" (p. 290). The review included studies in which bibliotherapy was provided in conjunction with no more than one session with a practitioner, thereby cutting across the first two of Glasgow and Rosen's (1978) categories. Twenty-two studies met the inclusion criteria. The authors concluded that "modest support was found for the efficacy of self-help materials in decreasing at-risk and harmful drinking" (p. 289).

In their review method, Apodaca and Miller (2003) made an important distinction between interventions aimed at individuals seeking treatment and those aimed at individuals identified through screening (so-called non-treatment-seekers). They found that effect sizes were considerably lower and more variable for the latter group. Despite the small effect sizes, when viewed from a public health perspective (Abrams et al., 1996), self-help interventions offer the chance of a significant population-level payoff as such interventions are low cost and could be provided to a wide range of individuals. Public health impact is typically conceptualized as the reach of the intervention × efficacy per unit cost (Abrams & Clayton, 2001). The low cost and potential for broad reach of self-help interventions, coupled with the high base rate of the behavior, suggests that such interventions can have a significant public health impact. This argument follows from the observation that the majority of individuals with drinking problems do not seek treatment (Institute of Medicine, 1990).

Motivating individuals to seek help is only the first in a series of steps needed to achieve a treatment outcome. Research on brief interventions in primary health care shows that practitioners are not always in favor of discussing alcohol with their patients through fear of damaging rapport and because of the scarcity of time available to conduct intervention where it is required (Beich, Gannik, & Malterud, 2002; Lock, Kaner, Heather, Gilvarry, & McAvoy, 2000). There is also evidence that it is difficult to maintain consistent involvement of key health service staff in the implementation of brief interventions; for example, service receptionists (Lock et al., 2000).

Qualitative Review of Self-Administered Treatments

Given the need to extend the reach of interventions for alcohol problems (U.S. Preventive Services Task Force, 2004), there is value in separately considering interventions that do not involve any contact with a health practitioner, which we take to include general practitioners, medical specialists, nurses, psychologists, counselors, and social workers. This category is equivalent to Glasgow and Rosen's (1978) *self-administered* classification. Effective interventions that are deliverable without the need for practitioner involvement may be more likely to be put into practice than those that require the ordinary systems of health care delivery to be modified substantially. Because of the heterogeneity in format of self-help and correspondence interventions revealed in the search for papers in this study, and the paucity of research evaluating them, we have not attempted a meta-analytic review. The purpose of this study was to critically review the evidence on self-administered treatments and to discuss future research needs.

Methods

Self-administered treatments were defined as materials or information supplied to individuals with the aim of reducing drinking or alcohol-related problems that did not involve contact with a health practitioner: doctor, nurse, psychologist, counselor, or social worker. Studies in which a health practitioner provided assessment or treatment for an alcohol or drug problem were excluded. To be eligible for inclusion, studies also had to have a randomly assigned control group; i.e., a group of individuals not exposed to an intervention or to only minimal materials such as educational pamphlets, which was assessed at the same follow-up time points as the experimental group(s). Accordingly, studies in which a self-help intervention served as a control condition (e.g., where compared with a practitioner-delivered intervention) were not included.

Studies were identified by: (a) searching of PubMed using the "Any Field" criterion; (b) searching of PsycINFO in the title, abstract, heading word, table of contents, and key concepts fields; and (c) by examining the reference lists of the papers identified in those searches. We searched for the following word combinations: alcohol and bibliotherapy, alcohol and self-help, alcohol and computer and intervention, alcohol and correspondence and intervention, alcohol and feedback and intervention, alcohol and motivational and intervention, alcohol and normative and intervention. The searches were conducted on April 1, 2004.

Only analyses of intervention group by time interaction effects and between-group comparisons adjusted for baseline differences are reported, which we take as an adequate test for a differential effect of intervention. Studies in which both the experimental and control conditions showed reductions in drinking but in which there were no significant differences between conditions were not taken as evidence of the efficacy of the interventions. We grouped the durations of outcome into the categories used by Moyer, Finney, Swearingen, and Vergun (2002) in their meta-analytic review of brief intervention efficacy trials: < 3 months, > 3–6 months, > 6–12 months, and > 12 months.

Results

A total of 1135 references were examined, of which 14 (describing 13 studies) were deemed eligible for inclusion in the review. The eligible papers are listed alphabetically and summarized in Table 11.1. They include two Ph.D. dissertations and 12 articles in peer-reviewed journals, spanning the period from 1986 to 2003.

Five of the studies include only college students as participants, recruited through undergraduate classes (Agostinelli, Brown, & Miller, 1995; Collins, Carey, & Sliwinski, 2002; Miller, 2001; Walters, Bennett, & Miller, 2000) or at a student health clinic (Kypri, 2002). The remaining studies involved members of the general population recruited through population surveys (Cunningham, Koski-Jannes, Wild, & Cordingley, 2002; Cunningham, Wild, Bondy, & Lin, 2001; Sobell et al., 2002), media advertisements (Heather et al., 1986; Hester & Delaney, 1997; Sitharthan et al., 1996), or a workplace (Walters & Woodall, 2003).

A broad range of criteria were used to define problem drinking, including average alcohol consumption above recommended limits (e.g., Agostinelli et al., 1995), a 7-day diary (e.g., Sitharthan et al., 1996), standard screening tests like MAST or the AUDIT (e.g., Hester & Delaney, 1997), and a combination of a standard screening questionnaire and a consumption measure (e.g., Heather et al., 1990).

Intervention Approaches The studies cover a range of intervention approaches. Two groups of intervention approaches, each applied to a range of populations and settings, could be discerned. Interventions based on motivational feedback and, in particular, normative comparison, in which a person's consumption levels were compared with a reference group, constituted the largest group (Agostinelli et al., 1995; Collins et al., 2002; Cunningham, Wild et al., 2001; Miller, 2001; Sobell et al., 2002, Walters et al., 2000, Walters & Woodall, 2003). A subgroup of these motivational

Table 11.1 Studies of Self-Administered Interventions for Problem Drinking

Study	Methods	Results and comments
Agostinelli et al., 1995	Design: Randomized controlled trial. Psychology students who screened positive for problem drinking were randomly assigned to: (A) mailed personalized feedback involving normative comparison (n = 12); or (B) assessment only control (n = 11)	Results: At 6 weeks follow-up, there were significant reductions in overall consumption and mean weekly BAC (but not peak BAC) in group A relative to B. Comment: The trial is small, and analyses do not control for baseline differences in alcohol consumption. The sample was highly self-selected, greatly limiting the generalizability of the results.
Collins et al., 2002	Design: Randomized controlled trial. Psychology students with hazardous drinking were randomly assigned to: (A) mailed normative feedback (n = 49); or (B) a psychoeducational brochure (n = 51)	Results: At 6 weeks follow-up, group A reported significantly fewer drinks per heavy drinking week and fewer binge episodes than group B. Differences were nonsignificant at 6 months follow-up. Comment: Attrition was high at 6 months follow-up, with 35 participants lost to follow-up.
Cunningham et al., 2002	Design: Randomized controlled trial (factorial design). Following a general population survey of drinking, volunteers were randomly assigned to: (A) assessment only control (n = 26); or (B) mailed personalized feedback alone (n = 21); or (C) self-help book alone (n = 22); or (D) mailed personalized feedback plus self-help book (n = 17)	Results: At 6 months follow-up condition B reduced the number of drinks per drinking day and number of binge episodes. Condition D had lower total consumption and number of binge episodes relative to groups A, B, and C. Comment: Analyses controlled for baseline drinking levels.
Cunningham, Wild, et al., 2001	Design: Posttest only with randomization by block into two conditions: (A) household was sent a normative feedback pamphlet (n = 472); or (B) no pamphlet was sent (n = 225). In the month following delivery of pamphlets, a general population survey was conducted and respondents were identified by postal code as coming from intervention or control condition households	Results: A three-way statistical interaction was observed: group A participants who were problem drinkers reduced their drinking (relative to group B), if they perceived themselves to be at high risk, but increased their drinking if they perceived themselves to be at low risk. Comment: Limited by posttest only design.

Note: BAC = blood alcohol concentration; MAST = Michigan Alcoholism Screening Test.

(continued)

Table 11.1 (continued)

Study	Methods	Results and comments
Heather et al., 1986	Design: Randomized controlled trial. Problem drinkers wanting to cut down their drinking were recruited through newspaper advertisements to: (A) a self-help manual (n = 126); or (B) a general information and advice booklet (n = 121)	Results: At 6 months follow-up, there were greater reductions in drinking during the preceding 7 days for those who received the manual (group A), relative to those who received the information booklet (group B). Comment: The external and internal validity of this study is limited by a low return rate of initial self-assessment questionnaires (31%) and high attrition at 6 months follow-up (47%).
Heather, Robertson, MacPherson, Allsop, & Fulton, 1987	Design: 12-month follow up of Heather et al., 1986, above. Assessed at 12-month follow-up: (A) self-help manual (n = 63); or (B) general information and advice booklet (n = 47)	Results: Reduced consumption in the group that received the self-help manual (group A relative to group B) was maintained at one year follow-up. Comment: Attrition at 12 months was high and differential by group (50% in A and 61% in B), which may have exaggerated the treatment effect size.
Heather et al., 1990	Design: Randomized controlled trial. Problem drinkers wanting to cut down their drinking were recruited through newspaper advertisements and randomly assigned to one of: (A) a general advice and information booklet (n = 32); (B) a behaviorally based self-help manual (n = 24); or (C) the manual plus an opportunity to make progress reports to answering service (n = 26); or (D) the manual plus an opportunity to make progress reports to an interviewer (n = 25)	Results: At 6 months follow-up, groups B, C, and D each reported significantly lower alcohol consumption than did group A. The differences between groups B, C, and D were nonsignificant. Comment: Attrition was relatively low (19%).

	Design	Results
Hester & Delaney, 1997	Design: Randomized controlled trial. Respondents to advertisements were screened for hazardous drinking and randomly assigned to: (A) eight weekly sessions of computerized assessment and feedback (n = 20); or (B) delayed intervention (n = 20)	Results: At 10 weeks follow-up, group A had significantly lower consumption than B. Comment: The authors also report analyses of within-group changes in consumption to 20 weeks and to 12 months but these comparisons are not considered to adequately test for a treatment effect.
Kypri, 2002	Design: Randomized controlled trial. University students visiting the student health service were screened for hazardous drinking and randomly assigned to: (A) Web-based assessment and personalized feedback (n = 51); or (B) a leaflet on the effects of alcohol (n = 53)	Results: Relative to group B, at 6 weeks follow-up group A reported significantly lower consumption and fewer problems. At 6 months follow-up reductions in problems were still statistically significant. Comment: Attrition was low: 10% at 6 months. Analyses controlled for baseline drinking. External validity is high: 94% of eligible students agreed to participate, and the trial occurred in a naturalistic setting in which it could be implemented long term.
Miller, 2001	Design: Randomized controlled trial. College students with hazardous drinking were randomly assigned to : (A) no assessment (n = 139); (B) assessment at one month and 3 months post-intervention (n = 140); or (C) a self-help CD-ROM (n = 136); or a self-help skills training program (n = 132)	Results: At 6 months follow-up, groups B, C, and D each reported significantly lower consumption and fewer alcohol-related problems than did group A. Groups B, C, and D did not differ significantly from each other. Comment: Groups C and D involved group sessions with trained facilitators so were ineligible interventions for this review. Group B may be considered a minimal self-help intervention.
Sitharthan et al., 1996	Design: Randomized controlled trial. Problem drinkers wanting to cut down their drinking were recruited through media advertisements to one of: (A) cognitive–behavioral therapy (CBT) by correspondence (n = 70); or (B) a minimal intervention consisting of five letters about the effects of alcohol and encouragement to complete and return drinking monitoring cards (n = 51)	Results: At 4 months follow-up group A had significantly lower alcohol consumption than group B. The differences remained at 6 and 12 months, despite group B receiving CBT prior to the later time points. Comment: the intervention was relatively intensive, involving five letters over a 4-month period.

(continued)

Note: BAC = blood alcohol concentration; MAST = Michigan Alcoholism Screening Test.

Table 11.1 (*Continued*)

Study	Methods	Results and comments
Sobell et al., 2002	Design: Randomized controlled trial. Problem drinkers wanting to reduce their drinking were recruited by newspaper advertisements to: (A) personalized feedback sent by mail (n = 414); or (B) educational pamphlet (n = 411)	Results: Both groups reduced their drinking but there were no significant differences between groups at one year follow-up.
Walters et al., 2000	Design: Randomized controlled trial. Psychology students (n = 37) were screened for hazardous drinking and randomly assigned to: (A) a 2-hour class on alcohol plus mailed motivational feedback (n = 12); or (B) mailed motivational feedback (n = 11); or (C) assessment only control (n = 14)	Results: At 6 weeks follow-up, group B reported a significantly lower volume consumed per month than group A. There were no other statistically significant effects. Comment: The sample size is small and there were several measures in which differences were nonsignificant; there was no adjustment for multiple comparisons to guard against Type I error.
Walters & Woodall, 2003	Design: Randomized controlled trial. Employees of a manufacturing firm were screened for hazardous drinking and randomly assigned to: (A) mailed feedback (n = 25); or (B) delayed intervention (n = 23)	Results: At 8 weeks follow-up, group A had lower alcohol consumption relative to B. Comment: No adjustment was made for pre-intervention differences between the groups. The study is limited by the fact that most participants were moderate drinkers (averaging 7 drinks per week) and only 7% of potential respondents participated

Note: BAC = blood alcohol concentration; MAST = Michigan Alcoholism Screening Test.

feedback approaches included studies relying on computers to deliver the assessment and feedback (Kypri, 2002; Hester & Delaney, 1997).

A second group of studies involved more complex interventions. In their experimental conditions C and D, Cunningham and colleagues (2002) used a self-help book called *Saying When* (Sanchez-Craig, Davila, & Cooper, 1996), which presents a five-step process following principles of motivational interviewing, cognitive–behavior therapy, and relapse prevention: (a) taking stock, (b) coping with temptation, (c) goal-setting, (d) developing strategies to meet goals, and (e) maintaining progress. Included in the book are forms to assist with self-monitoring of progress and some answers to frequently asked questions about drinking and alcohol-related problems.

In their experimental conditions (A in the 1986 study; B, C, and D in the 1990 study), Heather and colleagues used a 56-page manual titled *So You Want to Cut Down Your Drinking*, which was professionally printed in color with illustrations. The content followed principles of behavior therapy and relapse prevention with an emphasis on knowledge and skill acquisition. It included definitions of *alcoholism* and *problem drinking*, guidance on who should attempt controlled drinking versus abstinence, information on standard units and recommended weekly limits, a diary to record the previous week's drinking for the purpose of comparison, information on alcohol metabolism, the behavioral and emotional effects of different blood alcohol levels, the concept of tolerance, items on decisional balance, instruction in self-monitoring, a guided functional analysis of drinking behavior, limit setting, self-reinforcement, slowing drinking, drink refusal, and what to do in case of relapse. The control condition booklet called *Drinking and Alcohol Problems in Scotland* gave general information about drinking and alcohol-related problems illustrated by case studies.

The correspondence-based self-help materials tested by Sitharthan and colleagues (1996, condition A) consisted of five letters sent to participants over a 4-month period, beginning with information about the effects of alcohol and personalized feedback and followed by guidance in a range of cognitive–behavioral strategies that could be used to control their drinking. These included goal-setting, self-monitoring, problem-solving, planning for high-risk situations, dealing with temptation, relapse prevention, and planning a future lifestyle.

Efficacy in Reducing Drinking and Related Problems   Table 11.2 presents a summary of the post-intervention periods assessed in the reviewed studies. None of the studies examined outcomes for a period of greater than 12 months. Of the 13 studies reviewed, 11 presented evidence of intervention effects. The two exceptions were Sobell et al. (2002), in which there were

Table 11.2 Follow-up Assessments Conducted in the Reviewed Studies

	Assessment undertaken		
	(<3 Mos)	(>3–6 Mos)	(>6–12 Mos)
Agostinelli et al., 1995	✓	—	—
Collins et al., 2002	✓	x	—
Cunningham et al., 2001	—	✓	—
Cunningham et al., 2002	✓	—	—
Heather et al., 1986, 1987	—	✓	✓
Heather et al., 1990	—	✓	—
Hester & Delaney, 1997	✓	—	—
Kypri, 2002	✓	✓	—
Miller, 2001	—	✓	—
Sitharthan et al., 1996	—	✓	✓
Sobell et al., 2002	—	—	x
Walters et al., 2000	✓	—	—
Walters & Woodall, 2003	✓	—	—

✓ *Intervention effect; x no effect detected; — not assessed.*

small and inconsistent between-group differences, and Walters and Woodall (2003), in which a non-significant difference favored intervention.

Five trials showed that self-help interventions resulted in decreased consumption and/or alcohol-related problems in the intervention group relative to controls 6 months later (Cunningham et al., 2002; Heather et al., 1990, 1986; Kypri, 2002; Miller, 2001; Sitharthan et al., 1996). In two of these, the effects were present at 12 months (Heather et al., 1987; Sitharthan et al., 1996). In five trials, effects were limited to 10 weeks (Hester & Delaney, 1997), 6 weeks (Agostinelli et al., 1995; Collins et al., 2002), and one month (Cunningham, Wild et al., 2001; Walters et al., 2000), although it should be noted that in all but one of these (Collins et al., 2002), longer follow-up assessments were not undertaken.

Mailed manuals or feedback reports were the sole intervention in all but four of the studies. In addition to mailed self-help booklets, Heather et al. (1990) provided participants in one arm of their trial the opportunity to give progress reports on their drinking by leaving answering machine messages. Hester and Delaney (1997) screened individuals face-to-face, after which participants completed self-control training using an interactive computer program. In the trial described by Kypri (2002), all screening, assessment, feedback, and one of the follow-up assessments were conducted using an interactive Web interface, while the second assessment was by mail. In the study described by Miller (2001), two of the experimental arms (C, Alcohol 101 CD-ROM; and D, Alcohol Skills Training Program) did not meet eligibility criteria for this review. However, the multiple assessment group (B) could be considered to have received a minimal self-help intervention and was compared against a single assessment group (A). Both of these groups were screened by mail and then assessed with a Web survey.

Discussion

A small and heterogeneous group of self-administered interventions for problem drinking met the eligibility criteria for inclusion in this review. Only three of the trials included assessments of outcomes lasting more than 6 months. There was modest evidence supporting the use of minimal self-administered interventions for reducing problem drinking in the short term (up to 6 months). There was also some evidence of effectiveness for more intensive self-administered interventions for up to 12 months. These results are consistent with those of Apodaca and Miller (2003), who found small to medium effects of bibliotherapy with self-referred drinkers and more variable results for drinkers identified through screening.

There are a number of methodological factors that affect the reliability and generalizability of the results. Notably, many of the studies had small sample sizes: in six of the trials, there were fewer than 30 individuals included in each of the experimental arms analyzed. This exposes the review process to the risk of *publication bias* (Dickersin, 1990), also known as the *file-drawer* problem (Rosenthal, 1991). It has been shown that underpowered clinical trials with statistically significant findings are more likely to be reported in the scientific literature than studies with nonsignificant results (the latter often consigned to the file drawer; Dickersin, Chan, Chalmers, Sacks, & Smith, 1987). This is due to a variety of factors beyond the scope of this chapter (Dickersin, 1997). In a large systematic review, such as that conducted by Moyer et al. (2002), analyses can be conducted with and without the underpowered trials in order to estimate the extent of the bias. In this case, all six of the studies with fewer than 30 individuals per experimental arm yielded positive results. Caution is therefore advised in the interpretation of the findings.

In six of the trials, participants were recruited with advertisements offering help with drinking problems. One would therefore assume that these individuals had relatively high motivation to reduce their drinking. It is against this backdrop that the results from these studies should be interpreted.

One particularly interesting finding is that by Miller (2001), in which college students exposed to assessment alone (group B) reduced their drinking and related problems to an extent similar to those in groups that received intervention. This effect, sometimes called *assessment reactivity* or a *Hawthorne effect* (Mayo, 1933), is often observed clinically but has rarely been subjected to formal study in the alcohol research field. It underlines the value in at least assessing a patient's drinking, whether there is the capability of delivering intervention or not.

Cunningham and colleagues (2002) employed a factorial design to examine the effects of personalized feedback, a key component of motivational interviewing, and a self-help book, both separately and jointly. Participants who received personalized feedback reported better drinking outcomes than those who received no intervention, but the best outcomes were reported by individuals who received both personalized feedback and a self-help book.

The study by Cunningham et al. (2002) is arguably the most robust study of self-help materials for alcohol problems among the general population. Given the process by which participants were recruited—a probability sample from the general population—it can be concluded that personalized feedback and a self-help manual used proactively would be likely to benefit persons with problem drinking in the wider population, many of whom might not present for treatment.

The small area population study described by Cunningham, Wild et al. (2001) was the only study to experimentally examine a psychological mechanism—perceived risk—hypothesized to mediate the response to normative feedback. Problem drinkers tended to reduce their drinking if they received the intervention and perceived themselves to be at high risk of alcohol-related harm and to increase their drinking if they received the intervention but considered themselves to be at low risk of alcohol-related harm. This result has important implications for the way correspondence interventions are delivered but, because of its posttest-only design these findings need to be replicated.

A pilot study involving the provision of personalized assessment feedback for problem drinking on the Internet (Cunningham et al., 2000), showed that there is an audience for Internet-based interventions. The authors concluded that the next step was to determine whether receiving such personalized feedback materials on the Internet leads to changes in drinking behavior. Such a study was conducted by Kypri and colleagues (2004), with students attending a university health service. Electronic screening and brief intervention (e-SBI), involving assessment of drinking risk levels and personalized feedback delivered by computer, was found to produce significant reductions in hazardous drinking in the short and medium term. A process evaluation confirmed that the intervention was popular among students and suggested that the follow-up assessment (to which the control condition was exposed) may itself have encouraged moderation in drinking.

In the context of addiction medicine, the studies by Heather et al. (1986, 1990) and Sitharthan et al. (1996) are of the highest quality and relevance. Together they support the use of self-help manuals following cognitive–behavioral principles among individuals who are seeking help for problem drinking and are unwilling or unable to undergo face-to-face interventions.

Although there are some notable exceptions in the studies reviewed here, Glasgow and Rosen's (1978) conclusions concerning the lack of experimental rigor in this field arguably still apply. Of greatest concern are the small sample sizes and the high loss to follow-up in many studies, both of which can bias the conclusion one might draw from a review in favor of intervention. Another research need is for studies whose results can be sensibly generalized to the population and setting of interest. For example, experimental studies of normative feedback provided in the artificial context of an undergraduate psychology class are unlikely to produce results that generalize to clinical or general population settings. Accordingly, it is recognized that some experimental rigor may have to be sacrificed in order to promote ecological validity.

In researching this chapter, we were surprised at how difficult it was to find freely available and validated self-help materials on the Web, given the strong enthusiasm expressed for Web-based services of this kind (Kypri, Sitharthan, Cunningham, Kavanagh, & Dean, 2005). Two sites (http://www.alcoholhelpcenter.net and http: // www.alcoholscreening.org) stood out as being user-friendly, employing validated measures, and following proven principles of intervention, although it should be noted that efficacy data are not yet available for either site. In a large study of the latter of these sites, Saitz et al. (2004) found that it received over 115,925 visits per year, and over a 14-month period, screening questionnaires were completed by 39,482 adults (66% male). Two thirds (65%) screened positive for hazardous drinking on the AUDIT. A third of users visited a segment offering further help or referral for treatment. The study showed that a well-designed and resourced program can reach large numbers of hazardous drinkers and facilitate referral for further care.

From an evidence-based perspective, self-help interventions for problem drinking can best be described as promising. It is clear from this review that more research is needed in this area in order to develop and evaluate effective self-help interventions for the many problem drinkers who will never seek treatment.

Chapter Points

- Alcohol use runs the gamut from a small percentage of users who are alcohol dependent to a large minority who drink in a harmful or hazardous way to the majority who drink at low levels or who are abstinent.
- Binge drinking is on the rise in most countries and across all age groups, though most of this level of drinking is concentrated in individuals 18–25 years of age.
- Self-help materials have been used to supplement traditional treatment, stimulate interest in treatment, encourage maintenance of effective treatment, and help people cut down on their own.
- Many self-help approaches are based on the FRAMES system – generating Feedback based on assessment, emphasizing individual Responsibility for change, providing directed Advice to reduce drinking, offering a Menu of strategies for achieving goals, adopting an Empathic style, and promoting Self-efficacy.
- In a review of self-administered treatments that included no therapist contact, either for assessment or treatment, modest evidence was found supporting a treatment effect up to 6 months and some evidence of effectiveness up to 12 months.

References

Abrams, D. B., & Clayton, R. (2001). Transdisciplinary research to improve brief interventions for addictive behaviors. In P. M. Monti, T. A. Colby, & T. A. O'Leary (Eds.), *Adolescents, alcohol, and substance abuse* (pp. 321–341). New York: Guilford.

Abrams, D. B., Orleans, C. T., Niaura, R. S., Goldstein, M. G., Prochaska, J. O., & Velicer, W. (1996). Integrating individual and public health perspectives for treatment of tobacco dependence under managed health care: A combined stepped care and matching model. *Annals of Behavioral Medicine, 18*, 290–304.

Agostinelli, G., Brown, J. M., & Miller, W. R. (1995). Effects of normative feedback on consumption among heavy drinking college students. *Journal of Drug Education, 25*, 31–40.

American Psychiatric Association. (1994). *Diagnostic and statistical manual of mental disorders* (4th ed.). Washington, DC: Author.

Apodaca, T. R., & Miller, W. R. (2003). A meta-analysis of the effectiveness of bibliotherapy for alcohol problems. *Journal of Clinical Psychology, 59*, 289–304.

Babor, T., Caetano R., Casswell S., Edwards, G., Giesbrecht G., Graham K., et al. (2003). *Alcohol: No ordinary commodity—Research and public policy*. Oxford: Oxford University Press.

Beich, A., Gannik, D., & Malterud, K. (2002). Screening and brief intervention for excessive alcohol use: qualitative interview study of the experiences of general practitioners. *British Medical Journal, 325*, 870.

Breslow, R. A., & Smothers, B. A. (2005). Drinking patterns and body mass index in never smokers: National health interview survey, 1997–2001. *American Journal of Epidemiology, 161,* 368–376.

Collins, S. E., Carey, K. B., & Sliwinski, M. J. (2002). Mailed personalized normative feedback as a brief intervention for at-risk college drinkers. *Journal of Studies on Alcohol, 63,* 559–567.

Cunningham, J. A., Humphreys, K., & Koski-Jannes, A. (2000). Providing personalized assessment feedback for problem drinking on the Internet: A pilot project. *Journal of Studies on Alcohol, 61,* 794–798.

Cunningham, J. A., Koski-Jannes, A., Wild, T. C., & Cordingley, J. (2002). Treating alcohol problems with self-help materials: a population study. *Journal of Studies on Alcohol, 63,* 649–654.

Cunningham, J. A., Sdao-Jarvie, K., Koski-Jannes, A., & Breslin, F. C. (2001). Using self-help materials to motivate change at assessment for alcohol treatment. *Journal of Substance Abuse Treatment, 20,* 1–4.

Cunningham, J. A., Wild, T. C., Bondy, S. J., & Lin, E. (2001). Impact of normative feedback on problem drinkers: A small-area population study. *Journal of Studies on Alcohol, 62,* 228–233.

Cunningham, J. A., Wild, T. C., & Walsh, G. W. (1999). Interest in self-help materials in a general population sample of drinkers. *Drugs Education Prevention and Policy, 6,* 209–213.

Denny, C. H., Serdula, M. K., Holtzman, D., & Nelson, D. E. (2003). Physician advice about smoking and drinking: Are U.S. adults being informed? *American Journal of Preventive Medicine, 24,* 71–74.

Dickersin, K. (1990). The existence of publication bias and risk factors for its occurrence. *Journal of the American Medical Association, 263,* 1385–1389.

Dickersin, K. (1997). How important is publication bias? A synthesis of available data. *AIDS Education and Prevention, 9,* 15–21.

Dickersin, K., Chan, S., Chalmers, T. C., Sacks, H. S., & Smith, H., Jr. (1987). Publication bias and clinical trials. *Controlled Clinical Trials, 8,* 343–353.

Edwards, G., Arif, A., & Hadgson, R. (1981). Nomenclature and classification of drug and alcohol-related problems: A World Health Organisation Memorandum. *Bulletin of the World Health Organisation, 59,* 225–242.

Giesbrecht, N., Ialomiteanu, A., & Anglin, L. (2005). Drinking patterns and perspectives on alcohol policy: Results from two Ontario surveys. *Alcohol and Alcoholism, 40,* 132–139.

Glasgow, R. E., & Rosen, G. M. (1978). Behavioral bibliotherapy: A review of self-help behavior therapy manuals. *Psychological Bulletin, 85,* 1–23.

Grant, M., & Litvak, J. (1998). Beyond per capita consumption. In M. Grant & J. Litvak (Eds.), *Drinking patterns and their consequences* (p. 305). London: Taylor & Francis.

Hasin, D., Grant, B. F., Cottler, L., Blaine, J., Towle, L., Ustun, B., et al. (1997). Nosological comparisons of alcohol and drug diagnoses: A multisite, multi-instrument international study. *Drug and Alcohol Dependence, 47,* 217–226.

Hasin, D., Li, Q., McCloud, S., & Endicott, J. (1996). Agreement between DSM-III, DSM-III-R, DSM-IV and ICD-10 alcohol diagnoses in US community-sample heavy drinkers. *Addiction, 91,* 1517–1527.

Heath, D. B. (1998). Cultural variations among drinking patterns. In M. Grant & J. Litvak (Eds.), *Drinking patterns and their consequences* (pp. 103–128). Washington, DC: Taylor & Francis.

Heather, N., Kissoon-Singh, J., & Fenton, G. W. (1990). Assisted natural recovery from alcohol problems: Effects of a self-help manual with and without supplementary telephone contact. *British Journal of Addiction, 85,* 1177–1185.

Heather, N., Robertson, I., MacPherson, B., Allsop, S., & Fulton, A. (1987). Effectiveness of a controlled drinking self-help manual: One-year follow-up results. *British Journal of Clinical Psychology, 26,* 279–287.

Heather, N., Whitton, B., & Robertson, I. (1986). Evaluation of a self-help manual for media-recruited problem drinkers: Six-month follow-up results. *British Journal of Clinical Psychology, 25,* 19–34.

Hester, R. K., & Delaney, H. D. (1997). Behavioral self-control program for Windows: Results of a controlled clinical trial. *Journal of Consulting and Clinical Psychology, 65,* 686–693.

Institute of Medicine. (1990). *Broadening the base of treatment for alcohol problems.* Washington, DC: Institute of Medicine, Division of Mental Health and Behavioural Medicine.

Koski-Jannes, A., & Cunningham, J. (2001). Interest in different forms of self-help in a general population sample of drinkers. *Addictive Behaviors, 26,* 91–99.

Kypri, K. (2002). *Tertiary student hazardous drinking: Epidemiology and development of a brief intervention trial.* Unpublished doctoral dissertation, University of Otago, Dunedin.

Kypri, K., Saunders, J. B., & Gallagher, S. J. (2003). Acceptability of various brief intervention approaches for hazardous drinking among university students. *Alcohol and Alcoholism, 38,* 626–628.

Kypri, K., Saunders, J. B., Williams, S. M., McGee, R. O., Langley, J. D., Cashell-Smith, M. L., et al. (2004). Web-based screening and brief intervention for hazardous drinking: A double-blind randomised controlled trial. *Addiction, 99,* 1410–1417.

Kypri, K., Sitharthan, T., Cunningham, J. A., Kavanagh, D. J., & Dean, J. I. (2005). Innovative approaches to intervention for problem drinking. *Current Opinion in Psychiatry, 18,* 229–234.

Langley, J. D., Kypri, K., & Stephenson, S. (2003). Secondhand effects of alcohol use among university students: Computerised survey. *British Medical Journal, 327,* 1023–1024.

Lock, C. A., Kaner, E. F., Heather, N., Gilvarry, E., & McAvoy, B. R. (2000). Changes in receptionists' attitudes towards involvement in a general practice-based trial of screening and brief alcohol intervention. *British Journal of General Practice, 50,* 111–115.

Mayo, E. (1933). *The human problems of an industrial civilization.* New York: MacMillan.

Miller, E. T. (2001). Preventing alcohol abuse and alcohol-related negative consequences among freshmen college students: Using emerging computer technology to deliver and evaluate the effectiveness of brief intervention efforts. (Doctoral dissertation) *Dissertation Abstracts International: Section B: the Sciences & Engineering, 61*(8-B), 4417. University of Washington, Seattle, WA.

Miller, W. R., & Rollnick, S. (1991). *Motivational interviewing: Preparing people to change addictive behavior.* New York: Guilford.

Moyer, A., Finney, J. W., Swearingen, C. E., & Vergun, P. (2002). Brief interventions for alcohol problems: A meta-analytic review of controlled investigations in treatment-seeking and non-treatment-seeking populations. *Addiction, 97*, 279–292.

Naimi, T. S., Brewer, R. D., Mokdad, A., Denny, C., Serdula, M. K., & Marks, J. S. (2003). Binge drinking among US adults. *Journal of the American Medical Association, 289*, 70–75.

National Institute on Alcohol Abuse and Alcoholism. (2004, Winter). NIAAA council approves definition of binge drinking. *NIAAA Newsletter, 3*, 1–4.

Rehm, J., Room, R., Graham, K., Monteiro, M., Gmel, G., & Sempos, C. T. (2003). The relationship of average volume of alcohol consumption and patterns of drinking to burden of disease: An overview. *Addiction, 98*, 1209–1228.

Rehm, J., Room, R., Monteiro, M., Gmel, G., Graham, K., Rehn, N., et al. (2003). Alcohol as a risk factor for global burden of disease. *European Addiction Research, 9*, 157–164.

Richmond, R., Heather, N., Wodak, A., Kehoe, L., & Webster, I. (1995). Controlled evaluation of a general practice-based brief intervention for excessive drinking. *Addiction, 90*, 119–132.

Room, R. (2004). Disabling the public interest: Alcohol strategies and policies for England. *Addiction, 99*, 1083–1089.

Rosenthal, R. (1991). *Meta-analytic procedures for social research.* Newbury Park, CA: Sage.

Saitz, R., Helmuth, E. D., Aromaa, S. E., Guard, A., Belanger, M., & Rosenbloom, D. L. (2004). Web-based screening and brief intervention for the spectrum of alcohol problems. *Preventive Medicine, 39*, 969–975.

Sanchez-Craig, M., Davila, R., & Cooper, G. (1996). A self-help approach for high-risk drinking: Effect of an initial assessment. *Journal of Consulting and Clinical Psychology, 64*, 694–700.

Saunders, J. B., & de Burgh, S. (1998). The distribution of alcohol consumption. In M. Grant & J. Litvak (Eds.), *Drinking patterns and their consequences* (pp. 129–152). Washington, DC: Taylor & Francis.

Saunders, J. B., & Lee, N. K. (2000). Hazardous alcohol use: Its delineation as a subthreshold disorder, and approaches to its diagnosis and management. *Comprehensive Psychiatry, 41*, 95–103.

Sitharthan, T., Kavanagh, D. J., & Sayer, G. (1996). Moderating drinking by correspondence: An evaluation of a new method of intervention. *Addiction, 91*, 345–355.

Skinner, H. A., Allen, B. A., McIntosh, M. C., & Palmer, W. H. (1985). Lifestyle assessment: Applying microcomputers in family practice. *British Medical Journal, 290*, 212–214.

Skinner, H. A., Maley, O., Smith, L., Chirrey, S., & Morrison, M. (2001). New frontiers: Using the internet to engage teens in substance abuse prevention and treatment. In P. M. Monti, S. M. Colby, & T. A. O'Leary (Eds.), *Adolescents, alcohol and substance abuse: Reaching teens through brief interventions* (pp. 297–318). New York: Guilford.

Sobell, L. C., Sobell, M. B., Leo, G. I., Agrawal, S., Johnson-Young, L., & Cunningham, J. A. (2002). Promoting self-change with alcohol abusers: A Community-level mail intervention based on natural recovery studies. *Alcoholism: Clinical and Experimental Research, 26*, 936–948.

Sobell, M. B., Wilkinson, D. A., & Sobell, L. C. (1990). Alcohol and drug problems. In A. S. Bellack & M. Hersen (Eds.), *International handbook of behavior modification and therapy* (2nd ed., pp. 415–435). New York: Plenum.

Substance Abuse and Mental Health Services Administration. (2000). *1999 National Household Survey on Drug Abuse.* U.S. Department of Health and Human Services, Washington, DC.

Teesson, M., Dietrich, U., Degenhardt, L., Lynskey, M., & Beard, J. (2002). Substance use disorders in an Australian community survey. *Drug and Alcohol Review, 21,* 275–280.

Teesson, M., Hall, W., Lynskey, M., & Degenhardt, L. (2000). Alcohol- and drug-use disorders in Australia: Implications of the National Survey of Mental Health and Wellbeing. *Australian and New Zealand Journal of Psychiatry, 34,* 206–213.

Toll, B. A., Sobell, L. C., D'Arienzo, J., Sobell, M. B., Eickleberry-Goldsmith, L., & Toll, H. J. (2003). What do Internet-based alcohol treatment websites offer? *Cyberpsychology and Behavior, 6,* 581–584.

U.S. Preventive Services Task Force. (2004). Screening and behavioral counseling interventions in primary care to reduce alcohol misuse: Recommendation statement. *Annals of Internal Medicine, 140,* 554–556.

Walters, S. T., Bennett, M. E., & Miller, J. H. (2000). Reducing alcohol use in college students: A Controlled trial of two brief interventions. *Journal of Drug Education, 30,* 361–372.

Walters, S. T., & Woodall, W. G. (2003). Mailed feedback reduces consumption among moderate drinkers who are employed. *Prevention Science, 4,* 287–294.

World Health Organization. (1992). *ICD-10 international statistical classification of diseases and related health problems: Vol. 1.* Geneva: Author.

World Health Organization. (2002). *The World Health Report 2002, reducing risks, promoting healthy life.* Geneva: Author.

Author Note

Dr. Kypri gratefully acknowledges the support of the Alcohol Advisory Council of New Zealand and the Health Research Council of New Zealand.

CHAPTER 12

Self-Help Therapies for Cigarette Smoking Cessation

MITCHELL L. SCHARE AND
DESPINA D. KONSTAS

Smoking is a proven risk factor for the three leading causes of death in the United States: heart disease, cancer, and stroke. It is responsible for approximately 440,000 premature deaths in the United States each year and represents the single most preventable cause of death in our society (Centers for Disease Control and Prevention [CDC], 2002a). Nevertheless, it is estimated that 45.8 million Americans continue to smoke (CDC, 2004). Additionally negative effects of environmental smoke among non-smokers have been firmly established, with mortality rates estimated at up to 38,000 annually as a result of involuntary smoking (CDC, 2002a). In addition to premature mortality, smoking was responsible in the period from 1995 to 1999 for approximately $157 billion in annual health-related economic losses (CDC, 2002a).

Due to the well-known negative health consequences of smoking on the individual smoker, as well as to surrounding nonsmokers, and the economic costs of smoking, American society has waged a war against this behavior. According to the National Center for Chronic Disease Prevention and Health Promotion (CDC, 2006b), the implementation of social legislation, such as higher tobacco taxes and public smoking bans, have caused an increase in the number of smokers attempting to quit (estimated at 41.0% in 2000), yet only a few (4.7%) are successful at maintaining abstinence at

12 months. Furthermore, it is reported that there is a concurrent increase in the desire to quit among active smokers (70.0%; CDC, 2002b).

According to established research, most smokers (97%) quit on their own or with minimal help from a formal smoking cessation treatment (Cohen et al., 1989; Fiore et al., 1990; Lichtenstein & Glasgow, 1992). Furthermore, the majority of smokers who want to quit prefer to do so without having to participate in a clinic-based treatment (Fiore et al., 1990; U.S. Department of Health and Human Services [USDHHS], 1988). Individuals cannot or apparently do not commit to regular appointments, group meetings, or scheduled phone calls as activities typically associated with clinic programs. As a result, minimal interventions, meaning logistically simple programs such as self-help manuals, are thus considered "major" approaches in the field of smoking cessation treatment. Self-help interventions, which include pamphlets, manuals, audiotapes, videotapes, computer programs, etc., can reach many more people than interventions delivered by therapists. In addition, their low-cost nature allows these minimal interventions to target more diverse populations, including those at-risk populations such as youth, less educated, and smokers below the poverty level.

Lichtenstein and Glasgow (1992) have conceptualized smoking cessation interventions along a continuum from clinical to public health interventions. While intensive clinical interventions are efficacious with high cessation rates (e.g., 25 to 40% prevalent abstinence rates at 12-month follow-ups), as stated earlier, they are limited in the proportion of smokers they reach. On the other hand, public health interventions can reach a broad spectrum of smokers but have much more modest cessation rates. Therefore, while structured, clinic-based treatment programs are proven successful, their efficacy is limited by factors such as their inability to reach the broad smoking population, the desire of most smokers to quit on their own, low utilization, high dropout rate, high cost, and lack of third-party reimbursements (e.g., health insurance, governments, employers; Curry, Ludman & McClure, 2003; Niaura & Abrams, 2002).

The purpose of the present chapter is to describe the various forms of self-help currently available for smoking cessation. In reviewing these approaches it will be noted if effectiveness claims are based upon published research. Materials that do not report effectiveness data will be noted.

Smoking as a Physiological and Psychological Addiction

The addictive nature of smoking is conceptualized as having two equally important components: physiological and psychological factors that need to be addressed. While a very brief discussion of these factors follows, thorough reviews of the physiological factors can be found in Jaffe (1990), Julien (2001), and Taylor (1990), and, for the psychological factors, the reader is referred to Levinthal (2002) and Wikler (1948).

As indicated in the 1988 Surgeon General's Report (USDHHS, 1988), cigarettes and other forms of tobacco are addicting. Specifically, it is the chemical substance nicotine, found in cigarettes, that is primarily responsible for both the psychological and physiological addictive effects experienced by smokers. Tolerance of nicotine develops so that repeated use produces diminished effects, likely leading to an increase of nicotine intake (Jaffe, 1990). Physiological dependence on nicotine (c.f. Julien, 2001) is also demonstrated through the occurrence of withdrawal symptoms that often accompany prolonged periods of abstinence (American Psychiatric Association [APA], 2000).

Within a learning-based model, smoking is viewed as a behavior where nicotine itself serves as a positive reinforcer (via sensations such as euphoria, relaxation, warmth, etc.), in that the drug strengthens behavior leading to its own presentation (Goldberg, Spealman, & Goldberg, 1981). Nicotine may also serve as a negative reinforcer (via escape from negative states such as anxiety, anger, fatigue, etc.), leading to an increase in smoking behavior. In addition, there are a vast number of discriminative stimuli present in the environment (i.e., cues) that trigger the behavior of smoking, whether it be an experience of a particular emotion (e.g., boredom, anxiety, excitement), a particular time (e.g., between classes), a particular place (e.g., bar), or the presence of a particular person (e.g., fellow coworker who smokes). Conceptualizing smoking within a behavioral model becomes important, as most smoking cessation programs are based on such principles. It is the combination of the psychological and physiological effects of nicotine that helps to explain the difficulty that many smokers experience in quitting and maintaining abstinence.

Pharmacological Approaches to Self-Help

Pharmacological approaches to treat cigarette smoking have been studied for the past 30 years. The pharmacological therapies available are categorized as either nicotine replacement agents (e.g., gum, patch) or non-nicotine medication (i.e., bupropion, clonidine, fluoxetine). Medications are reported to reduce cravings for nicotine, though they do not replace it (Benowitz & Wilson Peng, 2000). The products that fall into the category of non-nicotine medication require prescriptions and physician monitoring to obtain and use these drugs and therefore will not be reviewed in this chapter as they cannot be conceptualized under the rubric of self-help.

Nicotine Replacement Therapies

The most popular pharmacological approach in the treatment of cigarette smoking involves nicotine replacement therapies. These therapeutic agents function to replace the nicotine formally obtained from tobacco while stopping the smoking behavior. Smokers learn to change their daily routines by not drawing out and lighting cigarettes while concurrently not experiencing withdrawal symptoms. Their nicotine levels are initially maintained and then slowly reduced.

Nicotine replacement agents are available in various forms. These include chewing gum, transdermal patch, nasal spray, oral inhaler, sublingual tablet, and lozenge. At the current time, only nicotine gum, lozenge, and the transdermal nicotine patch are available over-the-counter for consumer purchase.

Nicotine gum, transdermal patch, nasal spray, and inhaler are variable in their effects on withdrawal discomfort, urges to smoke, rates of abstinence, perceived helpfulness, or general efficacy, according to Hajek et al. (1999). When assessed as separate treatment groups, the 12-week abstinence rates for the use of gum, patches, sprays, and inhalers were 20, 21, 24, and 24%, respectively, among a population of 504 community volunteer smokers. The only difference among the products was the low usage compliance rate for the spray and inhaler groups. The authors offer several explanations for this low compliance rate including unpleasant side effects from usage and that these methods were considered to be embarrassing by the participants. Additionally, for the inhaler, participants were not taking forceful breaths as they had during clinical trials and thus did not receive enough nicotine.

Nicotine Gum Nicotine gum (or nicotine polacrilex; trademarked as Nicorette™) became available as a prescription treatment for tobacco dependence in 1984 and became available over-the-counter in 1995. The product's intent is to systematically and gradually decrease nicotine intake with a goal of terminating smoking in approximately 3 to 6 months. One major side effect of gum usage is mouth irritation (Lancaster, Stead, Silagy, & Sowden, 2000).

Researchers agree that nicotine gum is most efficacious when combined with a complementary behavior therapy treatment (Hall, Hall, & Ginsberg, 1990; Hughes, Goldstein, Hurt, & Shiffman, 1999). In studies with a minimum one-year follow-up, solely using nicotine gum, abstinence rates ranged from 8 to 38%, with a median of 11% (Schwartz, 1987). When nicotine gum was combined with behavior therapy, abstinence rates ranged higher from 12 to 49%, with a median of 29% (Schwartz, 1987). Notably, the average abstinence rate doubles when nicotine gum (or other nicotine replacement therapies) is combined with psychotherapeutic support (Hughes et al., 1999; Schwartz, 1987). However, the type and amount of therapeutic support to reach optimal results remains unclear and results of studies are mixed (e.g., Fagerstrom, 1984; Fortmann & Killen, 1995).

The necessary time period of actual gum usage in order to obtain optimal benefit is unclear. As marketed, the product instructions recommend a maximum of 6 months; however, some investigators recommend using the gum up to one year following cessation of smoking (Russell, Raw, & Jarvis, 1980). It appears that as the gum is used for a longer time period, higher quit rates are yielded (Hall et al., 1990).

As gum is advocated for longer term use, a question about potential addiction to the gum is raised (Hall et al., 1990). Among studies that assessed smokers who initially used the gum to quit, gum use has been reported in less than 5% of the participants 1 to 2 years after quitting (Hjalmarson, 1984; Raw, Jarvis, Feyerabend, & Russell, 1980). It should be noted that this 5% rate reflects a variety of regular and infrequent users of gum. Although prolonged use of the gum raises some concerns, research indicates that it does not increase health risks (such as cardiovascular or other diseases; Hughes et al., 1999). In addition, health risks for prolonged use of the gum are far less than those of continued smoking (Hall et al., 1990). Research has yet to elucidate the addictive potential of persisting with gum usage.

Nicotine Patch The patch, first marketed in 1996, delivers a consistent level of nicotine throughout the day through cutaneous application. The nicotine patch is discreet, as it may be placed on the body where it is not noticeable. The duration of patch usage varies considerably by manufacturers' instructions. A potential side effect of the transdermal patch is skin irritation (Lancaster et al., 2000).

As stated earlier, the nicotine patch is equally efficacious to the other nicotine replacement therapies. However, the efficacy of the patch, as with the gum, is better in controlled experimental settings than when smokers are allowed to self-administer the therapy in their home environments (Shiffman, Paty, Rohay, Di Marino, & Gitchell, 2000). Problems associated with home administration include noncompliance with the label directions resulting in underdosing, premature termination of use, and the unavailability of adjunctive behavioral treatment. One study reports that the use of a program consisting of telephone support and tailored cessation materials increased abstinence rates significantly for those who utilized the support in addition to the nicotine replacement therapy versus those who did not.

Killen, Fortmann, Davis, and Varady (1997) examined combined self-help behavioral treatments (a video-enhanced self-help manual versus a self-help manual only) with nicotine patch or placebo. The nicotine patch produced a (significantly) higher abstinence rate (36%) than placebo (20%) at 2 months follow-up. Other comparisons involving the nature of the manual were not significant. In contrast to the findings of Shiffman et al. (2000), this study indicates that self-help behavioral treatment did not enhance abstinence rates, although it could be argued that both groups did benefit from self-help instruction. Compliance with recommended patch use was associated with less relapse (measured at 2, 6, and 12 months) and suggests that regular usage as instructed will yield more efficacious outcomes. Regardless, adjunctive psychotherapy should still be sought to improve usage compliance.

Interestingly, in the psychotherapeutic literature, it is noted that the "amount of behavioral treatment establishes the base rate for quitting" and adding nicotine replacement therapies doubles the quit rate (e.g., Hughes et al., 1999). For example, in a study by Alterman, Gariti, and Mulvaney (2001), the level of intensity of behavioral treatment (high, moderate, and low) was combined with nicotine replacement therapy and examined. The most intense group (12 weeks of cognitive–behavioral therapy, 8 weeks of nicotine replacement, instructional videotapes, and four educational sessions with a nurse practitioner) had significantly higher abstinence rates at 26 and 52 weeks following the beginning of treatment than the low-intensity group (nicotine replacement for 8 weeks, instructional videotapes, and one educational session) and the moderate-intensity group (8 weeks of nicotine replacement, instructional videotapes, and four educational sessions; Alterman et al., 2001).

According to the guideline for treating tobacco use and dependence (Fiore et al., 2000), several forms of nicotine replacement therapies are effective—nicotine gum, the transdermal nicotine patch, the nicotine inhaler, and nicotine nasal spray. Therefore, the choice of treatment depends on smoker's preference, cost, and consequences (side effects) of treatment. The research literature suggests that nicotine replacement therapies are somewhat effective with minimal or no adjunctive behavioral treatment. Yet established practice guidelines for the treatment of nicotine dependence, such as those published by the American Psychiatric Association (1996), suggest that nicotine replacement strategies should be supervised by professionals and adjunctive psychotherapy should be encouraged even when products are available over-the-counter.

Self-Help Behavioral Therapies

Self-help behavioral therapies for smoking cessation include written leaflets, brochures and books, audiotapes, videotapes, telephone counseling, electronics, and Internet Web sites. These self-help therapies provide guidance through the process of quitting as well as teaching strategies of relapse prevention. The therapies can range from brief, unstructured motivational pamphlets to comprehensive, step-by-step instructional manuals encompassing all components implemented in therapist-directed cognitive–behavioral treatment groups. Typical components include self-monitoring, cigarette brand switching, nicotine fading, the identification of situational and affective triggers or cues to smoke, cognitive strategies such as self-talk, problem-solving methods in dealing with cravings, social support, stress management techniques, and assertiveness training. However, the structure, depth, and comprehensiveness of these treatment materials vary widely.

A 1991 population-based sample of 1,137 smokers at Group Health Cooperative collected data on the use of self-help materials. Smokers were identified from telephone surveys with a random sample of over 5,900 adults (Curry, McBride, Grothaus, Louie, & Wagner, 1995). Smokers responded to the question "Have you ever tried self-help quit smoking books, pamphlets, or guides?" Overall, 3% reported that they were currently using self-help materials, 28% reported using them in the past, and 69% said that they had never used them. Although this study only reports on the use of written self-help materials (the most readily available type), it demonstrates that over 30% of the sampled smokers had either currently or in the past consulted written resources to help them combat cigarette smoking.

Written Self-Help Smoking Cessation

Written self-help materials to aid smoking cessation may be considered along a number of varying dimensions. Resources may be as simple or brief as a single-page brochure with a few quitting suggestions to comprehensive manuals with smoking cessation strategies, exercises, and resources. Our review of current written materials finds them to generally fall into one of three categories: pamphlets (folded single sheets of paper), booklets (nonbound, and usually less than 50 pages), and books (bound manuals, typically of a hundred pages or more).

An important variable among these materials is the degree to which a specific technique is advocated and detailed for use. Most pamphlets and booklets advocate quitting with little specificity of a technique, though they may attempt to inform and educate the individual regarding issues of quitting and relapse. For example, Cummings, Emont, Jaen, and Sciandra (1988) reviewed the smoking booklets available at that time and found that the majority instruct smokers to prepare for quitting by gradually reducing the number of cigarettes smoked, usually by eliminating one or two cigarettes per day until a designated quit date or until the person is confident that he can quit. This gradual reduction is typically done with the rationale that the individual will have the opportunity to develop and employ coping skills that will be needed after quitting. However, specific detail to accomplish this successfully is often missing. While it is often suggested that cigarette reduction is expected to increase smokers' confidence in their ability to control their smoking behavior, the opposite argument can easily be made as well; an unsuccessful attempt to quit smoking could undermine a person's confidence in his ability to quit and reinforce his smoking habit.

Another dimension of written self-help resources is whether they are intended to be used as a sole guide to cigarette cessation or to be supplementary to another program or smoking treatment procedure. Often the pamphlets and booklets refer the reader to seek more information and guidance from professional resources in order to aid in smoking cessation and provide a short list of organizations, addresses, and phone numbers. In contrast, a number of the treatment books assessed are comprehensive in their treatment structure and plans. While additional resources to aid in quitting are often included, the manuals are typically written as stand-alone materials to be used by themselves. Thus, in looking at written materials, one can conclude they are highly variable in their length, structure, detail, and utility.

Review of Selected Manuals

Self-help manuals to quit smoking are readily available in a variety of local and Internet stores. Recently, we assessed the number of books available through an Internet retailer using "stop smoking" as the search term. This search returned 305 items. This points to the popularity of self-help treatment manuals for smoking and also makes daunting the possibility of reviewing all the available books on this topic. Rather, six best-selling smoking manuals found at two national booksellers were selected for review. It is interesting to note that the chosen manuals have several components in common and, while several of these techniques have been validated in research studies, none of these treatment guides appear to have been empirically evaluated.

Most of the reviewed books incorporate several standard aspects of cognitive behavioral quit smoking programs. Identifying patterns of smoking behavior through analyses of antecedent situations to smoking and cognitions regarding smoking are found in the manuals. Alternative behaviors (i.e., substitute behaviors) are suggested, as are discussions about possible weight gain. The manuals also address issues related to relapse prevention and suggest topics designed to keep the smoker motivated to stay quit, such as discussions of the health risks associated with continued smoking.

Typically included are resources for additional information and assistance with quitting and information on the nicotine replacement and non-nicotine replacement therapies. Two manuals associated with major public health organizations were chosen for a more through review in order to give the reader a clearer picture of these manuals.

Kicking Butts: Quit Smoking and Take Charge of Your Health (American Cancer Society, 2003). This manual outlines many options to quitting smoking and advocates using a combination of methods to stop. Its chapters are clearly labeled and divided into short, easily readable sections. In addition to the components of the quit smoking treatment described in the general review above, this book also includes cognitive restructuring and relaxation skills development. It addresses all nicotine replacement therapies as well as non-nicotine replacement therapies and highlights the advantages and disadvantages to each in a well-organized, easy-to-read chart. The book includes brief motivational activities mostly as checklists throughout the book and provides references to support groups, major organizations, and telephone counseling.

As for the actual quitting instructions, the authors recommend abrupt cessation (i.e., cold turkey) rather than gradual cigarette reduction. However, there are no clear steps or time frame to guide the smoker through the quitting process. The section on preparing to quit is full of many important but too brief techniques regarding stopping. The purpose of a daily checklist following quitting is unclear. In conclusion, while the book is rich with information on quitting options, there is a minimally defined quit plan. Lastly, the overall layout of the book lacks appeal, graphics, and color.

7 Steps to a Smoke-Free Life (Fisher & Goldfarb, 1998). This treatment manual is based on the Freedom from Smoking Program by the American Lung Association (ALA) and can be used to supplement nicotine replacement and non-nicotine replacement therapies. Its large print, numerous attractive illustrations, clearly labeled chapters, easily identifiable key points (enclosed within boxes), and workbook-like appearance contribute to its user-friendly appeal.

In addition to the components described earlier, this book includes cognitive restructuring, relapse prevention (addressed before and after quitting), information on healthy eating, and stress reduction techniques (e.g., relaxation, exercise, and meditation). Resources, primarily for ALA in each state, are provided as an independent chapter for a quick referral. While the chapter includes addresses and telephone numbers for ALA in each state, Internet site and e-mail addresses are not included (perhaps due to the 1998 publication date of this volume). The manual includes motivational activities throughout and provides space within the text for their completion. It also supplies the smokers with materials to assist them in quitting, such as the "Pack Tracks," which can be cut out of the book and used to keep track of the number of cigarettes smoked and the triggers (cues) for smoking.

As first elucidated by Curry (1993) and expanded by the current authors, written self-help manuals possess many positive and beneficial qualities: (a) the books can package effective cognitive–behavioral treatment components into an easily accessible format; (b) the level of detail may answer most typical questions regarding quitting; (c) they allow smokers to work through specific exercises within explicit timeframes; (d) the manuals are easily distributed to a limitless number of smokers through community resources or for profit businesses; (e) the treatment materials are available at low financial cost, especially when compared to psychotherapy or pharmacotherapy; (f) the programs can be tailored to the smokers' specific needs and interests by the program designers, as well as by the smokers themselves (e.g., they can change the order in which they complete recommended exercises or vary the length of time they take to complete the program); and (g) ex-smokers can easily keep the written materials for future reference when challenged by at-risk situations or if need arises to review or repeat an aspect of the program.

Efficacy of Written Self-Help Resources

An early review of studies evaluating the efficacy of self-help manuals to deliver behavioral smoking treatment found that when used alone, manuals yielded minimal effectiveness on smoking cessation (Glasgow & Rosen, 1978). More recent reviews (Curry, 1993; Curry et al., 2003) present mixed findings concerning the effectiveness of written manuals in the self-administration of behavioral treatments. The treatment programs evaluated in the studies below did not include the published manuals discussed in the previous section.

Curry (1993) conducted a review of 24 self-help programs for smoking cessation. The review concluded that when compared to self-help programs, group treatments produced higher abstinence rates. However, the group rates decreased over time, whereas the abstinence rates for self-help programs increased.

Perhaps due to the lack of conclusive evidence that self-help manuals alone are effective, recent research has focused on the effectiveness of adding supplemental procedures or making specialized modifications to the self-help manuals. Specifically, many studies have evaluated the use of self-help materials with nicotine replacement therapy and outreach telephone counseling (Curry et al., 2003; Fortmann & Killen, 1995; Killen et al., 1997), outreach telephone counseling and mailed reminders (Ossip-Klein, Carosella, & Krusch, 1997), and interactive individualized computer reports (Curry et al., 2003; Dijkstra, De Vries, & Roijackers, 1998; Velicer, Prochaska, Fava, LaForge, & Rossi, 1999). Additionally, studies have addressed the efficacy of self-help materials written specifically for certain issues or populations such as relapse prevention among heavier smokers (Fortmann & Killen, 1995), postpartum women (McBride, Scholes, et al., 1999), and reproductive age women undergoing cervical cancer screening (McBride, Curry, et al., 1999).

Higher abstinence rates were obtained for interventions using telephone counseling as an adjunct to a self-help treatment than those receiving the quit program alone among callers to a smokers' helpline (Zhu et al., 1996). Ossip-Klein et al. (1997) studied smokers 60 years or older receiving either mailed reminders or proactive telephone counseling as adjuncts to self-help materials and a telephone stop-smoking hotline. Abstinence rates were significantly higher among men who received the mailed reminders to call the hotline, whereas cessation rates among women were highest among those who received proactive telephone calls. However, studies of adjunctive outreach through telephone counseling in populations of non-volunteer smokers found either a short-term effect on abstinence that did not last (Curry et al., 1995; McBride, Scholes, et al., 1999) or had no benefit above control conditions (McBride, Curry, et al., 1999). Overall, these studies do not significantly challenge conclusions drawn from reviews that self-help manuals by themselves are of limited value. However, the addition of supplemental procedures to or special modifications of the self-help materials add incremental value to initial quit rates and abstinence rates.

In Curry et al.'s (2003) review of studies comparing self-help treatments, significant differences were not found among written interventions that differed with regard to degree of structure, type of quitting instructions, or personalized content among general samples of smokers. Nevertheless, self-help treatments that are personalized to individual characteristics (e.g., different stages of readiness to quit) are typically more effective than general self-help materials (e.g., Dijkstra, De Vries, & Roijackers, 1999). The authors conclude that personalized materials may reach the smokers that are less likely to be reached by generic, traditional materials. In terms of treatment participants, self-help treatments seem to be most effective for less addicted, more motivated, and confident smokers with a past history of staying abstinent for longer periods of time and with more social support. Not surprisingly, among studies with non-volunteer participants (who did not want to quit smoking), differences were not found between self-help treatments and control (no treatment) groups. In one study in which participants were randomized to either group or self-help treatment, abstinence rates did not differ among smokers who actively (completed workbook exercises, completed smoking tally forms) participated in either condition (Curry, Marlatt, Gordon, & Baer, 1988). Given the plethora of published literature on the issue of motivation and successful smoking cessation, it is likely that the efficacy of self-help materials is tied to the degree of motivation the smoker possesses to adhere to the guides.

Internet Self-Help

To put it mildly, the Internet is awash with self-help information regarding smoking. A Web-based Google search using the basic terms "quit, stop" and "smoking, cigarettes" yielded over 739,000 hits or sites in under a second! By adding the terms "treatment, manual, program, book" to the previous search, the total number was reduced to 102,000 sites, still an overwhelming number. The first 100 sites from this search were studied and sorted into categories.

The majority of sites fell into the general category of information provision, accounting for 64.5% of the sites rated. (Some sites were categorized into more than a single category.) Within this category were sites providing information, advice, articles, tips, and stories on quitting. Most of the sites had referrals to other resources for more detailed help and information on quitting programs. Often the more informative sites were those sponsored by various municipalities or public health organizations. Twelve of these sites offered quitting programs that varied in their detail and aims. A fairly comprehensive treatment program (a reproduction of a 50-page treatment manual) was offered at one site, while three others simply reproduced short booklets. One comprehensive treatment program found was specifically written for teen smokers, while three other programs were addressed to health care professionals (i.e., pharmacists, nurses, and medical hospital personnel) to help their patients stop smoking. Educational lesson plans were offered at two sites.

The other 35.5% of the sites were categorized as commercial ventures. The primary purpose of these sites was to sell a variety of merchandise and services related to smoking cessation. Most of the sites offered a variety of books, manuals, nonprescription and prescription pharmaceuticals, herbal remedies, tapes, cassettes, and programs to aid the viewer in stopping smoking. A few sites (six) were specific referrals to a therapist, clinic, or institutional setting's cessation program. Many sites offered a particular treatment manual; some as a published book, others as e-books. Interestingly, the published self-help manuals reviewed earlier were offered a number of times. One unusual site offered fetish pornography concerning "sexy smoking" but nothing relevant to smoking treatment.

As the study above shows, there is much information available on the Internet to aid one in quitting smoking. While a few free treatment programs were found, most sites were sources for information and referral to established therapy programs and treatment manuals. Clearly the buyer must beware of the thousands of untested and nontraditional methods to quit being proffered on the Web.

A few Web sites are dedicated to providing interactive therapy for smoking treatment, though none of these were readily found using the search discussed earlier. Parker-Pope (2003) reported preliminary data from two stop-smoking Web sites that claim that the results of Internet-based programs are as effective as one-on-one interventions with regard to abstinence rates. Forty-two percent of the users surveyed this past year of the smokeclinic.com Web site reported successful quitting. This is comparable to the short-term abstinence rates of many traditional interventions. Fifty percent of the 438 users surveyed 3 months after they signed up indicated that they had quit smoking for at least one week, while the majority of those people had quit for 2 months or more. However, the overall quit rate for this site is unclear due to 1,000 nonrespondents. Treatment programs available through the Internet are relatively new and have yet to offer much evidence of their success.

Audio & Video Self-Help Aids for Smoking Cessation

As described previously, the on-line search for smoking cessation materials rendered quit-smoking programs in audio format (tape and compact discs) as well as video format (tapes and DVDs). We felt it was important to acknowledge these materials as they appear as popular sellers among the search for smoking cessation materials in two national booksellers. Some audio and video treatment programs are similar to the commercially available books in that they are focused on cognitive–behavioral techniques and motivational issues in getting a person to decide to quit. However, they often lack essential detail for a comprehensive stop-smoking plan and have not been empirically evaluated as cessation programs on their own. Other programs review individuals' experiences in quitting, discuss the development of willpower, employ relaxation with music, and may contain pseudo-hypnotic suggestions to increase a quitter's motivation. None of these materials report any empirical validation of their efficacy.

Electronic Self-Help Aids for Smoking Cessation

The use of modern electronic combined with computer-based technology has allowed for the development of a cessation aid. The LifeSign Smoking Cessation Program is a program booklet and electronic device marketed as "the realistic way to quit smoking... gradually." The device is a credit card–size LifeSign™ computer whose purpose is to alter one's smoking patterns and gently ease one off cigarettes.

The LifeSign program guides one through three general steps to quitting: preparation, quitting and living as an ex-smoker. During the preparation stage, week one, the Lifesign computer is "programmed" to the smoker's behavior. The actual number and timing of cigarettes smoked are recorded by the device as the quitter simply keys in each cigarette consumed. During the second phase (quitting), typically lasting between 2 to 5 weeks, the computer alerts the smoker as to when he or she should initiate a cigarette. During this phase, the control of smoking is eased away from the smoker's conditioned cues to smoke. Additionally, the device slowly lengthens the time between cigarettes and reduces the number of cigarettes smoked. The program guide focuses on factual information, support, and a discussion of substitute behaviors. During the program's final phase, the guide offers information to the "ex-smoker" on living a healthy lifestyle. Of special note is a hotline support service offered to purchasers of the program at no additional cost.

Overall this program uses cognitive–behavioral techniques in helping people quit smoking within an innovative, easy-to-carry electronic device. The site also offers a video program and audio tape at additional cost as well as a number of specialized programs: for teens, pregnant women, and users of smokeless tobacco. A number of research citations found on the site (cf. Jerome, Perrone, & Kalfus, 1992; Prue, Riley, Orlandi, & Jerome, 1990) speak to the efficacy of the program to help some individuals totally stop smoking while reducing smoking considerably for many others.

Treatment Integrity of Self-Help Manuals

The issue with treatment integrity is an important one to consider when evaluating all smoking cessation methods, but it is especially a concern when examining self-help materials. The consideration of whether the self-help programs are ineffective due to participant misuse (e.g., not following directions) or due to limited or minimal use is important to consider. Curry (1993) reviewed the use of various self-help materials in 23 studies conducted between 1981 and 1993. The percentage manual usage ranged from 24 to 99 among those studies. However, it should be mentioned that manual usage and/or program adherence was determined by self-report. Typically, participants were asked what percentage of the material they read or used. These self-report data are limited in their accuracy due to a variety of potential memory lapses and reporting biases.

Manual usage was measured in a recent research study evaluating the effectiveness of the IQ* program, a self-help treatment program that will be described in detail later in this chapter (Konstas, 2005). Visual inspection of each treatment manual used by the participants was conducted to determine the participant's percentage of manual usage. This dependent variable was assessed in two ways. First, each component of the treatment manual was examined independently through participants' written comments, completion of graphs, motivational activities (including responses to daily activities), and self-monitoring sheets. This assessment provided the participant's percentage of using each of these treatment components. Second, a total percentage of manual usage was determined for each participant by adding all the components used and dividing by the total number of components available in the treatment manuals. The author reports that the participants' utilization of the manual was not related to the level of nicotine consumption, nicotine dependence, or motivation level.

Highly Structured Self-Help Smoking Program Development

As mentioned earlier, the majority of smokers (97%) quit on their own or with minimal help from a formal smoking cessation treatment (Cohen et al., 1989; Fiore et al., 1990; Lichtenstein & Glasgow, 1992), and most prefer to do so without having to participate in a clinic based treatment (Fiore et al., 1990; USDHH, 1988). Therefore, it is important to develop effective and successful treatments that allow smokers to quit on their own with minimal or no interactions with smoking treatment professionals.

Our review was unable to identify a comprehensive written program that fully reflected the depth of topics and activities and overall level of therapeutic attention a smoker could expect to receive during an in-office smoking treatment program. In our laboratory, we are currently evaluating a comprehensive program format called the IQ* (*I'm Quitting) program (Konstas, 2005). This manualized treatment is a highly structured, daily smoking cessation program designed to lead to complete cessation at the beginning of the 9th week of participation. Its goal is to entirely remove the need for therapist contact, yet to be friendly, encouraging, and provide the structure and daily activities of a typical treatment program. The program is a comprehensive, cognitive–behavioral smoking treatment package that requires the smoker to engage in a brief but relevant daily exercise to be completed in 10 minutes or less. An adjunctive Web site provides additional information and details on topics for those who choose to access this information.

The IQ* program encompasses many of the positive qualities of written self-help treatments mentioned earlier and stresses the motivational components. It packages effective behavioral techniques of nicotine fading and cigarette reduction, self-monitoring, functional analysis of and sensitization to antecedent stimuli (cues to smoke), and coping techniques for high-risk (and potential relapse) situations in a user-friendly format.

The topics build gradually over the weeks but are presented in a systematic manner. For example, on the third day of every week, the participants are instructed to graph their past and current level of smoking in order to reinforce reduction of nicotine intake and the number of cigarettes consumed.

Smokers are self-empowered throughout this program. Beginning with the welcome note, smokers learn that they are "in control of the quitting process" with much encouragement and positive reinforcement built into the IQ* program. Furthermore, participants are instructed to read, follow, and complete the activities within the manual—daily. Differing from the published manuals reviewed earlier in this chapter, smokers are actively discouraged from completing the activities out of order, as treatment components such as nicotine reduction, setting a quit date, and preparation for quitting are gradually introduced and timed to occur over subsequent weeks. The only exception to this notion is that the participants are explicitly allowed to totally quit smoking at any point they feel ready to do so. As an example, this may occur as participants have reduced their daily cigarette intake to very few and find this limitation frustrating.

During the program's evaluation period, the treatment is formatted in nine small, easy-to-carry booklets that only require a once weekly exchange. Purposely, the smoker gets the next week's materials (if compliant by coming to their exchange appointment) and the researchers obtain last week's data. Although the treatment is completed with minimal contact, pre and post measures were needed to obtain program assessment data.

Thirteen adults (24–64 years of age) interested in quitting smoking participated in the IQ* program and reported a mean age of smoking onset as 15 and nearly a 36-year history of smoking. Current daily cigarette smoking ranged from 15 to 30 cigarettes with an average of 20.85. At treatment completion and at one-month follow-up, a significant decrease in the amount of nicotine consumed was found among the 8 participants who either completed the smoking cessation program or quit smoking before completing the program. Specifically, the average drop from initial smoking rates among the program completers at program termination and at 7 weeks follow-up was 81.54 and 75.42%, respectively. The 8 participants also demonstrated a decrease in nicotine dependence (as determined by the Fagerstrom Test for Nicotine Dependence) and an increase in motivation level as determined by their stage of change level at treatment follow up (according to the percent changes calculated from baseline).

Among those participants who quit the program before completion (attrition rate of 38.46%), significant changes were not found between baseline and treatment follow-up regarding nicotine consumption, nicotine dependence, and motivation level. However, the program noncompleters did demonstrate an average drop of 27.78% from initial smoking rates at the time of their treatment termination.

Abstinence rates for program completers was 50%, with the overall abstinence rate for all program participants at 30.77%. Thus, the IQ* program was effective in decreasing the amount of nicotine consumed and nicotine dependence while increasing the motivation level among smokers motivated to quit. Regardless of abstinence, the program was most efficacious in decreasing smoking rates, nicotine consumption, and cigarette dependency, thus introducing harm-reduction behaviors to patients primarily through decreased smoking. A one-year follow-up is currently underway, as is another study of a modified version of the program with a goal of an increased number of participants.

Final Recommendations

The old expression *caveat emptor* certainly applies to the domain of self-help approaches to smoking cessation. However, this is not meant to imply that there are no good resources available. Smoking pharmaceuticals, particularly those of the nicotine replacement type, are useful for those wishing to quit by themselves. However, as research and clinical guidelines acknowledge, these approaches work best when their instructions are carefully followed and when monitored by a professional, preferably as part of a cognitive–behavior therapy program. In this regard, the efficacy of any self-help approach to smoking cessation may largely be based upon the motivation of the smoker as well as on the degree to which they attend to the self-help program.

The efficacy of popular smoking cessation programs as they appear in current published book forms is simply questionable. Research has demonstrated that these approaches are not as efficacious when used alone as when these resources are used with adjunctive telephone or computer support. Manuals with better structured programs, clear instructions, and motivational components are probably the better recommendations for those wishing to try this approach, but the authors feel that bigger, more comprehensive books may just become more confusing to the reader. Audio and video materials may be useful but in some cases have little structure to their programs and in most cases offer no research to back their efficacy. The LifeSign program was an interesting behaviorally based approach to cigarette smoking cessation that offered some efficacy data and would possibly help a program-compliant quitter.

As reviewed, there are many choices available for those wishing to quit smoking by themselves. However, most of these have not been empirically validated. Investigators may wish to focus on the determination of what key elements are most efficacious in bringing about smoking cessation and how these can best be structured. Issues involving compliance with program materials and their palatability have yet to be studied. These seem to be central variables to investigate. Why would a self-motivated individual choose one program over another? This key area of research has not been broached and calls out to clinical, health, and social psychologists to bring their expertise to this important topic of investigation.

Chapter Points

- In 2000, an estimated 41% of smokers were attempting to quit, with only 4.7% successful at maintaining abstinence at 12 months.
- Self-help approaches are considered a major treatment vehicle in reducing smoking as the majority of smokers who want to quit prefer non-clinic–based treatment.
- The combination of physiological and psychological effects of smoking, learned in an environment with multiple cues to smoke, produces dependence.
- Nicotine-replacement agents, including gum, patches, sprays, and inhalers, produce abstinence rates from 20 to 24%, a treatment outcome that is significantly improved by participating in a cognitive–behavioral program.
- Self-help treatment manuals and books alone have not been conclusively found to produce treatment effects. The effectiveness of these programs has been augmented with mailed reminders or telephone counseling.
- Differences between written intervention programs on degree of structure, type of quitting instructions, or personalized content did not improve outcome.
- Self-help programs are more effective for less addicted, more motivated individuals with more social support and more sustained prior quit periods. Self-help programs do not work for individuals who do not want to quit.
- Treatment Web sites offering books or manuals number in the tens of thousands. While none have been systematically evaluated, surveys of the effectiveness of two of these sites have substantiated quit rates for those individuals who responded to the survey.
- Audio- and visual-based programs, though commercially successful, have not been evaluated and are lacking in a programmatic approach to quitting.
- A field test, involving 13 individuals, and utilizing small, daily assignments, found a quit rate of 50% for program completers and a quit rate of 31% for all participants.

References

Alterman, A. I., Gariti, P., & Mulvaney, F. (2001). Short- and long-term smoking cessation for three levels of intensity of behavioral treatment. *Psychology of Addictive Behaviors, 15*, 261–264.

American Cancer Society. (2003). *Kicking butts: Quit smoking and take charge of your health.* Atlanta: Author.

American Psychiatric Association. (1996). *Practice guideline for the treatment of patients with nicotine dependence.* Washington, DC: Author.

American Psychiatric Association. (2000). *Diagnostic and statistical manual of mental disorders* (Text rev.). Washington, DC: Author.

Benowitz, N. L., & Wilson Peng, M. (2000). Non-nicotine pharmacotherapy for smoking cessation: Mechanisms and prospectus. *CNS Drugs, 13*, 265–285.

Centers for Disease Control and Prevention. (2002a). Annual smoking-attributable mortality, years of potential life lost, and economic costs—United States, 1995–1999. *Morbidity and Mortality Weekly Report, 51*, 300–303.

Centers for Disease Control and Prevention. (2002b). Cigarette smoking among adults—United States, 2000. *Morbidity and Mortality Weekly Report, 51*, 642–645.

Centers for Disease Control and Prevention. (2004). Cigarette smoking among adults—United States, 2002. *Morbidity and Mortality Weekly Report, 53*, 427–431.

Cohen, S., Lichtenstein, E., Prochaska, J. O., Rossi, J. S., Gritz, E. R, Carr, C. R., et al. (1989). Debunking myths about self-quitting: Evidence from 10 prospective studies of persons who attempt to quit smoking by themselves. *American Psychologist, 44*, 1355–1365.

Cummings, K. M., Emont, S. L., Jaen, C., & Sciandra, R. (1988). Format and quitting instructions as factors influencing the impact of a self-administered quit smoking program. *Health Education Quarterly, 15*, 199–216.

Curry, S. J. (1993). Self-help interventions for smoking cessation. *Journal of Consulting and Clinical Psychology, 61*, 790–803.

Curry, S. J., Ludman, E. J., & McClure, J. (2003). Self-administered treatment for smoking cessation. *Journal of Clinical Psychology, 59*, 305–319.

Curry, S. J., Marlatt, G. A., Gordon, J., Baer, J. S. (1988). A comparison of alternative theoretical approaches to smoking cessation and relapse. *Health Psychology, 7*, 545–556.

Curry, S. J., McBride, C., Grothaus, L. C., Louie, D., & Wagner, E. (1995). A randomized trial of self-help materials, personalized feedback and telephone counseling with nonvolunteer smokers. *Journal of Consulting and Clinical Psychology, 63*, 1005–1014.

Dijkstra, A., De Vries, H., & Roijackers, J. (1998). Long-term effectiveness of computer-generated tailored feedback in smoking cessation. *Health Education Research, 13*, 207–214.

Dijkstra, A., De Vries, H., & Roijackers, J. (1999). Targeting smokers with low readiness to change with tailored and nontailored self-help materials. *Preventive Medicine, 28*, 203–211.

Fagerstrom, K. O. (1984). Effects of nicotine chewing gum and follow-up appointments in physician-based smoking cessation. *Preventive Medicine, 13*, 517–527.

Fiore, M. C., Bailey, W. C., Cohen, S. J., Dorfman, S. F., Goldstein, M. G., Gritz, E. R., et al. (2000). *Treating tobacco use and dependence. Clinical practice guideline.* Rockville, MD: U.S. Department of Health and Human Services, Public Health Service.

Fiore, M. C., Novotny, T. E., Pierce, J. P., Giovino, G. A., Hatziandreu, E. J., Newcomb, P. A., et al. (1990). Methods used to quit smoking in the United States: Do cessation programs help? *Journal of American Medical Association, 263,* 2760–2765.

Fisher, E. B. & Goldfarb, T. L. (1998). *7 steps to a smoke-free life.* New York: John Wiley & Sons.

Fortmann, S. P. & Killen, J. D. (1995). Nicotine gum and self-help behavioral treatment for smoking relapse prevention: Results from a trial using population-based recruitment. *Journal of Consulting and Clinical Psychology, 63,* 460–468.

Glasgow, R. E., & Rosen, G. M. (1978). Behavioral bibliotherapy: A review of self-help behavior therapy manuals. *Psychological Bulletin, 85,* 1–23.

Goldberg, S. R., Spealman, R. D., & Goldberg, D. M. (1981). Persistent behavior at high rates maintained by intravenous self-administration of nicotine. *Science, 214,* 573–575.

Hajek, P., West, R., Foulds, J., Nilsson, F., Burrows, S., & Meadow, A. (1999). Randomized comparative trial of nicotine polacrilex, a transdermal patch, nasal spray, and an inhaler. *Archives of Internal Medicine, 159,* 2033–2038.

Hall, S. M., Hall, R. G., & Ginsberg, D. (1990). Pharmacological and behavioral treatment for cigarette smoking. *In M.* Hersen, R. M. Eisler, & P. M. Miller (Eds.), *Progress in behavior modification* (Vol. 25, pp. 86–118). Thousand Oaks, CA: Sage.

Hjalmarson, A. I. M. (1984). Effect of nicotine chewing gum in smoking cessation. A randomized, placebo-controlled, double-blind study. *Journal of the American Medical Association, 252,* 2835–2838.

Hughes, J. R., Goldstein, M. G., Hurt, R. D., & Shiffman, S. (1999). Recent advances in the pharmacology of smoking. *Journal of American Medical Association, 281,* 72–76.

Jaffe, J. M. (1990). Drug addiction and drug abuse. In A. G. Gilman, L. S. Goodman, T.W. Rall, & P. Taylor (Eds.), *Goodman and Gilman's the pharmacologic basis of therapeutics* (8th ed., pp. 522–573). New York: McGraw-Hill.

Jerome, A., Perrone, R., & Kalfus, G. (1992). Computer-assisted smoking treatment: A controlled evaluation and long-term follow-up. *Journal of Advancement in Medicine, 5,* 29–41.

Julien, R. M. (2001). *A primer of drug action: A concise nontechnical guide to the actions, uses, and side effects of psychoactive drugs.* New York: Henry Holt.

Killen, J. D., Fortmann, S. P., Davis, L., & Varady, A. (1997). Nicotine patch and self-help video for cigarette smoking cessation. *Journal of Consulting and Clinical Psychology, 65,* 663–672.

Konstas, D. (2005). *Self-directed smoking cessation program with minimal therapist contact.* Unpublished manuscript, Hofstra University, Hempstead, NY.

Lancaster, T., Stead, L., Silagy, C., & Sowden, A. (2000). Effectiveness of interventions to help people stop smoking: Findings from the Cochrane Library. *British Medical Journal, 321,* 355–358.

Levinthal, C. F. (2002). *Drugs, behavior and modern society* (3rd ed.). Boston: Allyn & Bacon.

Lichtenstein, E., & Glasgow, R. E. (1992). Smoking cessation: What have we learned over the past decade? *Journal of Consulting and Clinical Psychology, 60,* 518–527.

McBride, C. M., Curry, S. J., Lando, H. A., Pirie, P. L., Grothaus, L. C., & Nelson, J. C. (1999). Prevention of relapse in women who quit smoking during pregnancy. *American Journal of Public Health, 89,* 706–711.

McBride, C. M., Scholes, D., Grothaus, L. C., Curry, S. J., Ludman, E., & Albright, J. (1999). Evaluation of a minimal self-help smoking cessation intervention following cervical cancer screening. *Preventive Medicine, 29,* 133–138.

Niaura, R., & Abrams, D. B. (2002). Smoking cessation: Progress, priorities, and prospectus. *Journal of Consulting and Clinical Psychology, 70,* 494–509.

Ossip-Klein, D. J., Carosella, A., & Krusch, D. A. (1997). Self-help interventions for older smokers. *Tobacco Control, 6,* 188–193.

Parker-Pope, T. (2003, April 22). Getting "smober": Smokers who want to quit find some help on the web. *The Wall Street Journal,* D1.

Prue, D. M., Riley, A., W., Orlandi, M. A., & Jerome, A. (1990). Development of a computer-assisted smoking cessation program: A preliminary report. *Journal of Advancement in Medicine, 3,* 131–139.

Raw, M., Jarvis, M. J., Feyerabend, C., & Russell, M. A. H. (1980). Comparison of nicotine chewing-gum and psychological treatments for dependent smokers. *British Medical Journal, 281,* 481–482.

Russell, M. A. H., Raw, M., & Jarvis, M. J. (1980). Clinical use of nicotine chewing gum. *British Medical Journal, 280,* 1599–1602.

Schwartz, J. L. (1987). *Review and evaluation of smoking control methods: The United States and Canada, 1978–1985.* (NIH Publication No. 87-2940). Washington, DC: U.S. Government Printing Office.

Shiffman, S., Paty, J. A., Rohay, J. M., Di Marino, M. E., & Gitchell, J. (2000). The efficacy of computer-tailored smoking cessation material as a supplement to nicotine polacrilex gum therapy. *Drug and Alcohol Dependence, 64,* 35–46.

Taylor, P. (1990). Drug addiction and drug abuse. In A. G. Gilman, L. S. Goodman, T.W. Rall, & P. Taylor, (Eds.). *Goodman and Gilman's the pharmacologic basis of therapeutics* (8th ed., pp. 177–197). New York: McGraw-Hill.

U.S. Department of Health and Human Services. (1988). *The health consequences of smoking: Nicotine addiction. A report of the Surgeon General* (DHHS Publication No. CDC 88-8406). Washington, DC: U.S. Government Printing Office.

Velicer, W. F., Prochaska, J. O., Fava, J. L., LaForge, R. G., & Rossi, J. S. (1999). Interactive versus noninteractive interventions and dose-response relations for stage-matched smoking cessation program in a managed care setting. *Health Psychology, 18,* 21–28.

Wikler, A. (1948). Recent progress in research on the neurophysiologic basis of morphine addiction. *The American Journal of Psychiatry, 105,* 329–338.

Zhu, S. H., Stretch, V., Balabanis, M., Rosbrook, B., Sadler, G., & Pierce, J. P. (1996). Telephone counseling for smoking cessation: Effects of single-session and multiple-session interventions. *Journal of Consulting and Clinical Psychology, 64,* 202–211.

CHAPTER 13

Great Expectations

Self-Help Therapies for Dieting and Weight Loss

REBECCA Y. CONCEPCION AND
PATTI LOU WATKINS

Dieting to lose weight has become the norm for many people in America and other Westernized nations (Bish et al., 2005; Kruger, Galuska, Serdula, & Jones, 2004). Whether to improve their health or to obtain the look of the latest fashion model, cutting calories, fat, carbohydrates—or all of the above—is now the common denominator among friends and strangers. Indeed, dieting has turned into a national mentality in the United States, supported by the media and medical profession alike. In their efforts to lose weight, most Americans report attempting to do so on their own (Klesges, Mizes, & Klesges, 1987). Thus, sales of self-help books on dieting and weight loss are at an all-time high, with approximately $33 billion spent annually on various weight loss goods and services (Kruger et al., 2004).

In this chapter, we will first review current trends in obesity and over-weight status in the United States. In doing so, we will examine the health implications of these conditions as well as alternative views that question whether excess weight itself is actually a cause of disease. Next, we will review current trends in dieting, again presenting views that question the wisdom of this approach to enhancing health. Subsequently, we will review the history of self-help books promoting dietary approaches to weight loss, alongside current patterns in usage. At this point, we will examine empirical findings that speak to the efficacy of some of today's most popular diets. Following, we will weigh the benefits and limitations of self-help approaches to dieting and weight loss, ending with points for clinicians to consider when making recommendations for self-help resources in this area.

Obesity and Overweight

Prevalence and Demographics

Currently, over 97 million American adults are classified as overweight or obese; over 32% are obese and 66% are obese or overweight (Centers for Disease Control and Prevention [CDC], 2006e). The prevalence of overweight and obesity is highest in Mexican Americans (73.4%; 34.4%), followed by African Americans, non-Hispanic (69.6%; 39.9%), and lastly White Americans, non-Hispanic (62.3%; 28.7%) according to the American Obesity Association (AOA, 2002). Across gender and race, men have a higher prevalence of overweight than do women: 67% versus 62%, but women experience greater obesity rates than men: 34% versus 27.7%. However, with closer analysis of race by gender, African American women have the highest incidence of overweight at 78% and obesity at nearly 51%. Among men, Mexican Americans are the most likely to be overweight, 74%, and obese, nearly 30% (AOA, 2002). While rates of overweight and obesity tend to increase with age, rates among American children are at an all-time high, with 17% of youth between the ages of 2 and 19 years meeting this classification (CDC, 2006f).

Definitions, Health Implications, and Controversies

Obesity is defined as a body mass index (BMI) $\geq$ 30 kg/m^2 and overweight as a BMI of $\geq$ 25 kg/m^2 (World Health Organization [WHO], 2006; National Institutes of Health/National Heart, Lung and Blood Institute [NIH/NHLBI], 1998). Waist circumference is also used as a measure of relative risk for obesity-related morbidity with >40 inches (>102 cm) for men and >35 inches (88 cm) for women constituting the cutoff point for increased health risk (NIH/NHLBI, 2006). For children ages 2 to 19 years, the CDC uses the 95th percentile and greater of BMI by age and sex as a measure of overweight and explicitly avoids using the term obese (CDC, 2006a).

According to a review of studies that link risk behaviors and mortality (Mokdad, Marks, Stroup, & Gerberding, 2004), poor diet and lack of physical activity are soon to surpass tobacco use as the number one killer of Americans. Obesity, strongly linked to poor diet and lack of physical activity, has been associated with a host of conditions including hypertension, type 2 diabetes, dyslipidemia, gallbladder disease, cardiovascular disease, osteoarthritis as well as breast, colon, and prostate cancer, and all causes of mortality (Klein et al., 2004). Researchers have estimated that between 5.5 and 9.1% of the total health care expenses in the United States can be attributed to obesity, up to $92.6 billion in 2002 U.S. dollars (CDC, 2006d; Thompson & Wolf, 2001). These figures do not take into account the estimated $33 billion dollars (Weight-Control Information Network, 2004) spent annually on diet and exercise programs, including self-help books, specialty foods, and equipment that individuals access on their own in an effort to reduce weight.

The BMI method of weight classifications has served the medical profession for 20 years (Kuczmarskir & Flegal, 2000); however, the use of BMI is problematic in that it is an inaccurate method of assessing levels of body fat. As such, it may be an inappropriate method of classifying the health risks for many groups of people including the young and aged, the athletic, various racial groups, and those losing weight with and without the use of physical activity (CDC, 2006b; Prentice & Jebb, 2001). Just as an active and muscular person may be erroneously classified as obese based on BMI, a person who has lost muscle mass due to aging or poor health may be classified as having a normal BMI yet lack the associated body composition assumed with a healthy BMI. With the medical community strongly relying on this method of health-risk classification, it is probable that many people have been given misleading information about their health and recommendations—often dieting approaches—for improving their health status. In other words, many individuals may be convinced that they need to lose weight to improve health when, in actuality, they do not.

Ernsberger and colleagues (Cogan & Ernsberger, 1999; Ernsberger & Koletsky, 1999) take issue with the premise that obesity is a major cause of morbidity and mortality, declaring that obesity is overemphasized as a public health threat in the medical literature. They have argued against this well-ensconced position by exposing weaknesses in the literature used to support findings between obesity and poor health status. For instance, they state that the broader medical community seemingly ignores literature that demonstrates no link between obesity and increased mortality rates. That is, the stigma of obesity is evident in science and may be represented through selective reporting of the empirical evidence of this relationship. They, in fact, cite literature that has shown that individuals who are underweight suffer equal rates of morbidity and mortality that are comparable to individuals with obesity. Another issue raised by Ernsberger's group is the possibility that health problems associated with overweight and obesity may be a function of weight fluctuations from dieting or from harmful dieting practices themselves rather than poundage per se. Lastly, these researchers suggest that it may be the unhealthy behaviors, such as lack of physical activity or poor nutritional intake, that cause the disease state, not the relationship more commonly assumed in which the excess weight causes the disease state. In essence, bias in how research is conducted, interpreted, and disseminated—i.e., through a "thinness-biased lens"—(Cogan & Ernsberger, 1999, p. 187), may have created a weight-centered medical crisis that serves pharmaceutical companies, supplement manufacturers, and any person claiming to have the latest quick fix for weight loss, including purveyors of self-help programs.

Health at Every Size is a professional journal that addresses these concerns and presents research from the perspective that individuals may be both "fit and fat." Its mission statement purports that healthy bodies come in all sizes and shapes (Miller & Robinson, 2006). It further acknowledges that weight issues are ripe for exploitation. Empirical research has in fact shown that bias exists within the community of health care professionals who work with people who are obese (Teachman & Brownell, 2001). If so, are they more likely to conduct their practice based on research suggesting that obesity begets poor health while ignoring research questioning the link between weight and health status? Persons who are overweight and obese also seem to have internalized these social biases (Wang, Brownell, & Wadden, 2004). Thus, as a result of obesity bias from professionals, from like-others, and even from themselves, this group may overaccess therapies for weight-loss—including self-help programs—to the possible detriment of their health.

Dieting and Weight Loss

Prevalence and Demographics

The 2000 Behavioral Risk Factor Surveillance System (BRFSS) data shows that up to 46% of U.S. women and 33% of U.S. men are presently trying to lose weight (Bish et al., 2005). Currently, the weight-loss charge is practiced most frequently by Hispanic (50%), Caucasian and African-American (45–46%) women, followed by Hispanic (34%), Caucasian (32%), and African-American (31%) men based on data from over 180,000 participants in the BRFSS 2000 (Bish et al., 2005). Weight-loss strategies included eating fewer calories (56% of women, 53% of men). This strategy was most frequently used by non-Hispanic White women between the ages of 30 and 69 years, men over 50 years of age, and those who received a medical recommendation to lose weight (Bish et al., 2005). Physical activity was used by approximately 66% of men and women trying to lose weight. As with the strategy of cutting calories, physical activity was used most frequently by non-Hispanic White women (Bish et al., 2005). Although this combination of strategies is considered the most healthful and effective approach to weight loss, only 20% of respondents combined these in an effective manner by reducing calories and meeting the physical activity requirements of >150 min/week of leisure-time physical activity (Bish et al., 2005). Rather, most individuals choose simply to cut calories in an effort to lose weight.

While dieting was once the purview of adults, young children have now joined the ranks of dieters whereby 46% of 9–11 year olds are dieting (National Eating Disorders Association [NEDA], 2005a). Dieting has also increased among those on the other end of the age range, with 43% of women ages 60–69 years and 30% of women 70 years and older trying to lose weight. This is true for older men as well, with 37% of men in the 60–69 years age range and 26% of men 70 years and older also trying to lose weight (Bish et al., 2005). It is questionable as to the necessity of older people attempting weight loss as mortality related to obesity declines with age and is nearly absent by the time people reach their mid 70s (McTigue, Hess, & Ziouras, 2006). However, McTigue and colleagues recommend a careful evaluation of potential risks and benefits of weight loss for each individual patient. Perhaps more interesting are the findings that over 9% of adult men, nearly 29% of adult women (Bish et al., 2005), and 66% of high school-aged girls with normal BMIs were also trying to lose weight (Calderon, Yu, & Jambazian, 2004). These results are not surprising when 9% of adult men and over 25% of adult women of normal weight, BMI of 18.5 to 25, perceive themselves to be overweight (Paeratakul, White, Williamson, Ryan, & Bray, 2002). Such findings illustrate the problem of people dieting in hopes of meeting a potentially unrealistic ideal when their weight is already at what is considered a healthy level.

Definitions, Health Implications, and Controversies

According to the NEDA (2005b) dieting is defined as "Any attempts in the name of weight loss, 'healthy eating,' or body sculpting to deny your body of the essential, well-balanced nutrients and calories it needs to function to its fullest capacity." Although the majority of dieters, 71%, engaged in restrictive eating practices to improve their health (Paeratakul, White et al., 2002), research now questions whether dieting is health-enhancing as commonly believed or whether it is actually detrimental to physical and psychological well-being. The concern regarding the health effects of dieting lies in the difficulty of maintaining weight loss (Elfhag & Rossner, 2005). Weight cycling or yo-yo dieting, whether during childhood or adulthood, can cause ongoing stress on the cardiovascular and renal systems. Weight cycling can also cause vascular damage due to extreme fluctuations in circulating glucose and lipids and contribute to an increase in body fat and obesity (Montani, Viecelli, Prévot, & Dulloo, 2006). Montani et al. make the point that the physical impact of yo-yo dieting also affects people of normal weight who gain and lose weight throughout their lives. Because of the societal appearance standards for women and girls, they are at particular risk for the side effects of weight cycling. Additionally, the reduced calorie intake can cause dieters to receive inadequate nutrients such as calcium, thus increasing their risk for osteoporosis and related injury (NEDA, 2005b). Psychologically, dieting can lead to eating disorders such as binge eating, depression, and lowered self-esteem (Darby, Hay, Mond, Rodgers, & Owen, 2006; Grilo, & Masheb, 2000; NEDA, 2005b). However, the National Task Force on the Prevention and Treatment of Obesity's (2000) review of the literature suggests that these concerns have been exaggerated and makes the point that, "such concerns should not preclude attempts to reduce caloric intake and increase physical activity to achieve modest weight loss or prevent additional weight gain" (p. 2581).

Obesity and overweight are now acknowledged among researchers to be the result of multiple interacting variables including environmental, social, cultural, physiological, genetic, and behavioral variables (CDC, 2006c). In fact, a burgeoning body of literature attests to the unmodifiable influence of genetic endowment on body weight and shape (Montani et al., 2006). Nevertheless, many individuals still look to dieting as a means of altering their physiques. Some time ago, Brownell (1991b) suggested that people operate under a mistaken assumption that body weight and shape is completely under their control—that essentially, through individual effort and personal will, they can achieve any body type that they desire. Despite some recognition of these constraints in professional circles, the message has not trickled down to the lay public, evidenced by the vast and increasing number of dieters in the United States.

One needs only look to the mass media to understand this national obsession with dieting and weight loss. For instance, thinness is equated with both health *and* beauty in magazines, especially those targeting women and girls (Levine & Harrison, 2003). Similarly, Greenberg and Worrell (2005) found that articles and advertisements about dieting are 10 times more likely to appear in female-focused magazines than in male-targeted magazines. In addition to print media, television also projects a narrow range of desirable body types. Greenberg, Eastin, Hofschire, Lachlan, and Brownell (2003) found that, during the 1999–2000 television season, over 30% of women on television sitcoms were underweight, whereas in the real world, only 5% are underweight. In contrast, only 3% of women on television were obese, whereas in the real world, 25% are obese. Notably, the overweight women presented on television were the subject of jokes and had fewer positive relationships, friends, or love interests. Apart from these portrayals, television—and its celebrities—are also the direct source of information on self-help books, often those that promote dieting and weight loss (Kissling, 1995; Wilson, 2003).

Self-Help Dieting and Weight Loss Approaches

Only 16% of persons who are classified as overweight and half of those who are classified as obese have sought professional advice to lose weight (Bish, et al., 2005). In fact, 42% created their own version of a diet or used a plan that they had read or heard about from another source (Paeratakul, York-Crowe et al., 2002). Over 90% of college students attempted to lose weight without a formal program and to diet using their own approach (Klesges et al., 1987). These statistics give a sense of the number of people attempting to lose weight through self-help methods rather than professionally led programs. Furthermore, they speak to the importance of practitioners gaining an understanding of various popular self-help approaches to weight loss. While there are many self-help groups that promote weight loss through dieting (e.g., Weight Watchers and Overeaters Anonymous), our discussion will focus on media-based self-help approaches, specifically self-help books.

Historical and Current Trends

Starker (1989) takes a historical look at the self-help diet and weight loss industry in the United States, which began nearly a century ago with the publication of *Diet and Health With Key to the Calories* in 1918. This book was based upon the new science of nutrition, appearing a year after the American Dietetic Association was formed. Although grounded in this new science, its author, physician Lulu Hunt Peters, wrote specifically to appeal to laypersons. As such, she included colorful case examples along with humorous anecdotes and drawings. This formative work, which achieved best-seller status from 1922 through 1926, was followed by Victor Lindlahr's 1940 *You Are What You Eat*, an expression still common in today's vernacular. In contrast to its predecessor, this book focused on maintaining a "balanced diet" incorporating the appropriate vitamins and minerals, rather than one based simply on calorie-counting. According to Starker (1989), this best-selling book was reprinted in paperback as late as 1971. Another noteworthy self-help text of this early era was dietician Adelle Davis' 1954 *Let's Eat Right to Keep Fit*. Here, Davis provided readers with detailed nutritional information, criticizing "the typical American diet, with its excess salt and sugar, excessive processing, and its contamination by pesticides" (as cited in Starker, 1989, p. 99). She forewarned that unless preventive steps were taken immediately, Americans could expect to experience, among other disorders, increased rates of cardiovascular disease and cancer. Her insight proved to be prophetic as this is the state that Americans find themselves in today—*despite* the subsequent surge in self-help titles surrounding these topics.

Self-actualization was the Zeitgeist of the 1960s and 1970s, giving rise to an increased demand for self-help products, particularly in the areas of diet and weight loss. As Starker (1989) explains, "Being slim, healthy, and beautiful, was quite necessary, after all, to self-fulfillment and personal growth" (p. 100). In 1961, Herman Taller (1961), an obstetrician-gynecologist, published *Calories Don't Count*, perhaps the first of the "miracle" diets, states Starker. The so-called magic of this diet was to encourage the body to burn its own stored fat by consuming polyunsaturated fats. Other physicians followed suit with their own "proven" approaches to weight loss. Dr. Stillman's (1968) program, *The Doctor's Quick Weight Loss Diet*, was a high protein diet without carbohydrates that reached best-seller proportions in 1968. Still highly popular in the 21st century, *Dr. Atkins' Diet Revolution* (Atkins, 1972) made its debut in 1972. This book prescribed an initial one-week elimination of carbohydrates for rapid weight loss, and only small amounts thereafter. The goal was for dieters to achieve a state of ketosis in order to burn their own fat. While carbohydrates were denied, dietary fats such as bacon and eggs were permissible. Other popular self-help books appearing during this period included *The Save Your Life Diet* by psychiatrist David Reuben (1975), based on high fiber intake, *The Last Chance Diet* by osteopath Robert Linn and author Sandra Lee Stuart (1976) based on liquid protein intake, *The Scarsdale Diet* by physician Herman Tarnower and author Samm Sinclair Baker (1982), based on high protein intake with reductions in carbohydrates and especially fats, and *The Pritkin Program* by inventor and heart-attack survivor Nathan Pritkin and author Patrick McGrady, Jr. (1982), based on large consumption of vegetables along with increased exercise.

Self-help books on dieting and weight loss became firmly entrenched in American culture during the 1960s and 1970s. However, the 1980s saw an unprecedented demand for these products. Brownell (1991a) notes that the amount of money spent on diet foods, programs, and books nearly doubled in the 1980s from previous decades. Among the 1980s' bestsellers were Richard Simmon's (1980) *Never Say Diet* and *Jane Fonda's Workout Book* (Fondar & Schapiro, 1981). Kissling (1995) notes that this era was marked by numerous celebrity guides to weight loss, with books authored by the likes of Brooke Shields, Victoria Principal, Elizabeth Taylor, and Cher, among others. Regardless of author, Starker (1989) cites a 1984 report that found over 600 self-help books on weight loss in print at the time.

Starker (1989) attributes this trend to the baby boomers' entry into midlife. He remarks that members of this generation "had not yet surrendered their youth, beauty, and physical prowess, and the sudden awareness of the transitory natures of these characteristics only drove them to greater extremes in attempts to retain them" (p. 138). Thus, they sought solutions in the myriad of self-help books on these topics. Starker also connects the increased purchase of these products to changes in the structure of the American family. Specifically, from 1950 to 1980, households with married couples decreased by 55% and single-person households doubled. Starker speculates that the drive for physical self-improvement was spurred by the desire to appear physically attractive to potential dating partners. Titles such as *Thin Thighs in 30 Days* (Sterling, 1982) and *30 Days to a Flatter Stomach for Women* (Burstein, 1982) seem to confirm that weight loss efforts were undertaken for aesthetic, as well as health, reasons.

Brownell (1991b) offers further explanation as to why the self-help industry flourished as it did during the 1980s—particularly in the areas of dieting and weight loss. He states that "The concept of personal responsibility for health is deeply ingrained in our culture" (p. 304). Furthermore, this canon of personal responsibility is more pronounced in capitalistic societies with conservative governments in place. Thus, the 1980s marked a rejuvenation of this tenet in the United States. It also marked a time when cultural standards began to equate attractiveness, especially for women, with extreme thinness (Brownell, 1991a). As such, "This focus on individual responsibility reaches extremes in the search for the perfect body" (Brownell, 1991b, p. 304). Perini and Bayer (1995) concur that ours is a society based on the idea of self-determination in which "Americans have retained the ideal that we can achieve anything as long as we work hard enough for it" (p. 294). These authors note that while this is a concept rooted in masculinity, women in the 1980s began to assimilate the norms of traditional male culture, including individualism and its corollary, self-control. Perini and Bayer also stress that self-help diet books for women perpetuate the idea that weight loss is essential for aesthetic appeal, even if this message is couched in the rubric of health and fitness.

While published in 1989, Starker's treatise on self-help predicted that "such body-oriented issues as diet, nutrition, and exercise will remain popular topics for years to come" (p. 145). Indeed, he was correct. Seligman (1994) speaks to the costs of the 54 million copies of diet books sold in the early 1990s. In 2002, Polivy and Herman note the perennial popularity of self-help books, with diet books outselling those addressing other health-related topics. A 2006 search on Amazon.com for books using the key words "diet" and "weight loss" resulted in 5,726 and 231 relevant results respectively. Included in today's top 10 advice books are *The South*

Beach Diet and *The South Beach Diet Cookbook* by Agatston (2003, 2004), a newcomer to the diet book genre titled *French Women Don't Get Fat* by Guiliano (2004), *The Abs Diet* by Zinczenko and Spiker (2004), and *The Ultimate Weight Solution* by television talk show host, Dr. Phil McGraw (2003). The *Atkins* diet, an instant best-seller upon publication in 1972, and other "low carb" diets are enormously popular as well. Dr. Atkins' diet empire is still strong even after his death in 2003, with Amazon.com listing multiple versions of his diet book, cookbooks, shopping guides, and even CDs.

In spite of the popularity of self-help diet books, there is relatively little empirical evidence of their efficacy for weight loss or weight maintenance, not to mention their safety. This leaves health professionals uninformed and, thus, unable to make sound recommendations as to their use (Dansinger, Gleason, Griffith, Selker, & Schaefer, 2005; Hill & Astrup, 2003). Consumers are equally uninformed, thus possibly incurring harm from following these prescriptions (Brownell & Rodin, 1994). In an effort to remediate this problematic state of affairs, the following section presents an overview of scholarly articles speaking to the effectiveness of popular diets.

Empirical Evidence

Freedman, King, and Kennedy (2001) offer a characterization of popular diets, placing them into three distinct categories. The first is comprised of low-carbohydrate, high-fat and protein diets such as the *Atkins, Protein Power,* and *Life Without Bread* diets. The *Sugar Busters!* and *Zone* diets would also fall into this category, which we shall abbreviate as Low-Cho diets. The rationale behind these diets is that by greatly decreasing carbohydrate intake, insulin release will be decreased, resulting in greater satiety and weight loss through adipose metabolism, along with a decrease in serum triglyceride levels.

On the opposite end of the spectrum, Freedman et al. (2001) describe very high-carbohydrate, low- to very low-fat, and moderate protein diets, which we shall abbreviate as Low-Fat diets. These are exemplified by the *Ornish* and *Pritikin* programs. According to Freedman et al. (2001), these diets have traditionally been thought of more as a prescription to prevent cardiovascular disease rather than as a weight-loss approach for the general public. However, capitalizing on Americans' exponential weight gain, some authors of books promoting these diets have changed both the focus and the title to emphasize weight loss rather than heart disease reduction. These Low-Fat diets recommend eating high fiber and complex carbohydrates until one feels satiated. The fat intake is defined as <10% of total calories for very low-fat diets and 11–19% fat of total calories for low-fat diets. The rationale for these diets is that individuals will eat fewer calories, thus losing weight and body fat.

Lastly, Freedman et al. (2001) describe balanced nutrient reduction diets that are moderate in fat and protein intake while high in carbohydrate intake. We shall designate these as Bal diets, which are exemplified by the *Weight Watchers, Jenny Craig, Nutri-Systems, DASH,* and *USDA Food Guide Pyramid* diets. The *LEARN Program for Weight Maintenance* (Brownell, 2004) also utilizes this dietary approach and recommends that physical activity accompany these nutritional changes. Beyond these recommendations, the *LEARN* program also employs cognitive–behavioral principles for weight management including self-monitoring, reinforcement, and restructuring of negative thinking patterns. The rationale for these diets is that weight loss will occur when the body is in a state of negative energy balance produced through calorie reduction and concomitant increase in physical activity. The goal of these Bal diets "is to provide the greatest range of food choices to the consumer, to allow for nutritional adequacy and compliance, while still resulting in a slow but steady rate of weight loss (e.g., 1 to 2 lbs/wk)" states Freedman et al. (2001, p. 20S). Finally, Freedman et al. note that Bal diets, particularly in contrast to Low-Cho diets, are generally based on sound scientific principles and have been subjected to the most empirical scrutiny to date.

In the remainder of this section, articles will be reviewed that speak to the efficacy of diets within each of these three categories, either singly or in contrast to each other. Articles reviewed are of three types. The first consists of a single article (Anderson, Konz, & Jenkins, 2000) that predicts outcomes based on a nonclinical computer analysis of dietary protocols. The second consists of literature reviews (Bravata et al., 2003; Freedman et al., 2001; Katz, 2005) and the third consists of treatment outcome studies (Bacon et al., 2002; Dansinger et al., 2005; Gardner et al., 2007).

Computer Analysis   In lieu of direct administration of self-help dietary approaches to human participants, Anderson et al. (2000) opted to simulate these diets by entering suggested menu plans into a computer analysis. This analysis aimed to yield information on how closely each diet adhered to USDA Food Pyramid recommendations and to what extent each diet might impact coronary heart disease risk factors. These researchers chose to examine eight popular weight loss diets. Four of these fall into Freedman et al.'s Low-Cho diet category (i.e., the *Atkins, Protein Power, Sugar Busters!,* and *Zone* diets). Three fall into the Low-Fat diet category (i.e., the *Pritkin* and *Ornish* diets, along with *Dr. Anderson's High Fiber Fitness Plan*). Lastly, Anderson et al. (2000) examined the *American Dietetic Association's Exchange Diet* which might best be described as a Bal diet.

The researchers began by creating menus based on each diet author's recommendations, holding menus at a 2000 calorie limit. Upon analysis, they found that the *Atkins* diet was the highest in fat, saturated fat, and cholesterol and scored the poorest when compared to the USDA Food Pyramid. Not surprisingly, the *Atkins*, followed by the *Protein Power*, diet deviated the most from USDA Food Pyramid guidelines in terms of recommended servings of grains, vegetables, and fruits. Indeed, the *Atkins* diet stresses the avoidance of such foods. In contrast, the *Ornish* and *Pritkin* diets "most strongly encourage 'eating at the bottom' of the food pyramid" (Anderson et al., p. 584).

As for effects on cardiovascular risk factors, the *Atkins* diet was the worst and the *Ornish* diet was the best. The *Atkins* diet was implicated in increasing risk by virtue of the effects of low soluble fiber levels that would also increase serum cholesterol levels—the only diet in this analysis that contributed to cardiovascular risk for this reason. Based on their calculations, Anderson et al. (2000) state that "long-term use of the Atkins diet would increase serum cholesterol values by ~25%, while long-term use of the Ornish diet would decrease serum cholesterol concentrations by ~32%"(p. 586). They conclude that long-term use of the *Ornish* diet might decrease risk of heart disease by greater than 60% while long-term use of the *Atkins* diet might actually *increase* risk of heart disease by greater than 50%. Unfortunately, many consumers are seduced by the relatively rapid weight loss produced by the *Atkins* and other Low-Cho diets—weight loss that Anderson et al. (2000) contend is largely a function of water loss rather than fat. Anderson et al. conclude that the potential long-term hazards of Low-Cho diets outweigh any short-term benefits, thus obviating their use as a means of enhancing health. Based on their findings, this group instead recommends diets lower in fat and higher in both carbohydrates and fiber as the best means of reducing cardiovascular disease risk.

Literature Reviews   Freedman's group (Freedman et al., 2001) drew similar conclusions based on their review of literature dating from the 1960s. These researchers compared the claims made by popular diets to empirical studies that address the efficacy of various dietary approaches. They found that overweight people on Low-Cho diets eat less and lose weight when allowed to eat ad libitum. Like Anderson and colleagues (2000), Freedman et al. (2001) determined that Low-Cho diets produced weight reductions through a greater loss of body water than fat. However, at the conclusion of the diet, this water weight would be regained. This point is particularly salient given the possibility that individuals may not adhere to this dietary protocol in the long-term. Freedman et al. (2001) found that very few studies lasted long enough to truly address compliance, but dropouts in many of the studies were reported without explanation. They also found that, despite claims by Low-Cho diet proponents that caloric intake is inconsequential, this is not the case. Caloric balance is indeed the chief determinant of weight loss regardless of the diet's composition. Freedman et al. (2001) also warned of adverse effects associated with Low-Cho diets. These include ketosis as well as potential for increased cancer risk due to the lowered intake of fruits and vegetables. Low-Cho diets may also result in a host of side effects including constipation, diarrhea, nausea, fatigue, headache, insomnia, thirst, and halitosis. A final drawback to these diets is that they require supplementation with vitamins, specifically A, E, and B vitamins, as well as minerals and dietary fiber because of the lack of food variety, specifically fruits and vegetables.

In their review, Freedman et al. (2001) also assessed the worth of Low-Fat diets. As with Low-Cho diets, individuals adhering to these lose weight due to caloric reductions. However, in contrast to Low-Cho diets, weight reductions here are the result of a loss of body fat rather than water. As in Anderson et al.'s (2000) computer-based study, Freedman and colleagues (2001) found cardiovascular benefits associated with this dietary composition. These include a decrease in low-density lipoproteins and, in some cases, a decrease in plasma triglyceride levels and a reduction in blood pressure. Freedman et al. (2001) found few adverse effects for Low-Fat diets but noted that the American Heart Association recommends that persons with insulin-dependent diabetes mellitus avoid very low-fat diets. Another concern with these diets is that they require supplementing with vitamins E and B_{12} as well as zinc due to the limited animal protein sources. Individuals on Low-Fat diets typically reported having more than enough to eat and ate less when allowed to eat ad libitum. The high levels of dietary fiber likely contribute to feelings of satiety and thus may aid in compliance. One caveat, though, is that many of the studies of Low-Fat diets involved clinical populations who the authors admit may be more motivated to follow these relatively stringent protocols than members of the general population.

Finally, Freedman et al. (2001) spoke to Bal diets, which produce weight loss because, by reducing fat, a greater proportion of calories are removed. Specifically, "when dietary fat decreases from 34–36% to less than 30%, caloric intake significantly decreases and results in significant body weight reduction" (p. 21S). Unlike Low-Cho and Low-Fat diets, Bal diets are nutritionally sound with all food groups included at some level. Health-wise, improvements are seen in blood lipid levels and blood pressure, and no adverse effects were detected. Individuals on these diets generally reported being satiated and rated the diet highly in terms of palatability, although, once again, long-term compliance for the general public has yet to be assessed. Freedman et al. (2001) conclude that the best dietary approach for preventing weight gain, accomplishing weight loss, and maintaining this loss is one that is moderate in fat and low in calories. Such a diet—perhaps more aptly called a lifestyle—would incorporate a large amount of fruits, vegetables, and whole grains as well as low-fat dairy products. In concert with Anderson et al.'s (2000) conclusions, this diet would do best to reduce the risk of chronic disease. Finally, like Anderson's group, Freedman and colleagues (2001) discourage the use of Low-Cho diets, which, unfortunately, the general public has seized upon in recent years.

In a subsequent literature review, again dating from the 1960s, Katz (2005) reached many of the same conclusions as did Freedman et al. (2001) regarding the efficacy—and potential hazards—of various popular dietary approaches. That is, the evidence he gathered indicates that sustained weight loss is accomplished via caloric restriction, rather than dietary composition itself. While Low-Cho diets produce notable initial weight loss, this is attributable to loss of water and muscle protein, both undesirable effects. Katz (2005) also determined that "the more rapid the initial weight loss, in general the greater and more rapid the subsequent weight gain" (p. 66). That is, the methods used to achieve rapid initial weight loss are typically unsustainable. Supporting this statement, Katz noted high attrition and recidivism rates in studies of Low-Cho diets.

Additionally, Katz (2005) discussed the adverse side effects of Low-Cho diets, classifying them in terms of problems associated with high fat intake (e.g., worsened serum cholesterol levels), high protein intake (e.g., worsened renal functioning), and low carbohydrate intake. As to this last component, Katz (2005) listed 11 known ill effects of inadequate carbohydrate intake ranging from depression to increased cancer and cardiovascular disease risk. Thus, these diets appear damaging on many fronts. Katz (2005) concluded that more research must be done to identify a sustainable dietary approach that promotes both health and weight control. However, for the time being, he avers that "diets rich in fruits, vegetables, and whole grains; restricted in animal fats and trans fat from processed foods; limited in refined starches and sugar; providing protein principally from lean sources; and offering fat principally in the form of monounsaturated and polyunsaturated oils are linked to good health" (p. 74). Finally, Katz was equally adamant about the short-comings and ill effects of Low-Cho diets that the populace seems to prefer.

Bravata and colleagues (2003) reviewed the literature on Low-Cho diets, searching for empirical articles testing their effects between 1966 and 2003. These researchers also determined that weight loss was a result of caloric restriction as well as duration of the diet, rather than carbohydrate restriction per se. In contrast to Freedman et al. (2001) and Katz's (2005) literature reviews, Bravata's examination of empirical evaluations of Low-Cho diets failed to yield notable ill effects on health status. These researchers state "lower-carbohydrate diets were not associated with adverse effects on serum lipid levels, fasting serum glucose levels, or blood pressure" (p. 1847). Nevertheless, Bravata et al. (2003) stopped short of endorsing the widespread use of these diets. Rather, they enumerated a number of methodological weaknesses in the studies they reviewed.

First, they comment that relatively few studies reported on the metabolic variables on which they found no ill effects. In addition, these studies generally lacked any long-term follow-up, thus they were unable to determine both efficacy and harm that might be incurred over time. Bravata et al. (2003) also observe that most articles reported results only for participants who had completed the study, thus effects of the dietary interventions may have been overstated. On a related note, adherence to dietary protocols was often not assessed even among participants who completed the studies. For the most part, studies failed to include measures of exercise behavior, thus the impact of any changes in physical activity could not be assessed. Finally, Bravata et al. (2003) make an excellent point in light of obesity patterns in the United States. That is, information on race and ethnicity of participants in the studies reviewed was often lacking. Presumably, the majority of participants in these studies were White, non-Hispanic Americans, thus limiting the extent to which findings could be generalized to diverse groups in this country and abroad. Freedman et al. (2001) voice a similar concern, noting that the existing studies primarily examined dietary interventions among adults, with little research examining their effects on children and adolescents. This is worrisome given the increasing numbers of children and adolescents who embark on diets to lose weight.

Treatment-Outcome Studies   Because of the paucity of data on increasingly popular diets, Dansinger et al. (2005) set out to empirically evaluate the effects of the *Atkins, Zone, Weight Watchers,* and *Ornish* on weight loss and cardiovascular risk reduction, as well as adherence. The first two of these diets are of the Low-Cho variety while the *Weight Watchers* reflects the Bal diets, and the *Ornish* is representative of the Low-Fat diets. Participants were adult men and women of any age who were between 27 and 42 BMI and had at least one cardiovascular disease risk factor. Participants were randomly assigned to the four dietary conditions, which then met as a group for one hour on four occasions during the 2 months of active intervention. Each group was led by a dietician and physician who presented the rationale for the diet along with written materials and the official diet cookbook. They also provided diet-specific advice, reinforced positive dietary changes, and addressed barriers to adherence. Participants also received monthly telephone calls inquiring about adherence and assessing changes in medications, hospitalizations, and any adverse effects. Thus, the intervention in this study most closely resembled self-help as an adjunct to therapy rather than a pure self-help intervention. Individuals enrolled in this study received no monetary compensation for their participation.

Dependent variables were assessed at pretest, posttest (2 months), and follow-up (6 and 12 months). The researchers found that, in a year's time, all four diets resulted in a modest weight loss, with no significant difference among them. At year's end, all four diets also produced modest improvements in some, but not all, cardiovascular risk factors with some variation among the diets. Furthermore, no diet resulted in a significant worsening of any risk factor over the course of the year. However, adherence to dietary protocols did seem to be a problem, particularly for those assigned to the *Ornish* and *Atkins* diets, which only 50 and 53% of participants, respectively, completed. Attrition was still high among the other groups, with only 65% of participants in both the *Zone* and *Weight Watchers* diets completing the study. The two most common explanations for discontinuation was that the diet was too difficult to follow or that it was not meeting participants' expectations in terms of amount of weight lost. Even among those who completed the study, self-monitoring records revealed a clinically meaningful adherence level among only 25% of participants in each condition, with adherence diminishing as time progressed. Noteworthy is the fact that weight loss was significantly related to adherence levels in this study. Thus, the authors concluded that dietary adherence may be more salient than the diet itself in terms of producing weight loss and improvements in cardiovascular risk. While no adverse effects for any diet were encountered, Dansinger et al. (2005) did caution that their study was limited in its ability to elucidate long-term safety risks.

More recently, Gardner et al. (2007) conducted a similar study comparing four diets, the *Atkins, Zone,* and *Ornish* diets, but using the *LEARN* program, another Bal diet, in place of the *Weight Watchers* diet that Dansinger et al. (2005) had examined. This study also spanned 12 months, but participants here were restricted to premenopausal women ages 25 to 50 with BMIs between 27 and 40. Participants were randomized in blocks and assigned to one of the four experimental conditions. Again, the intervention more closely resembled self-help as an adjunct to therapy as participants attended one-hour classes once per week for 8 weeks. Classes were led by a dietician who covered approximately one eighth of the material in each self-help diet book during each meeting. Although the *LEARN* program is meant to be navigated across 16 weeks, it was covered in this accelerated time frame to match the intervention span of the other three groups. Additional contact with participants included e-mail and telephone prompts for appointments and additional contact throughout the study. In contrast to Dansinger et al., (2005) Gardner et al. (2007) offered participants increasing monetary incentives for completing assessments at 2, 6, and 12 months.

Gardner et al. (2007) aimed to assess the effects of these interventions on weight loss, which they dubbed their primary outcome. They also aimed to assess their effects on 11 metabolic measures, which they referred to as secondary variables. As in the Dansinger et al. (2005) study, all four diets assessed here resulted in weight loss over the course of a year. At 2- and 6-month assessments, weight loss for the *Atkins* diet was significantly greater than that for all other groups. This is consistent with reports of rapid initial weight loss on Low-Cho diets. However, by 12 months, the weight loss produced by the *Atkins* diet was significantly better than only the *Zone* diet. The weight loss produced by all diets was modest at best, with the *Atkins* resulting in the greatest loss, an average of 4.7 kg after one year. Modest improvements were also detected on the metabolic measures after one year, with the *Atkins* diet faring significantly better than the *Zone* in terms of BMI and triglycerides, better than the *Ornish* in terms of HDL and diastolic blood pressure, and better than all three other diets in terms of systolic blood pressure. In contrast to the Dansinger et al. (2005) study, far fewer individuals discontinued their participation throughout the course of Gardner et al.'s (2007) intervention. In all four diet groups, over 85% of participants attended over 75% of their assigned classes and retention at 12 months ranged from 76 to 88%, with no significant differences among groups. The authors add, however, that "adherence to the 4 sets of dietary guidelines varied within each treatment group and waned over time, especially for the Atkins and Ornish diets" (p. 976).

Gardner et al. (2007) concluded that concerns about the adverse effects of the *Atkins* diet were not confirmed, at least within the 12 months that their study entailed. They conceded that questions remain as to the source of weight loss—i.e., was it attributable to the composition of the diet itself, and if so, what dietary component? They acknowledged that questions about the long-term effects of these diets remain. While the authors extolled the external validity of their findings, one must remember that self-help diet books were used as an adjunct to therapy in a research setting where individuals were prompted and paid for their participation. The monetary incentives in this study might account for the much greater retention rates than those in Dansinger et al.'s (2005) study, where no such incentives existed. Such conditions vastly differ from those in which millions of Americans purchase these books and attempt to negotiate them on their own.

A final empirical study to be examined here is one that compared use of the *LEARN Program for Weight Control* manual to use of a manual espousing a nondieting approach to healthy eating, nutrition, physical activity, social support, and body acceptance (Bacon et al., 2002). Participants were obese (BMI > 30) women ages 30–45 years who had a chronic history of dieting. They were randomly assigned to either the dieting or nondieting condition, each of which entailed attending 24 weekly 90-minute sessions. Following this active treatment phase, participants could attend monthly aftercare sessions for 6 more months in which no new material was presented. The dieting group was led by a dietician, whereas the nondieting group was led by a counselor. Once again, the interventions resembled self-help as an adjunct to therapy rather than pure self-help.

Results revealed that only in the dieting group did significant weight loss occur, most of this happening by mid-treatment with no significant reductions thereafter. A significant reduction in BMI also occurred for the dieting group. In stark contrast, the nondieting group experienced virtually no change in these variables across time. However, *both* groups significantly improved in total cholesterol, LDL, triglycerides, and systolic blood pressure at 12 months. These changes occurred at mid-treatment for the dieting group and following aftercare for the nondieting group. Unfortunately, HDL values significantly worsened for both groups, more so for the nondieting group. Bacon et al. (2002) measured activity levels throughout their study, finding that there was a significant increase in energy expenditure for the nondieting group at 12 months, contrasting with a significant *decrease* for the dieting group.

Unlike many other studies assessing the effects of dietary approaches, Bacon et al.'s (2002) study included an assessment of psychological variables: eating disorder pathology, depression, and self-esteem. On the eating disorder measures, both groups improved significantly and similarly over time on some subscales, but the nondieting group significantly improved on a greater number, with the dieting group actually faring worse over time on cognitive restraint. The researchers, however, framed this as a successful outcome because this is a quality that dieting approaches attempt to imbue. Although both groups improved over time, the nondieting group exhibited significantly better scores on body image avoidance and disinhibiton than the dieting group. Furthermore, the nondieting group significantly improved over time and had significantly better scores on rigid control, whereas the dieting group's initial significant improvements disappeared by year's end. Both groups improved on depression and did not differ from each other on this variable. Regarding self-esteem, the nondieting group made a significant improvement although this did not occur until the 12-month assessment. The dieting group exhibited a significant improvement at the end of the 6-month treatment program, but this effect was not sustained at 12 months.

Last, but certainly not least, Bacon et al. (2002) assessed attrition levels throughout their study, finding significant differences between the two groups. While 33 and 41% of participants in the dieting group dropped out of the study at mid- and posttreatment, respectively, only 8% of participants dropped out of the nondieting group at mid-treatment, with no additional dropouts at posttreatment. Among those who remained in the study, significantly fewer participants (67%) in the dieting group attended sessions during the latter half of treatment than participants (76%) in the nondieting group. Similar proportions of participants did participate in the optional aftercare sessions, 50 and 53% for the dieting and nondieting groups, respectively. Participants also had the opportunity to complete a self-evaluation questionnaire. The researchers reported striking differences between the groups on the items, "I feel like I have failed the program" and "This program has helped me feel better about myself," with 38 and 35% of the dieting group endorsing the "failure" item at mid- treatment and 12-months, respectively, compared to 5 and 7% of the nondieting group at these junctures. On the "feel better" item, 51 and 78% of the dieting group endorsed this item at mid-treatment and 12 months compared to 93% of the nondieting group at both time periods.

Based on their findings, Bacon et al. (2002) urge practitioners to consider recommending nondieting interventions, at least to their larger women clients who have a history of failed dieting attempts. In this study, such an approach resulted in similar improvements in metabolic fitness variables as did a dieting approach. Furthermore, the nondieting approach resulted in greater improvements in psychological health, fewer attributions of failure, and seemingly related higher levels of adherence.

Advantages and Disadvantages

Generally speaking, self-help programs are less costly than professionally led psychological and medical interventions. This advantage is particularly meaningful for persons attempting to lose weight as most insurance programs do not cover weight-loss treatments (Downey, 2002). Furthermore, weight is inversely correlated with income in the United States. Thus, individuals classified as obese or overweight are likely to have fewer economic resources at their disposal. Fabricatore, Wadden, and Foster (2005) recognize that people of color are less likely to access health care even though they have higher rates of obesity and overweight than Caucasians in the United States. This same point can be made about American women, who have greater rates of obesity than their male counterparts but who have fewer financial means for treatment.

The availability of self-help resources in this area may also be advantageous as they eliminate the stigma of presenting oneself to a professional for assistance. Indeed, Fabricatore et al. (2005) report that health care professionals' attitudes toward obese patients are as negative today as they were 40 years ago. However, present-day practitioners are less likely to express this bias in an explicit manner. Thus, these authors suggest that patients' reluctance to seek formal weight loss treatment may stem from factors other than overt hostility on the part of practitioners. For instance, patients may encounter a more diffuse lack of empathy. In addition, they may be advised that their weight is problematic (in terms such as "fat" and "obese," which evoke negative emotional reactions) but offered little guidance for remedying this situation. Non-interpersonal elements of the health care setting may also deter persons from seeking professional care such as when chairs and medical equipment are too small for the patient or when scales are in plain view of other patients. All of these elements may conspire to evoke shame and embarrassment among persons of weight, leading them to seek private solutions for weight loss among the countless self-help books on this topic.

While the first chapter in this text lists enhanced self-efficacy among the psychological benefits of self-help therapies, Polivy and Herman (2002) suggest that this relationship is somewhat muddled when it comes to dieting and weight loss. Self-efficacy refers to confidence that one can successfully manage a task—in this case, lose weight. Polivy and Herman (2002) note that such efficacy, or confidence, is often based on a record of success or competence—in other words, some performance accomplishment. Bandura (1977) defined self-efficacy as the conviction that one can successfully execute the behavior required to produce the outcomes. Herein lies the problem with respect to weight loss. Polivy and Herman note that the "pernicious aspect of dieting is not that diets eventually fail, but that they do not fail before first succeeding" (p. 683). Indeed, Katz's (2005) literature review indicated that any diet that restricts calories will produce weight loss in the short term. However, the means used to achieve this initial weight loss is intrinsically unsustainable, with weight gain soon to follow. Low-Cho diets are the epitome of this problem because they tend to produce the largest initial weight losses, and they appear to be the least sustainable, perhaps due to their host of side effects.

Polivy and Herman lament that such initial success leads dieters to develop an unrealistic sense of self-efficacy. That is, if they keep trying—or try harder the next time—they will indeed achieve substantial and permanent weight loss. They speculate that such individuals persist in their dieting efforts because they attribute their inevitable failure to themselves rather than the inadequacy of the diet. Bacon et al.'s (2002) self-evaluation findings, reported in the previous section, poignantly illustrate this effect. Polivy and Herman suggest that if dieters do invoke an external attribution, it may be that this *particular* diet was "not for me" (p. 683), so they move on to the next self-help program that purportedly holds the key to lasting weight loss. Dieters certainly do not develop such notions in a social vacuum. Polivy and Herman assert that the diet industry thrives due to repeat customers. That is, "promoters of the diet in question have a vested interest in blaming the dieter rather than the diet" (p. 681). Dieters who fail to achieve (and maintain) the unrealistic weight loss that these programs promise—and the generalized happiness that such weight loss will certainly bring—can redeem themselves simply by trying harder next time.

The diet industry certainly seems to be one in which capitalistic motives usurp those of a therapeutic nature. Seligman (1994) accuses the industry with creating a public that is "discontent, even despairing, about their bodies, and willing—even eager—to spend a substantial portion of their earnings in the belief that they can and should become much thinner than they are" (p. 180). Wilson (2003) echoes this sentiment, stating that advertising strategies are devised to foster insecurity and inadequacy among recipients. This, of course, is followed by the unwavering promise that purchasing a certain product will ameliorate this distress. Seligman (1994) vehemently calls for an end to this practice, instigating for truth in advertising. For instance, he maintains that self-help diet books should disclose that long-term weight loss is an unlikely outcome. Instead, Brownell (1991b) observes that books make claims like "Lose Up to a Pound a Day and Never Gain it Back" (p. 305). Freedman et al. (2001) list "Not a single adverse reaction" as one of the "outrageous" claims found in Bantam Book's *Protein Power* and "Sugar is toxic!" (p. 40S) as an outrageous statement contained in Ballantine Book's *Sugar Busters!* Seligman (1994) goes so far as to say that those who author and promote these books are approaching a violation of the profession's "do no harm" oath (p. 197). Rosen, Glasgow, and Moore (2003) have long insisted that ineffective self-help programs are not necessarily benign—that these can actually lead to worsening of the problem. Katz (2003) warns that fad diets should be "presumed guilty" (p. 33) regarding their impact on health and that it is the responsibility of their authors to prove their program's efficacy, including lack of harm.

Unfortunately, numerous self-help diet books are created by individuals who are not even bound by professional ethics in the health-related fields. Starker (1989) states that "Anyone—even persons without an iota of nutritional training can design, develop, publish, and promote a diet ... all it takes is an idea and the ability to string some words together" (p. 4).

Kissling (1995) is particularly critical of self-help books on dieting and weight loss authored by celebrities who have no qualified expertise in this area. As such, messages and recommendations contained in these books may run counter to sound scientific evidence. For instance, these books often categorize foods as either good or bad—even "forbidden" (p. 215). In turn, ingestion of such foods is seen as abusive, weak, and/or sinful. Readers are counseled to be hypervigilant, lest they experience lapses in their efforts. Kissling (1995) quotes one book as warning "a dieter must be on National Guard duty twenty-four hours a day" (p. 214). Putterman and Linden (2004) cite a body of research linking this approach, known as *dietary restraint* or *restrained eating*, to a number of deleterious physical and psychological states. In fact, they acknowledge that dietary restraint may be etiologically involved in the onset of eating disorders.

"Looks do count" is another common theme that runs throughout celebrity-authored self-help books (Kissling, 1995, p. 213). That is, weight loss is to be pursued for aesthetic purposes, thus reinforcing unrealistic societal beauty standards and the idea that self-worth is necessarily contingent on body weight and shape, particularly for women. In their own examination of self-help books, Perini and Bayer (1995) encountered this same theme espoused by authors, even those of the non-celebrity variety. This focus on appearance also extended to muscularity in that books encouraged women to engage in strength training "because muscles are sexy!" as one book proclaimed (p. 300). Putterman and Linden (2004) produced empirical evidence showing that when weight loss is driven by appearance versus health concerns, female dieters report greater use of unhealthy practices (e.g., eliminating whole food groups) and a greater number of the aforementioned lapses in restraint. In addition, women participants who dieted to improve their appearance, rather than their health, experienced greater body dissatisfaction and lower self-esteem. Putterman and Linden (2004) further remark that drastic approaches to weight loss are also the least likely to work, setting dieters up to try ever harder, only to fail again and again.

Despite Kissling's (1995) critique of celebrity-authored self-help books, works continue to be published that rehash some of these same troubling themes. For instance, the back cover of talk show host Dr. Phil McGraw's *The Ultimate Weight Loss Solution* (2003) presents exaggerated claims in that it promises "permanent weight loss" with "immediate results." Messages about weight are moralistic in tone as exemplified by pejorative terms such as "fatties" and "couch potatoes." While the book touts good health as a consequence of weight loss, it simultaneously conveys the importance of weight loss for physical appearance; e.g., "You'll love what you start seeing in the mirror" (p. 207). It also places the blame for failure to lose weight squarely on the shoulders of the individual. McGraw (2003) refers to the statement "Because obesity runs in my family, I just can't lose weight" as a "handy excuse or justification for not losing weight" (p. 73) rather than acknowledging the empirically documented genetic limitations to weight loss. Along these lines, McGraw (2003) makes the statement, "Overweight people simply eat more calories, more fat, and more carbohydrates than normal-weight people do" (p. 181), which clearly contradicts scientific evidence regarding the influence of genetics on energy expenditure regulation, lipid metabolism, and other elements of weight and weight loss (Moreno-Aliaga, Santos, Marti, & Martínez, 2005).

An inherent limitation of the self-help genre is that it fails to address etiological factors beyond the individual's own psychological makeup. The self-help literature on dieting and weight loss presents perhaps the most glaring example of this critique. In this case, individuals must contend with both biological and sociocultural barriers to weight loss. In his aptly titled article, "Dieting and the Search for the Perfect Body: Where Physiology and Culture Collide," Brownell (1991a) cites early evidence for genetic influences on weight—which consequently places confines on the extent of weight loss one might realistically achieve. Research over the ensuing decades has reinforced this contention (e.g., Moreno-Aliaga et al., 2005). That is, the human body is *not* infinitely malleable because of biological forces beyond one's control. Brownell and colleagues (e.g., Horgen & Brownell, 2002) have also spoken of sociocultural barriers to weight loss—what they term, a "toxic environment" in which high-fat, high-calorie food is inexpensive, easily accessible, and heavily advertised. These authors raise the possibility that obesity is actually a normal response to this abnormal environment.

Despite the recognition that biological and sociocultural factors influence individuals' body weight and shape, Brownell (1991b) states that "Efforts on the management of obesity have focused almost entirely on changes the individual can make to lose weight" (p. 306). The focus on individual responsibility exemplifies the duty model of health care articulated by Winkler (1986) in which persons are expected to engage in positive health behaviors, with their resultant health status in their own hands. This lies in contrast to the rights model in which the broader social system is expected to create policies and environments which facilitate individuals' health status. Influenced by Winkler's (1986) writings, McFadden and Evans (1998) examined a random sample of articles describing obesity interventions from four leading behavior therapy and/or clinical psychology journals seeking to what extent these addressed macrolevel (e.g., cultural processes and social constructions) relative to microlevel (e.g., individual knowledge level and behavior) issues. As predicted, these articles largely attributed excess weight to individual behavior, and the interventions described therein reflected this perspective. Like Brownell

(1991b), McFadden and Evans (1998) deemed this problematic. As such, they advised against an overreliance on the duty model of health, which dictates that individuals have considerable control over their well-being. Such an emphasis may result in victim-blaming rather than recognizing the many social constraints on behavior change. That is, a bias toward personal responsibility may obscure the sociocultural factors that hamper individual choice. Evans (2005) subsequently stated that the target for treatment should never be the individual behavior alone. Rather, he contends that the individual must be considered in cultural context.

In his article "Personal Responsibility and Control Over Our Bodies: When Expectations Exceed Reality," Brownell (1991b) also warns against victim-blaming in the area of dieting and weight loss. McLellan (1995) argues that self-help books on this and other topics inherently do just that. Therefore, if weight loss is not achieved, the reader is at fault. McLellan (1995) laments that placing the onus solely on the individual does a major disservice, especially to those whose condition is a function of social oppression. Likewise, Evans (2005) remarks that some populations experience double jeopardy when their problems are a function of historical injustice and exploitation, but the proposed solutions rest solely upon individual behavior change. Kissling (1995) contends that self-help books that equate fitness, beauty, and self-esteem certainly contribute to "a climate of oppression by encouraging women to participate in the objectification of their own and other bodies" (p. 215). Perini and Bayer (1995) speak to this issue as well, stating that "The body is first and foremost to be understood as an object which is to be looked at and desired" (p. 299), with this theme rampant among the self-help books that these authors reviewed.

The language of self-blame is often incorporated in self-help books for diet and weight loss, as evidenced by the use of phrases such as *letting one's self go* (Kissling, 1995). Modern-day self-help books may not invoke overtly pejorative terms such as those found in books written in the early 1900s. For instance, Starker (1989) describes one book that used female case studies who were given "humorous" names such as "Ima Gobbler, Mrs. Sheesasite, Mrs.Weyaton, and Mrs. Knott Little" (p. 95). Nevertheless, the vocabulary used in more contemporary self-help guides still communicates that "the non-ideal female body is sick, lost, and disordered" (Perini & Bayer, 1995, p. 297). According to these authors, female readers are prompted to identify themselves as the problem in need of changing rather than question the sociocultural context in which they live.

Earlier in this chapter, we spoke of the cultural canon of personal responsibility as fueling the popularity of self-help books, with women increasingly buying into this notion, especially in the area of bodily transformation. Perini and Bayer (1995) are critical of this conception of the self-made *man* as it only applies to White men of economic means in our society. In essence, women, especially those of color and lower socioeconomic status, who embrace this Protestant ethic face greater societal barriers in their quest for success and are more likely to fall short in their efforts. When applied to overweight and obesity, this ideology sees these conditions as resulting from a lack of self-discipline, hard work, and moral character rather than resulting from dysfunctional social systems. Working from this presumption, Quinn and Crocker (1999) set out to explore the relationship between Protestant ethic ideology and psychological well-being for women who identified as "normal" weight or "overweight." In both correlational and experimental studies, these researchers found that self-perceived overweight women who embraced the Protestant ethic exhibited the poorest psychological well-being. Thus, messages about personal control espoused by the dieting self-help industry may propagate psychological distress and disordered attempts to lose weight.

Summary and Recommendations

This chapter has attempted to elucidate the long history of self-help dietary approaches to weight loss in the United States, culminating in an examination of popular programs in widespread use today. Contemporary approaches tend to fall into three categories; i.e., Low-Cho diets, Low-Fat diets, and Bal diets. The first of these, exemplified in large part by the *Atkins* diet, is the type with which Americans seem most enamored. Katz (2005) attributes this current preoccupation with Low-Cho diets to the failure of the previous decade's Low-Fat diets in fulfilling the public's great expectations. He suggests that "the public feels misled by promises that fat restriction would lead to weight loss" (p. 69). What the public neglects to understand, however, is that portion sizes have increased during this period when the population's weight has increased. Furthermore, a plethora of low-fat products arrived on the scene, many of which are high in sugar and calorie content without commensurate nutritional value. Nevertheless, a backlash seems to have occurred with respect to diets lower in fat, hence the present popularity of the *Atkins* diet and others of its ilk.

Unfortunately, Low-Cho diets appear to have the greatest number of drawbacks, weight loss aside. Although two recent experimental studies did not reveal adverse effects of the *Atkins* diet after one year, several literature reviews and a computer model suggested that long-term adherence to such a protocol may prove harmful. Perhaps it is fortunate then that many people who embark upon these types of diets are unable to stick with them in the long run. However, many individuals may berate themselves for failing to adhere to this or any type of diet or blame themselves when the amount or maintenance of weight loss falls short of expectations.

Across the literature reviewed, adherence has emerged as an issue taking predominance over dietary content itself. Regardless of diet, the greatest weight loss is associated with duration of and adherence to the protocol. If adherence is the key factor, then Bal diets seem to be the best recommendation. In addition, these appear to produce no adverse effects and, unlike both Low-Cho and Low-Fat diets, require no extraneous vitamin supplements. Bal diets seem to constitute a moderate and healthful approach in which all food groups are represented and nutritional adequacy is met. A self-help book that encompasses this approach is Brownell's (2004) *LEARN* program. Interestingly enough, it ranks 285,607th among sales on Amazon.com. Clearly it is not the first choice of consumers looking for a way to lose weight.

Even when utilized, Bal diets may have their short-comings, as Bacon et al.'s (2002) study showed. While the *LEARN* program resulted in weight loss and improved metabolic functioning, adherence was somewhat problematic, and both those who quit and those who completed the program often blamed themselves for a lack of—or limited—success. While some improvement in psychological variables occurred, the researchers cautioned that these changes may not be maintained if weight loss is not maintained. In contrast, a nondieting approach resulted in similar improvements in metabolic variables, greater improvements in psychological variables, fewer reports of self-blame, and much better adherence. These findings beg the question whether weight loss should be considered the "primary" variable, as Gardner et al. (2007) refer to it, in health-promotion interventions. Perhaps Gardner et al.'s "secondary" variables—i.e. metabolic fitness measures—should be accorded greater import when assessing the effectiveness of such interventions? Bacon et al.'s (2002) work also suggests that psychological variables be ascribed some significance in determining the worthiness of both dieting and nondieting approaches to health.

Overall then, each of the three diet approaches has its limitations, even under supervised research conditions. It is yet unknown whether these limitations would exist, or might even be magnified, when individuals attempt to use these diets under natural conditions. For now, practitioners might work with clients to let go of self-blame and the internalized bias they may have about their own weight. First, however, practitioners are advised to scrutinize themselves for any weight-biased beliefs they themselves may harbor. Such biases could adversely impact their interactions with clients in conspicuous or not so conspicuous ways. Practitioners can then assist clients concerned about their weight in processing the often conflicting information contained within the wide array of self-help books on this topic. "Nutrition and diet books that patients have discovered on their own are totally misleading and I spend a lot of time correcting bad information in these books," lamented an internist interviewed by Starker (1989, p. 156). Another exclaimed that readers "tend to believe that all that is in print is true!" Thus, practitioners are in a position to alert clients to potentially unhealthful content. For instance, they might help clients recognize that biological and environmental barriers to weight loss do exist and that dieting for the sake of aesthetics is often self-defeating. Practitioners can also work to modify the great expectations that the self-help industry perpetuates—that large and rapid weight loss is achievable, that such weight loss will be maintained, that no ill effects will occur, and that such weight loss will lead to a widespread transformation in the individual's life.

Finally, practitioners might question whether clients truly need to lose weight, as this chapter has pointed out that some individuals meeting criteria for overweight and obesity are actually fit and healthy. Furthermore, weight loss per se may not improve health to the extent that moderate diet and physical activity do. In addition, numerous individuals, particularly women, engage in dieting to lose weight when they are "normal" weight. Evans (1997) raises the possibility that practitioners may condone "unreasonable social standards of physical appearance and attractiveness" (p. 486), labeling a client's weight as problematic when, in actuality, it is not. Thus, practitioners must ask whether any attempt to lose weight is warranted for the individual in question, be it through self-help or some other modality of change.

If dieting is to be recommended, Bal diets seem to prevail in terms of a reasonably sustainable and healthful method. Although without the fanfare of currently popular diets, the federal government supplies many resources that support this dietary approach. These also come without the costs of best-selling self-help books. The National Institutes of Diabetes and Digestive and Kidney Disease's (2006) publication *Weight Loss for Life* addresses many points discussed in this chapter, including whether or not a person should even consider weight loss. It also provides a plan for healthy diet and exercise and how to find a safe and appropriate weight-loss program. Many other support materials are available in print or on the Web that may assist the public to think about their weight in a healthful way, tempering the great expectations that many people have—and have been fed by the diet industry—when it comes to weight loss. This chapter includes a listing of some of these resources.

Chapter Points

- Overweight and obesity are said to cause several health conditions, but controversy remains regarding the veracity of these claims.
- Nearly half of U.S. women and one third of U.S. men are trying to lose weight, primarily limiting caloric intake without concomitantly engaging in moderate physical activity.
- Many popular diets simplify the issues of body weight, shape, and size, omitting information about genetic and environmental constraints.
- Many self-help diet books state exaggerated information about the extent, immediacy, permanency, and consequences of weight loss.
- Many self-help diet books promote dangerous restrictive practices and weight loss for aesthetic purposes, both associated with psychosocial distress.
- Nonadherence and discontinuation of popular diet protocols are likely, perhaps linked to their unpalatability and/or failure to meet great expectations of weight loss.
- Research on self-help diet books is limited, rendering it difficult for practitioners to make sound recommendations, especially for more diverse racial and ethnic groups as well as children and adolescents, who are sparsely represented in empirical studies.
- Based on the extant empirical data, a balanced nutrient, moderate-fat reduction diet is the most healthful of popular dietary approaches.
- Practitioners are advised to thoroughly inspect any self-help book on dieting and weight loss that clients may use—and to carefully consider whether weight loss is truly a health-enhancing goal for the individual in question.

References

Agaston, A. (2003). *The South Beach diet: The delicious, doctor-designated, foolproof plan for fast and healthy weight loss*. Emmaus, PA: Rodale.

Agaston, A. (2004). *The South Beach cookbook*. Emmaus, PA: Rodale.

American Obesity Association. (2002). *AOA fact sheets: Obesity in minority populations*. Retrieved December 7, 2006, from http://www.obesity.org/subs/fastfacts/Obesity_Minority_Pop.shtml

Anderson, J. W., Konz, E. C., & Jenkins, D. J. A. (2000). Health advantages and disadvantages of weight-reducing diets: A computer analysis and critical review. *Journal of the American College of Nutrition, 19*, 578–590.

Atkins, R. C. (1972). *Dr. Atkins diet revolution*. New York: David McKay.

Bacon, L., Keim, N. L., Van Loan, M. D., Derricote, M., Gale, B., Kazaks, A., et al. (2002). Evaluating a "non-diet" wellness intervention for improvement of metabolic fitness, psychological well-being and eating and activity behaviors. *International Journal of Obesity, 26,* 854–865.

Bandura, A. (1977). Self-efficacy: Toward a unifying theory of behavioral change. *Psychological Review, 84,* 191–215.

Bish, C. L., Blanck, H. M., Serdula, M. K., Marcus, M., Kohl, H. W., & Khan, L. K. (2005). Diet and physical activity behaviors among Americans trying to lose weight: 2000 Behavioral Risk Factor Surveillance System. *Obesity Research, 13,* 596–607.

Bravata, D. M., Sanders, L., Huang, J., Krumholtz, H. M., Olkin, I., Gardner, C. D., et al. (2003). Efficacy and safety of low-carbohydrate diets: A systematic review. *Journal of the American Medical Society, 289,* 1837–1850.

Brownell, K. D. (1991a). Dieting and the search for the perfect body: Where physiology and culture collide. *Behavior Therapy, 22,* 1–12.

Brownell, K. D. (1991b). Personal responsibility and control over our bodies: When expectation exceeds reality. *Health Psychology, 10,* 303–310.

Brownell, K. D. (2004). *The LEARN program for weight management* (10th ed.). Dallas, TX: American Health.

Brownell, K. D., & Rodin, J. (1994). The dieting maelstrom. Is it possible and advisable to lose weight? *The American Psychologist, 49,* 781–791.

Burstein, N. (1982). *30 days to a flatter stomach for women.* New York: Bantam.

Calderon, L. L., Yu, C. K., & Jambazian, P. (2004). Dieting practices in high school students. *Journal of the American Dietetic Association, 104,* 1369–1374.

Centers for Disease Control and Prevention. (2006a). *BMI—Body mass index: About BMI for children and teens.* Retrieved November 11, 2006, from http://www.cdc.gov/nccdphp/dnpa/bmi/childrens_BMI/about_childens_BMI.htm

Centers for Disease Control and Prevention. (2006b). *Overweight and obesity: Contributing factors.* Retrieved December 7, 2006, from http://www.cdc.gov/nccdphp/dnpa/obesity/contributing_factors.htm

Centers for Disease Control and Prevention. (2006c). *Overweight and obesity: Defining overweight and obesity.* Retrieved November 11, 2006, from http://www.cdc.gov/nccdphp/dnpa/obesity/defining.htm

Centers for Disease Control and Prevention. (2006d). *Overweight and obesity: Economic consequences.* Retrieved December 7, 2006, from http://www.cdc.gov/nccdphp/dnpa/obesity/economic_consequences.htm

Centers for Disease Control and Prevention. (2006e). *Prevalence of overweight among adults: United States, 2003–2004.* Retrieved November 11, 2006, from http://www.cdc.gov/nchs/products/pubs/pubd/hestats/obese03_04/overwght_adult_03.htm

Centers for Disease Control and Prevention. (2006f). *Prevalence of overweight among children and adolescents: United States, 2003–2004.* Retrieved November 11, 2006, from http://www.cdc.gov/nchs/products/pubs/pubd/hestats/obese03_04/overwght_child_03.htm

Cogan, J. C., & Ernsberger, P. (1999). Dieting, weight, and health: Reconceptualizing research and policy. *Journal of Social Issues, 55*, 187–205.

Dansinger, M. L., Gleason, J. A., Griffith, J. L., Selker, H. P., & Schaefer, E. J. (2005). Comparison of the Atkins, Ornish, Weight Watchers, and Zone Diets for weight loss and heart disease risk reduction: A randomized trial. *Journal of American Medical Association, 293*, 43–53.

Darby, A., Hay, P., Mond, J., Rodgers, B., & Owen, C. (2007). Disordered eating behaviours and cognitions in young women with obesity: Relationship with psychological status. *International Journal of Obesity, 31*, 876–882.

Davis, A. (1954). *Let's eat right to keep fit.* Fort Worth: Harcourt, Brace and World.

Downey, M. (2002). Insurance coverage for obesity treatments. In D. H. Bessesen & R. Kushner (Eds.), *Evaluation and management of obesity*, (pp. 139–144). Philadelphia: Hanley and Belfus.

Elfhag, K., & Rossner, S. (2005). Who succeeds in maintaining weight loss? A conceptual review of factors associated with weight loss maintenance and weight regain. *Obesity Review, 6*, 67–85.

Ernsberger, P., & Koletsky, R. J. (1999). Biomedical rationale for a wellness approach to obesity: An alternative to focus on weight loss. *Journal of Social Issues, 55*, 221–260.

Evans, I. M. (1997). The effect of values on scientific and clinical judgment in behavior therapy. *Behavior Therapy, 28*, 483–493.

Evans, I. M. (2005). Behavior therapy: Regulation by self by others, and by the physical world. In C. R. O'Donnell & L. A. Yamauchi (Eds.), *Culture and context in human behavior change: Theory, research, and applications* (pp. 13–39). New York: Peter Lang.

Fabricatore, A. N., Wadden, T. A., & Foster, G. D. (2005). Bias in health care settings. In K. D. Brownell, R. M. Puhl, M. B. Schwartz, & L. Rudd (Eds.), *Weight bias: Nature, consequences, and remedies* (pp. 29–41). New York: Guilford.

Fonda, J., & Schapiro, S. (1981). *Jane Fonda's workout book.* New York: Simon and Schuster.

Freedman, M. R., King, J., & Kennedy, E. (2001). Popular diets: A scientific review. *Obesity Research, 9*(Suppl. 1), 1S–40S.

Gardner, C. D., Kiazand, A., Alhassan, S., Kim, S., Stafford, R. S., Balise, R. R., et al. (2007). Comparison of the Atkins, Zone, Ornish, and LEARN diets for change in weight and related risk factors among overweight premenopausal women: The A TO Z weight loss study: A randomized trial. *Journal of the American Medical Association, 297*, 969–977.

Greenberg, B. S., Eastin, M., Hofschire, L., Lachlan, K., & Brownell, K. (2003). Portrayals of overweight and obese individuals on commercial television. American Journal of Public Health, 93, 1342–1348.

Greenberg, B. S., & Worrell, T. R. (2005). The portrayal of weight in the media and its social impact. In K. D. Brownell, R. M. Puhl, M. B. Schwartz, & L. Rudd (Eds.), *Weight bias: Nature, consequences, and remedies* (pp. 42–53). New York: Guilford.

Grilo, C. M., & Masheb, R. M. (2000). Onset of dieting vs binge eating in outpatients with binge eating disorder. *International Journal of Obesity, 24*, 404–409.

Guiliano, M. (2004). *French women don't get fat: The secret of eating for pleasure.* New York: Knopf.

Heshka, S., Anderson, J. W., Atkinson, R. L., Greenway, F. L., Hill, J. O., Phinney, S. D., et al. (2003). Weight loss with self-help compared with a structured commercial program: A randomized trial. *Journal of the American Medical Association, 289*, 1792–1798.

Horgen, K. B., & Brownell, K. D. (2002). Confronting the toxic environment: Environmental public health actions in a world crisis. In T. A. Wadden & A. J. Stunkard (Eds.), *Handbook of obesity treatment* (pp. 95–106). New York: Guilford.

Katz, D. L. (2003). Pandemic obesity and the contagion of nutritional nonsense. *Public Health Review, 31*, 33–44.

Katz, D. L. (2005). Competing dietary claims for weight loss: Finding the forest through truculent trees. *Annual Review of Public Health, 26*, 61–88.

Kissling, E. A. (1995). I don't have a great body, but I play one on TV: The celebrity guide to fitness and weight loss in the United States. *Women's Studies in Communication, 18*, 209–216.

Klein, S., Burke, L. E., Bray, G. A., Blair, S., Allison, D. B., Pi-Sunyer, X., et al. (2004). Clinical implications of obesity with specific focus on cardiovascular disease: A statement for professionals from the American Heart Association Council on nutrition, physical activity, and metabolism. *Circulation, 110*, 2952–2967.

Klesges, R. C., Mizes, J. S., & Klesges, L. M. (1987). Self-help dieting strategies in college males and females. *International Journal of Eating Disorders, 6*, 409–417.

Kruger, J., Galuska, D. A., Serdula, M. K., & Jones, D. A. (2004). Attempting to lose weight: Specific practices among U.S. adults. *American Journal of Preventive Medicine, 26*, 402–406.

Kuczmarski, R. J., & Flegal, K. M. (2000). Criteria for definition of overweight in transition: Background and recommendations for the United States. *American Journal of Clinical Nutrition, 7*, 1074–1081.

Levine, M. P., & Harrison, K. (2003). Media's role in the perpetuation and prevention of negative body image and disordered eating. In J. Kevin Thompson (Ed.), *Handbook of eating disorders and obesity* (pp. 695–717). Hoboken, NJ: John Wiley & Sons.

Lindlahr, V. H. (1942). *You are what you eat.* New York: National Nutrition Society.

Linn, R., & Stuart, S. L. (1976). *The last chance diet: When everything else has failed.* New York: Lyle Stuart.

McFadden, A. S., & Evans, I. M. (1998). Behavioral health care: Have Winkler's admonitions regarding rights and duties been heeded? *The Behavior Therapist, 21*, 69–72.

McGraw, P. (2003). *The ultimate weight loss solution: The 7 keys to weight loss freedom.* New York: Free Press.

McLellan, B. (1995). *Beyond psychoppression: A feminist alternative therapy.* North Melbourne, Australia: Spinifex.

McTigue, K. M., Hess, R., & Ziouras, J. (2006). Obesity in older adults: A systematic review of the evidence for diagnosis and treatment. *Obesity, 14*, 1485–1497.

Miller, W. C., & Robinson, J. (Eds.). (2006). *Health at Every Size Journal*. Retrived October 28, 2006, from http://www.gurze.net/site12_5_00/newsletterhes.htm

Mokdad, A. H., Marks, J. S., Stroup, D. F., & Gerberding, J. L. (2004). Actual causes of death in the United States, 2000. *Journal of the American Medical Association, 291*, 1238–1245.

Montani, J. P., Viecelli, A. K., Prévot, A., & Dulloo, A. G. (2006). Weight cycling during growth and beyond as a risk factor for later cardiovascular diseases: The "repeated overshoot" theory. *International Journal of Obesity, 30*, S58–S66.

Moreno-Aliaga, M. J., Santos, J. L., Marti, A., & Martínez, J. A. (2005). Does weight loss prognosis depend on genetic make-up? *Obesity Reviews, 6*, 155–168.

National Eating Disorders Association. (2005a). *kNOw dieting: Risks and reasons to stop*. Retrieved December 7, 2006, from http://www.nationaleatingdisorders.org/p.asp?WebPage_ID=286&Profile_ID=41162

National Eating Disorders Association. (2005b). *Statistics: Eating disorders and their precursors*. Retrieved December 7, 2006, from nation aleating-disorders.org/p.asp?WebPage_ID=286&Profile_ID=41138

National Institutes of Health/National Heart, Lung and Blood Institute. (1998). *Clinical guidelines on the identification, evaluation, and treatment of overweight and obesity in adults: The evidence report*. Retrieved October 28, 2006, from http://www.nhlbi.nih.gov/guidelines/obesity/ob_gdlns.htm

National Institutes of Diabetes and Digestive and Kidney Diseases. (2006). *Weight loss for life* (No. 04-3700). Bethesda, MD: Author. Retrieved October 28, 2006, from http://win.niddk.nih.gov/publications/PDFs/WeightLossforLife_04.pdf

National Task Force on the Prevention and Treatment of Obesity. (2000). Dieting and the development of eating disorders in overweight and obese adults. *Archives of Internal Medicine, 160*, 2581–2589.

Paeratakul, S., White, M. A., Williamson, D. A., Ryan, D. H., & Bray, G. A. (2002). Sex, race/ethnicity, socioeconomic status, and BMI in relation to self-perception of overweight. *Obesity Research, 10*, 345–350.

Paeratakul, S., York-Crowe, E. E., Williamson, D. A., Ryan, D. H., & Bray, G. A. (2002). Americans on diet: Results from the 1994–1996 continuing survey of food intakes by individuals. *Journal of American Dietetic Association, 102*, 1247–1251.

Perini, G. M., & Bayer, B. M. (1995). Out of our minds, in our bodies: Women's embodied subjectivity and self-help culture. In C. W. Tolman & F. Cherry (Eds.), *Problems of theoretical psychology* (pp. 291–303). North York, England: Captus Press.

Peters, L. H. (1918). *Diet and health with key to the calories*. Chicago: Reilly and Lee.

Polivy, J., & Herman, P. (2002). If at first you don't succeed. False hopes of self-change. *The American Psychologist, 57*, 677–689.

Prentice, A. M., & Jebb, S. A. (2001). Beyond body mass index. *Obesity Reviews, 2*, 141–147.

Pritikin, N., & McGrady, P. M. (1982). *Pritikin program for diet and exercise*. New York: Putnam.

Putterman, E., & Linden, W. (2004). Appearance versus health: Does the reason for dieting affect dieting behavior. *Journal of Behavioral Medicine, 27*, 185–294.

Quinn, D. M., & Crocker, J. (1999). When ideology hurts: Effects of belief in the Protestant ethic and feeling overweight on the psychological well-being of women. *Journal of Personality and Social Psychology, 77*, 402–414.

Reuben, D. (1975). *Save your life diet: High-fiber protection from six of the most serious disease of civilization.* New York: Random House.

Rosen, G. M., Glasgow, R. E., & Moore, T. E. (2003). Self-help therapy: The science and business of giving psychology away. In S. O. Lilienfield, S. J. Lynn, & J. M. Lohr (Eds.), *Science and pseudoscience in clinical psychology* (pp. 399–424). New York: Guilford.

Seligman, M. E. P. (1994). *What you can change and what you can't: The complete guide to successful self-improvement.* New York: Knopf.

Simmons, R. (1980). *Never say diet book.* New York: Warner.

Starker, S. (1989). *Oracle at the supermarket.* New Brunswick, NJ: Transaction Publishers.

Stehling, W. (1982). *Thin thighs in 30 days.* New York: Bantam.

Stillman, I. M., & Baker, S. S. (1968). *The doctor's quick weight loss diet.* Boston: Prentice-Hall.

Taller, H. (1961). *Calories don't count.* New York: Simon and Schuster.

Tarnower, H., & Baker, S. S. (1982). *The complete Scarsdale medical diet plus Dr. Tarnower's lifetime keep slim program.* New York: Bantam Books.

Teachman, B. A., & Brownell, K. D. (2001). Implicit anti-fat bias among health professionals: Is anyone immune? *International Journal of Obesity, 25*, 1525–1531.

Thompson, D., & Wolf, A. M. (2001). The medical-care cost burden of obesity. *Obesity Reviews, 2*, 189–197.

Wang, S. S., Brownell, K. D., & Wadden, T. A. (2004). The influence of the stigma of obesity on overweight individuals. *International Journal of Obesity, 28*, 1333–1337.

Weight-Control Information Network. (2004, October). *Statistics related to overweight and obesity.* Retrieved November 19, 2006, from http://win.niddk.nih.gov/Statistics/index.htm

Wilson, N. (2003). Commercializing mental health issues: Entertainment, advertising, and psychological advice. In S. O. Lilienfield, S. J. Lynn, & J. M. Lohr (Eds.), *Science and pseudoscience in clinical psychology* (pp. 425–459). New York: Guilford.

Winkler, R. C. (1986). Rights and duty: The need for a social model. In N. J. King & A. Remenyi (Eds.), *Health care: A behavioral approach* (pp. 265–277). New York: Grune & Stratton.

World Health Organization. (2006). Global strategy on diet, physical activity, and health. Geneva, Switzerland: Author. Retrieved October 15, 2006 from http://www.who.int/dietphysicalactivity/publications/facts/obesity/en/

Zinczenko, D., & Spiker, T. (2004). *The abs diet: The six-week plan to flatten your stomach and keep you lean for life.* Emmaus, PA: Rodale.

Resources

American Dietetic Association
http://www.eatright.org/
216 West Jackson Boulevard
Chicago, IL 60606
(800) 877-1600, ext. 5000

American Obesity Association
http://www.obestiy.org/
1250 24th Street, NW, Suite 300
Washington, DC 20037
(800) 98-OBESE

American Society of Bariatric Physicians (ASBP)
http://www.asbp.org/
5600 S. Quebec, Ste. 109-A
Englewood, CO 80111
(303) 779-4833, (303) 770-2526
bariatric@asbp.org

The Council on Size and Weight Discrimination
http://www.cswd.org/
PO Box 305
Mt. Marion, NY 12456

Federal Trade Commission
http://www.ftc.gov/
Consumer Response Center
600 Pennsylvania Avenue, NW
Washington, DC 20580
(202) FTC-HELP

National Association to Advance Fat Acceptance
http://www.naafa.org/
NAAFA is a nonprofit human rights organization dedicated to improving the quality of life for fat people.
P.O. Box 22510
Oakland, CA 94609
(916) 558-6880

National Eating Disorders Association
http://www.nationaleatingdisorders.org

603 Stewart St., Suite 803
Seattle, WA 98101
(206) 382-3587
(800) 931-2237

National Institute of Diabetes and Digestive and Kidney Diseases
http://www2.niddk.nih.gov/
31 Center Drive
Bethesda MD 20892
(301) 496-3583

North American Association for the Study of Obesity
http://www.naaso.org/8630 Fenton Street, Suite 918
Silver Spring, MD 20910
(301) 563-6526

The Partnership for Healthy Weight Management
http://www.consumer.gov/weightloss/
A coalition of representatives from science, academia, the health care professions, government, commercial enterprises, and organizations whose mission is to promote sound guidance on strategies for achieving and maintaining a healthy weight.

Shape Up America!
http://www.shapeup.org/
Founded in 1994, Shape Up America! is a 501(c)3 not-for-profit organization committed to raising awareness of obesity as a health issue and to providing responsible information on healthy weight management.

Weight-Control Information Network (WIN)
http://www.win.niddk.nih.gov
WIN is the Federal Government's lead agency responsible for biomedical research on nutrition and obesity. WIN provides the general public, health professionals, the media, and Congress with up-to-date, science-based health information on weight control, obesity, physical activity, and related nutritional issues. 1 WIN WAY Bethesda, MD 20892-3665 (202) 828-1025 1 (877) 946-4627

CHAPTER 14

Preventing weight Gain with Internet Programs

RICHARD A. WINETT, DEBORAH F. TATE,
EILEEN S. ANDERSON, JANET R. WOJCIK AND
SHEILA G. WINETT

Two of the ten leading health indicators of *Healthy People 2010* (U.S. Department of Health and Human Services [USDHHS], 2000) focus on weight management and physical activity. Decades of research show the central role of these health behaviors for disease prevention (Koplan & Dietz, 1999) given their association with:

- type 2 diabetes and the metabolic sydrome (Ford, Giles, & Dietz., 2002; Harris et al., 1998; Mokdad et al., 2001, 1999);
- heart disease, particularly, the association with central obesity (Alexander, 2001; Melanson, McInnis, Rippe, Blackburn, & Wilson, 2001; Pi-Sunyer, 2002);
- stroke (Kurth et al., 2002);
- colon, breast, endometrial, esophagial, and renal cancers (Bianchini, Kaaks & Vainio, 2002; Calle, Rodriguez, Walker-Thurmond, & Thun, 2003; Friedenreich, 2001; see also Evenson, Stevens, Cai, Thomas, & Thomas, 2003; Kampert, Blair, Barlow, & Kohl, 1996; Lee & Blair, 2002; Vainio, Kaaks, & Bianchini, 2002);

- the loss of quality and years of life and premature death (Allison, Fontaine, Manson, Stevens, & VanItallie, 1999; Allison, Zannolli, & Narayan, 1999; Calle, Thun, Pertrelli, Rodriguez, & Heath, 1999; Fontaine, Redden, Wang, Westfall, & Allison, 2003; Mokdad, Marks, Stroup, & Gerberding, 2004); and
- the enormous burden placed on the health care system by the diseases associated with overweight and obesity (Manson & Bassuk, 2003; Must et al., 1999).

Most Americans and people in other developed countries are overweight (body mass index; BMI > 25) or moderately obese (BMI > 30) and are sedentary (Fielding, 2001; Flegal, Carroll, Ogden, & Johnson 2002; Hedley et al., 2004; Institute of Medicine, 2002; Rafferty, Reeves, McGee, & Pivarnik, 2002; USDHHS, 2002). Hill, Wyatt, Reed, and Peters (2003) predict by 2008 that about 75% of the U.S. population will be overweight and close to 40% will be obese.

This chapter addresses these problems by synthesizing a number of different theoretical and research domains including: (a) the determinants of overweight and obesity from a population perspective; (b) clinical and public health interventions; (c) long-term health behavior change strategies; (d) theoretically based guidelines for effective programs for preventing weight gain; (e) preliminary work on the prevention of weight gain; and (f) the viability of using Internet-based interventions alone or in therapeutic and supportive formats as a new approach to self-help for long-term health behavior changes. A final section of this chapter outlines a clinical research agenda.

Causes of the Obesity Epidemic

There are a number of plausible explanations for the growing epidemic of overweight and obesity. Genetic factors play a role. Some people are more susceptible to weight gain than other people given conducive environmental circumstances (Friedman, 2003). Changes in environmental and behavioral factors affect the entire population and likely most affect those at genetic risk (Booth, Chakravarthy, Gordon, & Spangenburg, 2002; Booth, Gordon, Carlson, & Hamilton, 2000; Chakravarthy and Booth, 2004). Technological changes reduce the necessity of physical activity in jobs and other aspects of daily life (Hill & Melanson, 1999; Hill & Peters, 1998). New cities and most suburbs are designed for cars and reduce the need for walking (King, Bauman, & Abrams, 2002; Reid, Schmid, Killingsworth, Zlot, & Raudenbush, 2003). Few people consistently exercise or engage in leisure-time physical activity and the small percentage of active people may be declining (Booth et al., 2002).

Pressure for work productivity and changes in family roles and family structure leave less time for formal meals and make fast food and snacks more convenient and attractive. The frequent consumption of fast food is associated with increases in body weight (French, Harnack, & Jeffery, 2000). Food is readily available and relatively inexpensive. More food is eaten outside the home and snack foods are heavily advertised and ubiquitous (French, Story, & Jeffery, 2001). Soft drinks and sweets are heavily promoted and amount to a substantial part (10% or more) of caloric consumption in the United States (Block, 2004). Agricultural policies encourage the overproduction of food and the need for the population to consume it (Nestle, 2003). Pricing strategies such as "super sizing" emphasize the "bargain" of larger quantities of food and the increase in portion sizes (Nestle, 2003; Nielsen & Popkin, 2003) are part of a "toxic environment" for gaining weight (Wadden, Brownell, & Foster, 2002). Vigilance and conscious efforts are needed to prevent weight gain (Peters, Wyatt, Donahoo, & Hill, 2002).

Clinical and Public Health Approaches to the Obesity Epidemic

Overweight and obesity are addressed by both clinical treatments and public health approaches. We will briefly describe these approaches and describe an alternative that bridges clinical and public health approaches.

Clinical Approaches

Higher dose, longer term behavioral interventions focusing on dietary changes and physical activity via lifestyle changes show modest weight loss (Andersen, Wadden et al., 1999; Anderson, Konz, Frederich, & Wood, 2001; Diabetes Prevention Program Research Group, 2002; Jeffery et al., 2000; Lowe, Miller-Kovach, & Phelan, 2001; Marcus, Dubbert, et al., 2000; Perri & Corsica, 2002; Riebe et al. 2003; Wing, 1999, 2000; Wing, Voorhees, & Hill, 2000). Weight loss of 5–10% that is maintained favorably impacts risk factors for heart disease (e.g., blood pressure and lipids), cancers (e.g., body fat), and diabetes (e.g., insulin resistance; see Perri & Corsica, 2002). Some people are successful in long-term weight loss on their own (McGuire, Wing, & Hill, 1999; Wing & Hill, 2001). But, many people are not very consistent or persistent in using existing strategies and are not successful (Serdula et al., 1999).

People who maintain a 5–10% loss for at least a year often use self-regulation strategies. They carefully monitor food consumption and physical activity, they frequently weigh themselves, and they adhere to a lower fat diet (Astrup, 2001; McGuire, Wing, & Klem, 1999; McGuire, Wing, Klem, & Hill, 1999). Methodologies to help and motivate people to use these effective weight-loss strategies can be delivered to people via the Internet (Tate, Jackvony, & Wing, 2003a; Tate, Wing, & Winett, 2001; see later). There also is an emphasis on physical activity and exercise for weight loss and preventing weight regain (Andersen et al., 1999; Jakicic, Winters, Lang, & Wing, 1999). Convenient, moderate intensity exercise or physical activity, primarily walking, can be maintained by overweight people, and such physical activity is linked to better long-term weight management (Jakicic, 2002; Jakicic, Wing, & Winters-Hart, 2002; Wing, 1999). Considerably more physical activity (60–90 min/day) than the current recommendation of 30 minutes per day may be required to help maintain weight loss among people with a history of overweight and obesity (Erlichman, Kerbey, & James, 2002; Fogelholm & Kukkonen-Harjula, 2000; Jakicic et al., 2001; Jakicic, Marcus, Gallagher, Napolitano, & Lang, 2003; Saris et al., 2003). A recent study, however, indicates that the caloric expenditure equivalent of only six to seven miles per week of walking (i.e., ~30 minutes per day of walking) is a threshold level that prevents weight gain (Slentz et al., 2004).

Traditional weight-loss programs are moderately effective and over time some people find weight loss easier to achieve (Klem, Wing, Lang, McGuire, & Hill, 2000). Weight-loss programs, however, have limitations and are not the first priority for decreasing the prevalence of overweight and obesity across the population.

Public Health Approaches

The problems of inactivity and overconsumption also are addressed through public health and ecological approaches and macrolevel analyses (Buchner & Miles, 2002; French, Story, & Jeffrey, 2001; Jeffery, 2001; King, Bauman, et al., 2002; King, Stokols, Talen, Brassington, & Killingsworth, 2002; Nestle & Jacobson, 2000; Powell, Bricker, & Blair, 2002; Sallis & Owen, 1997, 1999; Sallis, Owen, & Fotheringham, 2000; Wadden et al., 2002). Environmental design and public policies promote physical activity, especially walking (King, Stokols, et al., 2002; Reid et al., 2003). *Healthy People 2010* emphasizes increasing the number of children who walk or bike to school. Agricultural policies are being scrutinized (French et al., 2001; Nestle, 2003). Fruit and vegetable consumption needs to be encouraged. Marketing strategies leading to the purchase of large quantities of higher calorie foods need countervailing approaches (Nestle, 2003; Young & Nestle, 2002).

The history of reducing smoking prevalence shows public health approaches to food consumption and physical activity have comparable problems (Anderson & Hughes, 2000; Bayer, Gostin, Javitt, & Brandt, 2002). Politically and fiscally, it is difficult to change the car-dominated design of suburbs and cities and to change food production or marketing.

Large-scale change takes time, possibly decades. Providing access does not necessarily lead to high rates of walking across diverse groups of people. Design methods to assure some degree of use of walkways for daily functions (such as commuting to work on foot or shopping) are required (King, Stokols et al., 2002). Even in communities where walking is seemingly convenient and safe, sustained effort is required to increase walking (Reger et al., 2002). Similarly, lower calorie, convenience foods or fruits and vegetables when offered in direct competition to the usual high-calorie fast foods and snacks do not result in high purchase rates without subsidized changes in prices (Horgen & Brownell, 2002; Jeffery, French, Raether, & Baxter, 1994).

Individual approaches relying on self-regulation are complementary to public health approaches. One reason individual approaches are deemphasized is because the focus is weight loss requiring complex individual changes and an expensive set of interventions. Large-scale, individual weight-loss programs may be unrealistic. Large-scale individual programs can be feasible if they are inexpensive, focus on preventing weight gain, and use elements of self-help.

Preventing Weight Gain

Hill et al. (2003) and Jeffery and French (1999) point out that the annual mean weight gain across the population is small. Hill et al. (2003) estimated that among people 20–40 years old, the annual weight gain is 1.8–2.0 pounds/year. Data from the CARDIA study (Lewis et al., 2000), which investigated weight changes in African American and Caucasian males and females over 15 years, indicate that overall weight gain during young to middle adulthood averages ~1.5 pounds/year. The largest weight gain occurs in the 20s and then levels off. Weight gain is due to a small energy imbalance (energy gap) over many years. Hill et al. (2003) estimated mean energy accumulation accounting for both the metabolic costs of storing energy and considering their estimates for the 90th percentile for excess energy storage is only about 50 kcal/day (50 calories per day). Many people are consuming on average as little as 100 kcal more than expended each day to account for storage of 50 extra kcal per day needed to gain ~1.5 pounds/year (Hill et al., 2003). The energy imbalance appears small and correctable. We need conceptual and public policy shifts entailing less focus on weight loss and more focus on achieving the prevention of weight gain for people of normal weight (BMI 21–24) and harm reduction for people who are overweight (BMI 25–29).

If there is a balance between energy expenditure and energy consumption, weight remains the same. Balance is achieved through combinations of modest changes in consumption and physical activity. These figures provide a quantifiable public health goal that can be achieved, for example, by consistently walking one mile per day (~2000 pedometer steps, or walking 15–20 minutes all at one time or throughout the day), by eating slightly less at each meal, eating one less cookie per day, or consuming two fewer soft drink servings over a period of 3 days.

The recently launched America on the Move (www.americaonthemove. org), based on the data from Hill et al. (2003), encourages individuals and organizations to participate in this national program to affect energy balance. The main objectives are to increase pedometer step counts ~2000 or more steps per day and to decrease caloric intake by ~100 kcal per day. America on the Move is an open enrollment, public-health program and not a randomized controlled trial. Although it uses a Web-based format, it does not include the level of tailoring or personalization that are optimal for instructing and sustaining self-regulation strategies. Its preliminary data are, however, encouraging (Wyatt et al., 2004).

The prevention of weight gain with large groups of people has been tried in other formats. The best known of these programs is the randomized control study, Pound of Prevention (Jeffery & French, 1999). At the end of the 3-year Pound of Prevention trial, there were no differences between the intervention groups and the nontreated control group. All groups gained a small amount of weight. The Pound of Prevention trial tried to show the efficacy of a lower cost, lower dose (e.g., 2- to 4-page monthly newsletters), standard intervention. This approach has obvious appeal for reaching public health goals, but when objective outcome measures are used, few studies show its efficacy (Winett, 2004).

Jeffery and French (1999) made specific recommendations to improve weight gain prevention programs by: (a) increasing the frequency of contact; (b) making programs more tailored and interactive; (c) focusing more on physical activity and changes in eating patterns; (d) having provisions to respond to observed weight gain; and (e) maintaining motivation over the long term. In addition, studies have demonstrated the prevention of weight gain in smaller, targeted groups. These intervention used much higher doses (e.g., more and extended personal contact) than the Pound of Prevention trial (Hardeman, Griffin, Johnston, Kinmonth, & Wareham, 2000; Kuller, Simkin-Silverman, Wing, Meilahan, & Ives, 2001; Leermarkers, Jakicic, Viteri, & Wing, 1998; Polley, Wing, & Sims, 2002; Simkin-Silverman, Wing, Boraz, Meilahan, & Kuller, 1998; Simkin-Silverman et al., 2003). These studies and the conclusions reached by Jeffery and French (1999) show that the prevention of weight gain may be achievable in larger population segments. Our efforts are directed to cost-effectively reach large groups of people with interventions that have frequent contact, are tailored and interactive, respond quickly to weight gain, and remain engaging over long periods. The degree of contact, tailoring, and interactivity indicates a new generation of self-help interventions different from bibliotherapy and other traditional self-help modalities. The Internet appears to be an ideal medium to deliver these programs.

Internet Use

Access to the Internet is moving to universal coverage but there still is evidence of some continued digital divide (U.S. Department of Commerce [USDC], 2002). Groups prone to overweight or obesity (i.e., African Americans; Flegal et al., 2002) have somewhat lower rates of Internet use. One limitation of Internet-based interventions is that nonusers correspond closely to people at greater health risk.

Recent data based on 3553 telephone interviews indicate a dynamic picture. Internet users still tend to be younger, Caucasian, better educated, with higher incomes, and from suburban or urban areas (Lenhart, 2003). Internet users' levels and styles of Internet usage change frequently; some people use the Internet regularly on a daily or weekly basis, others use it more intermittently, and still others use it for a time and stop. Of those who do not currently use the Internet, younger African Americans and younger Hispanic Americans are more likely to intend to do so in the near future (Lenhart, 2003). There no longer is a gender gap for Internet access and use. Among users reporting annual incomes of more than $30,000, the proportion of Internet users who are Caucasian, African American, or Hispanic is similar to the general population. African Americans and people with disabilities still use the Internet at somewhat lower rates than other groups. The percentage of the population using the Internet has leveled off at about 60% because the number of new users is offset by the number of people discontinuing use (Lenhart, 2003).

The spread of Internet use parallels the spread of similar technological innovations. Internet use likely will increase as other communication modalities (i.e., cell phones and television) integrate Internet access. An Internet intervention is not a good match for engaging people with limited income and education as both access and literacy skills are likely to be barriers. These data do suggest that Internet use in lower middle income groups and minorities has increased in the last 2 years. The likelihood of attracting relatively diverse groups of people for an Internet-based intervention has improved (Lenhart, 2003).

Internet-based programs are not a panacea. It is one approach that can be used in conjunction with other public health and clinical efforts. Our collective experience shows that Internet-based programs work well with people who have incorporated Internet use into their daily lives (e.g., Tate et al., 2003a, 2003b). It is estimated that close to half of Internet users report seeking health information through the Internet (Baker, Wagner, Singer, & Bundorf, 2003). But, this is not the same as prolonged, programmatic use we envision for long-term weight gain prevention.

Long-Term Change

Programming for long-term maintenance is undergoing a marked shift. When programming is minimal at the end of treatment, eventually ceasing, relapse is predictable. Conversely, recent trials in physical activity show that when interventions continue, at least in some reasonable dose, then there are long-term health-behavior changes (Barlow, Kampert, Dunn, & Blair, 2001; Blair, Dunn, Marcus, Cooper, & Jaret, 2002; Dunn et al., 1999; Writing Group for the Activity Counseling Trial Research Group, 2001). Longer term, sustained interventions are more prominent in weight management with some evidence of efficacy at 18–24 months after post-test when interventions maintain contact, provide support, and emphasize such self-regulation strategies as enactive problem solving (Perri & Corsica, 2002).

These longer term interventions treat sedentary behavior and overconsumption of food as chronic problems needing continuous intervention, just as chronic diseases are treated (Glasgow et al., 1999). Such interventions need to be theoretically based, dynamic to deal with changing circumstances, and engaging enough to keep people focused on physical activity and nutrition for years.

Although the projects reported by Perri and Corsica (2002) show positive long-term results, they also highlight three important, continuing issues: (a) the difficulty of long-term program adherence, (b) the relatively high cost of providing longer term interventions, and (c) the need to articulate theoretically based strategies. Studies with long-term intervention indicate that specific self-regulatory strategies programmed in timely and appropriate ways and not simply didactically delivered content and contact are critical. With advanced technology and the Internet, the primary costs of continuing interventions are in the initial development. Advanced technology allows for fine-grained and, more importantly, ongoing, tailoring and strategy delivery. Mediated interventions, including print and Internet-based interventions, are more effective when there is sufficient tailoring to important variables theoretically tied to health-behavior changes (Kreuter, Stretcher, & Glassman, 1999; Marcus, Dubbert, et al., 2000; Marcus, Nigg, Riebe, & Forsyth, 2000; Marcus, Owen, Forsyth, Cavill, & Fridinger, 1998; Napolitano et al., 2003; Napolitano & Marcus, 2002).

Theoretical Base

Our theoretical base builds on recent work in behavioral maintenance and long-term change and social cognitive theory (SCT; Bandura, 1997, 2001; Marcus, Dubbert, et al., 2000; Marcus, Nigg, et al., 2000; Orleans, 2000; Rothamn, 2000; Rothman, Baldwin, & Hertel, 2004; Wing, 1999; 2000; Wing et al., 2000). Triadic SCT emphasizes the *dynamic interplay* of the self-system with behavioral competencies and the environment—key dimensions in long-term behavior change. In the face of predictable lapses and relapses, to recover and return to adherence people need a "resilient sense of self-efficacy" (Bandura, 1997). A resilient sense of self-efficacy is developed for a given set of health behaviors (e.g., being physically active and eating nutritiously) over time through a series of *mastery experiences*. Mastery experiences promote modification or differential use of self-regulation skills (i.e., planning, self-monitoring, problem solving, self-standards, goals, self-incentives), and some altered behavioral competencies. SCT indicates that process of behavior change and maintenance is enhanced through social support and cognizance of an individual's ecology. As described by Bandura (1997, 2001), the fourth generation of health behavior interventions attempts to embed a more dynamic approach to self-regulation (i.e., adaptive self-regulation skills) within a network of social influences germane to the individual's ecology to provide continued support (Winett, Anderson et al., 1999).

New behaviors need to be functionally valuable. Their value is enhanced if the initial expectations provided to people about outcomes are realistic (Rothman, 2000). Expectations about weight loss are usually unrealistic (Rothman, 2000). The idea of preventing weight gain is new and its value is likely to be unknown if not downplayed by diverse segments of people enamored with weight loss. There is little motivation to sustain change if outcome expectancies are neutral or negative (Williams, Anderson, & Winett, 2005). Rothman (2000) postulated that satisfaction with the experience of behavior change, a more global measure of outcome expectancies, is predictive of maintenance (Jeffrey et al., 2004; Rothman et al., 2004). Beginning with realistic expectations should increase satisfaction and facilitate long-term maintenance. The very dynamic, transactional nature of SCT has not always been appreciated (Bandura, 2001) and dynamic and long-term interventions that properly represent SCT theory have rarely been implemented.

The natural, extended, and dynamic course of health behavior change involves a series of episodes of adherence, lapses, relapses, and recovery as the individual faces new behavioral challenges and contexts (Rothman et al., 2004). Interventions need to plan for these predictable episodes and be long enough to provide individuals with the self-regulatory tools and supports to effectively problem solve and deal with minor and major set-backs through a series of personalized and tailored mastery experiences (Bandura, 1997; Kazdin, 2001).

Personal reidentification has value. Through reidentification, people see themselves as "regularly active people who pay attention to nutrition" and not people who are sedentary or "now and then" physically active, and eat whatever is available (Billings, 2000). Such "transformations" are part of self-systems and self-standards (Bandura, 2001).

Rothman et al. (2004) have postulated that interventions need to focus on different processes and SCT constructs throughout a long period of change. For example, to initially motivate behavior change, outcome expectancies appear critical. Without positive expectations or the avoidance of negative expectations, there is little reason to initiate change. Once the process of behavior change begins, self-efficacy and self-regulation processes need to be the focus of interventions. To maintain behaviors, self-regulation and active problem-solving for periods of decreased motivation and lapses are essential. This is because a person at this point should have little doubt that they can do the requisite behaviors but may see less reason to continue. One key difficulty is that very positive outcome expectancies that initially moti-vated behavior change may not match the experiences of actually doing the behaviors, leading to dissatisfaction and discontinuation of the behaviors. As stressed before, interventions need to be dynamic and long enough to address different SCT constructs and processes.

SCT represents a theoretical base for developing advanced technology Internet interventions, capitalizing on the cost efficiencies and reach of the Internet. But what evidence is there that computer-based and Internet delivered interventions can result in meaningful health behavior changes and what is their potential for long-term change? How have people used these interventions? How effective are these interventions when used alone in a solitary self-help format? As exemplars of feasibility and efficacy as well as reflecting on self-help issues, we briefly describe our recent work in nutrition, physical activity, and weight loss computer-based and Internet interventions and the SCT underpinnings of this work.

Studies

Computer-Based Nutrition and Exercise Interventions

The Virginia Tech group at the Center for Research in Health Behavior developed and field-tested a computer-based multimedia intervention: The *Nutrition For A Lifetime System* (*NLS*). Housed in a kiosk in supermarkets, the *NLS* helps shoppers alter their family food purchases to meet nutrition guidelines. The *NLS* uses pictures, graphics, narration, and interactions, and principally SCT-based planning, goal-setting, and feedback and oper-ates through a touch-screen monitor. Ten main programs (a new program is available each week) and a set of individualized maintenance programs are available for an additional 4 weeks.

The *NLS* focuses on small, cumulative, targeted changes within a food group to meet nutritional guidelines. A series of randomized control field studies with *NLS* demonstrated that *NLS* users decreased fat and increased fiber, fruits, and vegetables in their supermarket food purchases (Anderson et al., 1997; Anderson, Winett, Wojcik, Winett, & Bowden, 2001; Winett et al., 1997, 1991) and maintained some of these changes after contact with the program ended as assessed by participants' food shopping receipts (Rankin et al., 1998). Program acceptability and nutrition effects held across study participants from a range of SES groups (Anderson, Winett et al., 1997, 2001).

CRHB developed and tested measures of specific SCT variables operat-ing in the *NLS* (Anderson, Winett et al., 2001). In a unique empirical test of the theoretical model, Anderson, Winett et al. (2001) demonstrated that the *NLS* was effective in changing user's nutrition-related self-efficacy and outcome expectations that resulted in dietary changes.

NLS can be considered a self-help intervention in that once enlisted into the project, people followed their own schedule of access and use and there were no other program components. *NLS* was effective with its users with one major caveat. It is not clear what percentage of supermarket shoppers would regularly use *NLS*. Thus, the efficacy of *NLS* has been established but not its effectiveness.

Work with the *NLS* expanded through a project with rural high school students (Russ et al., 1998; Winett, Roodman, et al., 1999). In *Eat4Life*, we first modified the *NLS* template through formative work resulting in an Internet-based series of modules for 9th and 10th-grade girls and later expanded to include boys. These modules focus on modifying targeted nutrition practices and physical activity and exercise within and outside school. The modules provide each student with individualized content, planning mechanisms, and immediate feedback on progress in reaching a series of weekly and overall program goals (Winett, Roodman, et al., 1999). *Eat4Life* uses ethnically diverse on-screen models of both genders to relay information and provide feedback. Formative work tailored the *NLS* target food alternatives and strategies, identified acceptable alternatives to teens' fast-food fare, developed acceptable physical activities that provided health benefits, and found an appealing presentation format.

Eat4Life showed efficacy in helping girls reach nutritional goals com-pared to girls only involved in the standard health curriculum (Russ et al., 1998). A subsequent study with four cohorts of 9th and 10th-grade girls

($n = 250$) demonstrated that their weekly use (20 minutes) of the modules led to changes in target foods, reduction in calories and fat from fast food, and increases in frequency of activity and exercise compared to girls taking the regular health curriculum (Winett, Roodman, et al., 1999).

Eat4Life worked with captive groups of students who had to use the programs at designated times and places of access. In addition, there was classroom supervision and some reinforcement of program content in the classroom. Thus, *Eat4Life* can not be considered a stand-alone self-help intervention.

We also have conducted a series of studies on mediated approaches to exercise promotion using brief telephone or Internet-based contact and goal-setting and feedback primarily to promote walking (Lombard, Lombard, & Winett, 1995; Rovniak et al., 2005; Tate, 1997; Tate & Winett, 1996; Whiteley & Winett, 2002). Most participants in these projects were sedentary women and men. These programs involved assessment, feedback on specific assessment indices, goal selection, logs for recording walking (with some verification of walking), brief weekly contact by phone or by e-mail focusing on feedback on goal attainment, and selection of the next week's goal. Weekly, very brief phone contact was more effective in promoting walking than the same but less frequent contact (once every 2 or 3 weeks; Lombard et al., 1995). Tate (1997) modified this protocol and delivered the intervention via e-mail and examined the efficacy of providing tailored computer-automated feedback to promote the adoption of exercise. The tailored feedback was effective in increasing the number of days and minutes of exercise each week compared to standard messages.

Subsequent work refined the approach by providing a progressive paced walking program with more tailored instruction and feedback through an on-line "personal coach" (similar to the e-mail counselors used by Rovniak, 2003, and Tate et al., 2001, 2003a, 2003b; see below) and comparing the tailored SCT approach to an online didactic intervention. Results (Whiteley & Winett, 2002) indicated high adherence to the programs and increases in aerobic capacity of 10–15% as assessed with a standard one-mile walk test and estimated VO_{2max} (maximum oxygen consumption; Kline et al., 1987). Time, distance reported walking, and increases in fitness in this study are similar to outcomes of projects using extensive face-to-face contact (see King et al., 1992).

Of particular note is the recent study by Rovniak et al. (2005). She contrasted two paced walking interventions delivered by e-mail. One was a standard SCT intervention with feedback and goal-setting and limited, more standard use of personal coaching by e-mail. The other enhanced SCT intervention featured more tailored feedback and goal setting and electronically delivered personal coaching. She found that while the standard SCT group decreased their one-mile walk test time by 35 seconds, the enhanced SCT group reduced time by 86 seconds.

These mediated interventions combine aspects of self-help interventions (e.g., using program information to develop a personal plan, program access at any time or place) with more traditional therapeutic interventions (e.g., advice and corrective feedback from the coach or counselor). In practice, these interventions more closely describe a new generation of self-help approaches.

We are completing a project assessing the short and longer term (one year after pretest) efficacy of the Internet-based *Guide to Health* (*GTH*) program delivered within churches. *GTH* focuses on nutrition targets similar to *NLS* and has emphasis on soft drinks, sweets, portion sizes, fast food, and the importance of energy balance to weight management. Content for each individual is tailored based on initial assessments, personal goals for the overall program, and progress in the program. In addition, *GTH* expands on previous self-regulation components through planning templates for physical activity and fast-food consumption.

The *GTH* physical activity component revolves around a step count program using a pedometer provided to every participant. After a baseline period where mean steps per day are calculated, *GTH* users are provided with weekly goals that allow individual users to increase their baseline step counts by 3000 steps per day for 5 days per week in increments of 500 steps per week. The 3000 steps per day equates to about 1.5 miles or 30 minutes of walking or related physical activity meeting the Surgeon General's guidelines. *GTH* has other unique components including a physical activity planner to assist in increasing step counts and a fast-food meal planner for planning lower calorie and lower fat meals in a wide range of fast-food restaurants. *GTH* includes eight content or program modules and four maintenance modules. Maintenance modules primarily involve continued reporting with feedback on meeting nutrition and physical activity goals. Participants using the *GTH* have access to a new module on a weekly basis.

The *GTH* randomized trial involves 14 Baptist and United Methodist churches (Wojcik et al., 2003). Participants from five churches in the *GTH*-only condition accessed the 12-module, tailored, interactive *GTH* from home, work, or church. Participants in five churches received the *GTH* plus additional coordinated church-based supports (*GTH*-plus), while participants from four churches served as the wait-list control. Trained assessors, blind to condition, measured participants' height, weight, and waist and hip girths. At post-test (7–9 months after baseline) the resulting sample (*N* = 834) was 65% female; 19.3% African American; mean age = 52.2 years; mean BMI = 29.0. At post-test, participants in the control condition gained weight (N = 259; m = 1.34 lbs, sd= 7.73), whereas participants in the *GTH* treatment conditions lost weight (*GTH* only: N = 271, m = −.29 lbs, sd = 7.39; *GTH* plus: N = 303, m = −.88 lbs, sd = 7.34). The difference in weight gain observed between the control group and the two treatment groups was significant ($F_{(2,830)}$ = 6.50, p < .05; *GTH* only vs. control; p < .05; *GTH* plus vs. control p < .01; effect size = .29). Weight gain for the control condition closely followed secular trends reported by Lewis et al. (2000).

The supports used in the *GTH*-plus treatment follow Bandura's (2001) notion of tapping into social networks. Planned prompts (in church newsletters, as part of sermons) and feedback, goal-setting, and accountability are more salient within the social context. Internet interventions can be delivered in organizations that provide support and ongoing contact. This may be an ideal way to deliver self-help interventions. Individuals can work alone on their health behavior change program yet receive additional help and support from their organization. We also are planning to expand the role of an on-screen (virtual) counselor or coach revolving around self-regulatory strategies. We further discuss the use of virtual counselors and coaches later.

We conducted focus groups with *GTH* participants. As predicted by Reeves and Nass (1996), participants said the narrator's report on the audio track of their individual feedback and the narrator's perceived tone and use of words were very powerful. Participants said the very positive or less than positive feedback (we did not use negative feedback) had emotional meaning and motivated them. Building on these findings and those from Internet-based weight-loss programs (below), future programs will feature a virtual mastery counselor who has on-screen and audio presence and guides program users through tailored content and mastery experiences.

Internet Weight-Loss Programs

Randomized control trials have been conducted at Brown School of Medicine assessing the efficacy of delivering weight-loss programs via the Internet (Tate et al., 2001, 2003a, 2003b). Tate et al. (2001) hypothesized that using the Internet to deliver an SCT-based, structured behavioral weight-loss program would produce better weight loss than providing access to readily available educational, self-help weight-loss Web sites. The behavioral Internet program produced better weight loss (~9 pounds) than the education-only Web sites (~3.5 pounds) at 6 months. The study design did not allow the determination of the significance of the live counselor contact via e-mail in relation to the overall program. Such information is critical for the public health application of the Internet to the treatment of obesity since the counselor was expensive. A second, longer term study (Tate et al., 2003a) compared the efficacy of an SCT-based, Internet weight-loss program alone or with the addition of e-mail counseling from a human therapist over one year. This study confirmed that Internet approaches are viable for long periods and counselor feedback increases program efficacy. At one year, the Internet plus email counselor program group lost more weight (~9.5 pounds) than the basic Internet program group (~4.4 pounds). Although Internet programs with counseling from a human therapist makes treatment more effective, it is expensive.

The next step is developing an on-line weight-loss program with virtual counseling rather than a human therapist (Tate et al., 2003b). The initial study testing the feasibility and efficacy of the (virtual) computer-assisted, e-counseling approach found the computer-assisted program produced weight loss equivalent to the (real) counselor-assisted program at 3 months and both were better than the control. By 6 months, the real counselor-assisted program produced better weight losses than the virtual counselor group. Programming needs to make the virtual counselor as dynamic and interesting as the real counselor over extended time.

The series of studies at Brown School of Medicine show that static programs that resemble more traditional self-help program only result in minimal weight loss. Therapeutic interactions with a real or automated counselor increases efficacy.

The studies on using the Internet as a vehicle for weight-loss programs together with the computer and Internet-based studies on nutrition and physical activity do show that theoretically driven Internet programs are a means for helping many people prevent weight gain. We envision very long-term programs where there is a tailored and seamless approach to both maintaining weight and dealing in a very proactive way with smaller weight gains. The *GTH* study shows that the prevention of weight gain can be marketed within an overall nutrition, physical activity, and health program and not as weight management or even weight gain prevention. At the heart of such effective programs are key SCT based procedures that we call, following Bandura (1997), the Guided-Mastery Process.

Guided Mastery Process

The interventions revolve around the virtual mastery counselor and a specific set of SCT-based processes that we call the Guided-Mastery Process. A mastery counselor is a competent and successful model providing guidance in goal-setting, planning, and self-monitoring at each phase of behavior change (initiating behavior change, establishing new behaviors in one's repertoire, and behavioral maintenance) and serves as an exemplar of those behaviors (Bandura, 1997; Winett, 1986). The mastery counselor addresses the self-doubt and setbacks inherent in behavior change.

Indeed, a model's overall competence appears to be far more influential than other model characteristics (i.e., age, gender, and ethnic background). "Model competence is an especially influential factor when observers have a lot to learn and models have much they can teach them by instructive demonstration of skills and strategies" (Bandura, 1997, p. 101). The mastery counselor recounts his own past difficulties and shows how resilient self-efficacy, persistence, and specific strategies helped overcome these difficulties. The mastery counselor also models problem-solving skills (e.g., delineating alternatives and reaching decisions) and self-regulatory skills (e.g., planning, problem-solving, self-monitoring, and goal-setting)—skills particularly effective in behavior change (Bandura, 1997).

The guided-mastery process is woven throughout the content modules in our interventions via the mastery counselor and represents a theory-based approach to providing the tailoring, interactions, and frequent contact that is important for successful prevention of weight-gain efforts (Jeffery & French, 1999). This 10-step guide-mastery process was developed during 20 years of health promotion research focusing on the use of guided-mastery in many settings in a wide range of media (e.g., Anderson et al., 1997, 1993; E. Anderson et al., 2001; Fox, Nickols-Richardson, Winett, Herbert, & Wojcik, 2003; Lombard et al., 1995; Rovniak et al., 2005; Tate et al., 2001, 2003; Winett et al., 1997, 1993; Winett, Leckliter, Chinn, Stahl, & Love, 1985; Winett et al., 1991, 1992, 1999).

The steps are:

1. Evaluate outcome expectations for behavior change.
2. Gather information on progress toward goals in physical activity, fitness, and nutrition.
3. Evaluate progress toward goals (met or not met).
4. Provide feedback tailored as to the participant's preferred referent (self or others) and format (text, charts, or tables).
5. Model effective evaluation of current goals (realistic, too much challenge, not enough challenge).
6. Set new goals (keep, reduce, or increase current goals).
7. Model effective evaluation of a current plan (feasible, impractical).
8. Plan for achieving new goals (keep or modify current plan with prompts from guides) and enactment of other self-regulatory skills.
9. Obtain commitment to achieve a new goal.
10. Plan for evaluation of goal achievement.

These strategies follow directly from SCT and focus on increasing self-efficacy, positive and realistic outcome expectations, and use of self-regulatory strategies. A participant's continued use of the program allows the mastery counselor to anticipate a participant's problems and successes and highlight these areas with tailored guided-mastery content. As an ongoing and dynamic process, the steps allow for assessing changes across phases of change such as in outcome expectancies and satisfaction, or specific problems in self-regulation and providing new content and goals or skills to match such changes (Jeffrey et al., 2004; Rothman, 2000; Rothman et al., 2004).

Summary

The epidemic of overweight, obesity, and inactivity has been the impetus for a number of new initiatives such as Steps to a Healthier U.S. (USD-HHS, 2003) and the potentially large investment by the National Cancer Institute (USDHHS, 2004) and other National Institutes of Health divisions on the different dimensions of the energy balance. Transdisciplinary efforts also are likely to more precisely unravel the complexities of genetic and environmental factors, their interactions, and contributions to overweight and obesity (USDHHS, 2004). Most parsimoniously, the epidemic is explainable by a small, correctable energy imbalance between consumption and expenditure that is cumulative and results in added body weight and body fat year after year.

Interventions are needed to bridge the gap between intensive individual programs that are more appropriate for people at high risk (e.g., morbidly obese) and public health efforts. This prevention of weight gain requires sustained changes in food consumption and physical activity and interventions must be designed to reach diverse population segments. Theoretically based, tailored programs delivered via the Internet provide a way to engage people in ways that meet the guidelines of Jeffery and French (1999) for effective prevention of weight gain programs by: (a) increasing the frequency of contact; (b) making programs more tailored and interactive; (c) focusing more on physical activity and changes in eating patterns; (d) having provisions to respond to observed weight gain; and (e) maintaining motivation over the long term.

We note that the Internet-based programs that appear most efficacious are ones that closely follow a theory-driven therapeutic model. Similar to what has been found in applications for other areas such as psychological problems, health behavior changes seem best initiated and maintained by programs with tailored and interactive content, ongoing contact, guidance and support, and advice and corrective feedback from a real or virtual counselor (Tate & Zabinsky, 2004). There is little evidence that simply providing information on the Internet will lead to long-term health behavior changes. In many ways, effective self-help program delivered by the Internet resemble more effective programs delivered by providers (Tate & Zabinsky, 2004).

There are specific challenges for initiatives and interventions in the prevention of weight gain. Those interventions either embedded within sophisticated public health campaigns using social marketing strategies and paid advertisements (Randolph & Viswanath, 2004) or implemented and tested by groups and providers need to address these challenging efficacy, effectiveness, and dissemination questions:

- How can the prevention of weight gain be effectively marketed so that it is an appealing and valued, understandable, concrete, and achievable goal to different population segments?
- What are the specific theoretically based strategies that result in the prevention of weight gain for at least 3 years and how do the dynamics of program delivery, interactions, and dose conform to theory?
- For what population segments is prevention of weight gain more effective and are there optimal population segments and lifespan points for these interventions?
- What are appropriate levels of self-efficacy, outcome expectancies, and self-regulation skills for effectively using Internet health behavior change programs?
- How can the use of prevention of weight gain programs be more closely tied to every day practices such as the use of the Internet?
- How well do these programs work in this embedded mode with large groups of people?
- What are the personal qualities needed by virtual counselors to be most effective and what are the proper sequences of therapeutic strategies that need to be used?
- What supportive and guidance strategies can be used to help people stay engaged with their program for years given the chronic nature of weight gain and lack of physical activity?
- How can empirically validated programs be best popularized and widely disseminated?

Chapter Points

- Obesity is a major problem in the United States, with 40% of the population expected to be obese by 2008 with numerous associated health problems.
- A variety of environmental factors are associated with weight gain, requiring personal vigilance and conscious effort to mitigate these factors.
- Two approaches exist to address the obesity epidemic: high-dose, behavioral approaches that focus on dietary changes and physical

activity via lifestyle changes and public health approaches that emphasize environmental changes that encourage physical activity and the consumption of healthy foods.

- Large-scale, individually focused interventions are feasible if they focus on preventing weight gain and use elements of self-help.
- Weight gain is typically slow—1.5 lbs/year, and is produced by consuming small but excessive amounts of food consistently over time. Programs that target small increases in exercise and small decreases in food consumption will stabilize weight.
- Large-scale interventions to prevent weight gain use frequent contact, are tailored and interactive, respond quickly to weight gain, and remain engaging over the long term.
- Maintenance of lifestyle changes over the long term requires a resilient sense of self-efficacy produced by awareness of mastery experiences, maintained by social support and satisfaction with mastering weight control.
- Interventions should vary throughout the change process, with emphasis on outcome expectancies activating initial change, self efficacy and self-regulation predominating during the change process and active problem-solving used to deal with lapses.
- Effectiveness of these programs for producing healthy food consumption and increasing activity support the use of individualized goals, frequent tailored feedback, and support via telephone calls or e-mails.
- Internet-based weight-loss programs were more effective when regular feedback from a live counselor was provided compared to regular e-mail feedback or virtual counselor feedback.
- Individuals who serve as exemplars of how to lose weight (mastery counselors) had personal experience with the difficulties inherent in losing weight, and communicated both the types of difficulties encountered and ways of overcoming these difficulties.

References

Alexander, J. K. (2001). Obesity and coronary heart disease. *The American Journal of the Medical Sciences, 321*, 215–224.

Allison, D. B., Fontaine, K. R., Manson, J. E., Stevens J., & VanItallie, T. B. (1999). Annual deaths attributable to obesity in the United States. *The Journal of the American Medical Association, 282*, 1530–1538.

Allison, D. B., Zannolli, R., & Narayan, K. M. (1999). The direct health care costs of obesity in the United States. *American Journal of Public Health, 89*, 1194–1199.

American College of Sports Medicine. (2000). *ACSM's Guidelines for Exercise Testing and Prescription* (6th ed.). Baltimore: Williams & Wilkins. p. 323

Andersen, R. E., Wadden, T. A., Bartlett, S. J., Zemel, B., Verde, T. J., & Franckowiak, S. C. (1999). Effects of lifestyle activity vs. structured aerobic exercise in obese women: A randomized trial. *Journal of the American Medical Association, 281*, 335–340.

Anderson, E. S., Winett, R. A., Bickley, P. G., Walberg-Rankin, J., Moore, J. F., Leahy, M., et al. (1997). The effects of a multimedia system in supermarkets to alter shoppers' food purchases: Nutritional outcomes and caveats. *Journal of Health Psychology, 2*, 221–232.

Anderson, E. S., Winett, R.A., Moore, J. F., Taylor, C. D., Hook, R. J., Webster, D. A., et al. (1993). Efficacy of an HIV prevention video program for teens and parents. *Health Education Quarterly, 20*, 555–569.

Anderson, E. S., Winett, R. A., Wojcik, J. R., Winett, S. G., & Bowden, T. (2001). A computerized social cognitive intervention for nutrition behavior: direct and mediated effects on fat, fiber, fruits, vegetables, self-efficacy, and outcome expectancies among food shoppers. *Annals of Behavioral Medicine, 23*, 88–100.

Anderson, J. W., Konz, E. C., Frederich, R. C., & Wood, C. L. (2001). Long-term weight-loss maintenance: A meta-analysis of US studies. *The American Journal of Clinical Nutrition, 74*, 579–584.

Anderson, P., & Hughes, J. R. (2000). Policy interventions to reduce the harm from smoking. *Addiction, 95*(Suppl. 1), S9–S11.

Astrup, A. (2001). The role of dietary fat in the prevention and treatment of obesity. Efficacy and safety of low-fat diets. *International Journal of Obesity and Related Metabolic Disorders: Journal of the International Association for the Study of Obesity, 25*(Suppl. 1), S46–S50.

Baker, L., Wagner, T.H., Singer, S., & Bundorf, M.K. (2003) Use of the Internet and e-mail for health information: Results from a National survey. *Journal of the American Medical Association, 289*, 2400–2406.

Bandura, A. (1997). *Self-efficacy: The exercise of control*. New York: W.H. Freeman.

Bandura, A. (2001). Social cognitive theory; an agentic perspective. *Annual Review of Psychology, 52*, 1–25.

Barlow, C. E., Kampert, J. B., Dunn, A. L., & Blair, S. N. (2001). Project PRIME: Twenty-four month changes in physical activity [Abstract]. *Medicine and Science in Sports and Exercise, 33*, S100.

Bayer, R., Gostin, L. O., Javitt, G. H., & Brandt, A. (2002). Tobacco advertising in the United States: A proposal for a constitutionally acceptable form of legislation. *Journal of the American Medical Association, 287*, 2990–2995.

Bianchini, F., Kaaks, R., & Vainio, H. (2002). Overweight, obesity, and cancer risk. *The Lancet Oncology, 3*, 565–574.

Billings, J. H. (2000). Maintenance of behavior change in cardiorespiratory risk reduction: a clinical perspective from the Ornish program for reversing coronary heart disease. *Health Psychology, 19*, 70–75.

Blair, S. N., Dunn, A. L., Marcus, B. H., Cooper, K. H., & Jaret, P. (2002). *Active living*. Champaign, IL: Human Kinetics.

Block, G. (2004). Foods contributing to the energy intake in the U.S.: Data from NHANES III and NHANES 1999–2000. *Journal of Food Composition and Analysis, 17*, 439–447.

Booth, F. W., Chakravarthy, M. V., Gordon, S. E., & Spangenburg, E. E. (2002). Waging war on physical inactivity: using modern molecular ammunition against an ancient enemy. *Journal of Applied Physiology, 93*, 3–30.

Bouton, M. E. (2000). A learning theory perspective on lapse, relapse, and the maintenance of behavior change. *Health Psychology, 19*, 57–63.

Buchner, D., & Miles, R. (2002). Seeking a contemporary understanding of factors that influence physical activity. *American Journal of Preventive Medicine, 23*, 3–4.

Calle, E. E., Rodriguez, C., Walker-Thurmod, K., & Thun, M. J. (2003) Overweight, obesity, and mortality from cancer in a prospectively studies cohort of U.S. adults. *New England Journal of Medicine, 348*, 1625–1638.

Calle, E. E., Thun, M. J., Pertrelli, J. M., Rodriguez, C., & Heath, C. W., Jr. (1999). Body mass index and mortality in a prospective cohort of U.S. adults. *New England Journal of Medicine, 341*, 1097–1105.

Chakravarthy, M. V., & Booth, F. W. (2004). Eating, exercise, and 'thrifty" genotypes; connecting the dots toward an evolutionary understanding of modern chronic disease. *Journal of Applied Physiology, 96*, 3–10.

Diabetes Prevention Program Research Group. (2002). Reduction in the incidence of Type 2 diabetes with lifestyle intervention or metformin. *New England Journal of Medicine, 345*, 393–403.

Dunn, A. L., Marcus, B. H., Kampert, J. B., Garcia, M. E., Kohl, H. W., & Blair, S. N. (1999). Comparison of lifestyle and structured interventions to increase physical activity and cardiorespiratory fitness. *Journal of the American Medical Association, 281*, 327–334.

Erlichman, J., Kerbey, A. L., & James, W. P. (2002). Physical activity and its impact on health outcomes. Paper 2: Prevention of unhealthy weight gain and obesity by physical activity: An analysis of the evidence. *Obesity Reviews: An Official Journal of the International Association for the Study of Obesity, 3*, 273–287.

Evenson, K. R., Stevens, J., Cai, J., Thomas, R., & Thomas, O. (2003). The effect of cardiorespiratory fitness and obesity on cancer mortality in women and men. *Medicine and Science in Sports and Exercise, 35*, 270–277.

Fielding, J. E. (2001). *Increasing physical activity: A report on recommendations of the task force on community preventive services.* Atlanta: Centers for Disease Control and Prevention.

Flegal, K. M., Carroll, M. D., Ogden, C. L., & Johnson, C. L. (2002). Prevalence and trends in obesity among U. S. adults, 1999–2000. *Journal of the American Medical Association, 288*, 1723–1727.

Fogelholm, M., & Kukkonen-Harjula, K. (2000). Does physical activity prevent weight gain—A systematic review. *Obesity Reviews: An Official Journal of the International Association for the Study of Obesity, 1*, 95–111.

Fontaine, K. R., Redden, D. T., Wang, C., Westfall, A. O., & Allison, D. B. (2003). Years of life lost due to obesity. *Journal of the American Medical Association, 289*, 187–193.

Ford, E. S., Giles, W. H., & Dietz, W. H. (2002). Prevalence of the metabolic syndrome among U.S. adults: Findings from the Third National Health and Nutrition Survey. *Journal of the American Medical Association, 287*, 356–359.

Fox, L. D., Nichols-Richardson, S., Winett, R. A., Herbert, W. G. and Wojcik, J. R. (2003, March). A maintenance-oriented weight loss program. Paper presented at the Society for Behavioral Annual Meeting, Salt Lake City, UT.

French, S. A., Harnack, L., & Jeffery, R. W. (2000). Fast food restaurant use among women in the Pound of Prevention Study: Dietary, behavioral and demographic correlates. *International Journal of Obesity and Related Metabolic Disorders: Journal of the International Association for the Study of Obesity, 24*, 1353–1359.

French, S. A., Story, M., & Jeffery, R. W. (2001). Environmental influences on eating and physical activity. *Annual Review of Public Health, 22*, 309–335.

Friedenreich, C. (2001). Physical activity and cancer: lessons learned from nutritional epidemiology. *Cancer Epidemiology, Biomarkers and Prevention, 10*, 287–301.

Friedman, J. M. (2003). A war on obesity, not the obese. *Science, 299*, 856–858.

Glasgow, R. E., Wagner, E. H., Kaplan, R. M., Vinicor, F., Smith, L., & Norman, J. (1999). If diabetes is a public health problem why not treat it as one? A population-based approach to chronic disease. *Annals of Behavioral Medicine, 21*, 159–170.

Hardeman, W., Griffin, S., Johnston, M., Kinmonth, A. L., & Wareham, N. J. (2000). Interventions to prevent weight gain: A systematic review of psychological models and behaviour change methods. *International Journal of Obesity and Related Metabolic Disorders: Journal of the International Association for the Study of Obesity, 24*, 131–143.

Harris, M. I., Flegal, K. M., Cowie, C. C., Eberhardt, M. S., Goldstein, D. E., Little, R. R., et al. (1998). Prevalence of diabetes, impaired fasting glucose, and impaired glucose tolerance in U.S. adults. The Third National Health and Nutrition Examination Survey, 1988–1994. *Diabetes Care, 21*, 518–524.

Hedley, A. A., Ogden, C. L., Johnson, C. L., Carroll, M. D., Curtin, L. R., & Flegal, K. M. (2004). Prevalence of overweight and obesity among US children, adolescents, and adults, 1999–2002. *Journal of the American Medical Association, 291*, 2847–2850.

Hill, J. O., & Melanson, E. L. (1999). Overview of the determinants of overweight and obesity: Current evidence and research issues. *Medicine and Science in Sports and Exercise, 11*(Suppl.), S515–S521.

Hill, J. O., & Peters, J. C. (1998). Environmental contributions to the obesity epidemic. *Science, 280*, 1371–1374.

Hill, J. O., Wyatt, H. R., Reed, G. W., & Peters, J. C. (2003). Obesity and the environment: Where do we go from here? *Science, 299*, 853–855.

Horgen, K. B., & Brownell, K. D. (2002). Comparison of price change and health message interventions promoting healthy food choices. *Health Psychology: Official Journal of the Division of Health Psychology, American Psychological Association, 21*, 505–512.

Institute of Medicine. (2002). *Panel on dietary reference intakes for macronutrients*. Washington, DC: Academies of Sciences.

Jakicic, J. M. (2002). The role of physical activity in prevention and treatment of body weight gain in adults. *The Journal of Nutrition, 132*, 3826S–3829S.

Jakicic, J. M., Clark, K., Coleman, E., Donnelly, J. E., Foreyt, J., Melanson, E., et al. (2001). American College of Sports Medicine position stand. Appropriate intervention strategies for weight loss and prevention of weight regain for adults. *Medicine and Science in Sports and Exercise, 33*, 2145–2156.

Jakicic, J. M., Marcus, B. H., Gallagher, K. I., Napolitano, M., & Lang, W. (2003) Effect of exercise duration and intensity on weight loss in overweight, sedentary women: A randomized trial. *The Journal of the American Medical Association, 290*, 1323–1330.

Jakicic, J. M., Wing, R. R., & Winters-Hart, C. (2002). Relationship of physical activity to eating behaviors and weight loss in women. *Medicine and Science in Sports and Exercise, 34*, 1653–1659.

Jakicic, J. M., Winters, C., Lang, W., & Wing, R. R. (1999). Effects of intermittent exercise and use of home exercise equipment on adherence, weight loss, and fitness in overweight women: A randomized trial. *Journal of the American Medical Association, 282*, 1554–1560.

Jeffery, J. W. (2001). Public health strategies for obesity treatment and prevention. *American Journal of Health Behavior, 25*, 252–259.

Jeffery, R. W., Drewnowski, A., Epstein, L. H., Stunkard, A. J., Wilson, G. T., Wing, R. R., et al. (2000). Long-term maintenance of weight loss: Current status. *Health Psychology, 19*, 5–16.

Jeffery, R. W. & French, S. A. (1999). Preventing weight gain in adults: The Pound of Prevention study. *American Journal of Public Health, 89*, 747–751.

Jeffery, R. W., French, S. A., Raether, C., & Baxter, J. E. (1994). An environmental intervention to increase fruit and salad purchases in a cafeteria. *Preventive Medicine, 23*, 788–792.

Jeffery, R. W., Kelly, K. M., Rothman, A. J., Sherwood, N. E., & Boutelle, K. N. (2004). The weight loss experience: A descriptive analysis. *Annals of Behavioral Medicine, 27*, 100–106.

Kampert, J. B., Blair, S. N., Barlow, C. E., & Kohl, H. W. (1996). Physical activity, physical fitness, and all-cause and cancer mortality: A prospective study of men and women. *Annals of Epidemiology, 6*, 452–457.

Kazdin, A. E. (2001). *Behavior modification in applied settings*. Belmont, CA: Wadsworth.

King, A. C., Bauman, A., & Abrams, D. B. (2002). Forging trandisciplinary bridges to meet the physical inactivity challenge in the 21st century. *American Journal of Preventive Medicine, 23*, 104–106.

King, A. C., Blair, S. N., Bild, D. E., Dishman, R. K., Dubbert, P. M., Marcus, B. H., et al. (1992). Determinants of physical activity and interventions in adults. *Medicine and Science in Sports and Exercise, 24*(Suppl. 6), S221–S236.

King, A. C., Stokols, D., Talen, E., Brassington, G. S., & Killingsworth, R. (2002). Theoretical approaches to the promotion of physical activity: Forging a transdisciplinary paradigm. *American Journal of Preventive* Medicine, 23, 15–25.

Klem, M. L., Wing, R. R., Lang, W., McGuire, M. T., & Hill, J. O. (2000). Does weight loss maintenance become easier over time? *Obesity Research, 8*, 438–444.

Kline, G. M., Porcari, J. F., Hintermeister, R., Freedson, P. S., Ward, A., McCarron, R. F., et al. (1987). Estimation of VO_{2max} from a one-mile track walk, gender, age, and body weight. *Medicine and Science in Sports and Exercise, 19*, 253–259.

Koplan, J. P., & Dietz, W. H. (1999). Caloric imbalance and public health policy. *The Journal of the American Medical Association, 282*, 1579–1581.

Kreuter, M. W., Stretcher, V. J., & Glassman, B. (1999). One size does not fit all: The case for tailoring print materials. *Annals of Behavioral Medicine, 21*, 273–283.

Kuller, L. H., Simkin-Silverman, L. R., Wing, R. R., Meilahn, E. N., & Ives, D. G. (2001). Women's Healthy Lifestyle Project: A randomized clinical trail results at 54 months. *Circulation, 103,* 32–37.

Kurth, T., Gaziano, J. M., Berger, K., Kase, C. S., Rexrode, K. M., Cook, N. R., et al. (2002). Body mass index and the risk of stroke in men. *Archives of Internal Medicine, 162,* 2557–2562.

Lee, C. D., & Blair, S. N. (2002). Cardiorespiratory fitness and smoking-related total cancer mortality in men. *Medicine and Science in Sports and Exercise, 34,* 735–739.

Leermarkers, E. A., Jakicic, J. M., Viteri, J., & Wing, R. R. (1998). Clinic-based vs. home-based interventions for preventing weight gain in men. *Obesity Research, 6,* 346–352.

Lenhart, A. (2003). *The ever-shifting Internet population: A new look at Internet access and the digital divide. The Pew Institute and the American Life Project.* Washington, DC: The Pew Institute.

Lewis, C. E., Jacobs, D. R., Jr., McCreath, H., Kiefe, C. I., Schreiner, P. J., Smith, D. E., et al. (2000). Weight gain continues in the 90's: 10-Year trends in weight and overweight from the CARDIA Study. *American Journal of Epidemiology, 151,* 1172–1181.

Lombard, D. N., Lombard, T. N., & Winett, R. A. (1995). Walking to meet health guidelines: The effect of prompting frequency and prompt structure. *Health Psychology, 14,* 164–170.

Lowe, M. R., Miller-Kovach, K., & Phelan, S. (2001). Weight-loss maintenance in overweight individuals one to five years following successful completion of a commercial weight loss program. *International Journal of Obesity and Related Metabolic Disorders: Journal of the International Association for the Study of Obesity, 25,* 325–331.

Manson, J. E., & Bassuk, S. S. (2003). Obesity in the United States: A fresh look at its high toll. *Journal of the American Medical Association, 289,* 229–230.

Marcus, B. H., Dubbert, P. M., Forsyth, L. H., McKenzie, T. L., Stone, E. J., & Dunn, A. L. (2000). Physical activity behavior change: Issues in adoption and maintenance. *Health Psychology, 19,* 32–41.

Marcus, B. H., Nigg, C. R., Riebe, D., & Forsyth, L. H. (2000). Interactive communication strategies: Implications for population-based physical activity promotion. *American Journal of Preventive Medicine, 19,* 121–126.

Marcus, B. H., Owen, N., Forsyth, L. H., Cavill, N. A., & Fridinger, F. (1998). Physical activity interventions using mass media, print media, and information technology. *American Journal of Preventive Medicine, 15,* 362–378.

McGuire, M. T., Wing, R. R., & Hill, J. O. (1999). The prevalence of weight loss maintenance among American adults. *International Journal of Obesity and Related Metabolic Disorders: Journal of the International Association for the Study of Obesity, 23,* 1314–1319.

McGuire, M. T., Wing, R. R., Klem, M. L., & Hill, J. O. (1999). Behavioral strategies of individuals who have maintained long-term weight losses. *Obesity Research, 7,* 334–341.

Melanson, K. J., McInnis, K. J., Rippe, J. M., Blackburn, G., & Wilson, P. F. (2001). Obesity and cardiovascular disease risk: Research update. *Cardiology in Review, 9,* 202–207.

Mokdad, A. H., Bowman, B. A., Ford, E. S., Vinicor, F., Marks, J. S., & Koplan, J. P. (2001). The continuing epidemics of obesity and diabetes in the United States. *Journal of the American Medical Association, 286,* 1195–1200.

Mokdad, A. H., Marks, J. S., Stroup, D. F., & Gerberding, J. L. (2004). Actual causes of death in the United States, 2000. *Journal of the American Medical Association, 291,* 1238–1245.

Must, A., Spadano, J., Coakley, E. H., Field, A. E., Colditz, G., & Dietz, W. H. (1999). The disease burden associated with overweight and obesity. *Journal of the American Medical Society, 282,* 1523–1529.

Napolitano, M. A., Fotheringham, M., Tate, D., Sciamanna, C., Leslie, E., Ower, N., et al. (2003) Evaluation of an Internet-based physical activity intervention: A preliminary investigation. *Annals of Behavioral Medicine, 25,* 92–99.

Napolitano, M. A., & Marcus, B. H. (2002). Targeting and tailoring physical activity information using print and information technologies. *Exercise and Sports Sciences Reviews, 10,* 122–128.

Nestle, M. (2003). The ironic politics of obesity. *Science Magazine, 299,* 781.

Nestle, M., & Jacobson, M. F. (2000). Halting the obesity epidemic: A public health policy approach. *Public Health Reports, 115,* 12–24.

Nielsen, S. J., & Popkin, B. M. (2003). Patterns and trends in food portion sizes, 1977–1998. *Journal of the American Medical Society, 289,* 450–453.

Orleans, C. T. (2000). Promoting the maintenance of health behavior change: Recommendations for the next generation of research and practice. *Health Psychology, 19,* 76–83.

Perri, M. G., & Corisca, J. A. (2002). Improving the maintenance of weight lost in behavioral treatment of obesity. In T. A. Wadden & A. J. Stunkard (Eds.), *Handbook of obesity treatment* (pp. 357–375). New York: Guilford.

Peters, J. C., Wyatt, H. R., Donahoo, W. T., & Hill, J. O. (2002). From instinct to intellect: The challenge of maintaining healthy weight in the modern world. *Obesity Reviews: An Official Journal of the International Association for the Study of Obesity, 3,* 69–74.

Pi-Sunyer, F. X. (2002). The obesity epidemic: Pathophysiology and consequences of obesity. *Obesity Research, 10*(Suppl. 2), S97–S104.

Polley, B. A., Wing, R. R., & Sims, C. J. (2002). Randomized controlled trial to prevent excessive weight gain in pregnant women. *International Journal of Obesity and Related Metabolic Disorders: Journal of the International Association for the Study of Obesity, 26,* 1494–1502.

Powell, K. E., Bricker, S. K., & Blair, S. N. (2002). Treating inactivity. *American Journal of Preventive Medicine, 23,* 1–2.

Rafferty, A. P., Reeves, M. J., McGee, H. B., & Pivarnik, J. M. (2002). Physical activity patterns among walkers and compliance with public health recommendations. *Medicine and Science in Sports and Exercise, 34,* 1255–1261.

Randolph, W., & Viswanath, V. (2004). Lessons learned from public health mass media campaigns: Marketing health in a crowded media world. *Annual Review of Public Health, 25,* 419–438.

Rankin, J., Anderson, E. S., & Winett, R. A. (1998). Food purchase patterns at the grocery store and their relationship to family characteristics. *Journal of Nutrition Education, 30,* 81–88.

Reeves, B., & Nass, C. (1996). The media equation: How people treat computers, television, and new media like real people and places. Stanford, CA: CSLI Publications.

Reger, B., Cooper, L., Booth-Butterfield, S., Smith, H., Bauman, A., Wootan, M., et al. (2002). Wheeling walks: A community campaign using paid media to encourage walking among sedentary older adults. *Preventive Medicine, 35*, 285–292.

Reid, E., Schmid, T., Killingsworth, R., Zlot, A., & Raudenbush, S. (2003). Relationship between urban sprawl and physical activity, obesity, and morbidity. *American Journal of Health Promotion, 18*, 47–57.

Riebe, D., Greene, G. W., Ruggiero, L., Stillwell, K. M., Blissmer, B., Nigg, C. R., et al. (2003). Evaluation of a healthy-lifestyle approach to weight management. *Preventive Medicine, 36*, 45–54.

Rothman, A. J. (2000). Toward a theory-based perspective on lapse, relapse, and the maintenance of behavior change. *Health Psychology, 19*, 64–69.

Rothman, A. J., Baldwin, A. S., & Hertel, A. W. (2004). Self-regulation and behavior change: Disentangling behavioral initiation and behavioral maintenance. In K. Vohs & R. Baumeister (Eds.), *The handbook of self-regulation* (pp. 130–150). New York: Guilford.

Rovinak, L. S., Hovell, M. F., Wojcik, J. R., Winett, R. A., & Martinez-Donate, A. P. (2005). Enhancing theoretical fidelity: An e-mail based walking program demonstration. *American Journal of Health Promotion, 70*, 85–95.

Russ, C. R., Tate, D. F., Whiteley, J., Winett, R. A., Winett, S. G., & Pfglerer, J. (1998). *EAT4LIFE* program: A www-based health behavior intervention in a rural high school. *Journal of Gender, Culture, and Health, 2*, 232–239.

Sallis, J. F., & Owen, N. (1997). Ecological models. In K. Glanz, F. M. Lewis, & B. K. Rimer (Eds.), *Health behavior and health education: Theory, research, and practice*, (pp. 313–347). San Francisco: Jossey Bass.

Sallis, J. F., & Owen, N. (1999). *Physical activity and behavioral medicine.* Thousand Oaks, CA: Sage.

Sallis, J. F., Owen, N., & Fotheringham, M. J. (2000). Behavioral epidemiology: A systematic framework to classify phases of research on health promotion and disease prevention. *Annals of Behavioral Medicine, 22*, 294–298.

Saris, W. H., Blair, S. N., van Baak, M. A., Eaton, S. B., Davies, P. S., DiPletro, L., et al. (2003) How much physical activity is enough to prevent unhealthy weight gain? Outcome of the IASO 1st Stock Conference and consensus statement. *Obesity Review, 4*, 101–114.

Serdula, M. K., Mokdad, A. H., Williamson, D. F., Galuska, D. A., Mendlein, J. M., & Heath, G. W. (1999). Prevalence of attempting weight loss and strategies for controlling weight. *Journal of the American Medical Society, 282*, 1353–1358.

Simkin-Silverman, L. R., Wing, R. R., Boraz, M. A., & Kuller, L. H. (2003). Life cycle intervention to prevent weight gain during menopause: Results form a 5-year randomized clinical trial. *Annals of Behavioral Medicine, 26*, 212–220.

Simkin-Silverman, L. R., Wing, R. R., Boraz, M. A., Meilahn, E. N., & Kuller, L. H. (1998). Maintenance of cardiovascular risk factor changes among middle-aged women in a lifestyle intervention trial. *Women's Health, 4*, 255–271.

Slentz, C. A., Duccha, B. D., Johnson, J. L., Ketchum, K., Atken, L. B., Samsa, G. P., et al. (2004). Effects of the amount of exercise on body weight, body composition, and measures of central obesity: STRIDE—A randomized controlled trial. *Archives of Internal Medicine, 164*, 31–39.

Tate, D. F. (1997). *The effects of personalized goals and feedback in an email delivered walking intervention.* Unpublished master's thesis, Virginia Polytechnic Institute and State University. Blacksburg, VA.

Tate, D. F., Jackvony, E. H., & Wing, R. R. (2003a). Effects of Internet behavioral counseling on weight loss in adults at risk for Type 2 diabetes. *Journal of the American Medical Association, 289*, 1883–1836.

Tate, D. F., Jackvony, E. H., & Wing, R. R. (2003b). Internet counseling for weight loss: Computer vs. human counselors. *Obesity Research, 11*, S108.

Tate, D. F., Wing, R. R., & Winett, R. A. (2001). Using Internet technology to deliver a behavioral weight loss program. *Journal of the American Medical Association, 286*, 1172–1177.

Tate, D. F., & Zabinsky, M. F. (2004). Computer and Internet applications for psychological treatment: Update for clinicians. *JCLP/In Session, 60*, 209–220.

U.S. Department of Commerce. (2002). *A nation online: How Americans are expanding their use of the Internet.* Washington, DC: Economics and Statistics Administration, National Telecommunications and Information Administration.

U.S. Department of Health and Human Services. (2000). *Healthy People 2010: Understanding and improving health.* Washington, DC: U.S. Government Printing Office.

U.S. Department of Health and Human Services. (2002). *Physical activity is fundamental to disease prevention.* Retrieved June 2002, from http://aspe.hhs.gov/health/reports/physicalactivity/.

U.S. Department of Health and Human Services. (2003). *Steps to a healthier U.S.* Retrieved from http://www.healthierus.gov

U.S. Department of Health and Human Services. (2004). *The nation's investment in cancer research: A plan and budget proposal for 2005.* Washington, DC: The National Cancer Institutes.

Vainio, H., Kaaks, R., & Bianchini, F. (2002). Weight control and physical activity in cancer prevention: international evaluation of the evidence. *European Journal of Cancer Prevention: The Official Journal of the European Cancer Prevention Organisation (ECP), 11*(Suppl. 2), S94–S100.

Wadden, T. A., Brownell, K. D., & Foster, G. D. (2002). Obesity: Responding to the global epidemic. *Journal of Consulting and Clinical Psychology, 70*, 510–525.

Whiteley, J. A., & Winett, R. A. (2002, March). Internet-based program to promote fitness in women. Paper presented at the annual Society for Behavioral Medicine meeting, Washington, DC.

Williams, D. M., Anderson, E. S., & Winett, R. A. (2005). A review of outcome expectancy construct in physical activity research. *Annals of Behavioral Medicine, 29*, 70–79.

Winett, R. A. (1986). *Information and behavior: Systems of influence.* Hillsdale, NJ: Erlbaum.

Winett, R. A. (2004). Comments on challenges to improving the impact of worksite cancer prevention programs: Paradigm lost. *Annals of Behavioral Medicine, 25*, 287.

Winett, R. A., Anderson, E. S., Bickley, P. G., Walberg-Rankin, J., Moore, J. F., Leahy, M., et al. (1997). Nutrition for a lifetime system: A multimedia system for altering supermarket shoppers' purchases to meet nutritional guidelines. *Computers in Human Behavior, 13*, 371–382.

Winett, R. A., Anderson, E. S., Moore, J. F., Taylor, C. D., Hook, R. J., Webster, D. A., et al. (1992). Efficacy of an HIV prevention video program for teens and parents. *Health Education Quarterly, 20*, 555–569.

Winett, R. A., Anderson, E. S., Moore, J. F., Hook, R., Webster, D., Sikkema, K. S., Taylor, D., Dalton, J. F., Ollendick, T. H., Eisler, R. M. (1992). Family media approach to AIDS prevention, Results with a home-based parent-teen video program. *Health Psychology, 11*, 203–206.

Winett, R. A., Anderson, E. S., Whiteley, J. A., Wojcik, J. R., Winett, S. G., Rovniak, L., et al. (1999). Church-based health behavior programs: using social cognitive theory to formulate interventions for at-risk populations. *Applied and Preventive Psychology, 8*, 124–142.

Winett, R. A., Leckliter, I. N., Chinn, D. E., Stahl, B. N., & Love, S. Q. (1985). The effects of videotape modeling via cable television on residential energy conservation. *Journal of Applied Behavior Analysis, 18*, 33–44.

Winett, R. A., Moore, J. F., Wagner, J. A., Hite, L., Walker, W. B., Leahy, M., et al. (1991). Altering shoppers' supermarket purchases to meet nutrition guidelines: Interactive information systems. *Journal of Applied Behavior Analysis, 24*, 95–105.

Winett, R. A., Roodman, A., Winett, S. G., Bazjek, W., Rovniak, L., & Whiteley, J. A. (1999). Internet-based health behavior program: Effects of the Eat4Life program on high school girls' nutrition and exercise practices. *Journal of Gender, Culture, and Health, 4*, 239–254.

Wing, R. R. (1999). Physical activity in the treatment of the adulthood overweight and obesity: current evidence and research issues. *Medicine and Science in Sports and Exercise, 11*(Suppl.), S547–S552.

Wing, R. R. (2000). Cross-cutting themes in maintenance of behavior change. *Health Psychology, 19*, 84–88.

Wing, R. R., & Hill, J. O. (2001). Successful weight loss maintenance. *Annual Review of Nutrition, 21*, 323–341.

Wing, R. R., Voorhees, C. C., & Hill, D. R. (2000). Supplemental Issue: maintenance of behavior change in cardiorespiratory risk reduction. *Health Psychology, 19*, 1–90.

Wojcik, J. R., Anderson, E. S., Hohenshil, S. B., Winett, R. A., Winett, S. G., & Bowden, T. (2003, March). *Guide to health: An Internet-based intervention using step counts and pedometers to meet physical activity recommendations.* Paper presented at the Society for Behavioral Annual Meeting, Salt Lake City, UT.

Writing Group for the Activity Counseling Trial Research Group. (2001). Effects of physical activity counseling in primary care: The Activity Counseling Trial: Randomized controlled trial. *Journal of the American Medical Association, 286*, 677–687.

Wyatt, H. R., Peters, J. C., Reed, G. W., Grunwald, G. K., Barry, M., Thompson, H., et al. (2004) Using electronic step counters to increase lifestyle physical activity: Colorado on the move. *Physical Activity and Health, 1*, 181–190.

Young, L. R., & Nestle, M. (2002). The contribution of expanding portion sizes to the US obesity epidemic. *American Journal of Public Health, 92,* 246–249.

Author Note

Support for writing this chapter is from grant R01CA106250 from the NCI to Richard A. Winett at Virginia Tech and grants 1 RO1 DK 60058-01 from NIDDK and a Clinical Research Award ADA grant to Deborah F. Tate at the University of North Carolina School of Public Health.

CHAPTER 15

An Ecological Perspective on Self-Help
The Case of Diabetes

EDWIN B. FISHER, RUSSELL E. GLASGOW
AND JEANNE M. GABRIELE

Diabetes forces us to re-examine "self-help." The individual cannot do it alone. Diabetes requires medical treatment in order to avoid devastating complications like blindness and amputation and reduce risks of associated death through cardiovascular disease. Yet the individual's healthy eating, physical activity, weight management, and other behaviors are central to diabetes management. This chapter will review the established and potential benefits of self-help interventions as part of the range of resources and services individuals need in order to live life with diabetes. An ecological perspective that emphasizes the multiple levels of influence on behavior, from individual to organization, community and policy, provides the context within which self-help has an important role.

The first two sections of this chapter provide important frameworks with regard to the management of diabetes and the ecological perspective on self-management that frames self-help interventions. The chapter then reviews self-help interventions in diabetes and closely related areas such as weight loss. It concludes with discussion of the roles of self-help in diabetes management and their implications for our broader views about self-help and other approaches to behavior change.

Diabetes, Diabetes Management, and Diabetes Self-Management

With perhaps no disease is the individual's role so broad as in diabetes. Care of diabetes rests not only on healthy diet but also on sufficient physical activity; managing stress and negative mood; accommodating intercurrent illnesses; monitoring weight and blood sugar; medication management and adjustment in response to fluctuations in blood sugar; maintaining activities and interests of a healthy, satisfying life; and coordinating all of these through interacting with the health care system. All the while, the individual with diabetes must prepare for the vicissitudes of the disease, especially the fact that even with good metabolic control, complications can occur and, over time, become increasingly likely.

Diabetes is intrinsically progressive. Thus, added to the burdens of managing the disease itself are, often, the burdens of managing complications such as blindness, amputations, and sexual dysfunction as well as the other diseases to which diabetes often contributes such as kidney disease. Standing behind all of these, diabetes is a major risk factor for cardiovascular disease. Finally, there is no respite. Diabetes and most of its complications persist unto death—it is 24/7 for the rest of your life.

Managing the burdens and challenges of diabetes takes place in daily life, not in the clinic or operating room. Thus, the individual with diabetes has great responsibility to care for the disease, responsibility that professionals and others can lighten but not eliminate.

Diabetes management clearly requires health care and professional services. About 25% of adults with the disease go undiagnosed (Centers for Disease Control and Prevention, 2003). Early identification and treatment, with medication or with weight loss and physical activity can prevent or forestall the disease in those at risk (Diabetes Prevention Program Research Group, 2002). As the disease advances, medications to improve glucose metabolism or insulin become advantageous and, eventually, necessary to avoid the short-term impacts of high blood sugar and its long term impacts including cardiovascular disease, eye disease, and multiple other complications (The Diabetes Control and Complications Trial Research Group, 1995). The American Diabetes Association recommends that those with diabetes see their physicians at least three to four times each year to monitor their status, adjust medications and management plans, arrange for appropriate tests, and identify plans for other needed services or treatments. Thus, the individual cannot treat their own diabetes without help from physicians, other health professionals, and, as described below, responsive organizations and communities.

The Individual's Role

A variety of authors have articulated the role of the individual in diabetes management (Anderson & Funnell, 2000; Etzwiler, 1980, 1986; Hiss, 1986). The American Diabetes Association and the American Association of Diabetes Educators have used the term *self-management* for a number of years. For example, the American Diabetes Association criteria for registration of diabetes education programs refer to "Diabetes Self-Management Education" as "an integral component of diabetes care" (http://diabetes.org/uedocuments/ReviewCriteria_IndicatorListing_9-2003.pdf) and the American Association of Diabetes Educators describes itself as "dedicated to integrating successful self-management as a key outcome in the care of people with diabetes..." (http://www.aadenet.org/About Us/aboutus.shtml/). Some have advocated the term "co-management" to capture the collaborative relationship between the patient and provider in developing, implementing, and changing management plans Anderson & Funnell, 2000).

Most writers in the field agree on several key aspects of the patient's and professional's roles in diabetes management. First is the centrality of the patient's behavior. Second is the fact that the patient's behavior cannot be dictated or guaranteed by clinicians or by clinical interventions. In an important sense of the term, diabetes management is the responsibility of the patient once the clinical encounter or patient education has ended and the patient has returned to the daily world in which she lives. Third, and following from the first two, it is best that the responsibility of the patient be acknowledged throughout the interchanges of clinical care and patient education. This acknowledgement needs to confer to the patient substantial authority in decision-making and guiding disease management. Accordingly, the professional role becomes not that of a director but an expert consultant to the patient's disease management.

Self-Management Research in Diabetes

Two major, multisite clinical trials have stimulated substantial recognition of the importance of behavior and self-management in diabetes care and its prevention. The Diabetes Control and Complications Trial compared usual care to extensive patient education, follow-up, and support for intensive insulin management and related strategies involving diet and physical activity. Results of the intensive treatment demonstrated that controlling blood sugar reduces complications of diabetes (The Diabetes Control and Complications Trial Research Group, 1995). Teaching patients to implement intensive glucose management and follow up to maintain those management patterns over the several years of the program (The Diabetes

Control and Complications Trial Research Group, 1993) were effective in controlling blood sugar and reducing complications. In the Diabetes Prevention Program, behavioral interventions to achieve modest weight loss (7% of body weight) and modest exercise (150 minutes per week) among high-risk individuals reduced conversion to type 2 diabetes by 58% relative to controls (Diabetes Prevention Program Research Group, 2002). Similar findings were also achieved with lifestyle interventions in Japan (Pan et al., 1997) and Finland (Tuomilehto et al., 2001).

In addition to these major research programs, an emerging medley of smaller studies have included group and individual self-management interventions and have achieved improvements in self-efficacy, self-management behaviors, metabolic control, patient satisfaction, and quality of life (Anderson, Funnell, Barr, Dedrick, & Davis, 1991; Anderson et al., 1995; Aubert, Herman, Waters, Moore, Sutton, Peterson et al., 1998; Clement, 1995; Greenfield, Kaplan, Ware, Yano, & Frank, 1988; Muhlhauser & Berger, 1993; Pieber et al., 1995; Rubin, Peyrot, & Saudek, 1989, 1993), including among older type 2 patients and ethnic minorities (Anderson, Funnell, et al., 1991; Glasgow, Toobert, & Hampson, 1991; Glasgow et al., 1992). Summarizing these and other studies, two important meta-analyses showed that self-management interventions could be successful in promoting improved management patterns among adults with type 2 diabetes (Norris, Engelgau, & Narayan, 2001) and that they were associated with improved metabolic control (Norris, Lau, Smith, Schmid, & Engelgau, 2002).

Beyond the Self in Self-Management

Over 30 years ago, writing about self-control began advancing the idea that individuals could learn skills that enabled them to control their own behavior. For example, an influential book in the field published in 1974 was titled: *Self-Control: Power to the Person* (Mahoney & Thoresen, 1974). This view leads to the expectation that, once mastery of such skills is established, the individual becomes somewhat independent of the environment—"power to the person." But data do not support this view. In contrast, evaluations of self-management programs have frequently identified that benefits are short-lived, fading substantially by 6 months to one year after programs end. This is probably most pronounced in programs applying self-management to weight loss and smoking cessation. The most prevalent long-term result of these is relapse (Perri & Foreyt, 2004).

Although disappointing to the expectation that learning self-management skills can enable individuals to achieve and sustain goals like weight loss indefinitely, research does point the way toward improving long-term benefits. However, the path is not through stronger self-control or better self-management skills but through recognition of the critical role of the environment and the settings of individuals' lives in sustaining desired behavior patterns.

After controlling for the influence of a variety of program features, major meta-analyses of self-management programs in diabetes (Norris et al., 2001, 2002) found that the only program feature that was uniquely predictive of success was duration of contact. "Interventions with regular reinforcement are more effective than one-time or short-term education" (Norris et al., 2001, p. 583). This mirrors meta-analyses in smoking cessation. As Kottke and his colleagues noted in a major 1988 review of smoking cessation interventions (Kottke, Battista, & DeFriese), "Success was not associated with novel or unusual interventions. It was the product of personalized smoking cessation advice and assistance, repeated in different forms by several sources over the longest feasible period" (p. 2888).

More recently, AHRQ reviews of interventions for smoking cessation have identified variety and duration of treatment as predictors of success (Fiore et al., 2000). Similarly, a meta-analysis of 74 programs aimed at any one of a variety of health risks or health promoting behaviors (e.g., breast self-examination) found that number of different communication channels, as well as patient education and behavioral self-monitoring, were predictive of success (Mullen, Green, & Persinger, 1985).

The importance of varied and sustained interventions was also apparent in the Diabetes Control and Complications Trial, described above. The success of this program in showing that metabolic control matters rested on the adherence levels it achieved. In turn, these relied on effective patient education and sustained support for intensive management. Participants received: (a) extensive training in the skills they needed to implement the intensive treatment, (b) individualized plans for maximizing glucose control (e.g., providing choices between use of insulin infusion pumps versus multiple injections according to patient preference and need), and (c) ongoing support for maintaining their intensive management plan from a prestigious and dedicated team of professionals (Santiago, 1993; The Diabetes Control and Complications Trial Research Group, 1995). At the close of the Diabetes Control and Complications Trial (DCCT), the critical role of this staff support was summarized by one participant quoted in the *New York Times*: "The team was the strongest part of the program. They are really there to help us through the tough times".

Ecological Perspectives

Ecological perspectives in public health and health promotion offer an approach to understanding the factors surrounding the individual that can enhance—or impede—self-management. Ecological models articulate ways in which the individual and individual-level influences on behavior are embedded within several levels of social, organizational, and economic influences such as in Figure 15.1 (Stokols, 1996).

Ecological perspectives and the importance of sustaining diabetes management within the settings of individuals' daily lives lead to a view of self-management as entailing not only skills and choices of the individual but the services they receive, the support of their family, friends, work sites, organizations, and cultures, and the physical and policy environments of their communities and governments. From the perspective of the individual within the layers of ecological influences, self-management requires access to a variety of resources, including services provided by professionals, and supports for initiation and maintenance of healthy behavior.

The Diabetes Initiative of The Robert Wood Johnson Foundation has identified six resources and supports for self-management (RSSM): individualized assessment, collaborative goal setting, building skills, ongoing support for engagement in self-management, community resources, and continuity of quality clinical care (Fisher et al., 2005). RSSM have been developed through the 14 projects of the Initiative that demonstrate and evaluate promotion of diabetes self-management in both primary care and community settings (http://www.diabetesinitiative.org. The first author is the director of the national program office for this initiative and the second author is an active member of its national advisory committee.)

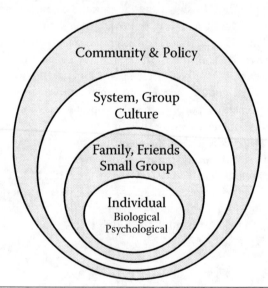

Figure 15.1 Multiple Layers of Influence on Behavior Illustrating an Ecological Perspective

Ecological perspectives and RSSM pose useful frameworks for thinking about self-help. Rosen and colleagues have described a continuum of therapist contact in treatment ranging from no contact to interventions that are totally therapist administered (Rosen, Glasgow, & Moore, 2003). The focus of this volume on self-help is on the "no contact" end of this continuum. Consideration of this and RSSM suggests that the level of direct therapist contact can vary for each of the categories of RSSM. For example, individualized assessment and collaborative goal-setting can be carried out in individual counseling with a live provider or through self-help manuals or Web-based formats. Assistance in identifying community resources can be delivered through counseling or through a local magazine or newspaper or TV station. Although provider contact will probably always be a central component of continuity of quality clinical care, many innovations in this area include self-help procedures including self-monitoring and reporting of results often through electronic linkages. For the purposes of this volume's focus on self-help, the following review focuses on interventions in each of the categories of RSSM that include minimal therapist contact. This literature is summarized in Table 15.1.

Individualized Assessment

This encompasses a variety of ways in which self-management may be tailored to the perspectives of the individual, including individuals' cultural perspectives. Although not the subject of appreciable controlled research, it is widely appreciated that before developing a disease management plan with an individual, discussion needs to explore the individual's perspectives regarding disease, the nature of disease, the role of the individual behavior in managing disease, or the individual's "personal models of illness" (Hampson, Glasgow, & Strycker, 2000, p. 30). Whatever disease management plan may emerge, it must make sense to the individual from these cultural and personal perspectives.

As can be seen in Table 15.1, computer-based individualized assessment has been implemented in primary care settings (Glasgow et al., 1997; Glasgow, Toobert, & Hampson, 1996). On the Web, a questionnaire on risk factors for diabetes led to a finding that 43.6% of users had elevated risk for diabetes (Baehring, Schulze, Bornstein, & Scherbaum, 1997). In a review of interactive behavior change technology (Glasgow, Bull, Piette, & Steiner, 2004), Glasgow and his colleagues identified a number of advantages of Web, e-mail and similar technologies in assessment of individuals such as their utility in gathering individual information much more efficiently than face-to-face contact, and, thereby, enabling the medical visit or other counseling opportunities to focus more on developing management plans.

Table 15.1 Recent Research on Minimal Contact Interventions Providing Resources & Supports for Self-Management of Diabetes

Individualized assessment	Computer-based individual dietary assessment and intervention within primary care included goal-setting, 15- to 20-minute problem-solving intervention, and two follow-up calls. These resulted in improved dietary behavior and cholesterol levels relative to controls (Glasgow et al., 1997, 1996).
	Questionnaire on diabetes risk factors turned into an interactive World Wide Web document. Feedback provided to Web site user; 43.6% of users found to have elevated risk for diabetes (Baehring, Schulze, Bornstein, & Scherbaum, 1997).
Collaborative goal-setting	In meta-analysis of self-management programs for chronic disease, inclusion of face-to-face contact was only predictor of outcomes (Warsi et al., 2004).
	Computer-based individual dietary assessment and intervention described above included review of patient-chosen goals with PCP (Glasgow et al., 1997, 1996).
	Touch-screen intervention in primary care facilitated setting priorities for care and goals for diet, physical activity, or smoking. Printouts for patients and providers. Well accepted by providers and by patients, including Latinos, older adults, and those with little formal education. Increased behavioral counseling received by patients. Other outcomes forthcoming (Glasgow et al., 2004).
	Touch-screen intervention prior to primary care visit that assessed diet and physical activity and provided feedback to patients. Patients then chose a goal related to physical activity, fat intake, or fruit and vegetable consumption and received mail and telephone support to reach goal. Patients goals in areas in which they needed improvement and showed behavioral changes related to their goals (Estabrooks et al., 2005).
	Computer-generated goal-setting intervention that provided an 11″ × 17″ color poster showing HbA1c status, goals along with personalized steps to aid in goal achievement, and discussion points for physicians; a personalized wallet card with baseline data and room to document subsequent values; and monthly postcards. Participants who received this intervention had greater reductions in HbA1c than participants who received standard care (Levetan, Dawn, Robbins, & Ratner, 2002).
Building skills	Face-to-face delivery of intervention, cognitive reframing, and including emphasis on exercise predict beneficial effects on metabolic control (HbA1) in meta-analysis (Ellis et al., 2004).
	Diabetes passport alone, without goal-setting, individualized assessment, or opportunities for building skills has minimal benefits in randomized trial (Simmonset al., 2004).
	Telephone counseling 2 times per week for first month, then weekly for months 2 and 3 (total = 16 calls, average call length = 25 min) led to 1.2 point reduction in GHb relative to 0.6 point increase in usual care (Oh et al., 2003).

Computer-based individual dietary assessment and intervention described above included 15- to 20-minute problem-solving session (Glasgow et al., 1997, 1996).

Touch-screen intervention in primary care discussed above (Glasgow et al., 2004) that facilitated setting priorities for care and goals for diet, physical activity, or smoking increased behavioral counseling received by patients.

Web-based computer-tailored nutrition intervention compared to generic nutrition information and no information control. Tailored intervention provided feedback about personal intake levels of fat, fruit, and vegetables and how these intake levels compared with recommendations and the average intake levels of peers. It also provided information about what changes to make and on how to make these changes. Computer-tailored intervention increased fruit and decreased fat intake (Oenema et al., 2005).

Adolescents who received Packy & Marlon, an interactive diabetes video game in which players play the role of animated characters who manage their diabetes by monitoring blood glucose, taking insulin injections, and choosing foods, had a decrease in urgent doctor visits and showed improvement in self-efficacy, communication with parents about diabetes, and self-care (Brown et al., 1997).

Take Charge of Diabetes, a multimedia CD-ROM program consisting of five modules (What is diabetes? How do you manage diabetes? What is blood sugar testing? Guidelines for nutrition and diabetes; and Making healthy choices and meal planning) associated with an increase in perceived diabetes knowledge in a pilot study of 7 patients with type 2 diabetes and three health professionals. Users had the option of listening to audio of information on screen and all participants reported using audio. Program found to be accurate, easy to use, and enjoyable (Castaldini, Saltmarch, Luck, & Sucher, 1998).

Building skills
(continued)

Intervention group that used computer kiosks in waiting rooms with audio-video sequences to communicate information, provide psychological support, and promote diabetes self-management skills had greater perceived susceptibility to diabetes complications than standard care group. Targeted individuals with low literacy rates. No between group differences on blood pressure, diabetes knowledge, weight, and HbA1c (Gerber et al., 2005).

Biweekly automated telephone disease management calls sent to 226 English-speaking and 30 Spanish-speaking patients in outpatient clinics for one year. Spanish-speaking selected self-care tips and dietary education modules more often than English-speaking patients. At 12 months, most Spanish-speaking and 25% of English-speaking patients continued to select each message type (Piette, 1999; Piette et al., 1999).

(continued)

Table 15.1 (continued)

Internet education Web site, consisting of basic weight-loss information and directory of selected Internet resources on diet, physical activity, self-monitoring, and other behavioral resources such as stress management, was associated with weight loss, reduction in waist circumference and caloric intake, and increase in exercise energy expenditure (Tate et al., 2001). Follow-up study (Tate et al., 2003, 2001) achieved weight loss through similar Internet education intervention plus a message board and weekly e-mail reminders to submit weight loss information.

A 6-month intervention using a computer-assisted diet education system (Diabeto) with personalized coaching to help diabetics self-monitor diets and balance meals increased diet knowledge and dietary habits and decreased caloric intake and HbA1c (Turnin, Beddok, Clottes, et al., 1992).

Eight-Week intervention in which adults with diabetes were assigned to either (a) an informational Web site with diabetes-specific articles and glucose tracking or (b) an interactive Web-based intervention that included informational Web site plus personalized physical activity plan, support from personal coach, tailored e-mails, peer support groups, and live chat. Both groups increased minutes of physical activity and walking. In the Internet condition, individuals who used the site three or more times had a greater change in activity than individuals who used the site less than three times. In the group receiving the informational Web site, no differences based on site usage were observed (McKay et al., 2001).

Ongoing follow-up and support for engagement in self-management

Meta-analyses (Norris et al., 2001, 2002) found that the only program feature that was uniquely predictive of success after controlling for the influence of all the other program features was duration of contact. "Interventions with regular reinforcement are more effective than one-time or short-term education" (Norris et al., 2001).

Failure to find duration of diabetes patient education programs a significant predictor of beneficial effects on metabolic control (HbA1) attributed by authors to lack of good measure of dose (Ellis et al., 2004).

Patients received intensive treatment for 8 weeks with and 8 weeks without the assistance of a computer program. When using the computer program, program provided recommendations for insulin adjustment. When not using the computer program, patients adjusted their own insulin using the same algorithm as the computer. Patients made more insulin dose adjustments and had higher diabetes knowledge scores when using the computer program. Both treatments resulted in improvements in blood glucose and hemoglobin (Boukhors et al., 2003).

Ongoing follow-up and support for engagement in self-management (continued)	Four-week randomized control trial comparing weekly communication of blood glucose data to health care provider by telephone or Accu-Chek Acculink Modem. No between-group differences in HbA1c, amount of time health care provider spent analyzing data, or the number of patient/health care provider attempts to make contact. Blood glucose data by phone had 6% error rate vs. no error rate by modem (Bergenstal et al., 2005)
	Nurse follow-up included attempted calls twice weekly for 1 month, then weekly. Actual contact averaged 16 calls over 12 weeks with average of 25 min per call. Significant reductions in GHb (8.8 to 7.6) and improved diet relative to controls (Kim & Oh, 2003).
	Computer-based individual dietary assessment and intervention described above included two follow-up phone calls by health educator to check progress in achieving dietary change goals (Glasgow et al., 1997, 1996).
	Clinic-based intervention to improve foot care (Litzelman, Slemenda, Langefeld, et al., 1993) included telephone and postcard follow-up.
	Ongoing phone calls from nurses reduced GHb relative to usual care (Weinberger et al., 1995). Phone calls were made at least monthly and included review of patient education, adherence, and general health status as well as problem-solving and access to care.
	Combination of automated phone calls through which patients reported self-monitored blood glucose levels and individually tailored phone follow-up by nurses resulted in improved GHb as well as increased self-efficacy and decreased depressed mood among lowincome and minority patients of Veterans Administration and community health centers (Piette et al., 1999; Piette, Weinberger, & McPhee, 2000; Piette, Weinberger, McPhee, Mah, et al., 2000).
	In the studies by Tate and colleagues described above, adding an e-counselor to the Internet education program doubled the amount of weight loss. The e-counselor sent individually tailored e-mails and provided feedback on self-management (Tate et al., 2003, 2001).
	Following a six-session group class focusing on empowerment, monthly newsletter to adults with diabetes was well accepted, especially by those having more problems with their diabetes (Anderson et al., 1994).
	Three-month intervention in which participants send blood glucose levels, medications and dosages, food intake, and exercise to health provider using a Web-based system. Providers provided recommendations based on data. Intervention resulted in improved HbA1c, triglycerides, and HDL cholesterol (Kwon et al., 2004).

Table 15.1 *(continued)*

Ongoing follow-up and support for engagement in self-management (continued)	Biweekly automated telephone disease management health assessment and self-care education calls with nurse follow-up based on reports resulted in more frequent glucose monitoring, foot inspections, visits to podiatrists and specialty clinics; fewer symptoms of poor glycemic control; and greater satisfaction with health care than usual care. Intervention used with both English- and Spanish-speaking diabetics (Piette et al., 2001; Piette, Weinberger, & McPhee, 2000).
	Twelve-week intervention in which patients accessed Web site by cell phone or Internet and input blood glucose levels every day. Recommendations were then sent to the patient by phone and Internet. Intervention resulted in decreased fasting glucose and postprandial blood sugar levels and increased satisfaction with care (Kim et al., 2005).
	Four-week randomized control trial comparing weekly communication of blood glucose data to health care provider by telephone or Accu-Chek Acculink Modem. No between group differences in HbA1c, amount of time health care provider spent analyzing data, or the number of patient/health care provider attempts to make contact. Blood glucose data by phone had 6% error rate vs. no error rate by modem (Bergenstal et al., 2005).
	Proactive call center treatment support using trained nonmedical telephonists supported by designed software and a nurse resulted in greater reduction in GHb levels than usual care at 12 months (Young et al., 2005).
	When offered monthly support group meetings over a 3- to 12-month period following 4-hour education program and individual consultations with dietitian, only 29/70 (41%) attended at least one meeting (Banister et al., 2004).
	Following a 6-month weight-loss intervention over interactive television, participants randomized to one of three conditions: frequent in-person support (biweekly meetings led by group therapist, self-monitoring, and peer phone and group contact), Internet support (bi-weekly interactive television sessions facilitated by group therapist, self-monitoring, and contact with other members via e-mail or chat room), or minimal Internet support (monthly interactive television sessions for 6 months, encouragement to self-monitor). Six months after randomization, all groups increased energy expenditure. Comparable and appreciable weight loss across all groups with differences in engagement among groups: Internet support (nonsignificant trend toward poorer retention, more frequent self-monitoring and obtaining peer support through e-mail and Internet), frequent in-person support (more frequent attendance; Harvey-Berino et al., 2004).

Community resources	Teaching adults how to set goals for and pursue acquisition and utilization of community resources was successful in increasing resource use and in maintaining physical activity levels (Riley, Glasgow, & Eakin, 2001).

Asheville Project in North Carolina trained pharmacists to provide ongoing education, training in self-monitoring of blood glucose, monitoring of status, goal-setting, and collaborative medication management with physicians for adults who had completed education from certified diabetes educators. Benefits included improved GHb, lipids, blood pressure and quality of life, satisfaction with pharmacy services, and reduced health care costs (Cranor et al., 2003; Cranor & Christensen, 2003).

Faculty and students of North Carolina Central University assisted a community-focused diabetes management program, Project DIRECT, in gaining community input into program planning and in developing community-based activities for diabetes management in African American churches that served the intended audience of Project Direct (Reid, Hatch, & Parrish, 2003).

Through linkages with community groups and organizations, The Cote-des-Neiges project in Montreal sought to develop community-based support for diabetes management including support groups, lobbying for improved medication coverage, group exercise sessions, and links to a local sports center. Although response to activities was positive, few activities were developed and implemented because of the short (one-year) project period (Nasmith et al., 2004).

Supplemental food programs for Native American groups are utilized by intended audiences but less effective than could be because (a) programs do not provide adequate amounts of healthy foods and (b) do not include education in healthy eating and preparation of healthy meals (Dillinger, Jett, Macri, & Grivetti, 1999).

Web-based resources offering chat rooms, discussion groups, and information pertinent to self-management have shown favorable acceptance and utilization among adults with diabetes (Goldberg et al., 2003; Zrebiec & Jacobson, 2001). |
| Continuity of quality clinical care | Health system instituted comprehensive approach to improving range of diabetes care services, including handouts and manuals, Web-based programs, telephone/nurse case management for those with GHb > 9, physician financial incentives for meeting testing guidelines, and patient incentives for annual eye exams. Improvements in all measures including reduction from 35 to 21% with GHb > 9.5 (Larsen et al., 2003).

Touch-screen intervention in primary care discussed above (Glasgow et al., 2004) provided printouts for PCPs of patient's dietary, physical activity, and smoking cessation goals. Increased completion of recommended laboratory tests. |

Collaborative Goal-Setting

Substantial research indicates both the importance of goal-setting in behavior and the value of interventions that focus on it (Locke, Saari, Shaw, & Latham, 1981). Anderson and his colleagues' work on empowerment in diabetes education emphasizes the importance of the individual in the process (Anderson & Funnell, 2000; Anderson et al., 1995). A classic demonstration of the benefits of involving patients in their care and planning was through a 20-minute patient activation intervention prior to outpatient visits. This included review of records, discussion of self-management issues, and instruction and rehearsal of how to ask questions of and negotiate with the PCP. This resulted in significant reductions in glycated hemoglobin (GHb)[1] relative to controls (Greenfield et al., 1988) at 12 weeks follow-up.

Both the importance of the individual and the possible limits of self-help interventions are suggested by one meta-analysis of self-management programs for chronic disease that found face-to-face contact to be the only predictor of outcomes (Warsi, Wang, LaValley, Avorn, & Solomon, 2004). However, interventions for collaborative goal-setting show how e-health procedures and face-to-face contact are not opposed or mutually exclusive but may be complementary. Several of the computer-based individual dietary assessments described under Individualized Assessment are intended to be completed in the waiting room prior to an outpatient visit and include displays for the primary care provider to prompt review of patient-chosen goals during the medical visit (Glasgow et al., 1997, 1996). These approaches have been well accepted by providers and by a wide variety of patients and have increased behavioral counseling received by patients and subsequent behavioral change relative to individuals' goals (Estabrooks et al., 2005; Glasgow et al., 2004). These methods can readily generate a set of prompts and assists for improved management, such as: (a) a display that combines current GHb status, personalized self-management goals, and personalized steps for goal attainment; (b) suggested discussion points for the clinician; and (c) a wallet card for monitoring progress. The combination of these led to greater reductions in GHb than standard care (Levetan, Dawn, Robbins, & Ratner, 2002).

---

[1] Glycated hemoglobin (GHb), also commonly referred to as glycosolated hemoglobin, HbA_{1c}, HbA1, or A1C, is a term used to describe a series of stable minor hemoglobin components formed slowly from the presence of glucose along with hemoglobin in the blood. "The rate of formation of GHb is directly proportional to the ambient glucose concentration" (Goldstein et al., 2004, p. 1765). Thus, GHb provides an estimate of metabolic or blood sugar control reflecting the previous 120 days. GHb is commonly used in the diabetes literature as a generic term to refer to the variety of individual tests employed.

Building Skills

A consensus document on self-management that was sponsored by The Robert Wood Johnson Foundation and the Center for the Advancement of Health noted that only an estimated 20% of skills in disease management are disease specific. This may be something of an underestimate for diabetes, given the complexity of its management. Nevertheless, the point is well taken that much of the skills to be taught in disease management are more general problem-solving skills, skills for resisting temptation, and skills for enhancing general patterns of healthy lifestyle, such as healthy diet and physical activity. For all of these, well-established principles of patient education and behavior change include the importance of focusing on concrete skills (e.g., how to read food labels for frozen and processed foods, estimating percentages of protein, carbohydrates, and fats in daily diet), modeling and demonstrating concrete skills, rehearsal of skills with opportunity for reinforcement as well as feedback to enhance performance, monitoring of implementation of skills in real-life settings and opportunity for further review of results, observation of practice, feedback to enhance performance, and reinforcement (Anderson, 1998; Hill-Briggs, 2003; Houston & Haire-Joshu, 1996; Perri et al., 2001).

Training skills generally requires working in detail regarding specific skills. Thus, successful self-management interventions often include a sequence of contacts in which skills are introduced, practiced, and reviewed with opportunities for real-world tests between sessions and, then, further review, practice, and skill enhancement. The absence of such steps illustrates their importance—a diabetes passport for monitoring self-management but without goal-setting, individualized assessment, or opportunities for building skills had minimal benefits in a randomized trial (Simmons, Gamble, Foote, Cole, & Coster, 2004).

As depicted in Table 15.1, a variety of e-health interventions have addressed skills through telephone, Web-based utilities, and combinations of these with live interactions with intervention staff. Several studies raise questions about the adequacy of programs that teach skills without some kind of direct contact with program staff. In one meta-analysis, face-to-face delivery of intervention, cognitive reframing, and inclusion of emphasis on exercise predicted beneficial effects on GHb (Ellis et al., 2004). Concerns about the adequacy of e-health interventions are also raised by limitations of findings of several studies, such as in a study that evaluated computer kiosks in waiting rooms that included video sequences to communicate information, provide psychological support, and promote diabetes self-management skills. Benefits of this package were found for greater recognition of susceptibility to diabetes complications but not in blood pressure, weight, or GHb (Gerber et al., 2005).

In contrast to those that rely solely on e-health interventions, other programs combine e-health with live counseling or instruction. Extending the work cited above under Goal-Setting, computer-based individualized assessment can guide teaching skills through face to fact contact (Glasgow et al., 2004, 1997, 1996). In another study, a 6-month intervention combined a computer-assisted diet education system (Diabeto) with personalized coaching to help individuals monitor their diets and balance meals. This improved dietary habits and decreased caloric intake and GHb (Turnin et al., 1992).

A study of the benefits of interactive components added to e-health interventions found mixed results. Adults with diabetes were assigned to either an informational Web site intervention with diabetes-specific articles and glucose tracking or to the informational Web site plus interactive features-personalized physical activity plan, support from a personal coach (via the Internet), tailored e-mails, peer support groups, and live chat (McKay, King, Eakin, Seeley, & Glasgow, 2001). Overall, there were no differences between the two groups in impacts. However, internal analyses indicated that, in the interactive Web-based intervention, individuals who used the site three or more times had a greater change in activity than individuals who used the site less than three times. In the group receiving only the informational Web site, no differences were found based on site usage. Thus, the interactive Web-based intervention was effective among those who used it, raising, however, the issue of how to encourage use of such interventions. Keeping participants engaged in self-management activities over time via the Internet (as well as other modalities) remains a challenge.

Healthy eating poses an especially challenging set of skills for diabetes management. The complexity of diet is exacerbated by the nuances of blood sugar control such as in the need to limit fruits that can be high in some types of sugars or the need to adjust diet in light of changes in blood sugar or other conditions such as current illness. In spite of this complexity, Web-based interventions have shown promise in dietary education for those with diabetes. In one study, a Web-based, individually tailored intervention provided feedback about personal intake levels of fat, fruit, and vegetables and how these intake levels compared with recommendations and the average intake levels of peers. It also provided information about what changes to make and on how to make these changes. Relative to control groups that received generic nutrition information or no information, the computer-tailored intervention increased fruit and decreased fat intake (Oenema, Tan, & Brug, 2005). Other interventions focused on weight loss include the work of Tate and colleagues, showing that an Internet education program, when combined with an electronic coach led to reduction in caloric intake and weight loss among obese adults with diabetes risk factors (Tate, Jackvony, & Wing, 2003; Tate, Wing, & Winett, 2001).

Anticipating a series of studies of telephone follow-up presented in the next section, a study in Korea examined telephone counseling 2 times per week for one month, then weekly for 2 more months, amounting to a total of 16 calls with an average call length of 25 min. This led to 1.2 point reduction in GHb relative to 0.6 point increase in usual care (Oh, Kim, Yoon, & Choi, 2003).

Ongoing Follow-Up and Support

As noted above, meta-analyses of self-management of diabetes (Norris et al., 2001, 2002), smoking cessation (Fiore et al., 2000; Kottke et al., 1988), and interventions in other areas of health promotion (Mullen et al., 1985) all note the importance of ongoing follow-up and support for behavior change. The content of Ongoing Follow-Up and Support may include continued assistance in refining problem-solving plans and skills, encouragement in the face of less than perfect performance and success, and assistance in responding to new problems that may emerge, assistance that may entail linking patients back to primary care providers or other parts of the disease management team.

As documented in Table 15.1, phone calls (Wasson et al., 1992; Weinberger et al., 1995) or the Internet (McKay, Feil, Glasgow, & Brown, 1998) can be important channels for ongoing support. Real-time modalities can be combined with e-health approaches such as in automated telephone monitoring of patients combined with nurse follow-up. This has been shown to reach low-income and minority patients; to elicit valid, self-reported blood glucose levels; and to achieve benefits not only in actual blood glucose levels but also in increased self-efficacy and reduced levels of depression (Piette, 1999; Piette, McPhee, Weinberger, Mah, & Kraemer, 1999; Piette, Weinberger, Kraemer, & McPhee, 2001; Piette, Weinberger, & McPhee, 2000; Piette, Weinberger, et al., 2000). This reflects research in other areas, such as smoking cessation, in which telephone counseling has been shown effective (Lichtenstein, Glasgow, Lando, Ossip-Klein, & Boles, 1996; Zhu et al., 1996).

The contributions of e-health follow up can be substantial. For example, adding an e-counselor to an Internet education program doubled the amount of weight loss. The e-counselor sent individually tailored e-mails and provided feedback on self-management (Tate et al., 2003, 2001).

Because chronic disease management is for the rest of your life, interventions to support that management need also to be extended for the rest of patients' lives. This point is so important and the challenge of providing sources of support for the rest of individuals' lives are so substantial that it is useful to give it separate attention. Successful self-management programs do not educate people so that they no longer need ongoing building of skills, follow-up, and support. Rather, successful programs *provide* ongoing services of these kinds. Also, changes in circumstances that have no direct relationship with diabetes, such as retirement, widowhood, marriage, and children moving out of the household or reduced physical ability with normal aging may nevertheless have substantial impacts on diabetes self-management, necessitating review and reinstitution of self-management plans. More fundamentally, and as noted in the beginning of the chapter, diabetes is progressive. It is normal for the clinical status of those with the disease to change and worsen over time. Thus, the whole set of services outlined here, including goal-setting, individualization of care, education about disease and the role of behavior in its care, building skills, follow-up and support, and attention to availability of resources needs to be repeated throughout the individual's life.

That diabetes is for the rest of your life also places a special priority within ongoing follow-up and support on monitoring and identifying changes in status. When changes in clinical status, as well as in the individual's circumstances and self-management patterns occur—as they naturally do given the progressive and lifelong nature of diabetes—they need to be recognized so that medical and self-management plans can be revised and the individual can be referred for additional instruction in key skills or any of the other RSSM that may be indicated. For example, a change in metabolic control may dictate clinical attention and a change in medication. Changes in physical activity with aging may trigger a booster on how to adjust physical activity patterns. Similarly, widowhood may occasion revisited instruction in how to maintain healthy eating patterns and recognition of increased need for encouragement and support from a support group, a community health worker, or some other source. Ongoing follow-up and support needs to identify emerging or renewed needs for the whole range of RSSM *and* promote appropriate utilization of them.

E-health modalities may be especially appropriate for this kind of monitoring changes in status and need for services and for promoting use of such services. E-health has helped link individuals with their providers, monitoring status, and triggering referral for appropriate services, whether a follow-up call from a nurse or an appointment for specialized services (Bergenstal et al., 2005; Kim, Yoo, & Shim, 2005; Kwon et al., 2004; Piette et al., 2001; Piette, Weinberger, & McPhee, 2000). This function of e-health stands at the connection between self-help and clinical care. It frees individuals to monitor and report their status without reliance on the health care system and, at the same time, links individuals to needed clinical and other types of care.

A critical need in developing effective approaches to ongoing follow-up and support is reaching those who may benefit from them. It has not been easy to identify ways to provide ongoing support that will be well accepted by those they are intended to reach. Anecdotally, a common experience among those who have conducted group programs such as for smoking cessation or weight loss is that participants request at the last scheduled meeting to keep getting together. Responding to this by arranging opportunities for further group meetings has almost always been met with near-zero attendance. Providing an example of such poor attendance at follow-up support groups, only 41% of participants attended even one optional, monthly support group meetings over a 3- to 12-month period following an initial program of individual consultations with a dietitian (Banister, Jastrow, Hodges, Loop, & Gillham, 2004).

One possible reason for poor attendance at follow-up or support meetings may be the inconvenience of having to attend according to the group's schedule rather than the individual's convenience. I may need support for managing my weight for the rest of my life, but I don't want to attend a group meeting at 8 p.m. on the second Tuesday of the month for the rest of my life. Convenience and the ability to access support when needed, not when scheduled, emerge as important features of ongoing follow-up and support. At the same time, it is important that follow-up and support be proactive in contacting individuals periodically, whether or not they seek out support, to keep individuals from falling through the cracks. Thus, ongoing follow-up and support need to include two features: easy, on-demand access and maintaining contact in a manner that is not contingent on the individual's efforts. These two features share maximizing convenience and minimizing effort of the individual.

E-health modalities may be especially useful in offering such a combination of easy access at the preference of the individual along with efficient contacting and prompting of individuals as needed, say every quarter if no other contact with the individual has occurred. As an example of prompting individuals, a proactive call center used nonprofessional trained individuals who were supported by computer-based algorithms and nurse backup to make follow-up phone calls. This resulted in greater reductions in GHb levels than usual care at 12-month follow-up (Young et al., 2005).

Blending in-person and Internet contact and devising the best schedule of contact pose substantial challenges. Several combinations of these were examined in a study that offered 6 months of weight-loss intervention provided through interactive television and then randomized participants to three 12-month follow-up conditions: (a) Internet support (bi-weekly interactive television chat sessions facilitated by group therapist, e-mail contact in alternate weeks, self-monitoring, and contact with other members via e-mail or chat room); (b) in-person support (bi-weekly in person meetings led by group therapist, personal contact in alternate weeks, self-monitoring, and peer phone and group contact); and (c) minimal Internet support (monthly interactive television sessions for 6 months, followed by no contact but encouragement of self-monitoring; Harvey-Berino, Pintauro, Buzzell, & Gold, 2004). Over the 18-month treatment and follow-up period and across all groups, maintenance of weight loss was quite good, ranging from 5.6 to 8.2% of body weight, but did not differ significantly among them. The different interventions led to somewhat different patterns of engagement. Although not significant, somewhat more individuals were lost to follow-up in the Internet support than in the in-person or minimal Internet support conditions. Those in the in-person support attended more group follow-up sessions than those in Internet support. However, this difference was reversed for self-monitoring and obtaining support from other group members (by e-mail, bulletin board, or chat room appointments) with the Internet support group exceeding the in-person support for these. Finally, both attendance (in-person support more frequent) and frequency of self-monitoring (Internet support more frequent) were correlated with weight loss. Thus, complex relationships among retention, type of engagement, and outcomes emerge. The complexity of these suggests no clear best treatment but, perhaps, advantages of approaches in which individuals may choose among modes, types, and frequencies of contact and support.

Community Resources

Teaching skills for disease management is of little utility if individuals lack access to the resources they need to carry out those skills. Thus, for example, convenient access to healthy foods and to attractive and safe settings for physical activity is necessary if healthy diet and healthy levels of physical activity are to be maintained. Research, especially using recently developed "geocoding" and spatial analysis, is showing substantial effects of geographic location of resources such as supermarkets and settings for safe, pleasant physical activity. For example, Baker and her colleagues studied access to stores selling fruits and vegetables in St. Louis, Missouri. Poor dietary intake was predicted not by distance to neighborhood grocery stores but by the quality of food selections available in neighborhood stores and by neighborhood average income (Baker et al., 2003).

Although most all who have thought about it recognize the importance of community resources for healthy eating, physical activity, and social encouragement of diabetes management, relatively little research addresses community resources in diabetes (Fisher et al., 2005). The literature on e-health in enhancing access to community resources reflects this. It is scant. As noted in Table 15.1, most published approaches to these issues have used community organization approaches to identifying community resources, training community members (e.g., pharmacists) to facilitate self-management, or developing advocacy efforts (Cranor, Bunting, & Christensen, 2003; Cranor & Christensen, 2003).

Web-based resources may integrate chat rooms, discussion groups, and general information. These have shown favorable acceptance and utilization among adults with diabetes (Goldberg, Ralston, Hirsch, Hoath, & Ahmed, 2003; Zrebiec & Jacobson, 2001). These could be expanded to provide assistance for locating community resources, facilitating information exchange about resources among participants, linking individuals with community resource providers, and linking community providers and agencies with each other. Existing agencies like supermarkets or, perhaps, municipal recreation agencies might develop or expand Web sites to promote and facilitate access to resources they provide.

Continuity of Quality Clinical Care

Misunderstanding has sometimes led to the perception that self-help is an alternative to or even opposed to clinical care. However, as noted in the initial part of this chapter, self-management and quality clinical care are not only compatible but really dependent on each other. Without sound clinical care, the individual's efforts may be misdirected; for example, in frustration over failure of dietary changes to lower cholesterol when cholesterol-lowering medications are indicated. But, without self-management, expert clinical care will fall far short of its potential, through failure to use prescribed medications or implement management plans or failure to complement clinical care with behavioral changes that greatly extend the benefits of medicine.

Wagner's Chronic Care Model (Wagner, 1998; Wagner, Austin, & Von Korff, 1996) provides an excellent framework for integrating resources and supports for self-management with key components of clinical care. The model details important features of how clinical care is organized, including evidence-based algorithms and protocols to guide clinical decision-making, information systems to monitor provision of care, design of delivery systems to prompt and support implementation of desired care elements, and organizational commitment to ensure resources for and consistency of interventions. It also includes self-management support along with community resources. One can view RSSM as expanding and detailing these last two. Together, then, the Chronic Care Model and RSSM provide a comprehensive view of how clinical care, the systems that support it, and a range of RSSM from clinical and community sources help individuals manage and live well with chronic diseases.

Self-help and e-health interventions can be employed at multiple points in the range of services comprised by the Chronic Care Model and RSSM. Web resources for patients have been included in general quality improvement initiatives in clinical care (Larsen, Cannon, & Towner, 2003), and computerized, touch-screen approaches to individualized assessment and collaborative goal-setting have been used to generate reminder lists and prompts for clinicians' encounters with patients (Glasgow et al., 2004).

One might wonder whether those expecting personalized clinical care would be disappointed by being asked to complete computer-based assessments. However, experience indicates that, far from making individuals feel dehumanized, well-designed e-health assessments and goal-setting utilities can be very detailed and responsive so that they make the individual feel better heard than by a hurried or distracted staff member or professional. Further, such e-health utilities may better inform and prepare both patients and clinicians so as to achieve efficiencies that then preserve more of the 12- or 15-minute encounter for substantive engagement and decision-making with patients rather than routine information gathering (Glasgow et al., 2004).

Discussion

Self-help and e-health approaches can play a substantial role in self-management of diabetes. They include contributions to key RSSM: individualized assessment, facilitation of goal-setting, building skills for diabetes management, providing ongoing support and encouragement, monitoring changes in status or circumstances, identifying needs for renewed treatment and revision of management plans, exchange of information about and linkage to community resources, and linkage with clinical providers.

A key point emerging from this review is that self-help is part of disease management, complementary to other components including clinical care. This is in important distinction from the idea that self-help constitutes an opposition to clinical or professional care or is somehow antithetical to or a replacement for clinical management. The complexity of diabetes and the needs of individuals with the disease make the complementarity among self-help and other dimensions of care especially clear. In their review of e-health and related approaches to health promotion in primary care, Glasgow and his colleagues (2004) have emphasized the complementarity between e-health and personal, face-to-face aspects of care. The high tech extends, makes more efficient, and enhances the value of personal, face-to-face care and counseling.

The complementarity of self-help and other aspects of care runs parallel to broader conceptual issues surrounding the causes of the behaviors that get labeled "self-management." Writing about behavior change sometimes poses an opposition between causes of behavior within the individual and those outside the individual. In reality, skills, preferences, propensities, or plans of the individual interact with opportunities, local or community resources, family and social characteristics, etc., in guiding the actions and lives of individuals. In parallel to this, the utility of self-help approaches interact with clinical care, patient education resources, community resources, etc., in guiding the management of diabetes and other health behaviors of individuals. Applying to both, a social ecological model (McLeroy, Bibeau, & Steckler, 1988) articulates how the layers of social influence, from family to policy, provide context for the actions and characteristics of the individual.

Recognizing the importance of contexts leads to a broader view of self-help. Consider the following alternative sets of resources available to an individual with diabetes:

- Resource Set A:
    - Good self-help interventions
    - Lack of patient education
    - Lack of opportunities for regular contact with the medical care provider
    - Episodic, reactive, and symptom-focused medical care
    - Lack of community resources for diabetes self-management such as healthy food or places for physical activity
- Resource Set B:
    - Good self-help interventions
    - Thorough and continuing patient education services readily available through several modes and channels (e.g., groups classes, individual education, on-line resources, etc.)
    - Responsive channels for initiating contact with the medical care provider and regular contact by provider to assess need for care, change of management plans, etc.
    - Medical care focused on regular management of diabetes, changing and updating management plans, as well as timely response to symptoms
    - Plentiful community resources for diabetes self-management such as healthy food or places for physical activity

With which set of resources is the individual better able to help herself? It would seem that self-help is advanced not just by self-help resources, component 1 in each of Resource Sets A and B, but by a range of self-help and other resources and services and the opportunity to choose among them. At this level, self-help is promoted by a range of RSSM—some self-help interventions, some not—and the opportunity to choose among them. Indeed, what is and is not self-help may depend on the level at which the question is considered as much as on the nature of a particular service chosen. An individual who chooses a non-self-help intervention (say a group class rather than a Web-based patient education intervention) from among Resource Set B may still be seen to be guiding her own management from a range of choices and, thus, engaging in self-help even if not at the moment using a specific self-help intervention. Non-self-help interventions and resources can be seen as part of a range of RSSM that, in their variety and accessibility, enable self-help. Self-help may depend more on that variety and accessibility of available choices than on the nature of any one service.

Turning to a population perspective raises questions about how large numbers of those of concern may be reached and enabled to manage diabetes and other chronic diseases effectively. Glasgow and colleagues' RE-AIM model (Glasgow, Vogt, & Boles, 1999) draws attention to aspects of interventions that will determine their population impacts, including their reach to intended audiences, effectiveness as used, adoption by multiple settings, consistency of implementation, and maintenance. These are especially important in diabetes, for which large numbers of individuals go undiagnosed and untreated and large numbers of those diagnosed receive insufficient patient education and RSSM. Self-help and the system-level view of self-help developed in the previous paragraph may enhance reach by providing multiple channels (as opposed to one size fits all) that enable people to find approaches that suit their preferences and circumstances. Among those multiple channels, the inclusion of effective and attractive self-help interventions may enhance the effectiveness of the entire set of available educational resources such as by increasing their appeal to those who would forego them if they were only available in group or individual classes. From this perspective, the most important sense of self-help may be the extent to which the preferences, circumstances and choices of a population are reflected in a range of RSSM that include self-help interventions and that are available to that population and enhance its ability to help itself.

Conclusions

The diverse challenges posed by diabetes and the many influences on diabetes self-management provide a rich terrain in which to examine self-help. Diabetes, a clearly biological disease, leads to consideration of the central role of behavior in diabetes management and the broad range of influences—from intrapersonal to family to community and policy—on those behaviors. Within this terrain, self-help interventions emerge as ecologically framed. In diabetes, self-help does not entail gaining independence from clinical care or the influence of the surround. Rather, it rests on the availability of a range of interventions (Fisher et al., 2005) that vary in the extent to which they employ intensive or direct contact with a provider (Rosen et al., 2003) but, together, provide individuals the resources they need to manage their disease and live their lives fully.

Chapter Points

- The self-management of diabetes requires numerous effortful behaviors to slow the progression of the disease, interact successfully with the health care system, and prepare for likely future complications.
- Studies targeting self-management of weight loss and increased exercise reduced conversion to type 2 diabetes by 58%.
- Self-management of diabetes is enhanced by reducing the responsibility on the individual and emphasizing environmental factors in the form of frequent and continuous support.
- Six resources and supports for self-management have been identified: individualized assessment, collaborative goal setting, building skills, ongoing support, community resources, and continuity of care.
- Assessment of progress toward patient-identified goals can be used to shape interactions between patients and health care providers by insuring that all aspects of care are covered and that treatment recommendations are based on both progress and problems while advancing toward goals.
- In skill building, focus on identifying concrete skills (e.g., how to read food labels), modeling and rehearsing skills, and monitoring skills implementation in daily life are requisite.
- Follow-up support, either through e-mail or telephone contact, is necessary to maintain change. Two essential features of support—easy, on demand access and maintenance of contact that is not continent on the individual's efforts—maximize outcomes. E-health and other self-help approaches may be especially useful in providing both these essential features of support.

References

American Association of Diabetes Educators, *About Us*, http://www.aadenet.org/ AboutUs/aboutus.shtml/. Accessed July 16, 2007.

American Diabetes Association, Review criteria and Indicator listing, http:// www.diabetes.org/uedocuments/ReviewCriteria_IndicatorListing_9- 2003.pdf. Accessed july 16, 2007.

Anderson, R. M. (1998). Educational principles and strategies. In M. M. Funnell, C. Hunt, K. Kulkarni, R. R. Rubin, & P. Yarborough (Eds.), *A core curriculum for diabetes educators* (pp. 5–26). American Association of Diabetes Educators, Chicago.

Anderson, R. M., Fitzgerald, J. T., Funnell, M. M., Barr, P. A., Stepien, C. J., Hiss, R. G., et al. (1994). Evaluation of an activated patient diabetes education newsletter. *Diabetes Educator, 20,* 29–34.

Anderson, R. M., & Funnell, M. M. (2000). Compliance and adherence are dysfunctional concepts in diabetes care. *Diabetes Educator, 26,* 597–604.

Anderson, R. M., Funnell, M. M., Barr, P. A., Dedrick, R. F., & Davis, W. K. (1991). Learning to empower patients: Results of professional education program for diabetes educators. *Diabetes Care, 14,* 584–590.

Anderson, R. M., Funnell, M. M., Butler, P. M., Arnold, M. S., Fitzgerald, J. T., & Feste, C. C. (1995). Patient empowerment. Results of a randomized controlled trial. *Diabetes Care, 18,* 943–949.

Aubert, R. E., Herman, W. H., Waters, J., Moore, W., Sutton, D., Peterson, B. L., et al. (1998). Nurse case management to improve glycemic control in diabetic patients in a health maintenance organization. A randomized, controlled trial. *Annals of Internal Medicine, 129,* 605–612.

Baehring, T. U., Schulze, H., Bornstein, S. R., & Scherbaum, W. A. (1997). Using the World Wide Web—A new approach to risk identification of diabetes mellitus. *International Journal of Medical Informatics, 46,* 31–39.

Baker, E. A., Williams, D., Kelly, C., Nanney, M. S., Vo, H., Barnidge, E., et al. (2003, November). *Access, income and racial composition: Dietary patterns aren't just a personal choice.* Paper presented at the American Public Health Association 131st Annual Meeting, San Francisco, CA.

Banister, N. A., Jastrow, S. T., Hodges, V., Loop, R., & Gillham, M. B. (2004). Diabetes self-management training program in a community clinic improves patient outcomes at modest cost. *Journal of the American Dietetic Association, 104,* 807–810.

Bergenstal, R. M., Anderson, R. L., Bina, D. M., Johnson, M. L., Davidson, J. L., Solarz-Johnson, B., et al. (2005). Impact of modem-transferred blood glucose data on clinician work efficiency and patient glycemic control. *Diabetes Technology and Therapeutics, 7,* 241–247.

Boukhors, Y., Rabasa-Lhoret, R., Langelier, H., Soultan, M., Lacroix, A., & Chiasson, J. L. (2003). The use of information technology for the management of intensive insulin therapy in type 1 diabetes mellitus. *Diabetes and Metabolism, 29*(6), 619–627.

Brown, S. J., Lieberman, D., Gemeny, B. A., Fan, Y. C., Wilson, D. M., & Pasta, D. J. (1997). Educational video game for juvenile diabetes: Results of a controlled trial. *Medical Informatics, 22,* 77–89.

Castaldini, M., Saltmarch, M., Luck, S., & Sucher, K. (1998). The development and pilot testing of a multimedia CD-ROM for diabetes education. *The Diabetes Educator, 24*, 285–286, 291–292, 295–286.

Centers for Disease Control and Prevention. (2003). Prevalence of diabetes and impaired fasting glucose in adults—United States, 1999–2000. *MMWR, 52*, 833–837.

Clement, S. (1995). Diabetes self-management education. *Diabetes Care, 18*, 1204–1214.

Cranor, C. W., Bunting, B. A., & Christensen, D. B. (2003). The Asheville Project: Long-term clinical and economic outcomes in a community pharmacy diabetes care program. *Journal of the American Pharmaceutical Association, 43*, 173–184.

Cranor, C. W., & Christensen, D. B. (2003). The Asheville Project: Short-term outcomes of a community pharmacy diabetes care program. *Journal of the American Pharmaceutical Association, 43*, 149–159.

Diabetes Prevention Program Research Group. (2002). Reduction of the incidence of type 2 diabetes with lifestyle intervention or metformin. *New England Journal of Medicine, 346*, 393–403.

Dillinger, T. L., Jett, S. C., Macri, M. J., & Grivetti, L. E. (1999). Feast or famine? Supplemental food programs and their impacts on two American Indian communities in California. *International Journal of Food Sciences and Nutrition, 50*, 173–187.

Ellis, S. E., Speroff, T., Dittus, R. S., Brown, A., Pichert, J. W., & Elasy, T. A. (2004). Diabetes patient education: A meta-analysis and meta-regression. *Patient Education and Counseling, 52*, 97–105.

Estabrooks, P. A., Nelson, C. C., Xu, S., King, D., Bayliss, E. A., Gaglio, B., et al. (2005). The frequency and behavioral outcomes of goal choices in the self-management of diabetes. *The Diabetes Educator, 31*, 391–400.

Etzwiler, D. D. (1980). Teaching allied health professionals about self-management. *Diabetes Care, 3*, 121–123.

Etzwiler, D. D. (1986). Diabetes management: The importance of patient education and participation. *Postgraduate Medicine, 80*, 67–72.

Fiore, M. C., Bailey, W. C., Cohen, S. J., Dorfman, S. F., Goldstein, M. G., & Gritz, E. R. (2000). *Treating tobacco use and dependence. Clinical practice guideline.* Rockville, MD: U.S. Department of Health and Human Services, Public Health Service.

Fisher, E. B., Brownson, C. A., O'Toole, M. L., Shetty, G., Anwuri, V. V., & Glasgow, R. E. (2005). Ecologic approaches to self management: The case of diabetes. *American Journal of Public Health, 95*, 1523–1535.

Gerber, B. S., Brodsky, I. G., Lawless, K. A., Smolin, L. I., Arozullah, A. M., Smith, E. V., et al. (2005). Implementation and evaluation of a low-literacy diabetes education computer multimedia application. *Diabetes Care, 28*, 1574–1580.

Glasgow, R., Toobert, D. J., & Hampson, S. (1991). Participation in outpatient diabetes education programs: How many patients take part and how representative are they? *The Diabetes Educator, 5*, 376–380.

Glasgow, R. E., Bull, S. S., Piette, J. D., & Steiner, J. F. (2004). Interactive behavior change technology: A partial solution to the competing demands of primary care. *American Journal of Preventive Medicine, 27*, 80–87.

Glasgow, R. E., La Chance, P. A., Toobert, D. J., Brown, J., Hampson, S. E., & Riddle, M. C. (1997). Long-term effects and costs of brief behavioural dietary intervention for patients with diabetes delivered from the medical office. *Patient Education and Counseling, 32,* 175–184.

Glasgow, R. E., Nutting, P. A., King, D. K., Nelson, C. C., Cutter, G., Gaglio, B., et al. (2004). A Practical Randomized Trial to Improve Diabetes Care. *Journal of General Internal Medicine, 19,* 1167–1174.

Glasgow, R. E., Toobert, D. J., & Hampson, S. E. (1996). Effects of a brief office-based intervention to facilitate diabetes dietary self-management. *Diabetes Care, 19,* 835–842.

Glasgow, R. E., Toobert, D. J., Hampson, S. E., Brown, J. E., Lewinsohn, P. M., & Donnelly, J. (1992). Improving self-care among older patients with type II diabetes: The "Sixty Something…" Study. *Patient Education and Counseling, 19,* 61–74.

Glasgow, R. E., Vogt, T. M., & Boles, S. M. (1999). Evaluating the public health impact of health promotion interventions: The RE-AIM framework. *American Journal of Public Health, 89,* 1322–1327.

Goldberg, H. I., Ralston, J. D., Hirsch, I. B., Hoath, J. I., & Ahmed, K. I. (2003). Using an internet comanagement module to improve the quality of chronic disease care. *Joint Commission Journal on Quality & Safety, 29,* 443–451.

Goldstein, D. E., Little, R. R., Lorenz, R. A., Malone, J. I., Nathan, D., Peterson, C. M., et al. (2004). Tests of glycemia in diabetes. *Diabetes Care, 27,* 1761–1773.

Greenfield, S., Kaplan, S. H., Ware, J. E., Yano, E. M., & Frank, H. (1988). Patients' participation in medical care: Effects on blood sugar control and quality of life in diabetes. *Journal of General Internal Medicine, 3,* 448–457.

Hampson, S. E., Glasgow, R. E., & Strycker, L. (2000). Beliefs versus feelings: A comparison of personal models and depression for predicting multiple outcomes in diabetes. *British Journal of Health Psychology, 5,* 27–40.

Harvey-Berino, J., Pintauro, S., Buzzell, P., & Gold, E. C. (2004). Effect of Internet support on the long-term maintenance of weight loss. *Obesity Research, 12,* 320–329.

Hill-Briggs, F. (2003). Problem solving in diabetes self-management: A model of chronic illness self-management behavior. *Annals of Behavioral Medicine, 25,* 182–193.

Hiss, R. G. (1986). The activated patient: A force for change in diabetes health care and education. *The Diabetes Educator, 12,* 600–602.

Houston, C. A., & Haire-Joshu, D. (1996). Application of health behavior models to promote behavior change. In D. Haire-Joshu (Ed.), *Management of diabetes mellitus: Perspectives of care across the lifespan,* (pp. 527–552). St. Louis: Mosby-Year Book.

Kim, H. S., & Oh, J. A. (2003). Adherence to diabetes control recommendations: Impact of nurse telephone calls. *Journal of Advanced Nursing, 44,* 256–261.

Kim, H. S., Yoo, Y. S., & Shim, H. S. (2005). Effects of an Internet-based intervention on plasma glucose levels in patients with type 2 diabetes. *Journal of Nursing Care Quality, 20,* 335–340.

Kottke, T. E., Battista, R. N., & DeFriese, G. H. (1988). Attributes of successful smoking cessation interventions in medical practice: A meta-analysis of 39 controlled trials. *Journal of American Medical Association, 259,* 2882–2889.

Kwon, H. S., Cho, J. H., Kim, H. S., Lee, J. H., Song, B. R., Oh, J. A., et al. (2004). Development of web-based diabetic patient management system using short message service (SMS). *Diabetes Research and Clinical Practice, 66*(Suppl. 1), S133–S137.

Larsen, D. L., Cannon, W., & Towner, S. (2003). Longitudinal assessment of a diabetes care management system in an integrated health network. *Journal of Managed Care Pharmacy, 9*, 552–558.

Levetan, C. S., Dawn, K. R., Robbins, D. C., & Ratner, R. E. (2002). Impact of computer-generated personalized goals on HbA(1c). *Diabetes Care, 25*, 2–8.

Lichtenstein, E., Glasgow, R. E., Lando, H. A., Ossip-Klein, D. J., & Boles, S. M. (1996). Telephone counseling for smoking cessation: rationales and meta-analytic review of evidence. *Health Education Research, 11*, 243–257.

Litzelman, D. K., Slemenda, C. W., Langefeld, C. D., et al. (1993). Reduction of lower extremity clinical abnormalities in patients with non-insulin-dependent diabetes mellitus: A randomized, controlled trial. *Annals of Internal Medicine, 119*, 36–41.

Locke, E. A., Saari, L. M., Shaw, K. N., & Latham, G. P. (1981). Goal setting and task performance: 1969–1980. *Psychological Bulletin, 90*, 125–152.

Mahoney, M. J., & Thoresen, C. E. (1974). *Self-control: Power to the person.* Monterey, CA: Brooks/Cole.

McKay, H. G., Feil, E. G., Glasgow, R. E., & Brown, J. E. (1998). Feasibility and use of an Internet support service for diabetes self-management. *Diabetes Educator, 24*, 174–179.

McKay, H. G., King, D., Eakin, E. G., Seeley, J. R., & Glasgow, R. E. (2001). The diabetes network Internet-based physical activity intervention: A randomized pilot study. *Diabetes Care, 24*, 1328–1334.

McLeroy, K., Bibeau, D., & Steckler, A. (1988). An ecological perspective on health promotion programs. *Health Education Quarterly, 15*, 351–377.

Muhlhauser, I., & Berger, M. (1993). Diabetes education and insulin therapy: When will they ever learn. *Journal of Internal Medicine, 233*, 321–326.

Mullen, P. D., Green, L. W., & Persinger, G. S. (1985). Clinical trials of patient education for chronic conditions: A comparative meta-analysis of intervention types. *Preventive Medicine, 14*, 753–781.

Nasmith, L., Cote, B., Cox, J., Inkell, D., Rubenstein, H., Jimenez, V., et al. (2004). The challenge of promoting integration: conceptualization, implementation, and assessment of a pilot care delivery model for patients with type 2 diabetes. *Family Medicine, 36*, 40–50.

Norris, S. L., Engelgau, M. M., & Narayan, K. M. (2001). Effectiveness of self-management training in type 2 diabetes: A systematic review of randomized controlled trials. *Diabetes Care, 24*, 561–587.

Norris, S. L., Lau, J., Smith, S. J., Schmid, C. H., & Engelgau, M. M. (2002). Self-management education for adults with type 2 diabetes: A meta-analysis of the effect on glycemic control. *Diabetes Care, 25*, 1159–1171.

Oenema, A., Tan, F., & Brug, J. (2005). Short-term efficacy of a web-based computer-tailored nutrition intervention: Main effects and mediators. *Annals of Behavioral Medicine, 29*, 54–63.

Oh, J. A., Kim, H. S., Yoon, K. H., & Choi, E. S. (2003). A telephone-delivered intervention to improve glycemic control in type 2 diabetic patients. *Yonsei Medical Journal, 44*, 1–8.

Pan, X. R., Li, G. W., Hu, Y. H., Wang, J. X., Yang, W. Y., An, Z. X., et al. (1997). Effects of diet and exercise in preventing NIDDM in people with impaired glucose tolerance: The Da Qing IGT and Diabetes Study. *Diabetes Care, 20,* 537–544.

Perri, M. G., & Foreyt, J. P. (2004). Preventing weight regain after weight loss. In G. A. Bray & C. Bouchard (Eds.), *Handbook of obesity* (pp. 185–199). New York: Marcel Dekker.

Perri, M. G., Nezu, A. M., McKelvey, W. F., Shermer, R. L., Renjilian, D. A., & Viegen, B. J. (2001). Relapse prevention training and problem-solving therapy in the long-term management of obesity. *Journal of Consulting and Clinical Psychology, 69,* 722–726.

Pieber, T. R., Brunner, G. A., Schnedl, W. J., Schattenberg, S., Kaufmann, P., & Krejs, G. J. (1995). Evaluation of a structured outpatient group education program for intensive insulin therapy. *Diabetes Care, 18,* 625–630.

Piette, J. D. (1999). Patient education via automated calls: A study of English and Spanish speakers with diabetes. *American Journal of Prevtive Medicine, 17,* 138–141.

Piette, J. D., McPhee, S. J., Weinberger, M., Mah, C. A., & Kraemer, F. B. (1999). Use of automated telephone disease management calls in an ethnically diverse sample of low-income patients with diabetes. *Diabetes Care, 22,* 1302–1309.

Piette, J. D., Weinberger, M., Kraemer, F. B., & McPhee, S. J. (2001). Impact of automated calls with nurse follow-up on diabetes treatment outcomes in a Department of Veterans Affairs Health Care System: A randomized controlled trial. *Diabetes Care, 24,* 202–208.

Piette, J. D., Weinberger, M., & McPhee, S. J. (2000). The effect of automated calls with telephone nurse follow-up on patient-centered outcomes of diabetes care: A randomized, controlled trial. *Medical Care, 38,* 218–230.

Piette, J. D., Weinberger, M., McPhee, S. J., Mah, C. A., Kraemer, F. B., & Crapo, L. M. (2000). Do automated calls with nurse follow-up improve self-care and glycemic control among vulnerable patients with diabetes? *American Journal of Medicine, 108,* 20–27.

Reid, L., Hatch, J., & Parrish, T. (2003). Commentary: The role of a historically Black university and the Black church in community-based health initiatives: The Project DIRECT experience. *Journal of Public Health Management Practice, 9* (Suppl.), S70–S73.

Riley, K. M., Glasgow, R. E., & Eakin, E. G. (2001). Resources for health: A social-ecological intervention for supporting self-management of chronic conditions. *Journal of Health Psychology, 6,* 693–705.

Rosen, G. M., Glasgow, R. E., & Moore, T. E. (2003). Self-help therapy: The science and business of giving psychology away. In S. O. Lilienfeld, S. J. Lynn, & J. M. Lohr (Eds.), *Science and pseudoscience in clinical psychology* (pp. 399–424). New York: Guilford.

Rubin, R. R., Peyrot, M., & Saudek, C. D. (1989). Effect of diabetes education on self-care, metabolic control, and emotional well-being. *Diabetes Care, 12,* 673–679.

Rubin, R. R., Peyrot, M., & Saudek, C. D. (1993). The effect of a comprehensive diabetes education program incorporating coping skills training on emotional wellbeing and diabetes self-efficacy. *The Diabetes Educator, 19,* 210–214.

Santiago, J. V. (1993). Lessons from the Diabetes Control and Complications Trial. *Diabetes, 42,* 1549–1554.

Simmons, D., Gamble, G. D., Foote, S., Cole, D. R., & Coster, G. (2004). The New Zealand Diabetes Passport Study: A randomized controlled trial of the impact of a diabetes passport on risk factors for diabetes-related complications. *Diabetic Medicine, 21,* 214–217.

Stokols, D. (1996). Translating social ecological theory into guidelines for community health promotion. *American Journal of Health Promotion, 10,* 282–298.

Tate, D. F., Jackvony, E. H., & Wing, R. R. (2003). Effects of Internet behavioral counseling on weight loss in adults at risk for type 2 diabetes: A randomized trial. *Journal of the American Medical Association, 289,* 1833–1836.

Tate, D. F., Wing, R. R., & Winett, R. A. (2001). Using Internet technology to deliver a behavioral weight loss program. *Journal of the American Medical Association, 285,* 1172–1177.

The Diabetes Control and Complications Trial Research Group. (1993). The effect of intensive treatment of diabetes on the development and progression of long-term complications in insulin-dependent diabetes mellitus. *The New England Journal of Medicine, 329,* 977–986.

The Diabetes Control and Complications Trial Research Group. (1995). Implementation of treatment protocols in the Diabetes Control and Complications Trial. *Diabetes Care, 18,* 361–376.

Tuomilehto, J., Lindstrom, J., Eriksson, J. G., Valle, T. T., Hamalainen, H., Ilanne-Parikka, P., et al. (2001). Prevention of type 2 diabetes mellitus by changes in lifestyle among subjects with impaired glucose tolerance. *The New England Journal of Medicine, 344,* 1343–1350.

Turnin, M. C., Beddok, R. H., Clottes, J. P., Martini, P. F., Abadie, R. G., Buisson, J. C. et al. (1992). Telematic expert system Diabeto. New tool for diet self-monitoring for diabetic patients. *Diabetes Care, 15,* 204–212.

Wagner, E. H. (1998). Chronic disease management: What will it take to improve care for chronic illness. *Effective Clinical Practice, 1,* 1–4.

Wagner, E. H., Austin, B. T., & Von Korff, M. (1996). Organizing care for patients with chronic illness. *Milbank Quarterly, 74,* 511–544.

Warsi, A., Wang, P. S., LaValley, M. P., Avorn, J., & Solomon, D. H. (2004). Self-management education programs in chronic disease: A systematic review and methodological critique of the literature. *Archives of Internal Medicine, 164,* 1641–1649.

Wasson, J., Gaudette, C., Whaley, F., Sauvigne, A., Baribeau, P., & Welch, H. G. (1992). Telephone care as a substitute for routine clinic follow-up. *Journal of the American Medical Association, 267,* 1788–1793.

Weinberger, M., Kirkman, M. S., Samsa, G. P., Shortliffe, E. A., Landsman, P. B., Cowper, P. A., et al. (1995). A nurse-coordinated intervention for primary care patients with non-insulin-dependent diabetes mellitus: Impact on glycemic control and health-related quality of life. *Journal of General Internal Medicine, 10,* 59–66.

Young, R. J., Taylor, J., Friede, T., Hollis, S., Mason, J. M., Lee, P., et al. (2005). Proactive call center treatment support (PACCTS) to improve glucose control in type 2 diabetes: A randomized controlled trial. *Diabetes Care, 28,* 278–282.

Zhu, S. H., Stretch, V., Balabanis, M., Rosbrook, B., Sadler, G., & Pierce, J. P. (1996). Telephone counseling for smoking cessation: Effects of single-session and multiple-session interventions. *Journal of Consulting and Clinical Psychology, 64,* 202–211.

Zrebiec, J. F., & Jacobson, A. M. (2001). What attracts patients with diabetes to an Internet support group? A 21-month longitudinal website study. *Diabetic Medicine, 18,* 154–158.

Author Note

Edwin B. Fisher, Ph.D., Department of Health Behavior and Health Education, School of Public Health, University of North Carolina at Chapel Hill.

Supported by the Diabetes Initiative of The Robert Wood Johnson Foundation, by training grant T32 HL07456 from the National Heart, Lung and Blood Institute, and by research grant DP000098 from the Centers for Disease Control and Prevention.

CHAPTER 16

Self-Administered Therapies in Primary Care

NORAH VINCENT, JOHN R. WALKER AND ALAN KATZ

Consumers of health services have been taking a more active approach to their own health care. For example, Sirovatka (2002) reports that 7 million hits are registered every month on the National Institute of Mental Health (NIMH) homepage. Self-administered treatment in the primary care setting is a promising approach to broaden the choice of treatments and improve the quality of service for those with a wide array of health problems. In this chapter, we review characteristics of patients and problems seen in primary care, discuss what is known about patient and provider receptivity to self-administered treatments, describe the evidence concerning the effectiveness of these treatments in primary care, and consider some of the promising models that have been evaluated. We conclude by discussing strategies to disseminate self-administered treatments (self-help) into primary care. For the purposes of this chapter, self-administered treatments are defined as media-based approaches such as manuals, self-help books, audiotapes, videotapes, computer programs, Internet sites, or interactive voice response systems that allow for individuals to help themselves with minimal assistance from a primary care provider (Williams, 2003).

Are Primary Care Patients Different From Those Seen in Other Health Settings?

The range of problems encountered in the primary care setting is even more diverse than those seen in specialty medical and mental health settings. Table 16.1 summarizes findings concerning common physical and mental health conditions in primary care. A number of these problems have been the focus of self-administered treatment approaches. Primary care patients with mental health complaints may differ in important ways from patients seeking help in specialty mental health clinics. For example, primary care patients often have subsyndromal problems and, in the initial

Table 16.1 Rank Ordering of Most Common Physical and Mental Health Problems in Primary Care

Ranking (1 = most common)	Physical health (urban setting)[a]	Physical health (chronic conditions)[b]	Mental health[c]	Mental health[d]
1	Upper respiratory infection	Orthopedic	Major depression	Major depression
2	Hypertension	Chronic sinusitis	Alcohol abuse/ dependence	Generalized anxiety disorder
3	Otitis media	Arthritis	Agoraphobia	Neurasthenia
4	Lower respiratory infection	Hypertension	Generalized anxiety disorder	Alcohol abuse/dependence
5	Sinusitis	Hay fever/ allergic rhinitis	Panic disorder	Somatization disorder
6	Diabetes	Hearing impairment	Social phobia	Dysthymia
7	Sprains, strains	Cardiovascular disease	Drug abuse or dependence	Panic disorder
8	Lacerations, contusions	Bronchitis	Specific phobia	Agoraphobia
9	Cardiovascular disease	Asthma	Bipolar disorder, obsessive– compulsive disorder	Hypochondriasis
10	Chronic rhinitis	Headache	Antisocial personality disorder	Agoraphobia without panic

Note: [a]Probst et al. (2002), [b]Collins (1997). [c]Olfson et al. (1997), [d]Ustun (1994).

stages of assessment and treatment, there is often considerable diagnostic uncertainty. A recent study of 1555 primary care patients (Rucci et al., 2003) revealed that 14.9% of the sample had a subthreshold mood disorder and 15.7% a subthreshold anxiety disorder. Further, primary care patients may have different attitudes toward psychological interventions than patients seen in specialty mental health settings, For example, Proudfoot et al. (2004) studied patients with major depressive disorder being followed in primary care, attending a mental health center, or receiving no treatment. Relative to those attending a mental health center or receiving no treatment, patients followed by a primary care physician were more likely to decline treatment with antidepressant medication, individual psychotherapy, or group therapy.

Other studies have compared primary care patients to patients attending specialty medical clinics. Longstreth et al. (2001) evaluated 245 patients with irritable bowel syndrome and found that those who were being followed by a primary care physician, relative to those who were being followed by a gastroenterologist and to non-treatment-seekers, were more anxious, smoked more frequently, and consumed more alcohol. Lest one think that primary care patients are a homogeneous group, studies have shown that patient demographics vary widely from one primary care practice to another (Peabody & Luck, 1998; Probst, Moore, Baxley, & Lammie, 2002; Roy-Byrne, Russo, Cowley, & Katon, 2003). Any intervention should consider the needs of the population served.

How Receptive are Primary Care Patients to Self-Administered Treatment?

Patients have preferences for the type of treatment that they receive and many individuals prefer behavioral over pharmaceutical methods to address health and mental health difficulties. For example, Van Schaik et al. (2004) reviewed the literature on preference in primary care for treatments of major depression. Six studies were included in the review and all showed that primary care patients preferred psychotherapy to antidepressant medication, by a factor of no less than 2:1. Arean and Miranda (1996) evaluated 131 primary care patients' views about the acceptability of psychological treatments for medical problems, stress, and depression. Among distressed patients (i.e., those achieving a t score > 60 on any subscale of the Symptom Checklist-90, SCL-90; Derogatis, 1977), 68% indicated a willingness to attend a psychological group treatment for a medical problem, 64% for stress, and 63% for depression. Level of somatic symptoms did not predict willingness to attend a psychological group treatment.

Consumers typically engage in a high level of self-administered treatment for various health problems. Segall and Goldstein (1989) inquired about treatment preference for a variety of physical ailments using a randomly selected community sample of 524 adults. Participants were asked "What type of treatment would you use if you experienced this condition?" The conditions included feelings of dizziness, bowel irregularity, constant tiredness, frequent headaches, rash or itch, shortness of breath, unexplained loss of weight, difficulty sleeping at night, loss of appetite, and stomach upset/indigestion. Respondents indicated that they were more likely to use self-administered treatment with stomach upset, bowel irregularity, and difficulty sleeping, while for weight loss, shortness of breath, and frequent headaches they were more likely to choose to visit a physician. Being younger, unmarried, and female were associated with the intention to engage in self-administered treatment for common health problems. In the United Kindgom, Graham, Franses, Kenwright, and Marks (2000) posted a survey on an Internet Web site to assess opinions about self-help for obsessive–compulsive disorder and agoraphobia. Surveys were sent by mail to those who agreed to participate and there was a 35% return rate. Participants indicated (with a yes or no response) whether they would like access to self-administered treatment through any of several different modalities. A total of 91% gave a positive response to the idea of accessing self-administered treatment by computer (of these, 43% indicated a computer to be based at home and 23% at the primary care clinic), 35% endorsed Internet access, 56% indicated access through an interactive voice-response system, and 62% endorsed access through print materials. Thus, even though the sample was recruited through the Internet and so may have been particularly receptive to new technology, sizeable numbers of respondents were receptive to print-based manuals, computer-assisted treatment, and telephone interactive voice-response systems.

Williams (2003) discussed predictors of outcome in self-help and indicated that those who have negative attitudes toward the self-help format, poor concentration and memory, and weak visual processing would be least likely to benefit from self-help. These authors suggest that those with an internal locus of control and more self-efficacy are the best candidates for self-administered treatments.

How Receptive Are Primary Care Physicians to Self-Administered Treatment?

Much less is known about the views concerning self-administered treatment among primary care physicians. Richards, Lovell, and McEvoy (2003) acknowledge that the general practitioner is often faced with limited remuneration or incentive for supporting self-help mental health care. Short consultations arising from pharmacological treatment are more economically rewarding. Pragmatically, primary care physicians are pressed for time, with the average primary care consultation being 15 minutes (Taylor, Jobson, Winzelberg, & Abascal, 2002). Primary care practices are often limited in physical space and support staff. There is an understandable lack of awareness and training about empirically supported self-administered treatments.

In order to consider provider opinions and concerns related to self-administered treatment in primary care, we conducted a focus group with five primary care physicians in a suburban practice in Winnipeg, Canada, a medium-sized city. The participants were 3 females and 2 males with from 2 to 15 years of practice who were graduates of Canadian or international medical schools. The focus group was one-hour in length and conducted by the third author (AK). Five questions were posed to the group, focusing on experiences with self-help, effectiveness of self-administered treatment, selection of self-help materials, use of Web sites, and barriers to the use of self-help in primary care. (See Table 16.2 for a summary of responses.) Analysis of the focus group transcript suggested that the participants were very supportive of self-administered treatments and viewed recommendations regarding self-help materials to be part of the physician–educator role. Brochures and other brief print materials were the most widely used resources and physicians indicated that they had limited knowledge of self-help resources. They recommended the development of a Website that centralized self-help resources for the purpose of increasing awareness of self-help materials. The group identified a number of barriers to the use of self-administered treatments described in Table 16.2. They also expressed concern about the quality of some of the information available on the Internet.

How Effective Is Self-Help in Primary Care?

Meta-analytic reviews of the efficacy of self-administered treatments (Bower, Richards, & Lovell, 2001; Cavanagh & Shapiro, 2004; Cuijpers, 1997; Gould & Clum, 1993; Scogin, Bynum, Stephens, & Calhoon, 1990) conclude that self-administered treatment is significantly more effective than no treatment for problems ranging from fears, depression, headache, insomnia, social skills, parent–child training, to sexual dysfunction. This effect extends to follow-up periods of several months. Surprisingly, several studies have found that self-administered treatment is as effective as therapist-administered treatment (Cuijpers, 1997; Gould & Clum, 1993; Marrs, 1995; Scogin et al., 1990) with the effect sizes for self-administered

Table 16.2 Physicians' Opinions Concerning Self-Administered Treatment in Primary Care: A Focus Group Study

Perceptions of efficacy of self-administered approaches	Physicians viewed this as an important issue but lacked information regarding the efficacy of self-administered approaches. Instead, physicians were generally satisfied that self-help was efficacious if patients returned for follow-up appointments, if patients told them that the material was helpful, or if patients showed improvement in their health condition after receiving self-help materials
Selection of self-administered materials	Physicians had very limited knowledge about the availability of self-administered resources for problems common in primary care. They were familiar with some self-help materials supplied to them by pharmaceutical representatives
Web site use in primary care	Physicians were receptive to considering the use of Internet sites for the provision of health-related treatment. There was limited knowledge about which sites were appropriate and which sites were popular with patients. There was concern about patients making premature diagnoses based on Web-site information and about poor quality information on some sites. Physicians felt that the use of Internet sites added time to the consultation appointment when patients have questions about the site but they may save time overall
Barriers to the use of self-help resources	Five barriers were identified and these were as follows: lack of knowledge about self-help resources, limited availability and few guidelines for the use of self-help materials, cost of self-help materials, lack of culturally sensitive self-help materials

treatment ranging from .96 to 1.08 and for self-administered treatment with additional minimal therapist contact ranging from 1.16 to 1.19, a nonsignificant difference (Gould & Clum, 1993; Scogin et al., 1990). Many of the larger studies have used participants recruited through the media or specialty mental health clinics. These individuals may be more receptive to psychological interventions than the primary care population (Proudfoot et al., 2004). Bower and colleagues (2001) conducted a meta-analysis of the effectiveness of self-help for anxiety and depressive disorders in primary care using a small sample of six studies. Results showed that the average effect size for self-administered treatments was only .41, with a range from −.18 to 1.18. A recent update of this literature shows that there have been few studies of the effectiveness of self-administered treatments in primary care and the quality of the studies varies widely. Many of the primary care investigations have lacked a well-defined sample (with very loose inclusion criteria), appropriate sample sizes, sophisticated statistical methods, and adequate randomization procedures (at times physicians chose which patients to approach about the study and which condition to assign).

Table 16.3 describes the 17 experimental investigations of the efficacy of self-administered treatment in primary care identified in our review of the literature. The studies focus on a range of problems: anxiety (41%, $n = 7$), mixed anxiety and depression (24%, $n = 4$), depression (12%, $n = 2$), chronic fatigue (6%, $n = 1$), hypertension (6%, $n = 1$), diabetes (6%, $n = 1$), and bulimia nervosa (6%, $n = 1$). A wide range of approaches are described in these studies including self-help brochures, booklets, and books; audiotape relaxation exercises; computer-based programs; and Web-based computer programs.

Models of Self-Administered Treatment in Primary Care Settings

Traditional Text Material

The most widely evaluated forms of self-administered treatment in primary care involve the use of traditional text materials. Kiely and McPherson (1986) studied the efficacy of six leaflets containing information on the causes, consequences, and control of stress. Patients were invited to participate by their primary care physician if they presented with stress-related problems. The package was administered to participants at the end of the consultation appointment and posttreatment assessment was conducted 12 weeks after recruitment. Those who received the bibliotherapy reported better health, less stress, and fewer consultations for psychological problems relative to controls. There were no group differences in the number of medications prescribed. Unfortunately, the randomization process in this study was unclear and there was no pretreatment data collection. It is difficult to determine whether the groups were similar in terms of general health and stress scores at the outset of the study.

Donnan and colleagues (Donnan, Hutchinson, Paxton, Grant, & Firth, 1990) created a self-help booklet and tape for those with chronic anxiety that provided education about anxiety, assistance with problem-solving, instruction on applied relaxation, suggestions for better coping with worry and panic attacks, and assistance in evaluating personal expectations. The audiotape duplicated information in the booklet and provided detailed instructions about relaxation exercises. Self-help participants, relative to controls, had greater pre-post test reductions in anxiety and depression and improvements in general health problems. Results from a 3-month follow-up revealed that self-help participants, relative to controls, had

Table 16.3 Effect Sizes of Self-Administered Treatments in Primary Care

Authors	n	Sample description	Dropout (%)	Self-help modality	Primary dependent variable	Effect size (Cohen's d)
Text-based materials						
Kiely & McPherson (1986)	27	Stress-related problem	3.7	12 weeks with 6 leaflets with information about stress vs. treatment as usual	stress improvement rating	Leaflet = .93 Treatment as usual could not be calculated
Milne & Covitz (1988)	22	Clinical anxiety (not diagnosed)	18	4 weeks with 35-page self-help manual (*Anxiety: How to Understand and Control Your Nerves*) vs. two-page informational leaflet vs. wait-list control	STAI	Manual: state = .35 trait = .04 Leaflet: state = .13 trait = .16 Waiting-list control: state = −.07 trait = .17
Donnan et al. (1990)	101	Chronic anxiety (not diagnosed)	39	6 weeks of 27-page self-help booklet and audiotape vs. treatment as usual	Leeds Self-Assessment Specific Anxiety Scale	NA
Sorby, Reavley, & Huber (1991)	64	DSM-III panic disorder, phobic avoidance, or generalized anxiety disorder diagnosis disorder	6	8 weeks with self-help booklet (*Anxiety: An Explanation and Self-Help Manual*) vs. treatment as usual	HAD-Anxiety subscale	Booklet = 7.88 Treatment as usual = 3.65

Study	N	Inclusion criteria	Intervention	Measure	Results
White (1995)	62	Anxiety disorder diagnosis (any); SCL-90-R ≥ 63; HAD ≥ 11	12 weeks of 79-page self-help booklet and relaxation audiotape (*Stresspac*) vs. advice-only vs. no treatment	HAD	*Stresspac* = 3.68 Advice only = 1.9 No treatment = 1.08
Holdsworth et al. (1996)	62	Mixed anxiety or depressive, anxiety, or depressive disorder	4 weeks with a 42-page self-help booklet (*Managing Anxiety and Depression: A Self-Help Guide*) vs. treatment as usual	HAD	NA
Chalder, Wallace, & Wessely (1997)	150	Chronic fatigue; Fatigue Questionnaire ≥ 4; fatigued for >6 months	12 weeks with self-help booklet (*Coping With Chronic Fatigue*) vs. no treatment	Fatigue measure	Booklet = 10.91 No treatment = 7.26
Reid, Maher & Jennings (2000)	45	Primary hypertension (controlled); systolic blood pressure ≤ 160 mmHG and/or diastolic blood pressure ≤ 95 mmHg	9 months of self-help booklet focusing on exercise and diet vs. treatment as usual (hypertensive medication)	systolic blood pressure	Booklet: -.53 Treatment as usual: -.44
Whitfield, Williams & Shapiro, 2001	42	Symptoms of anxiety and/or depression (physician selected)	6 sessions of self-help manual (*Mind Over Mood*) (no control group)	GHQ-28 (total)	1.38
Walsh, Fairburn, Mickley, Sysko, & Parides (2004)	91	Modified version of DSM-IV bulimia nervosa	15 weeks of guided self-help and placebo, guided self-help and fluoxetine, fluoxetine, or placebo	EDE (subjective bulimic episodes per month)	Self-help and placebo: .25 Self-help and Fluoxetine: .13 Fluoxetine: .63 Placebo: .54

(continued)

Table 16.3 (continued)

Authors	n	Sample description	Dropout (%)	Self-help modality	Primary dependent variable	Effect size (Cohen's d)
Computer-based programs						
White, Jones, & McGarry (2000)	33	Anxiety disorder diagnosis (any); HAD ≥ 8	15	Three sessions with *Stresspac* computer program (no control group)	HAD	1.30
Proudfoot et al. (2003)	167	Anxiety and/or depression; GHQ-12 ≥ 4; CIS-R ≥ 12	8.4	8 sessions with a computer program (*Beating the Blues*) vs. treatment as usual	BDI	*Beating the Blues = 1.21* Treatment as usual = .58
Proudfoot et al., (2004)	274	Depression, mixed anxiety and depression, or anxiety disorder; GHQ-12 ≥ 4; CIS-R >12	22	8 weeks of computerized CBT (*Beating the Blues*) vs. treatment as usual	BDI-II	*Beating the Blues = 1.19* Treatment as usual = .68
Marks et al. (2004)	93	DSM-IV agoraphobia, panic disorder with agoraphobia, social phobia, simple phobia; phobia subscale of Fear Questionnaire ≥ 4	27	10 weeks of computer-guided self-exposure (*Fear Fighter*) vs. clinician-guided self-exposure vs. stand-alone computer and audiotape-guided self-relaxation without exposure	Fear Questionnaire-Global Phobia scale (blind assessor rated)	*Fear Fighter = 2.09* Clinician-guided self-exposure = 1.92 Stand-alone computer and audiotape = .25

Web-based programs

Glasgow et al. (2003)	320	Type II diabetes	18	10 months of Internet-based tailored self-management vs. Internet-based peer support vs. Internet-based basic information	Kristal Fat and Fiber Behavior scale	Tailored self-management =.57 Peer support = .46 Basic information=.54
Interactive voice response						
Osgood-Hynes et al. (1998)	41	Major depression or dysthymia	32	12 session IVR adaptation of *COPE* (no control group)	HAM-D	1.3

Note: Effect sizes were calculated using Cohen's d (M pretreatment – M posttreatment/Sd pretreatment) and can be categorized as small (d = .2.), medium (d = .5), or large (d = .80) (Cohen, 1992). BDI = Beck Depression Inventory, BDI-II = Beck Depression Inventory II (Beck, Steer, & Brown, 1996); CIS-R = Clinical Interview Schedule—Revised (Lewis, 1994); Fear Questionnaire (Marks & Mathews, 1979); GHQ-12 = General Health Questionnaire (Goldberg, 1972); GHQ-28 = General Health Questionnaire (Goldberg & Hillier, 1979); HAD = Hospital Anxiety and Depression Scale (Zigmond & Snaith, 1983); HAM-D = Hamilton Rating Scale for Depression (Hamilton, 1967); Kristal Fat and Fiber Behavior scale (Kristal, Shattuck, & Henry, 1990); Leeds Self-Assessment Specific Anxiety and Depression scales (Snaith, Bridge, & Hamilton, 1970); SCL-90-R = Symptom Checklist 90—Revised (Derogatis, 1977); STAI = State-Trait Anxiety Inventory (Spielberger, O'Neil, & Hansen, 1970).

significant further improvements in depression but not in anxiety or general health problems. Although the assignment was described as random, it was actually nonrandom because practitioners selected patients and assigned them to conditions. These problems in design reduce confidence in the conclusions of the study.

Sorby, Reavley, and Huber (1991) evaluated the efficacy of their own self-help manual compared to treatment as usual for adult primary care patients with an anxiety disorder. The manual provided education about anxiety and avoidance, illustrated coping strategies, and materials to monitor progress. Participants were randomly assigned to the two study conditions and evaluated after 2, 4, and 8 weeks. Those in the self-administered condition showed more rapid improvement in anxiety than the control condition. Although not discussed in the report, tabulated data seemed to suggest that there were similar reductions in the dependent measures for both groups at the 8-week follow-up point. Milne and Covitz (1988) randomly assigned primary care patients with clinical anxiety to 4 weeks with a self-help manual, a two-page health educational leaflet, or a waiting list. The study found only a trend toward improvement in state and trait anxiety and in ratings of fear but was limited by a small sample size.

Holdsworth and colleagues (Holdsworth, Paxton, Seidel, Thomson, & Shrubb, 1996) evaluated the effectiveness of a self-help booklet on managing anxiety and depression compared to treatment as usual in primary care patients with anxiety, depression, or mixed anxiety and depression. Those in the self-administered treatment group showed greater improvement in anxiety and more reduction in the frequency of anxiolytic medication use. No improvements were found in areas of depressive symptoms, general health, or style of coping. At a 3-month follow-up, no significant group differences were observed, suggesting that improvements in anxiety were short-lived.

Another low-tech model of implementing self-administered treatments in a primary care setting involves the development of a self-help library within the clinic that stores self-help manuals, worksheets, and other materials. Whitfield, Williams, and Shapiro (2001) described an uncontrolled study of the use of a self-help room for primary care patients with symptoms of anxiety or depression who were waiting for an in-person mental health appointment. Nurses spent 20 minutes with participants to illustrate how best to use the manual *Mind Over Mood: Change How You Feel by Changing the Way You Think* (Greenberg & Padesky, 1995) and other materials. Participants were asked to use the room for 1-hour weekly appointments for 6 weeks. Only 22 of 42 patients actually attended, but there were significant pre-post treatment improvements in feelings of hopelessness, dysfunctional attitudes, and general health in the 20 patients that completed the treatment.

There has been very little research in primary care concerning self-administered treatments for problems other than stress, anxiety, and depression. Chalder, Wallace, and Wessely (1997) evaluated the efficacy of a self-help book, *Coping with Chronic Fatigue* (Chalder, 1995), in primary care patients with complaints of fatigue. Patients were recruited for the study if they were in the age range of 18–45 years with a duration of fatigue problems of greater than 6 months and if they exceeded a cutoff score on a fatigue questionnaire. Twelve percent fulfilled Oxford criteria for chronic fatigue syndrome and 52% had been given a psychiatric diagnosis. The book provided information about fatigue, self-monitoring, cognitive and behavioral coping strategies, activity pacing, suggestions to improve sleep, and a description of how to identify and challenge unhelpful thoughts. After 3 months, those who received the book experienced more improvement in both physical and mental fatigue and more improvement in general health than no treatment controls. At the follow-up point, 63% of those in the self-administered treatment group and 39% in the control group were considered to be relatively free of fatigue.

Reid, Maher, and Jennings (2000) examined the effectiveness a self-help booklet in primary care patients with hypertension who were well controlled on drug therapy. Participants were randomly assigned to continue to receive medication or to be discontinued and receive the booklet. The self-administered program focused on changing dietary intake and incorporating regular exercise, based on the stages of change model (Prochaska & diClemente, 1983). At 9 months follow-up, 71% of participants in the self-help group remained off of hypertensive medication and were well controlled; however, similar data for the control group were not provided. There were no group differences in systolic or diastolic blood pressure, total cholesterol, triglyceride, or body mass index. This study was interesting because it also examined some of the difficulties with practitioner implementation and patient acceptance of self-administered treatment. The ten primary care physicians in the project subsequently participated in a focus group to evaluate the acceptability of the self-help approach. Practitioners indicated that deterrents to offering lifestyle advice to patients were a view that patients were not motivated for change and that physicians lacked personal knowledge about how to promote such lifestyle changes. Impediments to adherence on the part of participants were also assessed and found to be the presence of family and work stress and a devaluing of the importance of self-help.

Computer-Based Programs

Stresspac   White and colleagues (1995) developed this program in print format and eventually created a computer-delivered version. The original Stresspac (SP) consisted of a self-help booklet and relaxation audiotape, primarily focused on the treatment of generalized anxiety. The program included cognitive therapy techniques based on work by Beck and Emery (1985) and Meichenbaum (1985), relaxation training based on protocols of Bernstein and Borkovec (1973), education and emphasis on exposure, and help with relapse prevention. White (1995) screened primary care patients using a structured clinical interview, the Anxiety Disorder Interview Schedule—Revised (DiNardo & Barlow, 1988), before random assignment to an advice only group (AO), a no-intervention control group (NI), or Stresspac (SP). Participants had a range of anxiety disorder diagnoses, the most common being generalized anxiety disorder and panic disorder. Those receiving Stresspac experienced more improvement in depression and anxiety relative to those in the control conditions. These results were maintained at a 12 month follow-up. Although there were no group differences in the number of general practitioner consultations, those assigned to Stresspac required significantly fewer subsequent therapy appointments (SP 3.8 appointments, AO 6 appointments, NI 5.4 appointments). Clinically significant improvement was seen in 38% of participants in SP, 10% in the AO condition, and 5% in the NI condition. A further 3-year follow-up study showed that those in the SP condition, relative to the control conditions, were more likely to rate themselves as better or much better (White, 1998). The authors concluded that Stresspac was superior to advice only and no treatment at all points in time. White, Jones, and McGarry (2000) subsequently created a computerized CD-ROM version of Stresspac, which they evaluated using primary care patients with anxiety disorders. The program was offered in the primary care clinic and a research assistant remained with the participant during all three computer sessions to provide assistance if needed. Clinically significant improvement was evident in 20% of participants at posttreatment and 50% of participants at follow-up. Comments suggested that participants appreciated the prompt availability of computerized help, the privacy of the interaction, the flexibility of appointment times, and the possibility of working on the program at convenient times, and 83% reported that they would recommend this program to others.

Beating the Blues   Proudfoot and colleagues (Proudfoot et al., 2004; Proudfoot, Goldberg, et al., 2003; Proudfoot, Swain, et al., 2003) evaluated a multimedia computerized package, *Beating the Blues*, in primary care patients with anxiety and/or depression. Proudfoot and colleagues (2004) randomly assigned 274 primary care patients with a depressive disorder, anxiety disorder, or mixed depressive–anxiety disorder to receive *Beating the Blues* or treatment as usual. Participants receiving *Beating the Blues* came to the clinic weekly to complete the program and a clinic nurse helped to troubleshoot the printouts and booked the next sessions. On average, nurses spent less than 5 minutes with each patient after the initial session. Printouts highlighting the session summary, homework tasks, progress report, and date of next session were made available to both patient and physician. Those in the *Beating the Blues* program had significant improvements on symptoms of depression and anxiety, attributions for aversive situations, and impairment in areas of work and leisure compared to those receiving treatment as usual.

The PACE Program   This program, focused on exercise and diet, provides one of the best models of self-help delivery in primary care. The Physician-based Assessment and Counseling for Exercise (PACE) program was developed in a survey format to enhance the activity level of adults in primary care settings (Long et al., 1996). Subsequent refinements of the program led to the development of the Patient-Centred Assessment and Counseling for Exercise plus Nutrition (PACE+) program, which was designed to promote physical activity and improve nutrition in adolescents and adults (Prochaska, Zabinski, Calfas, Saliis, & Patrick, 2000). The program can be completed in a relatively brief period of time (30–45 minutes) by patients and has been used in the primary care waiting room prior to an appointment with a physician. PACE+ was designed to screen for multiple behaviors and prioritize areas for change. The program has screening items to assess physical activity level and dietary behaviors (intake of fat, fruit, and vegetables) and to identify patients at risk for disturbed eating practices. Patients not meeting national guidelines for diet and exercise and who are ready to make changes are encouraged to select one physical activity and one dietary behavior to target for change. Patients who meet health guidelines are encouraged to create plans for relapse prevention. The PACE+ action and relapse-prevention plans identify the benefits of change, specific goals, strategies to reduce barriers to change, and persons who can support movement toward the goal. The program is unique in that it provides over 1000 combinations for each action or relapse-prevention plan, allowing for tailoring to the individual. Action and relapse-prevention plans are printed for the patient. A single-page provider summary report for review during the visit identifies the changes that the patient is planning and highlights areas of concern that may require more extensive discussion with the provider.

Prochaska and colleagues (2000) evaluated patient and provider satisfaction with the PACE+ program in a sample of 224 adolescents and 281 adults from 12 primary care clinics. The program was well liked and well understood by patients. The intervention was economical in terms of provider time, requiring an average of 5–8 minutes of discussion. Adolescents rated the program more favorably, with 68% of adolescents but only 45% of adults reporting that the program was helpful or very helpful in changing behavior. Unfortunately, behavior change was not assessed in this study. A sample of providers and office staff ($n = 28$) evaluated PACE+ and reported a high level of satisfaction with the program and with how it was integrated into the primary care setting. PACE+ stands out as an innovative approach to lifestyle intervention.

Interactive Voice-Response (IVR) Systems

The COPE Program   Other computer applications in primary care have occurred at a distance. Osgood-Hynes et al. (1998) evaluated the COPE program involving 12 sessions of telephone-accessed computer intervention plus a self-help booklet in patients with dysthymia or major depression recruited from primary care and mental health settings. The program included an introductory videotape, nine self-help booklets, and 11 toll-free calls to the interactive voice-response (IVR) system. Upon visiting the clinic to enroll, patients were screened and viewed the videotape, were informed about the COPE program, and participated in a trial run on the IVR system by making two telephone calls. The remaining calls into the system were completed from the patient's home. Patients were instructed to work through the self-help booklets at home and to call into the IVR when requested. The IVR contacts reinforced the homework, provided role-play opportunities, gave recommendations and feedback based on the patients' individual responses, and provided an opportunity to request clinical feedback for specific problems. Clinicians with the program provided feedback by recording responses on the system. The program description does not indicate that there is a mechanism for feedback to primary care providers concerning performance in the program The COPE IVR system contained more than 700 text segments and patients' responses determined which segments were heard. The IVR was available 7 days a week and was accessed by an ID number and password. Results were very promising in that 68% of participants completed the program and 64% of treatment completers had at least a 50% reduction in their depression scores. Patients who made more calls to the IVR system achieved better outcomes. While the COPE program with its IVR component is one of the more expensive ways to deliver self-administered treatment, it has demonstrated impressive outcomes.

Web-Based Systems

MySelfHelp.com   This is one of the most well developed Web-based programs, with modules for depression, grief, eating disorders, compulsive behaviors, guilt, self-esteem issues, and stress management (Bedrosian,

2004). The program is designed as a complement to work with a health service provider, although it may also be used as a freestanding self-help program. Providers are encouraged to refer patients to the Web site and, in turn, participants are encouraged to share summary information about their functioning with the health care provider. The program has been the focus of extensive input by mental health specialists. Considering the content on depression, for example, the program includes education about depression, evidence-based medication and psychological treatments, misconceptions about treatment, changing distorted thinking, changing basic beliefs and attitudes, behavioral activation, increasing compliance with treatment (pharmacological or psychological), and maintaining treatment gains. Unlimited access to all of the programs is provided for $15 per month. The Web site includes clinician guides to assist the clinician in using the program, including tip sheets about specific aspects of the program that may be of interest to specific patients. We are not aware of any published evaluations of MySelfHelp.com.

FearFighter.com   This program was developed to increase the availability of services for phobic anxiety by delegating many clinical tasks to the computer program and reducing therapist contact time. Access to the system is by ID number and password that are provided by the clinician (typically a general practitioner) and is provided for 13 weeks after the first login. The program provides feedback on progress to the patient and the clinician. While the program is currently being used in a number of primary care settings in the United Kingdom, the only large-scale evaluation was carried out in a specialty mental health clinic with recruiting advertisements in primary care offices or self-help services (Marks et al., 2004). Individuals who were screened by a clinician and found to have agoraphobia, social phobia, or specific phobia were assigned to the computer-guided self-exposure program (FearFighter; $N = 37$), clinician guided self-exposure with a similar emphasis ($N = 39$), and a computer- and audiotape-guided relaxation program ($N = 17$). The relaxation program had a significantly lower drop out rate (6%) than FearFighter (43%) and the clinician-guided programs (24%), which did not differ significantly from each other. Some participants who dropped out reported that they left the program because of technical problems, while others felt that they learned how to improve with self-exposure and it was too bothersome to attend again. Considering treatment completers, the two self-exposure conditions had comparable improvement and satisfaction at posttreatment assessment and one month follow-up, whereas the relaxation condition showed little clinical improvement in measures of phobic avoidance. Including both completers and dropouts, average therapist contact time was 76 minutes in the computer-guided relaxation program, 76 minutes in the FearFighter program, and 283 minutes in the clinician-guided program. This research group (Marks et al., 2003) also reported positive findings in an open trial of computer-guided treatment for phobic anxiety, depression, OCD, and generalized anxiety.

MoodGYM This Web-based program for depressed mood has been under development by a group at the Centre for Mental Health Research of the Australian National University (http://moodgym.anu.edu.au/). Following a preliminary open trial with promising results (Christensen, Griffiths, & Korten, 2002), a controlled trial was carried out with a sample of 525 individuals with elevated depression symptoms identified in a community epidemiological survey (Christensen, Griffiths, & Jorm, 2004). Three conditions were compared in the study: the MoodGYM Internet program, an Internet educational program concerning depression and its treatment (BluePages), and an active control condition. In the control condition, participants received weekly telephone calls over the 6-week duration of the study to discuss lifestyle and environmental factors that may have an influence on depression. Interestingly, a brief survey of intervention preference at the preassessment phase indicated that the telephone contact condition had the highest level of preference. Considering changes in depression from pre- to postassessment, effect sizes in an intent-to-treat analysis were 0.4, 0.4, and 0.1 for the MoodGYM, BluePages, and control conditions. For the completer analysis, effect sizes were larger: 0.6, 0.5, and 0.1, and for those with initial depression scores in the clearly clinically significant range the effect sizes for the three groups were 0.9, 0.75, and 0.25. The results of both the CBT (MoodGYM) and the educational (BluePages) program in this well-designed study were impressive. The program is currently under evaluation as a resource to primary care providers in Australia.

Diabetes Network Project Glasgow, Boles, McKay, Feil, and Barrera (2003) describe the evaluation of a Web-based program focused on diabetes self-management in a representative sample of primary care patients with type 2 diabetes. This was a challenging group due to their limited computer experience—the average age was 59 years and 83% had no or limited experience with use of the Internet. Brief Internet training (3–6 hours) was provided as part of the orientation to the study. Three levels of support were evaluated in the study. In the information only condition, participants completed assessments on-line and received automated dietary change goals based on their current dietary levels. They also had access through the Web site to an extensive collection of articles on medical, nutritional, and lifestyle aspects of diabetes. The articles gave information only and did not systematically instruct patients or provide individually tailored recommendations for behavior change. Participants in the remaining conditions received the information only program as a base with additional components. In the tailored self-management condition, participants had access to a professional coach who had expertise in providing dietary advice for diabetes. Access to the coach was provided twice each week. The coach negotiated dietary goals with the participants and provided advice and encouragement. Participants could enter individual data on food intake and blood glucose and receive graphical feedback on performance. Participants in the peer support condition had access to a peer-directed but professionally monitored forum where they could post messages concerning their experiences with coping with diabetes as well as chat discussions and topic forums related to coping with diabetes.

The outcome assessment considered changes from baseline assessment to follow-up after 10 months of access to the Internet resources. Participants in all three conditions showed improvement over time in behavioral (self-reported fat intake), psychosocial (depression, support, and barriers to change), and some biological outcomes (lipids). There were few differences among the conditions and the addition of coaching or peer support did not significantly improve results. The study did not include a condition involving treatment as usual, so it was not possible to rule out secular trends or placebo effects as an explanation for the change over time. The authors report, however, that the magnitude of change seen in this study are comparable to previous findings by the same research group with interventions using face-to-face coaching and considerably larger than the changes seen with treatment as usual. Glasgow and his colleagues have been very active in evaluating the use of interactive behavior change technology in primary care for a variety of health concerns and have produced some very helpful recommendations for research and practice (Glasgow, Bull, Piette, & Steiner, 2004; Glasgow, Goldstein, Ockene, & Pronk, 2004).

Stepped-Care Approach

The use of self-administered treatment is often advocated in models using a stepped-care approach. In stepped care, the first treatment offered to suitable patients is a low-cost, self-administered treatment. Higher levels of intervention (specialist consultation, brief individual treatment, group treatment, or longer term treatment) are reserved for patients who have not made good progress with lower levels of care. This approach has been used thus far in the treatment of eating disorders (Wilson, Vitousek, & Loeb, 2000), alcohol problems (Sobell & Sobell, 2000), generalized anxiety disorder (Newman, 2000), and panic disorder (Otto, Pollack, & Maki, 2000), although not in primary care settings. Scogin, Hanson, and Welsh

(2003) argue that self-administered treatments would make ideal first steps in stepped behavioral health care for mild to moderate depression in primary care settings. The success of such a stepped-care approach depends on the primary care provider's willingness to participate in self-administered treatment and the development of a user-friendly system to monitor patients' progress.

Advantages and Challenges of Formats for Delivering Self-Administered Treatments

There are promising studies in support of each of the approaches to providing self-administered treatment outlined above. A challenge for the future is to identify which approaches are most useful in which settings and for which populations and to develop models for dissemination. Table 16.4 describes advantages and challenges associated with each of the formats for delivering self-administered treatment. There is unlikely to be one right approach for every setting. With the tremendous increase in access to the Internet, this format may hold particular promise. At this point, it is possible to access self-administered treatments for depression, anxiety, and a variety of other health problems from anywhere in the world. While at one time computer and Internet use were limited to those who were technologically oriented, young, and prosperous, this is no longer the case. Health care providers, especially those who have been trained recently, are familiar with the use of the Internet to access information and research. The Internet has a very wide geographic reach and stores vast amounts of information that may be reviewed and printed as necessary. The quality of the information, however, varies from very high to dubious and it may be difficult for consumers to evaluate the source and the quality of information. A challenge for computer and Internet formats has been to develop economic models that support the dissemination of existing programs and the development of new and more sophisticated resources. As an example, the FearFighter program and other programs evaluated in a computer CBT clinic were very cost-effective, but the clinic closed when government funding ran out (Gega, Marks, & Mataix-Cols, 2004). The developers of the MySelfHelp.com Web site have received development support from the National Institute of Mental Health but they are still working to establish an economic model that will allow the program to become self-sustaining and to continue to develop new materials (Bedrosian, 2004).

Self-administered treatments that require the use of computer technology face specific challenges in primary care. Mitchell and Sullivan (2001) reviewed the literature on primary care computing between 1980 and 1997. While this review focused on computerized assessment, these findings may also apply to physicians' concerns about patients' use of computerized self-administered treatments. Most practitioners expressed concerns about the cost of computers, the amount of physician time involved in learning to use the computer programs, the confidentiality of health records, the negative effects on the physician–patient relationship (e.g., reluctance of patients to discuss problems if the material was to be entered into a computer), and a perception that computers might take over the role of a physician. Shakeshaft and Frankish (2003) argue that in many cases the initial introduction of computerized assessment in clinical settings resulted in an increase in physicians' workload and the gathering of unnecessary information. These authors speculate that the degree to which computer technologies are adopted in primary care in the future will depend on whether the creators can reduce the uncertainty associated with the technology, persuade physicians about the positive features, tailor the service and provide technical assistance to meet a particular need, and provide follow-up support. Involving primary care staff in the development of the resources and selecting academically oriented practices to pilot new approaches may facilitate the development of effective resources.

In contrast to the difficulty associated with establishing an economic model for computer- and Web-based programs, the traditional book publishing industry continues to be very active in publishing self-administered treatment materials. Most bookstores have a very large self-help section and books and related materials may now also be ordered through Internet booksellers. Unfortunately, only a small proportion of this information is directly accessible through primary care sites and many of the programs have not been thoroughly evaluated.

Dissemination of Self-Administered Treatments in Primary Care

The challenge of disseminating new knowledge and technologies into primary care settings is widely recognized. While there has often been a reliance on the publication of clinical trials to provide information to clinicians about improved assessment and treatment practices, it appears that the publication process (the evidence for evidence-based practice) has a limited impact on practice in the field (Majumdar, McAlister, & Soumerai, 2003; Stirman, Crits-Cristoph, & DeRubeis, 2004). Beyond the publication process, the next most commonly used approach to dissemination has been the use of continuing professional education for professionals. A systematic review of continuing medical education practices by Davis, Thomson, Oxman, and Haynes (1995) suggested that traditional professional education approaches involving seminars, lectures, and guidelines also have had limited impact on practice. As an example, the Hampshire Depression Project, a large clinical trial, examined whether education

Table 16.4 Advantages and Challenges of Different Approaches to Disseminating Self-Administered Interventions in Primary Care

Format	Advantages	Challenges[a]
Limited-production text materials	Material may be focused on local concerns and resources No computer resources required	Time consuming to produce and keep up to date Limited distribution Space required for inventory
Commercially available books	Existing distribution system through bookstores and Internet Very wide range of materials available	Challenge to become familiar with materials on a wide range of topics Quality of books varies, reading level varies More difficult to tailor the program to the needs of the patient
Computer-based programs (e.g., CD)	Easier to control distribution of materials Modest cost to patient Programs may be interactive and branching—responding to the patient's data and interests May include some audio and video material	Computer and printer access is required Younger people are more familiar with this format, older people are often less familiar Challenging to find an economic model to recover the cost of production and dissemination High initial development costs
Web-based programs	Very widely distributed (internationally) for those who have resources Ease of modifying and adding to content to keep up to date Modest cost to patient Programs may be interactive and branching—responding to the patient's data and interests May include some audio and video material Development tools are available in many health and educational settings	Computer, printer, and Internet access is required Younger people are more familiar with this format, older people are often less familiar Challenging to find an economic model to recover the cost of production and dissemination Variable quality in publicly available material High initial development costs

Table 16.4 (*continued*)

Format	Advantages	Challenges[a]
Interactive voice-response programs	Telephone technology is widely available Patients have evaluated interactive aspect positively Wide geographic reach within a region	Program development requires specialized skills and resources that are available on a limited basis High initial cost of development Programs are often supplemented by text material Long-distance telephone charges required for wider geographic distribution. This cost may be borne by the patient or the provider

Note: [a] A challenge for all of the approaches is limited evaluation of the interventions, particularly in primary care.

(a 4-hour interactive seminar with videotaped examples and availability of follow-up consultation) delivered to practice teams along with the use of clinical guidelines would improve recognition and treatment of depression in primary care. Results were disappointing: the sensitivity of detection of depression was 39% in the intervention group and 36% in the control group, a nonsignificant difference (Thompson et al., 2000).

On the other hand, a number of more active approaches to dissemination have been shown to have more impact on practice. For example, the involvement of local clinical opinion leaders in providing education about guidelines and identifying problems with the implementation of new practices have been shown to be effective when used as part of a comprehensive approach to quality improvement (Borbas, Morris, McLaughlin, Asinger, & Gobel, 2000). Active marketing approaches such as those used by the pharmaceutical industry have been shown to be very influential in introducing new medication treatments (Majumdar et al., 2003). Academic detailing, successfully used for many years in the pharmaceutical industry, is a method of disseminating new practices based on the model of marketing to physicians (detailing). This approach involves face-to-face education delivered to physicians with the goal of enhancing clinical decision-making (Soumerai, 1998). Academic detailing has been evaluated in controlled trials and found to outperform continuous quality improvement methods (i.e., employment of multidisciplinary teams to monitor local data regarding a practice change) and usual care in the pharmacological treatment of depression and hypertension (Goldberg et al., 1998). An important challenge is to obtain financial support for academic detailing provided by knowledgeable health care providers.

An alternative method of disseminating new practice approaches involves telemarketing directed at physicians. Gomel and colleagues (Gomel, Wutzke, Hardcastle, Lapsley, & Reznik, 1998) found that both telemarketing using a standardized sales script and academic detailing were each more successful than mailed promotional brochures in recruiting physicians to participate in a trial to provide self-administered treatment to hazardous drinkers in primary care. Telemarketing was significantly more cost-effective than academic detailing ($10.77/physician for telemarketing versus $58.96/physician for academic detailing).

The self-help clearinghouse has also been suggested as a model for dissemination of information about self-help support groups and possibly self-administered interventions. The mandate of the self-help clearinghouse is to provide technical assistance and information to health care consumers and professionals in developing and supporting self-help programs. The self-help clearinghouse movement has a long history but is relatively underutilized. Todres and Hagarty (1993) evaluated awareness of a self-help clearinghouse in Toronto and found that most self-help groups and professional helpers were unaware of its existence. However, the study increased subsequent awareness and utilization of the clearinghouse.

Finally, the media represents a powerful way to educate the public (including professionals) about the important health and practice issues. Paykel et al. (1997) described a large media campaign in the United Kingdom conducted between 1992 and 1996 to educate the public and healthcare professionals about the appropriate treatment of depression. The Defeat Depression Campaign involved the creation and provision of educational leaflets, books, audiotapes, newspaper and magazine articles, as well as television and radio interviews on the topic of depression. General practice education included consensus conferences, the development of management guidelines, and training videotapes. Public attitudes about the campaign were favorable.

While the producers of evidence-based treatments have often neglected working on disseminating these treatments, in recent years there has been greater emphasis on developing models for dissemination of improved health care practice (Stirman et al., 2004). There are evolving models of dissemination and calls for more active efforts to disseminate treatment innovations and to conduct research on the dissemination process. In the case of primary care, Williams (2003) suggests that a realistic plan to integrate self-administered treatments into primary care practices would involve providing an articulated model of service delivery to the physician, training staff to use the resources, finding a secure location for program materials, and clarifying who will provide information technology support. This is the approach taken in the PACE+ program described above.

Conclusion

Given that patients and practitioners are receptive to self-administered treatment, there is tremendous potential for the use of these interventions to improve the quality of service provided in primary care. The rapid pace of work in primary care settings, the diversity of problems seen, and the frequent comorbidity among problems suggests that approaches that address a broad range of concerns (such as stress management, coping with anxiety and/or depression, maintaining a healthy lifestyle, and dealing with chronic health conditions such as hypertension, diabetes, and back pain) are more likely to be accepted and maintained. There is also a need for more work on development and evaluation of programs designed specifically for primary care settings. Fortunately there are a number of promising models for continuing work in this area (Glasgow, Goldstein, Ockene, & Pronk, 2004).

Chapter Points

- Patients seen in primary care settings often present with chronic physical conditions and subsyndromal mental health problems.
- Patients in primary care settings are receptive to self-administered interventions, with preferences for printed materials, voice interactive telephone contact, and computer-assisted interventions.
- Experimental investigations in primary care have been largely confined to mental health problems, with several studies examining the effectiveness of self-help programs with diabetes, healthy lifestyles, and hypertension.
- The vast majority of studies examining the effectiveness of self-help interventions have utilized written materials, including books and pamphlets, with moderate success.
- Computer interactive programs utilized while at the office of a primary care physician are well received when targeting mental health problems and lifestyle changes.
- The importance of monitoring participation and symptom change was illustrated in a program conducted in the United Kingdom for anxiety problems.
- Dropouts were lowest in the least effective (relaxation) condition and highest in the most effective (exposure) condition.
- Discrepancies between outcomes within treatments were found in a study targeting mood disorders. Participants preferred the least effective telephone contact intervention, whereas the more effective, computer mediated information and treatment was least preferred.
- Individuals with type 2 diabetes and limited computer experience profited equally whether treated with on-line goal-setting plus feedback, information plus professional coaching, and information plus peer support.
- Effective dissemination of information has used both academic detailing (face-to-face education) and local opinion leaders to provide education about new practices in medicine. Telemarketing aimed at introducing physicians to self-help treatments for hazardous drinking was as effective as academic detailing at one fifth the cost.

References

Arean, P. A., & Miranda, J. (1996). Do primary care patients accept psychological treatments? *General Hospital Psychiatry, 18*, 22–27.

Beck, A. T., & Emery, G. (1985). *Anxiety disorders and phobias: A cognitive perspective*. New York: Basic Books.

Beck, A. T., Steer, R. A., & Brown, G. K. (1996). *Beck Depression Inventory manual* (2nd ed.). San Antonio, TX: Psychological Corporation.

Bedrosian, R. C. (2004, November). One-stop shopping: Designing a family of interactive self-help programs for comorbid problems. Paper presented at the meeting of the Association for the Advancement of Behavior Therapy, New Orleans, LA.

Bernstein, D. A., & Borkovec, T. D. (1973). *Progressive relaxation training.* Champaign, IL: Research Press.

Borbas, C., Morris, N., McLaughlin, B., Asinger, R., & Gobel, F. (2000). The role of clinical opinion leaders in guideline implementation and quality improvement. *Chest, 118*, 24S–32S.

Bower, P., Richards, D., & Lovell, K. (2001). The clinical and cost-effectiveness of self-help treatments for anxiety and depressive disorders in primary care: A systematic review. *British Journal of General Practice, 51*, 838–845.

Cavanagh, K., & Shapiro, D. A. (2004). Computer treatment for common mental health problems. *Journal of Clinical Psychology, 60*, 239–251.

Chalder, T. (1995). *Coping with chronic fatigue.* London: Sheldon Press.

Chalder, T., Wallace, P., & Wessely, S. (1997). Self-help treatment of chronic fatigue in the community: A randomized controlled trial. *British Journal of Health Psychology, 2*, 189–197.

Christensen, H., Griffiths, K. M., & Jorm, A. F. (2004). Delivering interventions for depression by using the Internet: Randomised controlled trial. *British Medical Journal, 328*, 265–269

Christensen, H., Griffiths, K. M., & Korten, A. (2002). Web-based cognitive behaviour therapy: Analysis of site usage and changes in depression and anxiety scores. *Journal of Medical Internet Research, 4*, e3.

Cohen, J. (1992). A power primer. *Psychological Bulletin, 112*, 155–159.

Collins, J. G. (1997). Prevalence of selected chronic conditions: United States, 1990–1992. *Vital Health Statistics, 194*, 1–89.

Cuijpers, P. (1997). Bibliotherapy in unipolar depression: A meta-analysis. *Journal of Behavior Therapy and Experimental Psychiatry, 28*, 139–147.

Davis, D. A., Thomson, M. A., Oxman, A. D., & Haynes, R. B. (1995). A systematic review of the effect of continuing medical education strategies. *Journal of the American Medical Association, 274*, 700–705.

Derogatis, L. R. (1977). *The SCL-90 Manual I: Scoring, administration and procedures for the SCL-90.* Baltimore: Clinical Psychometric Research.

DiNardo, P. A., & Barlow, D. H. (1988). *Anxiety Disorders Interview Schedule— Revised (ADIS-R).* Albany, NY: Phobia and Anxiety Disorders Clinic, State University of New York.

Donnan, P., Hutchinson, A., Paxton, R., Grant, B., & Firth, M. (1990). Self-help materials for anxiety: A randomized controlled trial in general practice. *British Journal of General Practice, 40*, 498–501.

Gega, L., Marks, I., & Mataix-Cols, D. (2004). Computer-aided CBT self-help for anxiety and depressive disorders: Experience of a London clinic and future directions. *Journal of Clinical Psychology, 60*, 147–157.

Glasgow, R. E., Boles, S. M., McKay, G., Feil, E. G., & Barrera, J. (2003). The D-Net diabetes self-management program: Long-term implementation, outcomes, and generalization results. *Preventive Medicine, 36*, 410–419.

Glasgow, R. E., Bull, S. S., Piette, J. D., & Steiner, J. F. (2004). Interactive behavior change technology. A partial solution to the competing demands of primary care. *American Journal of Preventative Medicine, 27,* 80–87.

Glasgow, R. E., Goldstein, M. G., Ockene, J. K., & Pronk, N. P. (2004). Translating what we have learned into practice. Principles and hypotheses for interventions addressing multiple behaviors in primary care. *American Journal of Preventative Medicine, 27,* 88–101.

Goldberg, D. (1972). *The detection of psychiatric illness by questionnaire* (Maudsley Monograph No. 21). London: Oxford University Press.

Goldberg, D. P., & Hillier, V. F. (1979). A scaled version of the GHQ. *Psychological Medicine, 9,* 139–145.

Goldberg, H. I., Wagner, E. H., Fihn, S. D., Martin, D. P., Horowitz, C. R., Christensen, D. B., et al. (1998). A randomized controlled trial of CQI teams and academic detailing: Can they alter compliance with guidelines. *Journal on Quality Improvement, 24,* 130–142.

Gomel, M. K., Wutzke, S. E., Hardcastle, D. M., Lapsley, H., & Reznik, R. B. (1998). Cost-effectiveness of strategies to market and train primary health care physicians in brief intervention techniques for hazardous alcohol use. *Social Science Medicine, 47,* 203–211.

Gould, R. A., & Clum, G. A. (1993). A meta-analysis of self-help treatment approaches. *Clinical Psychology Review, 13,* 169–186.

Graham, C., Franses, A., Kenwright, M., & Marks, I. (2000). Psychotherapy by computer: A postal survey of responders to a teletext article. *Psychiatric Bulletin, 24,* 331–332.

Greenberg, D., & Padesky, C. A. (1995). *Mind over mood: Change how you feel by changing the way you think.* New York: Guilford.

Hamilton, M. (1967). Development of a rating scale for primary depressive illnesss. *British Journal of Social and Clinical Psychology, 6,* 278–296.

Holdsworth, N., Paxton, R., Seidel, S., Thomson, D., & Shrubb, S. (1996). Parallel evaluations of new guidance materials for anxiety and depression in primary care. *Journal of Mental Health, 5,* 195–207.

Kiely, B. G., & McPherson, I. G. (1986). Stress self-help packages in primary care: A controlled trial evaluation. *Journal of the Royal College of General Practitioners, 36,* 307–309.

Kristal, A. R., Shattuck, A. L., & Henry, H. J. (1990). Patterns of dietary behavior associated with selecting diets low in fat: Reliability and validity of a behavioral approach to dietary assessment. *Journal of American Dietary Association, 90,* 214–220.

Lewis, G. (1994). Assessing psychiatric disorder with a human interviewer or a computer. *Journal of Epidemiology and Community Health, 48,* 207–210.

Long, B., Calfas, K. J., Wooten, W., Sallis, J. F., Patrick, K., Goldstein, M., et al. (1996). A multi-site field test of the acceptability of physical activity counseling in primary care: Project PACE. *American Journal of Preventive Medicine, 12,* 73–81.

Longstreth, G. F., Hawkey, C. J., Mayer, E. A., Joness, R. H., Naesdal, J., Wilson, I. K., et al. (2001). Characteristics of patients with irritable bowel syndrome recruited for three sources: Implications for clinical trials. *Alimentary Pharmacology Therapeutics, 15,* 959–964.

Majumdar, S. R., McAlister, F. A., & Soumerai, S. B. (2003). Synergy between publication and promotion: Comparing adoption of new evidence in Canada and the United States. *American Journal of Medicine, 115,* 467–472.

Marks, I. M., Kenwright, M., McDonough, M., Whittaker, M., & Mataix-Cols, D. (2004). Saving clinicians' time by delegating routine aspects of therapy to a computer: A randomized controlled trial in phobia/panic disorder. *Psychological Medicine, 34,* 9–18.

Marks, I. M., Mataix-Cols, D., Kenwright, M., Cameron, R., Hirsch, S., & Gega, L. (2003). Pragmatic evaluation of computer-aided self-help for anxiety and depression. *British Journal of Psychiatry, 183,* 57–65.

Marks, I. M., & Mathews, A. M. (1979). Brief standard self-rating for phobic patients. *Behaviour Research and Therapy, 17,* 263–267.

Marrs, R. W. (1995). A meta-analysis of bibliotherapy studies. *American Journal of Community Psychology, 23,* 843–870.

Meichenbaum, D. (1985). *Stress inoculation training.* New York: Pergamon.

Milne, D., & Covitz, F. (1988). A comparative evaluation of anxiety management materials in general practice. *Health Education Journal, 47,* 2–4.

Mitchell, E., & Sullivan, F. (2001). A descriptive feast but an evaluative famine: Systematic review of published articles on primary care computing during 1980–97. *British Medical Journal, 332,* 279–282.

Newman, M. G. (2000). Generalized anxiety disorder. In M. Biaggio & M. Hersen (Eds.), *Effective brief therapies: A clinician's guide* (pp. 157–178). San Diego: Academic Press.

Olfson, M., Fireman, B., Weissman, M. M., Leon, A. C., Sheehan, D. V., Kathol, R. G., et al. (1997). Mental disorder and disability among patients in a primary care group practice. *American Journal of Psyciatry, 154,* 1734–1740.

Osgood-Hynes, D. J., Greist, J. H., Marks, I. M., Baer, L., Heneman, S. W., Wenzel, K. W., et al. (1998). Self-administered psychotherapy for depression using a telephone-accessed computer system plus booklets: An open U.S.-U.K. study. *Journal of Clinical Psychiatry, 59,* 358–365.

Otto, M. W., Pollack, M. H., & Maki, K. M. (2000). Empirically supported treatments for panic disorder: Costs, benefits, and stepped care. *Journal of Consulting and Clinical Psychology, 68,* 556–563.

Paykel, E. S., Tylee, A., Wright, A., Priest, R. G., Rix, S., & Hart, D. (1997). The defeat depression campaign: Psychiatry in the public arena. *American Journal of Psychiatry, 154,* 59–65.

Peabody, J. W., & Luck, J. (1998). A comparison of primary care outpatient services in a veterans affairs medical center and a capitated multispecialty group practice. *Archives of Internal Medicine, 158,* 2291–2299.

Probst, J. C., Moore, C. G., Baxley, E. G., & Lammie, J. J. (2002). Rural-urban differences in visits to primary care physicians. *Health Services Research, 34,* 609–615.

Prochaska, J. O., & diClemente, C. C. (1983). Stages and processes of self-change of smoking toward an integrative model of change. *Journal of Consulting and Clinical Psychology, 51,* 390–395.

Prochaska, J. J., Zabinski, M. F., Calfas, K. J., Saliis, J. F., & Patrick, K. (2000). Interactive communication technology for behavior change in clinical settings. *American Journal of Preventive Medicine, 19,* 127–131.

Proudfoot, J., Goldberg, D., Mann, A., Everitt, B., Marks, I., & Gray, J. (2003). Computerized, interactive, multimedia cognitive behavioural therapy reduces anxiety and depression in general practice: A randomised controlled trial. *Psychological Medicine, 33*, 217–227.

Proudfoot, J., Ryden, C., Everitt, B., Shapiro, D., Goldberg, D., Mann, A., et al. (2004). Clinical efficacy of computerized cognitive-behavioural therapy for anxiety and depression in primary care: Randomized controlled trial. *British Journal of Psychiatry, 185*, 46–54.

Proudfoot, J., Swain, S., Widmer, S., Watkinds, E., Goldberg, D., Marks, I., et al. (2003). The development and beta-test of a computer-therapy program for anxiety and depression: Hurdles and preliminary outcomes. *Computers in Human Behavior, 19*, 277–289.

Reid, C. M., Maher, T., & Jennings, G. L. (2000). Substituting lifestyle management for pharmacological control of blood pressure: A pilot study in Australian general practice. *Blood Pressure, 9*, 267–274.

Richards, D. A., Lovell, K., & McEvoy, P. (2003). Access and effectiveness in psychological therapies: Self-help as a routine health technology. *Health and Social Care in the Community, 11*, 175–182.

Roy-Byrne, P., Russo, J., Cowley, D., & Katon, W. (2003). Panic disorder in public sector primary care: Clinical characteristics and illness severity compared with "mainstream" primary care panic disorder. *Depression and Anxiety, 17*, 51–57.

Rucci, P., Gherardi, S., Tansella, M., Piccinelli, M., Berardi, D., Bisoffi, G., et al. (2003). Subthreshold psychiatric disorders in primary care: Prevalence and associated characteristics. *Journal of Affective Disorders, 76*, 171–181.

Scogin, F., Bynum, J., Stephens, G., & Calhoon, S. (1990). Efficacy of self-administered treatment programs: Meta-analytic review. *Professional Psychology: Research and Practice, 21*, 42–47.

Scogin, F. R., Hanson, A., & Welsh, D. (2003). Self-administered treatment in stepped-care models of depression treatment. *Journal of Clinical Psychology, 59*, 341–349.

Segall, A., & Goldstein, J. (1989). Exploring the correlates of self-provided health care behaviour. *Social Science Medicine, 29*, 153–161.

Shakeshaft, & A. P., Frankish, C. J. (2003). Using patient-driven computers to provide cost-effective prevention in primary care: A conceptual framework. *Health Promotion International, 18*, 67–77.

Sirovatka, P. (2002). Hyman leaves NIMH stronger, richer. *Psychiatric Research Reports, 18*, 2.

Snaith, R. P., Bridge, G. W. K., & Hamilton, M. (1970). The Leeds scales for the self assessment of anxiety and depression. *British Journal of Psychiatry, 128*, 156–165.

Sobell, M. B., & Sobell, L. C. (2000). Stepped care as a heuristic approach to the treatment of alcohol problems. *Journal of Consulting and Clinical Psychology, 68*, 573–579.

Sorby, N. G. D., Reavley, W., & Huber, J. W. (1991). Self help programme for anxiety in general practice: Controlled trial of an anxiety management booklet. *British Journal of General Practice, 41*, 417–420.

Soumerai, S. B. (1998). Principles and uses of academic detailing to improve the management of psychiatric disorders. *Psychiatry in Medicine, 28*, 81–96.

Spielberger, C. D., O'Neil, H. F., & Hansen, D. N. (1970). *Anxiety, drive theory, and computer-assisted learning* (CAI Center Tech. Rep. No. 14). Florida State University, Tallahasse, FL.

Stirman, S. W., Crits-Christoph, P., & DeRubeis, R. J. (2004). Achieving successful dissemination of empirically supported psychotherapies: A synthesis of dissemination theory. *Clinical Psychology: Science and Practice, 11*, 343–359.

Taylor, B. C., Jobson, K. O., Winzelberg, A., & Abascal, L. (2002). The use of the Internet to provide evidence-based integrated treatment programs for mental health. *Psychiatric Annals, 32*, 671–677.

Thompson, C., Kinmonth, A. L., Stevens, L., Peveler, R. C., Stevens, A., Ostler, K. J., et al. (2000). Effects of a clinical-practice guideline and practice-based education on detection and outcome of depression in primary care: Hampshire Depression Project randomized controlled trial. *Lancet, 355*, 185–191.

Todres, R., & Hagarty, S. (1993). An evaluation of a self-help clearinghouse: Awareness, knowledge, and utilization. *Canadian Journal of Community Mental Health, 12*, 211–223.

Ustun, T. B. (1994). WHO collaborative study: An epidemiological survey of psychological problems in general health care in 15 centers worldwide. *International Review of Psychiatry, 6*, 357–364.

Van Schaik, D. J. F., Klijn, A. F. J., Van Hout, H. P. J., Van Marwijk, H. W. J., Beekman, A. T. F., De Haan, M., et al. (2004). Patients' preferences in the treatment of depressive disorder in primary care. *General Hospital Psychiatry, 26*, 184–189.

Walsh, B T., Fairburn, C. G., Mickley, D., Sysko, R., & Parides, M. K. (2004). Treatment of bulimia nervosa in a primary care setting. *American Journal of Psychiatry, 161*, 556–561.

White, J. (1995). Stresspac: A controlled trial of a self-help package for the anxiety disorders. *Behavioural and Cognitive Psychotherapy, 23*, 89–107.

White, J. (1998). Stresspac: Three-year follow-up of a controlled trial of a self-help package for the anxiety disorders. *Behavioural and Cognitive Psychotherapy, 26*, 133–141.

White, J., Jones, R., & McGarry, E. (2000). Cognitive behavioural computer therapy for the anxiety disorders: A pilot study. *Journal of Mental Health, 9*, 505–516.

Whitfield, G. E., Williams, C., & Shapiro, D. A. (2001). Assessing the take up and acceptability of a self-help room used by patients awaiting their initial outpatient appointment. *Behavioural and Cognitive Psychotherapy, 29*, 333–343.

Williams, C. (2003). New technologies in self-help: Another effective way to get better. *European Eating Disorders Review, 11*, 170–182.

Wilson, G. T., Vitousek, K. M., & Loeb, K.L. (2000). Stepped care treatment for eating disorders. *Journal of Consulting and Clinical Psychology, 68*, 564–572.

Zigmond, A. S., & Snaith, R. P. (1983). The Hospital Anxiety and Depression Scale. *Acta Psychiatrica Scandinavica, 67*, 361–370.

CHAPTER 17

Self-Help Therapies

Retrospect and Prospect

GEORGE A. CLUM AND PATTI LOU WATKINS

Where We've Been

The scientific research reviewed in the present compilation represents more than 30 years of studies that examine the effectiveness of self-administered treatment (SATs) programs. This research has progressed from treatment outcome studies evaluating the effects of such straightforward issues as self-administered desensitization for spider phobias and bibliotherapy for speech phobia to complex Internet-based interventions that incorporate virtual coaches and immediate feedback strategies. Controlled outcome studies have targeted everything from Axis I disorders (depression, panic disorders, bulimia nervosa) to habit disturbances (eating, smoking, drinking), children's problems (enuresis, conduct problems), and health problems (Diabetes control, sleep disturbances). Outcome studies have doubled in each of the last two decades from prior decades and the types of problems targeted have become increasingly complex.

The vast majority of these studies have dealt with the question of whether SATs are effective compared to no treatment, with fewer attempting to answer the question of whether SATs are effective compared to therapist directed treatments (TDTs) or drug treatments. Almost all of the studies reviewed have utilized interventions modeled after TDTs whose efficacy has been demonstrated, after adapting the interventions to a self-administered format. Again, in almost all instances, the interventions are based on learning principles consistent with a cognitive–behavioral treatment (CBT) paradigm. Given the adaptability of CBT strategies to the self-help format, it is not surprising that the majority of the studies reveal a therapeutic effect and that the level of the effect is one that recommends such approaches to studies of their effectiveness in the general health arena.

Our understanding of treatment effectiveness is generally limited to self-help books/bibliotherapy. While there is a growing literature on the effectiveness of computer/Internet-based treatment programs, to date such programs have been examined for a limited number of health problems. Nonetheless, the level of efficacy for those programs that have been evaluated and the potential for adapting strategies into this venue, known or suspected to be efficacious, has led to a proliferation of therapy-oriented Web sites. The task for individuals developing these sites is to evaluate them in controlled studies.

In addition to the question of efficacy, two additional questions bear close examination. The first is concerned with the durability of effects based on SATs and the second is concerned with factors associated with positive response. While the data on both of these questions is limited, more information is available to answer the first. Interestingly, the question of durability of effect seems to vary depending on the type of problem targeted by the intervention. A reading of the chapters in this book highlights the durability of effects for depression and a variety of anxiety disorders. While the follow-up periods in efficacy studies have been short, the data support the persistence of treatment effects with little degradation over periods of 6 months to several years (Hirai & Clum, 2006; Scogin, Jamison, & Davis, 1990). The persistence of treatment effects for these disorders may reflect the likelihood that individuals remain motivated to use strategies to keep them under control after treatment has concluded. In contrast, efficacy studies examining SATs for smoking, weight loss, and chronic health problems have identified high relapse and treatment degradation rates. Researchers (Chapter 14 in this text) into such health problems have accordingly emphasized the use of strategies such as continuous social support to maintain motivation at high levels during the follow-up period, which in many instances may mean as long as the targeted individuals are alive. It is clear that some target problems require intensive follow-up programs to sustain gains, while some require much less to maintain improvements.

Knowing who responds to SATs and who might be harmed could prove important in determining who should get such interventions and who should not. Surprisingly, few studies have addressed this question in anything more than a preliminary manner. Exclusionary criteria, based on common sense and clinical expertise, are a primary consideration in determining who receives SATs. Suicidal, acutely psychotic, and confused individuals would not be assigned to a SAT. Likewise, individuals with limited reading ability or attentional difficulties would not be assigned to read a self-help book or listen to self-help tapes. Another common-sense predictor, but one that has also received empirical support (Murray, Pombo-Carrill, & Bara-Carrill, 2003; Ost, Stridh, & Wolf, 1998), is individuals' attitudes toward using self-help materials exclusively or even in the context of other TDTs. Individuals who do not believe that SATs will be helpful to them are less likely to access and use such materials. Another variable expected to predict outcome in SATs is severity of the disorder, with more severe disorders more resistant to change. This expectation was confirmed in a study by McKendree-Smith (1998), who found that depressed and disabled older adults were not helped by an SAT. Concluding that individuals with severe levels of a targeted disorder should be guided to other forms of treatment, however, may be premature. For example, Otto, Pollack, and Maki (2001) noted that severity and comorbidity of a disorder are negative prognostic factors for SATs and TDTs alike. Until a great deal more data is available to address this question, our current conclusions must be based on common sense and clinical judgment.

Devising Effective Self-Help Programs

In one real sense we have no better idea today how to write a self-help book than we did 30 years ago. Similarly, we do not know what an effective Internet-based program for changing depression or other disorders should look like and how it might differ from one that was not effective. At present no study exists that has compared different ways of presenting the same self-help material. As empiricists, therefore, we must conclude that we simply do not know how to present therapeutic content in ways to maximize behavior change.

In another sense, however, information exists that serves as a guide to constructing effective self-help treatment programs. It is clear from examining the history of self-help that a typical progression occurs in demonstrating the effectiveness of a particular approach and its adoption into an effective self-help product. In Step 1, a treatment is conceived and its efficacy evaluated in a controlled study using individual therapists to deliver the treatment. Once established as efficacious by repeatedly validating the approach in multiple laboratories and clinics, the approach is adapted into a self-administered treatment format. This constitutes Step 2 in a program likely to lead to an efficacious self-help treatment. In Step 3, the SAT version of the efficacious treatment is subjected to empirical tests as rigid as those applied in Step 1. If validated, that version of the SAT is considered efficacious and preferable to other SH programs, even those designed from the same basic set of treatment prescriptions proven effective in Step 1. The basic difference is that the validated treatments have been shown to work, whereas the unvalidated ones have not.

This approach is cumbersome because no information is retrieved on what elements of the treatment program are necessary and sufficient and which are superfluous. Additionally, no information is provided on the venue of the treatment approach—e.g., book, tape, or Internet—likely to prove most effective. We do not know what steps are important and in what order they should be presented. This deficiency is largely related to the lack of formal assessment of the many self-help offerings that exist in a given domain, a deficiency that is at least partially remediable. Rather than call for publishers of self-help materials to evaluate their product, a call previously made (Rosen, 1987) that has gone largely unheeded, an alternative approach might be to provide the opportunity for users of self-help materials to evaluate their progress using whatever self-help program they choose. Such an opportunity might be provided by a Web site offering free assessment and feedback within specific domains; e.g., smoking cessation, depression, eating disorders, etc. In exchange for the free assessment, participants would be asked to provide information about variables associated with their identified problem, previous and current attempts to remedy their problem, degree of involvement with and completion of the self-help program chosen, and pre- and posttreatment outcome. Armed with information about the specific program being used, researchers could identify characteristics of self-help users, determine the amount of the program consumed and the practices employed, and evaluate and compare different programs. In this way, a real-life approach to evaluating specific programs within particular domains could be launched.

A second issue could also be addressed using this broad-stroke assessment service, related to the question of which content domains are necessary for addressing a particular problem and which are not. For programs using the Internet venue and, to a lesser extent, for other venues as well, assessments could be conducted after specific elements of a given SAT have been completed. For example, an Internet program devised by Hirai and Clum (2005) for the treatment of trauma-related consequences was divided into specific modules—information about PTSD, relaxation strategies, cognitive strategies, and exposure strategies. While not implemented in their study, assessments could easily be conducted to assess progress after completion of each module by having trauma sufferers access the assessment site after each module was completed. In this way, not only could SATs be evaluated but also their components. Internet-based SATs lend themselves to this type of particularized assessment. To the extent that specific book chapters or sequences of chapters constitute modules, self-help books and tapes could also be evaluated in this manner.

Information on the effectiveness of different venues on which SATs are offered could also be evaluated using this approach. Early results based on a meta-analytic summary by Gould & Clum (1993) suggests that audio- and videotapes are more effective than SATs offered in book form. Other data from this same study indicate that audio- or videotape-enhanced bibliotherapy confers some advantage over bibliotherapy alone. In no case, however, has the relative effectiveness of different venues been evaluated using the same material. Given that some SATs are offered in several different formats—e.g., via book or audiotape—and that the programs are nearly identical, the differential efficacy of specific venues could be evaluated.

A Blueprint for Developing Effective Self-Help Programs

As yet unanswered is the question of how to sequence treatment modules for programs that, as a whole, have demonstrated effectiveness. Which elements are necessary and which merely fillers? To begin to answer this question requires an analysis of effective programs developed to date, an examination of self-regulatory elements that have been found efficacious, and a logical analysis of how to sequence various treatment elements. With considerable humility and with the expectation of being proven wrong in the future when actual data become available to shed light on this question, we propose a potential model.

Four elements are considered essential in developing efficacious self-help programs: (a) a problem must be validly identified and progress in changing this problem evaluated; (b) the person with the problem must be motivated to change; (c) effective strategies of change must be effectively communicated and learned; and (d) application of these strategies in real-life situations must be undertaken; i.e., generalization must take place.

We have spoken previously (Chapter 3 in this text) of the importance of targeting validly identified problems with SATs. In all of the programs discussed in this book, formal evaluation of the target problem took place, either before the problem began to be addressed or, in rare instances (Febbraro, Clum, Roodman, & Wright, 1999), after the program had been completed. In addition, assessment of progress is an essential element of programs likely to prove effective. This assessment is important, not only to determine if progress is occurring but also as a treatment element in producing change. Febbraro and Clum (1998) summarized the research literature bearing on the importance of assessment in producing change in self-administered change programs. Two types of assessments can be distinguished: assessments of the target problem and assessments of the skills or techniques hypothesized to mediate problem reduction. Assessment of the target problem is important prior to beginning treatment to know that a problem exists. In this approach, the individual is compared to others with similar problems. Assessment is an effective change agent for several reasons. First, assessment acts as information to demonstrate whether or not the intended change has occurred. Assessment informs whether the individual seeking change is using the recommended strategies to produce that change. At what rate are the recommended strategies being employed? When the strategies are employed, do parallel changes in the target problem occur? Such information has a second effect of reinforcing the user, who sees that his performance on the recommended strategies is taking place at an increasing or high rate and that the recommended strategies are working. Such information motivates the decision-maker to continue the strategies or supplement them with additional strategies or determine that the particular strategy is not working and to switch to another strategy. Success in producing change on the target problem can affect the user's decision to stay with the program and even accelerate his involvement.

Motivation to begin an SAT begins with the evaluation of the problem. With some problems, such as anxiety and depression, intrinsic motivation often exists to reduce the symptoms associated with the problem. With such problems, the individual may need only to have confirmed that she has the problem and that the SAT being recommended fits the identified problem. In others, such as weight loss and substance abuse, motivation is less strong. With the latter problems, especially substance abuse, the technique of motivational interviewing has been used to motivate change, essentially by doing a cost–benefit analysis of the decision to continue the problem behaviors, to reduce such behaviors, or to eliminate them entirely. Such cost–benefit analyses are enhanced by the initial assessment, coupled with feedback on both the relative severity of the problem and a summary of the client-identified costs and benefits.

Another motivational strategy is based on the consideration of the extent to which the help-seeking individual believes that his problem can be helped and the amount of effort it will take. To produce change, information about the success of the program, the suitability of the program for this individual, and affirmations of both the possibility of change and the amount of effort necessary to produce it would also be provided. This information can be provided by individuals who have been helped by the program under consideration (audio- and videotapes of individuals making such attestations are most persuasive; case histories can be substituted if motivation is being provided in print) or they can be provided more generally by people who tell stories of their life-long struggle, successfully met head-on. Dr. Claire Weeke's (1990) story of her successful battle with agoraphobia and Dr. Kay Redfield Jamison's (1995) story of dealing with bipolar disorder are general examples of motivation-enhancing tales. Accordingly, SATs that are successful should be liberally sprinkled with examples of individuals with similar problems who have successfully used the techniques described. The chapter on approaches for stabilizing weight gain (Chapter 14 in this text) used a similar strategy, referred to as "mastery counselor" for increasing motivation to learn coping and deal with adverse situations.

Essential to developing successful SATs is recommending and teaching strategies that are both therapeutic and learnable in the self-administered format. The approach taken to date in selecting such techniques is to adopt those techniques taught in individually administered treatments of demonstrated effectiveness. Such adoption has been accomplished by providing information about the techniques, giving case examples of how such techniques have been employed, demonstrating their use in audio- or video-tapes, and providing forms to aid in the process of using such techniques. Chapter 9 in this text, for example, discusses studies in which techniques for treating sexual dysfunction are demonstrated by individuals using videotapes. All of these techniques are, in the absence of hard evidence to the contrary, of presumably equal value in assisting the program user in learning the strategies. Feedback systems have been employed on the Internet, asking program users to submit completed exercises or requiring that users complete mastery tests demonstrating acquisition of the knowledge and attesting to their completion of practice exercises (Hirai & Clum, 2005). Information on the use of homework in the context of SATs (e.g., McKendree-Smith, 1998) has shown a relationship between number of pages read and success in the program.

The last element of successful SATs, like their counterparts in therapist-administered treatments, provide instructions for and exercises in transmission of the newly learned strategies to the real world. This transition from the home laboratory to the individual's natural environment is best accomplished in incremental steps of ascending difficulty. The idea is to provide success experiences along the way so that motivation is maintained throughout this difficult process. As with all such recommended progressions, the individual applying them must be told of the expectation and informed of the reasonableness of the recommendation by being provided with either empirically supported evidence or sound arguments. Cooperation is best assured when the user is brought into the loop of knowledge and decision-making for all recommended applications.

Common-sense support for this progression is provided by the maxim of maximizing success experiences to the end-user. The answer to the previously asked question of how to sequence various therapeutic elements is also provided by this analysis. Thus, once suitability of the individual for the recommended SAT is completed, appropriate assessment to document change in place, and appropriate intervention elements determined, common-sense sequencing in which the individual is guided through learning the requisite skills, practicing them in controlled and low-demand conditions, and then guided through a series of increasingly difficult, real-world applications is then accomplished. When the therapeutic venue is bibliotherapy, such sequencing is very difficult to control, as the individual is free to skip sections, read others, apply recommendations whenever deemed necessary, and, in general, feel free to use or discard whatever elements are considered essential by the author. Such an approach may even be found to lead to the best outcomes, though available evidence suggests that the opposite is true—those individuals who access and apply the most elements are most likely to enjoy the greatest benefits.

In the world of the Internet, more control can be exercised by the therapist/researcher. In the program developed by Hirai and Clum (2005) for trauma victims, for example, the treatment program was divided into four modules. Progression to the next module was allowed only when the previous module had been mastered, as determined by passing a test requiring both knowledge and application of strategies. In such an approach, one can have some confidence that each of the modules has been accessed and that some mastery of skills has been obtained. Other approaches are also possible. For example, if one wanted to ensure that practice homework exercises had been carried out, one could require that assignments be returned to the therapist. Again, only then might the user be allowed to proceed to the next level.

Where We're Going

It is difficult to think of the arena of self-help as a nascent field of inquiry, given the numerous books and programs with which we have all become familiar. Yet that is exactly where this field is at present, at the beginning! We are only starting to answer the questions of whether and when SATs are effective and what elements of change produce the desired effects. We know almost nothing of who is likely to be positively disposed to such programs, how to enhance positive attitudes, and who is likely to actually get better using such venues. We have only a beginning knowledge of which problems are likely to improve, the degree of expectable improvement, and the permanency of change produced. Only recently have researchers begun to ask what strategies will reduce relapse and promote long-term change. Given these large gaps in knowledge, it is still important to ask, and try to answer, where do we go from here.

Targeting Interpersonal Behavior

To date, SATs have almost exclusively targeted individual symptoms, modifiable by the individual, working by himself or with minimal coaching, to produce change. However, it is axiomatic that numerous mental health problems are associated with or defined by problems of interpersonal behavior; in the most extreme example, personality disorders. Future SATs will target interpersonal behaviors, both because such behaviors are the identified problem and because such behaviors affect other individuals' ability to recover from mental illness. To illustrate when SATs might be used to target interpersonal problems, we next examine the application of self-help strategies to the construct of expressed emotion (EE), a construct that refers to a set of pernicious family behaviors directed toward the mentally ill family member.

Expressed emotion refers to the family's response to a family member's mental illness, with the response taking the form of excessive hostility or excessive emotional involvement. Using the Camberwell Family Interview (CFI) to assess this construct, EE has been linked to negative prognosis for a series of different psychiatric disorders, including schizophrenia (Brown, Birley, & Wing, 1972), depression (Hooley & Teasdale, 1989), and anxiety disorders (Chambless & Steketee, 1999). Modifications of EE within families have been linked to improved prognosis for these disorders.

The modification of EE is a task made for self-help treatment approaches. First, it is measurable using self-report instruments, such as the Expressed Emotion Questionnaire (Docherty, Serper, & Harvey, 1990). As such, individual family members or the patient himself can identify whether a problem exists and the severity of the problem. Moreover, improvement can be measured and feedback provided to the family member whose behavior is targeted. Second, EE is definable. The CFI specifies behaviors that are to be used by the trained clinician to define the construct. Because of its definable behaviors, family members can be taught what to modify. They can also be presented with information about the EE construct and how it relates to prognosis for affected individuals, thus increasing motivation to change. Case studies and video clips illustrating the problem can be presented and the family member invited to identify the behaviors and suggest modifications within the context of the case studies. Specific strategies for reducing behaviors reflective of EE can be introduced and practiced. Specific examples of the family member's mental illness can be illustrated from a series of video clips, with assignments to respond with non-hostile, low-involvement behaviors to the difficult behaviors.

Alternative Research Strategies

Throughout this text, authors have reviewed treatment outcome studies that rely on quantitative results to ascertain the value of various self-help approaches. However, Greenberg (1994) contends that quantitative studies such as these "repeatedly ask the wrong questions" when it comes to determining the worth of self-help programs. He argues that "A scientific study of their effects, even if it were to find them 'unhelpful,' is unlikely to deter people from buying them or psychologists from writing and profiting from them" (p. 44). From where we stand, Greenberg's logic is more than a bit skewed. That is, public popularity of self-help materials—no matter how great—in no way obviates the necessity of empirical evaluation. Greenberg does make a point, though, in that quantitative methods are limited in terms of the information that they are able to provide. For instance, one of the drawbacks of self-help books is their dependence on the consumer's willingness and/or ability to read the materials and follow through with any prescriptions contained therein (Ballou, 1995). Of the hundreds of outcome studies cited in this text, very few addressed this important question of treatment integrity. Alternative research methodologies may be better suited to addressing this, and other issues, surrounding self-help usage.

Qualitative research, consisting of in-depth interviews with participants, may help fill in the gaps in knowledge that quantitative designs are not equipped to do. For example, Grodin (1991), a self-described "qualitative media scholar," interviewed women readers of self-help books, as did Simonds (1992), who utilized such methods to determine *how* and *why* women read self-help books. Through this research, they learned that participants were active and critical consumers, selectively attending to some elements of self-help books while discarding information contained in other parts. Through similar qualitative research, Lichterman (1992) found that female readers of self-help may view their experience positively yet fail to assimilate "ideas or behavioral programs whole" (p, 438) from the material. From a treatment integrity standpoint, such information seems critical for researchers and clinicians working with this genre.

In addition to illuminating how and why people employ self-help programs, qualitative research may also provide information on the impact of these programs that quantitative methods cannot capture. Starker (1989) notes that researchers have paid little attention to individuals' reactions to self-help materials. While he presented narrative responses from self-help consumers as well as health care providers speaking to their clients' response to these programs, few studies cited in the present text even include quantitative measures of consumer satisfaction. Garvin, Striegel-Moore, Kaplan, and Wonderlich (2001) call for participants' input to determine which elements of self-help programs are beneficial and which are harmful. Indeed, Starker's findings include reports of harm incurred that quantitative measures and group averages might obscure.

Within the social sciences, qualitative research has been more the purview of sociology, communication, and women's studies than the field of psychology, as evidenced by the studies cited here (e.g., Grodin, 1991; Lichterman, 1992; Simonds, 1992). In the past decade, this form of inquiry has slowly become accepted in the field of sport psychology where investigators have come to realize its utility in devising effective interventions (e.g., Sparkes, 1998; Strean, 1998). Krahn and Putnam (2003), however, acknowledge clinical psychology's reluctance to include qualitative methods among its accepted research strategies, noting that few graduate training programs offer classes in these techniques. They, however, advocate for the expanded use of qualitative research that can deepen investigators' understanding of various phenomena. Fischer (2006) elaborates, stating that qualitative research addresses the what, when, and how of individuals' experiences. She further states that qualitative methods are best used when investigators "want to understand and characterize an experience or interaction in its own right, rather than explaining it in terms of independent variables [whether natural or experimental]" (p. xvii). While psychology has firmly established itself as an empirical discipline, members of the field now recognize that there are limits to the kind of information that traditional quantitative methods can produce (Fischer, 2006). Neither Fischer nor Krahn and Putnam (2003) suggest replacing quantitative methods with qualitative ones. In fact, the latter describe ways in which the two types of strategies might be combined, suggesting that such methodological pluralism makes for better science. Thus, it is our position that inclusion of qualitative research methods in the study of self-help can enhance our understanding of its great appeal and potential utility.

Another research strategy that might help inform those working in the area of self-help is the methodology known as single-case design. At a recent meeting of the Association for Behavioral and Cognitive Therapies, Ollendick (2006) remarked that, ironically, the field of behavior therapy, which was originally based on the study of the individual case, has now given way to a reliance on group research designs and randomized clinical control trials. Anderson and Kim (2003) remind readers that single-case designs constitute a practical method for evaluating individuals' progress in clinical settings. Hayes, Barlow, and Nelson-Gray (1999) have long promoted the use of single-case designs but have recently underscored their importance in this age of managed care where documentation of client progress is not just a matter of professional ethics but one of economics as well.

Research shows that practicing clinicians make ample use of self-help materials. For instance, Adams and Pitre (2000) found that 68% of therapists they surveyed used bibliotherapy with their clients. These authors expressed concern, however, that estimates of program effectiveness were based on subjective impressions rather than empirical data. We contend that it is time that recommendations for self-help materials are based on empirical evidence rather than "the collective wisdom of the professional community," as a review for the *Authoritative Guide to Self-Help Resources in Mental Health* (Norcross et al., 2000) states. We are encouraged by relatively new outlets for the publication of empirically based case studies (e.g., *Clinical Case Studies, Cognitive and Behavioral Practice*) as well as the acceptance of single-case designs by journals that typically publish group research. The *Journal of Clinical Psychology* and the *Journal of Clinical Psychology in Medical Settings* have published single-case design articles, including some which have specifically examined self-help interventions (e.g., Andersson & Kaldo, 2004; Gega, Marks, & Mataix-Cols, 2004).

One such article (Watkins, 1999) describes the use of bibliotherapy on patients presenting to a local medical clinic with panic disorder symptoms. The author documented their progress from baseline through treatment and follow-up using two separate A-B designs. Outcome data were comprised of self-report questionnaires with established reliability and validity as well as self-monitoring records. Treatment integrity data were comprised of self-monitoring records as well as qualitative telephone interviews. Treatment satisfaction was evaluated by a self-report measure as well as open-ended questions. Although A-B designs fall short of being able to establish that the treatment definitively caused the improvements in both participants' conditions, qualitative responses indicated that they were using the techniques as intended, lending credence to this explanation. Here, the participants described their actual use of cognitive restructuring, relaxation strategies, and exposure to feared situations. For example, one participant remarked "Find out what is in the situation that you are avoiding. It's not the restaurant itself, but fear of embarrassment. Get to the root of it" (Watkins, 1999, p. 362). The participant then described practicing coping techniques ahead of time before placing herself in the feared situation. A final element of this article involved relating participants' responses to patterns in the broader research literature, including experimental group designs assessing the efficacy of this particular self-help intervention.

In summary, we recommend not only an expansion of research in the area of self-help but an expansion of the research methods used to gather knowledge about these types of interventions. In doing so, we might adapt qualitative methods made popular by other fields of inquiry in the social sciences. We might also revisit single-case methodology that was once the linchpin of behavior therapy. Finally, we might fine tune our group experimental designs in an effort to address questions that remain about the effectiveness of self-help therapies.

The Need to Address Diversity Issues

In discussing the future of self-help therapies, we would be remiss if we did not address diversity—or the current lack thereof—in this field. One way that this issue may manifest itself is in terms of who is behind the development of self-help programs. While we did not systematically examine the gender, race, ethnicity, or sexual orientation of those who created the self-help programs cited throughout this text, Kissling (1995) found that most authors of the self-help books she reviewed were white, European American heterosexuals. Lack of diversity is also apparent when one considers the audiences to whom these materials are marketed and/or the populations on which they have been assessed. Mann and Kato (1996) describe two ways in which diverse populations have been marginalized in health psychology research. Either they are excluded from samples or they are included but overlooked with regard to data analysis. Watkins and Whaley (2000) describe how quite disparate results might be obtained when data are analyzed by gender. An examination of this text would certainly reveal that the research cited throughout overwhelmingly relied on participants who were White, with gender or sexual orientation either not specified or examined for potential differences in responsiveness.

This state of affairs is not surprising given that the American self-help movement arose from White Protestant heterosexual male ideology (DeFrancisco, 1995). As such, Perini and Bayer (1996) contend that the messages contained within self-help books apply "only to some—those of the masculinist culture, those with money in the bank, those whose skin is white" (p. 294). Rosenberg (2003) concurs, noting a lack of ethnic diversity in the content of self-help materials since the inception of this genre. DeFrancisco (1995) asserts that the self-help tradition has historic racial divides that mirror those of our broader society. Thus, people of diverse racial and ethnic backgrounds may be excluded from whatever benefits these materials might otherwise confer.

Kato (1996) identified two factors that might affect the ability of ethnic groups to benefit from traditional interventions. First, structural factors such as poverty or discriminatory policies may serve as a barrier. It has been noted previously in chapter 1 of this volume that self-help interventions are inherently lacking in their ability to affect needed changes in the sociocultural environment. Second, psychological factors such as health beliefs common to a culture may impinge on the success of a treatment. Certainly, beliefs about personal agency might impact how ethnically diverse individuals respond to a self-help intervention. One might also expect that people from collectivist cultures in which the good of the group supercedes personal development may be especially alienated from this mode of therapy unless specifically tailored to address these cultural nuances. Language itself may present another barrier for those who are not native English-speakers.

In a special issue of *Behavior Therapy* entitled *Thirty Years of Behavior Therapy: Promises Kept, Promises Unfulfilled*, Evans (1997) wrote that the field was well positioned to begin addressing the particular needs of ethnic minority groups. Over the ensuing decade, researchers seem to have heeded this suggestion. For instance, a special issue of *Cognitive and Behavioral Practice*, entitled *Culturally Sensitive CBT*, recently appeared. This issue presents research exploring the impact of race and ethnicity on the treatment process. One article describes the adaptation of a treatment manual for anxiety to a Native American population (De Coteau, Anderson, & Hope, 2006). The authors explain that the article is largely conceptual in that empirical data surrounding treatment of this population are still sparse. Nevertheless, it is our hope that articles such as this will spur further investigation into the use of manualized treatment approaches among ethnically diverse populations.

Race and ethnicity are not the only forms of diversity that the self-help field has yet to adequately address. Self-help materials, particularly those focusing on interpersonal relationships, often presume heterosexuality on the part of consumers. Simonds (1992) cites feedback from a lesbian reader who stated, "The feeling I had of being invisible to you was difficult to get past. Your book is very helpful and I ask that somewhere in it you acknowledge my existence" (p. 94). The reader suggested that the author of the self-help book simply add a clause to the introduction to "include me and others like me." In order to make interventions more welcoming to individuals of diverse sexual orientations, O'Hanlan (1996) recommends using inclusive language, with the term "partner," for instance, replacing heterosexist terms such as spouse, husband, and wife. Self-help materials, which often make use of illustrative vignettes, could include scenarios in which lesbian, gay, and bisexual characters appear. Even if symptom presentation and treatment strategies are the same for these groups as they are for heterosexuals, such representations may reduce the experience of marginalization.

We ask that the reader's comments, cited above, serve as a poignant reminder that self-help materials be made sufficiently inclusive or that they are specifically tailored to the diverse groups of individuals who populate the United States. Inattention to the differential experiences of oppressed groups in our society by those of us in privileged categories is quite common. Furthermore, it is often unintentional and usually not done out of malice (Johnson, 2001). It is our hope that this discussion will prompt investigators in this field to pay greater attention to the distinctive needs of others who may differ from themselves. As Mann and Kato (1996) avow, the goal of focusing on diversity issues is to provide effective care for *all* people.

Chapter Points

- Research on the effectiveness of SATs has accelerated over the last 30 years, with increases in both the complexity of the problems addressed and the approaches designed to address them.
- Durability of treatment effects varies by type of problem addressed, with those problems for which intrinsic motivation to change is high, having the best prognosis, and those problems where extrinsic motivation has to be provided having the highest relapse.
- A blueprint for designing effective SATs includes four elements: identifying and assessing the problem, increasing motivation, identifying change strategies, and applying these strategies to the real world.
- Future research will employ increasingly sophisticated technology and tailored treatments and will expand to address interpersonal behaviors, such as reflected in the construct of expressed emotion, as targeted problems.
- Research approaches should expand to include qualitative as well as quantitative strategies to enhance our knowledge of how people utilize self-help materials and what aspects of those materials are most helpful.
- SATs of the future should strive for greater inclusion of minority groups of all types to both make such offerings more palatable to individuals in those groups and to increase the effectiveness of the materials themselves.

References

Adams, S. J., & Pitre, N. (2000). Who uses bibliotherapy and why? A survey from an underserviced area. *Canadian Journal of Psychiatry, 45*, 645–650.

Anderson, C. M., & Kim, C. (2003). Evaluating treatment efficacy with single-case designs. In M. C. Roberts & S. S. Ilardi (Eds.), *Handbook of research methods in clinical psychology* (pp. 73–91). Malden, MA: Blackwell.

Andersson, G., & Kaldo, V. (2004). Internet-based cognitive behavioral therapy for tinnitus. *Journal of Clinical Psychology, 60*, 171–178.

Ballou, M. (1995). Bibliotherapy. In M. Ballou (Ed.). *Psychological interventions: A guide to strategies* (pp. 55–65). Westport, CT: Praeger.

Brown, G. W., Birley, J. L. T., & Wing, J. K. (1972). Influence of family life on the course of schizophrenic disorders: A replication. *British Journal of Psychiatry, 121*, 241–258.

Chambless, D. L., & Steketee, G. (1999). Expressed emotion and behavioral therapy outcome: A prospective study with obsessive-compulsive and agoraphobic outpatients. *Journal of Consulting and Clinical Psychology, 67*, 658–665.

De Coteau, T., Anderson, J., & Hope, D. (2006). Adapting manualized treatments: Treating anxiety disorders among Native Americans. *Cognitive and Behavioral Practice, 13*, 304–309.

DeFrancisco, V. L. (1995). Helping our selves: An introduction. *Women's Studies in Communication, 18*, 107–110.

Docherty, N. M., Serper, M. R., & Harvey, P. D. (1990). Development and preliminary validation of a questionnaire assessment of expressed emotion. *Psychological Reports, 67*, 279–287.

Evans, I. M. (1997). The effect of values on scientific and clinical judgment in behavior therapy. *Behavior Therapy, 28*, 483–493.

Febbraro, G. A. R., & Clum, G. A. (1998). Meta-analytic investigation of the effectiveness of self-regulatory components in the treatment of adult problem behaviors. *Clinical Psychology Review, 18*, 143–161.

Febbraro, G. A. R., Clum, G. A., Roodman, A. A., & Wright, J. H. (1999). The limits of bibliotherapy: A study of the differential effectiveness of self-administered interventions in individuals with panic attacks. *Behavior Therapy, 30,* 209–222.

Fischer, C. T. (2006). Introduction. In C. T. Fischer (Ed.), *Qualitative research methods for psychologists: Introduction through empirical studies* (pp. xivi–xlii). Boston: Elsevier.

Garvin, V., Striegel-Moore, R. H., Kaplan, A., & Wonderlich, S. A. (2001). The potential of professionally developed self-help interventions for the treatment of eating disorders. In R. H. Striegel-Moore & L. Smolak (Eds.), *Eating disorders: Innovative directions in research and practice* (pp. 153–172). Washington, DC: American Psychological Association.

Gega, L, Marks, I. M., & Mataix-Cols, D. (2004). Computer-aided CBT self-help for anxiety and depressive disorders: Experience of a London clinic and future directions. *Journal of Clinical Psychology, 60*, 147–157.

Gould, R. A., & Clum, G. A. (1993). A meta-analysis of self-help treatment approaches. *Clinical Psychology Review, 13*, 169–186.

Greenberg, G. (1994). *The self on the shelf: Recovery books and the good life.* Albany: State University of New York Press.

Grodin, D. (1991). The interpretive audience: The therapeutics of self-help book reading. *Critical Studies in Mass Communication, 8*, 404–420.

Hayes, S. C., Barlow, D. H., & Nelson-Gray, R. O. (1999). *The scientist-practitioner: Research and accountability in the age of managed care.* Boston: Allyn & Bacon.

Hirai, M., & Clum, G. (2005). An Internet-based self-change program for traumatic event related fear, distress, and maladaptive coping. *Journal of Traumatic Stress, 18*, 631–636.

Hirai, M., & Clum, G.A. (2006). A meta-analytic study of self-help interventions for anxiety problems. *Behavior Therapy, 37*, 99–111.

Hooley, J. M., & Teasdale, J. D. (1989). Predictors of relapse in unipolar depressives: Expressed emotion, marital distress, and perceived criticism. *Journal of Abnormal Psychology, 98*, 229–235.

Jamison, K. R. (1995). *An unquiet mind: A memoir of moods and madness.* New York: Alfred A. Knopf.

Johnson, A. G. (2001). *Privilege, power, and difference.* New York: McGraw-Hill.

Kato, P. M. (1996). On nothing and everything: The relationship between ethnicity and health. In P. M. Kato & T. Mann (Eds.), *Handbook of diversity issues in health psychology* (pp. 287–300). New York: Plenum.

Keeley, H., Williams, C., & Shapiro D. A. (2002). A United Kingdom survey of accredited cognitive behavior therapists attitudes towards and use of structured self-help materials. *Behavioural and Cognitive Psychotherapy, 30*, 193–204.

Kissling, E. A. (1995). I don't have a great body, but I play one on TV: The celebrity guide to fitness and weight loss in the United States. *Women's Studies in Communication, 18*, 209–216.

Krahn, G. L., & Putnam, M. (2003). Qualitative methods in psychological research. In M. C. Roberts & S. S. Ilardi (Eds.), *Handbook of research methods in clinical psychology* (pp. 176–195). Malden, MA: Blackwell.

Lichterman, P. (1992). Self-help reading as a thin culture. *Media, Culture, and Society, 14*, 431–447.

Mann, T., & Kato, P. M. (1996). Diversity issues in health psychology. In P. M. Kato & T. Mann (Eds.), *Handbook of diversity issues in health psychology* (pp. 3–18). New York: Plenum.

McKendree-Smith, N. (1998). *Cognitive and behavioral bibliotherapy for depression: An examination of efficacy and mediators and moderators of change.* Unpublished doctoral dissertation, University of Alabama, Tuscaloosa.

Murray, K., Pombo-Carril, M. G., & Bara-Carril, N. (2003). Factors determining uptake of a CD-ROM-based CBT self-help treatment for bulimia: Patient characteristics and subjective appraisals of self-help treatment. *European Eating Disorders Review, 11*, 243–260.

Norcross, J. C., Santrock, J. W., Campbell, L. F., Smith, T. P., Sommer, R., & Zuckerman, E. L. (2000). *Authoritative guide to self-help resources in mental health.* New York: Guilford.

O'Hanlan, K. A. (1996). Homophobia and the health psychology of lesbians. In P. M. Kato & T. Mann (Eds.), *Handbook of diversity issues in health psychology* (pp. 261–284). New York: Plenum.

Ollendick, T. H. (2006, November). *The evolution of cognitive and behavioral treatment and assessment: Past presidents' panel.* Paper presented at the 49th annual meeting of the Association for Behavioral and Cognitive Therapies, Chicago.

Öst, L. G., Stridh, B. M., & Wolf, M. (1998). A clinical study of spider phobia: Prediction of outcome after self-help and therapist-directed treatments. *Behaviour Research and Therapy, 36*, 17–35.

Otto, M. W., Pollack, M. H., & Maki, K. M. (2001). Empirically supported treatments for panic disorder: Costs, benefits and stepped care. *Journal of Consulting and Clinical Psychology, 69*, 556–564.

Perini, G. M., & Bayer, B. M. (1996). Out of our minds, in our bodies: Women's embodied subjectivity and self-help culture. In C. W. Tolman & F. Cherry (Eds.), *Problems of theoretical psychology* (pp. 291–303). North York, England: Captus Press.

Rosen, G. M. (1987). Self-help treatment and the commercialization of psychotherapy. *American Psychologist, 42,* 46–51.

Rosenberg, C. E. (2003). Health in the home: A tradition of print and practice. In C. E. Rosenberg (Ed.), *Right living: An Anglo-American tradition of self-help medicine and hygiene* (pp. 1–20). Baltimore: Johns Hopkins University Press.

Scogin, F., Jamison, C., & Davis, N. (1990). Two-year follow-up of bibliotherapy for depression in older adults. *Journal of Consulting and Clinical Psychology, 58,* 665–667.

Simonds, W. (1992). *Women and self-help culture: Reading between the lines.* New Brunswick, NJ: Rutgers University Press.

Sparkes, A. C. (1998). Validity in qualitative inquiry and the problem of criteria: Implications for sport psychology. *The Sport Psychologist, 12,* 363–386.

Starker, S. (1989). *Oracle at the supermarket.* New Brunswick, NJ: Transaction Publishers.

Strean, W. B. (1998). Possibilities for qualitative research in sport psychology. *The Sport Psychologist, 12,* 333–345.

Watkins, P. L. (1999). Manualized treatment of panic disorder in a medical setting: Two illustrative case studies. *Journal of Clinical Psychology in Medical Settings, 6,* 353–372.

Watkins, P. L., & Whaley, D. E. (2000). Gender role stressors and women's health. In R. M. Eisler & M. Hersen (Eds.), *Handbook of gender, culture, and health* (pp. 43–62). Mahwah, NJ: Lawrence Erlbaum.

Weekes, C. (1990). *Hope and help for your nerves.* New York: Signet Books.

Index